Grow Your Vocabulary

GROW YOUR VOCABULARY

by Learning the Roots of English Words

ROBERT SCHLEIFER

Random House New York

All rights reserved under International and Pan-American Copyright Conventions. No part of this publication may be reproduced in any form or by any means, electronic or mechanical, including photocopying, without permission in writing from the publisher. All inquiries should be addressed to Reference and Electronic Publishing, Random House, Inc., 201 East 50th Street, New York, NY 10022-7703. Published in the United States by Random House, Inc., New York, and simultaneously in Canada by Random House of Canada Limited, Toronto

Library of Congress Cataloging-in-Publication Data

Schleifer, Robert.
    Grow your vocabulary : by learning the roots of English words /
    Robert Schleifer.
        p.   cm.
        ISBN 0-679-74450-9
        1. Vocabulary.   2. English language—Roots.   I. Title.
    PE1449.S335   1995
    428.1—dc20   94-48243   CIP

Manufactured in the United States of America
First Edition
New York   Toronto   London   Sydney   Auckland

For Cy
who waited so long
for something like this

CONTENTS

PART II: HELPFUL HINTS 99

PART III: SUBJECTS 111

Professional Words 113

Specialty Words and Phrases 129

Picturesque Words and Expressions 141

FOREWORD

By George B. Wittmer, Doctor of Classical Rhetoric
University of Pittsburgh

Dissection:	1) fore- / -word
Analysis:	2) *fore-*[1]: before; *-word*: word
Reconstruction:	3) a word (*-word*) before (*fore-*)
Definition:	4) *n.* a short preliminary statement in a book or other published work, especially one written by someone other than the author.
Commentary:	5) A *foreword* is not just one word but a whole host of words appearing before the Preface and Introduction of a book, usually written by an authority in the field commenting upon the book as a whole. Nevertheless, these words generally do not constitute more than two or three pages and so, in comparison to the rest of the book, the *foreword* is just "a word before."

What you hold in your hands is, in my opinion, one of the finest and most innovative books on word roots and vocabulary-building to be written in the past fifty years.

The analysis of *foreword* above, provided by the author, is just one of hundreds of examples of a new and revolutionary system of word acquisition that makes tedious methods of memorization largely a thing of the past.

Through this unique system of dissection, analysis, reconstruction, definition, and occasional commentary (when necessary to show how the reconstructed meaning of a word evolved into its modern definition), over one thousand words are methodically broken down into their component roots, carefully analyzed, and then put back together again. This system presents a method that high school and college students and "word-loving" individuals can use to learn and remember new and difficult terms with an ease they may have never thought possible.

Having taught a variety of language-based courses at the university and college levels during the past twenty years, it has been my experience that one of the major obstacles students face in mastering

---

[1] The full meaning, construction, and language of origin of this and all other roots in this book can be found in the A CROSS-REFERENCE DICTIONARY, beginning on page 267.

their subjects is understanding the terms in their area of specialty. And the traditional way of teaching students new words—asking them to memorize word lists, encouraging them to read more, telling them to look up new words every time they come across them, and even teaching them isolated word roots—is simply not enough. What is needed is a quick and comprehensive system that they can employ every time they encounter a new and complex word. *Grow Your Vocabulary* is that system.

But more than this, the organization of *Grow Your Vocabulary* will enable those at home (as well as in school settings) to learn how multisyllabic English words are derived primarily from Latin and Greek words and elements. Its step-by-step analysis of how English roots have been "borrowed" from classical languages and its articulation of the principles governing this borrowing in an informative and easy to understand mini-course entitled HOW ENGLISH WORDS ARE CREATED: A SHORT COURSE make it eminently suitable for this purpose.

Many textbooks and college courses are devoted to teaching this information, but most do so in a highly technical manner that either presumes a working knowledge of Latin and Greek on the part of the student or requires that individual to devote an enormous amount of time to acquiring this knowledge. In *Grow Your Vocabulary*, however, this technical information is articulated in such a way as to meet the needs of nonclassical students and amateur etymologists, resulting in a work that should come as a refreshing alternative to standard texts in classrooms and libraries of high schools and colleges throughout this country.

In my own field of Classical Rhetoric, for example, students frequently struggle to grasp the linguistic underpinnings of our Greco-Roman heritage so that they can better understand such words as *circumlocution*, *elocution*, *solipsism*, and *syllogism* (all of which are dissected, analyzed, reconstructed, and defined in this book). But when they consider the prospects of taking Latin or Classical Greek courses, they are often overwhelmed by the complexities of these languages and the time commitment they will have to make just to learn the fundamentals. Yet they can quickly learn many of these fundamentals in *Grow Your Vocabulary*. The practical program of word analysis it presents will lead students to a markedly clearer understanding and retention of Latin and Greek terms while at the same teaching them the basics of the classical contribution to English words. And if they forget the meaning of some of these words they can often, with a little self-prodding, "reconstruct" them right on the spot.

The effectiveness of the practical program *Grow Your Vocabulary* presents is a remarkable achievement in a book of this kind. For not only will individuals learn new words, they will develop a system for remembering them and then of recalling these words should they forget them. In the process they will also learn the fundamentals of Latin and Greek. Moreover, by the use of subtle repetition and a host of learning aids, readers will learn and remember hundreds of the most common English roots in an easy and often enjoyable way—without their being aware that what they are accomplishing would, in a conventional manner, require hard study and constant drilling.

Grow Your Vocabulary is not a dry study of roots and words, nor is it limited to classical terms. Subtle humor and charming anecdotes run throughout its pages, and in a special SUBJECTS section it provides entertaining information on words with "animals" in them, words with "colors" in them, expressions derived from baseball, and other language-related topics. For the more serious reader, it includes coverage of the terminology in professional fields, such as photography, philosophy, biology, engineering, and medicine.

But in my opinion the culmination of this work, the *pièce de résistance* that draws it all together, is A CROSS-REFERENCE DICTIONARY, a combination dictionary-index that provides intensive, supplementary coverage and page citations for every root and difficult word in this book. This dictionary-index provides all levels of semantic and etymological information that both the serious student and casual reader will enjoy and learn from. I have found myself spending hours reading and rereading different entries in this part of the book with great pleasure.

As a thoroughly cross-referenced analytical work, *Grow Your Vocabulary* will invite reading as a "browser's dictionary." Hundreds of colorful and interesting words, such as *circumterrestrial* (that which surrounds the earth), *biblioklept* (a person who steals books), *gynecocracy* (rule by or government of women), *cervicide* (the killing of a deer), and *entomophobia* (the fear of insects), are liberally scattered throughout its pages. Its wealth of cross-referencing, letter-by-letter analyses of related terms, and delightful anecdotes will lead lovers of language through an enjoyable examination of how common, learned, and obscure English words can be easily comprehended once one understands the principles of word-building.

Grow Your Vocabulary is a book I can heartily and widely recommend, whether your interests are in improving your vocabulary, learning word roots, pursuing classical studies, understanding the fundamentals of English etymology, or simply browsing through some of the more intriguing and picturesque words the English language has to offer.

PREFACE

Dissection:	1) pre- / -face
Analysis:	2) *pre-*: before; *-face*: speaking
Reconstruction:	3) speaking (*-face*) before (*pre-*)
Definition:	4) *n.* a short preliminary statement in a book or other published work setting forth its purpose and scope, especially one written by the author or editor.
Commentary:	5) A *preface*, etymologically, is a Latin-derived equivalent of the native English *foreword* (< Old English *fore-*: before + *-word*: word; see FOREWORD on page xi for more details). Actually, *preface* is a much older term and was first recorded in Geoffrey Chaucer's *Second Nun's Tale* in 1386, predating *foreword* by almost 500 years. According to Henry Fowler's original 1926 *A Dictionary of Modern English Usage*, "F[oreword] is a word invented fifty years ago as a SAXONISM by anti-latinists, [sic] & caught up as a VOGUE WORD by the people who love a new name for an old thing." Today the major differences between a Foreword and Preface are that in a work that uses both, such as this one, the Foreword always precedes the Preface, it is usually written as an endorsement by a person other than the writer or editor, and it is generally briefer.

It may come as a surprise to learn that over a million words exist in the English language when we count all of the literary, scientific, business, and other miscellaneous jargon as well as the rich resources of our own mother tongue. But what is even more surprising is that perhaps 97 percent of these words—and in particular our more learned and technical vocabulary—can be dissected, analyzed, reconstructed, and defined in precisely the manner described for *preface* above and *foreword* on page xi. In other words, English words are to a great extent conglomerations of roots, and if you are familiar with these roots or can approximate their meanings, you will be able to understand, spell, remember, and explain the construction of most complex English words—even if you have just seen them for the first time!

Sound too good to be true? Then let me ask you a few questions:

Assuming for the moment that you didn't know the meanings of *foreword* and *preface* before reading about them in this book, do you think you would now have any difficulty remembering what they mean? Do you think you could ever forget that each one contains two primary roots, which, when combined, add up to the meaning of each word? Do you further think that with a modicum of reflection you could not recall or at least approximate the sense of each of their roots? And if by chance you forget what these words mean, do you think you would be unable to "reconstruct" their etymological meanings by recombining the senses or approximate senses of their roots and in so doing jog your memory about their modern definitions?

If you've answered no to these questions, then in the few minutes it took you to read the analyses of *foreword* and *preface*, you have learned how to "dissect" these words into their constituent roots, "analyze" these roots and assign a meaning to each of them, "reconstruct" the historical or etymological meaning of these words on the basis of the combined meanings of their roots, and use this reconstructed meaning to form a foundation for learning and remembering the modern definition of those words.

And with regard to spelling, let me ask you one more question:

If you remembered the meanings of these words but forgot how to spell them, do you think that after a moment's reflection about their roots you could ever misspell *foreword* as *forward*, or *preface* as *prefface*? In other words, by realizing that there's a "word" in *foreword*, which means "a word be*fore*," and a "pre-" in *preface,* which means "speaking before," how could you possibly misspell *word* as *ward* or *pre-* as *pref-*? And even if you forgot about these roots, as soon as you began dissecting and analyzing these words again, it would all come back to you. For, after all, the information is right in front of you. All you have to do is know *how* to look at it. And that is what this book is all about.

Moreover, should you forget any other particulars about these words (or in any other words that you will later dissect and analyze), you can use the particulars you do remember to fill in the gaps of what you don't remember—and thereby bring to mind the meanings of the roots, words, and even to a large extent, as we have seen, the spellings of the words.

Take the word *retrogression*. After reading chapter GRAD-, GRESS- in the COMMON ROOTS, you will instantly be able to dissect this word into:

retro- / gress- / -ion

You will then recall that *retro-* means "back, backward," *gress-* means "to step, to walk, to go," and *-ion* means "the act, means, or result of"; and with this information, you will be able to reconstruct *retrogression* into "the act, means, or result of (*-ion*) stepping, walking, or going (*gress-*) back or backward (*retro-*)," or more simply, "the act of (*-ion*) going (*gress-*) backward (*retro-*)." And either of these reconstructions will give you an excellent approximation of the modern definition of this word and a solid foundation with which to learn and remember its meaning.

But let's say you forgot (or never knew) the meaning of the key root in this word, *gress-*, "to step, to walk, to go," and recall only the meanings of the common prefix *retro-,* "back, backward," and the even more common suffix *-ion,* "the act, means, or result of." By using the method described above and simply filling in the missing part with some appropriate verb or verbs, you can still arrive at almost the identical reconstruction of *retrogression*, namely, "the act, means, or result of going or moving backward." And once you look up *retrogression* in a college or unabridged dictionary, as you should always do after reconstructing a word, and read its etymology and definition, this will lock into your memory the roots and meanings (and often the spelling) of this word, since it will largely confirm what you yourself have already mulled over and deduced. Moreover, the dictionary definition will further provide you with the evolution or "sense development" of the word, showing how its etymological or *reconstructed meaning* has evolved into its *modern definition*.

Thus, by comparing your reconstructed meaning of *retrogression* with its modern definition, you will see how the essentially neutral reconstruction of *retrogression* as the "the act, means, or result of stepping or going backward" evolved into the generally negative modern definition of "the act, means, or result of declining or deteriorating," with its even more specialized biological definition, "the act or result of returning to a less complex or more primitive state"—as, for example, a modern human being (*Homo sapiens sapiens*) retrogressing, at least in the movies, into a Neanderthal (*Homo sapiens neanderthalensis*). We will also analyze biological nomenclature in this book.

So right at the outset I should emphasize that while the reconstructed meaning of a word will often give you a close approximation of its modern definition and serve as your foundation for learning it, it will never give you the entire picture, and you must therefore *always* confirm your reconstruction with a good dictionary.

Nevertheless, dissecting, analyzing, reconstructing, defining, and, where necessary, providing a commentary on how the etymological or reconstructed meaning of an English word evolved into its modern definition is an effective system for learning and remembering new words—even after reading them just once!

But you might argue that the three words so far discussed—*foreword*, *preface*, and *retrogression*—are too simple and not a thorough test of this system.

Very well. Then consider the following scenario:

You're a student in Biology 101 sitting in class thinking about becoming a botanist when your teacher walks in and surprises the class by holding up five specimens of flowers labeled *Helianthus microcephalus*, *Helianthus decapetalus*, *Helianthus tuberosus*, *Helianthus angustifolius*, and *Helianthus giganteus*. Short of having a superhuman memory (which, unfortunately, few of us have), how can you possibly learn and remember what these different plants are and not get their names mixed up—*ever?*

Well, after spending even a few days with *Grow your Vocabulary*, you should be able to "dissect" *Helianthus* into:

heli- / anth- / -us

Then either through prior encounters with *heli-* in this book or with a little help from your dictionary, you will be able to determine that the first root *heli-* means "sun" (as in *Helios*, the Greek god of the sun, or *heliocentric*, of or having the belief that the sun is the center of the solar system or of some other physical or spiritual realm). Similarly, you will be able to determine that the second root *anth-* means "flower" (as in *anther*, the part of a flower that bears the pollen, or *anthology*, a collection of writings by one or various authors, or what reconstructs into "the act or process of gathering flowers," since the first anthologies were collections of sensitive short poems, rendered metaphorically as "flowers of verse"). And you will instantly recognize that the third root -us is a common Latin masculine suffix without meaning. So right off the bat (see this phrase under COMMON EXPRESSIONS DERIVED FROM BASEBALL), you will know that you are dealing with five species of sunflowers.

Then, with regard to the second term, *microcephalus*, by going through the same process, you can determine that *micr-* means "small or tiny" (as in *microscope*), -o- is a "connecting vowel" without meaning, *cephal-* means "head" (as in *encephalitis*, an inflammation in [*en-*] the head—hence, an inflammation of the brain), and -us, once again, is a Latin masculine suffix without meaning. So in less time than it takes to describe this process, you can reconstruct *Helianthus microcephalus* into "the sun- (*Heli-*) -flower (*anth-*) with a small (*micr-*) head (*cephal-*)," which indeed it is, having a flower head under two inches wide.

Similarly, you can reconstruct *Helianthus decapetalus* into "the sun- (*Heli-*) -flower (*anth-*) with ten (*deca-*) petals (*petal-*); *Helianthus tuberosus* into "the sun- (*Heli-*) -flower (*anth-*) full of (*-osus*) tubers (*tuber*)"—which I might add are edible and delicious, this being the scientific name for the Jerusalem artichoke. *Helianthus angustifolius* can be reconstructed into "the sun- (*Heli-*) -flower (*anth-*) with narrow (*angust-* [not to be confused with *august-*: royal, majestic]) leaves (*foli-*)"; and *Helianthus giganteus* can be reconstructed into the sun- (*Heli-*) -flower (*anth-*) characterized by (*-eus*) [being] giant (*gigant-*)," which it most certainly is, reaching a height of over ten feet.

So by identifying and understanding the roots in these words and combining their *meanings* into a more or less coherent English sentence, you will be able to fix in your mind which species is which *the first time you encounter their names.* And this will enable you to more effectively learn, remember, spell, and distinguish among these seemingly formidable botanical terms. From this procedure you will also learn important—and often critical—distinguishing characteristics about the appearance and anatomy of these plants, making further study about these plants easier.

Similarly, if you were a nursing student in Clinical Micropathology 358 studying abnormal conditions of the blood, you would have to be able to distinguish between such terms as *hemocytometer, hemagogue, hematorrhea, hematophagia, hematomyelitis,* and *hemocytopoiesis,* to name just a few. Regarding the last and most difficult term in this group, *hemocytopoiesis* (pronounced hē′mō·sīt′ō· poi·ē′sis), after spending a week or two with this book, you would be able to dissect this word into:

hem- / -o- / cyt- / -o- / poie- / -sis

In HOW ENGLISH WORDS ARE CREATED: A SHORT COURSE and chapter A-, AN-, you will learn that the first element in this word, *hem-*, is the Anglicized base of the Greek word *haima*, which means "blood," and you will be presented with a "formula" for converting the five-letter Greek *haima* into the three-letter English *hem-*. In chapter -CRACY, you will note that the second element -o- is an extremely common "connecting vowel" generally linking two Greek-derived roots, and in this chapter alone you will observe over forty words containing -o-. In chapter CORP -, CORPUS, CORPOR-, you will learn that the third element *cyt-* means "cell," and you will be presented with four moderately difficult words that use this root, including *cytology*, the scientific study of cells, and *leukocyte*, a white blood cell. In the entry for *poet* in A CROSS-REFERENCE DICTIONARY, you will recognize that from the fourth element, *poie-*, the shortened form *poe-* is derived, which means "to make or form," and that a poet, etymologically, is "one who makes or forms." And from the entries *synthesis* and *metathesis* you will learn that the fifth and final element, *-sis*, means "the act, process, condition, or result of"; and under the separate dictionary entry *-sis*, these and four other partially related words will be brought together, with further references to the closely related medical endings *-osis* and *-iasis*.

Thus, by time you spend a relatively brief period with this book, you will have come across so many instances of the roots in *hemocytopoiesis* (and I have cited only a few of them in the above paragraph) that it would be very difficult for you *not* to be able to reconstruct this word into "the act, process, or result of (*-sis-*) making (*poie-*) blood (*hem-*) cells (*cyt-*)." And once you look up this word in a medical or unabridged dictionary, as you should do, and read its definition as "the formation and development of blood cells in the body," how—in conjunction with your reconstruction—could you possibly forget what this word means?

And what you've just done for *hemocytopoiesis* you could just as easily have done for *hemagogue*, *hematophagia*, *hematomyelitis*, and every other *hem-* word highlighted above. For the roots in every one of these words crop up time and again in *Grow Your Vocabulary*. In fact, one pleasant result of using this book is that strange and seemingly unpronounceable technical terminology will no longer scare or intimidate you. For once you know the "trick," these words turn out to be little more than a number of simple roots strung together; and the rather startling fact of the matter is that after you become accustomed to dissecting, analyzing, reconstructing, and defining words, you may very well find that you have *less* difficulty learning and remembering highly complex technical terms than non-technical college and high school words.

Moreover, you need not be an "expert" or even a good amateur to use this system or parts of it. Even the most minuscule knowledge of word roots (so long as it is not incorrect) will help you more accurately understand and remember the meanings of words you read and hear—whether these are scholarly terms or everyday words. For example, if you are knowledgeable only about prefixes you can immediately perceive the differences between such words as *abduction*, *reduction*, *deduction*, *seduction*, *induction*, *production*, *reproduction*, and *introduction* (all covered in chapter DUC -, DUCT-). And even without knowing that *duct-* means "to lead or to bring" and *-ion* means "the act, means, or result of" (roots which are defined dozens of times in this book), by being familiar with the common prefixes in the above words (prefixes which are also covered time and again in this book), you can still come up with a surprisingly accurate reconstruction of these words. And what is most amazing is that you can accomplish this on the basis of what is, for the most part, no more than two letters per word!

But if you know nothing about prefixes but have a fair knowledge of what are loosely referred to as "suffixes," you can easily figure out the differences between such words as *cosmology*, *cosmography*, *cosmogony*, *cosmosophy*, *cosmocracy*, and *cosmolatry* (the roots of which are all analyzed in this book). Even without knowing that *cosm-* means "universe," by understanding the final elements in these words (technically known as "combining forms"), you can still determine that *cosmology* is the "scientific study of [—?—]," *cosmography* is the "scientific mapping of [—?—]," *cosmogony* is the "birth or creation of [—?—]," *cosmosophy* is the "wisdom or knowledge of [—?—]," *cosmocracy* is the "rule by or government of [—?—]," and *cosmolatry* is the "worship or adoration of [—?—]." And once you look up *cosm-* in A CROSS-REFERENCE DICTIONARY (if you haven't already guessed its meaning) and plug in "the universe" in place of each of those question marks, just think of how many new and colorful words you will have learned *and will not forget*.

So after you become acquainted with a number of roots in this book, you can decide how far you want to go with them. For example, if you're just interested in learning basic English roots and could care less whether they come from Latin, Classical Greek, Old English, Sanskrit, or Inuit, the guidelines outlined in the INTRODUCTION will tell you exactly how to accomplish this. But if you want to know where each root and word comes from and learn as much as you can about it, HOW ENGLISH WORDS ARE CREATED: A SHORT COURSE and A CROSS-REFERENCE DICTIONARY will offer a comprehensive approach for achieving these objectives. Or perhaps you just want to use this book for browsing as you go on a discursive safari to the nether regions of the English lexicon in search of exotic, picturesque, beguiling, and enigmatic words and expressions. Whatever your vocabulary or etymological needs, you can probably fulfill them with *Grow Your Vocabulary*.

SYMBOLS AND ABBREVIATIONS

(Note: Dates are approximate)

+	plus
*	hypothetical; not a real word or not documented
<	(which is) derived from; from
>	yields; which yields; yielding
?	(in etys.) perhaps, possibly
abstr.	abstracted
accus.	accusative
A.D.	< L. *annō Dominī*: in the year of the Lord, i.e., after the year 1
adj.	adjective, adjectival
adjs	adjectives
adv.	adverb, adverbial
agent.	agentival
alph.	alphabet
ALT., alt.	alternative
alter.	alteration
aspir.	aspirated
assim.	assimilated, assimilation
B.C.	before Christ, i.e., before the year 1
cf.	compare
charact.	characterized
Colloq.	colloquial
comb. form	combining form
compar.	comparative
condit.	condition
conj.	conjugation
conn.	connecting
ct.	contrast (used only in prefix and suffix tables)
decl.	declension, declensional

def.	definition
defs.	definitions
denom.	denominative
Derog.	derogatory
dim.	diminutive
DISS.	dissection
E., Eng.	Modern English (1500+)
e.g.	< L. *exemplī grātiā*: for example
equiv.	equivalent
esp.	especially
ety.	etymology
etys.	etymologies
ex.	example
fem., F	feminine
Fr.	French
fr.	from
freq.	frequentative
G., Gr.	Classical Greek (800 B.C.–200 A.D.)
gen.	genitive
Ger.	German
Gmc.	Germanic
Heb.	Hebrew
i.e.	< L. *id est*: that is
infin.	infinitive
infl.	influenced
Inflect.	inflectional
Ital.	Italian
L., Lat.	Latin (80 B.C.–200 A.D.)
LG.	Late Greek (200–600)
lit.	literally
LL.	Late Latin (200–600)

masc., M	masculine	pert.	pertaining
MD.	Middle Dutch (1100–1500)	pl., Plur.	plural
ME.	Middle English (1100–1500)	Port.	Portuguese
MF.	Middle French (1350–1550)	pp.	past participle
MG.	Medieval Greek (600–1500)	ppl.	past participial
Mid	Middle	prec.	preceding (entry)
misc.	miscellaneous	prep.	preposition
ML.	Medieval Latin (600–1500)	prob.	probably
ModE.	Modern English (same as E.)	prp.	present participle
ModG.	Modern Greek (1500+)	prpl.	present participial
ModL.	Modern Latin (same as NL.)	RECON.	reconstruction
myth.	mythology, mythological	rep.	representing
n.	noun	Sax.	Saxon
neut., N	neuter	sci.	science
NG.	New Greek (1500+)	SEC.	secondary
NL.	New Latin (1500+)	sep.	separation
no.	number (in Endnotes)	sing.	singular
Nom., nomin.	nominative	Sp.	Spanish
NormFr.	Norman French (1000–1200)	specif.	specifically
obs.	obsolete	Substand.	substandard
OE.	Old English (449–1100)	suf.	suffix
OF.	Old French (800–1350)	superl.	superlative
OL.	Old Latin (before 80 B.C.)	tech.	technically
ON.	Old Norse (before 1350)	translit.	transliteration
orig.	originally	ult.	ultimately
OS.	Old Saxon (before 1100)	usu.	usually
Pass.	passive	v.	verb; volume (in Endnotes)
Perf.	perfect	var.	variant

PRONUNCIATION KEY

English Vowels and Diphthongs

Symbol	Key Words	Pronunciation
a	bat, forecast	bat, fôr´kast
ā	bay, weight	bā, wāt
ä	bar, blotch	bär, bläch
e	met, head	met, hed
ē	meet, chlorine	mēt, klôr´ēn
i	bit, lymph	bit, limf
ī	bite, sky	bīt, skī
ō	hope, beau	hōp, bō
ô	horn, walk	hôrn, wôk
o͞o	hoop, flute	ho͞op flo͞ot
o͞o	hook, push	ho͞ok, po͞osh
u	bun, love	bun, luv
û	burn, fern	bûrn, fûrn
ou	out, cow	out, kou
oi	oil, boy	oil, boi

Schwas (shwäz)—Unstressed Vowels Often With Indistinct Sounds

Unstressed Vowel	Symbol (schwa)	Key Words	Pronunciation
a	ə	global, urban	glō´bəl, ûr´bən
e	ə	current, poem	kûr´ənt, pō´əm
i	ə	happily, denim	hap´ə•lē, den´əm
o	ə	carrot, bishop	kar´ət, bish´əp
u	ə	census, famous	sen´səs, fā´məs

Selected Consonants and Consonant Clusters

Symbol	Key Words	Pronunciation
g	get, dog	get, dôg
j	jet, dodge	jet, däj
ch	cheap, future	chēp, fyo͞o´chər
ng	long, singer	lông, sing´ər
sh (unvoiced)	ship, machine	ship, mə•shēn´
zh (voiced)	fusion, pleasure	fyo͞o´zhən, plezh´ər
th (unvoiced)	thin, ether	thin, ē´thər
th (voiced)	them, either	*th*em, ē´*th*ər

Latin and Greek Sounds Not Present in English Words

Language and Sound Approximations	Symbol	Key Words	Pronunciation
L. and G. *a* (articulate the *a* in E. *bola*)	ȧ	L. malus (bad)	mȧ´lo͝os
G. *ch* (aspirate the *ch* as in E. *chaos* or *loch*)	kh	G. cholē (bile)	khô•lā´
G. *y* (round lips for o͞o and pronounce ē)	ü	G. hydōr (water)	hü´dōr
G. *eu* (say e + o͞o in quick succession)	eo͞o	G. neuron (tendon)	neo͞o´rôn

For a detailed description of Latin and Greek pronunciation, see pages 175-79 and 229-34, respectively.

Syllabic Consonants

A syllabic consonant is a syllable pronounced with little or no perceptible vowel sound. In English words, these usually involve an *l, n,* or *m* and are designated as syllabic consonants by the presence of an apostrophe preceding them.

Symbol	Key Words	Pronunciation
'	beetle, cotton	bēt´'l, kät´'n

English Accentuation

Stress	Symbol	Key Words	Pronunciation
Primary	´	biscuit	bis´kit
Secondary	ˏ	benediction	ben´ə•dik´shən

Notes: 1) Every word of two or more syllables must have at least one primary accent. Words cannot have a secondary accent without a primary accent.
2) The alphabetical symbols in this pronunciation key always appear in roman typeface and when discussed in the text are enclosed in quotation marks.

INTRODUCTION

Dissection: 1) intro- / duct-/ -ion

Analysis: 2) *intro-*: in, into, within; *duct-*: to lead, to bring; *-ion*: the act, means, or
                       result of.

Reconstruction: 3) the act or result of (*-ion*) leading or bringing (*duct-*) into (*into-*).

Definition: 4) *n.* the preliminary part of a book or other work that generally defines and
                       explains the subject matter and thus serves as a guide to the main part of
                       the work.

Commentary: 5) An *introduction*, as the guide to a book or other work, "leads" or
                       "brings" one "into" the heart of the work and is therefore an essential
                       part. Unlike a Foreword or Preface, which also comes before the main
                       part of the work (both *fore-* and *pre-* mean "before") but functions to
                       prepare the reader to understand the work, the Introduction provides that
                       understanding and cannot be dispensed with without markedly affecting
                       the quality of the work.

Grow Your Vocabulary is a thoroughly cross-referenced language work containing approximately
850 roots of English words with an average of five to six derivative English words per root—resulting
in a vocabulary of over 4,500 entries.

This book is written for many different readers with a variety of goals and objectives. Whether
you're a high school or college student, a business professional, a scientist, or just a person who loves
words or word origins, this book can teach you the fundamentals of English etymology and enable you
to quickly and efficiently dissect, analyze, reconstruct, define, and, when necessary, provide commentaries for learned (lûr´nid; scholarly; erudite) and technical words. And in the process you will dramati-
cally increase your awareness of and confidence with words—and expand your vocabulary at an
unprecedented rate.

But to ensure that you not only learn these fundamentals but remember the details, this book is formatted into seven complementary parts (the five parts listed on page 3 plus the PREFACE and this
INTRODUCTION) in which, among other things, the same roots appear over and over again in different
contexts and in different words. So by merely reading this material you will, in effect, be reviewing it
and thereby learning without studying.

In fact, as a result of what I call "strategic redundancy," if you have spent even five minutes leafing
through this book, you already know this "system" for learning and remembering words, and now it is

1

just a matter of putting this knowledge into practice, fine tuning it, and seeing how far you want to go with it.

Specifically, this material is written and organized to serve six categories of readers, each coming from a different background and seeking various kinds and levels of information. These readers include:

1) high school and college students and other individuals seeking to improve their vocabularies and/or taking vocabulary-building courses.

2) educated adults seeking to understand the common roots that compose our vocabulary and how English words are constructed from an amalgamation of these roots.

3) educated adults seeking to understand the fundamentals of English etymology and how words change over time.

4) students and teachers of Latin and Greek and particularly of those courses emphasizing the classical components of English words.

5) students and professionals in a variety of fields and specialties, particularly medicine, biology, linguistics, writing, and the teaching of English.

6) browsers of difficult words and word lovers of all sorts—those persons fascinated by the rich and colorful vocabulary at the outer limits of the English lexicon.

Grow Your Vocabulary is intended for all of these audiences and is provided with many visual and discriminating features so that each of you can easily derive from this book exactly what you want without having to read or even skim material irrelevant to your needs.

With regard to your word-hoard (an Old English term for one's store or supply of words; hence, one's vocabulary), I have carefully selected every vocabulary entry in this book to approximate the reading level or desired reading level of one of three basic groups: high school students, college students, and postgraduate students or word lovers with a sophisticated interest in and knowledge of words. Specifically, of all the words and expressions discussed in this work, approximately 35 percent are essentially high school-level words, 45 percent are college- and graduate-level words, and 20 percent are highly technical, postgraduate-level words or what are more commonly referred to as "difficult" words—words that may be unfamiliar to even the most educated readers.

I have included difficult words for two reasons. The first—a major objective of this work—is to demonstrate how complex words are formed by the amalgamation of short elements which, in themselves, are not "difficult" elements but rather segments of "everyday" English, Latin, Greek, or other foreign words. This is repeatedly illustrated by showing you, as I have already done with *Helianthus microcephalus* and *hemocytopoiesis* in the PREFACE, that even the most intimidating words, when approached with the strategy of deciphering their constituent elements, become surprisingly easy for native speakers of English to understand and remember. The second reason is that many of these terms are colorful and entertaining words, for growing your vocabulary need not be a dry-as-dust proposition.

With regard to the coverage of the vocabulary entries, I have fully dissected, analyzed, reconstructed, and defined approximately 1,200 words; another 3,000 I have succinctly defined within parentheses and have at times partly or fully analyzed; and the remainder I have provided with partial analyses of selected roots, which can be found primarily in the HELPFUL HINTS.

In short, I have chosen a broad assortment of words to meet the particular needs of the six categories of readers described above; and if you, as part of one or more of these categories, focus upon the *principles* of vocabulary-building in conjunction with the particular roots and words that you seek, you will amaze yourself at how much you can learn and retain.

ORGANIZATION OF THE TEXT

This book is divided into five principal parts, each of which complements and supplements the others. These are:

Part I: COMMON ROOTS

Part II: HELPFUL HINTS

PART III: SUBJECTS

Part IV: HOW ENGLISH WORDS ARE CREATED: A SHORT COURSE

Part V: A CROSS-REFERENCE DICTIONARY

Part I: COMMON ROOTS consists of 18 chapters, which provide in-depth coverage of 36 common roots and describes, in detail, the dissection, analysis, reconstruction, definition, and commentary processes, followed by 24 exercise entries for each root or related roots.

Part II: HELPFUL HINTS is a partial answer key for the exercises in the COMMON ROOTS and provides the meaning and etymology of one root per exercise word.

PART III: SUBJECTS consists of three categories of specialized words and phrases, which are further divided into 36 subjects, each of which, through an illustrative example and a wide selection of exercise entries, provides additional practice in dissecting, analyzing, reconstructing, defining, and providing commentaries for English words.

Part IV: HOW ENGLISH WORDS ARE CREATED: A SHORT COURSE is a simplified, step-by-step presentation, which includes a large assortment of easy-to-understand charts and tables and illustrates how English words are constructed from native, Latin-, and Greek-derived roots to which prefixes, suffixes, and other roots are affixed in accordance with precise linguistic rules. This part serves both as a self-contained course in English etymology and as an explanation of the more technical Latin and Greek data presented in A CROSS-REFERENCE DICTIONARY and in the Technical Information and Detailed Example sections of the COMMON ROOTS.

Part V: A CROSS-REFERENCE DICTIONARY is a combination dictionary-index, which provides follow-up coverage and page references for thousands of words and roots discussed in this book. This Dictionary serves as both a reiteration and extension of the material presented throughout this book, and when used in conjunction with Part I: HOW ENGLISH WORDS ARE CREATED: A SHORT COURSE becomes a self-teaching primer for the study and application of English etymology.

Part I: Common Roots

The purpose of this part is to introduce you to 36 of our more common roots and to give you practice in dissecting, analyzing, reconstructing, defining, and, when necessary, providing commentaries for common and not-so-common English words.

In this part, I provide 18 chapters in which I thoroughly examine one to five roots per chapter on several levels of sophistication and provide at least 25 derivative English words for each root or root group, followed by three columns of exercises. Then after providing the definitions and etymologies for each of these "primary" or "chapter" roots, I gradually introduce and define 10 to 20 "secondary" roots and cross-refer these to more complex entries in A CROSS-REFERENCE DICTIONARY, which, in turn, often lead to other cross references. So within these 18 chapters, approximately 300 primary and secondary roots are cited and defined, almost all of which receive supplemental coverage in A CROSS-REFERENCE DICTIONARY. Thus, from the very first page of the COMMON ROOTS the cross-reference nature of this work becomes evident; but as you will see throughout this book, you always have a choice as to how many cross references you may wish to pursue and to what extent you may wish to pursue them.

Since this book assumes you have no prior knowledge of roots and etymology, I have purposely avoided an alphabetical listing of chapters and have instead arranged them in groupings that begin with those that are least complex and end with those that are most complex. The first group comprises eight chapters, each of which contains one relatively simple English root derived from a single form of a Latin or Greek word, and I therefore call this group "One-Root Derivatives." The second group comprises six somewhat more complex chapters that each contain two closely related English roots derived from two forms of a Latin or Greek word, and I call this group "Two-Root Derivatives." And the third group comprises four relatively complex chapters that each contain three to five closely related roots derived from a like number of forms of a Latin or Greek word, and I call this group "Three-Or-More-Root Derivatives." In each of these three categories, I present the roots alphabetically.

Within each chapter are six sections of information in which the primary roots are clearly highlighted and carefully analyzed from six different perspectives while the secondary roots are gradually and more subtly introduced throughout the chapter. These six sections are:

Section One: Roots and Definitions

Section Two: Memory Aid

Section Three: Technical Information

Section Four: Detailed Example

Section Five: Brief Analyses

Section Six: Exercises

Section One: Roots and Definitions

On the top of the first page of each chapter, one to five English roots are highlighted in boldface type with their definitions alongside.

When more than one root appears, they must meet the following criteria:

1) each root must be derived from the same classical or nonclassical word or different tense of that word.

2) each root must have the same or nearly the same English meaning.

While the Latin and Greek origins of these roots will only become apparent after you read the Technical Information section or the Analysis subsection of the Detailed Example (see pages 7-9), this classification of English roots is important in helping you to learn and remember the roots and for demonstrating that English roots are often derived unchanged or virtually unchanged from Latin and Greek bases.

Section Two: Memory Aid

Based on modern research in mnemonics (ni·män´iks; the art of improving the memory through word associations, formulas, visualization, rhyme schemes, and other techniques), the Memory Aid is designed—through a descriptive and often bizarre example—to fix in your mind both the spellings and definitions of each highlighted root and to serve as an introduction to each group of roots. For example, in chapter -AGOG-, you'll find the Memory Aid, as in all other chapters, immediately below the chapter root or roots and its definitions:

-agog- leader, leading, bringing

Memory Aid   Envision a *demagogue*, an unscrupulous, rabble-rousing leader of the people (see *dema-gogue* under BRIEF ANALYSES), leading a mob of yelling and jeering townspeople down Main Street and bringing them to the town square while inciting them with lies, half-truths, and inflammatory appeals.

In this Memory Aid, you'll notice that *demagogue* is in italics and the *agog* within it is underlined. The italics identify which word contains the chapter root, and the underlined letters within that word constitute that root. You'll also notice that leader, leading, and bringing are also underlined but are in roman type. This informs you that these words constitute the definition of the underlined italicized root. Thus, the underlined roots and words above can be translated into the sentence: "-*agog*- means 'leader, leading, bringing.'"

This, of course, is merely a recapitulation (a restatement or brief summary) of the chapter heading and definitions but is important in that it serves as your first review of this information and thus the first step in helping you learn and remember the roots.

The value of the Memory Aid, however, goes far beyond merely recapitulating words: it is designed to help you create a visual picture which has a vividness and detail approaching that of an actual experience. Human beings are by nature visual creatures. Bloodhounds, by contrast, are olfactory (äl·fak′tə·rē; of or pertaining to the sense of smell) animals. People are always impressed with how bloodhounds can track down a person through dense woods after a mere sniff of something that person was wearing. But what people don't generally realize is that we are just as impressive in our visual memory. If, for example, in witnessing a crime, an average person can get a clear glance of the perpetrator's face, six months later that person can normally pick out the perpetrator in a crowd of 100,000. I'd say that's as impressive as anything a bloodhound can do.

So to gain the most from these Memory Aids you must make a movie out of these stories. Don't just read them intellectually. Actually see the story happening, and use your own memories and experiences to embellish and exaggerate your picture. But above all, always make these pictures as bizarre and ridiculous as you can, for this will increase the likelihood that you will remember them and not confuse them with something similar. And if they make you cringe or shudder, all the better. This will further ensure that you do not forget them, and in the science of mnemonics shock value is actually a desirable and sought-after commodity (normally, an article of trade or commerce, but in this context, anything of value that can be turned to advantage). For example, if you've ever been in a car for hours in stop-and-go traffic, do you remember what any particular red light looked like? But if one of those red lights was fifty times its normal size and had caterpillars crawling all over it and red dye squirting out from the center and splattering all over your windshield, do you think you would ever forget it?

Thus, in the Memory Aid for Chapter -AGOG-, you should first of all try to picture a small town that you have actually visited or seen or that fits in with some stereotype for such a town—and then grossly exaggerate whatever features about it make it stand out for you, such as an old building, a vacant lot, Main Street, or the town church. Then perhaps imagine the *demagogue* as being ten (or even fifty) feet tall and wearing the most horrendous or ridiculous outfit, such as a suit of armor or loincloth, while looking down upon his yelling and jeering followers, whom you might further fancy turning into giant ants. And to tie in this picture with the other words in the Memory Aid, you might further "see" this *demagogue*-leader in the act of leading or bringing these half-human ant creatures to the "town square" by wrapping some kind of rope or net around them and dragging them on the ground "while inciting them with lies, half-truths, and inflammatory appeals."—Or if these images don't sit well with you, try some others, i.e., write another script.

Whatever your images, after you put them all together and create your movie, take out another thirty seconds, close your eyes if you can bring yourself to do so (this will be extremely helpful), and actually see these events occurring before your eyes; and as you view them, repeat to yourself some sentence or phrase with the key word and its definition, such as "The *demagogue*-leader is leading and bringing his people to town"—and see the whole scene playing out before you. Then in the future, if you ever forget the meaning of -agog-, all you have to do is try to think of a word containing -agog- and that will immediately bring to mind *demagogue*, and this will remind you of your movie, and you will again "see" the *demagogue*-leader in the act of leading and bringing those ant-people to the town square—and this will bring to mind your mnemonic sentence, "The *demagogue*-leader is leading and bringing his people to town." And even if there are gaps in your movie and sentence, you will still *feel* the meanings of -agog-, and this will enable you to provide a relatively accurate definition for it.

Section Three: Technical Information

The Technical Information is the next section after the Memory Aid, which is clearly identified and separated from the preceding and following sections.

Working in conjunction with the Memory Aid to optimize understanding and retention of the primary roots, the Technical Information describes how our seemingly arbitrary grouping of English letters called "roots" are derived from Latin, Greek, or other foreign words; and this knowledge reinforces the spelling and meanings of those English roots.

In addition, citations within the Technical Information direct your attention to semantically-related or potentially confusable words and bases from classical and nonclassical languages, and these are followed by a variety of English derivative from these languages. This achieves the dual objective of clarifying the spelling and meanings of the primary roots while expanding your knowledge in other directions. The Technical Information in chapter GRAD-, GRESS-, as a typical example, appears as follows:

Technical Information	***grad-*** is the base of the Latin verb *gradī* (grȧ´dē), "to step, to walk, to go." ***gress-*** is the base of Latin *gressus* (gres´sŏŏs), which is the past participle of *gradī*. A similar though unrelated Latin word also meaning "to walk" (or "to travel" but definitely not "to step") is *ambulāre* (ȧm·bŏŏ·lä´re), from which we derive such English words as *ambulance*, *ambulatory*, *somnambulism*, and *circumambulation*. And a Greek word meaning "to walk" is *patein* (pä·tān´), from which we derive only one common English derivative, *peripatetic*, a close synonym for the Latin-derived *itinerant*.

In the Technical Information, each primary root is always in *boldface italics*, and the definition of that root—about five to ten words after the first boldface root—is always within *quotation marks*. Thus, in the above example, if you look at the boldface root ***grad-*** and let your eyes wander to the quoted definition, "to step, to walk, to go," you will get a capsule view of ***grad-*** and its definition without having to read its Latin derivation in between. Furthermore, in those chapters that have two or more primary roots, the second root frequently appears immediately following these quotations and has the same meaning as the first root. In this example, ***gress-*** appears right after "to step, to walk, to go," which therefore also defines it, and ***gress-*** is accordingly presented as a synonym of ***grad-***, at least as far as English is concerned. In this manner, the definition within the first set of quotations consistently comes between the first and second boldface roots and applies to both of them. Again, if you wish to make the English roots and their definitions stand out from the etymology separating them, you can take your red pen or highlighter and circle or mark each boldface root and do the same for its definition in quotes.

Following this initial presentation of English roots, etymologies, and meanings, supplementary and often complex lexical (of or pertaining to the words or vocabulary of a language) and etymological information are provided. In this example, after the Latin words *gradī* and *gressus* are cited, they are compared with two other Latin and Greek words having similar meanings, which in turn are followed by six English derivative words from these Latin and Greek words—words you may look up in A CROSS-REFERENCE DICTIONARY if you want to learn their meanings and etymologies.

Here again, you can choose to what depth you want to go into this information, and for those of you who seek only basic vocabulary enrichment and consider the Technical Information too detailed or extraneous to your needs, I have formatted and isolated it in such a way that it can easily be skipped. Nevertheless, for the purpose of underscoring the meanings of the English roots presented in the Memory Aid and reiterated in the following three sections, I strongly suggest that you review this section at least once, and teachers using this work in classroom settings are urged to direct their students to do so.

Section Four: Detailed Example

The step-by-step analysis of one highlighted English word following the Technical Information is the heart of each chapter. In this section, a relatively common, multisyllabic English word is highlighted and provided with a pronunciation. Then, through our five-step process of Dissection, Analysis, Reconstruction, Definition, and Commentary, the word is dissected into its component parts, each part is analyzed and defined, the parts are then reconstructed into an "etymological meaning," and the word is defined and provided with a commentary either linking its etymological meaning with its modern definition or otherwise describing some entertaining and educational feature connected with this word. Consider, as a typical example, the Detailed Example of *pedagogue* in chapter -AGOG-.

DETAILED EXAMPLE

pedagogue (ped´ə·gäg´)

Dissection:	1) ped- / -agog- / -ue
Analysis:	2) **ped-** is derived from Greek *paidos* (pī·dôs´), which is the genitive of *pais* (pīs), "boy, child." **-agog-** is the base of Greek *-agōgos* (à·gō·gôs´), "leader, leading, bringing," which is derived from the Greek verb *agein* (à´gān), 'to drive, to lead.' **-ue** is a French "silent final ending." <u>Note</u>: Greek *paidos* becomes English *ped-* in the following manner: First, the *-os* of *paidos* drops off, leaving the base *paid-*. Then, in Latin, the Greek diphthong *-ai-* becomes *-ae-*, converting Greek *paid-* into Latin *paed-*. Finally, in English, the *-ae-* diphthong is reduced to *-e-*, yielding our simplified root *ped-*. (For further information, see PED-[1], PED-[2], and PED-[3] in the A CROSS-REFERENCE DICTIONARY.)
Reconstruction:	3) a leader (*-agog-*) of children (*ped-*); OR child (*ped-*) leader (*-agog-*).
Definition:	4) *n.* 1. a schoolteacher, particularly one who is old-fashioned, narrow-minded, and a stickler for rules and regulations. 2. any narrow-minded, pedantic instructor.
Commentary:	5) In ancient Greece, a *paidagōgos* (pī·dà·gō·gôs´) was a family slave who escorted (i.e., led, brought) little boys to and from school (little girls were not educated in those days). In some households, however, if the slave were himself properly educated, he also became a tutor or teacher for the boys of the family—expanding the meaning of *paidagōgos*. Moreover, as children of bygone times knew painfully well, teachers were often uncompromisingly strict and not infrequently a bit stuffy—hence, the pejorative connotations of *pedagogue*.

All Detailed Examples consist of five subsections or "steps":

Step 1: <u>Dissection</u> Through the use of slashes and hyphens, the highlighted word is separated into its constituent elements, which largely consist of prefixes, suffixes, bases, connecting vowels, combining forms, and silent endings (terms which are all defined in HOW ENGLISH WORDS ARE CREATED: A SHORT COURSE). In the example above, *ped-* is the first element (which is a base), *-agog-* is the second element (which is a combining form), and *-ue* is the final element (which is a silent ending). Through this dissection, you obtain a clear and isolated view of each element in the word, preparing you for the next task at hand: the *analysis* or defining of those elements.

Step 2: <u>Analysis</u> Once isolated, each English root is highlighted in *boldface italics* and defined within *quotation marks*, and the classical and nonclassical words and elements from which it derives are provided in *lightface italics*. Thus, in the example above if you're only interested in the English roots and their meanings, read ***ped-*** and look ahead to the first quotation, "boy, child"; then read ***-agog-*** and look ahead to the next quotation, "leader, leading, bringing"; and, finally, read ***-ue*** and note the final quotation, "silent ending." And, as in the Technical Information section, if you want this information to stand out, circle or highlight each boldface root and then do the same for its definition in quotes.

But if you are not content with just learning the English roots and their definitions and want to know where these roots derive from, read the information between each boldface italic root and its definition in quotation marks; and if you want to go even deeper into the origin of these and other English roots and words, read the supplementary information following the discussion of these roots. In this particular entry, this information begins after the cue, "<u>Note</u>" and ends with a directive to see PED-[1], PED-[2], and PED-[3] in A CROSS-REFERENCE DICTIONARY.

Step 3: <u>Reconstruction</u> The English roots that have been isolated in the Dissection and defined in the Analysis are now reassembled with their definitions (though not necessarily in their original order) to form a more-or-less coherent English sentence that illuminates the "etymological meaning" of the word and forms the foundation for its modern definition. Specifically, each root that appeared in boldface italics in the Analysis now appears in lightface italics in the Reconstruction *following* the definition of that root. In the example above, I have offered two slightly different reconstructions separated by a semicolon and "OR" to further illustrate that reconstruction is not an exact science and you usually have a certain degree of flexibility in how you reconstruct the roots and meanings in words.

Step 4: <u>Definition</u> The definition of the word is now provided to give you a clear understanding of the word and to illustrate how the modern definition is an outgrowth and refinement of the reconstructed meaning. This definition will enrich your vocabulary while simultaneously reinforcing the meanings of those roots that compose the reconstructed definition. And these roots will, in turn, help "lock in" the modern definition of the word.

Please note, however, that when defining a word it is important to phrase the definition in terms of that word's part of speech. Thus, *pedagogue*, which is a noun (note the abbreviation "*n.*" in the above example) must be defined as a noun, e.g. "a narrow-minded school-teacher," whereas *pedagogic*, an adjective, must be defined as an adjective, e.g., "of or pertaining to a narrow-minded schoolteacher." Much will be said about constructing adjective-, noun-, and verb-forming suffixes in HOW ENGLISH WORDS ARE CREATED: A SHORT COURSE.

Step 5: <u>Commentary</u> When the evolution of the reconstructed meaning of a word into its modern definition is not immediately evident, this "sense development" will be elaborated in the Commentary. Otherwise, some interesting (and often entertaining) aspect of word lore, etymology, or historical misinformation that directly affects the roots in question will be discussed. In the example above, it is not immediately clear why or how a "leader of children" (the reconstructed meaning) evolved into "any narrow-minded, pedantic instructor" (the CONNOTATION of the modern definition). So the Commentary traces the sense development of this word and elucidates this connection. But it goes even further, explaining that a pedagogue, who in ancient Greece was *paidagōgos*, was originally a family slave who later became, in certain households, the family tutor, and that tutors or teachers in those days "were often uncompromisingly strict and not infrequently a bit stuffy"—the sense which led to and underlies our modern connotation of *pedagogue*.

Section Five: Brief Analyses

This section is, to a large degree, a simplified version of the Detailed Example and reinforces the meanings of the primary roots in each chapter and helps make this system of word analysis easier to apply to new words. In this section, three to seven progressively more difficult words are dissected, analyzed, reconstructed, defined, and, where necessary, provided with a commentary—using the same numbering system as that of the Detailed Example.

Moreover, in addition to providing more advanced vocabulary study and reinforcing the meanings of the primary roots, this section introduces ten to twenty secondary English roots and provides cross references to a variety of English words derived from these roots—roots that are frequently and strategically repeated, with other illustrations of English words, throughout this book. A typical Brief Analyses is *cardialgia*, which appears in chapter CARDI-:

---

cardialgia 1) cardi-/alg-/-ia
(kär´dē·al´jē·ə, -jə) 2) *cardi-*: heart; *alg-*: pain (cf. NOST<u>ALG</u>IC); *-ia*: the state, condition, or result of (cf. ANEM<u>IA</u>).
3) the condition of (*-ia*) pain (*alg-*) in the heart (*cardi-*).
4) *n.* 1. a burning sensation beneath the midline of the chest, resulting from an upflow of acidic contents from the stomach into the esophagus; heartburn.
2. any pain in or near the heart.
5) *cardialgia*, while generally having nothing to do with the heart, is often perceived as a pain or discomfort in the heart.

Although the words *Dissection*, *Analysis*, *Reconstruction*, *Definition*, and *Commentary* never appear in the Brief Analyses, a glance at the Detailed Example will confirm that the format and numbering system are the same. The major differences between the Detailed Example and the Brief Analyses are that, besides being longer, the Analysis or second step of the Detailed Example provides the origins of the roots whereas the second step of the Brief Analyses does not. However, if you want to know where the roots in the Brief Analyses derive from, you need only look them up in A CROSS-REFERENCE DICTIONARY, which will divulge their full origin and direct you to any additional information. Moreover, the Brief Analyses provides one feature not included in the Detailed Example: after each secondary root it furnishes, in parentheses, a small capitalized English word derived from that root, with the letters of the root underlined for easy identification; and if you want to know the meaning and origin of that word or its underlined root, you can look it up in A CROSS-REFERENCE DICTIONARY as well.

Thus, in step 2 above, if you wish to know where the second root *alg-* comes from, you can consult A CROSS-REFERENCE DICTIONARY, where you will learn its language of origin, its full form in that language, and its original meaning. And if you want to know the definition and etymology of NOST<u>ALG</u>IC, which is derived in part from *alg-*, you can look up that word, too. (The first root *cardi-* is not cross-referenced to another word because it is the primary chapter root, and over thirty words and phrases derived from it can be found throughout the chapter.)

In some chapters, it sometimes happens that the same secondary root appears in more than one Brief Analyses entry. For example, in chapter LOQU-, LOCUT-, one Brief Analyses entry is *soliloquy* and another is *somniloquy*. Both of these words end in *-y*, and both *-y*'s are derived from the same Latin root. However, in citing a small capital English derivative for each of these roots in their respective entries, I use different words. In the entry of *soliloquy* I include EULOG<u>Y</u>, and in the entry or *somniloquy* I include AGON<u>Y</u>. While this may appear on the surface a tad (a small amount or trifle—perhaps a shortening of *tadpole*) confusing, it underscores one of the basic premises of this book: that the same roots turn up over and over again in different words.

Section Six: Exercises

The Exercises are the last in the six sections of information presented in each chapter. They are designed to help you focus on, understand, and remember the spellings and meanings of the primary roots as well as numerous other roots introduced throughout this book. Or put another way, the principles of word-building described in HOW ENGLISH WORDS ARE CREATED: A SHORT COURSE and exemplified in the first five sections of each chapter can now be actualized in a practical study.

The Exercises consist of three columns of eight words, each column presenting a substantially more difficult grouping of words. The left column includes words essentially on a high school level, the center column on a college and graduate level, and the right column on a highly technical and esoteric level—our "difficult" words. Again, the words in the third column are provided for their highly unusual and frequently entertaining meanings and to demonstrate that even the most obscure and complex words in the English language—words you may never encounter in normal reading—can just as easily be dissected, analyzed, reconstructed, and defined as the simpler words in the first two columns.

To do the Exercises, you are asked to "DISSECT, ANALYZE, RECONSTRUCT, DEFINE, and provide a COMMENTARY for three words in each column and [to] try to use each in an intelligent sentence." Thus, the Exercises complement the material presented in the other five sections by engaging your active participation in the process of word-building, and they are therefore extremely important to do.

But let's be honest. Unless you're in a school setting, most of you are not going to do them. So let me offer three alternatives:

1) Simply read through the exercises, but as you do, try to make an educated guess or approximation as to what each root and word means. Then after you've gone through, say, two to four words, turn to the HELPFUL HINTS following the common roots and check your approximations with that partial answer key.

2) Again, simply read through the exercises, but this time, as you consider each word, take a pencil or pen (I use an erasable red pen for this sort of thing) and "slash" each word between what you think are its different roots. Thus, you will give a two-root word one slash, a three-root word two slashes, a four-root word three slashes, and so on. Then, as in the first alternative, proceed to make an educated guess or approximation as to what each root and word means. And, finally, when you finish all the exercises, check your work with the HELPFUL HINTS and make any corrections by erasing your incorrect slashes, drawing in the correct ones, and repeating to yourself the meanings of those roots you have missed. If you do this little bit, you'll be amazed at how fast you learn these roots and master this system.

3) But if you still don't have the time or inclination to pursue the above alternatives, at least turn to the HELPFUL HINTS and read through this partial answer key. This will reinforce in your mind the form and meanings of the primary chapter roots and any other roots you may be partially familiar with, and it will teach you a number of new and interesting roots.

Part II: Helpful Hints

The HELPFUL HINTS works in conjunction with the COMMON ROOTS to help you learn and remember at least 24 "new" roots per unit, and it reinforces your knowledge of those roots you have previously encountered.

Specifically, the HELPFUL HINTS is a partial answer key to the Exercises provided at the end of each chapter in the COMMON ROOTS. The Hints identify and define one potentially difficult root per exercise and thereby help you through the Dissection and Analysis part of each exercise. After consulting the HELPFUL HINTS, you will then know at least two roots per exercise entry: the chapter root and the HELPFUL HINTS root. But any additional roots you are unfamiliar with you will have to look up in a college or unabridged dictionary. Thus, the HELPFUL HINTS will guide you over the more difficult hurdles in the Exercises and save you time in completing them, but it will not "give away" the answers. You will still have to do much of the work yourself.

For teachers who wish to assign the Exercises to classes, the Hints will not nullify the value of this endeavor. On the contrary, they will motivate students by giving them a head start and making the Exercises less imposing. But the students will still have to dissect, analyze, reconstruct, define, and provide commentaries for the Exercises. And just writing down these five steps will be a valuable learning experience. Moreover, many of the entries, particularly those in the third column, will open up new vistas of erudite roots and related words that should interest if not delight all but the most intellectually inert students.

Through the use of boldface type, italics, large and small parentheses, and underscoring, the Hints reveal both the English roots and their meanings, and the classical and nonclassical roots and words from which these roots derive. However, because of space limitations this information is highly compressed, and until you become familiar with the organization and structure of the Hints, they may be confusing. A typical HELPFUL HINTS entry reads as follows:

circum**nat**ant

< L. *nat(āre)*: to swim, float.

The exercise word always appears on the top line, and the boldface letters within it identify the English root that will be examined. The second line provides the etymology of that root. In the example above, circum**nat**ant is the exercise word, **nat** is the English root, and "< L. *nat(āre)*: to swim, float" is the etymology of **nat**, which is more properly recorded as *nat-*.

Whenever small parentheses appear in an etymology, they embrace the extraneous letters not found in the English root and thereby expose what is generally the "base" of that foreign word, which lies outside the parentheses. Thus, this Hint could be verbalized: "The '**n-a-t**' in circum**nat**ant is derived from Latin *nat-*, which is the base of *natāre*, which means 'to swim or float.'"

A slightly more complicated Hint would be:

circum**vent**

< L. *vent(us)* (*venīre*): to come.

When large parentheses appear around the second word of an etymology preceded by small parentheses in the first word, they generally embrace the infinitive or nominative of the first word, which is, respectively, the past participle or genitive of the second word. (If this seems hopelessly confusing to you, see HOW ENGLISH WORDS ARE CREATED: A SHORT COURSE for the definitions of these terms and a step-by-step explanation of their relationships.) Thus, this Hint could be verbalized: "The '**v-e-n-t**' in circum**vent** is derived from Latin *vent-*, which is the base of *ventus*, which is the past participle of *venīre*, which means 'to come.'"

Similarly, consider:

cardio**my**opathy

< G. *my(os)* (*mys*): mouse, <u>muscle</u>.

The only new feature introduced in this Hint is the underlining of <u>muscle</u>. Where the definition of a root has two or more meanings that are seemingly unrelated, I have underlined that meaning which pertains to the exercise word above. Thus, this Hint could be verbalized: "The '**m-y**' in cardio**my**opathy is derived from Classical Greek *my-*, which is the base of *myos*, which is the genitive of *mys*, which, in this context, means 'muscle.'"

Further, consider:

infanticide

< L. *fant(is)* (*fāns*) (*fārī*): to speak.

The etymology in this Hint is, in a sense, an extension of the previous Hint and could be verbalized: "The '**f-a-n-t**' in **infant**icide is derived from Latin *fant-*, which is the base of *fantis*, which is the genitive of *fāns*, which is the present participle of *fārī*, which means 'to speak.'"

Finally, consider:

aggradation

< L. *ag-* (*ad-*): to, toward.

In some Hints, a root and hyphen is followed by another root and hyphen within parentheses. This generally identifies both roots as being prefixes in which the first root is a variant or assimilated form of the second root. Thus, this Hint could be verbalized: "The '**a-g**' in **ag**gradation is derived from Latin *ag-*, which is an assimilated form of *ad-*, which means 'to or toward.'" But how do you know whether the first root is a variant or assimilated form of the second root? If you look to the exercise word above and note that it doubles the last letter of the first root, this tells you that that root is an assimilated prefix. But please note: if the second root on the second line (the one in parentheses) does not have a hyphen, then neither that root nor the one preceding it is a prefix, and the first root (still on the second line) can simply be stated to be the base of the second root. See "**hydr**opericarditis," the second to the last Hint in the HELPFUL HINTS for chapter CARDI-, for an example of this.

Finally, in some Hints you may observe brackets rather than parentheses in the etymologies. Brackets are used to embrace supplementary information closely related to but not actually part of the etymology of a given word. For example, if an English root is derived from the infinitive of a Latin verb (which is part of its etymology) but the past participle of that verb (which is not part of its etymology) is a much more common contributor to English words, I sometimes place that past participle in brackets to call your attention to this fact.

Part III: Subjects

In this Part, 36 SUBJECTS are presented to give you a glimpse of some of the specialized terminology and colorful words and expressions in the English language and to provide additional practice in dissecting, analyzing, reconstructing, defining, and providing commentaries for English words. These SUBJECTS are classified into three categories:

1) <u>Professional Words</u>, including words from such fields as biology, architecture, engineering, astronomy, law, philosophy, and medicine.

2) <u>Specialty Words and Phrases</u>, including words and phrases that have unusual etymologies, e.g., acronyms (words formed from the first or first few letters of two or more words), toponyms (words derived from place-names), proprietary terms (trademarks that have become words), words derived from classical mythology, words and phrases derived from the Bible, etc.

3) <u>Picturesque Words and Expressions</u>, including words with "colors" in them, words with "animals" in them, ninety-nine phobias, sixty-six manias, colorful expressions in the English language, common expressions derived from baseball, etc.

Within these three categories, each unit, which generally consists of one page, includes three sections of information:

1) Instructions modeled on the Dissection, Analysis, Reconstruction, Definition, and Commentary format of the Brief Analyses section of the COMMON ROOTS, but in some cases notably departing from this.

2) an Example of one subject word, illustrating how to work through the exercise entries.

3) 16-40 exercise entries.

The Instructions and exercise entries are self-explanatory. Within the Example, however—as within the Brief Analyses and other sections of the COMMON ROOTS—all italic roots not provided with etymologies are furnished with them (or with a reference as to where to find them) in A CROSS-REFERENCE DICTIONARY. And within the SUBJECTS as a whole, all exercise entries, subject headings, and highlighted words also appear in A CROSS-REFERENCE DICTIONARY.

Part IV: How English Words Are Created: A Short Course

In this Short Course I provide the fundamentals of how English words are born, borrowed, and constructed. By this time you should have a pretty good idea of how complex English words are fabricated from roots, which are often derived from Latin and Greek. But you may wonder: How did certain combinations of letters become roots? What exactly does it mean to be a root? And are there any underlying rules or principles upon which roots are fashioned? This part explores these questions and presents a framework within which we can classify and codify whole segments of roots to better understand and remember their individual forms and meanings.

This part is essentially divided into three subparts: "native sources," Latin, and Greek.

The first subpart, native sources, provides a brief history of the English language and includes within that description the influences of Latin and Greek. It then demonstrates how, by isolating the "base" of one of our simplest native words, *do*, and sequentially adding, removing, and substituting prefixes and suffixes, we can "create" all sorts of new words representing different parts of speech. From this approach we then develop a method that can be used not only to construct simple native words from native elements but can be employed with equal facility to create more complex "borrowed" words from Latin and Greek elements. Finally, at the end of this subpart, supplementary tables of native prefixes and suffixes are provided that serve both as a repository from which to create additional words and as a reference for use throughout this book and for any future study of etymology you may wish to pursue.

The Latin and Greek subparts are each divided into three clearly defined though unlabeled "sections." The first section covers the rudiments (roo´də·mənts; the first or fundamental elements or principles) of each language—its alphabet, pronunciation, and spelling conventions—and examines the principles behind the construction of its bases, prefixes, suffixes, connecting vowels, and combining forms, and shows how each of these forms join with other forms to create English words. This culminates in a description and model for finding the Latin or Greek word "behind" a derived English word, determining the base of that Latin or Greek word, deriving from this base an English root, and creating from this root one or more English words by attaching prefixes, suffixes, and other elements.

The second section of the Latin and Greek subparts consists, respectively, of three and four pages of prefix and suffix tables, similar to but generally more comprehensive than the tables of native roots.

Thus, if your objectives in reading this book are primarily to increase your vocabulary through a study of *English* roots and you seek only the fundamentals of Latin and Greek, you can stop reading after the first sections of the Latin and Greek subparts, right before their respective tables, and use the tables only as a reference. But if you would like to know precisely where our English roots originate and understand the network through which Latin and Greek words yield bases that become English roots, you should examine the prefix and suffix tables more closely and then read the more lengthy and complex third sections after the tables.

The third sections comprise a detailed, step-by-step examination of the Latin and Greek words, bases, and other elements within their respective grammatical units called declensions and, in the case of Latin, conjugations as well. This is very technical information, but I have tried to present it in the simplest manner possible and to organize it in such a way that you can learn these fundamentals without having to study this material. But this material is very detailed, and it will still require a high degree of motivation and dedication on your part to get through these pages. But the hours or days it takes to do so will reward you a thousand times over in the lifelong benefit and joy of being able to analyze and understand in depth the construction of the overwhelming majority of our more sophisticated and colorful English words.

What you may even find exhilarating in these sections is that after discussing each component of Latin and Greek grammar (and providing a simple table to summarize that discussion), we re-create several "new" English words based on that component and in a sense retrace the footsteps of those men and women during and after the Renaissance who literally sat down and combined Latin and Greek roots to coin learned English words. So in this Short Course you will actually find yourself partaking in the process of "creating" such words as *operate* and *hippopotamus* as if they never existed before; and by juggling endings and snipping off certain prefixes and suffixes and replacing them with other prefixes and suffixes, together we will convert these words into *cooperate* and *eohippus*, respectively, and then into *cooperative* and *mesohippus*—and onward to *uncooperative* and *protohippus* (all defined and explained in the text). So as far as practicable (able or capable of being put into practice—not to be confused with *practical*), you will actually experience what it's like to systematically coin English words as our ancestors did centuries ago and as scientists do today.

The only technical points in the Short Course that should be addressed at this time concern the presentation of etymologies within parentheses and, when present, brackets.

When a short string of English roots are separated by several parentheses, within which etymologies of each respective root appears, if you ignore everything within the parentheses and combine the roots outside of the parentheses, you will find that those roots invariably "add up" to the English word under discussion. Consider the following excerpt:

> To English *agr-* (< L. *agr-*, base of *agrī*, genitive of *ager*: field), we can add a connecting *-i-*, a second root *cult-* (< L. *cult-*, base of *cultus*, past participle of *colere*: to till, to cultivate), the noun-forming element *-ur-* (< L. *-ūr-*, base of *-ūra*: the act, process, condition, or result of), and a silent final *-e*, yielding *agriculture* . . . .-

All of the technical Latin data within the parentheses is explained in detail in the Short Course, so we need not go into this now. With regard to understanding how English roots combine to form words, if you simply delete the parenthetical data, the following simplified version will emerge:

> To English *agr-*, we can add a connecting *-i-*, a second root *cult-*, the noun-forming element *-ur-*, and a silent final *-e*, yielding *agriculture*.

Every letter in *agriculture* is thereby accounted for in the presentation of these roots, and I have tried my best to adhere to this pattern throughout this book. Thus, if your primary goal is to learn English roots, you can simply ignore or "remove" the technical Latin and Greek data within parentheses, and you will be left with only English roots, which will combine to form the word you are analyzing. One way of simulating (pretending or giving the appearance of—not to be confused with *stimulating*) this is by taking a red pen or highlighter and circling or marking those roots and definitions you wish to learn. Then when you return to this section at a later time, you need only look for your markings.

When brackets appear within parentheses, they often serve the same function as the parentheses described above, but with regard to how Latin and Greek words and elements, rather than English roots, derive. Thus, they generally take the etymological information one level deeper. Consider the following excerpt:

> A consonant (< L. *con-* [assimilated form of *com-*]: with, together + *son-* [base of *sonāre*]: to sound + *-ant-* [base of *-antis*, genitive of *-āns*]: present participial suffix equivalent in meaning to English *-ing*, as in "the laughing hyena") may be defined as . . . .

In this excerpt, we never identify the English roots but simply work with the Latin forms. This approach works fine in this example because the English roots are identical to their Latin antecedents, and by skipping the intermediate "English root" step we can provide further information about the Latin forms without cluttering up the example. Nonetheless, if you want to streamline this information, you can delete the bracketed information, in which case you will be left with the simple Latin forms and their definitions, as presented below:

> A consonant (< L. *con-*: with, together + *son-*: to sound + *-ant-*: present participial suffix equivalent in meaning to English *-ing*, as in "the laughing hyena") may be defined as . . . .

A more complicated example would be:

> Some of the French words adopted during this period include what have become . . . *city* (< NormFr. *citet*: city < L. *cīvitāt*- [base of *cīvitātis*, genitive of *cīvitās*]: citizenry, city < *cīv*- [base of *cīvis*]: citizen + -*i*-: connecting vowel + -*tāt*- [base of -*tātis*, genitive of -*tās*]: the quality, state, or condition of) . . . .

In this etymology—one of the most complicated in this book—you are immediately informed that English *city* derives from Norman French *citet*, which in turn derives from Latin *cīvitāt*-. At this point the etymology shifts from analyzing English *city* to analyzing Latin *cīvitāt*-, and provides such information as what this Latin root means, where it comes from, what each of its components are, and whence they derive. Specifically, within the brackets following *cīvitāt*- the full form of this root is provided, followed by the derivation of that form. And outside the brackets is a definition of *cīvitāt*-, followed, in succession, by its three constituent roots—*cīv*-, -*i*-, and -*tāt*-—followed, in turn, by their etymologies within brackets and their definitions outside the brackets.

Of course, if you do not wish to go into this etymology in such depth, you can ignore the bracketed material, in which case you would be left with:

> Some of the French words adopted during this period include what have become . . . *city* (< NormFr. *citet*: city < L. *cīvitāt*-: citizenry, city < *cīv*-: citizen + -*i*-: connecting vowel + -*tāt*-: the quality, state, or condition of) . . . .

Thus, after being informed that English *city* derives from Norman French *citet*, which in turn derives from Latin *cīvitāt*-, you are then provided with the components of *cīvitāt*-, specifically *cīv*-, -*i*-, and -*tāt*-, followed in each case by their definitions. But if you still find this information extraneous to your needs, you can ignore the parenthetical matter altogether, in which case you will wind up with:

> Some of the French words adopted during this period include what have become . . . *city* . . . .

Finally, in some etymologies you will see one or more letters in a Latin or Greek word within small parentheses. These are usually used to isolate the inflectional ending of a Latin or Greek word and thereby reveal its base, which in turn yields an English root. But in some cases they perform additional functions. Consider the following excerpt:

> . . . if we add the adjective- and noun-forming suffix -*oid*, "resembling, like" (< G. -*o(e)id(ēs)*: shaped-like < *eidos*: form, shape) to *aster*-, we get *asteroid*, which, etymologically, is "that which resembles a star."

In this example, the parentheses within -*o(e)id(ēs)* accomplish three things. First and most generally, they show which letters are not carried over into the English derivative -*oid*. Thus, if you remove the *e* and *ēs* from Greek -*o(e)id(ēs)*, this root will match English -*oid* exactly. Second and more specifically, the parentheses around *ēs* highlight the inflectional ending of Greek *-o(e)id(ēs)*, which if dropped will reveal the Greek base *-o(e)id-*. And third, the parentheses around *e* recall that through traditional Latinization and Anglicization (see the second line on the table on page 238), Greek *ei* becomes English *i* or *e*, and that in this case the *e* drops out.

While this information may, at this moment, seem highly complex and somewhat discouraging, by the time you get half way through the Short Course it will all become so clear to you that you may wonder why you ever thought it so difficult. So hang in there (see this phrase under COMMON EXPRESSIONS DERIVED FROM BOXING) and you can beat the count (ditto). Then you can come back and win by a knockout (ditto ditto).

In this Short Course we will thus cover a tremendous amount of material in a relatively short space, but, to continue the metaphor, you need not take it on the chin. The key to understanding this information is not to concentrate on individual examples—as I have just done at some length—but rather to focus initially on the basics and become as familiar as you can with the tables, which summarize these basics. It is not necessary or even desirable to try to learn everything in the text the first time through. Just read leisurely and don't even try to "study" this information. Then—and this is the trick to remembering this material—after you finish each section, leaf back over those pages you have just read and look at the tables as a kind of quick review, and state out loud to yourself a few of the principles on these tables, even if in just a whisper. Then after you finish a few sections, go back and do the same for all those sections, including the ones you have already looked over. Thus, by regularly reviewing these pages in a cumulative fashion, by the end of this Short Course you will not only learn hundreds of common prefixes, suffixes, and bases, but, more importantly, you will understand the principles underlying the construction of virtually every learned English word derived from Latin, Greek, and native sources.

Part V: A Cross-Reference Dictionary

In this Dictionary, thousands of prefixes, suffixes, bases, words, expressions, names, and other linguistic forms alluded to or briefly described in this book receive follow-up coverage on a multiplicity of levels. For many entries, such as the italic English words cross-referred from the COMMON ROOTS, the coverage is detailed and lengthy; for other entries it consists merely of cross references to other pages in the book or to other Dictionary entries where such coverage is provided. In short, the information contained in A CROSS-REFERENCE DICTIONARY is both a reiteration and an extension of the material presented throughout this book.

In addition, A CROSS-REFERENCE DICTIONARY functions as a self-contained standard and etymological dictionary. With its detailed definitions and step-by-step etymologies (often including a description of the "sense development" of the defined word), it provides a wealth of information that you can use to learn new words and develop an understanding of the fundamentals of word-building. And when this Dictionary is used in conjunction with the background material provided in HOW ENGLISH WORDS ARE CREATED: A SHORT COURSE, it becomes a self-teaching primer and introductory course for the study and application of English etymology.

Finally, A CROSS-REFERENCE DICTIONARY serves as a browser's dictionary of humorous, educational, technical, and outlandish words and roots. If you start reading almost any long entry in this Dictionary, you may be surprised and delighted to find how many new and interesting words it leads you to.

A CROSS-REFERENCE DICTIONARY includes eight major types of entries:

1) comprehensive word entries, providing for each entry one or more definitions followed by a dissection, analysis, reconstruction, and, when appropriate, a Secondary Dissection and Secondary Reconstruction, and often a commentary. Unlike the Detailed Example and Brief Analyses of the COMMON ROOTS and the Example of the SUBJECTS, the definitions in the Dictionary occur before the dissection, not after the reconstruction. This enables those of you who are interested solely in learning a word's definition to read just the first few lines of each entry without having to wade through its etymology.

2) comprehensive prefixes, suffixes, and combining forms, providing definitions, illustrative examples, variant forms, etymologies, and cross references—closely analogous in many entries to the format of the comprehensive word entries.

3) succinct root etymologies, providing analyses and definitions of selected English roots. These are furnished primarily for those roots introduced and defined in the COMMON ROOTS and SUBJECTS but not provided with etymologies .

4) homographic root entries, providing analyses and definitions of each homographic root in this book, followed by one to three derivative English words from each root.

5) special coverage of phobias and manias, providing pronunciations (where necessary), definitions, abbreviated yet thorough etymologies, and frequent commentaries. These entries correspond to the phobia and mania lists in the SUBJECTS.

6) special treatment of exercise entries, providing special markers for easy identification of and cross referencing to their corresponding COMMON ROOTS and HELPFUL HINTS.

7) dictionary-to-dictionary cross references, providing detailed coverage of contrasted words within Dictionary entries, and including supplementary listings of all Dictionary words defined within parentheses.

8) comprehensive index coverage, providing page references and cross references for all prefixes, suffixes, bases, words, expressions, names, concepts, headings, and other linguistic and structural matter in this book.

Thus, A CROSS-REFERENCE DICTIONARY provides a wealth of material, and some of you may initially find its appearance complex and intimidating. But this Dictionary is meticulously organized and consistent in its presentation of data, and once you become familiar with its organization it will become relatively easy to use—and you can glean from it exactly what you want.

Moreover, unlike other parts of this book, you need never read the entries in this Dictionary as though you were reading a chapter in a book. A CROSS-REFERENCE DICTIONARY is designed primarily to provide supplementary data for the words and roots cited in this book, and other than for browsing, you will never turn to it unless directed to do so from some other part of the book. And even then, it is up to you to determine whether your needs will be met by going there.

HOW TO USE THIS BOOK

There are many ways of using this book, and you need not restrict yourself to any one approach. How you read this book will depend on your time, mood, changing personal goals, and other factors.

For instance, you can browse through these pages as a leisurely pastime, perhaps reading a few entries in the COMMON ROOTS and SUBJECTS and following up on some of them in A CROSS-REFERENCE DICTIONARY as the fancy strikes you—and this is certainly an enjoyable and even educational approach to use, depending on how often you pick up this book. Or you can concentrate on learning *English* roots, pretty much ignoring everything else, at least until you have a fair understanding of these basic English forms. But if you are interested in knowing where these roots originate, you can explore their etymologies in the Technical Information and Detailed Example sections in the COMMON ROOTS as well as in the "analysis" sections of the comprehensive word entries in A CROSS-REFERENCE DICTIONARY.

If, however, your goal is to systematically learn as much as you can about all phases of words, I would propose the following procedure: First of all, if you haven't already, I strongly recommend that you read the PREFACE. More than anywhere else in this book, these few pages demonstrate in a concise manner some of the remarkable things you can do with a knowledge of roots and will, I hope, motivate you to read and use this book conscientiously.

Then, ironically (unless you're in a school setting), I *do not* recommend that you jump in and begin studying HOW ENGLISH WORDS ARE CREATED: A SHORT COURSE. Rather, I suggest that you spend a few days browsing through this book to become familiar with its organization and content so that you can determine which areas will be of greatest benefit to you. Then after this brief "orientation period," you can return to the beginning of this book and proceed with a more systematic review. In this manner, the material in the Short Course and the rest of this book will have more relevance and meaning for you— and you will remember more.

By this time you should be very much aware of how interrelated all the information is in this book. Thus, if you begin reading in one place and follow all of the cross references to where they will lead you, it may be hours before you return to your starting point—if, in fact, you ever get back there. With this in mind and for the purpose of simulating how you can use this book (and in this manner stimulating you to do so), I would like to take you on such a journey and in the process introduce many of the more intricate features of this work.

To begin, I will assume you have recently obtained a copy of this book and are currently leafing through the COMMON ROOTS and SUBJECTS. At some point you will inevitably come across the Technical Information section of chapter CORP-, CORPUS, CORPOR-, a typical section in this book. You will then observe:

Technical Information	*corp-* is the base of Latin *corpus* (kôr´pōōs), "body." *corpor-* is the base of Latin *corporis* (kôr´pô·ris), which is the genitive of *corpus*. However, Latin *corpus* (genitive: *corporis*), "body," is sometimes confused with Latin *cor* (genitive: *cordis*), "heart," which we see in *cordial, cordate,* and *misericord.* Also, a similar but unrelated Latin term meaning "body" but restricted exclusively to a "dead body" is *cadāver* (kà·dä´ wer), which we see in *cadaver, cadaverous,* and *cadaverine.* Finally, the Greek equivalent to Latin *corpus* (genitive: *corporis*) is *sōma* (genitive: *sōmatos*), which occurs in *chromosome, psychosomatic,* and *trypanosomiasis.*

Every italic English *word* in every Technical Information section in this book (as well as in every other section and subsection in the COMMON ROOTS) that is not provided with definitions and etymologies in the text will be provided with these in A CROSS-REFERENCE DICTIONARY. In this excerpt alone, for example, there are nine italic English words that receive full and comprehensive treatment in the Dictionary, and if you wish you can turn to these for in-depth, follow-up coverage of their meanings and etymologies.

Thus, if you were reading the second-to-the-last sentence (beginning with "Also") in this Technical Information section, you might very well say to yourself: "What in the world does *cadaverine* mean?" And since this word is in italics, you know that it is in A CROSS-REFERENCE DICTIONARY, which you could then turn to for the following entry:

> *cadaverine* (kə·dav´ə·rēn´, -ər·in) *n.* a colorless, syrupy, toxic PTOMAINE present in decomposing flesh and other substances. **[cadaver + -in- + -e]** < L. *cadāver*: dead body, corpse (< or akin to *cadere*: to fall; cf. INCIDENT) + *-īn(a)* (fem. of *-īnus*): pert. to, charact. by; also, a fem. abstract *n*-forming suffix having the basic meaning: the quality, state, or condition of + E. *-e*: silent final letter. **RECON:** *the quality, state, or condition of* (**-in-**) *a dead body* (**cadaver**). **SEC. DISS:** [cadaver + **-ine**] **Note:** L. *-īn(a)*: the quality, state, or condition of + E. *-e*: silent final letter > the E. *n*-forming suffix -INE², having, in this context, the medical and scientific meaning: an AL- KALOID or nitrogenous base of (that which is designated by the preceding base or roots). **SEC. RECON:** *an alkaloid of* (**-ine**) *a dead body* (**cadaver**); cf. PTOMAINE for a parallel but primarily Greek-derived secondary reconstruction, 22-25 (explanation of features in this entry), 93

After reading several Dictionary entries, the general organization of this as well as most other entries will become evident to you, but I would like to provide you with the specific breakdown of the different parts of this entry and call your attention to a few additional points.

First, of course, the headword appears, followed by its pronunciation, a part-of-speech label, and a generally succinct yet thorough definition.

Within the definition above, you'll notice that PTOMAINE is in small capitals. This means that *ptomaine* has its own entry in this Dictionary. So if you wonder what this word means or would like to learn its etymology, you can further turn to that entry. But if you already know the meaning of *ptomaine* or are not presently concerned about its meaning or etymology (or don't have the time), you can simply pass over this cross reference.

Now you have another choice: if all you are currently interested in is learning the meaning of *cadaverine*, you can stop reading after the definition and go back to the Technical Information or whatever sections or other entries interest you. But if you'd like to know what the roots of *cadaverine* are and where they come from, continue reading.

At the end of the definition, you'll notice "**[cadaver + -in- + -e]**." The boldface word and other elements in boldface brackets mark the beginning of the etymology section and identify the elements in *cadaverine*. This bracketed dissection corresponds to the Dissection step in the Detailed Example and Brief Analyses of the COMMON ROOTS and to the Dissection step in the Example of most SUBJECTS, in which I use lightface type and virgules (slashes) instead of boldface type and "+"s to separate the roots.

Following this dissection section is an analysis section (corresponding to but more comprehensive than the analysis step in the COMMON ROOTS and most SUBJECTS). Here, each Latin, Greek, Old English, or other etymon (an earlier form of a root or word from which a later form derives) is provided along with its meaning, with its inflectional ending (or other elements that do not appear in the English word) placed within *small* parentheses to set it off from what is generally the "base" of the etymon. In addition, for those of you who want to know where these non-English roots or words come from, additional in-depth etymological information is provided within *large* parentheses.

The parentheses thereby serve two important functions: First, they set off all secondary and tertiary (tûr´shē·er´ē; third in order, rank, degree, etc.) etymological data from the more immediate primary data. So if you ignore everything within large and small parentheses, the remaining italic letters in the etymons will match *exactly* the letters provided within the brackets, not counting Latinizations and Anglicizations (see HOW ENGLISH WORDS ARE CREATED: A SHORT COURSE for an explanation of this), revealing exactly where the boldface English letters come from. And second, the small parentheses isolate the nonessential parts of the etymon and call attention to the bases and other key elements of those etymons. Thus, for those of you who have no desire to delve into foreign languages but wish only to focus upon English roots, you can, once again, skip over the parenthetical data and be left with short English roots (or, in some cases, words) extracted from these etymons, followed by their definitions.

Near the beginning of the etymology of *cadaverine*, you'll notice "(< or akin to *cadere*: to fall; cf. INCIDENT)" within large parentheses. The small capitalized INCIDENT is yet another cross reference in this entry which directs you to turn to *incident* in A CROSS-REFERENCE DICTIONARY. This citation is included because within the entry of *incident* is an informative etymological comparison of ACCIDENT, OCCIDENT, and INCIDENT—terms which share the same etymological root as *cadaverine* and which are themselves listed as headwords in the Dictionary with their own cross references. In addition, DECIDUOUS, another English derivative of *cadere*, is introduced under INCIDENT with a directive to see that term in its own alphabetical order; and under *deciduous* is a cross reference to -OUS, which in turn directs you to DAN-GEROUS, CADAVEROUS, and CACOPHONOUS, all of which lead to still other cross references. So for those of you who are intrigued with word origins, there is almost no end to where one entry can lead.

But to return to *cadaverine*, after the analysis section (ending with "E. *-e*: silent final letter") is the reconstruction section (corresponding to the Reconstruction step in the COMMON ROOTS and most SUB-JECTS), which is introduced by the label "RECON:." In this section, I reconstruct the previously analyzed etymological information by formulating one more-or-less coherent sentence from the combined meanings of the individual roots and word in which an italicized definition of each of these elements is followed in parentheses by a boldface citation of that element. In the above entry, the reconstruction is rendered, "the quality, state, or condition of (**-in-**) *a dead body* (**cadaver**)."

In certain Dictionary entries where I feel it is important to do so, I then include what I call a "secondary dissection," introduced by the label "SEC. DISS:." In these sections I combine two or more of the roots presented in the primary bracketed dissection (which has no introductory label) to form a longer and more relevant affix (af´iks´; a prefix, suffix, or infix) or "combining form" for the word in question.

For example, in *cadaverine* you'll notice that after the label "SEC. DISS:" are the boldface brackets and elements, "[cadaver + **-ine**]." Within these brackets, the first element, *cadaver*, is in lightface, which indicates that I have not combined this element with any other element and it remains in the same form as it did in the initial bracketed dissection. The second element, **-ine**, however, is in bold-face, which indicates that this affix is an amalgamation of at least two of the roots initially displayed in the first bracketed dissection and is the root I am now going to discuss.

Following the second set of brackets is the boldface word "**Note:**" which signals that I am about to explain how I constructed this new boldface root. In this particular entry, I describe how I combined Latin *-īn(a)* with English *-e* to form English -INE[2] and what this new suffix means. Moreover, since the -INE[2] is in small capitals it too is defined and analyzed under its own headword, and the superscript "[2]" indicates that it is the second of at least two homographs (see pages 34-36 for a discussion of homographs), informing you exactly where to turn for further information about this suffix; and, of course, if you are so inclined, you can also turn to the closely related -INE[1] for still more information. Similarly, you can look up the small capitalized ALKALOID, where you will be referred to BELLADONNA, which will provide you with a parenthetical definition of *alkaloid* and bring into discussion caffeine, nicotine, MORPHINE, and cocaine.

After this secondary etymological analysis, I then provide the label "SEC. RECON:" which signals that I am about to reconstruct the roots highlighted in the bracketed secondary dissection in the same manner as I did for the roots highlighted in the primary dissection following the label "RECON:." For most entries, the secondary reconstruction, if indeed they have one, is the final component of the word's etymology.

However, in some entries I provide an additional commentary, which variously comprises an explanation of the sense development of the word (where this is not apparent from the reconstruction of the elements), a statement about the word's definition, an interesting anecdote about its usage, or a special directive to the reader. In the sample above, I provide yet another cross reference to a Dictionary entry that has a secondary reconstruction almost identical to that of *cadaverine* (which, coincidentally, is again *ptomaine*), which I now introduce by "cf." and follow with a brief explanation as to why I've included that cross reference.

Finally, after the commentary, I supply the page numbers and/or cross references showing which word or root elsewhere in the book prompted me to include this Dictionary entry.

Thus, the comprehensive word entries include a wealth of information that you can use for various purposes. In addition to such detailed entries, however, I also include "succinct root etymologies" for every English root cited in the COMMON ROOTS and SUBJECTS section that are not otherwise provided with etymologies.

For example, if your browsing takes you to chapter -AGOG- in the COMMON ROOTS, under the Brief Analyses entry *hypnagogic* you will observe:

---

hypnagogic
(hip′nə·gäj′ik)

1) hypn-/-agog-/-ic
2) *hypn-*: sleep (cf. HYPNOSIS); *-agog-*: leader, leading, bringing; *-ic*: pertaining to, characterized by (cf. ANGELIC).
3) characterized by (*-ic*) bringing (*-agog-*) sleep (*hypn-*).
4) *adj.* 1. of or associated with that state of consciousness immediately preceding sleep. 2. inducing sleep or drowsiness.
5) Hypnos was the Greek god of sleep. His son Morpheus (< Greek *morphē*: form, shape; cf. MORPHINE, MORPHOLOGY) was the classical god of dreams, his function being to form and shape images during sleep. The ancient Roman counterpart of Greek Hypnos was Somnus (< Latin *somnus*: sleep; cf. SOMNAMBULISM, SOMNILOQUY). And the twin brother of Hypnos was Thanatos (< Greek *thanatos*: death; cf. THANATOPHOBIA, EUTHANASIA)—the personification of death.

If you look under step 2 above, you will note that *hypn-* is the first root in *hypnagogic* and it means "sleep." Now this brief definition may be all that you need. But if you wish to know where *hypn-* comes from, you can look up this root in A CROSS-REFERENCE DICTIONARY where you will read:

---

hypn- < G. *hypn-*, base of *hypnos*: sleep, 47

Unlike the comprehensive word entries (such as *cadaverine*) in which I use small parentheses to isolate nonessential inflectional endings (which is done to save space and simplify what are often long and potentially confusing etymologies), in succinct root entries (such as *hypn-*) I dispense with the small parentheses and spell out each step. Thus, what appears in the *root* entry above as "*hypn-* < G. *hypn-*, base of *hypnos*: sleep" would appear in a *word* entry as "[**hypn-** . . .] < G. *hypn(os)*: sleep" (see excerpt of *hypnosis* on page 27). But both of these etymologies can be verbalized in the same manner, namely, "The English root *hypn-* is derived from Greek *hypn-*, which is the base of *hypnos*, which means 'sleep.'"

Similarly, if your browsing leads you to Engineering under the category entitled Professional Words in the SUBJECTS, you will note under Example:

---

centripetal (sen·trip´it'l)

Dissection:	1) centr- / -i- / pet- / -al
Analysis:	2) *centr-*: center; *-i-*: connecting vowel; *pet-*: to seek, to move toward; *-al*: pertaining to, characterized by.
Reconstruction:	3) characterized by (*-al*) seeking or moving toward (*pet-*) the center (*centr-*).
Definition:	4) *adj.* moving or directed inward toward a center or axis.
Commentary:	5) *centripetal* is the opposite of the more common *centrifugal*, a word derived from *centr-*: center + *-i-*: connecting vowel + *fug-*: to flee + *-al*: pertaining to, characterized by. Thus, while a centripetal force always "seeks" a center and propels objects (or people) toward it, a centrifugal force "flees" that center and propels objects (or people) toward its outer edge.

If you look under step 2 (which unlike the Brief Analyses but like the Detailed Example in the COM-MON ROOTS is labeled "Analysis"), you will note that *centr-* is the first root in *centripetal* and means "center." And if you look up *centr-* in A CROSS-REFERENCE DICTIONARY, you will read:

---

centr- < L. *centr-*, base of *centrum*: center (< G. *kentron*: the stationary point on a drawing compass; orig., spike, sharp point, goad for oxen < *kentein*: to prick, to goad oxen), 118

This is the same format as illustrated for *hypn-* above, though it may at first seem different because it is so much longer and contains a more detailed etymology. But if we remove the parenthetical information, we get the skeletal form:

---

centr- < L. *centr-*, base of *centrum*: center, 118

Now turning back to step 2 under *hypnagogic*, after the definition of "sleep," you'll notice the parenthetical "(cf. HYPNOSIS)." This is an example of a second English word (in addition to the Brief Analyses headword *hypnagogic*) that is derived in part from the root *hypn-*. The underlining highlights the root in question, a practice I have adopted for all *partially* analyzed English words in the Brief Analyses to make the referent roots immediately apparent. Furthermore, since *hypnosis* is in small capitals you know that it, too, will receive full coverage in A CROSS-REFERENCE DICTIONARY; and if you are interested in learning its etymology (including the meaning and origin of that somewhat odd-looking *-osis*), you can look up *hypnosis* in this Dictionary.

With this in mind, if you look at step 5 under *hypnagogic*, you will note six additional partially underlined words in small capitals. Each of these terms also receives comprehensive coverage in A CROSS-REFERENCE DICTIONARY, five of which further direct you to other entries in this book. Thus, if you are the type of person who likes—or could learn to like— etymological treasure hunts, you will find a wealth of clues to follow in these cross references.

But to return to step 2, if you look up *hypnosis* in the Dictionary you will see:

HYPNOSIS (hip·nō´sis) *n.* a sleeplike trance charact. by a heightened response to suggestion,
usu. induced by another person. **[hypn- + -o- +
-sis]** < G. *hypn(os)*: sleep + *-ō-*: conn. vowel
(orig., the base of denom. verbs ending in *-oun*)
+ *-sis*: the act, process, condition, or result of.
RECON: *the process of* (**-sis**) *sleep* (**hypn-**). SEC.
DISS: [hypn- + **-osis**] **Note:** G. *-ō-*: conn. vowel
+ *-sis*: the act, process, condition, or result of >
G. *-ōsis* > the E. *n*-forming suffix *-osis*, having,
in this entry, the modern medical meaning: a
diseased or abnormal state or condition of. SEC.
RECON: *an abnormal state of* (**-osis**) *sleep*
(**hypn-**), 47

The organization of this entry is essentially the same as that of *cadaverine* and is in no need of further comment. But other detailed word entries do show some variations in format, which are worth noting. For example, if you are reading chapter A-, AN- in the COMMON ROOTS and come across the Brief Analyses entry *anhydrous*, you will observe:

---

anhydrous	1) an-/hydr-/-ous
(an·hī´drəs)	2) *an-*: without, lacking, not; *hydr-*: water (cf. HYDROPHOBIA); *-ous*: full of, abounding in, characterized by (cf. DANGEROUS).
	3) characterized by (*-ous*) lacking (*an-*) water (*hydr-*).
	4) *adj.* without water, especially the water in a chemical crystal: *Lime is anhydrous calcium hydroxide.*

Looking at step 2, you'll note that *hydrophobia* is the first of two cross-referenced words in this subsection. If you look up this word in A CROSS-REFERENCE DICTIONARY, you will find:

HYDROPHOBIA (hī ´drə·fō´ bē·ə) *n.* **1.** an abnormal
fear or dread of water. **2.** rabies. **[hydr- + -o- +
phob- + -ia]** < G. *hydr-* (base of *hydōr*): water
+ *-o-:* conn. vowel + *phob(os)*: fear, panic, flight
(< *phobein* or *phebesthai*: to flee in fright) + *-ia*:
the act, process, condition, or result of. **RECON:**
the condition of (**-ia**) *fearing* (**phob-**) *water*
(**hydr-**). **SEC. DISS:** **[hydro- + -phobia]** **Note:**
G. *hydr-* (base of *hydōr*): water + *-o-:* conn.
vowel > G. *hydro-:* water > the E. comb. form
hydro-: water. Also note: G. *phob(os)*: fear,
panic, flight + *-ia*: the act, process, condition, or
result of > G. *-phobia* > the E. *n-*forming comb.
form -PHOBIA, having the modern medical meaning: one who has an irrational or intense fear or
dread of. **SEC. RECON:** *one who has an irrational fear or dread of* (**-phobia**) *water*
(**hydro-**). An extraordinary symptom of
advanced rabies is the inability to swallow, attempts at which can result in convulsions.
Hence, for some sufferers the mere fact of seeing or hearing that which induces them to swallow, as the sight or sound of running water, can
bring on convulsions; hence, the hydrophobe's
proverbial fear of water, 28-29. . . .

I would like to point out three differences in this entry with those of *cadaverine* and *hypnosis*.

First, if you look at the bracketed roots after "SEC. DISS:" you will see "**[hydro- + -phobia]**." In this
secondary dissection, both **hydro- + -phobia** are in boldface. This means that each of these combining
forms (not just one, as is the case in *cadaverine* and *hypnosis*) has united at least two of the roots initially displayed in the primary bracketed dissection (following *rabies* at the end of the second definition). Thus, the analysis following this secondary dissection will involve two stages.

In the first stage, I still introduce the first combining form *hydro-* with the boldface label, **"Note:."**
But in the second stage, following the analysis of *hydro-*, I introduce the second combining form *-pho-
bia* with the phrase, "Also note:," which is in lightface since it is not a section heading.

After analyzing *-phobia*, I proceed to the "SEC. RECON" in which I reconstruct this entire entry in
the same manner that I did in *hypnosis*. But in this particular entry I add one more feature. Immediately
following the last parenthetical boldface root "(**hydro-**)" is a sentence beginning, "An extraordinary
symptom of. . . ." Since these words begin after the completion of the secondary reconstruction (which
normally, when present, marks the close of the etymology), they signal the beginning of a commentary
about the entry—in this case, an explanation as to how a term that literally reconstructs into "the fear of
water" evolved into a synonym for rabies.

Unlike the final cross reference in *cadaverine*, which is introduced by "cf." (see page 22), commentaries are generally not introduced by any cross reference or marker nor do they employ special abbreviations or symbols in their text. Nevertheless, in those entries that include commentaries, it is feasible, should you so desire, to skip from the end of the last entry definition (preceding the initial boldface brackets and roots) to the beginning of the commentary section (following the last boldface root in parentheses) and thereby avoid all technical and etymological data.

The entries of *cadaverine*, *hypnosis*, and *hydrophobia*, despite their differences, are very similar, and this is further reflected in their modes of cross referencing words and roots.

For example, when a non-English italic root or word appears within an entry in A CROSS-REFERENCE DICTIONARY, it *usually* also appears as a separate headword in this Dictionary, depending on its frequency of use and other factors. But unlike an undefined English root in the COMMON ROOTS or SUBJECTS that is *always* provided with supplemental coverage, for Dictionary entries you can never be sure. For example, in the entry for *hydrophobia* eight Greek elements appear in italics: *hydr-*, *hydōr*, *-o-*, *phob(os)*, *phobein*, *phebesthai*, *-ia*, and *-phobia*. But you have no way of knowing which of these elements, if any, appear as a separate headword in the Dictionary. So if you seek additional information about any of these forms, you will just have to look in the Dictionary and see if it is there.

If you do find such a headword, it will either provide you with full coverage of that entry or direct you to some other place in the book where such coverage is provided. But if that element is not recorded as a headword, this tells you that it occurs only in A CROSS-REFERENCE DICTIONARY (and perhaps only in the entry you are reading), for I have not indexed roots and foreign words that are cited or described *only* within Dictionary entries (though I have cross-referenced italicized English words in the Dictionary and non-italicized English words that receive parenthetical definitions).

For example, if you look up the eight elements in the entry of *hydrophobia*, you will find *hydr-* recorded as a headword, complete with definition, etymology, a cross reference to HYDROPHOBIA, a definition-within-a-definition of *hydrocarbon*, and notations that it appears on page *28*, *71*, **101**, *101*, etc.; *hydōr* is also recorded in the Dictionary but does not provide a definition and instead simply directs you to page *101* and *102* and redirects you to the entry *hydr-*; *-o-* is similarly recorded as the headword *-o-*[1], but, after providing a brief definition, refers you to page **48**, *49*, **60**, *93*, etc., and to the entries ANTHROPOLOGY, GYNECOCRACY, and HYDROPHOBIA; *phob(os)* likewise appears in the Dictionary and provides several page references, including one to a HELPFUL HINTS entry and two to the COMMON ROOTS, and then cross-refers you to -PHOBE and -PHOBIA but does not itself furnish a definition or etymology; *phobein* and *phebesthai* are not recorded at all, which, of course, informs you that they only occur in one or more Dictionary entries, the only one you can be certain of is the one you have read it in, namely, *hydrophobia*; and *-ia* and *-phobia* are not only recorded as headwords but have relatively long and detailed entries, each having numerous cross references, derivative English words, and one providing a definition-within-a-definition.

So whenever you read an entry in A CROSS-REFERENCE DICTIONARY and desire further information about a word or root within that entry, look it up in the Dictionary to see if it is there. It does not have to be in small capitals to be cross referenced, and you will not know until you look.

In addition to the features so far discussed for *cadaverine*, *hypnosis*, and *hydrophobia*, other entries contain a variety of different kinds of information. For example, if in your reading you happen upon the Technical Information section in chapter BENE-, BEN- in the COMMON ROOTS, you will observe:

Technical Information	***bene-*** is derived from the Latin adverb *bene* (be´ne), "well." This adverb is closely related to the Latin adjective *bonus* (bô´nøøs), "good," from which we derive *bonus* and *bonbon*, and the Latin adjective *bellus* (bel´løøs), "beautiful, handsome," from which we derive *beldam* and *belladonna*. It is also identical in meaning to the common Greek combining form *eu-* (e$\overline{oo}$), "well," which we see in hundreds of English words, including *eulogy* and *euthanasia*. In English, however, both *bene-* and *eü-* have further adopted the adjectival meaning, "good"; and when followed by a vowel, particularly *i*, *bene-* drops its final *-e* and becomes the relatively uncommon variant ***ben-***. But *ben-* and *bene-* should not be confused with other classical and nonclassical roots and letter combinations that mirror these prefixes, as in the completely unrelated *beneath*, *benzaldehyde*, *Benelux*, and *Benjamin*.

Of the ten italic words in this excerpt (all of which receive in-depth coverage in A CROSS-REFERENCE DICTIONARY), the last one is *Benjamin*. If you're curious about what this name means and where it comes from, you can look it up in the Dictionary, where you will find:

> *Benjamin* (ben´ jə·min) a masculine name. Nicknames and diminutives: *Ben, Benny, Bennie, Benjy*, etc. [**Ben-** + **-jamin**] < Heb. *bin-*: son of + *-yāmīn*: the right hand (orig., south). RECON: *son of* (**Ben-**) *the right hand* (**-jamin**). In the Old Testament, Rachel, parturient (in the process of giving birth) and aware that she would soon die from her travail (trə·vāl´; childbirth), called her unborn child Benoni, or "son of my sorrow." But Jacob, the father, having prescience (presh´(ē)əns; foreknowledge) that this child would be his "son of the right hand" or favorite son, called him Benjamin, 30-31. . . .

This entry is similar to that for *hydrophobia* in that it includes a commentary after its reconstruction (though, in this case, the commentary follows the first and only reconstruction, not a secondary reconstruction, which it does not have or need). But the differences between this entry and those of *cadaverine*, *hypnosis*, and *hydrophobia* are much more significant.

First of all, *Benjamin* is a proper name, which in itself produces an unusual and novel Dictionary entry (see *Aristotle* for another proper name with an even more unusual commentary exploring some etymological liaisons among eight additional names). Instead of a real definition, therefore, the text simply notes that this is a masculine name and provides a few nicknames and diminutives. With regard to etymology, this entry is also simple and clear-cut, notwithstanding the spelling differences between the modern English roots and the transliterated Hebrew roots.

But most importantly, this entry exemplifies how short subdefinitions and, where necessary, pronunciations of potentially problematic words can be included within primary definitions and commentaries by placing them within parentheses following their respective terms. Specifically, in this example I define *parturient*, *travail*, and *prescience* in parentheses and further provide pronunciations of *travail* and *prescience*.

Now I think it is important to say a few words about why I have chosen a practice that may at first appear unnecessary, obtrusive, and stylistically cacophonous (see that word in A CROSS-REFERENCE DICTIONARY).

Grow Your Vocabulary has, as one of its primary goals, the task of enriching your vocabulary, and one of the best ways of achieving this is by introducing new words in real contexts in which definitions of those words are immediately presented and then continually available for reference and reinforcement. Who, for example, after reading this entry of *Benjamin* a few times would not recall the meaning of *parturient* or *travail*? And with regard to pronunciation, I believe that most people who have never encountered *travail* and *prescience* would pronounce them, respectively, *travel* and *pre-science*—a mortifying gaffe for, say, a person standing up at an important meeting and trying to make an important point. So unlike other books on vocabulary-building, *Grow Your Vocabulary* provides definitions and selected pronunciations for potentially problematic words whenever and wherever they occur—even, as you have no doubt noticed, in the PREFACE and this INTRODUCTION.

With this in mind, and to make this work even more useful and comprehensive, I have listed all of these words in their respective alphabetical order in A CROSS-REFERENCE DICTIONARY, with references to those entries in which they appear. Thus, if you look up *parturient*, *travail*, and *prescience* in their respective alphabetical listings, you would find the following cross references:

---

parturient, see under BENJAMIN

*   *   *   *   *   *

prescience, see under BENJAMIN

*   *   *   *   *   *

travail, see under BENJAMIN

However, in other situations in which a "sophisticated" word in a Dictionary entry has a particularly complicated definition or etymology that cannot be adequately covered within parentheses, I dispense with the parenthetical definition altogether, place the word in small capitals in the entry in which it appears, and create a detailed entry for it in its own alphabetical order in the Dictionary.

PTOMAINE under *cadaverine* (see page 22) is such an entry. It is a good choice for special coverage because most people have at some point heard or used this word, yet few people have a real fix on its definition. Moreover, its spelling is horrendous, its definition is confusing, and its etymology in many ways parallels that of *cadaverine*, the entry in which it appears. So for these reasons I thought it worthwhile to make *ptomaine* a separate entry.

But I only include dictionary-to-dictionary cross references when they meet certain criteria, some of which I have highlighted in the previous paragraph. By contrast, in the COMMON ROOTS I have adopted the practice of providing supplemental Dictionary entries for scholarly and out-of-the-ordinary terms whenever I think they may be of benefit to you. For example, if you were perusing (pə·rōō´zing; reading or examining) the Memory Aid in chapter AG-, ACT-, -IG- you would observe:

Memory Aid   Memorize the following sentence: **"The agile actor fumigated the stage."** Now visualize an agile actor on stage <u>do</u>ing a routine, <u>act</u>ing out a part, and <u>driv</u>ing a unicycle in circles. A mouse runs past him and two of his lickspittles follow the mouse across the stage. Undaunted, the <u>ag</u>ile <u>act</u>or fum<u>ig</u>ates the stage, then continues **to do, to act, to drive.**

Three words in this Memory Aid might perplex you as to their meaning or pique your curiosity about their etymologies: *lickspittles, fumigate,* and *undaunted.*

Whenever you encounter a new or curious word in the COMMON ROOTS that you would like to know more about, consider whether it might be in A CROSS-REFERENCE DICTIONARY. If it appears in the COMMON ROOTS in italics or small capitals, you *know* it will be in the Dictionary, but if it is in roman type you have no way of telling. So go ahead and check.

With this uncertainty, if you look up *lickspittles* in A CROSS-REFERENCE DICTIONARY, you will be pleased to find a short but entertaining entry for that word:

LICKSPITTLE (lik´spit´'l) *n.* a fawning, servile flatterer; toady. **[lick + spittle]** < E. *lick*: to lap up with the tongue (< OE *liccian*) + *spittle*: spit, saliva (prob. < a blend of OE *spitt(an)*: to spit + *(spæt)l* [var. of *spātl*]: saliva + E. *-e*: silent final letter). **RECON**: *to lap up* (**lick**) *spit* (**spittle**). In 1629, the then famous poet and playwright Sir William Davenant wrote in a work entitled *Albovine* what is now credited to be the first reference to what would later become *lickspittle*: "Lick her spittle / From the ground," 32, 87

In reading the definition of this word, "a fawning, servile flatterer; toady," an astute reader might ask, "Why isn't 'toady' also provided with a parenthetical definition? It too is an odd sort of word that is worth a little explication." The answer to this involves yet another feature of this Dictionary, which can be stated as a rule: "For those definitions that end in a semicolon followed by one final word, that final word is a synonym or near synonym for the headword and is also defined by the clause or phrase prior to the semicolon." Thus, *toady* is an approximate synonym of *lickspittle* and can also be defined as "a fawning, servile flatterer." Hence, you are getting one more word for your money.

As for *fumigate,* the second of the three potentially perplexing words in the Memory Aid above, if you look up this word in the Dictionary you will only be furnished with the following reference:

fumigate, 88

However, this boldface *word* (as opposed to a boldface *root*) should immediately alert you to the fact that this term is either a Detailed Example or Brief Analyses word within the COMMON ROOTS or an Example word within the SUBJECTS since these are the only entries in this book that appear in boldface roman type. So if you then turn to page agact-2, you will find *fumigate* under the Brief Analyses of chapter AG-, ACT-, -IG-.

---

fumigate
(fyōō´mə·gāt´)

1) fum-/-ig-/-at-/-e
2) *fum-*: smoke, vapor, fume (cf. PER<u>FU</u>ME); *-ig-*: to do, to act, to drive (cf. NAV<u>IG</u>ATE); *-at-*: to cause, to make, to function, to manage (cf. GENER<u>AT</u>E); *-e*: silent final letter.
3) to manage or cause (*-at-*) to drive (*-ig-*) smoke or fumes (*fum-*).
4) *v.* to permeate with smoke, vapor, or fumes, especially to rid of roaches, ants, bedbugs, or other vermin.

Once again, this four-step analysis of *fumigate* should satisfy most of you. But those of you who wish to know the derivation of the roots in *fumigate* can consult the cross references under step 2, namely, *fum-*, PER<u>FU</u>ME, *-ig-*, NAV<u>IG</u>ATE, *-at-*, and GENER<u>AT</u>E, which will not only provide you with definitions and etymologies of these roots and words, but will furnish you with a wealth of supplementary information and additional cross references.

Finally, with regard to *undaunted*, the third of the three entries in the Memory Aid, if you check A CROSS-REFERENCE DICTIONARY you will also be pleased to find the following short but information-packed entry:

UNDAUNTED (un·dôn´tid) *adj.* not intimidated, disheartened, or hesitant because of fear or opposition; fearless; intrepid. **[un- + daunt + -ed]** < E. *un-*: not, lacking, the opposite of + AF. *daunt(er)* (< OF. *donter*): to overcome, defeat (< L. *domitāre*, freq. of *domāre*: to tame, subdue) + E. *-ed* (in this context < OE. *-d, -ed, -od,* or *-ad*): ppl. suffix with the inflectional meaning: having been or having had (not to be confused with E. *-ed* [< OE. *-de, -ede, -ade,* or *-ode*], past tense suffix, as in *hopped* or *milked*). **RECON:** *not* (**un-**) *having been* (**-ed**) *overcome or defeated* (**daunt**); cf. DANGEROUS for a seemingly related but completely independent etymology, 33-34. . . .

Again, if you look up the italic roots in this entry, you will find a wide divergence of coverage in the Dictionary. For example, under the first root *un-*, you will not only receive a more complete definition of this prefix but will be presented with seven English words containing *un-*; and you will further be directed to the semantically similar and linguistically related Latin prefixes NON- and IN-[2]. And guess where that superscript "[2]" will lead some of you? As for the other roots in this entry, you will not find follow-up coverage for most of them since they are relatively rare, not cited very often in this book, or, in the case of -ed, fairly adequately covered in this entry.

On other occasions, while leafing through this book, you may observe two or more identical roots or words that are followed by different superscript numbers. These are called *homographs* (< G. *hom(os)*: same + -o-: connecting vowel + -*graph(os)*: written, drawn + E. -*s*: plural suffix), which may be defined as two or more words or roots that are spelled the same but have different origins, meanings, and sometimes pronunciations. For example, in the final sentence of the Analysis step of the Detailed Example of *pedagogue* in chapter -AGOG- (see page 8), you may recall the directive:

(For further information, see PED-[1], PED-[2], and
PED-[3] in A CROSS-REFERENCE DICTIONARY.)

In A CROSS-REFERENCE DICTIONARY, homographic root entries are treated essentially the same as succinct root entries cross-referred from the Brief Analyses of the COMMON ROOTS (see *hypn-* on page 25) or the Examples of the SUBJECTS (see *centr-* on page 26). The only difference is that the homographic root entries always include at least one (but usually three) English derivatives after their respective definitions to enable you to more effectively distinguish between the meanings and etymologies of the derivative English words of one homographic root from those of the other homographic root or roots. For example, if you look up *ped-* in A CROSS-REFERENCE DICTIONARY, you will find the following three homographs:

---

ped-[1] < L. *ped-*, base of *pedis*, gen. of *pēs*: foot: *pedestal*, PEDICURE, *pedometer* (pi·däm´i·tər, pə-; a device carried by a walker or jogger that records the number of steps taken), . . . **45**, *45*, **108**, *108*, see also under QUADRUPED

ped-[2] < G. *paid-*, base of *paidos*, gen. of *pais*: boy, child: PEDAGOGUE, PEDOPHILE, *pediatrics* (the branch of medicine dealing with the development, care, diseases, and treatment of children), *encyclopedia*, . . . *45*, 249-50

ped-[3] < L. *pēd-*, base of *pēdis*: louse (pl.: lice): *pediculosis* (the infestation with lice; also called *phthiriasis* [thə·rī´ə·sis]—not to be confused with *psoriasis*, a skin condition charact. by scaly, reddish patches), PEDICULOPHOBIA, . . . **102**

In each homographic entry, the English derivative words of each non-English root are listed in small capitals or italics immediately following the colon after the roman definition of that root. As with all other roots and words in this book, a derivative in small capitals will receive extensive, follow-up coverage in A CROSS-REFERENCE DICTIONARY or elsewhere in this book (though the word itself will not necessarily appear in small capitals in that location), but an italic English *word* in this Dictionary will receive only short parenthetical coverage within the same sentence or, if it is a common word, none at all.

The italic conventions used in A CROSS-REFERENCE DICTIONARY therefore differ substantially from those used in other parts of this book. In the COMMON ROOTS and SUBJECTS, italic *roots* that are not furnished with etymologies will *always* be provided with these in the Dictionary or elsewhere in this book; but in the Dictionary, italic *roots*, regardless of their coverage, may or may not be provided with follow-up etymologies, depending on how common those roots are and other factors. In further contrast, italic *words* in the COMMON ROOTS that are not furnished with definitions and etymologies will *always* be provided with these in the Dictionary or elsewhere in the book; but as we have just seen, italic *words* in the Dictionary will either receive short parenthetical definitions or none at all, but will *never* receive in-depth follow-up coverage in the Dictionary. And in the SUBJECTS, italic *words* will generally be provided with simple definitions and partial etymologies right in the text and will therefore not need nor usually receive follow-up coverage in the Dictionary.

This may all seem very confusing to you, but as you read the different parts of this book and become familiar with their general layout, you will develop a sense of which words and roots will receive follow-up coverage and which will not. Therefore, you need not attempt to memorize the information in the above paragraph.

For example, in the entry for PED-¹ the first English derivative cited after the definition "foot" is *pedestal*, which is in italics and in this case does not receive further coverage in this work. I have chosen this option for *pedestal* because I assume that most of you are familiar with this word and felt it was not worthy of further explication, though I do record *pedestal* in its own alphabetical order in the Dictionary and cross-refer it back to PED-¹ to show that it is a derivative of Latin *pēs*, "foot." The second derivative PEDICURE, however, is in small capitals and thus receives detailed follow-up coverage in this book. I have made the editorial decision that though this is only a slightly out-of-the-ordinary word, it is nonetheless an important word and deserves a definition and etymology. And the third derivative, *pedometer*—in distinction to *pedestal* and *pedicure*—has such a low frequency of use that few of you (unless you're a runner or racewalker) will know its meaning, and it therefore requires at least some follow-up coverage. Accordingly, I have provided it with a parenthetical definition and, because many people might mispronounce it "*ped´ō·mē´tər" or "*pē´dō·mē´tər," a pronunciation, too.

At the end of the entry for PED-¹, you'll notice that "45" appears in both boldface italics and lightface (normal) italics, and "108" appears in boldface roman and lightface italics. What this means is that PED-¹ appears at least twice on page 45, once in boldface italics and once in italics, and it appears at least twice on page 108, once in boldface roman and once in italics.

In PED-², the selection and rationale for the derivatives are a little different. Specifically, the first derivative, PEDAGOGUE, is not cross-referred to a Dictionary entry but rather, as you may recall, to the Detailed Example word in chapter -AGOG-. I have chosen this particular word because in the Analysis step of that Detailed Example, I provide a scholarly explanation as to how Greek *pais* evolved into English *ped-*, and I felt that a further cross reference to this telling information was important to make. But so as not to shortchange those of you with a less theoretical penchant (a strong liking or inclination for something) but who may still desire follow-up information, my second derivative, PEDOPHILE, is a cross reference to a more topical and straightforward Dictionary entry. And finally, my two remaining derivatives—*pediatrics* and *encyclopedia*—are much more common words, in which I provide a parenthetical definition for *pediatrics* for those of you who might be a little fuzzy about its meaning, and I include *encyclopedia* because I always find it encouraging to see children (*ped-*) in reference works (*encyclopedia*).

In PED-³, I include still other features not present in PED-¹ or PED-². Near the beginning of this entry, following the definition of Latin *pēdis*, "louse," I insert "(pl.: lice)," since I have found that most people don't realize that *louse* is the singular of *lice* but rather suppose it to be a separate insect, if, in fact, they even realize it is an insect. Then I proceed to cite a derivative of PED-³, *pediculosis*, followed by its definition in parentheses (for it would be ridiculosis [sic] not to do so), which further includes an almost humorous allusion to its jawbreaking synonym, *phthiriasis* (which, of course, necessitates a pronunciation of that term too) and which, in turn, leads to a caution not to confuse this word with the similar sounding *psoriasis* that many people will instantly mistake for *phthiriasis*, but whose meaning they may, in all likelihood, not know either—leading, in turn, to a subdefinition of *psoriasis*. And I wind up this entry by citing a second derivative of PED-³, PEDICULOPHOBIA. So in far less space than it took to write this, I have provided you with what I hope is an illuminating packet of related linguistic information.

In reading or scanning A CROSS-REFERENCE DICTIONARY, you will occasionally come across somewhat unusual "clumps" of partially underlined and partially boldface entries that appear as follows:

<u>biblio</u>**clast**, <u>50</u>, **101**
<u>biblio</u>**film**, <u>50</u>, **101**
<u>biblio</u>**gene**sis, <u>50</u>, **101**
<u>biblio</u>**gony**, <u>50</u>, **101**
<u>biblio</u>**gnost**, <u>50</u>, **101**
bibliographer, **48**, *90*
<u>biblio</u>**graphical**ly, <u>50</u>, **101**
<u>biblio</u>**graphy**, <u>50</u>, **101**
biblioklept, **49**
bibliokleptomania, **142**
<u>biblio</u>**latr**ist, <u>50</u>, **101**

With the exception of **bibliographer**, **biblioklept**, and **bibliokleptomania** (to be discussed in a moment), these are all combination Exercise-HELPFUL HINTS entries. As you know, at the end of each COMMON ROOTS chapter are three columns of exercises; and in each corresponding HELPFUL HINTS section, the meaning and etymology of one root in each exercise entry is provided.

The entries above are keyed to both the Exercises and their corresponding HELPFUL HINTS, both of which are immediately brought to your attention by their unique appearance. Specifically, the underlined, lightface portion of each headword identifies which root is covered in the chapter, and the boldface portion signifies which root is analyzed in the corresponding HELPFUL HINTS.

Similarly, the page numbers are coded to the Exercises and the HELPFUL HINTS: the underlined page number indicates the page in which the exercise entry appears, and the boldface page number indicates the page in which the corresponding HELPFUL HINTS unit appears.

The three exceptions in the list above are, as noted, **bibliographer**, **biblioklept**, and **bibliokleptomania**. These words are obviously not Exercise-HELPFUL HINTS entries since they are neither partially underlined nor partially boldface and no underlining appears in their page numbers. What the boldfacing does represent, however, is that these terms will appear in boldface in the text, which, as we have seen, means they are either Detailed Example or Brief Analyses words within the COMMON ROOTS, or Example words within the SUBJECTS.

It should thus be clear from the foregoing discussion how integrated the different parts of this book are and how every entry in A CROSS-REFERENCE DICTIONARY is included for a specific purpose. This is even true for those entries that do not have a page number, which immediately identifies them as a dictionary-to-dictionary cross reference, e.g., MONOZYGOTIC, which is cross-referred from the Dictionary entry DIZYGOTIC, which itself is cross-referred from the SUBJECTS entry *syzygy* in Astronomy under the category of Professional Words. In this context, the biological term *dizygotic* is associated with the astronomical term *syzygy* because they both derive from the Greek noun *zygon*, "yoke," an etymology which is clearly explained and qualified in their respective entries and elements.

In conclusion, now that you are familiar with the numerous features and conventions of this book, you can tailor your reading to suit your needs (pun intended). For example, if your primary objective is learning *English* roots, you should now be aware that you can avoid practically all of the technical information by skipping over the Technical Information and Detailed Example sections of the COMMON ROOTS and the even more recondite data provided within large and small parentheses in A CROSS-REFERENCE DICTIONARY. On the other hand, if your interest lies primarily in learning the fundamentals of English etymology, you would want to concentrate on HOW ENGLISH WORDS ARE CREATED: A SHORT COURSE and seek out the Technical Information and Detailed Example sections of the COMMON ROOTS as well as the more intricate parenthetical data in A CROSS-REFERENCE DICTIONARY. Or if you're one of those people who love obscure words, you would now know to go directly to the third column of Exercises in each of the COMMON ROOTS chapters and consult their corresponding HELPFUL HINTS; and you would probably also want to skim A CROSS-REFERENCE DICTIONARY for other esoteric headwords and references. There are many combinations and possibilities, and you should now be able to develop a regimen expressly adapted to your own needs and interests.

RATIONALE FOR THIS WORK

The logic behind the construction of *Grow Your Vocabulary* rests on a systematic and *repetitive* study of English words, word roots, and the classical and nonclassical sources from which these elements derive. Through the informative HOW ENGLISH WORDS ARE CREATED: A SHORT COURSE and motif (mō·tēf´; a recurrent theme or subject) of "dissection, analysis, reconstruction, definition, and commentary"—embellished with a wealth of secondary roots, cross references, illustrative examples, colorful anecdotes, and reinforcing exercises and answer keys—you can easily and effortlessly absorb much of the material in this book.

The pedagogic assumptions underlying the theory and construction of this work are that human beings generally do not recall the details of what they read and often do not retain what they believe they have learned. Thus, merely reading isolated examples of new words and new roots will not enable you to learn such material; and studying new roots and words only to the point of recall is not sufficient for long-term retention. To effectively remember complex data, you must "overlearn" what you have read and understood, or what may be described as learning material well beyond the point of mere recall.

It is overlearning that accounts for the fact that we can still recall the multiplication tables, rattle off the letters of the alphabet, and recall the names of many of our childhood friends; and it is the absence of overlearning which further explains how a student can successfully "cram" for an exam but two weeks later will have forgotten practically everything "learned."

Grow Your Vocabulary thus seeks to avoid this educational pitfall by systematically dissecting, analyzing, reconstructing, defining, and providing commentaries for hundreds of entries throughout this work, getting you to repeatedly review and participate in this process, and using the repetition inherent in this procedure and throughout this book as a means of enabling you to *overlearn* and remember what you have read and done. (For documentation and substantiation of this thesis, see REVIEW OF LITERATURE on page 41.)

A NOTE TO THE PROFESSIONAL

This book is written for a large and heterogeneous audience, consisting predominantly of intelligent and thoughtful lay readers with no background in word roots or etymology. It is not designed for nor directed to the professional linguist or lexicographer. Since the only "etymological" reference work most readers of this book possess is probably an old and musty desk or college dictionary (one reader has described his dictionary as "maggoty"), I have tried to present my material in a manner that is consistent with the treatment given in such dictionaries, though this treatment has often been standardized and in certain instances is less discriminating than one would like to see. For similar reasons, I have avoided highly technical etymologies and most linguistic terminology, and I have taken other minor liberties to make this information more accessible to the beginner.

Specifically, in my reconstructions I have sometimes added a definite or indefinite article, changed the part of speech of a word, made a singular word plural, or inserted an extra word or *-ing* to make the resulting sentence more intelligible. In my etymologies, I have routinely skipped intermediate stages in the development of complex words where to do otherwise would have only confused matters. Similarly, I have generally not distinguished between whether non-English roots were combined in their native tongue or in English to form combining forms and words, and in HOW ENGLISH WORDS ARE CREATED: A SHORT COURSE I have routinely presented this information as though the combining occurred in English. In certain words I have defined an *-i-* or *-o-* as a "connective vowel," when, more technically, these letters might have been expressed, respectively, as the variant ending of a primary or alternative Latin or Greek stem that merely *functions* as a connecting vowel; and I have adopted the almost universal practice of citing Latin past participles of intransitive verbs as though they were bona fide Latin forms.

Throughout this book, I have regularly cited the genitive singular, rather than the oblique stem or other hyphenated forms, as a vehicle for providing the base of certain nouns and adjectives. I think there is justification in this practice. In addition to the logic tendered on pages 192–94, oblique stems are not the perfect solution and have their own limitations. For example, in Latin, neuter nouns in the nominative and accusative cases have the same form, rendering the consistency of using the rubric, "the oblique stem of," for all nouns and adjectives problematic if not impossible; and if beginners need one aid in learning such a complex subject as etymology, it is consistency. Moreover, I have found that providing a stem with a hyphen is frustrating to beginners who need the closure of an entire word unless that stem is immediately followed by a specific ending that can be affixed to it to form a word. The genitive singular works admirably well in these instances. And if the beginner is made aware that the genitive is merely one representative of a whole declension of forms, most of which can also be used to elicit the substantival or adjectival stem—as I have taken pains to emphasize in this work—I see no objection to using this shorthand.

In short, without compromising the integrity of this work, I have slightly simplified and standardized certain noncritical data so as not to overwhelm and confuse readers with a baffling array of linguistic terms, variants, special forms, exceptions, anomalies, and miscellaneous etymological detritus.

I welcome any corrections or suggestions you may have for improvement of this book, however minor. Or if you would like to contact me for any other reason, I would be delighted to hear from you. You can reach me directly at P.O. Box 856, New York, N.Y. 10009.

ACKNOWLEDGMENTS

During my work on this project, I have had the opportunity to meet or speak with three eminent linguists and lexicographers, each of whom has generously shared his time and expertise with me: Professors George Szozkida, John Poulakos, and Frank Abate. And I have also benefited from the wisdom of Peter F. Skinner, a veritable Renaissance man whose breadth of scholarship is matched only by his endearing modesty and willingness to help. This transplanted Englishman often has on the tip of his tongue erudite information that has others scampering to reference libraries to unearth. To the foregoing, I should also add my uncle, Phillip Schleifer, a person fluent in more languages than I can keep track of, who has always been available to discuss sundry (sun´drē; various or diverse) etymological points of Dutch, German, French, Portuguese, Afrikaans, and other languages that have found their way into this book.

I also have warm feelings for Laurence Urdang, former Managing Editor of the Unabridged Random House Dictionary and former Editor-in-Chief of the Random House college dictionaries (and a person who has further benefited all of us in the field by authoring or editing over 125 lexicographic books and journals, including the popular *Verbatim*). Prior to entering graduate school in the early 1980's, I sent Mr. Urdang, who lives in Connecticut, a scribbled introductory note indicating my interest in etymology and lexicography. As a result of this, on his next trip to New York City (my home town), he made special arrangements to borrow an associate's office so we could meet and talk—which we did for two-and-a-half hours. I still can't believe he would spend all that time with a kid out of college who had to borrow a tie for the occasion. But I can say one thing for sure: Mr. Urdang's knowledge of Indo-European, Germanic, ancient Celtic, Hittite, Akkadian, and other areas of etymology is truly impressive; and despite his reputation in the field, I still don't believe he has yet received the recognition he deserves.

For their continual support, I also wish to thank Don Hauptman, author of the entertaining and educational *Cruel and Unusual Puns* and *Acronymania*; Lyn Grossman, a sparkling and meticulous copy editor who has been kind enough to review some of my technical data; Madeline Kripke, a collector of dictionaries who was generous enough to share with me some of her original lexicographic documents; and Dave Levner, President of Hypertext Corporation, who was always available to assist me with ticklish computer problems, often at his own inconvenience, and never with the slightest hint of impatience. With regard to my computer training, I must further thank Luann Totaro and especially "Moses" for spending countless hours teaching me how to use these contraptions and, in particular, how to program all of the special characters and diacritical marks needed for this book. And whenever my energy level drooped, I could always depend on Mary-Lynne Peluso, healthy life-style consultant and business production organizer, to help verify important facts and supply me with "brain formula" to get me through the day.

But, above all, I must thank two people who actually took the time to read portions of this manuscript and make useful and sometimes critical suggestions: Hugh Himwich, a dedicated Latin scholar and former publisher of the linguistic journal, *Sesquipedalian*, and my dizygotic brother Ronald (see that term in A CROSS-REFERENCE DICTIONARY), a Professor of English and truly innovative linguist, who helped me get this work out in time under the pressure of a horrendous deadline. And, of course, I cannot forget my editor on this project, Sol Steinmetz—a name that anyone in the field will instantly recognize—who waded through a morass of macrons, large and small parentheses, and roots and words spanning a period of over 2,500 years. Of course I, as the author, am ultimately responsible for any errors in this work.

Finally, I must thank the two people who started it all off: Peter Robert Margolin, an extraordinary geological scientist and the Physical Science editor of the Random House Unabridged Dictionary, and David L. Gold, a careful student of language whose modesty belies his erudition. I can only hope that this work comes close to meeting their high standards.

REVIEW OF LITERATURE

Bernt, Frank M., and Bugbee, Alan C., Jr. "Study Practices of Adult Learners in Distance Education: Frequency of Use and Effectiveness." Paper presented at the Annual Meeting of the American Educational Research Association, Boston, MA (April 1990), 19 pp.

Biggins, Catherine M., and Sainz, Jo-Ann. "Freshman Experience: The Needs of the Least Educated: How To Meet Their Problems and Help Them Persevere in Their College Program." Paper presented at the Northeast Regional Meeting of the Freshman Year Experience and Beyond: Foundations for Improving the Undergraduate Experience." White Plains, NY (April 1989), 26 pp.

Brainer, C. J., and Reyna, V. F. "Can Age X Learnability Interactions Explain the Development of Forgetting?" *Developmental Psychology* 26, no.2 (March 1990): 194–213.

Casey, M. B. "Effect of Training Procedures on the Overlearning Reversal Effect in Young Children." *Journal of Experimental Child Psychology* 20 (August 1975): 1–12.

Chasey, W. C. "Motor Skill Overlearning Effects on Retention and Relearning by Retarded Boys." *Research Quarterly* 48 (March 1977): 41–46.

Foriska, Terry J. "What Every Educator Should Know about Learning." *Schools-in-the-Middle* 3, no.2 (November 1993): 39–44.

Kratochwill, T. R., and others. "Effects of Overlearning on Preschool Children's Retention of Sight Vocabulary Words." *Reading Improvement* 14 (Winter 1977): 223–228.

Krueger, W. C. F. "The Effect of Overlearning on Retention." *Journal of Experimental Psychology* 12 (1929): 71–78.

Lopez, M. A. "Social Skills Training with Institutionalized Elderly: Effects of Pre-Counseling Structuring and Overlearning on Skill Acquisition." *Journal of Counseling Psychology* 27 (May 1980): 286–293.

Nelson, Thomas O., and others. "Overlearning and the Feeling of Knowing." *Journal of Experimental Psychology: Learning, Memory, and Cognition* 8, no.4 (July 1982): 279–288.

Postman, L. "Retention as a Function of Degree of Overlearning." *Science* 135 (1962): 666–667.

Postman, L. "Transfer of Training as a Function of Experimental Paradigm and Degree of First-List Learning." *Journal of Verbal Learning and Verbal Behavior* 1 (1962): 109–118.

Semb, G. B., and others. "Long-Term Memory for Knowledge Learned in School." *Journal of Educational Psychology* 85 (June 1993): 305–316.

Semb, George B., and Ellis, John A. "Knowledge Learned in College: What is Remembered?" Paper presented at the Annual Meeting of the American Educational Research Association, San Francisco, CA (April 1992), 28 pp.

Slate, John R., and Charlesworth, John, Jr. "Information Processing Theory: Classroom Applications." *Reading Improvement* 26, no.1 (Spring 1989): 2–6.

Spring, C., and others. "Learning to Read Words: Effects of Overlearning and Similarity on Stimulus Selection." *Journal of Reading Behavior* 11 (Spring 1979): 69–71.

Vockell, Edward L., and Mihail, Thomas. "Instructional Principles behind Computerized Instruction for Students with Exceptionalities." *Teaching Exceptional Children* 25, no.3 (Spring 1993): 38–43.

Wasim, M. "Effect of Repeated Learning and Overlearning on Recall." *Pakistan Journal of Psychology* (June 1974): 59–61.

PART I
COMMON ROOTS

ONE-ROOT DERIVATIVES

▪️**agog**▪️ leader, leading, bringing

Memory Aid   Envision) a *demagogue*, an unscrupulous, rabble-rousing <u>leader</u> of the people (see *dem-agogue* under BRIEF ANALYSES), <u>leading</u> a mob of yelling and jeering townspeople down Main Street and <u>bringing</u> them to the town square while inciting them with lies, half-truths, and inflammatory appeals.

Technical Information   *-agog-* is the base of the Greek masculine combining form *-agōgos* (à·gō·gôsʹ), "leader, leading, bringing." It is also the base of the feminine form *-agōgē* (à·gō·gāʹ) and the neuter form *-agōgon* (à·gō·gônʹ). All three forms in turn derive from the Greek verb *agein* (àʹgān), "to drive, to lead," which is closely related to the Latin verb *agere* (àʹge·re), "to do, to act, to drive" (see chapter AG-, ACT-, -IG-). But the *-ag-* in Greek *-agog-* (the entire base *-agog-* will always appear in English words) should not be confused with the *ag-* in Latin *agere* (the *-ere* will never appear in English words); nor should the *-a-* in *-agog-* be mistaken for any of various Greek and nonclassical pre-fixes represented by *a-*, as in *atom* and *asleep* (see chapter A-, AN-). And it is instructive to note that the English word *agog*, "very excited or in a state of eager anticipation," is neither derived from nor in any way related to *-agog-*, being from Old French *gogue*, "joke, jest."

DETAILED EXAMPLE

pedagogue (pedʹ ə·gägʹ)

Dissection: 1) ped- / -agog- / -ue

Analysis: 2) ***ped-*** is derived from Greek *paidos* (pī·dôsʹ), which is the genitive of *pais* (pīs), "boy, child." ***-agog-*** is the base of Greek *-agōgos* (à·gō·gôsʹ), "leader, leading, bringing," which is derived from the Greek verb *agein* (àʹgān), 'to drive, to lead.' **-ue** is a French "silent final ending." <u>Note</u>: Greek *paidos* becomes English *ped-* in the following manner: First, the *-os* of *paidos* drops off, leaving the base *paid-*. Then, in Latin, the Greek diphthong *-ai-* becomes *-ae-*, converting Greek *paid-* into Latin *paed-*. Finally, in English, the *-ae-* diphthong is reduced to *-e-*, yielding our simplified root *ped-*. (For further information, see PED-[1], PED-[2], and PED-[3] in the A CROSS-REFERENCE DICTIONARY.)

Reconstruction: 3) a leader (*-agog-*) of children (*ped-*); OR child (*ped-*) leader (*-agog-*).

Definition: 4) *n.* 1. a schoolteacher, particularly one who is old-fashioned, narrow-minded, and a stickler for rules and regulations. 2. any narrow-minded, pedantic instructor.

Commentary: 5) In ancient Greece, a *paidagōgos* (pī·dȧ·gō·gôs´) was a family slave who escorted (i.e., led, brought) little boys to and from school (little girls were not educated in those days). In some households, however, if the slave were himself properly educated, he also became a tutor or teacher for the boys of the family—expanding the meaning of *paidagōgos*. Moreover, as children of bygone times knew painfully well, teachers were often uncompromisingly strict and not infrequently a bit stuffy—hence, the pejorative connotations of *pedagogue*.

BRIEF ANALYSES

demagogue
(dem´ə·gäg´)

1) dem-/-agog-/-ue/
2) *dem-*: people (cf. <u>DEM</u>OCRACY); *-agog-*: leader, leading, bringing; *-ue*: silent ending.
3) a leader (*-agog-*) of the people (*dem-*).
4) *n.* a person, especially a political agitator, who seeks to gain popularity and power by inciting the passions and prejudices of the people.
5) In ancient Greece, *dēmagōgos* (dā·mȧ·gō·gôs´) referred, in particular, to the leaders of the popular party during the Peloponnesian War, who, because of the epithets hurled upon them, gave rise to the negative sense of this word—a word borrowed by John Milton in the 17th century and Anglicized to *demagogue*.

synagogue
(sin´ə·gäg´)

1) syn-/-agog-/-ue/
2) *syn-*: with, together (cf. <u>SYN</u>THESIS); *-agog-*: leader, leading, bringing; *-ue*: silent ending.
3) a bringing (*-agog-*) together (*syn-*).
4) *n.* 1. a building used by Jews for worship and instruction. 2. a Jewish congregation.
5) Originally, a *synagōgē* (sü·nä·gō·gā´; a 3rd century B.C. Greek translation of Hebrew *keneseth*, "assembly") was a "bringing together" of at least ten males over the age of thirteen to form a Jewish quorum, or *minyan*.

hypnagogic
(hip´nə·gäj´ik)

1) hypn-/-agog-/-ic
2) *hypn-*: sleep (cf. HYPNOSIS); *-agog-*: leader, leading, bringing; *-ic*: pertaining to, characterized by (cf. ANGELIC).
3) characterized by (*-ic*) bringing (*-agog-*) sleep (*hypn-*).
4) *adj.* 1. of or associated with that state of consciousness immediately preceding sleep. 2. inducing sleep or drowsiness.
5) Hypnos was the Greek god of sleep. His son Morpheus (< Greek *morphē*: form, shape; cf. MORPHINE, MORPHOLOGY) was the classical god of dreams, his function being to form and shape images during sleep. The ancient Roman counterpart of Greek Hypnos was Somnus (< Latin *somnus*: sleep; cf. SOMNAMBULISM, SOMNILOQUY). And the twin brother of Hypnos was Thanatos (< Greek *thanatos*: death; cf. THANATOPHOBIA, EUTHANASIA)—the personification of death.

galactagogue
(gə·lak´tə·gäg´)

1) galact-/-agog-/-ue
2) *galact-*: milk (cf. GALACTIC); *-agog-*: leader, leading, bringing; *-ue*: silent ending.
3) bringing (*-agog-*) milk (*galact-*).
4) *n.* any agent that induces or increases the flow of milk from a woman's breasts or an animal's mammae.
5) In medical terminology, *-agogue* is a prolific combining form having the technical meaning, "promoting or inducing the flow or expulsion of (that which is designated by the preceding base or elements)." For additional medical *-agogue* terms, see the entries in the third column under EXERCISES.

EXERCISES

DISSECT, ANALYZE, RECONSTRUCT, DEFINE, and provide a COMMENTARY for three words in each column, and try to use each in an intelligent sentence. Use a college or unabridged dictionary to check your work. The three columns are arranged in order of difficulty.

pedagogy	anagogy	hydragogue
pedagogics	isagoge	sialagogue
pedagogical	epagoge	cholagogue
pedagoguish	paragoge	emmenagogue
demagogy	agogic	lithagogue
demagoguism	isagogics	helminthagogue
demagoguery	psychagogue	dacryagogue
synagogical	mystagogue	dacryagogatresia

(Helpful Hints: Page 101)

bibli- book, books, bible

Memory Aid Think first of *bible*. Now actually "see" the *e* of *bible* dissolving into the final *i* of *bibli-* and then changing back into *e*. Then remember that the bible is still a <u>book</u> or, more accurately, a collection of <u>books</u> under one cover.

Technical Information *bibli-* is the base of Greek *biblion* (bi·blē´ôn), "book, little book"—originally a roll or scroll of papyrus (the inner bark or pith of the papyrus plant, used as an early type of paper). *biblion*, in turn, is a diminutive of *biblos* (bi´blôs), "papyrus," originally spelled and pronounced *byblos* (bü´blôs) after the Phoenician city of *Byblos*, from where it was produced and exported to Egypt and elsewhere. "Bible," as an alternative and less common meaning of *bibli-*, is a later development. The plural of Greek *biblion*, "book," is *biblia* (bi·blē´á), "books"; and *ta* (tá) *biblia*, "the books," eventually came to refer to the canonical books or scriptures. Then, during the Late Latin period, the Romans borrowed Greek *biblia* and appended *sacra* (sàk·rà), "holy," to it, forming the Latin phrase *biblia sacra*, "holy books." The *sacra* subsequently dropped out, leaving *biblia* alone to represent the holy books or "bible"—the *-a* being construed as a feminine singular (rather than neuter plural) suffix.

DETAILED EXAMPLE

bibliographer (bib´lē·äg´rə·fer)

Dissection: 1) bibli- / -o- / graph- / -er

Analysis: 2) **bibli-** is the base of Greek *biblion* (bi·blē´ôn), "book." **-o-** is a Greek "connecting vowel." **graph-** is the base of Greek *-graphos* (grä´fôs) "that which is written or drawn" OR "one who writes about or draws," which in turn is derived from the Greek verb *graphein* (grä´fān), 'to write, to draw.' **-er** is derived from Old English *-ere* (e´re), "one who or that which (performs the action designated by the preceding base)," which itself is derived from or akin to Latin *-ārius* (ä´ri·⊖⊖s), 'pertaining to, characterized by' OR 'one who or that which.'

Reconstruction: 3) one who (*-er*) writes or has written about (*graph-*) books (*bibli-*).

Definition: 4) *n.* 1. a person who compiles or works with bibliographies. 2. an expert in bibliography.

Commentary: 5) Bibliographies are essentially reference lists of or about books. Hence, the bibliographer, in part, compiles, annotates, or updates inventories of reference material about specific books. The *autobiographer*, in contrast, is one who (*-er*) writes (*graph-*) about the life (*bi-*) of [him- or her-] self (*aut-*); a *lexicographer*, whom Samuel Johnson characterized as "a harmless drudge," is one who (*-er*) writes (*graph-*) word books or dictionaries (*lexic-*); a *hagiographer*, also a drudge of sorts, is one who (*-er*) writes (*graph-*) about saints or those who are holy (*hagi-*); and a *pornographer*, in contradistinction, is one who (*-er*) writes about or draws (*graph-*) prostitutes (*porn-*).

BRIEF ANALYSES

biblical
(bib´li·kəl)
1) bibli-/-ic/-al
2) *bibli-*: book, books, bible; *-ic*: pertaining to, characterized by (cf. HISTOR<u>IC</u>); *-al*: pertaining to, characterized by (cf. HISTORIC<u>AL</u>).
3) pertaining to (*-al*) that which characterizes (*-ic*) the bible (*bibli-*).
4) *adj.* of, in, or in accord with the bible.
5) In this word, *bibli-* and *-ic* are sharing an *i*.

bibliophile
(bib´lē·ə·fīl´)
1) bibli-/-o-/phil-/-e
2) *bibli-*: book, books, bible; *-o-*: connecting vowel; *phil-*: loving, beloved (cf. DISCO<u>PHILE</u>); *-e*: silent final letter.
3) loving (*phil-*) books (*bibli-*).
4) *n.* a person who loves or admires books, especially a collector of rare or elegant books.

bibliophobe
(bib´lē·ə·fōb´)
1) bibli-/-o-/phob-/-e
2) *bibli-*: book, books, bible; *-o-*: connecting vowel; *phob-*: fear, dread, hate (cf. XENO<u>PHOBE</u>); *-e*: silent final letter.
3) fearing, dreading, or hating (*phob-*) books (*bibli-*).
4) *n.* a person who fears, dreads, or hates books.

biblioklept
(bib´lē·ə·klept´)
1) bibli-/-o-/klept-
2) *bibli-*: book, books, bible; *-o-*: connecting vowel; *klept-*: a thief (cf. <u>KLEPT</u>OMA-NIA).
3) a book (*bibli-*) thief (*klept-*).
4) *n.* a person who steals or has a compulsion to steal books.
5) *klept-* can further be dissected into two roots: *klep-* (< Greek *kleptein*), "to steal," and *-t-* (< Greek *-tēs*), "one who or that which" (cf. PO<u>ET</u>). Hence, a *biblioklept* is one who (*-t*) steals (*klep-*) books (*bibli-*).

bibliosoph
(bib´lē·ə·sof´)
1) bibli-/-o-/soph-
2) *bibli-*: book, books, bible; *-o-*: connecting vowel; *soph-*: wise (cf. <u>SOPH</u>ISTI-CATED).

3) book (*bibli-*) wise (*soph-*).
4) *n.* a person who is knowledgeable about books.
5) We also find *soph-* in *sophomore*, in which the *-mor-* is patterned after Greek *mōros*, "foolish, dull, stupid." By this reckoning, a sophomore is both wise and foolish—a rather apt description for a student in the second year of college. Such words or figures of speech that embody incongruities or seeming contradictions are called *oxymora*, the plural of the more common *oxymoron*, a term derived from the Greek words *oxys*, "sharp, keen, acid," and, once again, *mōros*, "foolish, dull, stupid." Hence, an oxymoron, etymologically, is both sharp and dull (or keen and stupid) and is itself an oxymoron. Oxymoronic figures of speech include *sight unseen, student teacher, jumbo shrimp, hateful love, final draft, uncommonly common*, and *pretty ugly*. Can you think of any more?

EXERCISES

DISSECT, ANALYZE, RECONSTRUCT, DEFINE, and provide a COMMENTARY for three words in each column, and try to use each in an intelligent sentence. Use a college or unabridged dictionary to check your work. The three columns are arranged in order of difficulty.

biblically	bibliology	bibliopole
bibliography	bibliotics	bibliomane
biblicism	bibliotist	bibliotaph
bibliotherapy	bibliotheca	biblioclast
biblicoliteracy	bibliogenesis	bibliognost
bibliographically	biblicality	bibliolatrist
bibliomania	bibliogony	bibliopegist
bibliofilm	bibliophilistic	bibliophagist

(Helpful Hints: Page 101)

cardi- heart

Memory Aid Think of _cardiac arrest_ (the sudden and complete cessation of the <u>heart</u>beat), _cardiolo-gist_ (a doctor specializing in the diagnosis and treatment of <u>heart</u> disease), _cardiovascu-lar_ (of or affecting the <u>heart</u> and blood vessels), or any other _cardi-_ word that will help you make the association between _heart_ and _cardi-_. (For more complete definitions and etymologies, see _cardiovascular_ under DETAILED EXAMPLE, and _cardiac_ and _cardiology_ under BRIEF ANALYSES.)

Technical Information _cardi-_ is the Latinized base of the Greek noun _kardia_ (kär·dē´å), "heart." The change in spelling from _k_ to _c_ is a standard Latinization of Greek _k_ that was later adopted for most English words of Greek ancestry, regardless of whether they passed through Latin on their journey to English (see HOW ENGLISH WORDS ARE CREATED: A SHORT COURSE for an explanation of this). Moreover, the _i_ in _cardi-_ is not a "connecting vowel" but is the final and an essential letter of the base. Thus, Greek-derived _cardi-_, "heart," should never be confused with English _card_, "a piece of stiff, flat paper or plastic" (< Middle English _carde_, ultimately < Greek _chartēs_: a sheet of papyrus; cf. BIBLI-), or with Latin-derived _cardin-_, as in _cardinal_ and _cardinalate_. Finally, it is instructive to note that Greek _kardia_ is cognate with and equivalent in meaning to Latin _cor_ (genitive: _cordis_), "heart," from which we derive dozens of English words including _courage_, _cordial_, _cordate_, and _misericord_.

DETAILED EXAMPLE

cardiovascular (kär´dē·ō·vas´kyə·lər, -kyoo)

Dissection: 1) cardi- / -o- / vas- / -cul-/ -ar

Analysis: 2) **_cardi-_** is the Latinized base of Greek _kardia_ (kär·dē´å, "heart." **_-o-_** is a Greek "connecting vowel (in this context representing 'and')." **_vas-_** is derived from Latin _vās_ (wäs), "vessel." **_-cul-_** is the base of the Latin diminutive suffix _-culus_ (koo´loos), "small, little, tiny." **_-ar_** is the base of Latin _-āris_ (ä´ris), "pertaining to, characterized by, having the nature of, like."

Reconstruction: 3) pertaining to (_-ar_) the heart (_cardi-_) and (_-o-_) small (_-cul-_) vessels (_vas-_).

Definition: 4) _adj._ of, relating to, or affecting the heart and blood vessels.

Commentary: 5) In multiple-base compounds describing two parts of the body, the connecting _-o-_ can be loosely interpreted as "and," the two primary bases can be translated around this "and," and the entire reconstruction can then be introduced by its

_51_

adjective-forming suffix, which is generally defined as "pertaining to." Thus, we have *cervicofacial*, "pertaining to the neck and face," *nephrocardiac*, "pertaining to the kidneys and heart," *hepatocystic*, "pertaining to the liver and gallbladder," and *oculogastric*, "pertaining to the eyes and stomach." However, if the first or second base is not part of the body but is a modification of or commentary upon the other base (which *is* part of the body), then this compound should be reconstructed in the usual manner without attributing any meaning to *-o-* or assuming that the word is necessarily an adjective, as in *lobotomy* or *erythrocyte*. For further examples of both types of compounds, see the entries in the first column under EXERCISES. Can you tell which are which?

BRIEF ANALYSES

cardiac
(kär´dē·ak´)

1) cardi-/-ac
2) *cardi-*: heart; *-ac*: pertaining to, characterized by (cf. ZODIAC).
3) pertaining to (*-ac*) the heart (*cardi-*).
4) *adj.* 1. of, relating to, or affecting the heart. 2. of or pertaining to the upper portion of the stomach, particularly that section which joins the esophagus. *—n.* 3. a person afflicted with heart disease.
5) The reference of "cardiac" to the upper portion of the stomach derives in all likelihood from the observation that this part of the body is on the heart or *cardiac* side of the stomach. As far as we know, it has no other relationship to the heart. Other *cardi-* words that refer to the upper portion of the stomach include *cardia, cardiospasm, cardioplasty,* and *cardiopyloric.*

cardiology
(kär´dē·äl´ə·jē)

1) cardi-/-o-/-logy
2) *cardi-*: heart; *-o-*: connecting vowel; *-logy*: the science, study, theory, or doctrine of (cf. BIOLOGY).
3) the science of (*-logy*) the heart (*cardi-*).
4) *n.* the branch of medicine involving the structure, function, diseases, and treatment of the heart.

cardialgia
(kär´dē·al´jē·ə, -jə)

1) cardi-/alg-/-ia
2) *cardi-*: heart; *alg-*: pain (cf. NOSTALGIC); *-ia*: the state, condition, or result of (cf. ANEMIA).
3) the condition of (*-ia*) pain (*alg-*) in the heart (*cardi-*).
4) *n.* 1. a burning sensation beneath the midline of the chest, resulting from an upflow of acidic contents from the stomach into the esophagus; heartburn. 2. any pain in or near the heart.
5) *cardialgia*, while generally having nothing to do with the heart, is often perceived as a pain or discomfort in the heart.

tachycardia	1) tachy-/cardi-/-ia
(tak´i·kär´dē·ə)	2) *tachy-*: fast, swift, rapid (cf. TACHYPHAGIA); *cardi-*: heart; *-ia*: the state, condition, or result of (cf. INSOMNIA).
	3) the condition of (*-ia*) having a fast (*tachy-*) heart (*cardi-*).
	4) *n.* an abnormally rapid heartbeat, generally above 100 beats per minute in adults at rest.
	5) In this word, *cardi-* and *-ia* are sharing an *i*.
bradycardia	1) brady-/cardi-/-ia
(brad´i·kär´dē·ə)	2) *brady-*: slow (cf. BRADYPHAGIA); *cardi-*: heart; *-ia*: the state, condition, or result of (cf. DEMENTIA).
	3) the condition of (*-ia*) having a slow (*brady-*) heart (*cardi-*).
	4) *n.* an abnormally slow heartbeat, generally below 60 beats per minute in adults who do not engage in regular physical activity.
	5) In this word, *cardi-* and *-ia* are sharing an *i*.

EXERCISES

DISSECT, ANALYZE, RECONSTRUCT, DEFINE, and provide a COMMENTARY for three words in each column, and try to use each in an intelligent sentence. Use a college or unabridged dictionary to check your work. The three columns are arranged in order of difficulty.

cardiotherapy	myocardium	cardioid
cardiophobia	pericardium	dextrocardial
cardiopulmonary	endocardium	diplocardiac
cardiohepatic	epicardium	cardiomyopathy
cardionephric	myocarditis	acardiohemia
cardiorenal	pancarditis	acephalocardia
cardioplegia	telecardiophone	hydropericarditis
cardiopathy	cardiotachometer	Anacardium

(Helpful Hints: Page 102)

-cide the killing of, the killer of

Memory Aid Imagine yourself in a dark, deserted alley of a large city, all alone at 4 A.M.—standing over a grossly mangled human body. You vigilantly look around to see if anyone is coming and then ask yourself: "Is this a *homicide* (<u>the killing of</u> a person)? . . . And if so, *who* is the *homicide* (<u>the killer of</u> the person)?" (For the derivation of these two meanings of *homicide*, see TECHNICAL INFORMATION below.)

Technical Information *-cide* is an English combining form composed of two elements: *-cid-* and *-e*. The first element *-cid-* is the base of Latin *-cīdere* (kē´de•re), which is a combining form of the Latin verb *caedere* (kī´de•re), "to kill, to cut," used only *within* words; and the second element *-e* is a typical English "silent final letter," without meaning. More technically, two derivatives of Latin *-cīdere* yield English *-cid(e)-*: *-cīdium* (kē´di•oom), "the killing of," and *-cīda* (kē´dà), "the killer of." Thus, *homicide* (< Latin *hom(ō)*: person + *-i-*: connecting vowel + *-cīd(ium)*: the killing of + English *-e*: silent final letter) means "the killing of a person," while *homicide* (< Latin *hom(ō)*: person + *-i-*: connecting vowel + *-cīd(a)*: the killer of + English *-e*: silent final letter) means "the killer of a person." *caedere*, the parent verb of *-cīdere*, also has the past participle *caesus* (kī´soos), whose base *caes-* (used in the sense of "to cut"), in conjunction with the surname of Julius *Caes(ar)*, is alleged to be the source of *Caesarian section*. And *caesus* has the variant *-cīsus* (kē´soos), which is also the past participle of *-cīdere*, and whose base *-cīs-* (also used in the sense of "to cut") appears in such words as *incision*, *excision*, *precision*, *decision*, and *circumcision*. Finally, English words containing *-cid-* (< Latin *-cīdere*, combining form of *caedere*: to kill, to cut) should not be confused with English words containing *-cid-* (< Latin *-cidere*, combining form of *cadere*: to fall), as in *accident*, *incident*, *occident*, and *deciduous* (but not *decide*).

DETAILED EXAMPLE

suicide (soo´ə•sīd´)

Dissection: 1) sui / -cide

Analysis: 2) *sui* is derived from Latin *suī* (soo´ē), "of oneself," which is the genitive of *sē* (sā), "self." *-cide* is an English combining form having two meanings: "the killing of" (< Latin *-cīd(ium)*: the killing of + English *-e*: silent final letter), and "the killer of" (< Latin *-cīd(a)*: the killer of + English *-e*: silent final letter). Both Latin forms, in turn, derive from Latin *-cīdere* (kē´de•re), which is a combining form of the Latin verb *caedere* (kī´de•re), 'to kill, to cut.'

Reconstruction:	3) the killing or killer (-*cide*) of oneself (*sui*).
Definition:	4) *n.* 1. the act of intentionally killing oneself. 2. a person who intentionally kills or attempts to kill himself or herself.
Commentary:	5) *suicide* is an Early Modern English coinage, first recorded in 1651. Prior to this time, its meaning was conveyed by the compound *self-homicide*. Indeed, in 1671 John Milton's nephew, Edward Phillips, inveighed against the word *suicide* on the grounds that it might be construed as the killing of pigs (< Latin *su(is)* [genitive of *sus*]: pig + -*i*-: connecting vowel + English -*cide*). Other "sui" words include *suid*, *Suidae*, *suimate*, *suiform*, and *suigenderism*. Can you figure out which have to do with pigs and which have to do with people? Answers not in A CROSS-REFERENCE DICTIONARY.

BRIEF ANALYSES

patricide
(pa´trə·sīd´, pā´-)

1) patr-/-i-/-cide
2) *patr*-: father (cf. PATRILINEAL); -*i*-: connecting vowel; -*cide*: the killing of, the killer of.
3) the killing or killer of (-*cide*) father (*patr*-).
4) *n.* 1. the act of intentionally killing one's father. 2. a person who intentionally kills his or her father.
5) If the victim of a murder is one's mother rather than one's father, the perpetrator and act is <u>matricide</u> (< Latin *māter*: mother); if the victim is one's brother, it is <u>fratricide</u> (< Latin *frāter*: brother); if one's sister, it is <u>sororicide</u> (sə·rôr´ə·sīd´; < Latin *soror*: sister); if one's wife, it is <u>uxoricide</u> (uk·sôr´ə·sīd´; < Latin *ūxor*: wife); if one's husband, it is <u>mariticide</u> (mə·rit´ə·sīd´; < Latin *marītus*: husband); and if one's child, it is <u>filicide</u> (fil´ə·sīd´; < Latin *fīlius*: son; *fīlia*: daughter) or <u>prolicide</u> (prō´lə·sīd´; < Latin *prōlēs*: offspring). For other acts of murder, see the entries in the first column under EXERCISES.

rodenticide
(rō·den´tə·sīd´)

1) rod-/-ent-/-i-/-cide
2) *rod*-: to gnaw (cf. ERODE); -*ent*-: one who or that which (cf. SUPERINTENDENT); -*i*-: connecting vowel; -*cide*: the killer of.
3) the killer of (-*cide*) that which (-*ent*-) gnaws (*rod*-).
4) *n.* a poison or other substance used to kill rodents, especially mice and rats.
5) The basis for classifying certain mammals—as squirrels, beavers, and rats—as rodents lies in these mammals' possession of a single pair of continuously growing incisors in their upper and lower jaws, designed to gnaw wood and other objects. Thus, a rodenticide, etymologically, is that which kills animals that gnaw. Similarly, that which kills deer or the act of killing a deer is <u>cervicide</u>

-cide

(sûr'və•sīd´; < Latin *cervus*: deer). The killer or killing of a dog is <u>cani</u>cide (kan´ə•sīd´; < Latin *canis*: dog); of a wolf is <u>lupi</u>cide (lōō´pə•sīd´; < Latin *lupus*: wolf); of a bear is <u>ursi</u>cide (< Latin *ursus*: bear); of a whale is <u>ceti</u>cide (sē´tə•sīd´; < Latin *cētus*: whale < Greek *kētos*); and of a fox, provided it is not killed by hounds, is <u>vulpi</u>cide (< Latin *vulpēs*: fox). For the killer or killing of other animals, see the entries in the third column under EXERCISES.

vermicide
(vûr'mə•sīd´)

1) verm-/-i-/-cide
2) *verm-*: worm (cf. <u>VERMICELLI</u>); *-i-*: connecting vowel; *-cide*: the killer of.
3) the killer of (*-cide*) worms (*verm-*).
4) *n.* a drug or other substance used to kill worms, especially intestinal worms; helminthicide.
5) Modern medicine is rife with chemicals and other agents used to kill viruses, fungi, bacteria, and other undesirable intruders and substances in the human body. For the names of a few categories of these agents, see the entries in the center column under EXERCISES.

EXERCISES

DISSECT, ANALYZE, RECONSTRUCT, DEFINE, and provide a COMMENTARY for three words in each column, and try to use each in an intelligent sentence. Use a college or unabridged dictionary to check your work. The three columns are arranged in order of difficulty.

infanticide	viricide	avicide
parenticide	fungicide	piscicide
giganticide	bactericide	cimicide
tyrannicide	spermicide	culicicide
femicide	taeniacide	pulicicide
genocide	streptococcide	muscacide
regicide	staphylococcide	macropicide
hereticide	treponemicide	pediculicide

(Helpful Hints: Page 102)

circum- around, about, surrounding

Memory Aid Think of _circumference_ (the line <u>surrounding</u> a circle), _circumscribe_ (to draw a line <u>around</u>), _circumcision_ (the cutting <u>around</u> and removal of the foreskin), or any other _circum-_ word in which something goes <u>around</u> or is in the position of <u>surrounding</u> something else. But remember that _circum-_ can also mean <u>about</u>, as in _circumforaneous_ (going <u>about</u> from market to market) and _circumambulation_ (a walking around or <u>about</u>). For more complete definitions and etymologies, see the entries under BRIEF ANALYSES, and see _circumambulation_ in A CROSS-REFERENCE DICTIONARY.

Technical Information _circum-_ is derived from the Latin prefix _circum-_ (kir´koom), "around, about, surrounding," which, without the hyphen, was originally the adverbial accusative (direct object) of the Latin noun _circus_ (kir´koos), "circle, ring, racecourse"—from which we derive _circus, circle, circulate,_ and, surprisingly, _search._ Latin _circus,_ in turn, is borrowed from or akin to Greek _kirkos_ (kēr´kôs), which is a metathesis (mə·tath´ə·sis) or transposition of the letters in _krikos_ (krē´kôs), "circle, ring." A Greek prefix almost identical in meaning to Latin _circum-_ is _peri-,_ "around, about, surrounding, near," which we see in _periscope_ and _perimeter;_ and the semantically similar Greek combining form _amphi-,_ "around, about, on both sides, of both kinds," is evident in _amphitheater_ and _amphibian._ But Greek _amphi-_ should not be confused with Latin _ambi-,_ "both, around, about," which we see in _ambivalent_ and _ambidextrous._

DETAILED EXAMPLE

circumnavigate (sûr´kəm·nav´ə·gāt´)

Dissection: 1) circum- / nav- / -ig- / -at- / -e

Analysis: 2) **circum-** is derived from the Latin prefix _circum-_ (kir´koom), "around, about, surrounding," which, in turn, is derived from the Latin noun _circus_ (kir´koos), 'circle, ring, racecourse.' **nav-** is the base of Latin _nāvis_ (nä´wis), "ship." **-ig-** is the base of Latin _-igere_ (i´ge·re), which is a combining form of _agere_ (à´ge·re), "to do, to act, to drive." **-at-** is the base of Latin _-ātus_ (ä´toos), 'having been or having had,' but is used in this entry with the English verbal sense: "to cause, to make, to function, to manage." **-e** is an English "silent final letter."

Reconstruction: 3) to cause (-_at-_) to drive (-_ig-_) a ship (_nav-_) around (_circum-_).

Definition: 4) _v._ 1. to sail or fly around (the earth, moon, an island, etc.). 2. to maneuver or steer around; circumvent; skirt: _to circumnavigate the rocks in a river._

circum-

Commentary: 5) While one who travels around the world *cirumnavigates* it, that which surrounds the earth is *circumterrestrial* or *circumterraneous*. Similarly, that which surrounds the moon is *circumlunar* and that which surrounds the sun is *circumsolar*. But if something surrounds not only the sun but all stars or any star, it is *circumstellar*. Likewise, if it surrounds a planet it is *circumplanetary*, though we may further specify which planet it surrounds, e.g., *circum-Mercurial* (Mercury), *circum-Cytherean* (sith´ə·rē·ən; Venus; Cytherea was an alternate name of Aphrodite, the Greek-derived equivalent of Latin *Venus*), *circum-Jovian* (Jupiter; *Jovis* functioned in Latin as the genitive of *Juppiter*: Jupiter), *circum-Saturnian* (Saturn), etc.

BRIEF ANALYSES

circumference
(sər·kum´fər·əns)
1) circum-/fer-/-ence
2) *circum-*: around, about, surrounding; *fer-*: to bear, to carry (cf. OF<u>FER</u>); *-ence*: the act, state, or result of ___ing (cf. PERSIST<u>ENCE</u>).
3) the result of (*-ence*) bear- (*fer-*) -ing (*-ence*) around (*circum-*).
4) *n.* 1. the line bounding a circle or any circular figure or surface. 2. the length of this line.

circumscribe
(sûr´kəm·skrīb´)
1) circum-/scrib-/-e
2) *circum-*: around, about, surrounding; *scrib-*: to scratch, to incise, to write (cf. SU<u>BSCRIBE</u>); *-e*: silent letter.
3) to scratch or incise (*scrib-*) around (*circum-*).
4) *v.* 1. to draw a line or circle around; encircle. 2. to restrict the boundaries or activities of; delimit.

circumcision
(sûr´kəm·sizh´ən)
1) circum-/-cis-/-ion
2) *circum-*: around, about, surrounding; *-cis-*: to cut, to kill (cf. IN<u>CIS</u>ION); *-ion*: the act, means, or result of (cf. DETENT<u>ION</u>).
3) the act, means, or result of (*-ion*) cutting (*-cis-*) around (*circum-*).
4) *n.* the act or result of excising the male foreskin, either as a religious rite or for purported hygienic reasons.
5) The foreskin is removed by surgically cutting around the glans or head of the penis while the infant is held by a medical apparatus, such as a *Circumstraint*— a trademark presumably contrived as a blend of *circum(cision)* and *(con)straint*. Other medical terms using *circum-* include *circumvascular* (surrounding a blood, lymph, or other vessel), *circumarticular* (surrounding a joint), *circumumbilical* (surrounding the umbilicus or bellybutton), and *circumorbital*

(surrounding the orbit or bony cavity of the eye). A *circumorbital hematoma* is a black eye.

circumforaneous

(sûr´kəm·fô·rā´
nē·əs)

1) circum-/for-/-an-/-e-/-ous

2) *circum-*: around, about, surrounding; *for-*: marketplace (cf. <u>FOR</u>UM); *-an-*: pertaining to, characterized by, belonging to (cf. AGRARI<u>AN</u>); *-e-*: connecting vowel; *-ous*: full of, abounding in, characterized by (cf. ARDU<u>OUS</u>).

3) characterized by (*-ous*) pertaining to (*-an-*) around (*circum-*) the marketplace (*for-*).

4) *adj.* going about or wandering from market to market.

5) Originally, *circumforaneous* alluded to the lifestyle of rogues, vagabonds, peddlers, and jugglers in their ramblings from market to market and fair to fair— a lifestyle evidenced by the existence of two earlier forms, *circumforaneal* and *circumforanean*. Other picturesque *circum-* words that are no longer in use (but might be fun to resurrect) include *circumnebulous* (cloudy all around), *circumvolitate* (to hover around, as a mosquito or flying saucer), *circumgyral* (in circling wreaths, as a puff of smoke), *circumsept* (to surround with a fence, hedges, barbed wire, etc.), and *circumvestite* (to wrap around in a garment, blanket, towel, etc.).

EXERCISES

DISSECT, ANALYZE, RECONSTRUCT, DEFINE, and provide a COMMENTARY for three words in each column, and try to use each in an intelligent sentence. Use a college or unabridged dictionary to check your work. The three columns are arranged in order of difficulty.

circumstance	circumjacent	circumboreal
circumstantial	circumscription	circumaustral
circumvent	circumfluent	circumlittoral
circumspect	circumduction	circumnatant
circumfuse	circumvolant	circumnutate
circumflex	circumvallate	circumscissle
circumaviate	circumvolution	circumneutrophilous
circumlocution	circumundulation	Begonia circumlobata

(Helpful Hints: Page 103)

▬cracy rule by, government of

Memory Aid   Think of *demo<u>cracy</u>* (<u>rule by</u> or <u>government of</u> the people), *aristo<u>cracy</u>* (<u>rule by</u> or <u>government of</u> aristocrats), *porno<u>cracy</u>* (<u>rule by</u> or <u>government of</u> prostitutes), or any other *-cracy* word among the 31 listed on these two pages. Or better yet, affix a connecting *-o-* + *-cracy* (together pronounced äk´rə•sē) to the end of your first name, and consider your home, workplace, school, or country club to be ruled by you. EXAMPLE: My home is a *Robocracy* (räb´äk´rə•sē). What's yours?

Technical Information   *-cracy* is an English combining form composed of two elements: *-crac-* and *-y*. The first element *-crac-* is an altered and Anglicized form of Greek *krat-* (krät), which is the base of the Greek noun *kratos* (krä´tôs), "strength, power, rule," which is itself the source of the often cited Greek verb *kratein* (krä´tān), "to rule." The second element *-y* is a derivative of Greek *-ia* (ē´à), "the act, process, condition, or result of." Hence, *-cracy*, etymologically, is "the act, process, condition, or result of ruling." A closely associated though entirely unrelated Greek-derived combining form also meaning "rule by or government of" is *-archy* (är´kē), which we see in dozens of English words, including *matriarchy*, *patriarchy*, and *hierarchy*. Thus *-cracy* and *-archy* are synonyms, both of which are available for future coinages depicting the control of power by persons, groups, or other entities—real or imaginary. (For an explanation of how Greek *krat-* + *-ia* evolved into English *-cracy*, see *kakistocracy* in the A CROSS-REFERENCE DICTIONARY.)

DETAILED EXAMPLE

democracy (di•mäk´rə•sē)

Dissection:	1) dem- / -o- / -cracy
Analysis:	2) ***dem-*** is the base of Greek *dēmos* (dā´môs), "people." ***-o-*** is a Greek "connecting vowel." ***-cracy*** is an English combining form, "rule by, government of," which is derived from two Greek elements: *krat-* (krät), the base of *kratos* (krä´tôs), 'strength, power, rule,' and *-ia* (ē´à), 'the act, process, condition, or result of.'
Reconstruction:	3) rule by or government of (*-cracy*) the people (*dem-*).
Definition:	4) *n.* 1. a form of government in which the people hold political power, either directly or through elected representatives. 2. a nation or state having this form of government. 3. any organization, club, enterprise, etc., in which the owners and participants collectively determine policy.

Commentary: 5) *dem-,* "people," turns up in many English words, the second most popular of which is *epidemic* (< Greek *epi-*: over, upon + *dēm(os)*: people + *-ik(os)*: pertaining to, characterized by). But what do we call an epidemic that affects animals rather than people? . . . An *epizootic* (ep´ə•zō•ät´ik; < Greek *epi-*: over, upon + *zō(ion)*: animal + *-o-*: connecting vowel + *-tik(os)*: pertaining to, characterized by). And if it affects plants? . . . An *epiphytotic* (ep´ə•fī•tät´ik; < Greek *epi-*: over, upon + *phyt(on)*: plant + *-o-*: connecting vowel + *-ik(os)*: pertaining to, characterized by). The *zo-* in *epizootic* we, of course, also see in *zoo* (which is an abbreviation of *zoological garden*) and *zodiac* (in which eight of the twelve constellations contain animals). But did you realize that the *phyt-* in *epiphytotic* also occurs in *neophyte* (a beginner, novice < Greek *ne(os)*: new + *-o-*: connecting vowel + *phyt(on)*: plant + English *-e*: silent final letter)? And that the *ne-* in *neophyte* occurs in hundreds of English words, including *neocracy* (nē•äk´rə•sē; a government of new and inexperienced leaders), *neo-Nazi,* and *neologism* (nē•äl´ə•jiz´m; a new word or a new meaning for an existing word < Greek *ne(os)*: new + *-o-*: connecting vowel + *log(os)*: word + *-ism(os)*: the act of)? And are you aware that the *log-* in *neologism* occurs in thousands of English words, including *logorrhea* (a running of the mouth, i.e., compulsive talkativeness) and *logophilia* (an unusual love of or attraction to words)? . . . Is there no end to where one root can lead us?

BRIEF ANALYSES

aristocracy
(ar´ə•stäk´rə•sē)

1) arist-/-o-/-cracy
2) *arist-*: best (cf. <u>A</u>RIST<u>OTLE</u>); *-o-*: connecting vowel; *-cracy*: rule by, government of.
3) rule by or government of (*-cracy*) the best (*arist-*).
4) *n.* 1. the hereditary nobility. 2. a form of government in which the hereditary nobility or any privileged class wields political power. 3. any class of people having considerable power and receiving high privileges in society: *the medical aristocracy.* 4. any group of individuals considered to be the best or finest in some field or endeavor: *an aristocracy of Olympian swimmers.*
5) In ancient Greece, *aristokratia* meant "rule of the best" and was used by Plato and Aristotle to denote a "government of a state by those best fitted for the task." But when this word passed into Middle French as *aristocratie* and English as *aristocracy,* it gained a secondary sense: "rule by the privileged or nobility" and, hence, "a ruling class of nobles."

gynecocracy
(gī´ni•käk´rə•sē´, jin´i-)

1) gynec-/-o-/-cracy
2) *gynec-*: woman, female (cf. <u>GYNEC</u>OLOGY); *-o-*: connecting vowel; *-cracy*: rule by, government of.

3) rule by or government of (-*cracy*) women (*gynec-*).

4) *n.* 1. rule by or government of women. 2. social and political supremacy of women.

5) The male counterpart to *gynecocracy* is *androcracy* (an·dräk´rə·sē; < Greek *andr-*: man, male + *-o-*: connecting vowel + *-cracy*: rule by, government of).

pornocracy

(pôr·näk´rə·sē)

1) porn-/-o-/-cracy

2) *porn-*: prostitute (cf. PORNOGRAPHER); *-o-*: connecting vowel; *-cracy*: rule by, government of.

3) rule by or government of (-*cracy*) prostitutes (*porn-*).

4) *n.* rule or domination by prostitutes or promiscuous women, especially within civil or religious governments.

5) Lest one think this a fanciful term, consider the following excerpt epitomizing the "pornocratic" papal court of the 10th century, recorded in Alfred Edersheim's 1860 translation of Kurtz's *History of the christian* [sic] *church* : "For half a century Theodora . . . and her equally infamous daughters, . . . filled the See of Peter with their paramours, their sons, and grandsons, . . . (the so-called Pornocracy)." You might also be interested to know that a member of a pornocracy is a *pornocrat*, a word first recorded in 1894.

EXERCISES

DISSECT, ANALYZE, RECONSTRUCT, DEFINE, and provide a COMMENTARY for three words in each column, and try to use each in an intelligent sentence. Use a college or unabridged dictionary to check your work. The three columns are arranged in order of difficulty.

bureaucracy	plutocracy	ochlocracy
autocracy	ethnocracy	dulocracy
theocracy	sociocracy	albocracy
technocracy	gerontocracy	bestiocracy
meritocracy	hierocracy	hetaerocracy
cosmocracy	hagiocracy	ptochocracy
arithmocracy	timocracy	pantisocracy
demonocracy	stratocracy	thalassocracy

(Helpful Hints: Page 103)

hyper- over, above, beyond; abnormally high; excessively

Memory Aid When they arrived at the birthday party and heard the loud booming music, the little children became _hyper_—running all <u>over</u> the place, throwing gumdrops and jellybeans <u>above</u> the heads of their parents, going <u>beyond</u> all boundaries of right and wrong, and, in general, exhibiting <u>abnormally high</u> energy levels while laughing <u>excessively</u>.

Technical Information _hyper-_ is derived from the Greek prefix _hyper-_ (hü´per), "over, above, beyond, excessively," which in turn is derived from the Greek adverb and preposition _hyper_. It is frequently contrasted with and should not be confused with Greek-derived _hypo-_, "under, below, beneath, less than normal," which we see in such words and phrases as _hypotensive_ (see under DETAILED EXAMPLE) and _hypodermic needle_. The Latin-derived counterpart to Greek _hyper-_ is _super-_, "over, above, beyond; higher in rank, position, power, etc.," which occurs in _superman_, _superintendent_, and over a thousand other words; and the Latin-derived counterpart to Greek _hypo-_ is _sub-_, "under, below, beneath; lower in rank, position, power, etc.," which we see in _subway_, _subscribe_, and, once again, in over a thousand English words.

Detailed Example

antihypertensive (an´tē•hī´pər•ten´siv, an´tī-)

Dissection: 1) anti- / hyper- / tens- / -iv- / -e <u>OR</u> anti- / hyper- / tens- / -ive

Analysis: 2) **anti-** is derived from the Greek prefix _anti-_ (an´ti), "against, opposed to, the opposite of (in English, also having the medical meaning: 'counteracting, preventing, curing')." **hyper-** is derived from the Greek prefix _hyper-_ (hü´per), "over, above, beyond, excessively." **tens-** is the base of Latin _tēnsus_ (tān´soos), which is the past participle of _tendere_ (ten´de•re), "to stretch, to extend." _-iv-_ is the base of Latin _-ivus_ (i•woos), "tending to (be), inclined to (be)," which when combined with English **-e**, "silent final letter," also means "one who or that which tends to or is inclined to."

Reconstruction: 3) opposed to (_anti-_) tending to (_-iv-_) stretch (_tens-_) excessively (_hyper-_); OR counteracting (_anti-_) that which tends to (_-ive_) stretch (_tens-_) excessively (_hyper-_).

Definition: 4) _adj._ 1. reducing or attempting to reduce hypertension or high blood pressure. —_n._ 2. a drug or other agent that reduces or attempts to reduce hypertension or high blood pressure.

Commentary: 5) In the late 17th century _tension_, which originally meant "the act or condition of stretching," became a synonym for _pressure_. Two hundred years later, in the

hyper-

late 19th century, *hyper-* was prefixed to *tension*, and *hypertension* became the technical term for abnormally high blood pressure. Then about a decade later, the adjective-forming suffix *-ive* was first substituted in this word for the noun-forming suffix *-ion*, and *hypertensive* was born. Finally, in the 1950's, *anti-* was prefixed to *hypertensive*, and *antihypertensive* became the medical term for any drug that reduces or attempts to reduce high blood pressure. Thus, if you have *hypertension* but do not take your *antihypertensive*, you will in all likelihood remain *hypertensive*. But if you take your *antihypertensive* and it works, you will become <u>normo</u>tensive (< Latin *norma*: a carpenter's square; hence, a rule or pattern; hence, a norm). If, however, you take too much of your *antihypertensive* or improperly combine it with other drugs, your blood pressure may drop too low and you will become <u>hypo</u>tensive (< Greek *hypo-*: under, below, beneath; less than normal). And if all of this baffles your doctor, who, in any case, may never have been able to determine the cause of your high blood pressure, he or she will label your condition *essential hypertension*, *primary hypertension*, or <u>idio</u>*pathic hypertension* (< Greek *idios*: one's own; hence, personal, private)—all of which really means, "I can't figure out the cause of your high blood pressure."

BRIEF ANALYSES

hyperbole
(hī·pûr′bə·lē)

1) hyper-/bole
2) *hyper-*: over, above, beyond; abnormally high; excessively; *bole*: to throw (cf. PARA<u>BLE</u>).
3) to throw (*bole*) over, above, or beyond (*hyper-*).
4) *n.* a word or figure of speech containing an absurd exaggeration, often used for rhetorical effect or to accentuate a point: Examples: *She's out of this world*; *I'm so hungry I could eat a horse*; *He's as large as a mountain*; *I perish for her touch*; *skyscraper*. . . . And what hyperboles can *you* think of?
5) *hyperbole* is often contrasted with *litotes* (lī′tə·tēz′, lit′ə·tēz′, lī·tō′tēz), a figure of speech in which an affirmative statement is made by the negation of its opposite, e.g., *He's not a bad athlete* means he's a good athlete. However, a better contrast for *hyperbole* would be *tapinosis* (tap′i·nō′sis), a figure of speech that belittles by diminution, such as referring to an aircraft carrier as a canoe. For additional *hyper-* words of related interest, see the entries in the third column under EXERCISES.

hypersonic
(hī′pər·sän′ik)

1) hyper-/son-/-ic
2) *hyper-*: over, above, beyond; abnormally high; excessively; *son-*: sound (cf. <u>SON</u>OGRAM); *-ic*: pertaining to, characterized by (cf. HISTOR<u>IC</u>).
3) characterized by (*-ic*) beyond (*hyper-*) sound (*son-*).

64   One-Root Derivatives

4) *adj.* of or traveling at a speed at least five times greater than that of sound, or slightly faster than one mile per second (3,600 mph).

hyperborean

(hī´pər·bôr´ē·ən)

1) hyper-/bore-/-an

2) *hyper-*: over, above, beyond; abnormally high; excessively; *bore-*: north wind, north (cf. AURORA BOREALIS); *-an*: pertaining to, characterized by, belonging to (cf. AGRARIAN).

3) pertaining to (*-an*) beyond (*hyper-*) the north wind (*bore-*).

4) *adj.* 1. of or pertaining to any far northern region. 2. (of climate) extremely cold; frigid. *—n.* 3. an inhabitant of a far northern region.

5) In Greek mythology, the Hyperboreans were a people living in a land of perpetual sunshine and warmth beyond the north wind. But because of the obvious association of the far north with snow and cold, the reference to sunshine and warmth has been thoroughly eclipsed by the modern definition of this word— a displacement further evidenced by such zoological and botanical names as *Plectrophenax hyperboreus*, McKay's snow bunting of western Alaska and the Bering Strait (a bird even whiter than the snow bunting or snowflake), and *Sparganium hyperboreum*, a rugged species of northern bur reed.

EXERCISES

DISSECT, ANALYZE, RECONSTRUCT, DEFINE, and provide a COMMENTARY for three words in each column, and try to use each in an intelligent sentence. Use a college or unabridged dictionary to check your work. The three columns are arranged in order of difficulty.

hypercritical	hyperemia	hyperbaton
hyperreactive	hyperoxemia	hyperthesis
hypervigilant	hyperlipemia	hypermetrical
hyperexcitability	hyperuricemia	hypercatalectic
hyperventilation	hypernitremia	hyperditone
hyperthermia	hypernatremia	hyperdiapente
hyperthyroidism	hyperkalemia	hyperdiapason
hyperpituitarism	hypercholesterolemia	hyperdiatessaron

(Helpful Hints: Page 65)

▰**ītis** the inflammation of

Memory Aid   Memorize the following sentence: "**The proctor** (a teacher or other person assigned to monitor students during an examination) **got proctitis** (the inflammation of the rectum or anus; see under BRIEF ANALYSES)." Now imagine yourself as a student sitting in a classroom taking your final exam—and looking around frantically as you realize that you don't know any of the answers. And as the proctor comes over to investigate and bends over to look at your paper, another student ignites a <u>flame</u> under the proctor's fundament, culminating in . . . proct<u>itis</u> for the proctor.

Technical Information   *-itis* is derived from the Greek suffix *-itis* (ē´tis), the feminine form of the adjective-forming suffix *-itēs* (ē´tās), "of, relating to, belonging to, or having the characteristics of." However, when this suffix was historically affixed to the base of Greek *arthr(on)*, "joint," and the resulting compound was preceded by *hē* (hā), "the," and followed by *nosos* (nô´sôs), "disease," the phrase, *hē arthritis nosos* (hā är•thrē´tis nô´sôs), "the disease of the joint," was born—which in time was shortened to simply *arthritis*, which was construed as a noun. And based on this model, Greek *nephritis* (ne•frē´tis), as just one of a number of anatomical *-itis* words, was also transformed from an adjective to a noun and came to mean "the disease of the kidney" (< Greek *nephr(os)*: kidney + *-itis*: [understood to mean] the disease of), which later yielded English *nephritis*. But in English and New Latin, the meaning of *-itis* further narrowed from "the disease of" to "the inflammation of," and particularly during the 19th century was freely attached to hundreds of different words and bases to form medical terms that had never existed in Greek, including every entry in the EXERCISES below save one nonmedical term (can you spot it?). And finally, in English, *-itis* developed several extended meanings, most notably, "an extreme enthusiasm for or compulsion to partake in some sport or activity" (reminiscent of the lighter side of English *-mania*), which we hear in such facetious coinages as *golfitis*, *movieitis*, *telephonitis*, and even *crossword puzzleitis*.

DETAILED EXAMPLE

poliomyelitis (pō´lē•ō•mī´ə•lī´tis)

Dissection: 1) poli- / -o- / myel- / -itis

Analysis: 2) ***poli-*** is the base of Greek *polios* (pô•lē•ôs´), "gray." ***-o-*** is a Greek "connecting vowel." ***myel-*** is the base of Greek *myelos* (mü•e•lôs´), "marrow, bone marrow," which is either derived from or akin to Greek *mys* (müs), 'muscle.' ***-itis*** is an English suffix, "the inflammation of," which is derived from Greek *-itis* (ē´tis), understood in this context to mean 'the disease of' (originally abstracted from the phrase *hē arthritis nosos*, 'the disease of the joint'), *-itis* being the feminine form of the adjective-forming suffix *-itēs* (ē´tās), 'of, relating to, belonging to, or having the characteristics of.'

Reconstruction: 3) the inflammation of (*-itis*) the gray (*poli-*) marrow (*myel-*).

Definition: 4) *n.* an infectious viral disease occurring primarily in children, characterized by the inflammation of nerve cells in the spinal cord that affect certain muscle groups and which, in acute cases, results in the paralysis and atrophy of those muscle groups with permanent deformities in one or more limbs; infantile paralysis.

Commentary: 5) *poliomyelitis*, commonly referred to as *polio*, is caused by a *poliovirus* but may be prevented by a *polio vaccine*. It was so named because it causes inflammation of the gray matter of the spinal cord. But if, instead, it causes inflammation of the gray matter of the brain, it is referred to as *polioencephalitis* (pō´lē•ō•en•sef´ə•lī´tis), and if it causes inflammation of both the gray matter of the brain and the gray matter of the spinal cord, it is called *polioencephalomyelitis* (pō´lē•ō•en•sef´ə•lō•mī´ə•lī´tis)—a word which, if you learn to say quickly and without hesitation, you will find to be a beautiful and almost musical conglomeration of syllables.

BRIEF ANALYSES

bronchitis
(brän•kī´tis)

1) bronch-/-itis
2) *bronch-*: windpipe, throat (cf. BRONCHIAL); *-itis*: the inflammation of.
3) the inflammation of (*-itis*) the windpipe (*bronch-*).
4) *n.* a chronic or acute inflammation of the inner lining of the bronchial tubes or bronchioles.

bursitis
(bər•sī´tis)

1) burs-/-itis
2) *burs-*: a bag, pouch (cf. BURSAR); *-itis*: the inflammation of.
3) the inflammation of (*-itis*) a pouch (*burs-*).
4) *n.* the inflammation of a bursa—a sac or pouchlike chamber, especially one containing a lubricating fluid that reduces friction in or near certain joints.
5) *bursitis* is sometimes confused with *arthritis*. While arthritis is the inflammation of a joint, bursitis is the inflammation of the sac or pouch in or near a joint.

phlebitis
(flə•bī´tis)

1) phleb-/-itis
2) *phleb-*: vein (cf. PHLEBOTOMY); *-itis*: the inflammation of.
3) the inflammation of (*-itis*) a vein (*phleb-*).

4) *n.* the inflammation of a vein, often occurring in a leg and accompanied by a thrombus or blood clot, resulting in pain, swelling, and stiffness, with potentially life-threatening complications.

5) Shortly after resigning from the Presidency in 1974 and faced with a subpoena to testify about Watergate, Richard Nixon developed a severe and debilitating phlebitis of the leg—a phlebitis perhaps resulting from or at least exacerbated by the stress related to the possibility of testifying. The subpoena was eventually withdrawn.

proctitis

(präk·tī´tis)

1) proct-/-itis
2) *proct-*: anus (cf. PROCTALGIA); *-itis*: the inflammation of.
3) the inflammation of (*-itis*) the anus (*proct-*).
4) *n.* the inflammation of the rectum or anus or both.

oophoritis

(ō´ə· fə·rī´tis)

1) oo-/phor-/-itis
2) *oo-*: egg, ovum (cf. PANHYSTEROSALPINGO-OOPHORECTOMY); *phor-*: bearing (cf. EUPHORIA); *-itis*: the inflammation of.
3) the inflammation of (*-itis*) egg (*oo-*) bearing (*phor-*).
4) *n.* the inflammation of the ovary; ovaritis.
5) In human beings, "egg-bearing" occurs in the ovaries. For other *-itis* terms referring exclusively to women, see the entries in the third column under EXERCISES. But note: one of these terms applies to men as well as women. Can you spot it?

EXERCISES

DISSECT, ANALYZE, RECONSTRUCT, DEFINE, and provide a COMMENTARY for three words in each column, and try to use each in an intelligent sentence. Use a college or unabridged dictionary to check your work. The three columns are arranged in order of difficulty.

appendicitis	pancreatitis	mastitis
tonsillitis	prostatitis	metritis
laryngitis	diverticulitis	colpitis
dermatitis	urethritis	coxitis
carditis	mephitis	thelitis
hepatitis	meningitis	trachelitis
sinusitis	cystitis	salpingitis
gastritis	gingivitis	endometritis

(Helpful Hints: Page 104)

TWO-ROOT DERIVATIVES

a-, an- without, lacking, not

Memory Aid 1) Think of <u>a</u>theist—a person <u>without</u> or <u>lacking</u> a god or gods; <u>not</u> a theist.

2) Think of <u>an</u>emia—literally, a condition in which a person is <u>without</u> or <u>lacks</u> blood (see *anemia* under DETAILED EXAMPLE). Now visualize several ghosts floating toward you—*without* any blood in their bodies!

Technical Information *a-* is derived from the Greek prefix *a-* (ȧ), "without, lacking, not." This prefix is very similar in meaning to our native *un-* and *-less*, and the Latin-derived *in-* and *non-*. For ease of pronunciation, however, *a-* becomes **an-** before a vowel or *h*. But the Greek prefixes *a-* and *an-* should not be confused with a number of common Latin and Greek roots that coincidentally begin with *a-* or *an-*, as in *agrarian, anthology, anthropology,* and *ancillary*; nor should Greek *a-* be mistaken for a variety of native and nonclassical prefixes that are also represented by *a-*, as in *asleep, arise, astern, akin,* and *ahimsa.*

DETAILED EXAMPLE

anemia (ə·nēˊmē·ə)

Dissection: 1) an- / -em- / -ia

Analysis: 2) **an-** is a form of the Greek prefix *a-* (ȧ), "without, lacking, not," used before a vowel or *h*. **-em-** is derived from Greek *haima* (hīˊmȧ), "blood." **-ia** is a borrowing from Greek *-ia* (ēˊȧ), "the state, condition, or result of." <u>Note</u>: Greek *haima* becomes English *-em-* in the following manner: First, the *-a* of *haima* drops off, leaving the base *haim-*. Then, following the prefix *an-*, the *h-* in *haim-* also drops off, creating the reduced base *-aim-*. In Latinization, the Greek diphthong *-ai-* characteristically becomes *-ae-*, converting Greek *-aim-* into Latin *-aem-*. And finally in English, the *-ae-* diphthong is reduced to *-e-*, yielding our simplified base *-em-*. (For additional *-emia* words, see the entries in the second column under EXERCISES in chapter HYPER-.)

Reconstruction: 3) the state, condition, or result of (*-ia*) lacking (*an-*) blood (*-em-*).

Definition: 4) *n.* a medical disorder due to a deficiency in the number of red blood cells or their hemoglobin content.

Commentary: 5) *anemia*, etymologically, is a misnomer. Anemia is a condition characterized by a *deficiency* in blood, not the *absence* of blood. But, evidently, the ancient Greeks who coined the word were either not very precise in their construction of this word or were unclear about the nature of this condition. A more logical choice might have been **hypemia* (< Greek *hypo-*: under, below, beneath; in English, also meaning: less than normal), **spanemia* (< Greek *spanos*: scarce), or *oligemia* (< Greek *oligos*: small, few, little), a word currently in use for a different though related condition.

BRIEF ANALYSES

atom
(at´əm)

1) a-/tom-
2) *a-*: without, lacking, not; *tom-*: divided, cut (cf. TONSILLEC<u>TOM</u>Y).
3) not (*a-*) cut (*tom-*).
4) *n.* the smallest characteristic component of an element, generally consisting of protons, neutrons, and electrons.
5) During the 5th century B.C., the Greek philosopher Leucippus and his follower Democritus postulated that all matter in the universe is composed of minute, indivisible particles that cannot be "cut or divided." They called such a particle *atomos* (ä´tô·môs). Their theory, though never accepted by the Greeks, was resurrected over 2000 years later in 1805 by the English chemist John Dalton. However, by 1896 it was discovered that atoms could, indeed, be cut or divided—a fact that was explosively demonstrated to the world on August 6, 1945 at Hiroshima.

atrophy
(a´trə·fē)

1) a-/troph-/-y
2) *a-*: without, lacking, not; *troph-*: food, nourishment (cf. MUSCULAR DYS<u>TROPH</u>Y); *-y*: the act, process, condition, or result of (cf. EULOG<u>Y</u>).
3) the condition or result of (*-y*) lacking (*a-*) nourishment (*troph-*).
4) *n.* 1. the wasting away of a muscle, organ, or other body part, as from disease or the lack of proper nutrition or exercise.
    –v. 2. (of a body part) to waste away.

anhydrous
(an·hī´drəs)

1) an-/hydr-/-ous
2) *an*-: without, lacking, not; *hydr*-: water (cf. HYDROPHOBIA); *-ous*: full of, abounding in, characterized by (cf. DANGEROUS).
3) characterized by (*-ous*) lacking (*an-*) water (*hydr-*).
4) *adj.* without water, especially the water in a chemical crystal: *Lime is anhydrous calcium hydroxide.*

anhedonia
(an´hē·dō´nē·ə)

1) an-/hedon-/-ia
2) *an*-: without, lacking, not; *hedon*-: pleasure (cf. HEDONIST); *-ia*: the state, condition, or result of (cf. THANATOPHOBIA).
3) the state, condition, or result of (*-ia*) lacking (*an-*) pleasure (*hedon-*).
4) *n.* a psychological condition in which a person is unable to find pleasure in those things that people normally find pleasurable.
5) In 1977, Woody Allen directed a movie originally entitled *Anhedonia.* However, his producers and marketing managers pleaded with him to change the name, arguing that no one would understand the title and sales would plummet. Woody finally capitulated and retitled the film. . . *Annie Hall*—the Academy Awards' "Best Picture of the Year."

EXERCISES

DISSECT, ANALYZE, RECONSTRUCT, DEFINE, and provide a COMMENTARY for three words in each column, and try to use each in an intelligent sentence. Use a college or unabridged dictionary to check your work. The three columns are arranged in order of difficulty.

amoral	amorphous	acephalous
atypical	analgesic	astomia
ahistorical	asphyxia	anotia
anarchy	anorexia	aphalangia
amnesia	alexia	anonychia
apathy	amentia	amastia
anesthesia	anomie	anorchia
asymmetry	anonym	anaphroditous

(Helpful Hints: Page 105)

bene-, ben- well, good

Memory Aid Imagine yourself to be the _beneficiary_ of an enormous sum of money. You've done well in life and helped many people, and now it feels good to be rich.

Technical Information _bene-_ is derived from the Latin adverb _bene_ (be´ne), "well." This adverb is closely related to the Latin adjective _bonus_ (bô´noos), "good," from which we derive _bonus_ and _bonbon_, and the Latin adjective _bellus_ (bel´loos), "beautiful, handsome," from which we derive _beldam_ and _belladonna_. It is also identical in meaning to the common Greek combining form _eu-_ (eōō), "well," which we see in hundreds of English words, including _eulogy_ and _euthanasia_. In English, however, both _bene-_ and _eü-_ have further adopted the adjectival meaning, "good"; and when followed by a vowel, particularly _i_, _bene-_ drops its final _-e_ and becomes the relatively uncommon variant **ben-**. But _ben-_ and _bene-_ should not be confused with other classical and nonclassical roots and letter combinations that mirror these prefixes, as in the completely unrelated _beneath, benzaldehyde, Benelux,_ and _Benjamin_.

DETAILED EXAMPLE

benediction (ben´ə·dik´shən)

Dissection: 1) bene- / dict- / -ion

Analysis: 2) **bene-** is derived from the Latin adverb _bene_ (be´ne), "well." **dict-** is the base of Latin _dictus_ (dik´toos), which is the past participle of _dīcere_ (dē´ke·re), "to say, to speak." **-ion** is the base of Latin _-iōnis_ (i·ō´nis), which is the genitive of _-iō_ (i·ō), "the act, means, or result of."

Reconstruction: 3) the act, means, or result of (_-ion_) speaking (_dict-_) well (_bene-_).

Definition: 4) _n._ 1. a blessing, especially one bestowed by the officiating minister, priest, rabbi, etc., at the close of a religious service. 2. the result of such a blessing; blessedness.

Commentary: 5) When we bless someone, we "speak well" of that person. But if we "speak ill" of a person, we are guilty of _malediction_ (< Latin _male_: badly, ill), which is a curse or slander. _ben(e)-_ and _mal(e)-_ form contrasting prefixes in English and can be found in such pairs as _benefactor, malefactor; benevolent, malevolent; benefic, malefic;_ and _benison_ and the now obsolete _malison_. For further information, see chapter MAL-, MALE-.

BRIEF ANALYSES

benefactor
(ben´ə·fak´tər)

1) bene-/fact-/-or
2) *bene-*: well, good; *fact-*: to make, to do (cf. FACTORY); *-or*: one who or that which (cf. PROTECTOR).
3) one who (*-or*) makes or does (*fact-*) good (*bene-*).
4) *n.* a person who confers a benefit, especially a financial benefit, to an individual, institution, group, or other body.

benevolent
(bə·nev´ə·lənt)

1) bene-/vol-/-ent
2) *bene-*: well, good; *vol-*: to wish (cf. VOLITION); *-ent*: a present participial suffix equivalent in meaning to *-ing*, as in "the marching band" (cf. RECUMBENT).
3) wish- (*vol-*) -ing (*-ent*) well (*bene-*).
4) *adj.* 1. having or expressing warm feelings and good will: *a benevolent attitude.* 2. performing or inclined to perform kind and generous acts: *a benevolent donation to charity.*

benefic
(bə·nef´ik)

1) bene-/-fic
2) *bene-*: well, good; *-fic*: making, doing, causing (cf. HORRIFIC).
3) making or doing (*-fic*) good (*bene-*).
4) *adj.* promoting or participating in that which is good or beneficial: *a benefic meeting of heads of state.*

benison
(ben´ə·zən, -sən)

1) ben-/-i-/-son
2) *bene-*: well, good; *-i-*: connecting vowel; *-son*: in this word, a contraction and alteration of *-diction*: the act, means, or result of speaking (cf. BENEDICTION).
3) the act or result of speaking (*-son*) well (*bene-*).
4) *n.* a blessing; benediction.
5) *benison* is an elegant and flowery synonym of *blessing*, found mainly in poetry, early English prose, and church services. Indeed, Samuel Johnson in his 1755 *A Dictionary of the English Language* includes a usage note that *benison* is ". . . not now used unless ludicrously." But *benison* has had something of a resurgence since Dr. Johnson's pontification, and the 20-volume *Oxford English Dictionary* currently asserts, without being ludicrous, that "[*benison*] is now common as a poetic or quaint form of *benediction*."

benedict
(ben´ə·dikt´)

1) bene-/dict-
2) *bene-*: well, good; *dict-*: to say, to speak (cf. DICTIONARY).
3) to speak (*dict-*) well (*bene-*).
4) *n.* a recently married man, especially one formerly self-proclaimed to be a confirmed bachelor.

5) *benedict* is actually an alteration of Shakespeare's Benedick, the sworn bachelor in *Much Ado About Nothing* who cavalierly courts and eventually marries Beatrice. Evidently, Shakespeare named his character after an early (though never fully recognized) meaning of *benedict*, "an inveterate bachelor sworn to celibacy," itself named after the proudly celibate St. Benedict, founder of the Benedictine order of monks in the early 6th century—whose name hearkens back to the Latin roots *bene-* + *dictus* (see BENEDICTION). Other names derived from these roots include *Bennett, Benson, Benoit, Benito, Benkovich, Benkowski*, and those reputedly curative plants, *herb bennet* and *Carduus benedictus* (the Blessed Thistle, of which Margaret implores Beatrice in *Much Ado About Nothing*: "Get you some of this distill'd Carduus benedictus and lay it to your heart").

EXERCISES

DISSECT, ANALYZE, RECONSTRUCT, DEFINE, and provide a COMMENTARY for three words in each column, and try to use each in an intelligent sentence. Use a college or unabridged dictionary to check your work. The three columns are arranged in order of difficulty.

benefit	benefice	benedicence
benefiting	beneficent	benevolist
benefiter	beneficence	beneficiate
beneficial	benefaction	beneficential
beneficiary	benedictional	benedictionale
beneficially	benefactive	benedictionary
benign	benedictory	benereceptor
benignly	benignity	benefactrices

(Helpful Hints: Page 105)

duc-, duct- to lead, to bring

Memory Aid Think of *induce* (a verb) and *induction* (a noun). Now imagine yourself all of eighteen years old listening to a sergeant of the United States Army trying to in<u>duc</u>e or <u>lead</u> you into the army by <u>bring</u>ing you to the nearest in<u>duct</u>ion center. But you are not sure if this is what you really want to do and keep asking yourself: "Should I be in<u>duc</u>ed to enlist in the in<u>duct</u>ion center? Is this really where I want my life to <u>lead</u>? Should I let the sergeant <u>bring</u> me there?"

Technical Information *duc-* is the Anglicized base of the Latin verb *dūcere* (dōō´ke•re), "to lead, to bring." *duct-* is the base of *ductus* (dook´ tōōs), which is the past participle of *dūcere*. A closely related verbal derivative of *dūcere* is *-ducāre* (doo. kä´ re), "to continue to lead or bring," whose base *duc-* we see in *educate* and *educable*. And a substantive (noun) derivative of *dūcere* is *dux* (dooks), "leader, commander, ruler," whose derivatives include *duke*, *duchess*, and *Il Duce*. But regardless of its immediate source, Latin-derived *duc-* must never be confused with the random letter combination *-duc-*, which occurs in such etymologically diverse words as *duckling*, *gweduc*, and *caduceus*.

DETAILED EXAMPLE

induction (in•duk´shən)

Dissection: 1) in- / duct- / -ion

Analysis: 2) *in-* is derived from Latin *in-* (in), "in, into, within." *duct-* is the base of Latin *ductus* (dook´tōōs), which is the past participle of *dūcere* (dōō´ke•re), "to lead, to bring." *-ion* is the base of Latin *-iōnis* (i•ō´nis), which is the genitive of *-iō* (i•ō), "the act, means, or result of."

Reconstruction: 3) the act, means, or result of (*-ion*) leading or bringing (*duct-*) into (*in-*).

Definition: 4) *n.* 1. the act or process of bringing or formally placing a person into an office, organization, position, etc. 2. enrollment in military service. 3. a form of reasoning in which a general conclusion is drawn from individual facts or instances: *Inferring that God exists from the presence of trees, planets, and galaxies is an example of induction or inductive reasoning.*

Commentary: 5) The *in-* in *induction* is a good example of how a prefix can determine the meaning of a word. For if we remove this *in-* and replace it with *de-* (< Latin *dē-*: away from, off, down), we get <u>deduction</u>, a word having the opposite meaning of *induction*, which reconstructs into "the act, means, or result of leading away from or down." If we then replace the *de-* with *re-* (< Latin *re-*: back, again), we

duc-, duct-

derive _reduction_, "the act, means, or result of leading or bringing back." Similarly, by substituting suffixes we can re-create _abduction_ (< Latin _ab-_: away, from), _conduction_ (< Latin _con-_: with, together), _introduction_ (< Latin _intrō-_: in, into, within), _seduction_ (< Latin _sē-_: apart, aside), _production_ (< Latin _prō-_: before, in front of; forward, forth), and _reproduction_ (< Latin _re-_: back, again + _prō-_: before, in front of; forward, forth—this word uses two prefixes). For additional _-duction_ words distinguished by their prefixes, see the entries in the third column under EXERCISES.

BRIEF ANALYSES

produce
(_v._ prə·dōōs´)
(_n._ präd´ ōōs, prō´dōōs)

1) pro-/duc-/-e
2) _pro-_: forward, forth (cf. PROGRESSIVE); _duc-_: to lead, to bring; _-e_: silent final letter.
3) bringing (_duc-_) forward or forth (_pro-_).
4) _v._ 1. to make, manufacture, create, or yield. –_n._ 2. agricultural yield, especially fresh fruits and vegetables.
5) In disyllabic (dī´si·lab´ik; two-syllable) English words that serve as both nouns and verbs, if the primary accent of the noun falls on the first syllable it frequently shifts to the second syllable when the word is used as a verb. Thus we have _con´duct_ (kän´dukt) _n._, and _con·duct´_ (kən·dukt´) _v._; _de´fect_ (dē´fekt) _n._, and _de·fect´_ (di·fekt´; to abandon or desert a country, cause, political party, etc.) _v._; and _in´cense_ (in´sens) _n._, and _in·cense´_ (in·sens´; to inflame with rage; enrage; infuriate) _v._

viaduct
(vī´ə·dukt´)

1) via/duct-
2) _via_: a way, road (cf. DEVIANT); _duct-_: to lead, to bring.
3) a leading (_duct-_) road (_via-_).
4) _n._ a bridge consisting of a number of short spans supported by arches and piers, used to carry a road or railway over a gorge or other low-lying landform.
5) Do not confuse _viaduct_ with _aqueduct_, a similar appearing structure traditionally used to transport water over land or water.

oviduct
(ō´vi·dukt´)

1) ov-/-i-/duct-
2) _ov-_: egg (cf. OVARY); _-i-_: connecting vowel; _duct-_: to lead, to bring.
3) to bring (_duct-_) the egg (_ov-_); OR egg (_ov-_) bringer (_duct-_).
4) _n._ either of a pair of tubes or ducts that transport an egg or reproductive cell from an ovary to the uterus; the fallopian tube of higher mammals.
5) When a woman _ovulates_ (äv´yə·lāts´), she discharges an _ovum_ (ō´vəm; egg cell) from an _ovary_ into an _oviduct_. If the ovum is fertilized—and all goes

well—she will eventually give birth to a live child. For this reason, human beings (and most other mammals) are said to be *viviparous* (vī·vip´ər·əs; bearing live young < Latin *vīv(us)*: alive + *-i-*: connecting vowel + *par(ere)*: to bear + English *-ous*: characterized by). However, non-mammals, such as chickens and alligators, generally lay eggs that hatch outside the body, and these animals are therefore said to be <u>*oviparous*</u> (ō·vip´ər·əs; < Latin *ōv(um)*: egg). Still other animals, as certain lizards, produce eggs that hatch within the body and are later delivered live, and these animals are said to be <u>*ovoviviparous*</u> (ō´vō·vī·vip´ər·əs; < Latin *ōv(um)*: egg + *vīv(us)*: alive). Finally, viviparous and ovoviviparous females, particularly human females, may be classified by how many offspring, if any, they have borne. If none, they are <u>*nulliparous*</u> (nul·lip´ər·əs; < Latin *nūll(us)*: none); if one, they are <u>*primiparous*</u> (prī·mip´ər·əs; < Latin *prīm(us)*: first) or <u>*uniparous*</u> (yoō·nip´ər·əs; < Latin *ūn(us)*: one); and if two or more they are <u>*multiparous*</u> (mul·tip´ər·əs; < Latin *mult(us)*: much, many).

EXERCISES

DISSECT, ANALYZE, RECONSTRUCT, DEFINE, and provide a COMMENTARY for three words in each column, and try to use each in an intelligent sentence. Use a college or unabridged dictionary to check your work. The three columns are arranged in order of difficulty.

conductor	ductile	adduction
misconduct	ductule	eduction
productivity	adducible	obduction
conductivity	educible	subduction
conducive	adductor	traduction
inducement	abductor	retroduction
deductive	conductance	circumduction
reproductive	inductance	superinduction

(Helpful Hints: Page 106)

grad-, gress- to step, to walk, to go

Memory Aid 1) Think of _graduate_—one who <u>step</u>s, <u>walk</u>s, or <u>go</u>es across a dividing line separating the undergraduates from the graduates. Now actually visualize yourself <u>step</u>ping, <u>walk</u>ing, or <u>go</u>ing across such a line and becoming a _graduate_.

2) Think of _regress_—to <u>step</u>, <u>walk</u>, or <u>go</u> (_gress-_) backward (_re-_), as to a former or less advanced state. Now as a graduate, visualize yourself <u>step</u>ping, <u>walk</u>ing, or <u>go</u>ing back across that line and _regressing_ into an _undergraduate_.

Technical Information _grad-_ is the base of the Latin verb _gradī_ (grȧ´dē), "to step, to walk, to go." **gress-** is the base of Latin _gressus_ (gres´sŏŏs), which is the past participle of _gradī_. A similar though unrelated Latin word also meaning "to walk" (or "to travel" but definitely not "to step") is _ambulāre_ (ȧm·bŏŏ·lä´re), from which we derive such English words as _ambulance_, _ambulatory_, _somnambulism_, and _circumambulation_. And a Greek word meaning "to walk" is _patein_ (pä·tān´), from which we derive only one common English derivative, _peripatetic_, a close synonym for the Latin-derived _itinerant_.

DETAILED EXAMPLE

aggression (ə·gresh´ən)

Dissection:	1) ag- / gress- / -ion
Analysis:	2) **ag-** is an assimilated form of the Latin prefix _ad-_ (ȧd), "to, toward" (see AD- for further information). **gress-** is the base of Latin _gressus_ (gres´sŏŏs), which is the past participle of _gradī_ (grȧ´dē), "to step, to walk, to go." **-ion** is the base of the Latin suffix _-iōnis_ (i·ō´nis), which is the genitive of _-iō_ (i·ō), "the act, means, or result of."
Reconstruction:	3) the act or result of (_-ion_) stepping, walking, or going (_gress-_) to or toward (_ag-_).
Definition:	4) _n._ the act of attacking or assaulting a person, group, or thing, either physically or psychologically.
Commentary:	5) Aggression is clearly a form of attack, and when we attack someone we "go toward" that person, either literally or figuratively.

BRIEF ANALYSES

gradual
(graj´ŏŏ·əl)

1) grad-/-u-/-al

2) _grad-_: to step, to walk, to go; _-u-_: connecting vowel; _-al_: pertaining to, characterized by (cf. LOGIC<u>AL</u>).

3) pertaining to or characterized by (*-al*) stepping, walking, or going (*grad-*).

4) *adj.* occurring or changing very slowly, often by degrees or steps.

gradation
(grā·dā´shən)

1) grad-/-at-/-ion

2) *grad-*: to step, to walk, to go; *-at-*: having, having been (cf. INSENS<u>A</u>TE); *-ion*: the act, means, or result of (cf. EXPLOS<u>ION</u>).

3) the act, means, or result of (*-ion*) having (*-at-*) stepped, walked, or gone (*grad-*).

4) *n.* a gradual, often imperceptible, change from one thing to another: *Can you detect the gradation of colors in the rainbow?*

degradation
(deg´rə·dā´shən)

1) de-/grad-/-at-/-ion

2) *de-*: away from, off, down (cf. <u>DE</u>BASE); *grad-*: to step, to walk, to go; *-at-*: having, having been; *-ion*: the act, means, or result of.

3) the act, means, or result of (*-ion*) having (*-at-*) gone (*grad-*) down (*de-*).

4) *n.* 1. the result or condition of being lowered in esteem, honor, dignity, etc.
2. the gradual wearing away of land through erosion.

egress
(ē´gres´)

1) e-/gress-

2) *e-*: out, out of (cf. <u>E</u>JECT); *gress-*: to step, to walk, to go.

3) to step, walk, or go (*gress-*) out of (*e-*).

4) *n.* 1. the act of leaving or going out of. 2. an exit.

5) P.T. Barnum was always annoyed when sightseers were reluctant to leave his crowded museum in New York City, preventing others from entering. So one day, next to the cage with a female tiger he put up a sign, "Tigress." Then, adjacent to the tigress, over an exit door, he put up another sign, "To the Egress." Unwary patrons, thinking that this passageway led to a female egret or some sort of exotic animal, would walk through the doors and find themselves out on the street.

transgression
(trans·gresh´ən)

1) trans-/gress-/-ion

2) *trans-*: over, across, beyond (cf. <u>TRANS</u>CENDENTAL MEDITATION); *gress-*: to step, to walk, to go; *-ion*: the act, means, or result of.

3) the act, means, or result of (*-ion*) stepping (*gress-*) across (*trans-*).

4) *n.* the act of breaking a law, violating an oath, committing a sin, etc.

5) When we commit an illegal or immoral act, we "step across" a boundary we are not supposed to cross.

digitigrade
(dij´i·tə·grād´)

1) digit-/-i-/grad-/-e

2) *digit-*: finger, toe (cf. <u>DIGIT</u>AL); *-i-*: connecting vowel; *grad-*: to step, to walk, to go; *-e*: silent final letter.

3) to step or walk (*grad-*) on the fingers or toes (*digit-*); OR finger or toe (*digit-*) walking (*grad-*).

4) *adj.* walking on the toes without the heels touching the ground, characteristic of cats, dogs, and most other quadrupeds: *Digitigrade animals often appear taller than they actually are.*

saltigrade

(sal´ti·grād´, sôl´-)

1) salt-/ -i-/grad-/-e
2) *salt-*: to jump or leap about (cf. SOMER<u>SAULT</u>); *-i-*: connecting vowel; *grad-*: to step, to walk, to go; *-e*: silent final letter.
3) to step, walk, or go (*grad-*) by jumping or leaping about (*salt-*).
4) *adj.* having legs adapted for leaping, as certain animals: *Beware of the salti-grade spiders.*
5) *saltigrade* and *digitigrade* are but two of a number of *-grade* "walking words." For others, see the entries in the third column under EXERCISES.

EXERCISES

DISSECT, ANALYZE, RECONSTRUCT, DEFINE, and provide a COMMENTARY for three words in each column, and try to use each in an intelligent sentence. Use a college or unabridged dictionary to check your work. The three columns are arranged in order of difficulty.

progression	ingress	plantigrade
digression	aggradation	pinnigrade
regressive	biodegradable	pronograde
graduation	gradeability	tardigrade
retrogression	gradine	dorsigrade
congressional	gradiometer	orthograde
undergraduate	gressorial	vermigrade
centigrade	intergradation	unguligrade

(Helpful Hints: Page 106)

loqu-, locut- to speak

Memory Aid The ventri<u>loqu</u>ist walked on stage and tried <u>to speak</u> without opening his mouth. But his e<u>locut</u>ion (manner of <u>speak</u>ing; see definition under BRIEF ANALYSES) was so dismaying that no one could hear a word he was saying. So the audience began to chant, "Speak! Speak!" and the ventriloquist, bewildered, became very meek. But when the audience calmed down and the ventriloquist did speak, everyone present knew what to critique: the ventri<u>loqu</u>ist's e<u>locut</u>ion is weak when he tries <u>to speak</u>. (See *doggerel* in A CROSS-REFERENCE DICTIONARY.)

Technical Information *loqu-* is the base of the Latin verb *loquī* (lô´kwē), "to speak." *locut-* is the base of Latin *locutus* (lô·kōō´tōōs), which is the past participle of *loquī*. English *locut-*, however, should not be confused with English *loc-* (< Latin *locus*: a place, site), which never ends in *-ut* and appears in such words as *locale* and *collocate*. Also, since speaking is such an integral part of human existence, Latin has further provided us with the synonymous roots *dict-* (< Latin *dictus*, past participle of *dīcere*: to say, to speak), which we see in *dictionary* and *benediction*, and *fa-* (< Latin *fārī*: to speak), which occurs in *affable* and *infantry*. Similarly, Greek has furnished us with the synonymous roots *pha-* and *phat-* (both < Greek *phanai*: to speak), which we see in *aphasia* and *phatic* (not to be confused with *phallic*), and the sometimes synonymous roots *leg-*, *log-*, and *lec-* (all < Greek *legein*: to gather, to choose, to speak), which occur in *prolegomenon*, *gynecology*, and *analects*.

DETAILED EXAMPLE

ventriloquist (ven·tril´ə·kwist)

Dissection:
1) ventr- / -i- / loqu- / -ist

Analysis:
2) ***ventr-*** is the base of Latin *ventris* (wen´tris), which is the genitive of *venter* (wen´ter), "belly." ***-i-*** is a Latin "connecting vowel." ***loqu-*** is the base of the Latin verb *loquī* (lô´kwē), "to speak." ***-ist*** is derived from Greek *-istēs* (is´tās), "one who (performs the action designated by the preceding base)," which in turn is derived from *-is-* (is), base of denominative verbs ending in *-izein* (i´zān) + *-tēs* (tēs), 'one who or that which' (see *denominative* and *-ist* in A CROSS-REFERENCE DICTIONARY).

Reconstruction:
3) one who (-*ist*) belly (*ventr-*) speaks (*loqu-*).

Definition:
4) *n.* a person who practices or performs ventriloquism, the art of speaking with little or no lip movement so that the voice appears to emanate from another

loqu-, locut-

source, usually a hand-operated dummy with whom that person pretends to engage in conversation.

Commentary: 5) Why is a ventriloquist a "belly-speaker" and not, for instance, a "nose-speaker" or "silent-speaker" (cf. *oxymoron* in chapter BIBLI-)? For the answer, we may turn to Thomas Blount's 1656 edition of *Glossographia, or a dictionary interpreting such hard words . . . as are now used*, in which the author cites both the literal and extended meanings of ventriloquist: "*Ventriloquist*, one that hath an evil spirit speaking in his belly, or one that by use and practise [sic] can speak as it were out of his belly, not moving his lips." Thus, "belly-speaking" was originally believed to be an actual phenomenon observed in possessed individuals. Bishop Francis Hutchinson, in his 1718 *An historical essay concerning witchcraft*, further explains: "There are also many [possessed] that can form Words and Voices in their Stomach, which shall seem to come from others rather than the Person that speaks them. Such people are call'd Engastriloques, or Ventriloquists." An engastriloque, as any fellow in the street will tell you, is an obscure 18th century synonym for ventriloquist (< Greek *en-*: in, within + *gastr(os)*: stomach, belly + *-i-*: connecting vowel [technically, the dative ending of *gastri*] + Latin *loqu(ī)*: to speak + English *-e*: silent final letter—hence, "to speak within the belly" or "belly-speaker").

BRIEF ANALYSES

eloquent
(el´ə·kwənt)

1) e-/loqu-/-ent
2) *e-*: out, out of (cf. ERODE); *loqu-*: to speak; *-ent*: a present participial suffix equivalent in meaning to *-ing*, as in "a cry<u>ing</u> baby" (cf. NOC<u>ENT</u>).
3) speak- (*loqu-*) -ing (*-ent*) out (*e-*).
4) *adj.* 1. of or characteristic of speech or writing that is articulate, graceful, penetrating, and persuasive. 2. deeply or vividly expressive: *a story eloquent with heartbreak.*

colloquial
(kə·lō´kwē·əl)

1) col-/loqu-/-i-/-al
2) *col-*: with, together (cf. COLL<u>INEAR</u>); *loqu-*: to speak; *-i-*: connecting vowel; *-al*: pertaining to, characterized by (cf. PRODIG<u>AL</u>).
3) characterized by (*-al*) speaking (*loqu-*) together (*col-*).
4) *adj.* of or designating those words, phrases, and expressions characteristic of everyday conversation, as distinguished from slang, jargon, cant, formal speech or writing, etc.; conversational; informal: *"Take care!" is a colloquial expression.*

elocution
(el´ə·kyo͞o´shən)

1) e-/locut-/-ion
2) *e-*: out, out of (cf. <u>E</u>JECT); *locut-*: to speak; *-ion*: the act, means, or result of (cf. EXPLOS<u>ION</u>).

3) the act, means, or result of (*-ion*) speaking (*locut-*) out (*e-*).

4) *n.* 1. a manner or style of speaking or reading aloud, especially before an audience. 2. the art of public speaking.

soliloquy
(sə·lil´ə·kwē)

1) sol-/-i-/loqu-/-y

2) *sol-*: alone (cf. SOLIPSISM); *-i-*: connecting vowel; *loqu-*: to speak; *-y*: the act, process, or condition of (cf. EULOG<u>Y</u>).

3) the act or condition of (*-y*) speaking (*loqu-*) alone (*sol-*).

4) *n.* 1. in drama, a device by which a character reveals his or her thoughts to the audience but not to the other characters, as by thinking aloud or addressing the audience, especially when no other characters are on stage. 2. the act of talking to or conversing with oneself, regardless of the presence of others.

somniloquy
(säm·nil´ə·kwē)

1) somn-/-i-/loqu-/-y

2) *somn-*: sleep (cf. SOMNAMBULISM); *-i-*: connecting vowel; *loqu-*: to speak; *-y*: the act, process, or condition of (cf. AGON<u>Y</u>).

3) the act or condition of (*-y*) sleep (*somn-*) speaking (*loqu-*).

4) *n.* 1. the act or condition of talking while asleep or in a sleeplike trance; sleep talking. 2. the words, phrases, sentences, etc., uttered while in this state.

EXERCISES

DISSECT, ANALYZE, RECONSTRUCT, DEFINE, and provide a COMMENTARY for three words in each column, and try to use each in an intelligent sentence. Use a college or unabridged dictionary to check your work. The three columns are arranged in order of difficulty.

colloquy	obloquy	grandiloquent
colloquium	allocution	magniloquent
colloquia	interlocutor	somniloquent
locution	interlocutory	stultiloquent
interlocution	circumlocutory	breviloquent
circumlocution	locutory	multiloquent
locutionary	soliloquacious	pleniloquent
loquacious	somniloquacious	pauciloquent

(Helpful Hints: Page 107)

mal-, male- (mal, malum) bad, badly, ill (disease, sickness)

Memory Aid The _mal(e)_ chauvinist pig is a <u>bad</u> man who acts <u>badly</u> with <u>ill</u> intent. Moreover, when he 'stands alone' and speaks 'in phrases' (see TECHNICAL INFORMATION for the relevance of these quotes), some say he is a walking <u>disease</u> or <u>sickness</u>. Now picture a crude, sloppy, overweight male wearing a dirty T-shirt and holding a beer in one hand (with perhaps a few drops clinging to his chin and the remainder landing on his partially exposed beer belly) walking into an elegant club or restaurant (or sports arena) and carrying on in whatever manner will fix in your mind the key words "bad, badly, ill; disease and sickness."

Technical Information *mal-* is derived from the Latin adjective *malus* (mȧ´lŏŏs), "bad." *male-* is derived from the Latin adverb *male* (mȧ´le), "badly, ill," which in turn is derived from *malus* and has no relationship to English *male*, as in *male chauvinist pig*. In medical and quasi-medical terminology, however, **mal** and its Latin neuter form **malum** generally 'stand alone in phrases' (see MEMORY AID for a tie-in to these quotes) in which they signify "disease or sickness," as in *mal de mer* (see under BRIEF ANALYSES) and *malum venereum*, a scientific name for syphilis. Interestingly, a Greek combining form similar in meaning to *mal-* and *male-* but far more prevalent in medical terminology is *dys-* (düs), "bad, difficult," which appears in such words and phrases as *dysmenorrhea* and *muscular dystrophy*; and a more literary Greek word that also means "bad" but which seldom appears in medical terminology is *kakos* (kä´kôs), whose base *kak-* and its Latinized form *cac-* turn up in *kakistocracy* and *cacophonous*.

DETAILED EXAMPLE

malediction (mal´ə•dik´shən)

Dissection: 1) male- / dict- / -ion

Analysis: 2) ***male-*** is derived from the Latin adverb *male* (mȧ´le), "badly, ill," which in turn is derived from the Latin adjective *malus* (mȧ´lŏŏs), "bad." ***dict-*** is the base of Latin *dictus* (dik´tŏŏs), which is the past participle of *dīcere* (dē´ke•re), "to say, to speak." ***-ion*** is the base of Latin *-iōnis* (i•ō´nis), which is the genitive of *-iō* (i•ō), "the act, means, or result of."

Reconstruction: 3) the act, means, or result of (-*ion*) speaking (*dict-*) ill (*male-*).

Definition: 4) *n.* 1. a curse or the invoking of a curse; imprecation; execration. 2. a malicious, false, and injurious statement about another; slander.

Commentary:

5) When we curse someone, we "speak ill" of that person. But when we "speak well" of a person, we bestow a *benediction* (< Latin *bene*: well), which is a blessing. *mal(e)-* and *ben(e)-* form contrasting prefixes in English and can be found in such pairs as *malefactor, benefactor; malevolent, benevolent;* and *malefic, benefic.* For further examples, see chapter BENE-, BEN-.

BRIEF ANALYSES

malefactor
(mal´ə·fak´tər)

1) male-/fact-/-or
2) *male-*: bad, badly, ill; *fact-*: to do, to make (cf. STUPEFACTION); *-or*: one who or that which (cf. DEFECTOR).
3) one who (*-or*) does (*fact-*) bad (*male-*).
4) *n.* a person who breaks the law or does harm or evil to another or others; criminal; evildoer.

malevolent
(mə·lev´ə·lənt)

1) male-/vol-/-ent
2) *male-*: bad, badly, ill; *vol-*: to wish (cf. VOLITIVE); *-ent*: a present participial suffix equivalent in meaning to *-ing*, as in "an exasperating problem" (cf. AMBIVALENT).
3) wish- (*vol-*) -ing (*-ent*) ill (*male-*).
4) *adj.* 1. wishing harm or evil to another or others: *the malevolent destruction of property*. 2. producing or responsible for harm or evil: *the malevolent forces of nature*.

malefic
(mə·lef´ik)

1) male-/-fic
2) *male-*: bad, badly, ill; *-fic*: making, doing, causing (cf. PROLIFIC).
3) making or doing (*-fic*) bad (*male-*).
4) *adj.* causing or responsible for that which is evil or harmful: *the malefic shifting of crustal plates of the San Andreas fault.*

malaria
(mə·ler´ē·ə)

1) mal-/aria
2) *mal-*: bad, badly, ill; *aria*: air (cf. ARIA).
3) bad (*mal-*) air (*aria*).
4) *n.* any of a group of infectious, usually cyclical, diseases characterized by bouts of severe chills, fever, and sweating, caused by the infestation and destruction of red blood cells by one of four species of protozoa, which are transmitted to humans by the bite of an infected anopheles (ə·näf´ə·lēz) mosquito.
5) During the barbarian invasions following the fall of the Roman Empire, great expanses of cultivated Italian fields were abandoned and eventually became swampland, resulting in the proliferation of the anopheles mosquito and, hence,

mal-, male- (mal, malum)

malaria. But the Italians did not see the causal relationship between the mosquito and the disease, believing the latter to derive from the "bad air" or *mala aria* emanating from the swamps—a phrase that was later contracted to *mal'aria* and, ultimately, *malaria*. In England, however, the term *malaria*, also known as *marsh fever*, did not arrive until the mid-18th century, the disease prior to that time being commonly referred to as *ague* (ā´gyo͞o; ultimately < Latin (*febris*) *acū(ta)*: (fever) acute); and America's *swamp fever* and its medical equivalent, *paludism* (pal´yə•diz´ ´m; < Latin *palūd(is)*: swamp, marsh + English -*ism*: in this context, "an abnormal medical condition of") was not added to this lot for another 130 years, until the late 19th century. Finally, in modern malariology (the scientific study of malaria), the disease is often classified by the number of days in each cycle plus the first day of the following cycle, e.g., if a cycle lasts two days the disease is called *tertian malaria* or simply *tertian* (tûr´shən; < Latin *terti(us)*: third + -*ān(us)*: pertaining to, characterized by), and if a cycle lasts three days the disease is called *quartan malaria* or simply *quartan* (Latin *quart(us)*: fourth + -*ān(us)*: pertaining to, characterized by). As Andrew Boorde explained in 1547: "A fever quartayne . . . doth infeste a man every thyrd day, that is to say two dayes whole and one sycke."

mal de mer

(mȧl də me*r*)

1) mal/de/mer
2) *mal*: disease, sickness; *de*: of, from (cf. LA VILLA REAL DE LA SANTA FÉ DE SAN FRANCISCO DE ASIS); *mer*: sea (cf. MERMAID).
3) sickness (*mal*) of (*de*) the sea (*mer*).
4) *n*. seasickness.

EXERCISES

DISSECT, ANALYZE, RECONSTRUCT, DEFINE, and provide a COMMENTARY for three words in each column, and try to use each in an intelligent sentence. Use a college or unabridged dictionary to check your work. The three columns are arranged in order of difficulty.

malfunction	malign	grand mal
malnutrition	malaise	petit mal
malpractice	malignity	mal du pays
maladroit	malinger	mal du siècle
dismally	malism	mal del pinto
malicious	malfeasance	mal de la rosa
malignant	malocclusion	malum coxae
malodorous	antimalarial	malum coxae senilis

(Helpful Hints: Page 107)

THREE-OR-MORE-ROOT DERIVATIVES

---

ag-, act-, -ig- to do, to act, to drive

Memory Aid Memorize the following sentence: **"The agile actor fumigated the stage."** Now visualize an agile actor on stage doing a routine, acting out a part, and driving a unicycle in circles. A mouse runs past him and two of his lickspittles follow the mouse across the stage. Undaunted, the agile actor fumigates the stage, then continues **to do, to act, to drive.**

Technical Information *ag-* is the base of the Latin verb *agere* (à´ge•re), "to do, to act, to drive." *act-* is the base of Latin *āctus* (äk´toos), which is the past participle of *agere*. *-ig-* is the base of Latin *-igere* (i´ge•re), which is a combining form of *agere* used only within words. But the Latin root *ag-* should not be mistaken for the Latin prefix *ag-* (which is an assimilated form of *AD-*) in such words as *aggression* and *aggravation*; nor should the Latin root *ag-* be confused with the Greek combining form *-agog-* (see chapter -AGOG-) or the Greek letter combination *-ag* in *agnostic* and *agony*. And remember that the Latin combining form *-ig-* always appears within a word and must not be mistaken for the Latin or nonclassical letter combination *ig-* that appears at the beginning of a word, as in *ignore, iguana,* and *igloo.*

DETAILED EXAMPLE

reactionary (rē•ak´shə•ner´ē)

Dissection: 1) re- / act- / -ion / -ary

Analysis: 2) *re-* is derived from Latin *re-* (re), "back, again, anew." *act-* is the base of Latin *āctus* (äk´toos), which is the past participle of *agere* (à´ge•re), "to do, to act, to drive." **-ion** is the base of Latin *-iōnis* (i•ō′nis), which is the genitive of *-iō* (i•ō), "the act, means, or result of." **-ary** is derived from Latin *-ārius* (ä′ri•ⴲs), "pertaining to, characterized by, or having the nature of" OR "one who or that which is characterized by or performs (the action designated by the preceding base or elements)."

Reconstruction: 3) pertaining to or characterized by (*-ary*) the act or result of (*-ion*) driving (*act-*) back (*re-*); OR one who or that which is characterized by (*-ary*) the act of (*-ion*) driving (*act-*) back (*re-*).

Definition: 4) *adj.* 1. of or relating to a person or ideology that opposes social or political change and advocates the return to a former, more conservative state of affairs. —*n.* 2. a person who holds such views.

Commentary: 5) The reactionary, etymologically, drives backward. The opposite of the reactionary is the *progressive*, who tends to or is inclined to (*-iv-*) step (*gress-*) forward (*pro-*). The *liberal* is characterized by (*-al*) that which is free (*liber*); and the *conservative* possesses (*-at-*) a tendency or inclination to (*-iv-*) thoroughly (*con-*) preserve (*serv-*).

BRIEF ANALYSES

actor
(ak′tər)
1) act-/-or
2) *act-*: to do, to act, to drive; *-or*: one who or that which (cf. CREAT<u>OR</u>).
3) one who (*-or*) does, acts, or drives (*act-*).
4) *n.* 1. a person who acts in a play, movie, television show, etc. 2. a person who does or participates in something; a doer.

agile
(aj′əl, -īl)
1) ag-/-il-/-e
2) *ag-*: to do, to act, to drive (cf. A<u>G</u>ENDA); *-il-*: able to, capable of, or inclined to (cf. DOC<u>IL</u>E); *-e*: silent final letter.
3) able to or inclined (*-il-*) to do, act, or drive (*ag-*).
4) *adj.* able to move quickly or think in a shrewd and dexterous manner; deft; nimble.

fumigate
(fyōō′mə•gāt′)
1) fum-/-ig-/-at-/-e
2) *fum-*: smoke, vapor, fume (cf. PER<u>FUM</u>E); *-ig-*: to do, to act, to drive (cf. NAV<u>IG</u>ATE); *-at-*: to cause, to make, to function, to manage (cf. GENER<u>AT</u>E); *-e*: silent final letter.
3) to manage or cause (*-at-*) to drive (*-ig-*) smoke or fumes (*fum-*).
4) *v.* to permeate with smoke, vapor, or fumes, especially to rid of roaches, ants, bedbugs, or other vermin.

intransigent

(in·tran´si·jənt)

1) in-/trans-/-ig-/-ent

2) *in-*: not, without (cf. <u>IN</u>ELIGIBLE); *trans-*: over, across, beyond (cf. <u>TRANS</u>AT-LANTIC); *-ig-*: to do, to act, to drive (cf. PROD<u>IG</u>AL); *-ent*: a present participial suffix equivalent in meaning to *-ing*, as in "a sitting duck" (cf. DESPOND<u>ENT</u>), OR a substantive suffix meaning: one who or that which (cf. SUPERINTEND<u>ENT</u>).

3) not (*in-*) driv- (*-ig-*) -ing (*-ent*) across (*trans-*); OR one who (*-ent*) does not (*in-*) drive (*-ig-*) across (*trans-*).

4) *adj.* 1. refusing to compromise or give in; stubborn; inflexible. —*n.* 2. a stubborn, inflexible person who refuses to compromise or give in, especially in politics.

5) *Los intransigentes* ("the uncompromisers") was a label originally applied in the early 1870's to a radical faction within the Spanish Republican party—a faction whose members were forever unwilling to "drive across" to compromise with their adversaries.

abreaction

(ab´rē·ak´shən)

1) ab-/re-/act-/-ion

2) *ab-*: away, from, away from (cf. <u>AB</u>DUCT); *re-*: back, again (cf. <u>RE</u>CAPTURE); *act-*: to do, to act, to drive; *-ion*: the act, means, or result of (cf. DETENT<u>ION</u>).

3) the act, means, or result of (*-ion*) doing or acting (*act-*) away (*ab-*) again (*re-*).

4) *n.* the psychological release of tension and anxiety by actively recalling and reliving a repressed emotional experience; catharsis.

5) Sigmund Freud and his associate Joseph Breuer first recorded the German term *Abreagierung* in their 1895 *Studien über Hysterie* (*Studies in Hysteria*), of which *abreaction* is an English element-by-element "loan translation." In other words, the English roots ab-/re-/act-/-ion were modeled upon and correspond, respectively, to the German roots ab-/re-/-agier-/-ung. (For a German loan translation of an Italian word, see *zwieback* under *biscuit* in chapter BI-, BIN-, BIS-.)

EXERCISES

DISSECT, ANALYZE, RECONSTRUCT, DEFINE, and provide a COMMENTARY for three words in each column, and try to use each in an intelligent sentence. Use a college or unabridged dictionary to check your work. The three columns are arranged in order of difficulty.

agent	counteractive	exiguous
actress	ambiguous	levigate
actual	litigate	fustigate
inactive	mitigate	remigate
reactive	castigate	suffumigate
transaction	exigency	cutireactive
interaction	reagent	seroreactive
enactment	redactor	agitatrix

(Helpful Hints: Page 108)

bi-, bin-, bis- two, twice, double

Memory Aid Memorize the following sentence: **"The <u>bi</u>lingual looked through the <u>bin</u>oculars at a <u>bis</u>cuit."** Now exaggerate the size and appearance of these objects so you can better visualize this ridiculous picture; and note that a bilingual speaks <u>two</u> languages, a biscuit was originally baked <u>twice</u>, and binoculars have <u>double</u> lenses. (For more complete definitions and etymologies, see the entries under BRIEF ANALYSES.)

Technical Information *bi-* is derived from Latin *bi-* (bi), which is a combining form of *bis* (bis), "two, twice, double." Before vowels, however, *bi-* becomes **bin-**, which is technically a derivative of Latin *bīnī* (bē´nē), "two each, two at a time, double," which is itself a derivative of Latin *bis*. English **bis-**, however, is generally considered to be a variant of *bi-* (rather than the reverse) and normally occurs before *c* or *s*. But all of these forms, regardless of derivation, usually appear at the beginning of words and should not be confused with such Greek roots as *bi-* (< Greek *bios*: life), which we see in *biology* and *autobiographer*, or with the *bi-* in *bibli-* (< Greek *biblion-*: book, bible), which we see in *bibliographer* and *biblical*. And Latin *bi-* should never be mistaken for the identical letter combination *-bi-* that occurs in thousands of English words, such as *ambidextrous* and *bikini*.

DETAILED EXAMPLE

bicentennial (bī´sen·ten´ē·əl)

Dissection: 1) bi- / cent- / -enn- / -i- / -al

Analysis: 2) *bi-* is a combining form of Latin *bis* (bis), "two, twice, double." *cent-* is the base of Latin *centum* (ken´toom), "hundred." *-enn-* is a combining form of Latin *ann(us)* (àn´noos), "year." *-i-* is technically extracted from the Latin noun-forming suffix *-ium* (i·oom) but serves here as and may be considered a "connecting vowel." *-al* is the base of Latin *-ālis* (ä·lis), "pertaining to, characterized by" OR "one who or that which pertains to."

Reconstruction: 3) pertaining to or characterized by (*-al*) two (*bi-*) hundred (*cent-*) years (*-enn-*); OR that which pertains to (*-al*) two (*bi-*) hundred (*cent-*) years (*-enn-*).

Definition: 4) *adj.* 1. pertaining to a 200th anniversary or its celebration. 2. lasting for or occurring every 200 years. —*n.* 3. a 200th anniversary or its celebration.

Commentary: 5) If we remove the *bi-* from *bicentennial*, we get *centennial*, which is a 100th anniversary. If we then affix the combining form *semi-* (< Latin *sēmi-*: half) to the beginning of *centennial*, we derive *semicentennial*, which is a 50th anniversary. And if we then replace the *semi-* with *sesqui-* (< Latin *sēsqui-*: one and a half), we come up with *sesquicentennial*, which is a 150th anniversary. Following this model, we can re-create *tricentennial* (< Latin *trēs*: three), a 300th anniversary; *quadricentennial* (< Latin *quattuor*: four), a 400th anniversary; *quincentennial* (< Latin *quīnque*: five), a 500th anniversary; *sexcentenary* (< Latin *sex*: six, not to be confused with Latin *sexus*: sex), a 600th anniversary; *septicentennial* (< Latin *septem*: seven), a 700th anniversary; *octocentennial* (< Latin *octō*: eight), a 800th anniversary; and *millennial* (< Latin *mille*: thousand), a rare synonym and adjectival form of the more common *millennium*, a 1000th anniversary or period of 1000 years. Remarkably, no term for a 900th anniversary has been documented, though if and when it is, it will in all likelihood turn out to be *novicentennial* (< Latin *novem*: nine).

BRIEF ANALYSES

biscuit
(bis´kit)

1) bis-/-cuit
2) *bis-*: two, twice, double; *-cuit*: cooked, baked (cf. CUISINE).
3) cooked or baked (*-cuit*) twice (*bis-*).
4) *n.* a type of bread baked in small, soft cakes, raised and lightened with baking powder, soda, or yeast.
5) A biscuit was originally "twice baked" as a means of preserving it, being returned to the oven after its initial baking to make it hard, dry, and flat. In Medieval Latin, this "hardtack" was referred to as *panis bis coctus*, "bread twice baked," of which the *panis* eventually dropped out, leaving *bis coctus*, "twice baked," which in turn passed on to Middle French where it became *bescuit* and ultimately *biscuit*. Interestingly, another type of bread that is also "twice baked" is zwieback (pronounced at least nine different ways), which is first baked in a loaf and then cut into slices and toasted. Indeed, *zwieback* is a German element-by-element "loan translation" of Italian *biscotto* (*cotto* being the Italian equivalent of Middle French *cuit*), in which the German elements *zwie* and *back* were modeled upon and correspond, respectively, to the Italian elements *bis-* and *cotto*. So *biscuit* and *zwieback* are etymologically as well as semantically related. (For an English loan translation of a German word, see *abreaction* in chapter AG-, ACT-, -IG-)

bilingual
(bī·ling´gwəl)

1) bi-/lingu-/-al
2) *bi-*: two, twice, double; *lingu-*: tongue (cf. LINGUIST); *-al*: pertaining to, characterized by (cf. IMMORTAL).
3) characterized by (*-al*) two (*bi-*) tongues (*lingu-*).

4) *adj.* 1. capable of speaking two languages fluently: *a bilingual secretary.*
2. written or spoken in two languages: *a bilingual newsletter.* *—n.* 3. a person who speaks two languages fluently.

5) The most important anatomical structure in the articulation of speech and, hence, language is the tongue. For this reason, *language* and *tongue* have long been used synonymously to denote any system of speech common to a particular people, nation, geographical area, etc.

binocular
(bi·näk´yə·lər, bī-)

1) bin-/ocul-/-ar

2) *bin-*: two, twice, double; *ocul-*: eye (cf. OCULIST); *-ar*: pertaining to, characterized by (cf. LUNAR).

3) characterized by (*-ar*) two (*bi-*) eyes (*ocul-*).

4) *adj.* having or involving two eyes that can be jointly focused to provide depth perception: *Human beings and most animals have binocular vision.*

5) If you doubt that binocular vision provides depth perception, close one eye and focus upon two objects one of which is clearly in front of the other, and they will appear to be touching.

EXERCISES

DISSECT, ANALYZE, RECONSTRUCT, DEFINE, and provide a COMMENTARY for three words in each column, and try to use each in an intelligent sentence. Use a college or unabridged dictionary to check your work. The three columns are arranged in order of difficulty.

bicycle	bicameral	bipedal
bimonthly	bilabial	bimanual
combination	bicuspid	bicorporeal
bimetallic	bimester	binaural
biracial	biliteral	bicephalous
binary	bifoliate	bicaudal
bisect	bissextile	biligulate
bisexual	bifurcation	bimastic

(Helpful Hints: Page 92)

corp-, corpus, corpor- body

Memory Aid   Memorize the following sentence: **"The <u>corpse</u> constituted the <u>corpus</u> of the <u>corporation</u>"** (see *corpus*, definition 4, under BRIEF ANALYSES). Now imagine yourself walking up a majestic stairway to the entrance to a large *corporation*, passing through the front doors into an imposing but deserted corridor, slowly walking down this corridor into a stately boardroom—and observing to your horror: a decomposed <u>corpse</u> or <u>body</u> atop the <u>corporate</u> table.

Technical Information   *corp-* is the base of Latin *corpus* (kôr´pŏŏs), "body." *corpor-* is the base of Latin *corporis* (kôr´pô·ris), which is the genitive of *corpus*. However, Latin *corpus* (genitive: *corporis*), "body," is sometimes confused with Latin *cor* (genitive: *cordis*), "heart," which we see in *cordial*, *cordate*, and *misericord*. Also, a similar but unrelated Latin term meaning "body" but restricted exclusively to a "dead body" is *cadāver* (kà·dä´wer), which we see in *cadaver*, *cadaverous*, and *cadaverine*. Finally, the Greek equivalent to Latin *corpus* (genitive: *corporis*) is *sōma* (genitive: *sōmatos*), which occurs in *chromosome*, *psychosomatic*, and *trypanosomiasis*.

DETAILED EXAMPLE

corpuscle (kôr´pə·s'l, kôr´pus·əl)

Dissection: 1) corpus / -cl- / -e

Analysis: 2) ***corpus*** is derived from Latin *corpus* (kôr´pŏŏs), "body." ***-cl-*** is abstracted from Latin *-cul-* (kŏŏl), which is the base of the Latin diminutive suffix *-culus* (kŏŏ´lŏŏs), "small, little, tiny." ***-e*** is an English "silent final letter."

Reconstruction: 3) tiny (*-cl-*) body (*corpus*).

Definition: 4) *n.* 1. an independent or semi-isolated body cell, especially a free-floating blood cell. 2. any minute particle, as a proton, neutron, or electron.

Commentary: 5) Two types of blood cells are the red blood cell or *erythrocyte* (i·rith´rə·sīt´; < Greek *erythr(os)*: red + *-o-*: connecting vowel + *kyt(os)*: hollow vessel, receptacle, cell + English *-e*: silent final letter) and the white blood cell or *leukocyte* (lōō´kə·sīt´; < Greek *leuk(os)*: white + *-o-*: connecting vowel + *kyt(os)*: hollow vessel, receptacle, cell + English *-e*: silent final letter). We also see *erythr-*, "red," in *erythrophobia* (i·rith´rə·fō´bē·ə), an irrational fear of the color red (see -PHOBIA); and we see *leuk-*, "white," in *leukemia*, a common form of cancer characterized by an excessive proliferation of white blood cells (cf. ANEMIA).

corp-, corpus, corpor-

English *cyt-*, "cell," appears in hundreds of English words, including *cytoplasm*, the protoplasm or living semifluid surrounding the nucleus of a cell (see *plas(sein)* in CARDIOPLASTY + *-m(os)* in SOMNAMBULISM), and *cytology*, the scientific study of the structure, function, formation, and pathology of cells (see *-logy* in BIOLOGY; and cf. *cyst-* in HEPATOCYSTIC).

BRIEF ANALYSES

corpus
(kôr´pəs)

1) corpus
2) *corpus*: body.
3) body (*corpus*).
4) *n.* 1. a large and often comprehensive collection of writings or data in a particular field or by a specific author: *the corpus of early Germanic law.* 2. the principal or financial holdings of a person or business as distinguished from the interest or income derived from it. 3. a body of words, sentences, or other spoken or written forms that provides the basis for a linguistic analysis: *a corpus of over one million English words to be studied and analyzed.* 4. the main body or principal part of something: *The corpus of our disagreement was over time, not money.*
5) *corpus* frequently turns up in medical and, to a lesser extent, in legal two-word phrases. A well-known legal phrase is *habeas corpus*, literally, "thou shalt have the body"—the opening words in a writ directing a prison guard to bring a recently detained or imprisoned person (i.e., that person's live *body*) before a judge or court to show justification why he or she is being held. *habeas* is derived from Latin *habēre* (past participle: *habitus*), "to have, to hold," which in turn yields the Latin frequentative verb *habitāre*, "to dwell, to reside," the base of which we see in *habitant*, *inhabitable*, and *cohabit*. For additional legal and medical phrases that incorporate *corpus*, see the entries in the third column under EXERCISES.

incorporeal
(in´kôr·pôr´ē·əl)

1) in-/corpor-/-e-/-al
2) *in-*: not, without (cf. INELIGIBLE); *corpor-*: body; *-e-*: connecting vowel; *-al*: pertaining to, characterized by (cf. DIGITAL).
3) characterized by (*-al*) without (*in-*) a body (*corpor-*).
4) *adj.* without a body or form; immaterial; spiritual.
5) Note: *in-*, "not, without" (as in *incurable*, *incompetent*, *insane*, and *insomnia*), should not be confused with *in-*, "in, into, within" (as in *inflammable*, *induction*, *incumbent*, and *incarcerate*). Interestingly, owing to this distinction, *incorporeal* and *incarnate* (endowed with a body or human form < Latin *in-*: in, into, within + *carn(is)*: flesh + *-at(us)*: having been, having had + English *-e*: silent final letter) turn out to be almost exact opposites.

corposant

(kôr´pə·sant´, -zant´)

1) corp-/-o-/sant-
2) *corp-*: body; *-o-*: connecting vowel; *sant-*: holy, sacred (cf. S<small>ANTA</small> F<small>E</small>).
3) holy (*sant-*) body (*corp-*).
4) *n.* a luminous electrical discharge sometimes observed on the tips of steeples, masts, sailyards, and other pointed objects during electrical storms.
5) Purportedly, this word derives from the fanciful resemblance of this electrical discharge to the halo presumed to exist above the heads of saints. For this reason, *corposant* is more popularly known as *St. Elmo's fire* (or occasionally *St. Ulmo's fire*), named after a 3rd-century bishop and patron saint of sailors. But *corposant* today is often referred to as simply an "electrical glow," though in former times it was described as a flickering or "rolling" fire, as evidenced by the now archaic *furole* (< French *f(e)u*: fire + *ro(u)l(er)*: to roll + *-e*: silent final letter). In scientific nomenclature, this phenomenon is known as *corona discharge*, the first term *corona* (< Greek *koronē*: crown) alluding, once again, to the fanciful shape of the discharge—bringing us full circle to the poetic *corposant*.

E<small>XERCISES</small>

D<small>ISSECT</small>, A<small>NALYZE</small>, R<small>ECONSTRUCT</small>, D<small>EFINE</small>, and provide a C<small>OMMENTARY</small> for three words in each column, and try to use each in an intelligent sentence. Use a college or unabridged dictionary to check your work. The three columns are arranged in order of difficulty.

corps	corporality	corpus juris
corpse	corporeity	corpus callosum
corporation	incorporeity	corpus delicti
incorporate	bicorporeal	corpus luteum
corporatism	tricorporate	corpus striatum
corporative	corpuscularity	corpus cavernosum
corpulent	corporification	Corpus Juris Civilis
incorporable	corpusculiferous	Corpus Juris Canonici

(Helpful Hints: Page 109)

fact-, -fect-, fac-, -fic-, -fy   to make, to do

Memory Aid   1) Perhaps a *facile* (easy <u>to make</u> or <u>to do</u>; see definition under BRIEF ANALYSES) way to remember these five roots is to link them phonetically (with regard to speech sounds or their representation in a language).

2) Thus, if you look closely at these roots, you'll notice that the major difference among them is their single vowel, which in each case is the second letter. In English, we have six vowels: *a, e, i, o, u,* and *y*—a list you probably already know by heart. So in considering these six vowels by number and letter while viewing the five roots on the top of this page, imagine the first vowel *a* in *fact-* becoming the second vowel *e* in *-fect-*; then imagine the first vowel *a* in *fac-* becoming the third vowel *i* in *-fic-*; and finally, imagine the third vowel *i* in *-fic-* becoming the sixth (and rhyming) vowel *y* in *-fy* (the *o* and *u*—as in *ouch!*—we can ignore). Thus, we have *fact-*|-*fect-* (*a > e*) and *fac-*|-*fic-*|-*fy* (*a > i > y*).

3) Of course, the best way to remember these roots is to truly understand the relationships among them, as described in the TECHNICAL INFORMATION below.

Technical Information   *fac-* is the base of the Latin verb *facere* (fȧ´ke•re), "to make, to do." *fact-* is the base of Latin *factus* (fȧk´tŏŏs), which is the past participle of *facere*. *-fic-* is the base of Latin *-ficere* (fĭ´ke•re), which is a combining form of *facere* used only with prefixes or initial combining forms, as in *officious* and *orifice*. However, in many English words, *-fic* is derived from Latin *-ficus* (fĭ´kŏŏs), "making, doing, causing, producing" (< Latin *-fic(ere)* + *-us*: adjectival suffix), and serves as an adjective-forming suffix defined as "making, doing, causing, or producing," as in *terrific* (see under BRIEF ANALYSES) and *horrific*. And in an even greater number of words, English *-fy* (< Latin *-ficāre*: to make, to do < *-fic(us)* + *-āre*: verbal suffix) serves as a verb-forming suffix with the related meanings, "to make, to do, to cause, to become," as in *pacify* and *petrify*. Moreover, when *-fy* occurs within words, it often takes the form of *-fic-*, which, in combination with *-at-* and *-ion*, yields the noun-forming suffix *-fication*, "the making, causing, or production of," as in *calcification* and the more technical words in the third column under EXERCISES. Finally, *-fect-* is the base of Latin *-fectus* (fek´tŏŏs), which is the past participle of *-ficere* used only with prefixes, as in *imperfect* (see under BRIEF ANALYSES) and *defector*.

DETAILED EXAMPLE

stupefaction (stŏŏ´pə•fak´shən, styŏŏ´-)

Dissection: 1) stup- / -e- / fact- / -ion

Analysis: 2) *stup-* is the base of Latin *stupēre* (stoo•pā′re), "to be numbed or stunned." *-e-* is a Latin "connecting vowel." *fact-* is the base of Latin *factus* (făk′toos), which is the past participle of *facere* (fă′ke•re), "to make, to do." *-ion* is the base of Latin *-iōnis* (i•ō′nis), which is the genitive of *-iō* (i•ō), "the act, means, or result of."

Reconstruction: 3) the act, means, or result of (*-ion*) making (*fact-*) numb (*stup-*).

Definition: 4) *n*. 1. a dazed or benumbed condition with little or no sensibility, often resulting from a drug overdose, major injury, or traumatic emotional event. 2. the state or condition of being utterly bewildered or confounded, as by a supposed encounter with a ghost or extraterrestrial.

Commentary: 5) *stupefaction* is the abstract noun of the verb *stupefy*, "to benumb or bewilder." The concrete noun is *stupefacient* (stoo′pə•fā′shənt), which is a drug or other agent that causes stupefaction. But *stupefacient* (< Latin *-i-*: connecting vowel + *-ent(is)*, genitive of *-ēns*: one who or that which) may also be used as an adjective, equivalent in meaning to *stupefying*, "causing or inducing stupefaction," as in the sentence, "The stupefacient lecture made my brain wither and eventually put me to sleep." However, if the lecture only tends to put you to sleep but doesn't actually do so, then it is *stupefactive* (< Latin *-īv(us)*: tending to, inclined to + English *-e*: silent final letter). But if the lecture is neither stupefacient nor stupefactive but you are nonetheless stupefied, then perhaps you are just plain stupid.

BRIEF ANALYSES

imperfect
(im•pûr′fikt)

1) im-/per-/-fect-
2) *im-*: not, without (cf. IMMORTAL); *per-*: through, throughout, completely (cf. PERFUME); *-fect-*: to make, to do.
3) not (*im-*) making or doing (*-fect-*) completely (*per-*).
4) *adj*. 1. not finished or complete: *an imperfect deck of cards*. 2. having or characterized by having defects, faults, or weaknesses: *imperfect coordination*.

terrific
(tə•rif′ik)

1) terr-/-i-/-fic
2) *terr-*: to frighten, scare, or terrify (cf. TERRIFY); *-i-*: connecting vowel; *-fic*: making, doing, causing, producing.
3) making (*-fic*) frightened (*terr-*).
4) *adj*. 1. [*Colloq*.] great, wonderful, marvelous. 2. [*Substand*.] intense, severe, unbearable: *a terrific heat wave*.
5) Originally, *terrific*—like *horrific*—meant "causing terror, frightening." But over the centuries it gradually "weakened" and by 1809 was first recorded to mean "intense, severe, excessive"; and by 1930, if not earlier, it had substan-

tially "meliorated" or become elevated in meaning, having developed the sense, "splendid, wonderful."

facile
(fas´'l)

1) fac-/-il-/-e
2) *fac-*: to make, to do; *-il-*: able to, capable of, tending to, or inclined to (cf. DOCILE); *-e*: silent final letter.
3) able or inclined to (*-il-*) make or do (*fac-*).
4) *adj.* 1. easy to make or do: *a facile assignment.* 2. moving, thinking, speaking, etc., with ease and grace: *a facile charmer.*

vinify
(vin´ə•fī´)

1) vin-/-i-/-fy
2) *vin-*: wine (cf. VINEGAR); *-i-*: connecting vowel; *-fy*: to make, to do.
3) to make (*-fy*) wine (*vin-*).
4) *v.* to make wine by fermenting the juice of grapes or other fruit.

EXERCISES

DISSECT, ANALYZE, RECONSTRUCT, DEFINE, and provide a COMMENTARY for three words in each column, and try to use each in an intelligent sentence. Use a college or unabridged dictionary to check your work. The three columns are arranged in order of difficulty.

horrify	edify	cornification
difficulty	artifice	dulcification
facility	confection	lignification
acidify	facsimile	lapidification
pacific	artifact	saponification
defection	refectory	nidification
inefficient	putrefactive	thurification
manufacture	abortifacient	devitrification

(Helpful Hints: Page 109)

PART II

HELPFUL HINTS

-agog- (from page 47)

pedagogy
< G. -ia: act, process, or result of.

pedagogics
< E. -ics: sci. of < G. -ik(a).

pedagogical
< L. -āl(is): pert. to, charact. by.

pedagoguish
< OE. -isc: like, characteristic of.

demagogy
< G. -ia: act, process, or result of.

demagoguism
< E. -ism: practice of < G. -ism(os).

demagoguery
< E. -rie: practice of < OF. -(e)rie.

synagogical
< L. -ic(us): pert. to, charact. by.

anagogy
< G. an(a)-: up, upward.

isagoge
< G. (e)is-: into.

epagoge
< G. ep(i)-: over, upon, besides.

paragoge
< G. par(a)-: beside, alongside.

agogic
< G. -ik(os): pert. to, charact. by.

isagogics
< E. -ics: study of < G. -ik(a).

psychagogue
< G. psych(ē): soul, spirit, life.

mystagogue
< G. myst(ēs): religious initiate.

hydragogue
< G. hydr- (hydōr): water.

sialagogue
< G. sial(on): saliva.

cholagogue
< G. chol(ē): bile.

emmenagogue
< G. emmēn(a): menses.

lithagogue
< G. lith(os): stone.

helminthagogue
< G. helminth(os): worm.

dacryagogue
< G. dakry(on): teardrop.

dacryagogatresia
< G. trēs(is): perforation.

bibli- (from page 50)

biblically
< OE. -lī(ce): in the manner of.

bibliography
< G. -ia: act, process, or result of.

biblicism
< E. -ism: beliefs of < G. -ism(os).

bibliotherapy
< G. therap(euein): to treat, cure.

biblicoliteracy
< L. lit(t)er(a): letter (of alph.).

bibliographically
< OE. -lī(ce): in the manner of.

bibliomania
< G. ma(i)n(esthai): to go mad.

bibliofilm
< OE. film(en): membrane, skin.

bibliology
< G. log(os): word, speech.

bibliotics
< E. -ics: study of < G -ik(a).

bibliotist
< G. ist(ēs): one who practices.

bibliotheca
< G. thēkē: case, cover, box.

bibliogenesis
< G. genē-: to be born, become.

biblicality
< L. -tās: quality or condit. of.

bibliogony
< G. gon(os): procreating.

bibliophilistic
< G. ·ist(ēs): one who.

bibliopole
< G. pōl(ein): to offer for sale.

bibliomane
< G. ma(i)n(esthai): to go mad.

bibliotaph
< G. taph(os): burial, tomb.

biblioclast
< G. klas- (klan): to break.

bibliognost
< G. (gi)gnōs(kein): to know.

bibliolatrist
< G. latr(euein): to worship.

bibliopegist
< G. pēg(nynai): to fasten, bind.

bibliophagist
< G. phag(ein): to eat, devour.

cardi- (from page 53)

cardiotherapy
< G. *therap(euein)*: to treat, cure.

cardiophobia
< G. *phob(os)*: fear, panic, flight.

cardiopulmonary
< L. *pulmōn(is)* (*pulmō*): lung.

cardiohepatic
< G. *hēpat(os)* (*hēpar*): liver.

cardionephric
< L. *nephr(os)*: kidney, kidneys.

cardiorenal
< G. *rēn(ēs)*: kidneys.

cardioplegia
< G. *plēg(ē)*: a blow, stroke.

cardiopathy
< G. *path(os)*: suffering, feeling.

myocardium
< G. *my(os)* (*mys*): mouse, <u>muscle</u>.

pericardium
< G. *peri-*: around, about.

endocardium
< G. *end(on)*: in, within.

epicardium
< G. *epi-*: over, upon, on.

myocarditis
< E. *-itis*: the inflammation of.

pancarditis
< G. *pan*, neut. of *pas*: all, every.

telecardiophone
< G. *tēle-*: far, far off, afar.

cardiotachometer
< G. *tach(os)*: speed.

cardioid
< G. *-o(e)id(ēs)*: shaped like.

dextrocardial
< G. *dextr-* (*dexter*): right.

diplocardiac
< G. *diplo(os)*: twofold, double.

cardiomyopathy
< G. *my(os)* (*mys*): mouse, <u>muscle</u>.

acardiohemia
< G. *haim(a)* [*haimatos*]: blood.

acephalocardia
< G. *kephal(ē)*: head.

hydropericarditis
< G. *hydr-* (*hydōr*): water.

Anacardium occidentale
< G. *ana-*: up, back, <u>similar to</u>.

-cide (from page 56)

infanticide
< L. *fant(is)* (*fāns*) (*fārī*): to speak.

parenticide
< L. *par(ere)*: to bring forth, beget.

giganticide
< G. *gigant(os)* (*gigās*): giant.

tyrannicide
< G. *tyrann(os)*: master, tyrant.

femicide
< L. *fēm(ina)*: woman, female.

genocide
< G. *gen(os)*: race, kind.

regicide
< L. *rēg(is)* (*rēx*): king.

hereticide
< E. *heret(ic)*: heretic.

viricide
< L. *vīr(us)*: slime, poison.

fungicide
< L. *fung(us)*: fungus, mushroom.

bactericide
< G. *baktēr(ion)*: a little staff.

spermicide
< G. *sperm(a)*: a seed, germ.

taeniacide
< G.. *tainia*: band, ribbon.

streptococcide
< G. *strept(os)*: twisted, twined.

staphylococcide
< G. *staphyl(ē)*: cluster of grapes.

treponemicide
< G. *nēm(a)* [*nēmatos*]: thread.

avicide
< L. *av(is)*: bird.

piscicide
< L. *pisc(is)*: fish.

cimicide
< L. *cimic(is)* (*cimex*): bedbug.

culicicide
< L. *culic(is)* (*culex*): gnat.

pulicicide
< L. *pulic(is)* (*pulex*): flea.

muscacide
< L. *musca*: a fly.

macropicide
< G. *p(ous)* (*podos*): foot.

pediculicide
< L. *pēd(is)*: louse (pl: lice).

circum- (from page 59)

circumst**a**nce
< L. *st(āre)*: to stand.

circumstanti**al**
< L. *-āl(is)*: pert. to, charact. by.

circum**vent**
< L. *vent(us)* *(venīre)*: to come.

circum**spect**
< L. *spect(us)* *(specere)*: to look.

circum**fuse**
< L. *fūs(us)* *(fundere)*: to pour.

circum**flex**
< L. *flex(us)* *[flectere]*: to bend.

circum**a**viate
< L. *av(is)*: bird.

circum**locut**ion
< L. *locūt(us)* *(loquī)*: to speak.

circum**jac**ent
< L. *jac(ēre)*: to lie, rest.

circum**scrip**tion
< L. *scrīpt(us)* *(scrībere)*: to write.

circum**flu**ent
< L. *flu(ere)*: to flow.

circum**duct**ion
< L. *duct(us)* *(dūcere)*: to lead.

circum**vol**ant
< L. *vol(āre)*: to fly.

circum**vall**ate
< L. *vall(um)*: rampart, wall.

circum**volut**ion
< L. *volūt(us)* *(volvere)*: to roll.

circum**und**ulation
< L. *und(a)*: a wave, surge.

circum**bore**al
< L. *bore(ās)*: the north wind.

circum**austr**al
< L. *aust(e)r*: the south wind.

circum**littor**al
< L. *lītor(is)* *(lītus)*: shore.

circum**nat**ant
< L. *nat(āre)*: to swim, float.

circum**nut**ate
< L. *nūt(āre)*: to nod (repeatedly).

circum**sciss**le
< L. *sciss(us)* *(scindere)*: to cut.

circum**neutr**ophilous
< L. *neut(e)r*: not either, neither.

Begonia circum**lob**ata
< G. *lob(os)*: lobe, vegetable pod.

-cracy (from page 62)

bureaucracy
< F. *bureau*: office, department.

autocracy
< G. *aut(os)*: self, oneself.

theocracy
< G. *the(os)*: god.

technocracy
< G. *techn(ē)*: art, skill.

meritocracy
< L. *merit(um)*: a worthy act.

cosmocracy
< G. *kosm(os)*: universe, world.

arithmocracy
< G. *arithm(os)*: number.

demonocracy
< G. *daimōn*: divine spirit.

plutocracy
< G. *pl(o)ut(os)*: wealth, riches.

ethnocracy
< G. *ethn(os)*: nation, people.

sociocracy
< L. *soci(us)*: companion.

gerontocracy
< G. *geront(os)*: old man.

hierocracy
< G. *hier(os)*: holy, sacred.

hagiocracy
< G. *hagi(os)*: holy, sacred.

timocracy
< G. *tīm(ē)*: honor, worth.

stratocracy
< G. *strat(os)*: army, host.

ochlocracy
< G. *ochl(os)*: a crowd, mob.

dulocracy
< G. *d(o)ul(os)*: a slave.

albocracy
< L. *alb(us)*: white.

bestiocracy
< L. *bēsti(a)*: beast.

hetaerocracy
< G. *hetair(a)*: female consort.

ptochocracy
< G. *ptōch(os)*: beggar, pauper.

pantis**ocracy
< G. *is(os)*: equal.

thalassocracy
< G. *thalass(a)*: sea.

hyper- (from page 65)

hyper**cri**tical
< G. *kri(nein)*: to discern, judge.

hyper**re**active
< L. *re-*: back, again, anew.

hyper**vigil**ant
< L. *vigil(āre)*: to be watchful.

hyperex**cit**ability
< L. *cit(āre)*: to excite, rouse.

hyper**vent**ilation
< L. *vent(us)*: wind.

hyper**therm**ia
< G. *therm(ē)*: heat; *therm(os)*: hot.

hyper**thyr**oidism
< G. *thyr(eos)*: oblong shield.

hyper**pituit**arism
< L. *pītuīt(a)*: phlegm, mucus.

hyper**em**ia
< G. *(h)aim(a)*: blood.

hyper**ox**emia
< G. *ox(ys)*: sharp, keen, <u>acid</u>.

hyper**lip**emia
< G. *lip(os)*: fat.

hyper**ur**icemia
< G. *(o)ur(on)*: urine.

hyper**nitr**emia
< E. *nitr(ogen)*: nitrogen.

hyper**natr**emia
< E. *natr(ium)*: (obs.) sodium.

hyper**kal**emia
< NL. *kal(ium)*: potassium.

hypercholes**ter**olemia
< G. *ster(eos)*: firm, hard, solid.

hyper**ba**ton
< G. *ba(inein)*: to step, walk.

hyper**the**sis
< G. *(ti)the(nai)*: to put, place.

hyper**metri**cal
< G. *metr(on)*: a measure.

hypercata**lec**tic
< G. *lēk- (lēgein)*: to leave off.

hyperdi**tone**
< G. *ton(os)*: vocal pitch, tone.

hyperdia**pente**
< G. *pente*: five.

hyperdia**pason**
< G. *pasōn*, gen. pl. of *pas*: all.

hyperdia**tessaron**
< G. *tessarōn (tessares)*: four.

-itis (from page 68)

ap**pend**icitis
< L. *pend(ere)*: to cause to hang.

tonsillitis
< L. *tōnsill(ae)*: tonsils.

laryngitis
< G. *laryng(os) (larynx)*: voice box.

dermatitis
< G. *dermat(os) (derma)*: skin.

carditis
< G. *kardi(a)*: heart.

hepatitis
< G. *hēpat(os) (hēpar)*: liver.

sinusitis
< L. *sinus*: a bend, fold, hollow.

pan**creat**itis
< G. *kreat(os) (kreas)*: flesh, meat.

gastritis
< G. *gastr(os) (gastēr)*: stomach.

urethritis
< G. *(o)urēthr(a)*: urethra.

mephitis
< ? Oscan *Mefīt(ei)*: a goddess.

meningitis
< G. *mēning(es)*: membranes.

cystitis
< G. *kyst(is)*: bag, sac, <u>bladder</u>.

gingivitis
< L. *gingiv(a)*: gum (of teeth).

pros**tat**itis
< G. *(hi)sta(nai)*: to set, stand.

divertic**ul**itis
< L. *-cul(um)*: a place of or for.

mastitis
< G. *mast(os)*: breast.

metritis
< G. *mētr(a)*: uterus.

colpitis
< G. *kolp(os)*: bosom, <u>vagina</u>.

coxitis
< L. *cox(a)*: hip, hipbone.

thelitis
< G. *thēl(ē)*: nipple.

trachelitis
< G. *trachēl(os)*: uterine neck.

salpingitis
< G. *salping(os)*: trumpet.

endometritis
< G. *end(on)*: in, within.

a-, an- (from page 71)

amor**al**
< L. *mōr(is)* (*mōs*): custom, usage.

atyp**ical**
< G. *typ(os)*: a figure, model.

a**histor**ical
< G. *histor(ia)*: knowledge.

an**arch**y
< G. *arch(os)*: first, chief, ruler.

amne**sia**
< G. *(mi)mnē(skesthai)*: to recall.

apath**y**
< G. *path(os)*: suffering, feeling.

an**esthe**sia
< G. *aisthē-*: feeling, sensation.

a**sym**metry
< G. *sym-* (*syn-*): with, together.

a**morph**ous
< G. *morph(ē)*: form, shape.

an**alg**esic
< G. *alg(os)*: pain, suffering.

a**sphyx**ia
< G. *sphyx(is)*: pulse, heartbeat.

an**orex**ia
< G. *orex(is)*: desire, appetite.

a**lex**ia
< G. *lex(is)*: word, speech.

a**ment**ia
< L. *ment(is)* (*mēns*): mind.

a**nom**ie
< G. *nom(os)*: law, custom.

an**onym**
< G. *onym(a)*: a name, noun.

a**cephal**ous
< G. *kephal(ē)*: head.

a**stom**ia
< G. *stom(a)* [*stomatos*]: mouth.

an**oti**a
< G. *ōt(os)* (*ous*): ear.

a**phalang**ia
< G. *phalang(os)* (*phalanx*): digit.

an**onych**ia
< G. *onych(os)* (*onyx*): claw, nail.

a**mast**ia
< G. *mast(os)*: breast.

an**orch**ia
< G. *orch(is)*: testicle.

an**aphrodit**ous
< G. *Aphrodit(ē)*: Aphrodite.

bene-, ben- (from page 74)

bene**fit**
< MF. *-f(a)it* < L. *-fact(um)*: deed.

benefit**ing**
< OE. *-ende*: doing, performing.

benefit**er**
< OE. *-er(e)*: one who, that which.

benefic**ial**
< L. *-āl(is)*: pert. to, charact. by.

benefici**ary**
< L. *-ārius*: pert. to, charact. by.

beneficial**ly**
< OE. *-lī(ce)*: in the manner of.

beni**gn**
< L. *-gn(us)*: born < *gignere*.

benign**ly**
< OE. *-lī(ce)*: in the manner of.

bene**fice**
< L. *-fic(us)*: making, doing.

benefic**ent**
< L. *-ent(is)* (*-ēns*): -ing.

benefic**ence**
< L. *-ent(is)* (*-ēns*): -ing + -ia.

bene**fact**ion
< L. *fact(us)* (*facere*): to make.

bene**dict**ional
< L. *dict(us)* (*dīcere*): to speak.

benefact**ive**
< L. *-īv(us)*: tending to.

benedict**ory**
< L. *-ōrius*: tending to.

benigni**ty**
< L. *-tās*: quality or condit. of.

benedic**ence**
< L. *-ent(is)* (*-ēns*): -ing + -ia.

bene**vol**ist
< L. *vol(ēns)* (*velle*): to wish.

benefici**ate**
< E. *-at-*: to cause, become.

bene**fic**ential
< L. *-fic(us)*: making, doing.

bene**dict**ionale
< L. *dict(us)* (*dīcere*): to speak.

benediction**ary**
< L. *-ārium*: a thing which.

bene**cept**or
< L. *cept(us)* (*capere*): to seize.

benefac**trices**
< L. *-tricēs*, pl. of *-trix*: she who.

duc-, duct- (from page 77)

conduct**or**
< L. *-or*: one who, that which.

misconduct
< OE. *mis(se)-*: bad, wrong.

product**iv**ity
< L. *-īv(us)*: tending to.

conductiv**ity**
< L. *-tās*: quality or condit. of.

conducive
< L. *con- (com-)*: with, together.

induce**ment**
< L. *-ment(um)*: act or result of.

deductive
< L. *dē-*: away from, off, down.

reproductive
< L. *re-*: back, again, anew.

duct**ile**
< L. *-il(is)*: tending to.

duct**ule**
< L. *-ul(us)*: small, little, tiny.

adduci**ble**
< L. *-b(i)l(is)*: tending to.

educible
< L. *ē- (ex-)*: out, out of.

adductor
< L. *ad-*: to, toward, near.

abductor
< L. *ab-*: away, from.

conductance
< L. *con- (com-)*: with, together.

induct**ance**
< L. *-ent(is) (-ēns)*: -ing + -ia.

adduction
< L. *ad-*: to, toward, near.

eduction
< L. *ē- (ex-)*: out, out of.

obduction
< L. *ob-*: to, toward, over.

subduction
< L. *sub-*: under, below, beneath.

traduction
< L. *trā(ns)-*: over, across, beyond.

retroduction
< L. *retrō-*: back, backward.

circumduction
< L. *circum-*: around, surrounding.

superinduction
< L. *super-*: over, above, beyond.

grad-, gress- (from page 80)

progression
< L. *prō-*: in front of; forward.

digression
< L. *di- (dis-)*: away, from, apart.

regressive
< L. *re-*: back, again, anew.

gradu**ation**
< L. *-āt(us)*: having been.

retrogression
< L. *retrō-*: back, backward.

congressional
< L. *con- (com-)*: with, together.

undergraduate
< OE. *under-*: below, subordinate.

centigrade
< L. *cent(um)*: hundred.

ingress
< L. *in-*: in, into, toward.

aggradation
< L. *ag- (ad-)*: to, toward.

biodegradable
< G. *bi(os)*: life.

gradeabili**ty**
< L. *-tās*: quality or condit. of.

grad**ine**
< L. *-īn(us)*: pert. to; that which.

gradio**meter**
< G. *met(ron)*: a measure.

gress**or**ial
< L. *-or*: one who, that which.

intergradation
< L. *inter-*: between, among.

plantigrade
< L. *plant(a)*: sole of the foot.

pinnigrade
< L. *pinn(a)*: feather, wing, fin.

pronograde
< L. *prōn(us)*: prone, horizontal.

tardigrade
< L. *tard(us)*: slow, tardy.

dorsigrade
< L. *dors(um)*: back (of toes).

orthograde
< G. *orth(os)*: straight, upright.

vermigrade
< L. *verm(is)*: worm.

unguligrade
< L. *ungul(a)*: claw, hoof, talon.

loqu-, locut- (from page 83)

colloquy
< L. *col-* (*com-*): with, together.

colloquium
< L. *-ium*: n-forming suffix.

colloquia
< L. *-ia*, pl. of *-ium* (see prec.).

locution
< L. *-iōn(is)*: the act or result of.

interlocution
< L. *inter-*: between, among.

circumlocution
< L. *circum-*: around, about.

locutionary
< L. *-ārius*: pert. to, charact. by.

loquacious
< E. *-acious*: tending to.

obloquy
< L. *ob-*: to, toward, <u>against</u>.

allocution
< L. *al-* (*ad-*): to, toward.

interlocutor
< L. *-or*: one who, that which.

interlocutory
< L. *-ōrius*: tending to.

circumlocutory
< L. *circum-*: around, about.

locutory
< L. *-ōrium*: a place for.

soliloquacious
< L. *sōl(us)*: alone, solitary.

somniloquacious
< E. *-acious*: tending to.

grandiloquent
< L. *grand(is)*: great, grand.

magniloquent
< L. *magn(us)*: great, large.

somniloquent
< L. *somn(us)*: sleep, slumber.

stultiloquent
< L. *stult(us)*: foolish, stupid.

breviloquent
< L. *brev(is)*: short, brief.

multiloquent
< L. *mult(us)*: much, many.

pleniloquent
< L. *plēn(us)*: full, complete.

pauciloquent
< L. *pauc(us)*: few, little.

mal-, male- [mal, malum] (from page 86)

malfunction
< L. *funct(us)* (*fungī*): to perform.

malnutrition
< L. *nūtrit(us)* (*nūtrīre*): to nourish.

malpractice
< G. *prāk-* (*prassein*): to do.

maladroit
< Fr. *droit*: right, straight.

dismally
< OF. *dis*: days < ML. *diēs*.

malicious
< L. *-iti(a)*: the quality of.

malignant
< L. *-gn(us)*: born < *gignere*.

malodorous
< L. *odor*: odor, stench, scent.

malign
< L. *-gn(us)*: born < *gignere*.

malaise
< OF. *ais(e)*: comfort, ease.

malignity
< L. *-tās*: quality or condit. of.

malinger
< OF. ?*(he)ingre*: sick, haggard.

malism
< E. *-ism*: the doctrine of.

malfeasance
< OF. *fais-* < L. *facere*: to make.

malocclusion
< L. *-clūs(us)* (*claudere*): to shut.

antimalarial
< G. *anti-*: opposed to, <u>curing</u>.

grand mal
< OF. *grand* < L. *grand(is)*: great.

petit mal
< OF. *petit*: small, little, tiny.

mal du pays
< Fr. *pays*: country, land.

mal du siècle
< F. *siècl(e)*: century.

mal del pinto
< Sp. *pint(o)*: spot < L. *pi(c)t(us)*.

mal de la rosa
< Sp. *ros(a)*: rose < L. *ros(a)*: rose.

malum coxae
< L. *cox(a)*: hip, hipbone.

malum coxae senilis
< L. *sen(ex)*: old, aged; an elder.

ag-, act-, -ig- (from page 89)

agent
< L. -*ent(is)* (-*ēns*): -ing; <u>one who</u>.

act**ress**
< OF. -*ess(e)*: female; she who.

act**ual**
< L. -*āl(is)*: pert. to, charact. by.

inactive
< L. *in-*: not, without.

reac**tiv**e
< L. -*īv(us)*: tending to.

transaction
< L. *trāns-*: over, across, beyond.

interaction
< L. *inter-*: between, among.

enactment
< OF. *en-*: in, into < L. *in-*: into.

counteractive
< OF. *contre-* against, opposite.

ambiguous
< L. *ambi-*: both, around, about.

litigate
< L. *līt(is)* (*līs*): lawsuit.

mitigate
< L. *mīt(is)*: mild, soft.

castigate
< L. *cast(us)*: clean, pure.

exi**gency**
< L. -*ent(is)* (-*ēns*): -ing + -*ia.*

reagent
< L. *re-*: back, again.

redactor
< L. *red-* (*re-*): back, again.

exi**guous**
< L. -*uus*: adj. suffix; pert. to.

levigate
< L. *lēv(is)*: smooth, polished.

fustigate
< L. *fūst(us)*: a stick, cudgel.

remigate
< L. *rēm(us)*: oar.

suffumigate
< L. *sub-*: under, <u>from under.</u>

cutireactive
< L. *cut(is)*: skin.

seroreactive
< L. *ser(um)*: whey, <u>serum.</u>

agita**trix**
< L. -*trix*: female; she who.

bi-, bin-, bis- (from page 92)

bi**cycle**
< G. *kykl(os)*: circle, wheel.

bi**monthly**
< OE *mōn(a)th*: month.

combination
< L. *com-*: with, together.

bi**metallic**
< G. *metall(on)*: mine, quarry.

bi**racial**
< Ital. *razz(a)*: race, lineage.

bin**ary**
< L. -*ārius*: pert. to, charact. by.

bi**sect**
< L. *sect(us)* (*secāre*): to cut.

bi**sexual**
< L. *sex(us)*: sex.

bi**camera**l
< G. *kamar(a)*: chamber, vault.

bi**labia**l
< L. *lab(ium)*: lip.

bi**cuspid**
< L. *cuspid(is)* (*cuspis*): a point.

bi**mester**
< L. *mē(n)s(is)*: month.

bi**liter**al
< L. *lit(t)er(a)*: letter (of alph.).

bi**foliate**
< L. *foli(um)*: a leaf.

bis**sextile**
< L. *sext(us)*: sixth.

bi**furc**ation
< L. *furc(a)*: a fork.

bi**ped**al
< L. *ped(is)* (*pēs*): foot.

bi**man**ual
< L. *man(us)*: hand.

bi**corpore**al
< L. *corpor(is)* (*corpus*): body.

bi**naur**al
< L. *aur(is)*: ear.

bi**cephal**ous
< G. *kephal(ē)*: head.

bi**caud**al
< L. *caud(a)*: tail.

bi**lig**ulate
< L. *li(n)g(ere)*: to lick.

bi**mast**ic
< G. *mast(os)*: breast.

corp-, corpus, corpor- (from page 95)

corps
< ME. *corps* < L. *corpus*: body.

corpse
< E. *-e*: silent final letter.

corpor**ation**
< L. *-āt(us)*: having been.

incorporate
< L. *in-*: in, into, within.

corpor**atism**
< E. *-ism*: the practice of.

corpor**ative**
< L. *-īv(us)*: tending to.

corpu**lent**
< L. *-lent(us)*: abounding in.

incorpor**able**
< L. *-b(i)l(is)*: tending to.

corpor**ality**
< L. *-āl(is)*: pert. to, charact. by.

corpor**eity**
< L. *-tās*: quality or condit. of.

incorporeity
< L. *in-*: not, without.

bicorporeal
< L. *bi(s)*: two, twice, double.

tricorporate
< L. *tri- < trēs*: three.

corpus**cularity**
< L. *-cul(us)*: small, little, tiny.

corporific**ation**
< L. *-iōn(is)*: act or result of.

corpusculi**ferous**
< L. *fer(re)*: to bear, to carry.

corpus **juris**
< L. *jūris (jūs)*: law, right.

corpus **callosum**
< L. *call(um)*: tough skin.

corpus de**licti**
< L. *-līct(us) (linguere)*: leave.

corpus **luteum**
< L. *lūte(us)*: golden-yellow.

corpus **striatum**
< L. *stri(a)*: channel, groove.

corpus **cavernosum**
< L. *cavern(a)*: cavern, cave.

corpus juris **civilis**
< L. *cīv(is)*: citizen.

corpus juris **canonici**
< ML. *canōn*: sacred writings.

fact-, -fect-, fac-, -fic-, -fy (from page 98)

horrify
< L. *horr(ēre)*: to tremble.

diffi**culty**
< L. *-ul- (-ilis)*: tending to.

facili**ty**
< L. *-tās*: quality or condit. of.

acidify
< L. *acid(us)*: sour < *acēre*.

pacific
< L. *pāc(is) (pāx)*: peace.

defection
< L. *dē-*: away from, off, down.

inefficient
< L. *-ent(is) (-ēns)*: -ing.

manufac**ture**
< L. *ūr(a)*: process or result of.

edify
< L. *(a)ed(ēs)*: temple, house.

artifice
< L. *art(is) (ars)*: skill, craft.

confection
< L. *con- (com-)*: with, together.

fac**simile**
< L. *simile*: likeness < *similis*.

artifact
< L. *art(is) (ars)*: skill, craft.

refect**ory**
< L. *-ōrium*: a place for.

putrefactive
< L. *putr(ēre)*: to rot, decay.

a**bort**ifacient
< L. *ort(us) (orīrī)*: to be born.

cornification
< L. *corn(ū)*: horn (of animal).

dulcification
< L. *dulc(is)*: sweet, pleasant.

lignification
< L. *lign(um)*: wood, firewood.

lapidification
< L. *lapid(is) (lapis)*: stone.

saponification
< L. *sāpōn(is) (sāpō)*: soap.

nidification
< L. *nīd(us)*: a nest.

thurification
< L. *thūr(is) (thūs)*: incense.

de**vitr**ification
< L. *vitr(um)*: glass.

PART III
SUBJECTS

PROFESSIONAL WORDS

architecture

INSTRUCTIONS 1) Dissect two words from each column below into their prefixes, suffixes, bases, and other elements.

2) Analyze and define each element in each word.

3) Reconstruct the etymological meaning of the word.

4) Define the word and cite its part of speech. Consult a college, unabridged, or architectural dictionary.

5) If not apparent from the definition, provide a brief commentary explaining the sense development of the word. Otherwise, include some interesting anecdote about the roots and meaning of this or one or more related terms.

EXAMPLE

interfenestral (inˊtər·fə·nesˊtrəl)

Dissection: 1) inter- / fenestr- / -al

Analysis: 2) *inter-*: between, among; *fenestr-*: an opening in a wall; window; *-al*: pertaining to, characterized by.

Reconstruction: 3) pertaining to (*-al*) between (*inter-*) windows (*fenestr-*).

Definition: 4) *adj.* situated or placed between windows, as an ornamental motif.

Commentary: 5) Another word that uses *fenestr-*, "window," is *defenestration*, "the act of throwing someone or something out of a window." This word was made famous by the "Defenestration of Prague," a meeting of imperial commissioners at Prague, Czechoslovakia in 1618 in which two Roman Catholic emissaries and their secretary were thrown out a window by Protestant insurgents, triggering the Thirty Years' War.

ARCHITECTURAL TERMS

Parthenon	capital	zoophorus	architrave
colonnade	pilaster	terrazzo	entablature
fenestration	dentil	pediment	coplanarity
polyhedra	corbel	entasis	crenellation

art

INSTRUCTIONS
1) Dissect two words from each column below into their prefixes, suffixes, bases, and other elements.
2) Analyze and define each element in each word.
3) Reconstruct the etymological meaning of the word.
4) Define the word and cite its part of speech. Consult a college, unabridged, or art dictionary.
5) If not apparent from the definition, provide a brief commentary explaining the sense development of the word. Otherwise, include some interesting anecdote about the roots and meaning of this or one or more related terms.

EXAMPLE

ultramarine (ul´trə•mə•rēn´)

Dissection:
1) ultra- / mar- / -in- / -e

Analysis:
2) *ultra-*: beyond, on the other side of; *mar-*: sea; *-in-*: pertaining to, characterized by; *-e*: silent letter.

Reconstruction:
3) pertaining to (*-in-*) the other side of (*ultra-*) the sea (*mar-*).

Definition:
4) *n.* 1. a blue pigment prepared from lapis lazuli (lap´is lazh´ə•lē, laz´(y)oo•lē), a characteristically deep-blue semiprecious stone. 2. a similar pigment prepared from other sources. 3. a deep-blue color.

Commentary:
5) In the Middle Ages, lapis lazuli was imported to Europe from Persia and other countries "on the other side of the sea," or what in Medieval Latin was referred to as *ultrāmarīnus.*

ART TERMS

glaucous	fulvous	castaneous	subfuscous
cyaneous	fuscous	sepia	rubiginous
ferruginous	aquamarine	orpiment	testaceous
verdigris	pyrography	amaranthine	incarnadine

astronomy

INSTRUCTIONS 1) Dissect two words from each column below into their prefixes, suffixes, bases, and other elements.

2) Analyze and define each element in each word.

3) Reconstruct the etymological meaning of the word.

4) Define the word and cite its part of speech. Consult a college, unabridged, or astronomy dictionary.

5) If not apparent from the definition, provide a brief commentary explaining the sense development of the word. Otherwise, include some interesting anecdote about the roots and meaning of this or one or more related terms.

EXAMPLE

syzygy (siz´ə•jē)

Dissection: 1) sy- /zyg-/ -y

Analysis: 2) *sy-*: with, together; *zyg-*: a yoke; *-y*: the act, process, condition, or result of.

Reconstruction: 3) the act, process, condition, or result of (*-y*) yoking (*zyg-*) together (*sy-*).

Definition: 4) *n.* the alignment of three celestial bodies, as the sun, moon, and earth during a full moon or new moon.

Commentary: 5) The three *y*'s in *syzygy* make this word one of the great spelling demons. But as you can see from the analysis above, the *y*'s are not arbitrary or accidental. The *sy-* is a shortened form of Greek *syn-*, "with, together," from which we derive such words as *system* and *systole* (sis´tə•lē), the normal contraction of the heart during a heartbeat; and *zyg-* is the base of Greek *zygon*, "yoke," from which we derive *zygote*, a fertilized egg cell before cell division, and *zygodactyl*, a bird with two opposing pairs of toes, as the parrot or cuckoo; cf. also DIZYGOTIC.

ASTRONOMY TERMS

nova	ecliptic	chondrite	spectroscopy
umbra	apogee	perihelion	declination
pulsar	aphelion	perigee	occultation
quasar	anthelion	penumbra	perturbation

biology

INSTRUCTIONS
1) Dissect two words from each column below into their prefixes, suffixes, bases, and other elements.
2) Analyze and define each element in each word.
3) Reconstruct the etymological meaning of the word.
4) Define the word and cite its part of speech. Consult a college, unabridged, or biology dictionary.
5) If not apparent from the definition, provide a brief commentary explaining the sense development of the word. Otherwise, include some interesting anecdote about the roots and meaning of this or one or more related terms.

EXAMPLE

phagocytosis (fag´ō•sī•tō´sis)

Dissection:
1) phag- / -o- / cyt- / -osis

Analysis:
2) *phag-*: to eat, devour; *-o-*: connecting vowel; *cyt-*: a cell; *-osis*: the act, process, condition, or state of.

Reconstruction:
3) the act or process of (*-osis*) eating (*phag-*) cells (*cyt-*).

Definition:
4) *n.* the process by which certain cells and cellular organisms ingest other cells or microorganisms, either for the purpose of neutralizing them or for nourishment.

Commentary:
5) *phag-*, "to eat, devour" (< G. *phagein*), occurs in hundreds of words, often appearing in the adjective-forming compound *-ophagous* (äf´ə•gəs), "eating or devouring." Thus, *carpophagous* means "fruit-eating" (< G. *karpos*: fruit); *creophagous* means "flesh-eating" (< G. *kreas*: flesh), a synonym for the much more common *carnivorous* (< L. *carn(is)*: flesh + *-i-*: connecting vowel + *vor(āre)*: to devour + E *-ous*: characterized by); and *anthropophagous* means "human-eating or cannibalistic" < G. *anthrōpos*: human being).

BIOLOGY TERMS

paleontology	mitochondria	fructivorous	ectomorph
hexagynous	frugivorous	racemose	endomorph
sagittate	archegonium	bryology	mesomorph
aristate	angiosperm	gymnosperm	plumigerous

engineering

Instructions 1) Dissect two words from each column below into their prefixes, suffixes, bases, and other elements.

2) Analyze and define each element in each word.

3) Reconstruct the etymological meaning of the word.

4) Define the word and cite its part of speech. Consult a college, unabridged, or engineering dictionary.

5) If not apparent from the definition, provide a brief commentary explaining the sense development of the word. Otherwise, include some interesting anecdote about the roots and meaning of this or one or more related terms.

Example

centripetal (sen·trip´it'l)

Dissection: 1) centr- / -i- / pet- / -al

Analysis: 2) *centr-*: center; *-i-*: connecting vowel; *pet-*: to seek, to move toward; *-al*: pertaining to, characterized by.

Reconstruction: 3) characterized by (*-al*) seeking or moving toward (*pet-*) the center (*centr-*).

Definition: 4) *adj.* moving or directed inward toward a center or axis.

Commentary: 5) *centripetal* is the opposite of the more common *centrifugal*, a word derived from *centr-*: center + *-i-*: connecting vowel + *fug-*: to flee + *-al*: pertaining to, characterized by. Thus, while a centripetal force always "seeks" a center and propels objects (or people) toward it, a centrifugal force "flees" that center and propels objects (or people) toward its outer edge.

Engineering Terms

kinetics	dynamometer	coefficient	entropy
rectifier	commutator	convection	dielectric
litharge	oscilloscope	thermocouple	kinematics
enthalpy	hygrometer	transducer	solenoid

fashion and fabrics

INSTRUCTIONS
1) Dissect two words from each column below into their prefixes, suffixes, bases, and other elements.
2) Analyze and define each element in each word.
3) Reconstruct the etymological meaning of the word.
4) Define the word and cite its part of speech. Consult a college, unabridged, or textile dictionary.
5) If not apparent from the definition, provide a brief commentary explaining the sense development of the word. Otherwise, include some interesting anecdote about the roots and meaning of this or one or more related terms.

EXAMPLE

multifilamentous (mul´tə•fil´ə•men´təs)

Dissection:
1) mult- / -i- / fil- / -a- / -ment / -ous

Analysis:
2) *mult-*: much, many, more than two; *-i-*: connecting vowel; *fil-*: thread; *-a-*: connecting vowel; *-ment*: the act, means, or result of; *-ous*: full of, abounding in, like.

Reconstruction:
3) full of or abounding in (*-ous*) the result of (*-ment*) many (*mult-*) threads (*fil-*).

Definition:
4) *adj.* of or pertaining to yarn or other material composed of many threads or fibers.

Commentary:
5) In Greek legend, Dionysius, the "Elder" Syracusan tyrant, seated his envious flatterer Damocles at a banquet beneath a sword suspended by a single hair to demonstrate the perils of being ruler. This filipendulous (< L. *fil(um)*: thread + *-i-*: connecting vowel + *pend(ēre)*: to hang + E. *-ulous*: tending to, characterized by) *sword of Damocles* has thus come to signify any imminent danger or threat.

FASHION AND FABRIC TERMS

polyester	diaphanous	serigraphy	baldachin
lingerie	gossamer	sericulture	seersucker
millinery	cerement	mercerization	grenadine
couturier	mannequin	polymerization	marquisette

film and filmmaking

INSTRUCTIONS
1) Dissect two words from each column below into their prefixes, suffixes, bases, and other elements.
2) Analyze and define each element in each word.
3) Reconstruct the etymological meaning of the word.
4) Define the word and cite its part of speech. Consult a college, unabridged, or media dictionary.
5) If not apparent from the definition, provide a brief commentary explaining the sense development of the word. Otherwise, include some interesting anecdote about the roots and meaning of this or one or more related terms.

EXAMPLE

cinemicrography (sin´ə•mī•kräg´rə•fē)

Dissection: 1) cine- / micr- / -o- / graph- / -y

Analysis: 2) *cine-*: motion picture; *micr-*: small, minute, of or through

a microscope; microscopic; *-o-*: connecting vowel; *graph-*: to write, to draw; *-y*: the act, process, or result of.

Reconstruction: 3) the act, process, or result of (*-y*) drawing (*graph-*) motion pictures (*cine-*) through a microscope (*micr-*).

Definition: 4) *n.* the filming through a microscope of minute structures or life forms, as the protozoa in a body of water.

Commentary: 5) *cine-*, "motion picture," is a modern English combining form abstracted from *cinema*, which is a borrowing of French *cinéma*, which is itself abstracted from French *cinématographe*, "a motion picture projector or camera," which in turn yields English *cinematograph*. The classical source of these words is Greek *kinē-*, base of *kinein*, "to move," from which we derive such English words as *kinetics*, *kinesics*, and *telekinesis*.

FILM AND FILMMAKING TERMS

cinematography	Technicolor	Oscar	chiaroscuro
asynchronous	CinemaScope	gaffer	Cinerama
superimpose	animation	auteur	docudrama
documentary	pixilation	cineaste	film noir

interior design

INSTRUCTIONS 1) Dissect two words from each column below into their prefixes, suffixes, bases, and other elements.
2) Analyze and define each element in each word.
3) Reconstruct the etymological meaning of the word.
4) Define the word and cite its part of speech. Consult a college, unabridged, or interior design dictionary.
5) If not apparent from the definition, provide a brief commentary explaining the sense development of the word. Otherwise, include some interesting anecdote about the roots and meaning of this or one or more related terms.

EXAMPLE

iridescent (ir´i•des´ ’nt)

Dissection: 1) irid- / -e- / -sc- / -ent

Analysis: 2) *irid-*: rainbow; *-e-*: connecting vowel; *-sc-*: to begin, start, become, or emit light (in the manner prescribed by the preceding base); *-ent*: a present participial suffix roughly equivalent to *-ing*, as in "a sitting duck."

Reconstruction: 3) light emit- (*-sc-*)-ing (*-ent*) of the rainbow (*irid-*).

Definition: 4) *adj.* 1. having or displaying an interplay of changing rainbowlike colors, particularly when viewed from different angles or through a prism. —*n.* 2. a fabric, trimming, or other material exhibiting such colors.

Commentary: 5) Iris was the Greek goddess of the rainbow, shuttling the gods' messages to earth via her beautiful iridescent bridge. From her name, we derive such words as *iris* (a plant with showy, multicolored flowers), *iris* (the colored part of the eye, having different colors in different people), and *iridium* (a metallic element named after its iridescent compounds).

INTERIOR DESIGN TREMS

cabriole	antimacassar	Kurdistan	credenza
linoleum	secretary	bombé	jalousie
wainscot	hassock	boudoir	têt-à-têt
candelabrum	chandelier	portiere	vis-à-vis

law

1) Dissect two words from each column below into their prefixes, suffixes, bases, and other elements.
2) Analyze and define each element in each word.
3) Reconstruct the etymological meaning of the word.
4) Define the word and cite its part of speech. Consult a college, unabridged, or law dictionary.
5) If not apparent from the definition, provide a brief commentary explaining the sense development of the word. Otherwise, include some interesting anecdote about the roots and meaning of this or one or more related terms.

EXAMPLE

contravention (kän´trə·ven´shən)

Dissection:	1) contra- / vent- / -ion
Analysis:	2) *contra-*: against, opposite, opposed to, counter; *vent-*: to come; *-ion*: the act, means, or result of.
Reconstruction:	3) the act, means, or result of (*-ion*) coming (*vent-*) against (*contra-*).
Definition:	4) *n.* an action counter to or in violation of another action, law, contract, etc.; transgression, infringement.
Commentary:	5) To a great extent, the prefix *contra-* determines the meaning of this word. For if we replace the *contra-* with *pre-*, we get *prevention*, which is, etymologically, "the act of coming before." If we then replace the *pre-* with *con-*, we derive *convention*, "the act of coming together"; and if we replace the *con-* with *inter-*, we get *intervention*, "the act of coming between." Can you think of any more *-vention* words?

LEGAL TERMS

abrogation	primogeniture	defeasance	tortfeasor
abjuration	libelant	malfeasance	holograph
gravamen	legatee	misfeasance	appellant
subrogation	usufructuary	nonfeasance	recusation

literature and rhetoric

INSTRUCTIONS
1) Dissect two words from each column below into their prefixes, suffixes, bases, and other elements.
2) Analyze and define each element in each word.
3) Reconstruct the etymological meaning of the word.
4) Define the word and cite its part of speech. Consult a college or unabridged dictionary, or a glossary of literary and rhetorical terms.
5) If not apparent from the definition, provide a brief commentary explaining the sense development of the word. Otherwise, include some interesting anecdote about the roots and meaning of this or one or more related terms.

EXAMPLE

periphrasis (pə•rif´rə•sis)

Dissection: 1) peri- / phra- / -sis

Analysis: 2) *peri-*: around, about, surrounding, near; *phra-*: to speak; *-sis*: the act, process, condition, or result of.

Reconstruction: 3) the act or result of (*-sis*) speaking (*phra-*) around (*peri-*).

Definition: 4) *n.* a wordy and roundabout way of expressing an idea or making a point; circumlocution.

Commentary: 5) *circumlocution* is the Latin-derived equivalent of the Greek-derived *periphrasis*. It is constructed from the roots *circum-*: around, about, surrounding + *locut-*: to speak + *-ion*: the act, means, or result of. Hence, the act or result of (*-ion*) speaking (*locut-*) around (*circum-*).

LITERATURE AND RHETORICAL TERMS

alliteration	parataxis	metonymy	polysyndeton
assonance	anadiplosis	apophasis	prosopopoeia
metaphor	syllepsis	litotes	epithalamion
anaphora	asyndeton	oxymoron	prothalamion

medicine

INSTRUCTIONS

INSTRUCTIONS 1) Dissect two words from each column below into their prefixes, suffixes, bases, and other elements.
2) Analyze and define each element in each word.
3) Reconstruct the etymological meaning of the word.
4) Define the word and cite its part of speech. Consult a college, unabridged, or medical dictionary.
5) If not apparent from the definition, provide a brief commentary explaining the sense development of the word. Otherwise, include some interesting anecdote about the roots and meaning of this or one or more related terms.

EXAMPLE

oophorectomy (ō´ə·fə·rek´tə·mē)

Dissection: 1) oo- / phor- / ec- / tom- / -y

Analysis: 2) *oo-*: egg; *phor-*: bearing, carrying; *ec-*: out of, from, forth; *tom-*: a cutting; *-y*: the act, process, condition, or result of.

Reconstruction: 3) the act or process of (*-y*) cutting (*tom-*) out (*ec-*) that which bears or is bearing (*phor-*) the egg (*oo-*).

Definition: 4) *n.* the surgical excision or removal of one or both ovaries; ovariectomy.

Commentary: 5) In human females, that which bears (*phor-*) the egg (*oo-*) is the egg-bearer or ovary, represented by the combining form *oophor-*.

MEDICAL TERMS

carcinoma	taeniasis	iatrogenic	bromhidrosis
sarcoma	narcohypnia	trichorrhea	blepharospasm
epithelioma	obdormition	typhlology	nephrolithotomy
torticollis	horripilation	vasectomy	onychocryptosis

nutrition and dietetics

INSTRUCTIONS
1) Dissect two words from each column below into their prefixes, suffixes, bases, and other elements.
2) Analyze and define each element in each word.
3) Reconstruct the etymological meaning of the word.
4) Define the word and cite its part of speech. Consult a college, unabridged, or biochemistry dictionary.
5) If not apparent from the definition, provide a brief commentary explaining the sense development of the word. Otherwise, include some interesting anecdote about the roots and meaning of this or one or more related terms.

EXAMPLE

cholesterol (kə·les´tə·rôl´, -rōl´)

Dissection: 1) chole / ster- / -ol

Analysis: 2) *chole*: bile; *ster-*: firm, hard, solid; *-ol*: an alcohol.

Reconstruction: 3) a solid (*ster-*) bile (*chole*) alcohol (*-ol*).

Definition: 4) *n.* a solid fatty "alcohol" found in blood, bile, brains, and other animal tissues, serving as a precursor of vitamin D$_3$ and various steroid hormones. In excess amounts, cholesterol contributes to atherosclerosis or the formation of plaque on the inner lining of arterial walls.

Commentary: 5) In 1815, what we now call cholesterol was styled *cholesterine* in France, the *-ine* later suggesting that cholesterol contains nitrogen, which it does not. Then in 1859 it was discovered that cholesterol contains a hydroxyl group in its molecule and is therefore an alcohol—a substance that usually ends in *-ol*. Hence, in the early 1890's the *-ine* in *cholesterine* (and the *-in* in its later variant *cholesterin*) was replaced by *-ol*, and *cholesterol* was born.

NUTRITION AND DIETETICS

calciferol	levulose	riboflavin	ergosterol
glycogen	dextrose	glucagon	albumin
phospholipids	polypeptide	anabolism	albumen
coenzym	disaccharide	catabolism	tocopherol

philosophy

INSTRUCTIONS 1) Dissect two words from each column below into their prefixes, suffixes, bases, and other elements.
2) Analyze and define each element in each word.
3) Reconstruct the etymological meaning of the word.
4) Define the word and cite its part of speech. Consult a college, unabridged, or philosophy dictionary.
5) If not apparent from the definition, provide a brief commentary explaining the sense development of the word. Otherwise, include some interesting anecdote about the roots and meaning of this or one or more related terms.

EXAMPLE

transcendentalism (tran´sen•den´t'l•iz´m)

Dissection: 1) trans- / -scend- / -ent- / -al / -ism

Analysis: 2) *trans-*: over, across, beyond; *-scend-*: to climb; *-ent-*: a present participial suffix equivalent in meaning to *-ing*, as in "a boring speech"; *-al*: pertaining to, characterized by; *-ism*: the beliefs, theory, school, or doctrine of.

Reconstruction: 3) the beliefs, theory, school, or doctrine (*-ism*) characterized by (*-al*) climb- (*-scend-*) -ing (*-ent-*) beyond (*trans-*).

Definition: 4) *n.* any of various philosophical doctrines proclaiming that reality is essentially mental or spiritual and that the intuitive, not the empirical, is one's guide to inner truth and understanding.

Commentary: 5) *-scend-*, "to climb," and its variants *scans-* and *-scens-*, turn up in many words, including *ascend*, which etymologically is "to climb toward," *ascension*, "the act of climbing toward," *descend*, "to climb down," *descendant*, "one who climbs down," *condescend*, "to thoroughly climb down," and *scansorial*, "characterized by tending to climb," as certain mountain goats.

PHILOSOPHY TERMS

ontology	teleology	sophistry	isagogics
epistemology	pantheism	telegnosis	maieutic
theosophical	palingenesis	metempsychosis	hermeneutic
casuistry	dysteleology	a posteriori	propaedeutic

photography

INSTRUCTIONS 1) Dissect two words from each column below into their prefixes, suffixes, bases, and other elements.

2) Analyze and define each element in each word.

3) Reconstruct the etymological meaning of the word.

4) Define the word and cite its part of speech. Consult a college, unabridged, or photography dictionary.

5) If not apparent from the definition, provide a brief commentary explaining the sense development of the word. Otherwise, include some interesting anecdote about the roots and meaning of this or one or more related terms.

EXAMPLE

photogravure (fō´tō·grə·vyŏŏr´, fō´tə-)

Dissection: 1) phot- / -o- / grav- / -ur- / -e

Analysis: 2) *phot-*: light, photograph, photography; *-o-*: connecting vowel; *grav-*: to carve, incise; *-ur-*: the act, process, condition, or result of; *-e*: silent letter.

Reconstruction: 3) the act or process of (*-ur-*) carving or incising (*grav-*) a photograph (*phot-*).

Definition: 4) *n.* 1. a photoengraving process by which the elements of a photograph are etched into a printing plate or cylinder from which reproductions are made. 3. the plate or cylinder itself. 2. a print made from such a plate or cylinder.

Commentary: 5) A highly productive form of photogravure is *rotogravure*, named after the German firm *Roto(gravur Deutsche Tiefdruck Gesellschaft) + (photo)gravure*—the "*Roto*" derived from Latin *rota*, "wheel, roller." This process, extremely popular during the early 20th century for producing the "fancy" pictorial sections in many newspapers, consisted of etching the image of a photograph onto a copper cylinder and running off reproductions on a high-speed rotary press.

PHOTOGRAPHY TERMS

tripod	positive	radiograph	collodion
spectrogram	negative	resolution	thiosulfate
exposure	heliograph	fixative	kallitype
emulsion	daguerreotype	monochromatic	hologram

SPECIALTY WORDS AND PHRASES

acronyms
(words formed from the first or first few letters of two or more words)

INSTRUCTIONS
1) Analyze two acronyms from each column below. Do so by citing those words from which each acronym derives, and place parentheses around those letters in each word that do not form part of the acronym.
2) Define the acronym and cite its part of speech. Consult a college or unabridged dictionary.
3) Provide the history of the acronym, i.e., indicate approximately when it was coined, what its background is, and why it is relevant today. If necessary, consult an encyclopedia or other references.

EXAMPLE

laser (lā′zer)

Analysis:
1) *l(ight) a(mplification)* [by] *s(timulated) e(mission)* [of] *r(adiation).*

Definition:
2) *n.* an instrument that produces an amplified or highly intense beam of light by exciting atoms to a high energy level with the subsequent stimulation and emission of photons or electromagnetic radiation.

History:
3) The laser was first introduced in 1960 as a modification of the earlier microwave or high-frequency radio wave *maser*, itself an acronym for *m(icrowave) a(mplification)* [by] *s(timulated) e(mission)* [of] *r(adiation).* Laser beams generate pinpoints of intense heat and are used in medicine to cut and repair minute body tissues, such as detached retinas. They are also used in industry to transmit television and other electromagnetic signals.

ACRONYMS

radar	snafu	UNICEF	NIMBY
sonar	yuppie	NATO	YAVIS
scuba	cyborg	OPEC	SWAK
loran	parsec	NAFTA	POSSLQ
Anzac	alnico	GATT	WYSIWYG

portmanteau words
(blends of two or more words)

INSTRUCTIONS   1) Analyze two portmanteau words from each column below. Do so by citing those words from which each portmanteau derives, and place parentheses around those letter in each word that do not form part of the blend. Use a "+" sign to join the words.

2) Define the portmanteau and cite its part of speech. Consult a college or unabridged dictionary.

3) Provide the history of the portmanteau, i.e., indicate approximately when it was coined, what its background is, and why it is relevant today. If necessary, consult an encyclopedia or other references.

EXAMPLE

smog (smäg)

Analysis: 1) *sm(oke) + (f)og*

Definition: 2) *n.* an unhealthy and sometimes irritating mixture of smoke and other pollutants in fog or haze, often enveloping large metropolitan areas and industrial centers.

History: 2) *smog*, surprisingly, is not a new word. It was introduced in London in 1905 by Dr. H. A. des Vœux of the Coal Smoke Abatement Society in a paper presented at a meeting of the Public Health Congress entitled "Fog and Smoke." In referring to the London fog, des Vœux explained that "it required no science to see that there was something produced in great cities which was not found in the country, and that was smoky fog . . . or 'smog.'" Indeed, all one need do to verify his observations is to visit Los Angeles or New York City.

PORTMANTEAU WORDS

brunch	splatter	quasar	telethon
motel	newscast	pulsar	camcorder
chortle	glasphalt	beefalo	slanguage
liger	bookmobile	cattalo	dancercise
tiglon	travelogue	contrail	infomercial

clipped forms

INSTRUCTIONS 1) Cite the "full forms" from which two "clipped forms" in each column below derive, and place parentheses around those letters that do not form part of the clipped form.
2) Dissect each full form into its prefixes, suffixes, bases, and other elements.
3) Analyze and define each element in the full form.
4) Reconstruct the etymological meaning of the full form.
5) Define the full form and cite its part of speech.
6) If not apparent from the definition, provide a brief commentary explaining the sense development of that form. Otherwise, include some interesting anecdote about the roots and meaning of this or one or more related terms.

EXAMPLE

flu (flo͞o)

Full form: 1) (in)flu(enza)

Dissection: 2) in- / flu- / -enz- / -a

Analysis: 3) *in-*: in, into; *flu-*: to flow; *-enz-*: a present participial suffix equivalent in meaning to *-ing*, as in "the talking donkey"; *-a*: the act, process, condition, or result of.

Reconstruction: 4) the process or result of (*-a*) flow- (*flu-*) -ing (*-enz-*) into (*in-*).

Definition: 5) *n.* a common contagious disease caused by any of a number of closely related viruses and generally characterized by fever, running nose, congestion, sore throat, and a variety of minor aches and pains.

Commentary: 6) The medieval Romans believed that human fate and personality were determined by the influence of the stars, or *influentia*. This term became *influenza* in Italian and later narrowed in meaning to any epidemic caused by this influence and then to one specific epidemic, the flu.

CLIPPED FORMS

gym	disco	memo	wig
zoo	pants	photo	perk
exam	plane	cello	quack
stereo	possum	curio	piano

proprietary terms
(trademarks that have become words)

INSTRUCTIONS
1) Define two words from each column below, and cite each one's part of speech. Consult a college or unabridged dictionary.
2) Provide the history of the word, i.e., indicate approximately when the word was introduced as a trademark, by whom or what company, and in which country. If feasible, analyze and reconstruct the word.
3) Explain why the trademark evolved into a common English word.

EXAMPLE

aspirin (as´pə•rin, -prin)

Definition:
1) *n.* a white crystalline powder, acetylsalicylic acid, commonly used in tablet form as an analgesic (pain reliever), anti-inflammatory, and antipyretic (a substance used to reduce fever).

History:
2) In 1899, Hermann Dreser of Germany introduced *Aspirin* as a brand name for a synthetic form of acetylsalicylic acid, which was hitherto derived from spirea blossoms. He therefore constructed this name from Greek *a-*: without, lacking (though often construed as German *a(cetyl)* or *a(cetylirte)*: acetylated) + New Latin *Spir(aea)*: spirea (though often construed as German *Spir(säure)*: salicylic acid) + *-in*: a chemical suffix generally denoting any of various neutral compounds or pharmaceuticals. Hence, a neutral compound or pharmaceutical (*-in*) without (*a-*) spirea (*Spir-*).

Explanation:
3) *aspirin* is considerably easier to read, write, pronounce, and remember than *acetylsalicylic acid*. Also, for over a half century, *aspirin* was the major brand name for this extremely popular medication.

PROPRIETARY TERMS

(Note: some of the following terms are no longer trademarks)

escalator	Kleenex	cellophane	mimeograph
Scotch tape	Frisbee	Band-Aid	Photostat
Vaseline	Coke	Teflon	Xerox
thermos	Jell-O	Ping-Pong	Teletype

eponyms
(words derived from persons' names)

INSTRUCTIONS 1) Define two eponyms from each column below, and cite each one's part of speech. Consult a college or unabridged dictionary.

2) State each eponym's source, i.e., the person's full name, nationality, and birth and death dates.

3) Explain why the eponym was named after this person, i.e., provide its historical and, if relevant, its etymological background. If necessary, consult an encyclopedia or biographical dictionary.

EXAMPLE

guillotine (gil´ə•tēn´, gē´ə-)

Definition: 1) *n.* an apparatus for beheading a person, consisting of a heavy horizontal blade that falls freely between two upright posts.

Source: 2) Joseph Ignace Guillotin, France, 1738–1814.

Background: 3) On October 10, 1789 Joseph Guillotin, a French physician, proposed that the cruel and disgraceful state hangings and sword executions be replaced by swift and painless "machine" decapitations. His proposal, after nineteen months of deliberation, was accepted by the French National Assembly in May, 1791; and on April 22, 1792 a highwayman named Peletier was the first individual to be decapitated by the guillotine, then called *La Louisette* or *La Petite Louison* in honor of its designer, Dr. Antoine Louis, and Louis XVI. Thus, Guillotin did not invent the guillotine—nor did he conceive, construct, or perish by it. He merely proposed its use, based on similar contraptions in use as early as the Middle Ages in Italy, Germany, Scotland, China, and even France.

EPONYMS

silhouette	Doberman	bowdlerize	boycott
chauvinism	saxophone	Celsius	nicotine
sandwich	bloomers	Fahrenheit	sadism
sideburns	lynch	Mae West	masochism

toponyms
(words derived from place-names)

INSTRUCTIONS

1) Define two toponyms from each column below, and cite each one's part of speech. Consult a college or unabridged dictionary.

2) State each toponym's provenance or place of origin, being as specific as possible.

3) Explain why the toponym was named after this place,
i.e., provide its historical and, if relevant, its etymological background. If necessary, consult an encyclopedia or gazetteer (gaz´i•tēr´; a geographical dictionary).

EXAMPLE

blarney (blär´nē)

Definition:
1) *n.* 1. smooth, flattering talk used to cajole or wheedle.
2. misleading or deceptive talk; humbug; poppycock.

Provenance:
2) the Blarney stone in Blarney Castle, situated in the village of Blarney, five miles northwest of the city of Cork in County Cork, Ireland. This triangular stone is positioned twenty feet below the battlements on the southern wall of the donjon or central tower of the castle.

Background:
3) Blarney Castle was constructed in 1446 by Cormac McCarthy. On the Blarney stone is the inscription, "Cormac Mac Carthy *fortis me fieri fecit* A.D. 1446" (a strong man caused me to be made). Allegedly, to commemorate the astute political persuasiveness of McCarthy (or one of his descendants), the legend arose that whoever was brave enough to kiss the stone would be rewarded with similar gifts of persuasion and eloquence. The stone, however, is difficult to reach; today, the customary manner is to hang from the heels from a walkway above.

TOPONYMS

cantaloupe	bikini	shanghai	antimacassar
tarantula	champagne	bourbon	dungarees
tuxedo	sardonic	Scotch	denims
bayonet	copper	tequila	jeans

words derived from classical mythology

1) Dissect two words from each column below into their prefixes, suffixes, bases, and other elements.
2) Analyze and define each element in each word.
3) Reconstruct the etymological meaning of the word.
4) Define each word and cite its part of speech. Consult a college, unabridged, or mythological dictionary.
5) Explain how each word derived its current meaning, i.e., provide the mythological and, if relevant, the historical background of the word.

EXAMPLE

jovial (jō´vē·əl)

Dissection: 1) jov- / -i- / -al

Analysis: 2) *jov-*: Jupiter; *-i-*: connecting vowel; *-al*: pertaining to, characterized by.

Reconstruction: 3) pertaining to or characterized by (*-al*) Jupiter (*jov-*).

Definition: 4) *adj.* having or characterized by a hearty, joyous good humor; convivial; jolly.

Background: 5) The ancient Romans named the planets after their gods and goddesses, based, in part, on real or fancied resemblances between each planet and deity. Hence, they called the most majestic planet *Juppiter* or *Jupiter*, and used *Jovis* as a functional genitive. The Romans also believed in astrology and calculated that persons born under the sign of Jupiter would be joyful and optimistic, or *jovi-ālis*, a sense that we still retain in *jovial*.

MYTHOLOGICAL TERMS

museum	amazon	Junoesque	gorgonize
tantalize	titanic	plutonium	Acherontic
volcanic	aegis	stentorian	Procrustean
protean	panic	hymeneal	terpsichorean
hermetic	atropine	aphrodisiac	hermaphrodite

words and phrases derived from the bible

INSTRUCTIONS 1) Define two entries from each column below, and cite each one's part of speech. Consult a college, unabridged, or biblical dictionary.

2) Identify the biblical source of the entry, providing, where possible, the book, chapter, and verse where it is cited.

3) Explain how the entry derived its current meaning, i.e., provide the biblical and, if relevant, the historical background of the entry.

4) Analyze and define each element of those entries in the first and second columns.

5) Reconstruct the etymological meaning of those entries in the first and second columns.

EXAMPLE

doubting Thomas

Definition: 1) *n.* a person who often or habitually refuses to believe anything without firsthand proof or physical evidence; skeptic.

Source: 2) the apostle (Saint) Thomas: John 20: 24–29.

Background: 3) Thomas, one of the twelve apostles, refused to believe that Christ had risen from the dead after his crucifixion until Christ appeared to him in person: "But Thomas, one of the twelve, called Didymus, was not with them when Jesus came. The other disciples therefore said unto him, We have seen the Lord. But he said unto them, Except I shall see in his hands the print of the nails, and put my finger into the print of the nails, and thrust my hand into his side, I will not believe."

BIBLICAL WORDS AND PHRASES

maudlin	veronica	Judas kiss	land of Nod
sodomy	Aceldama	Adam's apple	good Samaritan
simony	Gehenna	Adam's ale	potter's field
calvary	gethsemane	raise Cain	bain-marie

foreign words and phrases in the English language

INSTRUCTIONS
1) Look up two entries from each column below in a college or unabridged dictionary and indicate their pronunciations. Use the pronunciation key provided in this book or any other system that *you* can understand.
2) Identify the language from which the entry is borrowed. (Hint: each one is from a different language.)
3) Analyze and define each element in the entry.
4) Reconstruct the etymological meaning of the entry.
5) Define the entry and cite its part of speech.
6) Provide a brief commentary or interesting anecdote about the roots and meaning of this or one or more related terms.

EXAMPLE

esprit de l'escalier

Pronunciation: 1) e·sprē´d<del>oo</del>·les·skəl·yā´, eh-SPREE-duh-lehs-skol-YAY

Language: 2) French

Analysis: 3) *esprit*: spirit, wit; *de*: of; *l'*: the; *escalier*: staircase.

Reconstruction: 4) wit (*esprit*) of (*de*) the (*l'*) staircase (*escalier*).

Definition: 5) *n.* a witty repartee (rep´ər·tē´, -tā´, -är-) one thinks of after the opportunity to present it has passed.

Commentary: 6) Have you ever thought of a great repartee while walking down a staircase after leaving a party? If so, you've experienced *esprit de l'escalier* or what's known in German as *Treppenwitz* (< *Treppen*: staircases + *Witz*: wit). But you can still salvage your belated brilliance. For in recounting the evening's events to a friend, you can "correct" your oversight, beginning with the phrase, "And then I said . . . ."

FOREIGN WORDS AND PHRASES

faux pas	origami	cumshaw	salud	auto da fe
jihad	al fresco	schnorrer	skoal	mazel tov
kayak	apartheid	sahib	bhakti	non sequitur
batik	babushka	aloha	hoi polloi	Schadenfreude

common nouns and their collateral adjectives
(adjectives that represent nouns but have entirely different forms)

INSTRUCTIONS 1) Research and record at least one collateral adjective for each common noun below.

   One method of investigation: Look up each noun in an English–Latin dictionary, and then consult a college or unabridged dictionary to see if any English adjectives begin with the initial letters or bases of the corresponding Latin nouns.

2) Dissect two collateral adjectives from each column below into their prefixes, suffixes, bases, and other elements.

3) Analyze and define each element in the collateral adjective.

4) Reconstruct the etymological meaning of the collateral adjective.

5) Define the collateral adjective and cite its part of speech.

EXAMPLE

bird

Collateral adjs.	1) avian, avine, <u>ornithological</u>, volucrine
Dissection:	2) ornith- / -o- / -log- / -ic- / -al
Analysis:	3) *ornith-*: bird; *-o-*: connecting vowel; *-log(y)*: the science, study, theory, or doctrine of; *-ic-*: pertaining to, characterized by; *-al*: pertaining to, characterized by.
Reconstruction:	4) characterized by (*-ic-*) pertaining to (*-al*) the study of (*-log-*) birds (*ornith-*).
Definition:	5) *adj.* of or relating to the branch of zoology that deals with birds.

COMMON NOUNS

mother	winter	earth	hand	dog
father	spring	moon	foot	cat
brother	summer	sun	nose	wolf
sister	fall	star	mouth	bear

PICTURESQUE WORDS AND
EXPRESSIONS

phobias

INSTRUCTIONS 1) Dissect two words from each column below into their prefixes, suffixes, bases, and other elements.

2) Analyze and define each element in each word.

3) Reconstruct the etymological meaning of the word.

4) Define the word and cite its part of speech. Consult a college or unabridged dictionary.

5) Provide an interesting commentary about the roots and meaning of this or one or more related terms.

EXAMPLE

entomophobia (ent´ə∙mō∙fō´bē∙ə)

Dissection: 1) entom- / -o- / phob- / -ia

Analysis: 2) *entom-*: insect; *-o-*: connecting vowel; *phob-*: fear, dread, hatred; *-ia*: the act, state, or condition of.

Reconstruction: 3) the state or condition of (*-ia*) fearing or dreading (*phob-*) insects (*entom-*).
Note: The roots *phob-* + *-ia* yield the combining form *-phobia*: a mental disorder characterized by an intense or irrational fear, dread, or hatred of. Hence . . .

Definition: 4) *n.* a mental disorder characterized by an intense or irrational fear, dread, or hatred of (*-phobia*) insects (*entom-*).

Commentary: 5) *entom-* can further be dissected into *en-*: in, into + *tom-*: to cut. Hence, insects are "cut-in (animals)," or what the Greeks called *entom(a)* (*zōa*) in allusion to their segmented, antlike bodies. Similarly, the Romans called these creatures *insect(um)* (*animale*), which is an element-by-element translation of the singular of *entom(a)* (*zōa*) and is itself the source of English *insect*—a word totally supplanting our native 16th- and 17th-century *cut-waist*.

PHOBIAS

claustrophobia	hydrophobia	xenophobia	gametophobia
acrophobia	thanatophobia	demophobia	androphobia
agoraphobia	taeniophobia	haptophobia	gynephobia
arachnophobia	ophidiophobia	pantophobia	maieusophobia

ninety-nine phobias

AEROPHOBIA: air
ZOOPHOBIA: animals
MELISSOPHOBIA: bees
EROTOPHOBIA: sex
APIPHOBIA: bees
NEPHOPHOBIA: clouds
OCHLOPHOBIA: crowds
HEMATOPHOBIA: blood
AMATHOPHOBIA: dust
AILUROPHOBIA: cats
DROMOPHOBIA: streets
ANGINOPHOBIA: choking
GALEOPHOBIA: cats
PSYCHROPHOBIA: cold
HIPPOPHOBIA: horses
HYGROPHOBIA: moisture
NYCTOPHOBIA: night
SCIAPHOBIA: shadows
EOSOPHOBIA: dawn
BLENNOPHOBIA: slime
ORNITHOPHOBIA: birds
BATHOPHOBIA: depths
MYSOPHOBIA: dirt
DENDROPHOBIA: trees
PEDOPHOBIA: children
PHAGOPHOBIA: eating
COPROPHOBIA: feces
OMMATOPHOBIA: eyes
PHOBOPHOBIA: fear
ANTHOPHOBIA: plants
PYREXIOPHOBIA: fever
OPHRESIOPHOBIA: smell
CHIONOPHOBIA: snow

FEBRIPHOBIA: fever
PYROPHOBIA: fire
ICHTHYOPHOBIA: fish
ANTLOPHOBIA: floods
HOMICHLOPHOBIA: fog
THERMOPHOBIA: heat
SITOPHOBIA: food
HYLOPHOBIA: forests
BATRACHOPHOBIA: frogs
PHASMOPHOBIA: ghosts
PARTHENOPHOBIA: girls
HYALOPHOBIA: glass
CIBOPHOBIA: food
URANOPHOBIA: heaven
STYGIOPHOBIA: hell
OIKOPHOBIA: houses
LYSSOPHOBIA: insanity
CHRONOPHOBIA: time
ACAROPHOBIA: mites
PHOTOPHOBIA: light
DIPSOPHOBIA: drinking
ONEIROPHOBIA: dreams
CHREMATOPHOBIA: money
KONIOPHOBIA: dust
MUSOPHOBIA: mice
GYMNOPHOBIA: nudity
ONOMATOPHOBIA: names
BELONEPHOBIA: needles
CARCINOPHOBIA: cancer
HOMILOPHOBIA: sermons
LALIOPHOBIA: speaking
COITOPHOBIA: coitus
ODONTOPHOBIA: teeth

ALGOPHOBIA: pain
THALASSOPHOBIA: the sea
PENIAPHOBIA: poverty
CREMNOPHOBIA: cliffs
CYNOPHOBIA: dogs
OMBROPHOBIA: rain
POTAMOPHOBIA: rivers
HARPAXOPHOBIA: robbers
ODYNOPHOBIA: pain
HAMARTOPHOBIA: sin
HYPNOPHOBIA: sleep
SIDEROPHOBIA: stars
GERONTOPHOBIA: elders
MYRMECOPHOBIA: ants
HELIOPHOBIA: sunlight
BRONTOPHOBIA: thunder
HODOPHOBIA: travel
PHENGOPHOBIA: daylight
TOCOPHOBIA: childbirth
EMETOPHOBIA: vomiting
ANEMOPHOBIA: wind, drafts
SELENOPHOBIA: the moon
HELMINTHOPHOBIA: worms
GRAPHOPHOBIA: writing
NECROPHOBIA: corpses
RHABDOPHOBIA: magic
PEDICULOPHOBIA: lice
POGONOPHOBIA: beards
PHARMACOPHOBIA: drugs
LIMNOPHOBIA: lakes
ERGASIOPHOBIA: work
THEOPHOBIA: God
BASIPHOBIA: walking

(For further information, consult A CROSS-REFERENCE DICTIONARY)

manias

INSTRUCTIONS 1) Dissect two words from each column below into their prefixes, suffixes, bases, and other elements.

2) Analyze and define each element in each word.

3) Reconstruct the etymological meaning of the word.

4) Define the word and cite its part of speech. Consult a college or unabridged dictionary.

5) Provide an interesting commentary about the roots and meaning of this or one or more related terms.

EXAMPLE

bibliokleptomania (bib´lē·ə·klep´tō·mā´nē ə, -tə-)

Dissection: 1) bibli- / -o- / klep- / -t- / -o- / man- / -ia

Analysis: 2) *bibli-*: book, books, bible; *-o-*: connecting vowel; *klep-*: to steal; *-t-*: one who or that which; *-o-*: connecting vowel; *man-*: to rage, go mad; *-ia*: the act, state, or condition of.

Reconstruction: 3) the act or condition of (*-ia*) one who (*-t-*) rages (*man-*) to steal (*klep-*) books (*bibli-*). **Note:** The roots *klep-* + *-t-* + *-o-* yield the combining form *klepto-*: stealing. Also note: *man-* + *-ia* yield the combining form *-mania*, having the modern medical meaning: a mental disorder characterized by an extreme preoccupation with or enthusiasm or compulsion for. Hence . . .

Definition: 4) *n.* a mental disorder characterized by a preoccupation with or compulsion for (*-mania*) stealing (*klepto* -) books (*bibli-*).

Commentary: 5) *klep-*, "to steal" (< G. *kleptein*), turns up in *cleptobiosis*, a zoological term denoting a symbiotic relationship in which the members of certain species of insects and other arthropods, particularly ants, thrive by habitually stealing the food collected by kindred species. However, if they take the food on the sly, the relationship is known as *lestobiosis* (< G. *lēistēs*: a pirate). I think these terms would apply just as well to humans as to ants.

MANIAS

megalomania	ornithomania	cynomania	chrematomania
pyromania	ichthyomania	Beatlemania	ablutomania
egomania	nostomania	choreomania	ailuromania
dipsomania	zoomania	balletomania	coprolalomania

sixty-six manias

HYDROMANIA: water
HIPPOMANIA: horses
EREMIOMANIA: stillness
GYNECOMANIA: women
LETHEOMANIA: narcotics
SITOMANIA: food
ANTHOMANIA: flowers
CLINOMANIA: bed rest
ERGASIOMANIA: work, activity
PORIOMANIA: impulsive travel
LOGOMANIA: talking
HYPNOMANIA: sleep
NOCTIMANIA: night
MONOMANIA: one subject
DROMOMANIA: traveling
ENTOMOMANIA: insects
HODOMANIA: travel
PHAGOMANIA: eating
ONIOMANIA: buying
OINOMANIA: wine
ECDEMOMANIA: wandering
DORAMANIA: fur
DOROMANIA: gift giving
PHARMACOMANIA: medicines
THANATOMANIA: death
GAMOMANIA: marriage
PLUTOMANIA: wealth, riches
HAMARTOMANIA: sin
PHRONEMOMANIA: thinking
ERGOMANIA: work
AGORAMANIA: open spaces
GRAPHOMANIA: writing
HELIOMANIA: sun

MESMEROMANIA: hypnotism
ELEUTHEROMANIA: freedom
HYDRODIPSOMANIA: drinking water
EROTOMANIA: sexual desire
OLIGOMANIA: a few subjects
MELOMANIA: music
BRUXOMANIA: gritting teeth
ENTHEOMANIA: religion
PHILOPATRIDOMANIA: homesickness
THALASSOMANIA: the sea
XENOMANIA: foreigners
CHIONOMANIA: snow
PHOTOMANIA: light
TOMOMANIA: surgery
MYTHOMANIA: tall tales, lies
ERYTHROMANIA: red, blushing
HEDONOMANIA: pleasure
PHANEROMANIA: picking at growths
SIDERODROMOMANIA: railroad travel
AMENOMANIA: elation, gaiety
SCRIBOMANIA: writing
GYMNOMANIA: nudity
HOMICIDOMANIA: murder
APHRODISIOMANIA: sexual desire
CACODEMONOMANIA: demonic possession
TRICHOTILLOMANIA: hair plucking
KATHISOMANIA: sitting
OPHIDIOMANIA: snakes
KINESOMANIA: movement
NECROMANIA: corpses
MENTULOMANIA: masturbation
CHEROMANIA: elation, gaiety
OPSOMANIA: a special food

(For further information, see A CROSS-REFERENCE DICTIONARY)

words with numbers in them

1) Dissect two words from each column below into their prefixes, suffixes, bases, and other elements.
2) Analyze and define each element in each word.
3) Reconstruct the etymological meaning of the word.
4) Define the word and cite its part of speech. Consult a college or unabridged dictionary and, if necessary, an encyclopedia or other references.
5) If not apparent from the definition, provide a brief commentary explaining the relevance of the word's number. Otherwise, include some interesting anecdote about the roots and meaning of this or one or more related terms.

EXAMPLE

quintessence (kwin·tes´əns)

Dissection: 1) quint- /ess- / -ence

Analysis: 2) *quint-*: fifth; *ess-*: to be; *-ence*: the state of ___ing.

Reconstruction: 3) the state of (*-ence*) fifth (*quint-*) be- (*ess-*) -ing (*-ence*).

Definition: 4) *n.* 1. the purist and most concentrated essence of a substance. 2. the highest form or most perfect embodiment of a being, thing, quality, stereotype, etc.

Commentary: 5) In the fifth century B.C., Empedocles of Acragas, the Greek philosopher, proclaimed that the universe is composed of four primal elements: fire, earth, air, and water. While highly perceptive at the time, this analysis did not fully satisfy Aristotle, who, writing a century later, explained that while these four *material* elements could define all earthly substances, a fifth *immaterial* element must define all heavenly phenomena. He called this element *pemptē ousia* or "fifth being," a phrase that nearly two millennia later was translated into Medieval Latin *quīnta essentia* and eventually became English *quintessence*.

NUMBERS IN WORDS

decimate	octopus	quarantine	hendecagon
millennium	protagonist	primogeniture	deuterogamy
Decalogue	decathlon	Pentecost	quadrumanous
sextet	triathlon	Septuagint	nonagenarian

words with colors in them

INSTRUCTIONS 1) Dissect two words from each column below into their prefixes, suffixes, bases, and other elements.

2) Analyze and define each element in each word.

3) Reconstruct the etymological meaning of the word.

4) Define the word and cite its part of speech. Consult a college or unabridged dictionary and, if necessary, an encyclopedia or other references.

5) If not apparent from the definition, provide a brief commentary explaining the relevance of the word's color. Otherwise, include some interesting anecdote about the roots and meaning of this or one or more related terms.

EXAMPLE

chrysanthemum (kri•san´thə•məm)

Dissection: 1) chrys- / anthem- / -um

Analysis: 2) *chrys-*: gold; *anthem-*: flower; *-um*: Latin neuter suffix.

Reconstruction: 3) gold (*chrys-*) flower (*anthem-*).

Definition: 4) *n.* any of a large genus of daisies and daisylike flowers of the composite family, typically consisting of relatively large white "ray" flowers surrounding a disk of tiny yellow "tube" flowers.

Commentary: 5) The common "oxeye daisy" has the scientific Latin name, *Chrysanthemum leucanthemum.* The *leuc-* in the second word means "white," which we see in its original Greek form in *leukocyte,* a white blood cell, and *leukemia,* a cancer of the white blood cells. Thus, *Chrysanthemum leucanthemum* translates to "gold flower, white flower," which is exactly what we see when we look at it.

COLORS IN WORDS

blanket	chlorine	Gwendolyn	candidate
iodine	leukemia	denigrate	Colorado
chrome	melancholy	Melanesia	edelweiss
albino	Argentina	glaucoma	rhododendron
Melanie	rubeola	verdigris	Xanthippe

words with animals in them

INSTRUCTIONS
1) Dissect two words from each column below into their prefixes, suffixes, bases, and other elements.
2) Analyze and define each element in each word.
3) Reconstruct the etymological meaning of the word.
4) Define the word and cite its part of speech. Consult a college or unabridged dictionary and, if necessary, an encyclopedia or other references.
5) If not apparent from the definition, provide a brief commentary explaining the relevance of the word's animal. Otherwise, include some interesting anecdote about the roots and meaning of this or one or more related terms.

EXAMPLE

hippopotamus (hip´ə•pät´ə•məs)

Dissection: 1) hipp- / -o- / potam- / -us

Analysis: 2) *hipp-*: horse; *-o-*: connecting vowel; *potam-*: river; *-us*: Latin masculine suffix.

Reconstruction: 3) river (*potam-*) horse (*hipp-*).

Definition: 4) *n.* one of two species of large, semiaquatic African mammals having a broad head, short legs, and a thick-skinned, almost hairless body.

Commentary: 5) The ancient Greeks who coined *hippopotamus* greatly admired the horse. They watched their spectacles in the *hippodrome*; they named important deities after the horse, e.g., *Hippolyta* (queen of the Amazons); they created mythological creatures that embodied horses, e.g., *hippocampus* (a half-horse, half-dolphin sea mammal); and they "founded" mythological habitats in memoriam of horses, e.g., *Hippocrene* (the sacred fountain of the Muses, created by the winged horse Pegasus). Therefore, it is not surprising that the Greeks should have defined the hippopotamus in terms of the horse.

ANIMALS IN WORDS

cancer	canary	Adolf	dandelion
muscle	lupine	Debra	Antarctica
porcupine	halibut	Ursula	formication
Beverly	cynosure	Melissa	Xanthippe

shape words
(words ending in -iform)

INSTRUCTIONS 1) Dissect two words from each column below into their prefixes, suffixes, bases, and other elements.

2) Analyze and define each element in each word.

3) Reconstruct the etymological meaning of the word.

4) Define the word and cite its part of speech. Consult a college or unabridged dictionary.

5) Provide an interesting commentary about the roots and meaning of this or one or more related terms.

EXAMPLE

vermiform (vûr´mə·fôrm´)

Dissection:	1) verm- / -i- / -form
Analysis:	2) *verm-*: worm; *-i-*: connecting vowel; *-form*: having the form of; shaped like.
Reconstruction:	3) worm (*verm-*) shaped (*-form*).
Definition:	4) *adj.* 1. resembling or shaped like a worm. 2. long, slender, and wavy.
Commentary:	5) *verm-*, "worm," provides the base of a number of rather creepy words, including *vermicelli* (thin "wormlike" spaghetti), *vermiculation* (architectural or other designs in the shape of little worms or their tracks), *vermigrade* (crawling or creeping like a worm), and, of course, *vermiform appendix* (the full name of the human appendix, which looks very much like a worm).

SHAPE WORDS

oriform	cruciform	bursiform	cuneiform
oviform[1]	claviform	ensiform	selliform
oviform[2]	pisiform	eruciform	stelliform
filiform	pisciform	aciform	scrotiform
piliform	dolioform	aciniform	scalpriform
reniform	dolabriform	acinaciform	monilliform

terms of divination
(prophetic words ending in -mancy)

INSTRUCTIONS 1) Dissect two words from each column below into their prefixes, suffixes, bases, and other elements.
2) Analyze and define each element in each word.
3) Reconstruct the etymological meaning of the word.
4) Define the word and cite its part of speech. Consult one or more unabridged dictionaries.
5) Provide an interesting commentary about the roots and meaning of this or one or more related terms.

EXAMPLE

oneiromancy (ō·nī´rə·man´sē)

Dissection: 1) oneir- / -o- / manc- / -y

Analysis: 2) *oneir-*: dream; *-o-*: connecting vowel; *manc-*: to divine, foretell; *-y*: the act, process, condition, or result of.

Reconstruction: 3) the act or process of (*-y*) divining or foretelling by (*manc-*) dreams (*oneir-*).

Definition: 4) *n.* the art or practice of foretelling the future through the interpretation of dreams.

Commentary: 5) An *oneirocritic* (an interpreter of dreams) engages in *oneirocriticism* (the interpretation of dreams) when he performs *oneiromancy*. However, if he also practices *oneiroscopy* (the diagnosis of mental states through the analysis of dreams) and resorts to *oneiropompism* (the "sending" of dreams), which may induce *oneirodynia* (disturbed sleep or nightmares), he may himself be experiencing *oneirism* (a distorted, dreamlike sense of reality) and may have to suspend his *oneirocrisy* (oneirocriticism). After all, a good *oneiroscopist* (one who practices oneiroscopy) and a credible *oneiromantic* (one who foretells the future through the interpretation of dreams) should be an *oneirologist* (a scientist who studies dreams) as well as an *oneirocritic* (an interpreter of dreams).

TERMS OF DIVINATION

necromancy	oneiromancy	myomancy	ophiomancy
bibliomancy	gastromancy	pyromancy	ornithomancy
rhabdomancy	capnomancy	amniomancy	omphalomancy
graptomancy	osteomancy	hippomancy	astragalomancy

colorful expressions in the English language

INSTRUCTIONS
1) Choose two expressions from each column below, and cite each expression's common, figurative meaning.
2) Record the expression's original, literal meaning, and provide its historical background. If necessary, consult an idioms dictionary or any other references for this information.
3) Compose a short, humorous paragraph using at least ten of the expressions below.

EXAMPLE

beat around the bush

Figurative meaning:
1) 1. to talk around an issue without getting to the point; periphrase. 2. to be evasive or hesitant; stall for time.

Literal meaning:
2) to strike or beat the ground around shrubs with a club or stick. This practice, no longer in vogue, was current in 15th-century England when nocturnal bird hunters would flush birds out of bushes by cautiously beating around the bush with a bat while holding a light.

Humorous paragraph:
3) He's *a spitting image* of his father and *a hard nut to crack*. But if I stay *as cool as a cucumber* and *handle him with kid gloves*, I'll be sitting *in the catbird seat*. After all, this is no *pie in the sky* and I'm not *wet behind the ears*. But if there's *a fly in the ointment* and this doesn't *pan out*, I may have to *pay through the nose* and *eat crow*.

COLORFUL EXPRESSIONS

in a pig's eye	knock on wood	eat crow	suck the hind teat
warts and all	have a jag on	dog days	pay through the nose
tickled pink	a pig in a poke	harp on	fly in the ointment
I smell a rat	a spitting image	pan out	wet behind the ears
out to lunch	pie in the sky	wing it	a hard nut to crack
shake a leg	down the tubes	hard up	handle with kid gloves
go bananas	the Big Apple	rat race	as cool as a cucumber
feet of clay	a can of worms	cry wolf	in the catbird seat

common expressions derived from baseball

INSTRUCTIONS
1) Choose two expressions from each column below, and cite each expression's common, generally figurative meaning.
2) Record the expression's original, baseball meaning. If necessary, consult a sports dictionary or other references for this information.
3) Compose a short, humorous paragraph using at least ten of the expressions below.

EXAMPLE

hit-and-run

Common meaning:
1) of or relating to the driver of a motor vehicle who flees the scene of an accident without stopping to report it or render assistance.

Baseball meaning:
2) of or designating a prearranged play in which a base runner begins to run to the next base before the ball is pitched and the batter makes every effort to hit the ball to ensure that the runner reaches that base without being tagged out.

Humorous paragraph:
3) You must *cover all the bases* if you expect to *get to first base* with your new job. You're now in *the big leagues*, and I can no longer *go to bat for* you. But if you're ever *off base* and get *sent to the showers*, *touch base* with me and I'll *pinch hit for* you. But if you're *out of bounds* or *out in left field*, it'll be *a close call* and I may *strike out*.

BASEBALL EXPRESSIONS

out of bounds	go to bat for	touch base	right off the bat
doubleheader	the big leagues	raincheck	cover all the bases
in the lineup	pinch hit for	southpaw	come off the bench
a close call	ballpark figure	off base	get to first base
strike out	out in left field	farm out	send to the showers
a hard call	in there pitching	in a slump	out of one's league
bush-league	batting average	Bronx cheer	right up one's alley
extra innings	Who's on first?	charley horse	one down, two to go

common expressions derived from boxing

INSTRUCTIONS 1) Choose two expressions from each column below, and cite each expression's common, generally figurative meaning.
2) Record the expression's original, boxing meaning. If necessary, consult a sports dictionary or other references for this information.
3) Compose a short, humorous paragraph using at least ten of the expressions below.

EXAMPLE

throw in the towel

Common meaning:

1) 1. to give up; surrender; acknowledge defeat. 2. to die.

Boxing meaning:

2) (of a ringside manager) to signal his desire to stop the bout by throwing a towel into the ring when his fighter is taking a beating and in jeopardy of being seriously injured.

Humorous paragraph:

3) You've been *down and out* lately, and at the interview next week you may *meet your match* and be *knocked for a loop*. But if you *come out swinging* and *roll with the punches* you can still *knock 'em dead*. Just keep *on your toes*, *hang in there*, and when they *square off* give 'em the ol' *one-two*. Then they'll be *down for the count* and you can *make a clean break*.

BOXING EXPRESSIONS

meet your match	beat the count	on the ropes	come out swinging
pull no punches	answer the bell	polish it off	down for the count
knock 'em dead	blow-by-blow	hang in there	at the drop of a hat
ahead on points	evenly matched	a mismatch	roll with the punches
take your lumps	out like a light	on your toes	knocked for a loop
the main event	one-two (punch)	hard-nosed	win by a knockout
knockout drops	pack a wallop	go toe to toe	make a clean break
a good matchup	a split decision	a cover-up	don't count me out
down but not out	down and out	boxer shorts	no skin off my nose
make a comeback	a fighting chance	the Real McCoy	The bigger they are

collective nouns of venery
(hunting terms)

INSTRUCTIONS
1) Speculate as to which members of the animal kingdom are described by each collective noun below.
2) Confirm or reject your speculations by consulting a college or unabridged dictionary.
3) Choose two collective nouns from each column below, and using traditional "venereal" phraseology, specify what kind of animals are described by each, e.g., *a pack of wolves*, *a flock of sheep*, *a swarm of bees*, *a colony of ants*.
4) Provide the etymology of the collective noun and explain why this noun is an appropriate choice to describe the group of animals it is associated with.

EXAMPLE

school

Speculation: 1) see INSTRUCTIONS above

Confirmation: 2) see INSTRUCTIONS above

Venereal phrase: 3) a school of fish

Explanation: 4) This *school* is derived from Dutch *school* (or Middle Dutch *schōle*) and has absolutely no relationship with its homograph *school*, "an institution for learning," which is derived from Greek *scholē*. Dutch *school* means "group, troop, crowd" and is cognate with Old English *scolu*, which is believed by some etymologists to yield Modern English *shoal*, a synonym for the piscine (of or relating to fish) *school*. But this *shoal* should not be confused with its homograph *shoal*, "a sand bar or shallow place in a body of water," which is derived from Old English *sceald*, "shallow." Hence, Dutch-derived *school* and its cognate *shoal* (< ?Old English *scolu*) are appropriate collective nouns for large numbers of swimming or feeding fish since these animals often appear in crowded groups or troops.

TERMS OF VENERY

pride	bevy	sloth	gaggle	parliament
plague	covey	cast	army	murmuration
murder	troop	pod	skein	exaltation
bouquet	crash	cete	clowder	ostentation

outlandish terms

INSTRUCTIONS 1) Dissect two words from each column below into their prefixes, suffixes, bases, and other elements.

2) Analyze and define each element in each word.

3) Reconstruct the etymological meaning of the word.

4) Define the word and cite its part of speech. Consult *Webster's New International Dictionary, Unabridged* (2nd or 3rd editions) or *The Oxford English Dictionary*.

5) If not apparent from the definition, provide a brief commentary explaining the sense development of the word. Otherwise, include some interesting anecdote about the roots and meaning of this or one or more related terms.

EXAMPLE

retromingent (re´trō•min´jənt, -trə-)

Dissection:	1) retro- / ming- / -ent
Analysis:	2) *retro-*: back, backward, behind; *ming-*: to urinate; *-ent*: a present participial suffix equivalent in meaning to *-ing*, as in "a cry<u>ing</u> baby."
Reconstruction:	3) urinat- (*ming-*) -ing (*-ent*) backward (*retro-*).
Definition:	4) *adj.* urinating backward.
Commentary:	5) Male lions, tigers, elephants, and house cats are, under most circumstances, retromingent. A human being, I imagine, can also be retromingent when adopting a suitable position.

OUTLANDISH TERMS

pornocracy	logorrhea	googolplex	cisvestite
pogonotomy	onychophagist	pseudocyesis	pygalgia
callipygian	coprophagous	gynecomastia	nosism
lycanthropy	bdellatomy	psomophagist	merkin
ignivomous	borborygmus	chthonophagia	cimicine
bibliophagist	philematology	omphalopsychite	Ucalegon

155

PART IV

HOW ENGLISH WORDS ARE CREATED: A SHORT COURSE

HOW ENGLISH WORDS ARE CREATED: A SHORT COURSE

English is the richest and most universal language the world has ever known. It is indeed a global language spoken today by almost a billion people on every continent on earth, and it is the mother tongue of about ten percent of the world's population. It is the principal language of the United States, Britain, Australia, New Zealand, Canada, the Bahamas, and numerous small nations. And it is an "official language" of dozens of other countries and territories, including India, Nigeria, Hong Kong, Ghana, and Liberia. But what is even more remarkable, English has become the lingua franca (any language used as a means of communication between speakers of different languages) of the world—ranging from the common speech of millions to the international language of trade, finance, and technology in almost every country and on almost every level of society, even extending beyond terra firma ("solid ground," as distinguished from water or air).

For example, when the spacecraft *Voyager* embarked on its intragalactic journey to Jupiter and beyond in the late 1970's, it carried a recorded message addressed to extraterrestrial beings, beginning with a statement from the Secretary-General of the United Nations—in English. When a Norwegian tourist enters a Japanese shop, the tourist and shopkeeper generally converse, not in Norwegian or Japanese, but in English; when a Russian airplane comes in for a landing in a Pakistani airport, the pilot converses with the control tower not in Russian or Urdu (an official language of Pakistan), but in English; and if the pilot veers a little to the west and decides instead to land in China, do you think they speak in Russian or Chinese over the airways? Again it's English—as though a cold war had never existed.

But English is not limited to the skies. When multinational corporations meet to discuss business strategy, they usually conduct their meetings in English; when Israeli and Arab leaders meet to consider peace initiatives they speak not in Hebrew or Arabic, but in English; when tiny schoolchildren throughout the non-English speaking world begin to learn their first foreign language, it is almost always English; and in such countries as India, in which almost 200 different languages are spoken (such as Hindi, Bengali, Gujarati, and Tamil), and Nigeria, in which over 250 languages are spoken (such as Hausa, Ibo, Efik, and Kanuri), the people often use English just to communicate from village to village.

But if you really want to get a sense of the universality of English, the next time you're watching the news and see a protest or demonstration in, say, Somalia, Bangladesh, Kenya, Ethiopia, or the

Philippines and then see one of the participants being interviewed, pay attention to what language that person is speaking. Then look closely and see in what languages the banners and signs in the background are written. And then ask yourself, if the situation were reversed and you were being interviewed at a demonstration in this country, how likely would it be for you to speak in or hold up a banner in Somali, Bengali, Swahili, Amharic, or Tagalog (the principal languages of the countries mentioned above)—and then you will begin to appreciate the unique position of English in the world today and how fortunate you are to speak this global tongue.

But where do all of the words in this global tongue come from? And what patterns and themes can we find in all of this?

English words derive from practically every language on earth and include such linguistic gems as *igloo* and *husky* from Inuit (in´yōō·it; a synonym and now preferable term for *Eskimo*), *zombie* and *chimpanzee* from Bantu (a grouping of over 500 closely related African languages, including Kikongo, Zulu, and Swahili), *skunk* and *squash* from Algonquian (an American Indian language family, including Cree, Blackfoot, Cheyenne, Shawnee, and Chippewa), and *commando* and *trek* from Afrikaans (af´ri·käns´, -känz´; not a native African language but a direct descendant of Dutch brought to southern Africa by Dutch settlers in the 17th century).

But probably 90 percent of all English words derive from three primary sources: Anglo-Saxon (referred to in this book as "native sources"), Latin, and Classical Greek (referred to in this book as simply "Greek"). And these are the sources we will address in this Short Course.

NATIVE SOURCES

Native sources refer to those Germanic words brought to Britain in 449 and the centuries following by the invasions of the Angles, Saxons, and Jutes from what is now northern Germany and Denmark—invasions that would ultimately eradicate virtually all of the pre-existing Celtic languages and establish English (< OE. *Engl(e)*: the Angles + *-isc*: belonging to) as a new tongue. These Germanic words form the essential or "core" vocabulary of English and constitute practically all of our simple nouns, verbs, adjectives, pronouns, prepositions, and conjunctions; and these are the words that, in their modern form, make up the overwhelming majority of our daily speech. Some of these words in their modern form are illustrated below.

ENGLISH WORDS FROM NATIVE SOURCES

NOUNS	mother	father	dog	cat	house	home
VERBS	do	go	walk	run	hit	fight
ADJECTIVE	good	bad	strong	clean	red	dark
PRONOUNS	I	me	you	he	she	it
PREPOSITIONS	in	on	to	at	by	for
CONJUNCTIONS	and	but	if	as	when	though

As you can see, native words are our short, simple words that practically everyone knows, so I shall therefore refrain from discussing them in any depth.

In fact, if you examine the preceding sentence you'll find that of the twenty-six words mentioned, twenty-one are from native sources and only five—*native*, *simple*, *practically*, *refrain*, and *discussing*—are from non-native sources, these being Latin (via French) and Greek (via Latin). But even of these five non-native words, four of them employ the native endings *-e*, *-ly*, and *-ing*, which further demonstrates how fundamental the Germanic element is in our language.

In addition, you might have noticed from both the illustrative sentence and the table above that every word is either one or two syllables long. This is generally another characteristic of native words, that unless they use prefixes or suffixes or are compounded with other words—such as *everybody*, *however*, *notwithstanding*, *heretofore*, *upside-down*, etc.—they are usually only one or two syllables long. But short words are also characteristic of many of our "borrowed" words—as we have already seen with such words as *igloo* and *trek*—so you should be very careful when using this factor to help identify native words.

Historically, the English language is divided into three broad periods: Old English, Middle English, and Modern English.

Old English (OE.: 449–1100)

Old English, also called Anglo-Saxon (named after the Angles and Saxons), was the first period of spoken and, later, written English and is traditionally considered to have begun in the year 449 with the first of the major invasions of Britain by the Angles, Saxons, and Jutes; and it is generally regarded to have ended about 1100. However, because language evolves gradually over centuries and dating this evolution is at best an arbitrary exercise, different texts assign different closing dates to this period, and you may see such dates ranging from 1066 to 1200. In any event, it was not until at least a century or two after these momentous (of great and far-reaching importance or significance) invasions that Old English began to take shape as a language of its own and become distinct from its Germanic mother tongue on the Continent.

Old English, in distinction to Modern English, was a complex and highly inflected language with a vocabulary, grammatical form, and a multiplicity of case endings that we would not recognize as English today. The following excerpt from an Old English manuscript, dated about 890, illustrates this.

Hīe	sōna	compedon	wið	heora	gewinnan,
They	immediately	battled	against	their	enemies,

þe	hīe	oft	ær	norðan	onhergedon;
who	them	often	before	from north	raided;

and	Seaxan	þā	siġe	ġeslōgon.
and	Saxons	the	victory	won.

This was our "pure" native language, unembellished with foreign borrowings. But this state was not to last very long, for during the Old English period three events occurred, which added new words to the language and forever altered its course in history.

The first began in the year 597 after Pope Gregory the Great had sent St. Augustine of Rome (not to be confused with the more famous 4th century bishop and philosopher, St. Augustine of Hippo, a seaport in northern Africa) to England with about forty monks to convert the heathen to Christianity, beginning the systematic Christianization of England. During this period many words from Greek, which was the language of the New Testament, were brought to England in their Latinized form, which is to say, their case endings and other Greek earmarks had been given corresponding Latin forms. Then in England they were further Anglicized, or given English sounds and forms. Thus, such Modern English words as *school* (< OE. *scōl* < L. *schola* < G. *scholē*: leisure, discussion, lecture, school), *meter* (< OE. *meter* < L. *metrum* < G. *metron*: measure), *bishop* (< OE. *bisceop* < LL. *episcopus* < G. *episkopos*: overseer), and *devil* (< OE. *dēofol* < LL. *diabolus* < G. *diabolos*: Devil, Satan, slanderer), while originally Greek, entered English in their Latinized form and were then Anglicized to conform to the norms of English—a process we will describe in detail later on. But what is important to realize at this point is that a pattern of borrowing Latinized Greek words was established in Old English and later reinforced in Middle English and Modern English in which even those words passing directly from Greek into English were Latinized before taking on English form; and this process continues unabated to this day.

The second "event" occurred in 787 when the Vikings from Scandinavia (particularly the Danes and Norwegians) began a systematic series of invasions of England and came to dominate England politically, if not culturally, for almost three centuries. During this period, English adopted many basic Scandinavian words that ordinarily are never borrowed when one language is influenced by another but were in this case because Danish and Norwegian, also derived from Germanic, were extremely similar to Old English. Such words include what have become Modern English *take* (< ON. *tak(a)*: to take + E. *-e*: silent final letter), *sister* (< ON. *systir*: sister—replacing the closely related OE. *sweoster*), *sky* (< ON. *sky*: that which is above; cloud), *window* (< ON. *vindauga*: window < *vind(r)*: wind + *auga*: eye; hence, "eye of the wind"—in those days windows did not have glass), and, most surprisingly, *they* (< ON. *their*, *they*—replacing OE. *hīe*). *They* is surprising because this is one of the most fundamental words in the English language.

The third and by far the most significant event that occurred during the Old English period was the Norman Conquest of 1066 in which the descendants of the Norsemen from Scandinavia who had invaded and settled in France around 900 and adopted the French language (hence, the French deletion of the *-se-* from *Norseman*) attacked and defeated the English and imposed their young and extremely Latinate Norman-French language upon the English. This was the official beginning of the French influence on English which for the next four centuries was to have a profound effect upon the English language. Some of the French words adopted during this period include what have become Modern English *cattle* (< NormFr. *catel*: personal property < L. *capitāl-*, base of *capitāle*: property, cattle; originally, the neuter of *capitālis*: of the head < *capit-* [base of *capitis*, genitive of *caput*]: head + *-ālis*: pertaining to); *castle* (< NormFr. *castel*: castle < L. *castell-* [base of *castellum*]: fortress < *cast(r)-* [base of *castrum*]: fort, military camp + *-ell-* [base of *-ellum*]: small, little); *city* (< NormFr. *citet*: city < L. *cīvitāt-* [base of *cīvitātis*, genitive of *cīvitās*]: citizenry, city < *cīv-* [base of *cīvis*]: citizen + *-i-*: connecting vowel + *-tāt-* [base of *-tātis*, genitive of *-tās*]: the quality, state, or condition of); and *beef* (< NormFr. *boef*: ox, beef < L. *bov-* [base of *bovis*, genitive of *bōs*]: ox, bull, cow).

Middle English (ME.: 1100–1500)

Middle English is traditionally considered to have lasted from 1100 to 1500, though some sources cite 1066 (the year of the Norman Conquest) and others 1150 or even 1200 (after elements of the early Norman-French language had been incorporated into English) as the beginning of this period; and many cite 1475 (the year before William Caxton brought printing to England) for the end of this period. As with Old English, the dating is arbitrary, and the changes from Old English to Middle English happened extremely gradually and were imperceptible to the people at the time. What is far more important to recognize is that during the Middle English period most of the strange vocabulary and inflectional endings that make Old English unintelligible (not capable of being understood; incomprehensible) to us disappeared, and Middle English begins to look very much like what we would expect of an earlier form of our language. The following excerpt is from a poem written about 1365 and illustrates the extensive changes from the Old English excerpt on page 161.

In	a	somer	sesun	whon	softe	was	the	sonne,
In	a	summer	season	when	soft	was	the	sun,

I	schop	me	in-to	a	schroud	a	scheep	as	I	were
I	put	me	into	a	cloak	a	shepherd	as if	I	were

Though Norman French was declared the official language of England after the Norman Conquest, it never replaced English but rather coexisted with it, and the lasting Norman French contribution to English is relatively small. Beginning about 1200, however, English—still in many ways a crude and undeveloped language—began borrowing from French at an accelerated rate but this time from the more sophisticated French of Paris, which had become the commercial and cultural center of Europe. But, again, this influx of French words supplemented rather than supplanted the existing stock of native words, resulting in virtually doubling the size of the English lexicon. As one illustration of this growth, a modern analysis of all the words used in the writings of Geoffrey Chaucer, indisputably the greatest writer during the Middle English period, reveals that 48 percent of his words were derived from French. As one consequence of the massive French borrowing during this and the Norman-French period, English developed a wealth of paired synonyms for common nouns and verbs—the original and simpler word being of native heritage and its synonym being from French. Ten of these pairs are illustrated below:

NATIVE / FRENCH-DERIVED SYNONYMS

Native Word	French-Derived Equivalent	Native Word	French-Derived Equivalent
begin	commence	ask	demand
wish	desire	yearly	annual
buy	purchase	shun	avoid
try	attempt	meet	assemble
room	chamber	foe	enemy

Since French is derived from Latin, and all of the French-derived words above are either from Norman French or Old French, pre-dating 1300, the French forms of these words (not shown in the table) are very close in structure and meaning to their parent Latin; and it is fair to say that we are essentially talking about Latin here. So from these two centuries of French borrowing alone, Latin-derived words have already doubled the size of the English vocabulary. And this is just the beginning!

Modern English (E.: 1500–present)

Modern English is traditionally considered to have begun in 1500 (often cited as 1475, the year before William Caxton brought printing to England) and in its later period is the English we speak today. In its earlier period, referred to as Early Modern English, the vocabulary was still considerably smaller than today, and the language was sprinkled with what we now perceive as archaisms (är´kē· iz´ 'mz, -kā-; words commonly used in and marked by the characteristics of an earlier period, such as *thou*, *thee*, *ye*, *methinks*, etc.)—words which are very much evident in the writings of Shakespeare.

The most significant event during this period, however, was the Renaissance or "Revival of Learning," which began in Italy in the 14th century and swept over Europe during the next 200 years, marking the transition from the medieval world to the modern world. During this period, English accelerated a process it had begun in late Middle English of borrowing words directly from Latin and Greek to fill real or perceived gaps in the language. With the blossoming of science, technology, and literature, thousands of additional classical words were incorporated into English in a frenzy to enrich its vocabulary. During this time, English borrowed such words from Latin as *ēducātiōnis*, *suppressiōnis*, and *turgidus*, forming, respectively, *education*, *suppression*, and *turgid* (swollen, distended, pompous); and from Greek it borrowed *kritērion*, *katastrophē*, and *isoskelēs*, forming, respectively *criterion*, *catastrophe*, and *isosceles* (of or pertaining to a figure having two equal sides, generally said of certain triangles).

Even more significantly, English developed a process of coining terms that never existed in Latin or Greek by combining the roots of Latin and Greek words in ways that would have raised the eyebrows of Aristotle and Cicero. This resulted in a proliferation of English words and established a trend that more than anything else is responsible for the astronomical growth of the English vocabulary in the second half of the 20th century—and which forms the basis of this book. For example, the Latin-derived word *reciprocal*, which one might reasonably surmise was borrowed from Latin *reciprocālis*, a word that never existed in Latin, was in fact created in the mid-16th century from the Latin roots *reciproc-* (base of *reciprocus*: returning, alternating) + *-āl-* (base of *-ālis*: pertaining to, characterized by). Similarly, Greek-derived *anthropology*, which one might assume was borrowed from Greek *anthrōpologia*, a word that never existed in Greek, was in fact created at about the same time from the Greek roots *anthrōp-* (base of *anthrōpos*: human being) + *-o-*: connecting vowel + English *-logy*: the science, study, theory, or doctrine of (< G. *-log-* [base of *logos*: word, thought, reason, reckoning, discourse] + *-ia*: the act, process, condition, or result of). Thus, since the Renaissance it has become increasingly difficult to tell which Latin- and Greek-derived English words actually had prior forms in their respective classical languages and which were coined in English by combining elements from these languages.

To summarize this brief history of the English language, we can represent its three periods in the diagram on the following page:

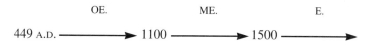

OE.   ME.   E.

449 A.D. ⟶ 1100 ⟶ 1500 ⟶

The Latin Influence

The second major source of words in English is of course Latin, whose elements are "borrowed," rather than "inherited" and are therefore imposed upon our native foundation. With few exceptions, such as the occasional substitution of the Latin-derived plural ending *-a* or *-i* (as in *memoranda* or *fungi*) for the conventional English plural *-s* or *-es*, Latin has had no effect on the grammatical structure of English.

Latin is an older language than English, having experienced its Golden and Silver Ages from about 80 B.C. to A.D. 200, during which time Cicero, Caesar, Vergil, Lucretius, Tacitus, and Juvenal lived and wrote (compare this to English, which did not even emerge as a distinct language until at least a century or two after the first Germanic invasions of A.D. 449 and did not develop a written form until the 7th or 8th century). The Golden and Silver Ages make up the period we call Classical Latin, which we generally designate simply as "Latin" (L.). Then from about 200 to 600, Latin underwent a certain degree of simplification in its form and structure (as did English during its transition from Old English to Middle English), and we call this period "Late Latin" (LL.). And from about 600 to 1500 this trend accelerated while Latin became increasingly replaced by its modern "Romance" descendants, such as French and Spanish, and eventually ceased to be a spoken language except in Roman Catholic Church debate and certain academic settings. It is during these centuries that Latin became what is now unflatteringly referred to as a "dead language," and we designate the period 600 to 1500 as "Medieval Latin" (ML.)

Finally, at about 1500 with the coming of the Renaissance to England, Latin was resurrected from the dead, during which time thousands of "new" Latin words were coined by combining Latin elements in ways that had hitherto (hi*th*′ər·to͞o; up until this time) never been combined. In this book I designate this period as "New Latin" (NL.), sometimes referred to in English dictionaries as "Modern Latin" (ModL.). These four periods in the evolution of Latin are illustrated below.

THE FOUR PERIODS OF THE LATIN LANGUAGE

L.   LL.   ML.   NL

80 B.C. ⟶ A.D. 200 ⟶ 600 ⟶ 1500 ⟶

New Latin words are unique on this timeline because they are coined by combining elements from Latin, Late Latin, or Medieval Latin (or from Latinized Greek words) to denote a thing or concept that in most cases has no other name. However, in the etymologies of English dictionaries, words are generally only labeled New Latin or Modern Latin when they have a Latinate ending or fill a need in the international scientific community, such as naming a new species of insect. If they do not meet these criteria, they are generally considered "Modern English" and no distinguishing label is provided. For example, if you look up *centripetal* (sen·trip´i·t´l; moving or directed inward toward a center or axis—the opposite of *centrifugal*) in a college or unabridged dictionary and turn to its etymology, it will first inform you that this word derives from "NL. *centripetus*: center-seeking," which immediately tells you that this word was constructed after 1500; and it will then provide the Latin words, "*centrum*, center + *petere*, to seek," from which this word derives—though it is up to you to extrapolate from these data the four elements that compose *centripetal*. (You will probably also have look up the suffix *-al* in its respective alphabetical order since English dictionaries, with one notable exception, are notorious for omitting etymologies of suffixes within entries.) On the other hand, if you look up *acupuncture* in the same dictionary, it will omit any *initial* etymological label and one-word derivative and will simply inform you that this word derives from "L. *acus*, needle + E. *puncture*." It is then up to you to figure out that this word was coined after 1500, which is actually quite easy, for if it was coined prior to 1500, "ME." or some other initial label would have to be inserted before the "L." In short, the distinction between "New Latin" words and "Modern English" words that were coined after 1500 from existing Latin elements is a very fine and sometimes arbitrary distinction indeed.

In contrast to these words, if you look up *impute* (to ascribe or attribute something to someone or something, especially that which is negative or unfavorable) in a college or unabridged dictionary, it will inform you that this word derives from "L. *imputāre*," of which the "L." tells you that this word existed in Latin between approximately 80 B.C. and A.D. 200; and that dictionary will then provide the two roots that compose Latin *imputāre*, namely, "*in-*, in, into + *putāre*, to think, reckon, prune, cleanse, etc." (The fact that these dictionaries do not provide a definition for Latin *imputāre* generally means that this word, in at least one of its senses, has the same meaning as English *impute*.) So *impute*, unlike *centripetal* and *acupuncture*, was borrowed wholesale from Latin and was not created from Latin elements in English. Thus, by carefully reading dictionary etymologies, you can determine a great deal about the history of a word.

With regard to assessing the "difficulty" of English vocabulary, we can classify words derived from Latin into three categories:

1) short, simple words derived from Latin at a very early stage of English. These borrowings consist primarily of those words adopted from Norman French and Old French after the Norman Conquest of 1066 but also include some words introduced to Britain during the Roman occupation from A.D. 43 to A.D. 410 and others brought by the invading Angles, Saxons, and Jutes, who had previously picked up these words on the Continent. Such words, then, have been in the language so long that they have become thoroughly Anglicized and in many ways appear indistinguishable from native words. A few of these borrowings include *street*, *wall*, *wine*, *cheese*, *fork*, *joy*, *kitchen*, and *cry*.

2) considerably more sophisticated but still relatively well-known words borrowed in late Middle English or early Modern English, either directly from Latin or from Latin via French, but only slightly modified from their earlier form. Such words tend to be three or more syllables, such as *classical*, *reception*, *component*, *definition*, *permeate*, *consequent*, and *reprehensible*.

3) learned and highly technical terms either borrowed directly from Latin in Modern English or constructed from Latin roots in Modern English or New Latin. Such words tend to

be four or more syllables and include scholarly and technical terms such as *soliloquy*, *somniloquy*, *filipendulous*, *circumforaneous*, *ovoviviparous*, and *stupefaction* (all covered in this book).

If you slowly pronounce the words in the last two categories and then compare them to the words in the first category (and to the native terms on page 160), you will actually be able to feel that distinctive and expressive Latinate quality. So if you pay attention to how words are constructed and pronounced, with a little practice you will be able to pick out Latin-derived words in your reading and in speech.

The Greek Influence

Our third major source of words in Modern English is Greek, which, like Latin, is a borrowed rather than inherited language and therefore has no effect on the grammatical structure of English, other than the occasional substitution of a Greek-derived plural ending, such as *-a* (as in *phenomena* and *criteria*), for the conventional English plural *-s*.

Greek is a much older language than Latin and English, having achieved its classical literary form during the millennium (a period of a thousand years) from about 800 B.C. to A.D. 200, during which time Homer, Plato, Aeschylus, Sophocles, Euripides, and Xenophon lived and wrote (again, compare this to Latin, which entered its classical period at about 80 B.C. and to English, which we like to pretend originated in A.D. 449 but in reality did not become a distinct language for at least another century or two). This was the glorious period of Classical Greek, which we designate today simply as "Greek" (G.)—not, of course, to be confused with Modern Greek. Then, like Latin, from approximately A.D. 200 to 600 Greek underwent a certain degree of simplification in its form and structure, and we label this period "Late Greek" (LG.). And from about A.D. 600 to 1500 this trend accelerated, and we designate this period as "Medieval Greek" (MG.).

Then, around 1500, two divergent developments occurred. One was the emergence of Modern Greek (ModG.), which does not concern us, and the other, as we have seen, was the resurrection of Classical Greek during the Renaissance—which is extremely important to us. During this period, Classical Greek contributed thousands of borrowed words to English, and thousands more were coined in English from individual roots in Greek. In both cases, this was essentially the first time that Greek elements were adopted directly into English without first passing through Latin, but because Greek words had for so many centuries been Latinized prior to adoption into English, they continue to be Latinized. I therefore designate this period as "New Greek" (NG.)—a label not otherwise used in this sense, but which I feel is valuable because it describes a process parallel to that which was simultaneously occurring in Latin. These five stages in the development of Greek are illustrated below.

The Five Periods of the Greek Language

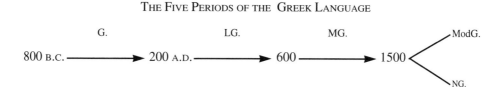

167

If you compare this diagram with the one for Latin on page 165, you will notice that they are almost identical, the only significant differences being that Greek's classical period began around 800 B.C. whereas Latin's began in 80 B.C., and Classical Greek has a modern descendant, Modern Greek, whereas Latin has none (unless you care to include the Romance languages here, which include Italian, French, Spanish, Portuguese, Romanian, Sardinian, and others).

New Greek words, in a process similar to that for New Latin words, are coined by combining elements from Greek, Late Greek, or Medieval Greek, generally when no prior word exists to denote a particular thing or concept. But since New Greek words are invariably Latinized before they pass into English, they are designated in dictionary etymologies as "New Latin," rendering the rubric (roo´brik; a heading or title; also, any directive or rule of conduct, procedure, order, etc.) "New Greek" superfluous (soo·pûr´floo·əs; unnecessary or needless); and you will never see this term in your readings. Moreover, if the resulting word does not maintain a Latinate ending or is not used in science, it will not receive the New Latin label either.

For example, if you look up *Helianthus* in a college or unabridged dictionary and turn to its etymology, you will first note the label "NL." (or ModL.), which immediately informs you that this word was coined after 1500; and since no other form of this word appears immediately after that designation, this further tells you that this word initially appeared in the same form as it is currently used in English (cf. *centripetal* on page 166 for an example of a NL. word that has changed slightly in form). After this primary etymology you will then note the Greek words, "*hēlios*, sun + *anthos*, flower" from which *Helianthus* derives—revealing that this word, in essence, is not a Latin-derived word but a Greek-derived word, or what I designate as New Greek. Similarly, if you look up *telephone* (a word that could hardly have existed in classical Greek, the phone being invented in 1861 by an obscure German named Philip Reis but credited to Alexander Graham Bell fifteen years later), the same dictionary will not provide a New Latin label for this word but will simply state that it was constructed from the Greek elements "*tēle-*, far, far off + *phōnē*, sound, voice," which again tells you that this word was coined in Modern English since no "ME." or other earlier label is supplied. Likewise, if you look up the partially related *phonograph*, you will be informed that this word is derived from the Greek words "*phōnē*, sound, voice + *graphein*, to write, to draw, to scratch," which not only tells you that this word was coined in Modern English but suggests that a phonograph, etymologically, produces "scratched" sound, which indeed is a picturesque description of how early (and even some modern) phonographs may have struck the listener. However, this is not what Thomas Edison had in mind when he invented the phonograph in 1877. In point of fact, the combining form *-graph* generally denotes "an instrument that writes, draws, or records," as in *telegraph* or *electrocardiograph*; and its related combining form *-gram* denotes "that which is written, drawn, or recorded," as in *telegram* or *electrocardiogram*.

From the standpoint of assessing the "difficulty" of English vocabulary, we can classify words derived from Greek into two categories:

1) relatively well-known words borrowed in late Middle English or early Modern English either directly from Greek or from Greek via Latin, but in both cases Latinized before entering English. Such words are often three or more syllables and include *epidemic*, *democracy*, *biology*, *hierarchy*, *hippopotamus*, and *nostalgic* (all covered in this book).

2) learned and highly technical terms either borrowed in Modern English directly from Greek or, more commonly, constructed from Greek roots in Modern English or New Latin. Such terms are usually four or more syllables, are almost always Latinized, and generally have not become common words. Some examples are *euthanasia, hyperborean, cinemicrography, thanatophobia, kakistocracy,* and *bibliokleptomania* (all also covered in this book).

Greek, more than Latin, has become the language of science, and Greek-derived words form the core of our scientific terminology—particularly in medicine and biology. Leaf through any medical dictionary and you will find about 65 percent of the words are derived from Greek, 30 percent from Latin, and a paltry 5 percent from native sources. Some of the terms you may come across that are covered in this book include *cholesterol, gynecology, hydrophobia, phagocytosis, trypanosomiasis,* and *panhysterosalpingo-oophorectomy.*

Moreover, with regard to the technical names of plants and animals, while such designations are usually referred to as "Latin names," most of these names are in fact derived from Greek elements that have only been Latinized to fit the norms of classification. Thus *Helianthus microcephalus* (the small-headed sunflower described in detail in the PREFACE) is constructed from the Latinized Greek roots *hēli-, anth-, micr-, cephal-,* and *-us.* But if these roots were not Latinized, they would be *hēli-, anth-, mikr-, kephal-,* and *-os,* and the resulting term would be **Hēlianthos mikrokephalos* (the un-Latinized Greek letters are underlined). For a detailed description of the changes in Latinization, see the tables on page 236.

Up to this point, I have emphasized the different periods in English, Latin, and Greek and shown some of the historical and linguistic interactions between these periods. This is important for providing an overview of these languages and developing a perspective on their evolution. However, with regard to analyzing and understanding English words, knowing whether a word was borrowed wholesale during Latin, Late Latin, or Medieval Latin, or whether it was coined from individual elements in Middle English, Modern English, or New Latin is, at best, of only theoretical interest and, at worst, irrelevant and confusing. Similarly, knowing whether a word was borrowed from Greek, Late Greek, or Medieval Greek or at what period of English its elements were combined is of dubious (of doubtful value, quality, or outcome; questionable) benefit. In this book we are primarily interested in learning English roots (and their sources) so that we can effectively dissect, analyze, reconstruct, and define English words, and knowing at what period in Latin or Greek such words were borrowed or at what point in time their elements were combined in English will generally not aid in this process. On the contrary, it will hinder the process by bringing in too much information too soon and obscuring the main issue at hand—learning what those roots mean and how they combine with other roots to form English words. So when dissecting and analyzing words our primary concerns are: what are the roots, what do they mean, from what language (not from what period of a language) do they derive, and what was their prior form in that language.

Word-Building

In analyzing and reconstructing words—whether these are from native sources, Latin, Greek, or any other language—the most important element is the base, which we may define as any morpheme or meaningful group of letters to which prefixes, suffixes, and other roots can be affixed. A base therefore provides the central meaning of a word that all other elements in that word modify or qualify. But native bases differ from Latin and Greek bases in one fundamental way: whereas native bases are invariably English words, Latin and Greek bases are never Latin or Greek words. Or put another way, while we cannot find a base in English that *is not* a word, we cannot find a base in Latin or Greek that *is* a word. Thus, while it might appear that English bases have little in common with Latin and Greek bases, the procedure with regard to word-building upon these bases is all but identical, and if we can word-build with one we can do so with the others.

Word-building in our native English will of course be much easier since we already know our basic grammar and vocabulary and can dispense with most of the material we will cover in our discussion of Latin and Greek. For example, consider the word *blood*. By treating it as a base, we can add a variety of prefixes, suffixes, and other roots and words to it, creating such words and phrases as *bloody, bloodless, unbloodied, bloodletting, bloodshot, blood brother, blood poisoning, bloodcurdling, bloodthirstily, bloodhound, red-blooded, flesh and blood, in cold blood,* and dozens of others. What we take for granted in this process is that we understand every one of these words and phrases without even having to think about them.

Now compare these English "blood" words with the corresponding Greek *hem-* and *hemat-* words scattered throughout this text, such as *hemal, hematic, hemagogue, hematorrhea, hemapoiesis, hemangioma, hemocytometer, hematophagia, hematomyelitis,* and *hemacytopoiesis.* Do you know without thinking what every one of these words mean? Can you figure each of them out? And can you identify the prefixes, bases, and suffixes in these words as easily as in the "blood" words? These are silly questions, but they do point out why any practical study of word roots must emphasize Latin and Greek roots and give only a passing nod to native words. Nevertheless, by initially working with native words, we can establish a model that we can readily apply to Latin- and Greek-derived words. So let us take a simple native word and see what we can do with it.

How about *do*? This is a good choice because *do* is about as simple a base as we can find and will demonstrate that what we can do with the simplest of native bases we can also do with the most complex of Latin and Greek bases.

Do is derived from Old English *dō*, which is the first person singular (as in, "I do") of the infinitive *dōn*, which means "to do or to cause." Now to *do* we can add a prefix, which for our purposes may be defined as any morpheme or meaningful letter or group of letters affixed to the *beginning* of a base which modifies that base and thereby alters the meaning of the word.

Thus, if we add the prefix *re-* (< L. *re-*: back, again) to *do* (< OE *dōn*: to do, to cause), we get *redo*, which may be dissected into "re-/do" and can be reconstructed into "to do (*do*) back (*re-*)" or "to do or cause (*do*) again (*re-*)." And when we look up the modern definition of *redo* in a dictionary, we learn it means "to do over or to do again" which is almost exactly the same as its reconstructed meaning. If we then want to verbalize the dissection, analysis, reconstruction, and definition of this word, as if explaining this process to a friend, we can describe this process in the following manner: "*redo* consists of two roots: *re-* and *do*. The *re-* is derived from the Latin prefix *re-*, which means 'back or again,' and the *do* is derived from Old English *do-*, which is the first person singular of the infinitive *dōn*, which means 'to do or to cause.' So when we put these two roots together we get 'to do (*do*) back (*re-*)' or 'to do or cause (*do*) again (*re-*).' And this is almost exactly what *redo* means, for when we redo something, we do it again or do it back."

If we then replace the *re-* with *un-* (< OE. *un-*: not, without; the reversal or removal of), we get *undo*, which dissects into "un-/do" and reconstructs into "to do or cause (*do*) the reversal or removal of (*un-*)." And when we look up the modern definition of *undo* in a dictionary, we find it means "to reverse, cancel, annul, or take apart," which is essentially the same as our reconstructed meaning.

To *undo*, which consists of a prefix and a base, we can now add a suffix, which for our purposes may be defined as any morpheme affixed to the *end* of a base which modifies that base and thereby alters the meaning of the word. In this respect, a suffix is almost identical to a prefix. But a suffix does something that a prefix can never do and which, in most words, is far more important than simply modifying the base: A suffix determines the part of speech of a word—whether it will be an adjective, noun, verb, adverb, interjection, etc.

Thus, if we add the noun-forming suffix *-er* (< OE. *-ere*: one who or that which) to *undo*, we get *undoer*, which dissects into "un-/do/-er" and reconstructs into "one who (*-er*) does or causes (*do*) the reversal or removal of (*un-*)," which turns the verb *undo* into the noun *undoer*. If we then replace the noun-forming suffix *-er* with the verb-forming suffix *-ing* (< OE. *-ende*: present participial suffix having the inflectional meaning: be<u>ing</u>, hav<u>ing</u>, do<u>ing</u>, perform<u>ing</u>, or manifest<u>ing</u> that which is designated by the preceding base), we get *undoing*, which in such sentences as, "She's undoing the bad he has done," converts the noun *undoer* into the verb *undoing*. And if we replace the verb-forming suffix *-ing* with the adjective-forming suffix *-able*, we convert the verb *undoing* into the adjective *undoable*.

So by adding and removing prefixes and suffixes, we have converted our simple two-letter *do* into six different words. And we will use the same process when we get to Latin and Greek words.

From this example, you can see how words are constructed from a base to which prefixes and suffixes are added. But a base need not always have prefixes and suffixes. Sometimes it can stand alone as we saw with *do*. Or it may have only one prefix, as we observed with *undo* and *redo*. Then again, it may lack a prefix and have only a suffix, as we noted in *doing* and *doer*. And, of course, it may have both a prefix and a suffix as we saw in *undoable*.

But a word may also have a variety of prefixes, suffixes, and even bases. For example, the essentially Latin-derived *transcendentalism* has 1 prefix, 1 base, and 3 suffixes; the Latin-Greek-French *antidisestablishmentarianism* has 3 prefixes, 1 base, and 6 suffixes; the Greek *bibliokleptomania* has 0 prefixes, 3 bases, 2 connecting vowels, and 1 suffix, and the medical Greek monstrosity *panhysterosalpingo-oophorectomy* has 1 prefix, 6 bases, 2 connecting vowels, and 1 suffix. So all sorts of variations are possible, but each word must have at least one base.

The Tables

Below and on the following two pages are detailed tables of native prefixes and suffixes. Since native bases (which are also English words) run into the tens of thousands, it is neither practical nor particularly helpful to include a table for them. But since there are relatively few native prefixes and suffixes and these turn up in *thousands* of English words, it makes a great deal of sense to tabulate them. Moreover, while native bases are always English words, prefixes and suffixes seldom are, and some of these—such as the first three prefixes or the last four suffixes in the following tables—may actually be "new" to you though you have used them countless times before.

Since suffixes, unlike prefixes and bases, determine the part of speech of a word, I have further categorized these on the basis of whether they are adjective-forming, noun-forming, or verb-forming suffixes; and as far as practicable, I have also tried to subclassify suffixes with similar meanings to make them easier to remember and to illustrate similar patterns of word-building using different roots—patterns that will become particularly helpful when we get to Latin and Greek.

While native adjective- and noun-forming suffixes are very much evident in Modern English words, native verb-forming suffixes, which characteristically ended in *-an* and *-ian* in Old English, routinely dropped off in Middle English, occasionally leaving one or sometimes two letters behind as reminders of these previous forms. One such suffix is illustrated in the verb-forming suffix table.

NATIVE PREFIXES

English Prefix	Etymology	English Derivatives	Compare (cf.) or Contrast (ct.)
a-[1]	< OE. *an, on*: on, in, into, at	ashore, afoot, afire, afar	ct. E. *a-[2], a-[3]* ; G. *a-*
a-[2]	< OE. *of-*: of, off, away, from	anew, akin, afresh	ct. E. *a-[1], a-[3]* ; G. *a-*
a-[3]	< OE. *ā-*: out, up	arise, awake, ashamed	cf. L. *ex-*; G. *ex-*
be-	< OE. *bī-*: by, near, at, beside.	between, betwixt, betroth	cf. E. *by-*; L. *ad-*; G. *pros-*
	1) around, about, thoroughly	beset, bemuse, bemoan	cf. L. *circum-*; G. *amphi-*
	2) forming verbs fr. nouns and adjs.	befriend, belittle, becloud	cf. L. *-ātus*; G. *-izein*
	3) removal or departure of	behead, bereave (bereft)	cf. L. *ex-*; G. *ex-*
by-	< OE. *bī-*: by, near, at, beside	bystander, byway, byword	cf. E. *be-*; L. *ad-*; G. *pros-*
for-	< OE. *for-, fær-*: away, apart, off	forget, forbear, forgo	cf. L. *ab-, dis-*; G. *apo-*
fore-	< OE. *fore-*: before, in front of	forenoon, forebear, forego	cf. L. *prae-*; G. *pro-*
mis-	< OE. *mis-*: bad, badly; wrong(ly)	misbehave, misprint	cf. G. *dys-, kak-* (E. *cac-*)
off-	< ME. *off-*: from, away from, apart	offset, offspring, offbeat	cf. L. *ab-, sē-*; G. *apo-*
out-	< OE. *ūt-*: out, outside, from, forth	outside, outward, outlive	cf. G. *ex-, ekto-*; L. *ex-*
un-	< OE. *un-*: not, without, reversal of	unkind, untruth, unfold	cf. L. *in-[2], non-*; G. *a-*
under-	< OE. *under-*: below, beneath	underground, underling	cf. L. *sub-*; G. *hypo-*
with-	< OE. *with-*: against, opposite, away	withstand, withdraw, within	cf. L. *contrā-*; G. *anti-*
	(in ME.: together, alongside)	with, withal, wherewithal	cf. L. *com-*; G. *syn-*

I. Adjective-forming suffixes having the basic meaning: "pertaining to, belonging to, characterized by; having the nature, quality, or form of; full of, like."

English Suffix	Etymology	English Derivatives	Compare (cf.) or Contrast (ct.)
-y	< OE. -ig: full of, characterized by	sleepy, windy, holy	ct. L. -ia; G. -ia (E. -y)
-ly	< OE. -lic: having the form of	brotherly, heavenly	ct. OE. adv. -līce (E. -ly)
-ish	< OE. -isc: having the quality of	boyish, foolish, greenish	cf. L. -ālis (E. -al)

II. Past participial suffixes having the essential meaning: "having, having been, possessing, or characterized by (that which is designated by the preceding base or elements)."

-ed	< OE. -d, -ed, -od, -ad	(had) walked, renowned	cf. L. -ātus, -ītis, -itus
-en	< OE. -en: having or had_____	spoken, broken, fallen	ct. OE. -en: made of

III. Adjective-forming suffix having the basic meaning: "made of, consisting of, having the form or appearance of."

-en	< OE. -en: made of	golden, wooden, leaden	ct. OE. -en: ppl. suffix

IV. Present participial suffix having the essential meaning: "being, having, doing, performing, or manifesting (that which is designated by the preceding verb base)."

-ing	< ME. -ing < OE. -ende: -ing	singing, running, swimming	cf. L. -āns, -antis (E. -ant)

V. Adjective-forming suffix having the basic meaning: "tending to (be), inclined to (be), characterized by, having the quality of, like."

-some	< OE. -sum: same + E. -e	quarrelsome, tiresome	cf. L. -idus, -īvus, etc.

VI. Adjective-forming suffix having the basic meaning: "full of, abounding in; or characterized by that which fills."

-ful	< OE. -ful, -full: full	thankful, helpful, handful	cf. L. -ōsus (E. -ous, -ose)

VII. Adjective-forming suffix having the basic meaning: "lacking, without; or lacking the ability to be evaluated, determined, performed, etc."

-less	< OE. -lēas: -less	childless, helpless, countless	cf. OE. un-; L. nōn-; G. a-

VIII. Adjective-forming and adverb-forming suffixes having the basic meaning: "to, toward, in the direction of."

-ward(s),	< OE. -weard: to, toward	forward, backward	cf. L ad-; G. pros-
-ling	< OE. -ling, -lang < ?var. of long	darkling, sideling, middling	ct. OE. n-forming -ling
-erly	< OE. -er(ne): direction of + -līc: -ly	easterly, southerly, westerly	alt. ety: < OE. -ling: long

IX. Adjective-forming suffix having the basic meaning: "multiplied or increased by (that amount designated by the preceding base)."

-fold	< OE. -feald, pp. fealdan: to fold	twofold, fourfold, manifold	cf. L. plicāre (> E. -ply)

I. Abstract noun-forming suffixes: nouns describing "the quality, state, or condition of," but which sometimes also denote "the act, means, result, or process of." Abstract nouns, such as *love*, *philosophy*, and *stupefaction*, differ from concrete nouns, such as *house*, *tree*, and *Tyrannosaurus rex*, which denote a person or thing.

English Suffix	Etymology	English Derivatives	Comments
-ness	< OE. *-ness, -nes, -nyss, -nys*	kindness, wilderness	cf. G. *-ia, -eia*; L. *-ia, -or*
-ship	< ME. *-schipe* < OE. *scipe*	friendship, kinship, lordship	also: office or position of
-hood	< ME. *-hode, -hade* < OE. *hād*	knighthood, womanhood	OE. *-hād* > E. *godhead*
-dom	< OE. *-dōm* < or akin to *dōm*: doom	freedom, wisdom, kingdom	also: rank or domain of

II. Nouns of agency: "a person or thing connected with," or "one who or that which (performs the action designated by the preceding base or elements)."

-er	< OE. *-ere* < or akin to L. *-ārius*	boxer, player, outsider	cf. L. *-or*: agent. suffix
-yer	< ME. *-ier* < OF. *-ier* < L. *-ārius*	lawyer, sawyer, bowyer	used before *w* and vowels
-ard, -art	< ME. *-ard* < OF. *-ard, -art* < Gmc.	coward, bastard, braggart	usually pejorative
-ster	< ME. *-ster* < OE. *-istre, -estre*	gangster, spinster, youngster	orig. fem., then mas.
-ling	< OE. *-ling* < ?-(e)l + -ing, -ung*	hireling, underling, gosling	usually pejorative

III. Nouns of place: "a place, town, village of or for (that which is designated by the preceding base or elements)."

-ton	< OE. *tūn*: walled-in place, town	Boston, Washington	cf. L. *-ārium*; G. *-eion*
-burgh, -burg	< OE. *burg, burh*: fortified town	Pittsburgh, Gettysburg	cf. Edinburgh (ed´'n·bûr´ō)
-bury	< OE. *-byrig*, dative of *burg*: town	Canterbury, Waterbury	ct. E. *bury* < OE. *brygan*
-thorp, -thorpe	< OE. *thorp*: village, hamlet	Linthorp, Oglethorpe	cf. OF. *-ville* < L. *vīlla*: farm
-ing	< ?OE. *-ing*: place, river; ON. *-eng*	Hastings, Reading	ct. OE. *-ende* > ME. *-ing*

IV. Diminutive nouns: nouns denoting that which is "small, little, tiny, or young" with reference to the base noun.

-ock	< ME. *-ok* < OE. *-oc, -uc*: small	bullock, hillock, buttock	cf. L. *-ellus*; G. *-iskos*
-le	< ME. *-le* < *-el* < OE. *-el, -il, -ol*	icicle, bramble, dimple	ct. OE. *-lian*: freq. suffix

NATIVE VERB-FORMING SUFFIXES

Native verb-forming suffixes, when present, are frequently just shadows of inflected verb endings that existed in Old English but which all but vanished in Middle English, occasionally leaving one or sometimes two letters behind as reminders of these previous forms. One such suffix is presented below. It is best defined in relationship to its preceding base or word but often has one or more of the following meanings: "to cause, to become, to cause to become, to make, to form, to induce, or to render."

English Suffix	Etymology	English Derivatives	Comment
-en	< ME. *-en*, based on OE. *-nian*	frighten, strengthen, lengthen	ct. OE. pp. *-en*

LATIN

Word-building with Latin roots is essentially the same as word-building with native roots. However, since Latin is a foreign language we must first understand the principles of its alphabet, pronunciation, and grammar before we can start creating or, more accurately, re-creating Latin-derived English words.

The Latin Alphabet

The Latin alphabet, also called the Roman alphabet, is essentially the same as the English alphabet. In fact, the English alphabet is derived from the Latin alphabet and has introduced but minor modifications over the centuries. The primary differences are that initially, in ancient Rome, there was no *j* or *w*; *k* was all but unknown, and *y* and *z* were adopted only near the end of the Roman Republic in imitation of Greek words using those letters. Moreover, the letter *v* initially represented both the consonant *w* and the vowel *u*—the *u* itself not appearing until the second century A.D. And the letter *i* represented a consonant subsequently recorded as *j* as well as a vowel.

However, most modern Latin texts have minimized (to reduce to a minimum or the smallest possible amount, extent, degree, etc.; also, to belittle or disparage by representing as having the least possible importance or significance) these differences by using a *v* for the consonant *w* and a *u* for the vowel; and they have standardized the *j* as a replacement for *i* when it represents a consonant and have restricted the *i* to its use as a vowel.

In short, we may consider the Latin alphabet to be the same as ours with the qualification that there is no *w* in this alphabet, and *k*, *y*, and *z* are extremely rare.

Latin Pronunciation

Latin, unlike English, is a phonetic language: every letter is pronounced in every word (there are no "silent" letters), and each letter is pronounced the same way every time it is used. Thus, Latin pronunciation is extremely easy to learn, and whereas a non-native speaker of English could spend years trying to learn how to properly pronounce every common English word, in the next few minutes you will learn everything you need to know about pronouncing Latin words.

However, since tape recorders did not exist in ancient Rome, we cannot know for sure how the Romans pronounced their words. Most of what we know or think we know is based on intelligent speculation derived, in part, from the study of comparative linguistics, the examination of ancient manuscripts, and the analysis of early Roman poetry to determine its scansion or where its short and long vowels occurred. Nevertheless, different authorities suggest different pronunciations, and all we will do is acknowledge the most widely held theory.

To simplify the question of pronunciation, we will divide English, Latin, and Greek speech sounds into three categories: consonants, vowels, and diphthongs. A consonant (< L. *con-* [assimilated form of *com*-]: with, together + *son*- [base of *sonāre*]: to sound + *-ant*- [base of *-antis*, genitive of *-āns*]: present participial suffix equivalent in meaning to English *-ing*, as in "the laughing hyena") may be defined as any speech sound made by temporarily blocking the passage of air through the mouth with the tongue, teeth, or lips. In English, all of our letters with the exception of our vowels are consonants. A vowel (< OF. *vouel* < L. [*littera*] *vōcālis*: [letter] sounding < *vōc*- [base of *vōcis*, genitive of *vōx*]: sound, voice + *-ālis*: pertaining to, characterized by) may be defined as any speech sound made by permitting the free passage of breath through the mouth and is generally represented in English by the letters *a, e, i, o, u*, or sometimes *y*. A diphthong (dif´thäng, dip´-; < G. *di*-: two + *phthong*- [base of *phthongos*]: voice, sound) may be defined as a speech sound made by automatically and imperceptibly gliding the tongue from one vowel to another within the same syllable, as the *oi* in *toy* or the *ou* of *cow*.

Latin Consonants

Latin consonants are the simplest speech sounds to distinguish by ear and are essentially pronounced the same way as in English, with the following exceptions and qualifications:

1) *v* is always pronounced like *w*, as in *wine*; never *v*, as in *vine*.
   vēna (wā´nȧ) "vein"
   vermis (wer´mis) "worm"

2) *j* is always pronounced like *y*, as in *year*; never *j*, as in *jury*.
   jacere (yȧ´ke·re) "to throw"
   Juppiter (yoo´pi·ter) "Jupiter"

3) *g* is always pronounced hard, as in *get*; never soft, as in *gene*
   genius (ge´ni·oos) "guardian spirit"
   gingīva (gin·gē´wȧ) "gum (of the mouth)"

4) *c* is always pronounced hard, as in *call*; never soft, as in *cite*.
   cella (kel´lȧ) "cell"
   causa (kau´sȧ) "reason, cause"

5) *t* is always pronounced like the *t* in *ten*; never the *t* in *nation*.
   sectiō (sek´ti·ō) "section"
   inductiō (in·dook´ti·ō) "a leading into"

6) *x* is always pronounced like *ks*, as in *fax*; never *gz*, as in *exonerate*, or *z*, as in *xylophone*.
   expurgāre (eks·poor·gä´re) "to cleanse, purge"
   dexter (deks´ter) "right"

7) *qu* is always pronounced like *kw*, as in *quiz*; never kyoo, as in *queue* (a line or file, as of people waiting to be served; also, a pigtail) or *cue*.
   quantus (kwȧn´toos) "how much"
   quaerere (kwī´re·re) "to ask, to seek"

8) *b* is pronounced like *p* before *s* or *t*, as in *lips*; never *b*, as in *dibs*.
   absentis (ȧp·sen´tis) "to be away"
   obtrūdere (ôp·troo´de·re) "to obtrude"

9) *z* is pronounced like *dz*, as in *adz* (an axlike tool); never *z*, as in *zebra*.

    zōna (dzō´nȧ) "belt, girdle"

    zōdiacus (dzō·di´ȧ·ko͝os) "zodiac"

Latin Vowels

Latin has five vowels, each of which can be pronounced long or short. A few of our finer dictionaries and any decent Latin textbook identify all long Latin vowels with a macron (mā´krän; a short horizontal line placed above a vowel to indicate that it has a long sound < G. *makron*, neuter of *makros*: long, large), and this tells you exactly how to pronounce the vowel. But if your dictionary or textbook does not provide macrons, you will not know what sound value to attribute to these vowels nor will you know where to accent many of these words, and I would strongly suggest you purchase a better reference. The five Latin vowels, along with what we believe to be their pronunciations, are described below.

Latin Vowels

SHORT VOWELS		LONG VOWELS	
Vowel	*Pronunciation*	*Vowel*	*Pronunciation*
a	ȧ (as in bola)	ā	ä (as in bar)
e	e (as in bet)	ē	ā (as in bay)
i	i (as in bit)	ī	ē (as in bee)
o	ô (as in bought)	ō	ō (as in blow)
u	o͝o (as in book)	ū	o͞o (as in boom)

With regard to the short vowels, while English *a* generally represents the *a* of *rat*, Latin *a* represents the *a* of *bola* (bō´lȧ; in South America and other areas, one or more ropes, often formed into an elongated "ʏ" with a heavy ball fastened to two or three legs, for throwing at and entangling the legs of cattle or game animals), a sound similar to but slightly longer than the English *a* in *above*. Latin *e* and *i*, as far as we can tell, were pronounced the same as our vowels in *bet* and *bit*, respectively. But while English short *o* generally represents the *o* of *pot*, Latin *o* was probably pronounced with a sound closer to the *o* in *port*, and we should enunciate it with a sound intermediate between these two *o*'s. Finally, while English short *u* generally represents the *u* in *but*, Latin *u* represents the *oo* in *book*.

With regard to the long vowels, you'll notice that the macron above each Latin vowel, with the exception of *o*, imparts to that vowel a sound completely different from what a macron imparts to the corresponding English vowel. Thus, while English *ā* represents the *a* in *day*, Latin *ā* represents the *a* in *bar*; and while English *ē* represents the *e* in *beet*, Latin *ē* represents the *a* in *bay*. Equally confusing, English *ī* represents the *i* in *bite* while Latin *ī* represents the *e* in *bee*; and English *ū* represents the *u* in *cute* while Latin *ū* represents the *oo* in *boom*. But before you bemoan the superannuation (so͞o´pər·an´yo͞o·ā´shən; the quality or state of being old, antiquated, or out of date) of the Latin system, you should realize that every other language that uses the Roman alphabet observes the same or similar vowel representation as Latin: English, not Latin, is the anomaly (ə·näm´ə·lē; a deviation or digression from what is considered normal or standard).

Thus, in this book you will have to distinguish between the *symbols* used in the pronunciation key to represent the sounds of English, Latin, Greek, and other languages (see pp. xxiii–xxiv) and the specific letters themselves, which in Latin and Greek (and certain other languages) employ macrons to represent long sounds. For example, the ē and ī in Latin *verērī*, "to fear, to stand in awe of" (from which we derive the words *revere* and *reverend*) are *not* pronounced, respectively, "ē" and "ī" since they are Latin characters and not pronunciation symbols. Instead, they are pronounced "ā" and "ē" in accordance with the sounds described in the table of Latin vowels above. So Latin *verērī* should be articulated "we·rā´rē" (remember that Latin *v*'s are pronounced like English "w"; and that first *e* is pronounced "e," as in *wet*, not "ē," as in *we*). If this all seems a bit confusing, it should be of some consolation to know that Greek vowels are for the most part pronounced the same as Latin vowels. So once you understand the pronunciation and representation of Latin vowels, you will also understand the pronunciation and representation of most Greek vowels.

Diphthongs

Diphthongs in Latin words are pronounced in a specific manner, and these pronunciations remain constant in all words. While there are six diphthongs in Latin, for our purposes we need only know three, which are described below.

LATIN DIPHTHONGS

Diphthong	Pronunciation	Latin Word and Pronunciation
ae	ī (as in eye)	*taedium* (tī´di·oom) "weariness, disgust"
au	ou (as in mouse)	*taurus* (tou´roos; *not* tô´rəs) "ox, bull, cow"
oe	oi (as in boil)	*amoenitās* (à·moi´ni·täs) "pleasantry"

As with vowels, in English we generally attribute different sounds to these diphthongs. While Modern English *ae* is typically pronounced "ē," as in *Aesop*, *algae*, and *Pangaea* (pan·jē´ə; a hypothetical supercontinent believed to have comprised all of the continents and islands of earth and to have split into two smaller supercontinents about 200 million years ago < G. *pan-*: all + *gaia*: earth), Latin *ae* is pronounced "ī," as in *eye* and *bile*. While English *au* is regularly pronounced "ô," as in *taught* and *bought*, Latin *au* is pronounced "ou," as in *mouse* and *cow*. And while English *oe* is usually pronounced "ē," as in *subpoena* and *coelacanth* (sē´lə·kanth´; a creature considered to have been one of the missing links between fish and amphibians and believed to have become extinct 70 million years ago but found swimming off the coast of southeastern Africa in 1938 and later near the Comoro islands, northwest of Madagascar), Latin *oe* is pronounced "oi," as in *boil* and *spoil*. (English *oe* is also sometimes pronounced "e," as in *Oedipus*; or "i," as in *coelenterate* [si·len´tə·rāt], any of a phylum of invertebrates, including the corals and jellyfishes, having a single opening for ingestion and excretion).

Latin Accentuation

Knowing where to accent Latin words is perhaps the hardest part of Latin pronunciation to learn, but even this is not particularly complicated if you learn three basic rules. But first you should be familiar with three terms:

ultima (ul´ti·mə) *n.* the last syllable in a word. **[ultima]** < L. *ultima* (fem. of *ultimus)*: farthest, last. RECON: *last* (**ultima**).

penult (pē´nult, pi·nult´) *n.* **1.** the next to the last syllable in a word. **2.** the next to the last entity in any group or series. **[pen- + ult-]** < L. *p(a)en(e)*: almost, scarcely + *-ult(ima)* (fem. of *ultimus*): farthest, last. RECON: *almost* (**pen-**) *last* (**ult-**).

antepenult (an´tē·pē´nult, -pi·nult´) *n.* the second to the last syllable in a word, i.e., the third syllable from the end of a word. **[ante- + pen- + ult-]** < L. *ante-*: before, in front of + *p(a)en(e)*: almost, scarcely + *ult(ima)* (fem. of *ultimus*): farthest, last. RECON: *in front of* (**ante-**) *almost* (**pen-**) *last* (**ult-**).

The rules for pronouncing Latin words are as follows:

1) Words of two syllables are accented on the penult (which, in this case, is also the first syllable):

> *mundus* (moon´doos) "world"
> *cīvis* (kē´wis) "citizen"

2) Words with more than two syllables are accented on the penult *if* the penult is long. A syllable is long if it contains a long vowel, a diphthong, or has a short vowel followed by two or more consonants or *x*:

(long vowel)	*sentīre* (sen·tē´re) "to feel, to perceive"
(diphthong)	*applausus* (àp·plou´soos) "applauded"
(double consonant)	*ineptus* (in·ep´toos) "inept"
("x")	*reflexus* (re·flek´soos) "bent back"

3) Words with more than two syllables are accented on the antepenult *if* the penult is short:

> *facere* (fà´ke·re) "to make, to do"
> *fortissimus* (for·tis´si·moos) "strongest, bravest"

For our purposes, the most important thing to consider about Latin accentuation is whether to accent a three-syllable verb on the first syllable or the second syllable. If the second syllable is short, as in *tendere*, "to stretch, to extend," accent the first syllable (ten´de·re), but if the second syllable is long, as in *tenēre*, "to have, to hold," accent the second syllable (te·nā´re).

Latin Bases

Latin bases, like native bases, are the most important parts of words and provide their central meaning, to which prefixes, suffixes, and other endings are attached. However, while native bases are invariably also complete words, as we saw with *do*, Latin bases are never complete words, at least not in Latin, though in some cases they do become English words. For example, Latin *factus*, the past participle of *facere*, "to make, to do," has the base *fact-*, which, as a derivative of the neuter form *factum*, "that which is done, deed," becomes the English word *fact*. But for the most part Latin bases only become English roots, which in turn appear as parts of words, as English *fact-* in *factory*, *manufacture*, *malefactor* (a person who breaks the law or does harm or evil to another or others; criminal; evildoer), and *artifact* (any object crafted by hand, especially by a prehistoric or nonliterate people). Because

Latin bases do not generally become English words, this explains why, if you've ever looked in an English word-root book, the Latin-derived roots (as well as the Greek-derived roots) often appear as meaningless combinations of letters and dashes, such as *lect-*, *somn-*, *loqu-*, *-bl-*, and *-ig-*, the dash or dashes indicating where letters have been dropped from the original Latin word and to which side other elements can be attached to form words.

The key, then, to understanding such roots is to *know* the Latin words and bases from which they derive, and to be familiar with the *process* through which they are derived. If you open any decent dictionary and read the etymology of a Latin-derived English word you will immediately "learn" the Latin word from which the English word derives, but this will not tell you *how* the Latin base, which yields the English root, is derived nor, in many cases, even what it is. You must therefore ascertain (as ́ər·tān ́, *not* a·sûr ́ t'n; to determine or discover with certainty, as by examination or investigation) this information on your own. But this is not difficult and the process for doing so can be summarized in one short sentence: *A Latin base can be extracted from a Latin word by removing that word's inflectional ending.* Thus, whenever you see a Latin word, if you can recognize and "remove" its inflectional ending, you will be left with its base, which, in turn, will yield an English root, to which you can attach additional roots to build English words. And if you know the meaning of the Latin word (which the dictionary will tell you), you will also know the meaning of the Latin base and the English root since these usually retain the same meaning. Below is a listing of the most common Latin inflectional endings that can be removed from Latin words to reveal their bases.

LATIN INFLECTIONAL ENDINGS THAT CAN BE REMOVED
FROM LATIN WORDS TO REVEAL THEIR BASES

-a   -ae   -us   -um   -is   -ī   -ēs   -ū
-āre   -ēre   -ere   -īre   -ārī   -ērī   -īrī

Whenever you look up an English word in a dictionary and encounter a Latin word in its etymology, you can therefore extract the base of that Latin word by removing one of these endings; and this base, sometimes with slight modification, will become an English root, which will form the foundation of that English word, and to which you can attach prefixes, suffixes, and other roots to "re-create" that English word or to form additional words. Thus, if you look up *selection* in a college dictionary, you will learn, either directly or indirectly, that this word is derived from Latin *lēctus*, a form of a verb meaning "to gather, to choose, to read." From the table above, you will note that *-us* is one of the "Latin inflectional endings that can be removed from Latin words to reveal their bases." Thus, by removing this ending you will be left with the Latin base *lēct-*, which, with the removal of the macron over the *ē*, will yield the English root *lect-*. By then adding the prefix *se-*, "apart, aside," and the suffix *-ion*, "the act, means, or result of," you can re-create *selection*, which, etymologically, means "the act, means, or result of (*-ion*) choosing (*lect-*) apart (*se-*)."

To understand and re-create such words, however, you need not memorize the above list. When we explore the structure of Latin nouns, adjectives, and verbs, you will learn exactly what all of these endings mean, where they come from, and how they are used; and as you begin browsing entries in A CROSS-REFERENCE DICTIONARY (and reading etymologies in college and unabridged dictionaries), you will quickly get a feel for recognizing and removing these endings whenever you see them.

Latin Prefixes

Prefixes, as we have seen, function to modify the base of a word and thereby alter its meaning. But while in Latin, as with native sources, there are thousands of bases, a relative handful of Latin prefixes modify these bases, and it is possible to learn practically every one of them with a minimum of work. Accordingly, the table on page 184 comprises the 31 most common Latin-derived prefixes used in English, which account for over 95 percent of all Latin-derived prefixes you will encounter in your reading. Thus, by learning these prefixes—half of which you probably already know—you will be able to understand at least partially the etymologies and meanings of tens of thousands of words that contain these prefixes. But, again, you needn't memorize or study this table. Just look it over and then consider it a reference you can come back to time and again as we proceed to analyze and create words in the remainder of this Short Course and throughout this book.

Two technical points, however, are important to understand about Latin prefixes. First, while Latin is a highly inflected language with a multiplicity of inflectional endings for every noun, adjective, and verb, Latin prefixes are almost entirely uninflected. However, they do sometimes drop or change their final letter (or even add an occasional letter) in response to the first letter of the following base or root. This is primarily due to a linguistic process known as *assimilation*, a word derived from English *as-* (< L. *as-*, an assimilated form of the prefix *ad-*): to, toward + *simil-* (< L. *simil-*, base of *similis*): like, similar + *-at-* (< L. *-āt-*, base of *-ātus*: past participial suffix of verbs ending in *-āre*): having, having been, possessing, or characterized by + *-ion-* (< L. *-iōn-*, base of *-iōnis*, genitive of *-iō*): the act, means, or result of. Hence, "the result of (*-ion*) having been (*-at-*) similar (*simil-*) toward (*as-*)."

As you can see from this etymology, the word *assimilation* is itself an example of assimilation, which may be defined as that process by which the last sound in a prefix becomes identical or more similar to the first sound of the following root or element. In the word *assimilation*, if the *as-* were not assimilated it would be *ad-*, and *assimilation* would be **adsimilation*, which at one time it probably was. But as speakers of language tend to slur their speech over time, that *-d-* would have become an *-s-*, making the word much easier to pronounce. Indeed, if you quickly repeat **adsimilation* a few times and then do the same for *assimilation*, you will experience this yourself. Similarly, we spell and pronounce **adcident* as *accident* and **disferent* as *different*; and we pronounce *cupboard* as kub´ərd, though interestingly, its spelling has not yet changed to reflect its pronunciation, something of an anomaly in assimilation. For further examples of assimilation, see *ad-*, *com-*, *in-*[1], and *in-*[2] in A CROSS-REFERENCE DICTIONARY.

The second technical point: In many Latin words that use prefixes, the prefixes sometimes drop their specific meanings and are used instead to intensify the base and other elements of the word, imparting the basic meaning, "completely, thoroughly, throughout, or utterly." Some of the more common Latin prefixes that double as "intensives" are *com-*, *dē-*, *dis-*, *ex-*, *in-*[1], *ob-*, and *per-*. By comparison, we also use intensives in English, but instead of calling upon prefixes to do this work, we generally insert a separate word (usually an adjective) before a more substantial word (usually a noun) to emphasize our point. These are most conspicuous in the use of oaths and curses, as in the sentence: "You owe me five ____ dollars." (Fill in whatever intensive comes to mind.)

Latin Suffixes

Suffixes, like prefixes, modify a base. But their most important feature, as we have seen, is that they determine the part of speech of a word. Therefore, when evaluating suffixes we should first determine if they are adjective-forming, noun-forming, or verb-forming suffixes and then classify them accordingly. Moreover, word-building in Latin is so precise that certain suffixes can only be affixed to noun bases, others only to adjective bases, others only to noun and adjective bases, and still others to only verb bases. And with regard to verb bases, the process becomes even more specific: some suffixes can only be affixed to infinitive bases and others only to past participial bases. Accordingly, in the adjective- and noun-forming suffix tables on pages 185–87, I have also indicated to which bases Latin-derived suffixes can be affixed.

Latin suffixes, while rigid with regard to where they can be used, sometimes display a surprising flexibility in how they can be used. The most frequently used adjective-forming suffixes sometimes double as noun-forming suffixes. This occurrence is part of a process known as *functional shift*, which may be defined as a change or "shift" in the grammatical role or "function" of a word or root in a particular construction or context. What this means is that a word can change its part of speech depending on how it is used. In English, which is an excellent language for demonstrating this process, we can turn almost any noun into a verb simply by using it differently in a sentence. For example, we can read a *book*, but we can also *book* a criminal; we can blink an *eye*, but we can also *eye* a person; and we can put food into our *stomachs*, but can we *stomach* the food? Similarly, we can turn adjectives into nouns by speaking of *red* pens and *blue* pens but then asking a co-worker, "Hand me the *red*, not the *blue*." And we can turn nouns into adjectives by wondering about a *mystery* and then meeting the *mystery* man. Latin can do the same things, but on a much more limited scale, and the "shift" is generally restricted to using certain adjective-forming suffixes as noun-forming suffixes, as illustrated, in part, in the adjective table.

Latin-derived suffixes, surprisingly, are much more prevalent in English than native suffixes. But their number is still relatively low, and I have consolidated them on three separate tables: one for adjectives, one for nouns, and one for verbs. The adjective table comprises the 21 most common Latin-derived adjective-forming suffixes; the noun table comprises the 28 most common Latin-derived noun-forming suffixes; and the verb table comprises the three most common Latin-derived verb-forming suffixes. Together, these suffixes constitute over 95 percent of all Latin-derived suffixes in English and occur in over one hundred thousand English words.

Latin Connecting Vowels

Latin words occasionally contain two or more bases in addition to other roots. In these words, sometimes referred to as multiple-based compounds, a connecting *-i-* (or, rarely, another vowel) is generally used to unite these bases. Thus, in *centrifugal*, an *-i-* is used to join *centr-* (< L. *centr-*, base of *centrum*: center) and *fug-* (< L. *fug-*, base of *fugere*: to flee); and in *multiparous* (mul·tip´ər·əs; of or pertaining to a woman who has borne more than one child), an *-i-* is used to connect *mult-* (< L. *mult-*, base of *multus*: much, many) and *par-* (< L. *par-*, base of *parere*: to bring forth, give birth to). However, if either the final letter of the first base or the initial letter of the second base is a vowel, than that vowel links the two bases and a connecting -*i*- is not necessary. Thus, in *benediction,* the second *e* of *bene*- serves as the connecting vowel, and this word is derived entirely from the three roots *bene*- (< L. *bene*: well) + *dict*- (< L. *dict*-, base of *dictus*, past participle of *dīcere*: to say, to speak) + -*ion* (< L. -*iōn*-, base of -*iōnis*, genitive of -*iō*: the act, means, or result of).

Latin Combining Forms

Technically, a combining form is a base, a special form of a base, or a combination of roots that occurs in conjunction with other forms. Thus, any Latin base can be considered a combining form if it can bond with other roots. But there are certain restrictions to how bases can bond with other roots. For example, the Latin verb *agere*, "to do, to act, to drive," has the base *ag*-, to which roots can be affixed. But these can only be affixed to the terminal or back side of *ag*-. If we wish to attach a prefix or other root to the initial or front side of *ag*-, we must use an alternative base to *ag*-, which is -*ig*-. The process of obtaining -*ig*- from *agere* is as follows: *agere* has the combining form -*igere*, to which prefixes and other word-initial elements can be affixed; and just as *ag*- is the base of *agere*, -*ig*- is the base of -*igere*. To verbalize this process, we can simply state: "-*ig*- is the base of -*igere*, which is a combining form of *agere*." (For a more detailed explanation of this process, see Phonetic Shift on page 217; and for eleven English words with -*ig*- in them, see chapter AG-, ACT-, -IG- in COMMON ROOTS.)

More commonly, however, a combining form, especially in English, is considered to be a base linked with a connecting vowel that is treated as one unit, as though it were a solitary base. Thus, in *centrifugal* and *multiparous* above, *centri*- (not *centr*-) and *multi*- (not *mult*-) are considered "combining forms," and this is the way English dictionaries usually represent them. But this is not a very accurate way to present a base and a following vowel, which is an unrelated element simply inserted to join two bases. For this reason and to avoid any ambiguity as to what is and what is not a base, in this book I always separate a root from its connecting vowel, unless otherwise noted.

How to Create English Words from Latin Words

We now have all of the information we need to create English words, and the secret to doing so can be summarized as follows:

1) Note the Latin word.

2) Identify its inflectional ending.

3) Remove that inflectional ending to reveal its base.

4) Create an English root from this base, which, in most cases, simply involves removing any macrons, if present.

5) Add one or more prefixes, suffixes, connecting vowels, combining forms, etc., to this root to create an English word.

These steps are outlined on the following page, using the Latin word *vīvere*, "to live," as an example.

Latin Word	Inflectional Ending	Latin Base	English Root	English Word
vīvere (to live)	-ere	vīv-	viv-	re**viv**al

Thus, we begin with the Latin verb *vīvere*, "to live." We immediately identify and remove its inflectional ending *-ere*, revealing its base *vīv-*. We then remove the macron from this base, yielding the English root *viv-*. To this root we add the prefix *re-* (< L. *re-*: back, again) and the adjective- and in this case noun-forming suffix *-al* (< L. *-āl-*, base of *-ālis*: pertaining to, characterized by), yielding the English word *revival*.

LATIN-DERIVED PREFIXES

English Prefix	Etymology	English Derivatives	Compare (cf.) or Contrast (ct.)
ab-, abs-, a-	< L. *ab-*: away, from, away from	abduct, abstruse, avert	cf. L. *dē-*, *dis-*; G. *apo-*
ad-, a- (assim.)	< L. *ad-*: to, toward, at, near	advent, ascribe, accident	cf. G. *pros-*; L. *in-*[1]
ambi-, amb-	< L. *ambi-*: both, around, about	ambidextrous, ambagious	cf. G. *amphi-*; L. *circum-*
ante-	< L. *ante-*: before, in front of	antebellum, antepenult	cf. G. *pro-*; ct. G. *anti-*
circum-	< L. *circum-*: around, about	circumference, circumfuse	cf. G. *peri-*, *amphi-*
cis-	< L. *cis-*: on this side of	cisatlantic, cisalpine	ct. L. *trāns-*; cf. G. *peri-*
com-, co- (assim.)	< L. *com-*: with, together	complex, cognition	cf. G. *syn-*; ME. *with-*
contra-	< L. *contrā-*: against, opposite	contradict, contravene	cf. Fr. *counter-*; G. *anti-*
de-	< L. *dē-*: away from, off, down	depress, depend, decrepit	cf. L. *ab-*; G. *kata-* (E. *cata-*)
dis-, di- (assim.)	< L. *dis-*: away, from, apart	dismiss, digress, different	cf. L. *sē-*; ct. G. *di-*, *dis-*
ex-, e- (assim.)	< L. *ex-*: out, out of, from, forth	excision, elocution, effort	cf. G. *ex-*; OE. *ūt-* (E. out-)
in-[1], im- (assim.)	< L. *in-*: in, into, within	incise, impel, irruption	ct. L. *in-*[2]; G. *en-*
in-[2], im- (assim.)	< L. *in-*: not, without	ineligible, imperfect	ct. L. *in-*[1], *non-*; G. *a-*
infra-	< ML. *infra-*: under, below	infrared, infrastructure	ct. L. *ultrā-*, *super-*
inter-	< L. *inter-*: between, among	international, interlocutor	cf. LL. *intrā-*; L. *intrō-*
intra-	< LL. *intrā-*: inside, within	intramural, intrauterine	cf. L. *inter-*, *intrō-*
intro-	< L. *intrō-*: in, into, within	introduce, introspection	cf. LL. *intrā-*; L. *inter-*
non-	< L. *nōn-*: not, without	nonhuman, nonsense	cf. L. *in-*[2]; G. *a-*; OE. *un-*
ob-, o- (assim.)	< L. *ob-*: to, toward, against	obvious, omit, oppress	cf. L. *ad-*; G. *pros-*
per-	< L. *per-*: through, throughout	perfume, perambulate	cf. L. *trāns-*; ct. G. *peri-*
post-	< L. *post-*: behind, after	postmeridian, postprandial	cf. L. *ante-*; ct. prae- (E. pre-)
pre-	< L. *prae-*: before, in front of	preview, predict, preprandial	ct. L. *post-*; cf. OE. *fore-*
pro-	< L. *prō-*: before; forward, forth	proclivity, propensity	cf. G. *pro-*; L. *prae-*
re-, red-	< L. *re-*: back, again, anew	reverse, recoil, redintegrate	cf. L. *retrō-*; G. *ana-*
retro-	< L. *retrō-*: back, backward	retrogression, retrospective	cf. L. *re-*; G. *ana-*
se-, sed-	< L. *sē-*: apart, aside	secede, separate, seditious	cf. L. *dis-*; OE. *for-*
semi-	< L. *sēmi-*: half	semicircle, semiformal	cf. G. *hēmi-*; OF. *demi-*
sub-, sus- (assim.)	< L. *sub-*: under, below, beneath	submarine, sustain, succumb	cf. G. *hypo-*; ct. L. *super-*
super-, sur-	< L. *super-*: over, above, beyond	superfluous, surface	cf. G. *hyper-*; ct. L. *sub-*
trans-, tra-	< L. *trāns-*: over, across, beyond	transatlantic, traduce	cf. G. *meta-*; ct. L. *cis-*
ultra-	< L. *ultrā-*: beyond, on far side	ultramarine, ultraviolet	ct. ML. *infra-*; G. *meta-*

I. Adjective-forming suffixes having the basic meaning: "pertaining to, characterized by, having the nature of, like, belonging to"; also forming nouns, generally with the meaning: "one who or that which (performs the action designated by the preceding base or elements)." These suffixes are usually affixed to noun or adjective bases.

English Suffix	Etymology	English Derivatives	Comments
-al	< L. *-āl-*, base of *-ālis*: pert. to	gradual, immortal, manual	our most common L. suf.
-ar	< L. *-ār-*, base of *-āris*: pert. to	lunar, muscular, agrarian	used esp. with *l* in base
-ic	< L. *-ic-*, base of *-icus*: pert. to	civic, acidic, vocalic	cf. G. *-ikos*; ct. G. *-tikos*
-an, -ane	< L. *-ān-* (base of *-ānus*) + E. *-e*	urban, urbane, American	often denotes: natives of
-ine, -in-	< L. *-īn(us)* or *-in(us)* + E. *-e*	canine, feminine, femininity	often used in animal adjs.
-ile, -il	< L. *-īl-* (base of *-īlis*) + E. *-e*	juvenile, virile, civil	ct. L. *-ilis*: tending to
-ary, -ari-	< L. *-āri(us)* or *-ār(is)*	lapidary, military, agrarian	cf. L. *-ārium* (E. *-ary*)

II. Adjective-forming suffixes having the basic meaning: "able to (be), capable of (being), tending to be, inclined to be." These suffixes are usually affixed to infinitive or past participial bases.

-ble, -bil-	< L. *-b(i)l(is)*: tending to + E. *-e*	affable, educable, visibility	*-ble > -bil-* within words
-ile, -il-	< L. *-il(is)*: tending to + E. *-e*	agile, docile, facility	ct. L. *-īlis*: pert. to

III. Adjective-forming suffixes having the basic meaning: "tending to (be), inclined to (be), characterized by, having the quality of; full of, abounding in."

-id	< L. *-id-*, base of *-idus*: charact. by	vivid, torpid, fluidity	affixed to infin. bases
-ive, -iv-	< L. *-īv-* (base of *-īvus*) + E. *-e*	aggressive, reflective	affixed to ppl. bases
-ory, -or-	< L. *-ōr(ius)*: tending to, inclined to	amatory, amatorially	affixed to ppl. bases
-ulous	< L. *-ul(us)*: tending to + *-ōs(us)*	pendulous, tremulous	affixed to infin. bases
-itious	< L. *-ici-* (base of *-īcius*) + *-ōs(us)*	fictitious, factitious	affixed to ppl. bases
-acious	< L. *-āc-* (base of *-ācis*) + *-i-* + *-ōs(us)*	vivacious, voracious	affixed to infin. bases

IV. Adjective-forming suffixes having the basic meaning: "full of, abounding in, characterized by, like." These suffixes are affixed to noun or adjective bases.

-ous, -ose,-os-	< L. *-ōs-* (base of *-ōsus*) + E. *-e*	glorious, bellicose, bellicosity	ct. L. *-ulus* (E. *-ulous*)
-lent	< L. *-lent-*, base of *-lentus*	violent, fraudulent, corpulent	ct. L. prp. *-entis* (E. *-ent*)

V. Past participial suffixes having the essential meaning: "having, having been, possessing, or characterized by (that which is designated by the preceding base or elements)."

-ate, -at-	< L. *-āt-* (base of *-ātus*) + E. *-e*	adequate, inanimate, creation	ct. L. *-ātus* (noun, verb)
-ite, -it-	< L. *-īt(us)* or *-it(us)* + E. *-e*	finite, composite, erudition	ct. G. *-itēs* (E. *-ite*)

VI. Present participial suffixes having the essential meaning: "being, having, doing, performing, or manifesting (that which is designated by the preceding verb base)," equivalent in meaning to English participles ending in *-ing*. Frequently, these suffixes yield nouns, having the general meaning: "one who or that which (performs the action designated by the preceding base or elements)."

-ant	< L. *-ant-*, base of *-antis*, gen. of *-āns*	militant, repugnant, servant	cf. L. *-antia* (E. *-ance*)
-(i)ent	< L. *-(i)ent(is)*, gen. of *-(i)ēns*	apparent, affluent, resilient	ct. L. *-lentus* (E. *-lent*)

I. Abstract noun-forming suffixes: nouns describing "the quality, state, condition; act, means, result, or process of." Abstract nouns, such as *justice*, *euphoria*, and *solitude*, differ from concrete nouns, such as *boy*, *girl*, and *Nephelococcygia* ("Cloud Cuckoo Land, " the abode of the birds in Aristophanes' *The Birds*), which denote a person or thing.

A. Abstract nouns, particularly those emphasizing "the quality, state, or condition of," but which can also mean "the act, means, result, or process of."

English Suffix	Etymology	English Derivatives	Comments
-ia	< L. *-ia*: the state or condition of	inertia, insomnia	affixed to n. or adj. bases
-y	< L. *-ia*: the state or condition of	injury, controversy	affixed to n. or adj. bases
-ine, -in-	< L. *-īn-* (base of *īna*) + E. *-e*	medicine, indoctrinate	affixed to infin. or n. bases
-ice, -it-	< L. *-it(ius)*, *-it(ia)*, *-it(ium)*	service, novice, novitiate	affixed to adj. bases
-or	< L. *-or*: quality, state, condition of	ardor, torpor, pallor	affixed to infin; ct. L. n. *-or*
-ty, -t-	< L. *-tās*: the state or condition of	gravity, society, societal	affixed to adj. bases
-tude, -tud-	< L. *-tūd(ō)* + E. *-e*: silent ending	attitude, longitudinal	affixed to adj. bases
-mony, -mon-	< L. *-mōn(ia)* or *-mōn(ium)*: quality of	matrimony, matrimonial	affixed to n. or adj. bases

B. Abstract nouns, particularly those emphasizing "the act, means, result, or process of, " but which can also mean "the quality, state, or condition of."

-ion	< L. *-iōn-*, base of *-iōnis*, gen. of *-iō*	location, diction, injection	affixed to infin. or ppl. bases
-ment	< L. *-ment-*, base of *mentum*	testament, resentment	affixed to infin. bases
-men	< L. *-men*: the act or result of	specimen, gravamen	affixed to infin. bases
-ure, -ur-	< L. *-ūr-*, base of *-ūra*: the act of	pressure, rupture, conjectural	affixed to ppl. bases

C. Abstract nouns, particularly those emphasizing "the act, process, condition, or result of being full of, abounding in, or characterized by."

-lence, -lency	< L. *-lent-* (base of *-lentus*) + *-ia*	violence, corpulency	ct. L. prp. *-entia* (E. *-ent*)

D. Abstract noun-forming suffixes + present participial endings; hence, "the act, process, condition, or result of being, having, doing, performing, or manifesting (that which is designated by the preceding base or elements)."

-ance, -ancy	< L. *-ant(is)* (gen. of *-āns*) + *-ia*	attendance, militancy	cf. L. *-antis* (E. *-ant*)
-ence, -ency	< L. *-ent(is)* (gen. of *-ēns*) + *-ia*	conference, dependency	cf. L. *-entis* (E. *-ent*)
-(i)ence, -(i)ency	< L. *-(i)ent(is)* (gen. of *-(i)ēns*) + *-ia*	eloquence, efficiency	cf. L. *-(i)entis* (E. *-(i)ent*)

E. Abstract noun-forming suffix with the basic meaning: "the quality, state, condition; act, means, result, or process of: tending to be or inclined to be (that which is designated by the preceding base or elements).

-acity	< L. *-āc(is)* (gen. of *-āx*) + *-itās*	vivacity, voracity, pugnacity	cf. L. *-tās* (E. *-ty*)

II. Nouns of agency: "a person or thing connected with" or "one who or that which (performs the action designated by the preceding base or elements)."

-ary	< L. *-ārius* (adj. suf. used as n.)	dictionary, lapidary	affixed to n. or adj. bases
-or	< L. *-or*: one who, that which	actor, inventor, competitor	affixed to ppl. bases

III. Nouns of place: "a place, dwelling, or abode of (that which is designated by the preceding base or elements)."

-ary, -arium	< L. *-ārium*, neut. of *-ārius*: pert. to	library, aviary, aquarium	affixed to n. or adj. bases

(continued on following page)

Engl. Suffix	Etymology	English Derivatives	Comments
-ory, -orium	< L. *-ōrium*, neut. of *-ōrius*: pert. to	dormitory, auditorium	affixed to ppl. bases
-ium	< L. *-ium*, often neut. of *-ius*	colloquium, consortium	ct. G. *-ium*, *-eum*, *-ion*
-ate, -at-	< L. *-āt(us)*: 4th decl. suf. + E. *-e*	senatorial, cardinalate	cf. L. pp. *-ātus* (> E. *-ate*)

IV. Diminutive nouns: nouns denoting that which is "small, little, tiny, or young" with reference to the base noun. These suffixes are usually affixed to noun bases.

-ule, -le, -ul-	< L. *-ul(us)*, *-ul(a)*, or *-ul(um)*	capsule, scruple, scrupulous	*-le* > *-ul-* within words
-cule, -cle, -cul-	< L. *-cul(us)*, *-cul(a)*, or *-cul(um)*	animalcule, muscular	*-cle* > *-cul-* within words
-el, -ellum	< L. *-ell(us)*, *-ell(a)*, or *-ell(um)*	morsel, novel,	ct. L. *-ēla* > E. *sequel*, etc.
-il, -ille	< L. *-ill(us)*, *-ill(a)*, or *-ill(um)*	pupil, fibril, pistil, pastille	ct. L. *-īlis* and *-ilis* (E. *-ile*)
-ole, -ola	< L. *-ol(us)*, *-ol(a)*, or *-ol(um)*	vacuole, escarole, cupola	ct. L. *oleum*: oil (> E. *-ole*)

LATIN-DERIVED VERB-FORMING SUFFIXES

I. Latin past participial suffixes used as verb-forming suffixes in English, best defined in relationship to their preceding base or elements, i.e., "to cause, to become, to cause to become, to make, to do, to act, to form, to produce, to provide, to function, to manage, etc."

English Suffix	Etymology	English Derivatives	Comment
-ate, -at-	< L. *-ātus*, pp. of *-āre*: infin. ending	navigate, generate, fumigation	ct. L. pp. *-ātus* (E. *-ate*)
-ite, -it-	< L. *-ītus*, pp. of *-īre*: infin. ending	unite, ignite, attrite, reuniting	ct. G. *-itēs*: one who (E. *-ite*)

II. Verb-forming suffix derived from Latin *facere*, "to make, to do," freely attached to classical and nonclassical words and bases.

-fy	< L. *-ficāre* < *-ficus* < *-ficere* < *facere*	dignify, mummify, Frenchify	*-fy* > *-fic-* within words

UNDERSTANDING LATIN

Latin is a highly inflected language or what is sometimes referred to as a *synthetic* language. What this means is that the significance or meaning of a phrase or sentence in Latin is determined primarily by its case endings or other changes in the spellings and pronunciations of the words. English, by contrast, is a highly distributive or *analytic* language. What this means is that the significance or meaning of a phrase or sentence in English is determined primarily by its word order in that phrase or sentence. Consider, for example, the following sentence:

The frog kisses the queen

In this sentence, the word order determines the meaning: the frog is doing the kissing, and the queen is receiving the kissing. And without inserting extra words into this sentence, we cannot change the word order and retain its meaning. We can switch *queen* and *frog* but then the meaning—the queen kisses the frog—will be completely different. This is the only word order that makes sense for the meaning we want.

In Latin, however, this sentence can be expressed in six different ways by simply changing the order of the Latin words for "frog," "queen," and "kisses" without introducing any extra words into the sentence or making any other changes. In Latin, the inflectional endings—not the word order—determines the meaning of a phrase or sentence.

Rana osculatur rēgīnam	Rēgīnam osculatur rana	Osculatur rana rēgīnam
Rana rēgīnam osculatur	Rēgīnam rana osculatur	Osculatur rēgīnam rana

In Latin, *rana* is the proper form for "frog" only when it is used as the subject of a sentence. If we want to use "frog" as the object of a sentence, as in "The queen kisses the frog," we would have to use the form *ranam*. Similarly, *rēgīnam* is the proper form for "queen" only when used as the object of a sentence. If we want to use "queen" as the subject of a sentence, again as in "The queen kisses the frog," we would have to use the form *rēgīna*. And *osculatur* is the proper form for "kiss" regardless of who is giving or receiving it, since Latin verbs do not change their form based on subject, object, gender, or amphibians.

Thus, in Latin it doesn't much matter in what order you place your words, so long as you get your endings or inflections right—which is strikingly different from English, in which word order means just about everything. In fact, in Latin you can even use word orders that would be nonsensical in English, such as "Frog queen kisses" or "Kisses queen frog," just so long as the endings are right. Therefore, in understanding Latin and how English words are derived from Latin, we must pay special attention to these endings. And when these endings affect large numbers of nouns, adjectives, and pronouns in similar ways, we place them in groups called *declensions*.

Latin Declensions

In Latin, there are five declensions. Declensions and the selection of words that go into them are determined primarily by three factors: case (the various forms that nouns, adjectives, and pronouns take to show their relationship to other words in a phrase or sentence), gender (whether they are masculine, feminine, or neuter), and number (the form that their plural and singular forms take).

In English, we do not have a system of declensions as do Latin, Greek, and many other languages. But we do have three cases: subjective, objective, and possessive. *I*, for example, is in the subjective case because it always forms the subject of a sentence, as in "I hit the omnibus" (the original and now pretentious form of *bus*); *me* is in the objective case because it always forms the object of a sentence, as in "The omnibus hit me"; and *my* is in the possessive case because it shows possession, as in "My omnibus arrives in five minutes." And while gender is not evident in these examples, each of the pronouns *I*, *me*, and *my* has its own distinctive plural form. Thus, if we wanted to establish a system of English declensions, we could begin by placing all of these words along with their plural forms in the following paradigm (par´ə·dīm´; a model or table showing the different inflected forms of a word < G. *para-*: beside, alongside + *deig-* [base of *deiknynai*]: to show + *-ma*: the result of).

ENGLISH DECLENSIONS OF *I*

Case	Singular	Plural
Subjective	I	we
Objective	me	us
Possessive	my	our

In Modern English, a declension such as this, in which each word has a completely different form in every case and number, is extremely rare. Nevertheless, we can find other English words that are "declined" in a similar manner and place them all in this declension, which we can name, "The First Declension." Two other members of this declension would be *he* (with its forms *him*, *his*, and *they*) and *she* (with its forms *her* and *they*).

A much more typical English declension, however, might be created for such nouns as *dog*, which is declined in the following manner:

ENGLISH DECLENSIONS OF *DOG*

Case	Singular	Plural
Subjective	dog	dogs
Objective	dog	dogs
Possessive	dog's	dogs'

Most English nouns fall into this category, such as *book*, *paper*, *pen*, and *chichevache*, and we can name this declension, "The Second Declension."

But now consider the declension for *goose*.

ENGLISH DECLENSIONS OF *GOOSE*

Case	Singular	Plural
Subjective	goose	geese
Objective	goose	geese
Possessive	goose's	geese's

This declension is unusual in that its nouns primarily change their internal vowels, rather than their endings, to form their plurals, and we can name this declension, "The Third Declension." In this group we would place *mouse*, *tooth*, *foot*, *louse*, *man*, and *woman* (with their respective plurals, *mice*, *teeth*, *feet*, *lice*, *men*, and *women*).

Thus, the primary consideration in determining which words go into which declensions is their case endings, and English, as we have seen, has three cases—the subjective, the objective, and the possessive. Latin has six primary cases—the subjective (called the nominative; näm´ə·nə·tiv), objective (called the accusative), possessive (called the genitive; jen´i·tiv), dative (dā´tiv), ablative (ab´lə·tiv), and vocative (väk´ə·tiv). These are all listed and described below in the order in which they usually appear in Latin grammar books.

Case	Description	English Sentence
Nominative (E. subjective)	Subject of sentence	*I* am not getting a haircut.
Genitive (E. possessive)	Indicates possession	It is not *Ronald's* decision.
Dative	Indirect object	Hand the fishing line *to Ben*.
Accusative (E. objective)	Direct object	Give Nancy *the hoe*.
Ablative	Indicates removal, sep., etc.	Come *out of the backyard*.
Vocative	Direct address	*Cy*, stop laughing.

Fortunately, 99 percent of the time you need only be concerned with one or two cases: the nominative and, when this is not sufficient to identify a word's base, the genitive. (The dative, accusative, and ablative can usually also be employed to determine a word's base, but for reasons to be discussed shortly we shall restrict ourselves to the genitive.) Within these cases, you will consider—depending on declension—the masculine, feminine, or neuter forms in their singular and sometimes plural forms. But please note: because the nominative masculine singular is the basic form cited in English dictionaries and Latin grammar books, whenever a Latin (or Greek) word is mentioned in this book without specifying or implying its case, gender, and number, it too will be the nominative masculine singular.

Latin Nouns

Latin nouns that yield English words occur in all five declensions but are primarily concentrated in the first three declensions. Therefore, we shall examine in some detail these three declensions. But the fourth and fifth declensions also provide English with some extremely important derivatives, so we shall briefly cover them as well.

While Latin declensions, collectively, have over 50 case endings, we need only learn a fraction of these. Specifically, of the first three declensions, the first is by far the easiest to understand and includes only two case endings we need to know; the second is a little tricky but still has only five endings of importance to us; and the third, while furnishing English with a wealth of words and derivatives, contains only three endings we must learn. The fourth and fifth declensions include, respectively, three and one case ending with which we should be acquainted.

Thus, in this Short Course, we will only cover the bare essentials of Latin grammar—what we need to know to establish a foundation for understanding English etymology and word-building. The following description of these declensions is therefore intended to enable you, with the least amount of work, to understand precisely where and how our roots are derived; and this description will also serve as a reference for the rest of this book and for any future study of etymology you may wish to pursue. But you need not memorize this information or distinguish between the different declensions to effectively dissect, analyze, and reconstruct words. If you understand the *principles* of tearing down Latin words to their bases and then deriving from them English roots to which prefixes, suffixes, connecting vowels, and other roots can be attached, it doesn't really matter whether a particular Latin noun belongs to the first, second, third, or fiftieth (if such existed) declension. Indeed, in over 99 percent of the examples in this book—even my most complicated ones—no mention is ever made of "declension" simply because it is not necessary to do so and does not add to the effectiveness of the analysis. But by understanding the composition of these declensions, you will perceive how marvelously structured language is and how all Latin nouns and their English derivatives radiate from these nuclei of original forms. And with this understanding you may very well gain a new perspective on language and etymology that you might otherwise never acquire.

Latin First Declension Nouns

Latin first declension nouns are almost exclusively feminine. These nouns are the simplest words you will be working with because you need only concern yourself with one case, the nominative, and one gender, the feminine.

First declension feminine nouns always end in -a in the nominative singular, and some of these words, such as Latin *antenna*, "sail yard (on a ship)," and *vertebra*, "joint of the spine," have been borrowed unchanged into English, where their definitions may or may not have been slightly altered during their passage from Latin. But for the most part, it is the base of Latin words that forms the foundation of English words, and the base of first declension feminine nouns can be found by simply dropping their final, inflectional -a. Thus, Latin *herba*, "grass, plant, herb," has the inflectional ending -a and the resulting base *herb-*, which becomes the English word *herb*. Similarly, Latin *cella*, "small room, storeroom," has the inflectional ending -a and the resulting base *cell-*, which becomes English *cell*. We can represent these in a table:

LATIN FIRST DECLENSION FEMININE NOUNS YIELDING ENGLISH WORDS

Nominative Singular	Inflectional Ending	Latin Base	English Word
herba (grass, plant, herb)	-a	herb-	herb
cella (small room, storeroom)	-a	cell-	cell

It is rare for English words to be formed simply by dropping the hyphen from a Latin base. Usually, we must first derive an English root from a Latin base, and then add either a prefix or suffix (or any combination of these or additional elements) to this root to form an English word. Two typical Latin words that yield Latin bases, which in turn yield English roots, are *fēmina*, "woman," and *causa*, "reason, purpose, cause," as outlined below.

LATIN FIRST DECLENSION FEMININE NOUNS YIELDING ENGLISH ROOTS

Nominative Singular	Inflectional Ending	Latin Base	English Root
fēmina (woman)	-a	fēmin-	femin-
causa (reason, purpose, cause)	-a	caus-	caus-

It is a simple matter to create English words from these roots. For example, to English *femin-* (< L. *fēmin-*, base of *fēmina*: woman), we can add the adjective-forming element *-in-* (< L. *-īn-*, base of *-īnus*: pertaining to, characterized by) and a silent final *-e*, creating the English word *feminine*. And this word then reconstructs into "pertaining to or characterized by (*-in-*) a woman (*femin-*)," which forms the basis for our modern definition of *feminine*, which emphasizes, in one of its senses, those qualities traditionally associated with women, such as sensitivity and tenderness. We can verbalize this dissection, analysis, and reconstruction of *feminine* in the following manner: "*feminine* consists of three elements: *femin-*, *-in-*, and *-e*. The *femin-* is derived from Latin *fēmin-*, which is the base of *fēmina*, which means 'woman.' The *-in-* is an adjective-forming element derived from Latin *-īn-*, which is the base of *-īnus*, which means 'pertaining to or characterized by.' And the *-e* is a silent English letter without meaning. Thus, when we put these three elements together we get 'pertaining to or characterized by (*-in-*) a woman (*femin-*).'"

Now to *feminine*, we can further add the prefix *un-* (< OE. *un-*: not, without; the reversal or removal of), creating the four-element word *unfeminine*. Or if we replace the prefix *un-* with *ultra-* (< L. *ultrā*: beyond, on the other side of), we get *ultrafeminine*. And by playing with our prefixes and suffixes, we can derive such words as *femininity*, *feminism*, *defeminize*, *antifeminist*, and *effeminate* (i·fem´i·nit; a generally disparaging reference to a man or boy possessing those more gentle or passive qualities traditionally attributed to women).

Similarly, to English *caus-* (< L. *caus-*, base of *causa*: reason, purpose, cause), the second English root in the table above, we can add a silent final *-e*, forming the word *cause*. And if we then add the prefix *be-* (< OE. *bī-*: by) to *cause*, we, of course, derive *because*, which reconstructs into "by (*be-*) reason (*caus-*)," which if you think about it is a fairly good definition of *because*. If we then remove that *be-* and final *-e*, bringing us back to *caus-*, and add the adjective-forming suffix *-al* (< L. *-ālis*: pertaining to, characterized by), we wind up with *causal*, as in "The causal agent of the disease is a virus." Other *caus-* words we can create include *causation*, *causality*, and the legalistic *causidical* (of or pertaining to the pleader or the pleading of a case in court).

One other form of first declension nouns we need to understand is the nominative *plural*. As we now know, the nominative singular ends in *-a*, and its base can be found by dropping that ending. In like manner, the nominative plural ends in *-ae*, and its base can be found by dropping the *-ae*. Thus, while *fēmina* is the nominative singular, *fēminae* (fā´mi·nī) is the nominative plural, and its base is also *fēmin-*, which becomes the English root *femin-*. Similarly, *antenna* is the nominative singular, *antennae* is the nominative plural, and its base is *antenn-*, which becomes the English root *antenn-*. This is all illustrated in the table below.

LATIN FIRST DECLENSION FEMININE PLURAL NOUNS

Nom. Sing.	Nom. Plural	Inflect. Ending	Latin Base	English Root
fēmina (woman)	fēminae	-ae	fēmin-	femin-
antenna (sail yard)	antennae	-ae	antenn-	antenn- (antenna)

The nominative plural is important to us because the *-ae* sometimes appears in English words as an alternative or replacement plural ending for our native *-s* or *-es*. Thus, we have both *antennas*, which usually refer to those metal rods and wires that transmit or receive radio and television waves, and *antennae*, which more properly denote the sensory appendages on the heads of certain insects and other animals. And bear in mind that while the Latin diphthong *ae* is pronounced "ī," the English diphthong *ae* is pronounced "ē." So while Latin *antennae* is pronounced "ăn·te´nī," English *antennae* is pronounced "an·ten´ē"—though it is so often mispronounced "an·ten´ī" that in all likelihood this will become an accepted pronunciation of *antennae* just as *vertebrae* (vūr´tə·brā´) has become an accepted pronunciation of what is more properly articulated as "vūr´tə·brē´."

Finally, you'll notice on the table that after *antenna*, beneath the "Nom. Sing." heading (on the left), the definition "sail yard" is provided in parentheses whereas after *antenn-*, beneath the "English Root" heading (on the right), the definition "antenna" is provided in parentheses. This indicates that the modern definition of English *antenn-* has significantly changed from its earlier meaning in Latin, and in those instances in which the *semantic shift* from a Latin (or Greek) word to its derivative root in English has been substantial, I provide a definition of the evolved English root in parentheses so that you can observe this "sense development."

Latin Second Declension Nouns

While first declension nouns are almost exclusively feminine, second declension nouns are either masculine or neuter, and each of these genders has a few different endings with which you should be familiar.

Second declension masculine nouns characteristically end in *-us* in the nominative singular, and some of these nouns, such as *fungus*, "fungus, mushroom," and *radius*, "rod, beam, spoke of a wheel," have entered English unchanged—in form if not meaning. But it is the base of second declension nouns that generally provides the key to forming English words, and this base can be found by dropping the *-us*. Moreover, when we remove these endings, some of these nouns, such as *digitus*, "finger, toe," and *pāgānus*, "villager, peasant, civilian," emerge as English words, yielding, respectively, *digit* and *pagan*.

Most often, Latin second declension masculine nouns—like first declension feminine nouns—become English words only after first discarding their inflectional endings and becoming Latin bases, which in turn become English roots to which we can attach prefixes, suffixes, and other roots. Two typical masculine nouns are *fūmus*, "smoke, vapor, fume," and *socius*, "partner, companion," as described in the following table.

LATIN SECOND DECLENSION MASCULINE NOUNS YIELDING ENGLISH ROOTS

Nominative Singular	Inflectional Ending	Latin Base	English Root
socius (partner, companion)	-us	soci-	soci-
fūmus (smoke, vapor, fume)	-us	fūm-	fum-

We can again create English words from these roots. To English *soci-* (< L. *soci-*, base of *socius*: partner, companion), we can add the adjective- and noun-forming suffix *-al* (< L. *-ālis*: pertaining to or characterized by), forming the word *social*, which reconstructs into "pertaining to or characterized by (*-al*) partnering or companioning (*soci-*)," which is precisely what we do at a social dance and in other more intimate social encounters. And if we add to *social* the noun-forming suffix *-ist* (< G. *-ist-*, base of *-istēs*: one who), we get *socialist*, or "one who (*-ist*) is characterized by (*-al*) partnering or companioning (*soci-*)." If we then remove this *-ist* and add the prefix *anti-* (< G. *anti-*: against, opposed to, the opposite of), we obtain *antisocial* (of or pertaining to one who is unable or unwilling to "partner or companion" with others in a manner considered normal or socially acceptable). And if we remove this *anti-* and replace it with *psych-* (< G. *psych-*, base of *psychē*: breath, spirit, soul, mind) and add a connecting *-o-*, we derive *psychosocial* (of or pertaining to the interaction of psychological and social factors in one's mental development, personality, world view, etc.). Other *soci-* words we can create by juggling prefixes and suffixes include *society, socialite, societal, association,* and *dissociate* (to break down or dissolve an association; in psychiatry, to undergo a process in which the psyche breaks down or dissolves into multiple personalities).

Similarly, to *fum-* (< L. *fūm-*, base of *fūmus*: smoke, vapor, fume), the second English root in the table above, we can add the prefix *per-* (< L. *per-*: through, throughout) and the silent final letter *-e*, forming *perfume*, or that which "smokes or fumes (*fum-*) throughout (*per-*)," since perfume originally denoted the fumes from a burning substance, such as incense or burning leaves. Or if we remove the *per-* and following the *fum-* insert *-ig-* (< L. *-igere*, combining form of *agere*: to do, to act, to drive) and *-at-* (< L. *-āt-*, base of *-ātus*: past participial suffix with the inflectional meaning: having been or having had, but used in this word as a verbal suffix with the general meaning: to cause, to make, to function, to manage), we get *fumigate*, or "to manage or cause (*-at-*) to drive (*-ig-*) smoke or fumes (*fum-*)," which is exactly what we do when we fumigate an area. Then if we replace the *-ate-* with *-ant* (< L. *-ant-*, base of *-antis*, genitive of *-āns*: present participial suffix with an inflectional meaning equivalent to English *-ing*, but used in this word as a noun-forming suffix with the general meaning: one who or that which), we come up with *fumigant* or "that which (*-ant*) drives (*-ig-*) the fumes (*fum-*)." Finally, by removing the *-ig-* and *-ant* and adding one or more additional elements to the remaining *fum-*, we can construct such words as *fumy* (emitting or full of fumes; vaporous), *fumarole* (the opening in the top of a volcano through which the smoke and fumes escape), and *fumatorium* (an airtight room or chamber for fumigating fruits, vegetables, and other products with toxic gases).

Not all Latin second declension masculine nouns, however, end in *-us* in the nominative singular. Two other endings exist, but we need only be concerned with one of these, *-er*. This occurs in such Latin words as *ager*, "field," and *liber*, "book" (not to be confused with *līber*: free). To find the bases of such words, we cannot simply remove the *-er*'s and expect the remaining letters to constitute their bases. This will not work because the *-er*'s are not inflectional endings nor do the letters preceding them constitute a base. Rather, the *-er*'s are inherent parts of these words that cannot be removed. Therefore, to find the bases associated with these words, we have to look to other forms of these words that possess inflectional endings that *are* attached to bases and then remove those endings to reveal the bases.

In Latin, when the nominative singular case cannot reveal the base of a word, usually the genitive, dative, accusative, and ablative—but not the vocative singular—cases can, and we sometimes refer to these cases as "oblique" cases. Therefore, to find the base we are looking for, we need only remove the inflectional ending of any word in any one of these oblique cases, which will leave us with the base not only for that particular word but for every form of that noun with the exceptions of the nominative singular and vocative singular forms, which, as far as we're concerned, do not have bases. For example, consider all of the singular and plural forms of the Latin noun *ager*, "field," below:

Case	Singular	Inflect. Ending	Plural	Inflect. Ending
Nominative (subjective)	**ager**	(none)	agrī	-ī
Genitive (possessive)	**agrī**	-ī	agrōrum	-ōrum
Dative (indirect object)	agrō	-ō	agrīs	-īs
Accusative (direct object)	agrum	-um	agrōs	-ōs
Ablative (removal, sep.)	agrō	-ō	agrīs	-īs
Vocative (direct address)	ager	(none)	agrī	-ī

To find the common base for any of these words, with the exception of the nominative singular and the vocative singular, all we have to do is locate a word under the "Singular" or "Plural" column, look immediately over to the right under the "Inflect. Ending" column for its inflectional ending, remove this inflectional ending, and we will be left with the base. For example, if we gaze over at the accusative plural form (the fourth entry in the fourth column), we will observe that its form is *agrōs*, and the fifth column will inform us that its inflectional ending is *-ōs*. By removing this *-ōs*, we will reveal its base *agr-*, which therefore constitutes the base not only of *agrōs* but for every form in this declension, excepting, of course, the nominative singular and the vocative singular. To verify this, you can remove the inflectional ending from any other word in this table, and you will also wind up with *agr-*.

The only problem with this system is that, without the aid of this table, you will have to memorize a variety of similar yet different case endings, and this can become very confusing, not to mention time-consuming. Therefore, in most English dictionaries—and throughout this book—whenever we cannot determine the base of a noun or adjective from its nominative singular form, we will *always* turn to the genitive singular form (usually spoken of as simply "the genitive") to provide us with a form of that word from which we can easily find the base. The genitive is a good choice because it is the most "regular" and precisely consistent form of the word that will reveal the base. But in most situations, the other oblique cases will do as well, as we have already seen from the example of *agrōs*. Therefore, it should be understood that we are using the genitive only as a convenience, and when I refer to a noun or adjectival base as being "the base of the genitive," you should always be aware that it is also the base of most if not all of the other oblique forms.

With this background, we can now return to second declension nouns ending in *-er*. To find the base of an *-er* noun (or, more properly speaking, the base of a related form of that noun in the same declension), we need only find its genitive and remove its ending. This method is actually quite simple because the genitive ending of all second declension *-er* nouns is *-ī* (see the table above). Therefore, by removing this *-ī*, we can always uncover the base of the word, which will in turn yield an English root, often without change. Specifically, the genitive of *ager*, "field," is *agrī*; and by removing this *-ī*, we uncover its base *agr-*, which then becomes English *agr-*. Similarly, the genitive of *liber*, "book," is *librī*; and by removing its *-ī*, we reveal its base *libr-*, which becomes English *libr-*. This is all illustrated in the table below.

Latin Second Declension Masculine Nouns Ending in -ER

Nominative Singular	Genitive Singular	Inflect. Ending	Latin Base	English Root
ager (field)	agrī	-ī	agr-	agr-
liber (book)	librī	-ī	libr-	libr-

Even without bothering to construct an English word, we can verbalize these roots and bases in the following manner: "English *agr-* is derived from Latin *agr-*, which is the base of *agrī*, which is the genitive of *ager*, which means 'field.'" Similarly, we can aver (ə·vūr´; to assert or affirm with confidence; declare to be true): "English *libr-* is derived from Latin *libr-*, which is the base of *librī*, which is the genitive of *liber*, which means 'book.'" You'll notice that in both examples, I have used the genitive (singular) to identify the base. To be entirely accurate, I should have stated: "English *agr-* is derived from Latin *agr-*, which is the base of the nominative plural *agrī*, the dative singular *agrō*, the dative plural *agrōrum*, the accusative singular *agrum*," and all the way down the list for every singular and plural form in this table, with the exceptions of the nominative singular and vocative singular forms. And I should then have done the same for *liber*. Since this would be ludicrous (loo´di·krəs; absurd and ridiculous in a laughable and often derisive way), I have confined my analysis to the genitive, and this is the procedure we will use throughout this book.

Now let's construct some words. To English *agr-* (< L. *agr-*, base of *agrī*, genitive of *ager*: field), we can add a connecting *-i-*, a second root *cult-* (< L. *cult-*, base of *cultus*, past participle of *colere*: to till, to cultivate), the noun-forming element *-ur-* (< L. *-ūr-*, base of *-ūra*: the act, process, condition, or result of), and a silent final *-e*, yielding *agriculture*—which reconstructs into "the act or result of (*-ur-*) cultivating (*cult-*) a field (*agr-*)." Or to the base *agr-* we can instead affix the adjective-forming element *-ari-* (a variant of *-ary* used within a word < L. *-āri-*, base of *-ārius*: of, pertaining to, characterized by), and the adjective-forming suffix *-an* (< L. *-ān-*, base of *-ānus*: pertaining to, characterized by, belonging to), yielding *agrarian* (of or relating to land, the cultivation of land, or agriculture), as in *agrarian rights*. Or if we go back to *agr-* and append a connecting *-i-* and then tack on *business*, we get *agribusiness*, which may help us more effectively pursue our agrarian rights. But if we have no interest in business and no concern for agriculture, we can toss out the *business* and replace it with *-cide*, resulting in *agricide* (the abuse and destruction of agricultural land through the overuse of *agrichemicals* or by other negligent or improper farming methods). But if we espouse the agrarian movement and seek to optimize farm production, we can remove the *culture* from *agriculture* and affix the *-mation* from *automation*, producing *agrimation* (the use of robots and other sophisticated electronic apparatus to perform farm operations).

To *libr-* (< L. *libr-*, base of *librī*, genitive of *liber*: book), the second English root in the table above, we can add the noun-forming suffix *-ary* (< L. *-āri-*, base of *-ārium*: a place for, neuter of *-ārius*: pertaining to, characterized by), yielding *library*, or "a place for (*-ary*) books (*libr-*)." If we then remove the noun-forming suffix *-ary* and attach the adjective-forming element *-ari-* (< L. *-āri-*, base of *-ārius*: pertaining to, characterized by), and then tack on the normally adjective-forming suffix *-an* (< L. *-ān-*, base of *-ānus*: pertaining to, characterized by, belonging to; but used in this word as a noun-forming suffix with the basic meaning: one who or that which), we derive *librarian*. And if we then remove this *-arian* and travel to Italy where we pick up the diminutive suffix *-etto*, "small, little, tiny," we obtain *libretto* (a small book containing the text of a musical work, especially an opera). Speaking of diminutives, if we discard the Italian diminutive -etto and replace it with the English diminutive -el (< L. -el(l)-, base of -ellus: small, little, tiny), and suppress the preceding r in libr-, we wind up with libel—originally a formal written charge by a plaintiff, then a little book, then any defamatory statement written about another.

Second declension nouns, you'll recall, also have neuter forms as well as masculine forms. The neuter nouns always end in -um in the nominative singular, and their bases can be found by dropping this -um. However, some second declension neuter nouns have entered English with this ending intact and have yielded such words as forum (any meeting hall, assembly, etc., in which issues of public concern are discussed), ovum (an egg cell), and serum (the clear yellowish part of the blood, most notable as the liquid that oozes out of a blood clot). Other second declension nouns have dropped the -um before entering English, yielding document (< L. documentum: example, proof, lesson), verb (< L. verbum: word, verb), and insect (< L. insectum: insect).

But for the most part, as we have seen with the majority of Latin words so far examined, second declension neuter nouns become English words only after discarding their inflectional endings to reveal their bases, which then become English roots to which we can attach a variety of different roots. Two such nouns are bellum, "war," and grānum, "seed, grain." These are illustrated in the following table.

LATIN SECOND DECLENSION NEUTER NOUNS ENDING IN -UM

Nominative Sing.	Inflectional Ending	Latin Base	English Root
bellum (war)	-um	bell-	bell-
grānum (seed, grain)	-um	grān-	gran-

To English bell- (< L. bell-, base of bellum: war), we can add the adjective-forming element -ic- (< L. -ic-, base of -icus: pertaining to, characterized by), the adjective-forming suffix -ous (< L. -ōsus: full of, abounding in, characterized by, like), and a silent final -e, yielding bellicose, which both etymologically and lexically (with respect to the words or vocabulary of a language) mean "warlike." Or if we replace the -e with a connecting -i- and add the noun-forming suffix -ty (< L. -tās: the quality, state, or condition of), we get bellicosity, "the quality or state of (-ty) full of (-os-) war (bell-)." Now if we go back to the original Latin word bellum and insert the prefix ante- (< L. ante-: before, in front of), we derive antebellum, an English word that reconstructs into "before (ante-) the war (bellum)," particularly the Civil War. And if we replace the ante- with post- (< L. post-: behind, after), we get postbellum, a word which, though opposite in meaning, likewise reconstructs into "after (post-) the war (bell-) particularly the Civil War." However, Latin bellum, "war," should not be confused with Latin bellus and bella, "beautiful," which we see in such words as belle (an attractive and charming woman or girl, especially the prettiest or most alluring at a dance or social gathering—generally used in the phrase, "the belle of the ball"), belladonna (a poisonous European plant of the nightshade family), and beldam (an old woman, especially an ugly or hideous one; see beldam in A CROSS-REFERENCE DICTIONARY for an explanation of how "beautiful" became "ugly").

In the same way, to gran- (< L. grān-, base of grānum: seed, grain), the second English root in the table above, we can add the noun-forming suffix -ary (< L. -āri-, base of -ārium: a place for, neuter of

-ārius: pertaining to, characterized by), yielding *granary*, a place for storing grain—just as *library* is a place for storing books. Or if we remove the *-ary*, infix the element *-ul-* (< L. *-ul-*, base of *-ulus*: a diminutive suffix having the basic meaning: small, little, tiny), and append a silent final *-e*, we get *granule*, a small grain. And *grain*, itself, is a descendant of Latin *grān-*, the base of *grānum*—the *i* being inserted during its passage through Old French into Middle English. Similarly, by swapping suffixes we can come up with the relatively common *granular* and *granulate*, or we can construct the more colorful and esoteric *granivorous* (eating or feeding upon seeds or grain), *granuliform* (having the shape or form of small grain or granules), and *granuliferous* (bearing or producing small grain or granules).

Before leaving second declension masculine and neuter nouns, there is one final matter we should consider. Have you ever wondered why certain English words, such as *focus* or *fungus*, have the alternative plural forms *foci* (fō′sī) and *fungi* (fun′jī, fung′gī) in addition to the standard *focuses* and *funguses*? Or why *rostrum* (a stage, pulpit, or other raised platform for public speaking) and *ovum* (an egg cell) have the alternative plural forms *rostra* and *ova*? And do you ever become confused as to whether such words as *alumnus* (a former student or graduate of a university or other school, especially a male graduate) and *curriculum* (the courses, or a particular group of related courses, offered at a university or other school) take an *-i* or an *-a* (or even an *-ae*) to form their plurals?

Well, these are all plural endings directly derived from second declension masculine or neuter nouns, and once you understand the principles of their formation, you will never confuse these plurals again—or at least you will always be able to figure out which is which.

Essentially, these principles are as follows: Latin second declension masculine nouns end in *-us*, and their bases can be found by dropping this *-us*. To form their plurals, an *-ī* is simply added to their bases, and in English this *-ī* drops its macron to become our plural *i*. Two Latin nouns that illustrate this process are *focus*, "fireplace, hearth (the floor of a fireplace, usually consisting of a flat slab of stone partially extending into the room)," and *fungus*, "mushroom." These are shown below.

Latin Second Declension Masculine Plural Nouns

Nominative Singular	Latin Base	Plural Ending	Latin Plural Word	English Plural Words
focus (fireplace, hearth)	foc-	-ī	focī	foci, focuses
fungus (mushroom)	fung-	-ī	fungī	fungi, funguses

You might wonder how Latin *focus*, "fireplace, hearth," came in English to refer to that area upon which one's interests or pursuits are concentrated. As far as we know, Johann Kepler, the German astronomer, first used *focus* in 1604 to refer to the "burning point" at which heat rays meet and are concentrated in a lens or mirror, presumably in allusion to a fire burning in a fireplace. This meaning was then extended to the site at which light or any other rays meet, as in a camera, and this sense later evolved into our more common definition of *focus* as the center of attention of one's interests or pursuits.

With regard to the plural forms, *rostra* and *ova*, the principles of their formations are as follows: Latin singular neuter nouns of the second declension, as we also know, end in *-um*, and their bases can be found by dropping this *-um*. To form their plurals, an *-a* is simply attached to their bases, which we carry over into English as our plural *-a*. For these examples, then, the starting point of this process is the Latin etymons (earlier forms of roots or words from which later forms derive) of English *rostra* and *ova*, which are, respectively, *rōstrum* and *ōvum*. This process is illustrated below.

LATIN SECOND DECLENSION NEUTER PLURAL NOUNS

Nominative Singular	Latin Base	Plural Ending	Latin Plural Word	English Plural Words
rōstrum (snout, beak)	rōstr-	-a	rōstra	rostra, rostrums
ōvum (egg)	ōv-	-a	ōva	ova (egg cells)

You might also wonder how Latin *rōstrum*, "snout, beak," came to refer to a stage or other raised platform for public speaking. In ancient Rome, the prows or projecting tips of warships, unlike today, were hooked and used as battering rams. Evidently, they looked like beaks to the Romans, who called them *rōstra*, the plural of *rōstrum*. In time, the Romans developed the practice of cutting *rostra* out of captured ships as symbols of victory, and in 338 B.C. they adorned their famous platform for public speakers in the Forum with numerous *rōstra* as a sign of Roman greatness. Thus, the name of that which adorned their platform became transferred to the name of the platform itself—a sense which passed unchanged into English.

Latin Third Declension Nouns

While Latin first declension nouns are primarily feminine, and second declension nouns are masculine or neuter, third declension nouns are masculine, feminine, or neuter, and have a wide array of endings in their nominative singular.

Some of these nouns, like those of the first and second declensions, have been adopted essentially unchanged into English. Such English words include *genus* (jē´nəs; any class or group, especially a zoological or botanical category ranking below a family or subfamily and above a species), *opus* (a musical composition or other work by one artist, usually numbered in the order of publication), and *omen* (a sign or event supposed to portend good or evil or prophesy something about the future, as a big, beautiful bird landing on one's windowsill).

In some words, the nominative singular of the third declension ends in *-is*. In these instances, this ending can be dropped to yield a Latin base which, in turn, becomes an English root. Such Latin words include *avis*, "bird," and *cīvis*, "citizen," as illustrated below.

LATIN THIRD DECLENSION NOUNS YIELDING ENGLISH ROOTS

Nominative Singular	Inflectional Ending	Latin Base	English Root
avis (bird)	-is	av-	av-
cīvis (citizen)	-is	cīv-	civ-

To English *av-* (< L. *av-*, base of *avis*: bird), we can add a connecting *-i-* and the adjective-forming suffix *-an* (< L. *-ān-*, base of *ānus*: pertaining to, characterized by), forming *avian* (ā´vē·ən; of or pertaining to birds)—a "collateral adjective" for *bird* just as *canine* is a collateral adjective for *dog*, and *lunar* is a collateral adjective for *moon*. If we then remove the *-an* and attach the noun-forming suffix *-ary* (< L. *-āri-*, base of *-ārium*: a place for), we derive *aviary* (ā´vē·er´ē; a large cage, building, or other enclosure for housing birds, as in a zoo). In place of the *-ary*, we can then add *-at-* (< L. *-āt-*, base of *-ātus*: past participial suffix with the inflectional meaning: having been or having had) and the agentival suffix *-or* (< L. *-or*: one who or that which), yielding *aviator* or, etymologically, one who flies like a bird. And if we replace the *-tor* with *-trix* (< L. *-trix*: a feminine, noun-forming suffix having the basic meaning: a female of, or she who), we wind up with the now outdated and demeaning *aviatrix* (ā´vē·ā´ triks; a female aviator).

Similarly, to *civ-* (< L. *cīv-*, base of *cīvis*: citizen), the second English root in the table above, we can add the adjective-forming suffix *-ic* (< L. *-ic-*, base of *-icus*: pertaining to, characterized by), yielding *civic* (of or pertaining to a citizen or citizenship). If we then add an *-s* to the *-ic*, we obtain *civics* (the branch of political science dealing with the rights and responsibilities of citizens—though, etymologically, the *-ic* here is actually derived from Greek *-ikos* and only passes through Latin *-icus*). If we then discard this noun-forming suffix *-ics* and replace it with the adjective-forming suffix *-il* (< L. *-īl-*, base of *-īlis*: pertaining to, characterized by), we get *civil*. And by tacking on a connecting *-i-* and the normally adjective-forming suffix *-an* (< L. *-ān-*, base of *-ānus*: pertaining to, characterized by, belonging to, but used in this word as a noun-forming suffix with the basic meaning: one who or that which), we come up with *civilian*. Similarly, by adding different suffixes and even words to *civil*, we can construct such words and compounds as *civilize, civilization, civil rights, civil liberties,* and *civil disobedience.*

Despite these examples, we can rarely determine the base of a third declension Latin noun from its nominative singular. With few exceptions, we can do this only when the nominative ends in *-is*, which it seldom does. However, the genitive always ends in *-is* regardless of its gender, so by finding the genitive and by removing its final *-is*, we can almost always uncover the base of a third declension noun, which will in turn yield a derivative English root.

For example, the feminine noun *lēx*, "law," has the genitive *lēgis*. By dropping this *-is*, we expose its Latin base *lēg-*, which yields the English root *leg-*. Similarly, the masculine noun *rēx*, "king," has the genitive *rēgis*, and by discarding its *-is*, we reveal the Latin base *rēg-* and its derivative English root *reg-*. And the neuter noun *opus*, "work, labor," has the genitive *operis*, which in dropping its *-is*, yields both its base *oper-* and the identical English root *oper-*. This is all represented in the table below.

LATIN THIRD DECLENSION NOUNS YIELDING LATIN BASES AND ENGLISH ROOTS

Nominative Singular	Genitive Singular	Inflect. Ending	Latin Base	English Root
(F) lēx (law)	lēgis	-is	lēg-	leg-
(M) rēx (king)	rēgis	-is	rēg-	reg-
(N) opus (work, toil)	operis	-is	oper-	oper-

As usual, we can add prefixes, suffixes, and other elements to the English roots in the last column to create English words. To *leg-* (< L. *lēg-*, base of *lēgis*, genitive of *lēx*: law), we can affix the prefix *il-* (< L. *il-*, an assimilated form of *in-*: not, without) and the adjective-forming suffix *-al* (< L. *-āl-*, base of *-ālis*: pertaining to, characterized by), forming *illegal*. If we wish to verbalize the dissection, analysis, and reconstruction of this word, we would state: "*illegal* consists of three roots: *il-, leg-,* and *-al*. The *il-* is derived from Latin *il-*, which is an assimilated form of *in-*, which means 'not, without.' The *leg-* is derived from Latin *lēg-*, which is the base of *lēgis*, which is the genitive of *lēx*, which means 'law.' And the *-al* is derived from Latin *-āl-*, which is the base of *-ālis*, which is an adjective-forming suffix meaning 'pertaining to or characterized by.' Thus, when we put all of these elements together, we get 'pertaining to or characterized by (*-al*) without (*il-*) law (*leg-*).'" By switching prefixes and suffixes, we can create such additional "leg-" words as *illegality*, *legitimate*, *illegitimate*, *privilege*, and *legist* (lē´ jist; a scholar or expert in law). Then if we return to the original Latin genitive *lēgis* and Anglicize it by removing its macron and adding the appropriate roots, we can produce *legislature* and *overlegislate*; and by using the Anglicized nominative *lex*, we can form the legal phrases *lex non scripta* (unwritten law, hence common law) and *lex talionis* (the law of punishment in kind; hence, the law of retaliation; hence, an eye for an eye).

In the same way, to *reg-* (< L. *rēg-*, base of *rēgis*, genitive of *rēx*: king), the second English root in the table above, we can add the adjective-forming suffix *-al* (< L. *-ālis*: pertaining to, characterized by), yielding *regal*, which, etymologically and lexically, means "pertaining to or characterized by (*-al*) a king (*reg-*)," though it has developed the additional senses of "magnificent or splendid" or that which is befitting of a king, making *regal* a synonym for *royal*. However, if we remove the *-al* of *regal* and add a connecting *-i-* and the combining form *-cide* (< L. *-cīd-* [base of both *-cīdium*: the killing of AND *-cīda*: the killer of] + E. *-e*: silent final letter), we turn *regal* into *regicide* (the act of killing a king, or one who kills a king). And if we drop the *-i-* and *-cide* and replace them with *-alia* (< L. *-ālia*, a plural noun-forming suffix, often used in the names of ancient Roman festivals < *-āl-* [base of *-ālis*: pertaining to, characterized by] + *-i-*: connecting vowel + *-a*: neuter plural suffix), we derive *regalia* (ri·gā´lē· ə; the signs and symbols of royalty, as the crown and scepter, or the ceremonial attire or finery of royalty). Finally, if we substitute the noun-forming suffix *-ty* (< L. *-tās*: the quality, state, or condition of) for the terminal *-a* of *regalia*, we wind up with *regality*, a rare synonym for the much more common *royalty*, which itself derives, through Middle French, from Latin *rēg-*, making *royalty* and *regality*, as well as *royal* and *regal*, linguistic *doublets* (two or more words in a language that are derived through different routes from a common source).

With regard to *oper-* (< L. *oper-*, base of *operis*, genitive of *opus*: work, toil), the third English root in the table above, we can add *-at-* (< L. *-āt-*, base of *-ātus*: past participial suffix with the inflectional meaning: having been or having had, but used in this word as a verbal suffix with the general meaning: to cause, to make, to function, to manage) and a silent final *-e*, creating *operate* or, etymologically, "to cause or make (*-at-*) work (*oper-*)." If we then prefix this word with *co-* (< L. *co-*, an assimilated form of *com-*: with, together), we derive *cooperate* or "to cause or make (*-at-*) work (*oper-*) together (*co-*)." And if we insert the adjective-forming element *-iv-* (< L. *-īv-*, base of *-īvus*: tending to, inclined to) between the *-at* and *-e*, we form *cooperative*, which, with the addition of the prefix *un-* (< OE. *un-*: not, without; the reversal or removal of), becomes *uncooperative*—which is what you will be if you do not carefully read this book.

Now before leaving third declension nouns, we must examine one more area that is relevant to English words: plural forms. But to do so, we must now consider an additional factor that was not critical to know when constructing English words from third declension singular nouns: gender. Fortunately, in this declension both masculine and feminine nouns use the same plural ending and can be classified together, so we need only learn two plural forms—one for masculine and feminine nouns, and the other for neuter nouns.

Latin third declension nouns, as we have seen, have a genitive that ends in *-is*, and their bases can almost always be found by dropping this *-is*. To form their plurals, an *-ēs* is simply attached to their bases, and in English this *-ēs* drops its macron to become our plural *-es*. Thus, Latin *index*, "informer, indicator," has the genitive *indicis* with the resulting base *indic-*. By adding an *-ēs* to this base, we form the Latin plural *indicēs*, which becomes the English plural *indices*, an alternative to *indexes*. Similarly, Latin *cortex*, "tree bark, rind, shell," has the genitive *corticis* with the resulting base *cortic-*. By attaching an *-ēs* to this base, we form the Latin plural *corticēs*, which becomes English *cortices*, the plural of *cortex* (the outer layer or part, as of a plant or internal organ of a person or animal, e.g., the *adrenal cortex*). This can all be seen in the table below.

LATIN THIRD DECLENSION MASCULINE AND FEMININE PLURAL NOUNS

Nom. Singular	Gen. Sing.	Latin Base	Plural Ending	Latin Plural Word	English Plural Words
index (indicator)	indicis	indic-	-ēs	indicēs	indices, indexes
cortex (tree bark)	corticis	cortic-	-ēs	corticēs	cortices

I have selected these Latin words because their plural forms yield English words with essentially no change. This, however, is not a common occurrence, and as we have repeatedly seen, it is usually Latin bases which yield English roots to which prefixes and suffixes can be attached. But these examples will emphasize an important point about Latin and English pronunciation.

You should recall that the first declension feminine plural ending *-ae*, as in *antennae*, is pronounced "ī" in Latin but "ē" in English, yielding Latin "ȧn·te´nī" but English "an·ten´ē." Similarly, Latin *-ēs* is pronounced "ās" in Latin, but its English derivative *-es* is pronounced "ēz." Moreover, when *c* precedes these endings it is hard in Latin (like the *k* in *kiss*— Latin *c*'s are always hard) but soft in English (like the *s* in *see*). Thus, while Latin *indicēs* is pronounced "in´di·kās," English *indices* is pronounced "in´di·sēz´"; and while Latin *corticēs* is pronounced "kôr´ti·kās," English *cortices* is pronounced "kôr´ti·sēz´" Other English plurals of this ilk (type or class) include *appendices* (ə·pen´di·sēz´), an alternative plural of *appendix*, and *vertices* (vûr´ti·sēz´), an alternative plural of *vertex* (the highest point, as of a mountain or the head, or the apparent highest position of a star or other celestial body).

Finally, Latin *neuter* nouns of the third declension form their plurals by attaching an *-a* to the base of the nominative singular (which, again, is found by dropping the *-is* of the genitive singular), and this *-a* passes unchanged into English. Thus, Latin *opus*, "work, labor" has the genitive *operis* and the base *oper-*. By adding an *-a* to this base, we form the Latin plural *opera*, which passes unchanged into English as the plural of *opus*. Similarly, Latin *genus*, "birth, origin, race, kind, species," has the genitive *generis* and the base *gener-*. By adding an *-a* to this base, we form the Latin plural *genera*, which also passes unchanged into English as the plural of *genus*. This can all be viewed in the table below.

LATIN THIRD DECLENSION NEUTER PLURAL NOUNS

Nom. Singular	Gen. Sing	Latin Base	Plur. Ending	Latin Plur. Word	English Words
opus (work, labor)	operis	oper-	-a	opera	opera
genus (kind, species)	generis	gener-	-a	genera	genera

It is interesting to note that English *opera*, though originally a Latin plural noun, has become singular in English, at least in its more popular usage. Thus, if we want to refer to more than one opera, we must now add an -s to opera, creating, in effect, the double plural *operas*. The plural *genera*, which in Latin is pronounced "ge´ne·rȧ" (with a hard *g* as in *get*) in English is pronounced "jen´ər·ə" (with a soft *g* as in *Gemini*). Its singular *genus* refers in English to any class of things with common attributes but is more specifically used in scientific terminology to designate the first word in biological names that denote one or more species of animals or plants that forms a major subdivision of a family or subfamily. Through scientific convention, the genus designation always appears in italics with its first letter capitalized, and the species name, the second word in scientific classifications, also appears in italics but never has its first letter capitalized, even if it is a proper name. Thus, in *Homo sapiens*, *Homo* is the genus, and *sapiens* is the species. The family name for genera of related animals also has its conventions. It always appears in roman typeface (never in italics), its first letter is always capitalized, and it characteristically ends in -idae (< NL. *-idae*, plural of *-idēs* [< G. *-idai*, plural of *-idēs*]: the descendants or offspring of), which is affixed to the declensional base of the word that designates the genus, which is usually represented as the base of the genitive. So Latin *homō*, "human being," which is a third declension noun, has the genitive *hominis* and the base *homin-*. By affixing the ending -idae to this base, capitalizing the first letter, and romanizing the entire word, we get Hominidae, the human family, of which *Homo sapiens* is the only surviving species. Other family names include Canidae, the dog family, Felidae (fē´lə·dē), the cat family, and Orycteropodidae (ô·rik´tə·rō·päd´ə·dē´), the aardvark family—of which the aardvark, like human beings, is the only surviving species.

Latin Fourth Declension Nouns

The Latin fourth declension, like the third declension, contains masculine, feminine, and neuter nouns. However, unlike the third declension, it is a relatively small declension but does provide English with a few important derivatives. For our purposes, fourth declension masculine and feminine nouns can be treated together, while fourth declension neuter nouns will be examined separately.

Masculine and feminine nouns of the fourth declension always end in *-us* in the nominative singular (like masculine nouns of the second declension), and their bases can be found by dropping this *-us* or, in many cases, just the *-s*, or sometimes both—and these bases in turn form English roots. Thus, Latin *manus*, "hand," has the dual bases *manu-* and *man-*, which form English roots of the same spelling; and Latin *tribus*, "tribe," has the single base *trib-*, which also forms an English root of the same spelling. These forms are represented below.

LATIN FOURTH DECLENSION MASCULINE AND FEMININE NOUNS

Nominative Singular	Inflectional Ending	Latin Bases	English Roots
(F) manus (hand)	-u or -us	manu- or man-	manu- or man-
(M) tribus (tribe)	-us	trib-	trib-

To *manu-* (< L. *manu-*, base of *manus*: hand), we can add the adjective-forming suffix *-al* (< L. *-āl-*, base of *-ālis*: pertaining to, characterized by), forming *manual*, which functions as both an adjective and noun. If we then append the noun-forming suffix *-ism* (< G. *-ism-*, base of *-ismos*: the act or the result of the act of), we get *manualism* (the practice and advocacy of sign language, rather than lipreading and other oral and mechanical methods, as the primary means of communication among persons who are deaf). To *man-* (< L. *man-*, the second or alternate base of *manus*: hand), we can insert a connecting -*i*-, the root *cur*- (< L. *cūr*-, base of *cūra*: care, concern), and a silent final -*e*, forming *mani-cure*. And if we replace the connecting -*i*- with a connecting -*a*-, and the *cur*- with the diminutive element -*cl*- (< L. -*c(u)l*-, base of -*culus*: small, little, tiny), we obtain *manacle* (an old-fashioned device for shackling the hands, very much like handcuffs but having a relatively long metal chain used to connect each cuff). To *manacle* we can further add the negative prefix *un*- (< OE. *un*-: not, without; the reversal or removal of), forming *unmanacle*, which is what we may have to do with our intellects to contend with the Latin ablative (ab´lə·tiv; the Latin case indicating removal, separation, etc.; see page 190) *manū* in *manuscript*, *manufacture*, and *manumission* (a releasing or freeing, as from slavery or bondage). The *Emancipation Proclamation*, issued by Abraham Lincoln in September, 1862 to free the slaves is, etymologically, "the act, means, or result of (-*ion*) having (-*at*-) shouted (*clam*-) forth (*pro*-) the result of (-*ion*) having (-*at*-) taken (-*cip*-) the hand (*man*-) from (*e*-)."

With regard to *trib*- (< L. *trib*-, base of *tribus*: tribe), the third English root in the table above, we can add a silent -*e*, forming *tribe*. Or instead we can attach the adjective-forming suffix -*al* (< L. -*āl*-, base of -*ālis*: pertaining to, characterized by), creating *tribal*. And if we then append the noun-forming suffix -*ism* (< G. -*ism*-, base of -*ismos*: the act or the result of the act of), we get *tribalism* (the beliefs of or identification with and loyalty toward one's tribe or group), not to be confused with *tribadism*. Similarly, by adding the appropriate affixes to *trib*-, we can create *tribute* (a gift, payment, or other acknowledgment of appreciation, respect, or subjugation), *tribunal* (a court, committee, or seat of justice), *tributary* (a branch of a river or stream that flows into a larger body of water; also, a nation or state that pays tribute to a more powerful nation or state), and *contribution*, *distribution*, and *retribution* (repayment or retaliation for something done, as punishment for a crime).

As for the neuter nouns of the fourth declension, they always end in -*ū* in the nominative singular, and this ending can be dropped to find their bases, which often pass unchanged into English. Thus, *cornū*, "horn," has the base *corn*-, which yields the English root *corn*-; and *genū*, "knee," has the base *gen*-, which yields the English root *gen*-. These are illustrated below.

LATIN FOURTH DECLENSION NEUTER NOUNS

Nominative Sing.	Inflectional Ending	Latin Base	English Root
cornū (horn)	-ū	corn-	corn-
genū (knee)	-ū	gen-	gen-

From English *corn*- (< L. *corn*-, base of *cornū*: horn), we can simply drop the hyphen and produce *corn*, "a horny growth, as on the foot," which should not be confused with *corn*, the grain crop, which is derived from Old English *corn*. Then if we add the French diminutive -*et*, we get *cornet*, an instrument very much like a trumpet, which should also not to be confused with *coronet*, a small crown (< G. *korōn*- [base of *korōnē*]: crown + Fr. -*et*: a diminutive suffix having the basic meaning: small, little, tiny). If we then remove the -*et* from *cornet* and add the initial root *un*- (< L. *ūn*-, base of *ūnus*: one—this base has no relationship with the OE. prefix *un*-: not, without) and insert a connecting -*i*-, we derive *unicorn* (a mythological creature represented as a horse with a single horn growing out of its forehead). And if we replace the *un*- and -*i*- with *bi*- (< L. *bi*-, combining form of *bis*: two, twice, double), we come up with *bicorn*, a mythological creature in early French and English literature, usually depicted as a grotesquely obese animal that existed solely by devouring virtuous husbands. The bicorn, interestingly, has a counterpart in the Chichevache (chich´ə·väsh´), a mythological creature cited in early English literature that existed solely by devouring virtuous women and is usually depicted as a grotesquely underweight cow verging on starvation. As Geoffrey Chaucer wrote in 1386 in *The Clerk's Tale*, "O noble wyves, ful of heigh prudence, Lat noon humylitee youre tonge naille, ... Lest Chichevache yow swelwe in hire entraille!" If this is unclear to you, the 15th century monk and poet, John Lydgate, sums it up in one sentence: "*Chichevache* etith wymmen goode." In Greek mythology, a goat by the name of Amalthaea suckled Zeus as an infant, and as an adult Zeus made sure that one of her horns was always filled with whatever its owner wanted, a horn that is usually represented in art as overflowing with fruit, flowers, and grain. We call this overflowing horn the horn of plenty, or *cornucopia* (< L. *cornū*: horn + *cōpiae*: of plenty [the genitive of *cōpia*: plenty] < *co-* [an assimilated form of *com-*]: with, together + *(o)p-* [the base of *opis*, genitive of *ops*] wealth, riches + *-i(a)*: the act, process, condition, or result of + *-ae*: genitive suffix).

With regard to *gen-* (< L. *gen-*, base of *genū*: knee), the second English root in the table above, if we add a connecting *-i-* and the diminutive element *-cul-* (< L. *-cul-*, base of *-culum*: small, little, tiny), followed by *-at-* (< L. *-āt-*, base of *-ātus*: past participial suffix with the inflectional meaning: having been or having had) and a silent final *-e*, we get *geniculate* (jə·nik´yə·lit, -lāt´; having kneelike knots or joints, as on a shrub or tree). If we then replace the *-e* with the noun-forming suffix *-ion* (< L. *-iōn-*, base of *-iōnis*, genitive of *-iō*: the act, means, or result of), we turn the adjective *geniculate* into the noun *geniculation* (the state or condition of being geniculate). Then if we return to the original Latin word *genū* and Anglicize it by removing its macron and append *flect-* (< L. *flect-*, base of *flectus*, past participle of *flectere*: to bend) to it and reinstate the *-ion* (< L. *-iōn-*, base of *-iōnis*, genitive of *-iō*: the act, means, or result of), we get *genuflection* (the act of bending the knees and lowering the body, as a sign of respect or reverence). Finally, if we substitute the adjective-forming suffix *-ory* (< L. *-ōrius*: pertaining to one who or that which [< *-or*: one who + *-ius*: adjectival suffix]) for the noun-forming suffix *-ion*, we derive the seldom heard *genuflectory* (of or pertaining to genuflection) in which, if we replace its adjective-forming *-ory* with the noun-forming suffix *-or* (< L *-or*: one who or that which), we wind up with *genuflector* (one who genuflects)—a not very laudatory (praiseworthy, commendable) appellation (name, title, or designation).

Latin Fifth Declension Nouns

Latin fifth declension nouns, like fourth declension nouns, constitute a very small group of nouns but also supply English with some important derivatives. Grammatically, its nouns—like those of the first declension—are almost exclusively feminine. The nominative singular (and plural) always ends in *-ēs*, and this ending can be dropped to reveal its base, which then becomes an English root. Thus Latin *diēs*, "day," has the base *di-*, which yields the English root *di-*; and Latin *fidēs*, "faith, trust," has the base *fid*, which yields the English root *fid-*. These are shown below.

LATIN FIFTH DECLENSION NOUNS

Nominative Sing.	Inflectional Ending	Latin Base	English Root
(M) diēs (day)	-ēs	di-	di-
(F) fidēs (faith, trust)	-ēs	fid-	fid-

To *di-* (< L. *di-*, base of *diēs*: day), we can add the adjective-forming suffix *-al* (< L. *-āl-*, base of *-ālis*: pertaining to, characterized by), forming *dial* or "pertaining to (*-al*) day (*di-*)"—the sense development being that *dial* was originally short for *sundial*, an indicator that marked the hours of a day, which in this short form came to represent any knob or switch used to indicate or control the gradations on a machine or contrivance, such as a radio or television. If we then replace the *-al* on *dial* with the adjective- and noun-forming suffix *-ary* (< L. *-āri-*, base of *-ārius*: pertaining to, characterized by), we get *diary*, a book in which we record our daily thoughts and activities. If we then detach the *-ary* and exchange it for the obscure element *-urn-* (< L. *-urn-*, base of *-urnus*: a seldom used adjectival suffix often associated with time) and reinstate the adjective-forming suffix *-al* (< L. *-āl-*, base of *-ālis*: pertaining to, characterized by), we turn up *diurnal* (of or pertaining to day or daytime), the opposite of *nocturnal*. And if we prefix this word with the equally obscure element *ho-* (< L. *ho-*, a shortened form of *hoc*: this) and make a slight change in spelling, we derive *hodiernal* (of or pertaining to this day). A variety of other unusual but useful *di-*, "day," words exist, and three of these you may wish to work into conversation are *postmeridian* (of or pertaining to the afternoon—not to be confused with *post meridiem*, the phrase for which P.M. stands), *quotidian* (daily, ordinary, commonplace), and *circadian* (of or relating to biological rhythms recurring over 24-hour periods, as in the sentence, "Writing this book has wreaked havoc on my circadian rhythms").

Similarly, to English *fid-* (< L. *fid-*, base of *fidēs*: faith, trust), the second English root in the table above, we can affix the obscure element *-el-* (< L. *-ēl-*, base of *-ēlis*, an adjectival suffix of uncertain origin, perhaps modeled upon *-ālis*, with the *ē* of *fidēs* replacing the *ā* of *-ālis*) followed by a connecting *-i-* and the noun-forming suffix *-ty* (< L. *-tās*: the quality, state, or condition of), yielding *fidelity*. Or if we remove the *-ity* and prefix this word with *in-* (< L. *in-*: in, into, within), we turn *fidelity* into *infidel*. And if we drop the *-el* and replace the prefix *in-* with the prefix *per-* (< L. *per-*: through, throughout) and add the noun-forming suffix *-y* (< L. *-ia*: the act, process, or condition of), we wind up with *perfidy* (a deliberate and willful breach of trust or faith, as in marriage). Other words in this group include *confident*, *diffident* (lacking confidence; timid, shy), and *fiduciary* (fi·dōō´shē·er´ē; of or designating that which is held in trust for someone or something, as property; or pertaining to that which has value because the public has confidence in it, as paper money).

Latin Adjectives

Latin adjectives occur in three declensions, which are adopted from the five declensions used for nouns. These include the first and second declensions (which are classified together) and the third declension.

As in English, Latin adjectives modify, limit, or describe certain nouns. But while English adjectives always retain one form regardless of who or what they are modifying (e.g., a *small* boy, a *small* girl, a *small* table), Latin adjectives change their inflectional endings to agree with the case (nominative, genitive, dative, etc.), gender (masculine, feminine, or neuter), and number (singular or plural) of the noun they are modifying. For example, an adjective that modifies a nominative masculine singular noun must use a nominative masculine singular ending, and an adjective that modifies a genitive feminine plural noun must use a genitive feminine plural ending. Thus, with six cases, three genders, and two numbers, the permutations (the different possible combinations or arrangement of the elements of a set) are considerable, and this is one reason Latin is such a difficult language to learn.

But since we are not seeking to learn Latin or to construct Latin phrases or sentences, we need not normally concern ourselves with agreement of adjectives with nouns. We need to learn only a very few case endings, and most of these we already know since they are borrowed from the first, second, and third noun declensions. So working with Latin adjectives will be as much a review of old material as an introduction to new, and when we dissect, analyze, and reconstruct English words derived from Latin adjectives we will do so in the same manner that we have been doing for nouns. Therefore, if any of the following information is unclear to you, please check those previous sections that describe first, second, and third declension nouns.

Latin First and Second Declension Adjectives

Latin first and second declension adjectives are classified together because they use the feminine endings of the first declension and the masculine and neuter endings of the second declension. So together these two declensions supply the endings for all three genders.

As you know, first declension *feminine* nouns end in *-a* in the nominative singular and *-ae* in the nominative plural; second declension *masculine* nouns regularly end in *-us* in the singular and *-ī* in the plural; and second declension *neuter* nouns end in *-um* in the singular and *-a* in the plural. These constitute six different endings, of which the proper one must be attached to the base of any Latin adjective that falls within the category we call "first and second declension Latin adjectives" to enable it to agree with the noun it is modifying. If, for example, an adjective is to modify a feminine plural noun, in this category of adjectives it must attach the feminine *-ae* plural ending to its base, since this is the only feminine plural ending in this group. Similarly, if an adjective in this category must modify a neuter singular noun, it must attach the neuter singular ending *-um* to its base since this is the only neuter singular ending in this group. So regardless of what gender or number the original adjective is in, you must now affix the appropriate ending to its base so it agrees with the noun it is modifying. The six possible endings are shown below for the Latin adjective *firmus*, "firm."

LATIN FIRST AND SECOND DECLENSION ADJECTIVAL FORMS OF *FIRMUS*

Gender and Number	Adjective Base	Adjectival Ending	Latin Adjective
Masculine singular	firm-	-us	firmus
Feminine singular	firm-	-a	firma
Neuter singular	firm-	-um	firmum
Masculine plural	firm-	-ī	firmī
Feminine plural	firm-	-ae	firmae
Neuter plural	firm-	-a	firma

When presenting a Latin adjective in the etymology of an English word, English dictionaries invariably provide only the masculine singular form since the Latin word is cited in isolation (it is not in a phrase or sentence) and there are no other words for it to agree with. Therefore any one of these six Latin endings would do as well as any other one in showing the origin of the English word. But through tradition, the masculine form is the one that is cited, and this is the form I have been using—and will continue to use—in this book.

For example, the base of all the adjectives shown in the table above is *firm-*, from which we derive the English root *firm-* (not shown in the table). Now consider the following etymology: "To the English root *firm-* (< L. *firm-*, base of *firmus*: firm), we can add the prefix *af-* (< L. *af-*, an assimilated form of *ad-*: to, toward), forming the word *affirm*." This is a typical example of the type of analysis I provide in this Short Course and is structurally similar to that provided in dictionary etymologies. But note the opening statement: "To the root *firm-* (< L. *firm-*, base of *firmus*: firm) . . ." I have used the masculine form! To be entirely accurate, I should have written, "To the root *firm-* (< L. *firm-*, base of the masculine singular *firmus*, the feminine singular *firma*, the neuter singular *firmus*, the masculine plural *firmī*," and so on down the list since *firm-* is the base of all of these forms. But this would be ridiculous. So in providing etymologies of English words, we simply choose one form to cite, and, for better or worse, this has traditionally been the masculine.

Of course, in those few English phrases that use Latin adjectives, such as *terra firma* (firm earth, i.e., solid ground as opposed to water or air), the adjective must agree with the noun, and in this example *firma* is used because it agrees with *terra*, which is a first declension feminine singular noun. But for the most part, you need not concern yourself with agreement of forms, and when you analyze and reconstruct Latin adjectives you will generally do so by using the masculine form.

But not all nominative masculine singular adjectives end in *-us*. As you will recall from our discussion of second declension masculine nouns, some masculine nouns end in *-er* in the nominative singular, but you cannot drop the *-er* to get a word's base. So in those cases in which an adjective ends in *-er*, you will first have to find its genitive, which always ends in *-ī*, and then drop the *-ī* of that genitive to get its base. Thus, for *sacer*, "holy, sacred," its genitive is *sacrī-*, and its base is *sacr-*. To this base, then, you must affix the appropriate adjectival ending from the table below—with the exception of the nominative masculine singular *-er* which is not an inflectional ending and cannot be used—to form an adjective that will agree in case, gender, and number with whatever noun it is modifying, e.g., the nominative feminine singular, the nominative neuter plural, etc.

LATIN FIRST AND SECOND DECLENSION ADJECTIVAL FORMS OF *SACER*

Gender and Number	Adjective Base	Adjectival Ending	Latin Adjective
Masculine singular	(none in nomin.)	(none available)	sacer
Feminine singular	sacr-	-a	sacra
Neuter singular	sacr-	-um	sacrum
Masculine plural	sacr-	-ī	sacrī
Feminine plural	sacr-	-ae	sacrae
Neuter plural	sacr-	-a	sacra

The only difference between this paradigm and the one for *firmus* is that the nominative masculine singular, which ends in *-er*, is not constructed upon the paradigm base, which is *sacr-*. Everything else is the same. The base of all of these forms—with the exception of the nominative masculine singular—is *sacr-*, which yields the English root *sacr-*, to which we can add prefixes and suffixes to form a variety of English words. However, since we express Latin adjectives in the masculine singular form but there is no way to account for the base of a masculine singular *-er* word without citing its genitive form, we must always include a reference to this genitive in our etymologies.

For example, consider the opening line in a typical construction for an adjective beginning in *sacr-*, such as *sacrifice*: "To *sacr-* (< L. *sacr-*, base of *sacrī*, genitive of *sacer*: sacred, holy), we can add. . . ." Thus, by expressing the adjective in the nominative masculine singular, we must bring into discussion the genitive *sacrī*. By contrast, if we were to use the nominative feminine singular, we could simplify the opening line to: "To *sacr-* (< L. *sacr-*, base of *sacra*: sacred, holy), we can add . . . . " Such is a drawback of the male gender.

Latin Third Declension Adjectives

Latin third declension adjectives use the masculine, feminine, and neuter endings of third declension nouns. Specifically, the nominative singular ends in *-is* for the masculine and feminine and *-ēs* for their plurals. And the neuter, which practically never occurs in English derivatives, ends in *-e* in the nominative singular and *-ia* in the plural. These constitute four different endings (two if we discount the neuter forms), and any one of them must be attached to the base of any Latin adjective that falls within the category we call "third declension Latin adjectives" to enable it to agree with the noun it is modifying. For example, if an adjective in this category is to modify a neuter singular noun, then it must attach the neuter singular ending *-e* to its base since this is the only available option. A simplified paradigm for the adjective *fortis*, "strong, brave," is presented below.

LATIN THIRD DECLENSION ADJECTIVAL FORMS OF *FORTIS*

Gender and Number	Adjective Base	Adjectival Ending	Latin Adjective
Masculine singular	fort-	-is	fortis
Feminine singular	fort-	-is	fortis
Neuter singular	fort-	(-e)	(forte)
Masculine plural	fort-	-ēs	fortēs
Feminine plural	fort-	-ēs	fortēs
Neuter plural	fort-	(-ia)	(fortia)

As with first and second declension adjectives, English dictionaries invariably provide only the masculine singular form, so this is the form we should be familiar with. But with third declension adjectives, the feminine singular form, which ends in *-is*, is identical to the masculine form, so we need not make a distinction here. The Latin adjective *fortis* not only illustrates this but also provides English with many common derivatives. For example, to the English root *fort-* (< L. *fort-*, base of *fortis*: strong, brave) we can add a connecting *-i-*, the root *-fic-* (< L. *-fic-*, base of *-ficāre*: to make or do repeatedly [< *-ficere*, combining form of *facere*: to make, to do]), a second root *-at-* (< L. *-āt-*, base of *-ātus*: past participial suffix with the inflectional meaning: having been, having had), and the noun-forming suffix *-ion* (< L. *-iōn-*, base of *-iōnis*, genitive of *-iō*: the act, means, or result of), resulting in *fortifica-*

tion, or "the act, means, or result of (*-ion*) having (*-at-*) repeatedly made (*-fic-*) strong (*fort-*)." If we then add the prefixes *un-* (< OE. *un-*: not, without; the reversal or removal of) and *com-* (< L. *com-*: with, together; also used intensively, i.e., completely, thoroughly, throughout) and replace the *-ification* with the suffix *-able* (< L. *-ā-*: connecting vowel + *-b(i)l(is)*: tending to be, inclined to be + E. *-e*: silent final letter), we get *uncomfortable*, or "tending to be (*-able*) not (*un-*) completely (*com-*) strong (*fort-*)." And if we replace the prefixes *un-* and *com-* with the single prefix *ef-* (< L. *ef-*, an assimilated form of *ex-*: out, out of) and exchange the combining form *-able* for the native suffix *-less* (< OE. *-lēas*: -less < *lēas*: free from, lacking, without), we convert *uncomfortable* into *effortless*. Other words derived from *fort-* include *fort*, *forte* (fôrt, but now commonly pronounced fôr′tā; a person's strong point, or an area in which one excels), *fortitude*, *discomfort*, *fortress*, and *fortissimo* (a musical directive to sing or play an instrument very loudly < Ital. *fort-* [base of *forte*: strong, loud < L. *fortis*: strong, brave] + *-issimo* [< L. *-issimus*]: a superlative suffix having the basic meaning: of the highest degree or order; most).

There is also another class of third declension adjectives in which the nominative masculine singular ends in *-er* (similar to those second declension masculine nouns and adjectives that end in *-er*). To find the base of these adjectives, we must first find the genitive, which ends in *-is* (this should not be confused with the second declension genitive, which ends in *ī*), and then drop the *-is* or *-s* of that genitive. Thus, for *ācer*, "sharp, sour," the genitive is *acris*, and its base is *acr-* or *acri-*. To this base, then, we must affix the appropriate adjectival ending from the table below—with the exception of the nominative masculine singular *-er* which is not an inflectional ending and cannot be used—to form an adjective that will agree in case, gender, and number with whatever noun it is modifying.

LATIN THIRD DECLENSION ADJECTIVAL FORMS OF *ĀCER*

Gender and Number	Adjective Base	Adjectival Ending	Latin Adjective
Masculine singular	(none in nomin.)	(none available)	ācer
Feminine singular	ācr- or ācri-	-is	ācris
Neuter singular	ācr-	(-e)	(ācre)
Masculine plural	ācr-	-ēs	ācrēs
Feminine plural	ācr-	-ēs	ācrēs
Neuter plural	ācr-	(-ia)	(ācria)

As is the case of second declension adjectives whose nominative masculine singular ends in *-er*, we can express the base of *ācer* only with regard to its genitive. As an example, we can verbalize *acrimonious* (harsh or bitter in speech or behavior) in the following manner: "*acrimonious* consists of three roots: *acri-*, *-moni-*, and *-ous*. The *acri-* is derived from Latin *ācri-*, which is an alternative base of *ācris*, which is the genitive of *ācer*, which means 'sharp or sour.' The *-moni-* is derived from Latin *-mōnia*, which means 'the quality, state, or condition of.' And the *-ous* is derived from Latin *-ōsus*, which is an adjective-forming suffix meaning 'full of, abounding in, characterized by, or like.' So when we put all of these roots together we get, 'full of or abounding in (*-ous*) the quality, state, or condition of (*-moni-*) sharp or sour (*acri-*).'"

Comparison of Adjectives

One other category of Latin-derived adjectives that has produced a wealth of English derivatives involves the "comparison" of adjectives, or what may be defined as "the three degrees to which an adjective can modify a noun." This is illustrated in English by such triplets as *big, bigger, biggest* and *pretty, prettier, prettiest.* These degrees even have names: the first is the *positive*, which simply denotes an amount, quality, or quantity of something, or what we can designate as "some"; the second is the *comparative*, which denotes "more" of that amount, quality, or quantity and therefore involves the *comparison* of two things, concepts, or people; and the third is the *superlative*, which denotes the "most" of that amount, quality, or quantity and therefore involves the comparison of three or more things, concepts, or people.

In English, the positive can have various endings, but, as you can see, the comparative regularly ends in *-er* and the superlative in *-est.* With regard to word-building, English comparatives and superlatives can therefore be formed by simply adding *-er* or *-est* to the end of suitable words, and in this manner we can turn *sweet* into *sweeter* or *sweetest*, and *dark* into *darker* or *darkest.*

Latin also has regular endings. When represented in the masculine singular form, the positive usually ends in *-us*, the comparative in *-ior*, and the superlative in *-issimus.* Therefore, Latin comparatives and superlatives can be formed by adding *-ior* and *-issimus*, respectively, to the base of the positive. For example, the Latin adjective *lātus*, "wide, broad," has the base *lāt-*. To this base, we can add the comparative suffix *-ior*, forming *lātior*, "wider, broader," or we can add the superlative suffix *-issimus*, forming *lātissimus*, "widest, broadest." Similarly, Latin *longus*, "long," has the base *long-*, to which we can add the comparative suffix *-ior*, forming *longior*, "longer," or the superlative suffix *-issimus*, forming *longissimus*, "longest." These and other "regular" adjectives are illustrated below.

LATIN COMPARISON OF REGULAR ADJECTIVES

Positive	Comparative	Superlative
lātus (wide, broad)	lātior (wider, broader)	lātissimus (widest, broadest)
longus (long)	longior (longer)	longissimus (longest)
fortis (strong, brave)	fortior (stronger, braver)	fortissimus (strongest, bravest)
lentus (slow)	lentior (slower)	lentissimus (slowest)
altus (high)	altior (higher)	altissimus (highest)

English has not borrowed or constructed many words from these regular Latin comparatives and superlatives, and most of the ones it has are of a highly specialized nature. For example, English *latissimus* (< L. *lātissimus*: widest, broadest < *lāt-* [base of *lātus*]: wide, broad + *-issimus*: a superlative suffix having the basic meaning: of the highest degree or order; most) turns up in the names of a number of muscles, the most notable being the *latissimus dorsi* (< L. *lātissimus*: widest, broadest + *dorsī*, genitive of *dorsum*: the back; hence, "the broadest of the back"), either of two broad, flat muscles in the back that draws an arm backward and downward. Similarly, *longissimus* (< L. *longissimus*: longest < *long-* [base of *longus*]: long + *-issimus*: a superlative suffix having the basic meaning: of the highest degree or order; most), turns up in *longissimus capitis* (< L. *longissimus*: longest + *capitis*, genitive of *caput*: the head; hence, "the longest of the head"), the muscle responsible for keeping the head erect and drawing it backward or to one side.

In addition to their appearance in anatomical terms, Latin superlatives are commonly used by the Italians for musical directives, and besides *fortissimo* (a directive to sing or play an instrument very loudly), we have derived such terms from them as *pianissimo* (a directive to sing or play an instrument very softly or quietly), *lentissimo* (a directive to sing or play an instrument very slowly), and *altissimo* (a directive to sing or play an instrument in a very high range, specifically the second octave above the treble staff).

In English, besides our "regular" formations, such as *big, bigger, biggest* and *pretty, prettier, prettiest*, we also have "irregular" formations, such as *good, better, best*; and *bad, worse, worst*. Latin, too, has a number of irregular formations. In fact, Latin irregulars furnish English with far more derivatives than do its regulars. Below are five sets of irregular Latin adjectives that have supplied English with a variety of derivative words.

LATIN COMPARISON OF IRREGULAR ADJECTIVES

Positive	Comparative	Superlative
bonus (good)	melior (better)	optimus (best)
malus (bad)	pējor (worse)	pessimus (worst)
magnus (great)	major (greater)	maximus (greatest)
superus (above)	superior (higher)	suprēmus (highest)
parvus (small)	minor (smaller)	minimus (smallest)

Without reading the caption of the table or the preceding paragraph, you might think that this table contains both English and Latin words, for five of these words—*bonus, major, minor, superior,* and *minimus* (the medical name of the pinky or small toe) have come down to us unchanged. And the others have just required minor surgery with a little post-operative care. For example, if we take Latin *pessimus*, "worst," (the second word in the third column), and remove its inflectional ending *-us*, we expose its Latin base *pessim-*, which in turn becomes the English root *pessim-*, to which we can add the noun-forming suffix *-ist* (< G. *-ist-*, base of *-istēs*: one who), forming *pessimist* (a person who generally looks negatively or unfavorably upon events or conditions). Likewise—but with one minor step added—we can take Latin *optimus*, "best," (immediately above *pessimus* in the table), convert it into its neuter form *optimum*, remove its *-um* ending to reveal its base *optim-*, derive from this base English *optim-*, and add *-ist* (< G. *-ist-*, base of *-istēs*: one who) to this base, yielding *optimist*. And to both *pessimist* and *optimist* we can attach the adjective-forming suffix *-ic* (< G. *-ik-*, base of *-ikos*: pertaining to, characterized by), forming, respectively, *pessimistic* and *optimistic*. Similarly, by making minor changes and substitutions in the three remaining words in this column, *maximus, suprēmus,* and *minimus*, we can, respectively, turn these words into English *maximal, supreme,* and *minimal*. And what we've done in this column, we could just as easily have done in the other two.

In English, there are many words that cannot form comparatives and superlatives simply by adding *-er* or *-est*, such as *powerful* and *rapid*. For these words, we have to use the slightly cumbersome phrases *more powerful* and *most powerful*, or *more rapid* and *most rapid*. Similarly in Latin, some words do not lend themselves to the regular or irregular inflectional endings needed to compare adjectives, and for such words, as *ēgregius*, "remarkable" (from which we derive *egregious* [i·grē´jəs]: remarkably bad), Latin inserts its adverbs *magis*, "more," or *maximē*, "most," before the positive to achieve the same effect as our "more" or "most." In certain cases, however, Latin lacks only one of the three degrees in the comparison of adjectives and must resort to such circumlocution (a wordy and roundabout way of expressing an idea or making a point) in only this degree. But from the other two degrees, we still derive ample English words. Consider, for example, the four incomplete sets of adjectives below, which include one preposition, *ante*, as the form from which Latin *anterior* was developed since the "proper" Latin positive **anterus* does not exist.

LATIN INCOMPLETE COMPARISON OF ADJECTIVES AND PREPOSITION

Positive	Comparative	Superlative
juvénis (young, youthful)	jūnior (younger)	————
senex (old, old man)	senior (older)	————
————	prior (former)	prīmus (first)
ante (before, in front of)	anterior (more in front of)	————
————	ulterior (farther)	ultimus (farthest)

Again, without reading the caption, you might think that half of the words in this table are in English, for five of them—*jūnior*, *senior*, *prior*, *anterior*, and *ulterior*—have come to us essentially unchanged. As for the others, if you look to the lower right, you'll note Latin *ultimus*, "farthest." If we replace its masculine *-us* ending with a feminine *-a*, it becomes Latin *ultima*, which in turn yields English *ultima* (the last syllable in a word), a word we already met in conjunction with *penult* and *antepenult*. If you now look catty-corner (diagonally) to the upper left, you will see *juvenis*, "young, youthful." This is almost certainly a third declension adjective because it ends in *-is*, an inflectional ending which if removed reveals the Latin base *juven-* and, hence, the English root *juven-*. To this root, then, we can add the adjective-forming element *-il-* (< L. *-īl-* base of *-īlis*: pertaining to, characterized by) and a silent final *-e*, yielding *juvenile*. And if we discard the *-il-* and replace it with another adjectival-forming element *-at-* (< L. *-āt-*, base of *-ātus*: past participial suffix with the inflectional meaning: having been or having had) and then prefix this entire form with *re-* (< L. *re-*: back, again), we derive *rejuvenate*. If we then wish to create a Latin-Old English hybrid, we can replace the final *-e* of *juvenile* with *-ed* (< OE. *-ed*: a past participial suffix with the inflectional ending: having been or having had) and add a second prefix *un-* (< OE. *un-*: not, without, the reversal or removal of), forming *unrejuvenated*.

If you look below *juvenis*, you will see *senex*, "old, old man." Since this word has an odd ending, it is probably a third declension word, and either through intelligent guesswork or with a little help from your dictionary, you can determine that its genitive is *senis* and its base and resulting English root are *sen-*. To this root, we can then add the same adjective-forming element *-il-* (< L. *-īl-* base of *-īlis*: pertaining to, characterized by) and *-e* that we affixed to *juven-* above, but instead of turning up *juvenile*, this time we get *senile*. And if we replace the *-il-* with the noun-forming element *-at-* (< L. *-āt-*, base of *-ātus*: the office or holder of the office of; originally, a past participial suffix with the inflectional meaning, "having been or having had," but later becoming, in certain words, a substantive [noun] suffix), we derive *senate*—the etymology of which gives you some idea of the age and sex of the people who first composed (and to a great extent still do compose) these bodies.

Finally, if you glance over to the right side of the table, above *ultimus*, you will observe *prīmus*, "first." If we remove its obvious masculine ending *-us*, this will reveal its Latin base *prīm-*, which, after dropping the macron above *ī*, becomes English *prim-*. And if to this root we add the adjective-forming suffix *-ary* (< L. *-ārius*: pertaining to, characterized by), we turn up *primary*. If we then substitute the adjective-forming suffix *-al* (< L. *-āl-*, base of *-ālis*: pertaining to, characterized by) for the adjective-forming suffix *-ary*, we derive *primal*, a word which structurally is very similar to *primary* but semantically is quite different. If we then wish to get a little fancy, we can remove the *-al* from *primal* and attach a connecting *-i-*, the root *grav-* (< L. *grav-*, base of *gravis*: heavy), the adjective-forming suffix *-id* (< L. *-id*, base of *-idus*: tending to be, inclined to be), and a final feminine *-a* (< L. *-a*: feminine singular suffix of the first declension), resulting in *primigravida* (prī′mi·grav′i·də; a woman pregnant for the first time), or "she (*-a*) who tends to be (*-id*) first (*prim-*) heavy (*grav-*)."

Latin Verbs

With regard to the development of English vocabulary, Latin verbs fall within four broad categories: present active infinitives (referred to in this book as simply "infinitives"), perfect passive participles (referred to in this book as "past participles"), present active participles (referred to in this book as "present participles"), and gerundives. And every Latin verb has numerous forms and generally one base in each of these four categories. Thus, while Latin nouns and adjectives, regardless of their number of inflectional endings, usually have one base per word, Latin verbs characteristically have four.

Moreover, within each of these four categories of verb forms, Latin verbs are divided into four groupings or *conjugations* based on similarities in their inflectional endings. Thus, conjugations serve the same function for verbs as declensions serve for nouns and adjectives, and it is important that we learn the fundamentals of these forms. Of the four categories of verb forms, the infinitive is the primary and most important one. This is the form upon which the three other categories are based and is therefore the form with which we must begin.

Infinitives

Infinitives are the "to" forms of verbs, represented in English by such phrases as "to walk" or "to go." In Latin, however, only one word is used, and its inflectional ending both identifies the word as being an infinitive and determines to which of the four conjugations it belongs. The "regular" infinitives of the four conjugations can always be identified by the last three letters in each verb, which are as follows:

LATIN REGULAR INFINITIVE ENDINGS

First Conjugation	Second Conjugation	Third Conjugation	Fourth Conjugation
-āre	-ēre	-ere	-īre

Thus, we can immediately identify the Latin verb *clāmāre*, "to call out, cry out, shout," as a first conjugation verb from its *-āre* ending. Likewise, we can identify *monēre*, "to warn, to advise," as a second conjugation verb from its *-ēre* ending. *Scrībere*, "to scratch, to incise, to write," is clearly a third conjugation verb because of its *-ere* ending (though it is easy to confuse this conjugation with the previous *-ēre* conjugation); and *audīre*, "to hear," is unmistakably a fourth conjugation verb because of its unique *-īre* ending. If we remove the infinitive endings from each of these words, we reveal the word's "infinitive base"; and by removing the macron, if present, from this base we derive an English root. This is all described in the table below.

LATIN INFINITIVES YIELDING LATIN BASES AND ENGLISH ROOTS

Conjugation	Infinitive Word	Inflect. Ending	Infin. Base	English Root
First	clāmāre (to call out)	-āre	clām-	clam-
Second	monēre (to warn)	-ēre	mon-	mon-
Third	scrībere (to write)	-ere	scrīb-	scrib-
Fourth	audīre (to hear)	-īre	aud-	aud-

With regard to word building, the English roots derived from Latin verbs are no different from the roots derived from Latin nouns and adjectives, and to each of them we can add prefixes, suffixes, and other roots to form English words. For example, to *clam-* (< L. *clām-*, base of *clāmāre*: to call out, cry out, shout), the first English root in the table above, we can attach the noun-forming suffix *-or* (< L. *-or*: the quality, state, or condition of), yielding *clamor* (klam´ər; a loud noise or uproar). If we then add the adjective-forming suffix *-ous* (< L. *-ōsus*: full of, abounding in, characterized by, like) to this word, we derive *clamorous*. To *mon-* (< L. *mon-*, base of *monēre*: to warn, to advise), the second English root in the table above, we can attach a connecting *-u-* and the noun-forming suffix *-ment* (< L. *-ment-*, base of *-mentum*: the act, means, or result of), forming *monument*. And by appending to this word the adjective-forming suffix *-al* (< L. *-āl-*, base of *-ālis*: pertaining to, characterized by), we derive *monumental*. To *scrib-* (< L. *scrīb-*, base of *scrībere*: to scratch, to incise, to write), the third English root in the table above, we can add the prefix *in-* (< L. *in-*: in, into, within) and a silent final *-e*, yielding *inscribe*. Or if we replace the *in-* with *trans-* (< L. *trāns-*: over, across, beyond), we obtain *transcribe*. Finally, to *aud-* (< L. *aud-*, base of *audīre*: to hear), the fourth English root in the table above, we can attach a connecting *-i-* and *-bl-* (< L. *-b(i)l-*, base of *-bilis*: tending to be, inclined to be), followed by a silent final *-e*, yielding *audible*. And if we prefix this word with *in-* (< L. *in-*: not, without), we convert *audible* into *inaudible*.

These are just a few examples of how infinitives of Latin verbs have produced English words. But in addition to these regular infinitive verbs, there is a closely related group called "deponent" verbs (which include present *passive* infinitives as distinguished from the present *active* infinitives we have been calling "infinitives") that have also produced a number of English derivatives. What is odd about these verbs is that while their inflectional endings are passive in construction, their meanings are active. From our point of view, once we learn their inflectional endings (which are very similar to the infinitives we have just covered), we can treat them the same as regular infinitives. For the sake of comparison, in the following table I have placed the infinitive endings of deponent verbs below the infinitive endings of regular verbs.

Latin Inflectional Endings of Two Verb Forms

Verb Form	First Conjugation	Second Conjugation	Third Conjugation	Fourth Conjugation
Infinitive (regular verbs)	-āre	-ēre	-ere	-īre
Infinitive (deponent verbs)	-ārī	-ērī	-ī	-īrī

With the exception of the third conjugation, the only difference between the infinitive endings of regular and deponent verbs is the final letter, which is always *-ī* for deponent infinitives and *-e* for regular infinitives. And in the third conjugation, the deponent *-ī* stands alone, "replacing" the entire regular infinitive *-ere*. So it should not be difficult to learn these forms.

Thus, the Latin verb *luctārī*, "to struggle," can immediately be identified as a first conjugation deponent verb from its *-ārī* ending; *verērī*, "to fear," can likewise be identified as a second conjugation deponent verb from its *-ērī* ending; *gradī*, "to step, to walk, to go," is unmistakably a third conjugation deponent verb because of its unique *-ī* ending; and *sortīrī*, "to cast lots," can quickly be recognized as a fourth conjugation deponent verb from its *-īrī* ending. If we remove the deponent ending from each of these words, this will reveal each word's deponent (or infinitive) base, which will often become an English root without change. This is summarized in the table below.

Latin Deponent Verbs Yielding Latin Bases and English Roots

Conjugations	Infinitive	Inflect. Ending	Infin. Base	English Root
First	luctārī (to struggle)	-ārī	luct-	luct-
Second	verērī (to fear)	-ērī	ver-	ver-
Third	gradī (to step, walk, go)	-ī	grad-	grad-
Fourth	sortīrī (to cast lots)	-īrī	sort-	sort-

As with regular infinitives, we can add prefixes, suffixes, and other roots to each of these English roots to form English words. For example, to English *luct-* (< L. *luct-*, base of *luctārī*: to struggle), we can add the prefix *re-* (< L. *re-*: back, again) and the adjective-forming suffix *-ant* (< L. *-ant-*, base of *-antis*, genitive of *-āns*: present participial suffix equivalent in meaning to E. *-ing*, as in "the whirling dervish"), producing *reluctant*. Or if we remove the *re-* and replace it with the prefixes *in-* (< L. *in-*: not, without) and *e-* (< L. *ē-*, variant of *ex-*: out, out of) and substitute a connecting *-a-*, the root *-bl-* (< L. *-b(i)l-*, base of *-bilis*: tending to, inclined to), and silent final *-e* for the suffix *-ant*, we derive *ineluctable* (incapable of being avoided; inescapable, inevitable), which is a very serviceable word. Similarly, to *ver-* (< L. *ver-*, base of *verērī*: to fear), the second English root in the table above, we can attach the prefix *re-* (< L. *re-*: back, again) and the silent final *-e*, yielding the verb *revere* (to regard with great respect tinged with fear or awe; venerate). And if we remove the final *-e* from this verb and replace it with the adjective-forming suffix *-ent* (< L. *-ent-*, base of *-entis*, genitive of *-ēns*: present participial suffix equivalent in meaning to E. *-ing*), we convert the verb *revere* into the adjective *reverent*.

To *grad-* (< L. *grad-*, base of *gradī*: to step, to walk, to go), the third English root in the table above, we can simply attach a silent final *-e*, yielding *grade*, which, etymologically, means a degree or step, as reflected in rank, seniority, prestige, etc. Or if we remove the -e, affix the element -at- (< L. -āt-, base of -ātus: past participial suffix with the inflectional meaning: having been or having had) and the noun-forming suffix -ion (< L. -iōn-, base of -iōnis, genitive of -iō: the act, means, or result of), and then prefix this whole formation with de- (< L. dē-: away from, off, down), we get *degradation*, which, etymologically, is "the act, means, or result (-ion) of having gone (-at-) down (de-)." Finally, to *sort-* (< L. sort-, base of sortīrī: to cast lots), the last English root in the table above, we can simply drop the hyphen, forming English *sort*. Or if we like obscure words, we can attach a connecting -i-, the root *leg-* (< L. leg-, base of legere: to gather, to choose, to read), and a silent final -e, yielding *sortilege* (the divination or prophecy of the future by casting and gathering lots).

Phonetic Shift

Before proceeding to other verb forms, I should say something about one more area concerning Latin spelling and pronunciation: *phonetic shift*. When certain Latin verbs and verb bases occur in other than first position within a word (usually following a prefix), their first vowel is sometimes "shortened" or "weakened," often becoming another vowel. This process is called phonetic shift because of the "shift" in the *phōnē* or sound (cf. *telephone* and *phonograph*) of the vowel. We should not, however, be particularly surprised with this process because we do the same thing in English. For example, when we convert the verb *pronounce* to the noun *pronunciation*, we shorten the "ou" sound in *pronounce* to the "u" sound in *pronunciation*; and when we convert the verb *crystallize* into the noun *crystallization*, we shorten the "ī" sound in *crystallize* to the "i" sound in *crystallization*—though in this case we retain the same letter.

In Latin, there are five sound shifts we should be familiar with, and each one typically occurs within a verb and is accompanied by a spelling change. The resulting verb or verb base containing the weakened vowel then becomes a combining form and can effectively bond with other roots. These changes are summarized below.

PHONETIC SHIFT OF LATIN VOWELS

Initial Sound	Weakened to	Occurrence	Latin Verb / Combining Form
a	i	Before a single consonant	facere / -ficere (to make, to do)
a	e	Before two consonants	facere / -fectus (to make, to do)
e	i	Before a single consonant	tenēre / -tinēre (to have, to hold)
ae	ī	Occasionally before a consonant	caedere / -cīdere (to kill, to cut)
au	ū	Usually before a consonant	claudere / -clūdere (to shut, to close)

It is not necessary to memorize these vowel changes or those situations in which they occur, but you should at least be aware of their existence so that when you see them in this book and in dictionary etymologies, you have some idea of what is going on. For several examples of this process in operation, see chapters AG-, ACT-, -IG- and FACT-, -FECT-, FAC-, -FIC-, -FY in the COMMON ROOTS.

Past Participles

The past participle, after the infinitive, is the next most important verb form we must be familiar with. It may be briefly—and nontechnically—defined as a verb form that serves as an adjective and describes an action that has occurred in the past. In English, we may speak of a "fallen" tree or a "defeated" enemy. In Latin, the past participles we are primarily concerned with are generally passive in meaning and can be translated as "having been or having had (that which is designated by the preceding verb base)." But past participles of deponent verbs are active in meaning and can be translated as "having (that which is designated by the preceding verb base)." However, for our purposes, it is not important to make this distinction in derivative English words, and we can treat all past participles the same. In like manner, I might add that the historical existence of certain past participial forms, such as *dormitus* and *cessus*, has been seriously questioned by scholars. Nevertheless, since they appear in every college and almost every unabridged dictionary, I have chosen to use them in this work without comment.

In Latin, past participles are created by adding one of four specific endings to each of the infinitive bases of the four conjugations. For the sake of comparison and continuity, I have added these endings to the last line of what is essentially the same table in which I presented the infinitive endings of regular and deponent verbs on page 216.

LATIN INFLECTIONAL ENDINGS OF THREE VERB FORMS

Verb Form	First Conjugation	Second Conjugation	Third Conjugation	Fourth Conjugation
Infinitive (regular verbs)	-āre	-ēre	-ere	-īre
Infinitive (deponent verbs)	-ārī	-ērī	-ī	-īrī
Past Participle	-ātus	-itus	-tus	-ītus

All of these forms end in -*tus* and are distinguished by whether an -*ā*, -*i*, no additional inflectional letter, or an -*ī* precedes the -*tus*. Past participial endings are therefore immediately recognizable, but it is not particularly important to remember which ending goes with which conjugation so long as you recognize that these endings form past participles. However, for the sake of more effectively describing the word-building processes, I will initially refer to specific conjugations in the following discussion.

The Latin verb *clāmāre*, "to call out, cry out, shout," is a first conjugation infinitive verb because it ends in -*āre*. If we remove the -*āre*, we expose its base *clām*-, and by attaching the first conjugation past participial ending -*ātus* to this base, we derive its past participle *clāmātus*, "having been called out." Similarly, *habēre*, "to have, to hold," is a second conjugation infinitive verb because it ends in -*ēre*; its base is *hab*-, and by attaching the second conjugation past participial ending -*itus* to this base, we derive its past participle *habitus*. Likewise, we can recognize *scrībere*, "to scratch, to incise, to write," as a third conjugation infinitive verb from its -*ere* ending. By removing this ending, we reveal its base *scrīb*-, and by appending the third conjugation past participial ending -*tus* to this base we derive its past participle *scrīptus*. Finally, we can determine that *dormīre*, "to sleep," is a fourth conjugation infinitive verb from its -*īre* ending; its base is *dorm*-, and by appending the fourth conjugation past participial ending -*ītus* to this base, we derive its past participle *dormītus*. These forms are all tabulated below.

Conjugation	Infinitive	Inflect. Ending	Infin. Base	PP. Ending	Past Participle
First	clāmāre (to call out)	-āre	clām-	-ātus	clāmātus
Second	habēre (to have, hold)	-ēre	hab-	-itus	habitus
Third	scrībere (to write)	-ere	scrīb-	-tus	scrīptus
Fourth	dormīre (to sleep)	-īre	dorm-	-ītus	dormītus

You may notice from this table that *scrīb-*, the base of *scrībere*, "to scratch, to incise, to write," in combination with the past participial base *-tus* yields the past participle *scrīptus* rather than **scrībtus*. This is an example of an "irregular" past participial formation (if you quickly repeat *scrībtus* several times, you will see how it evolved into *scrīptus*), and, unfortunately, with the exception of the first conjugation, irregular past participial formations occur so frequently that they sometimes seem to be the norm rather than the exception. Thus, *cēdere*, "to go, to yield," yields the past participle *cessus*; *cadere*, "to fall," yields the past participle *casus*; *frangere*, "to break," yields *fractus*; and so on. But every past participle ends in *-us* (and most of the irregulars end in *-sus*), and since all past participles have a certain feel about them, you may surprise yourself with how fast you become familiar with these irregular forms.

Just as infinitive words have an "infinitive base" that can be found by removing their infinitive endings (see page 215), past participles have a "past participial base" that can be found by removing their past participial *-us* ending. (Remember, Latin verbs, unlike nouns and adjectives, characteristically have four different bases per word, and past participial bases constitute the second of these bases.) Thus, *clāmātus*, the past participle of *clāmāre*, "to call out, cry out, shout," has the past participial base *clāmāt-*; *habitus*, the past participle of *habēre*, "to have, to hold," has the past participial base *habit-*; *scrīptus*, the past participle of *scrībere*, "to scratch, to incise, to write," has the past participial base *scrīpt-*; and *dormītus*, the past participle of *dormīre*, "to sleep," has the past participial base *dormīt-*. All of these forms—and their derivative English roots—are shown in the table below.

Conjugation	Infinitive	Infin. Base	Past Participle	PP. Base	English Root
First	clāmāre (to call out)	clām-	clāmātus	clāmāt-	clamat-
Second	habēre (to have, hold)	hab-	habitus	habit-	habit-
Third	scrībere (to write)	scrīb-	scrīptus	scrīpt-	script-
Fourth	dormīre (to sleep)	dorm-	dormītus	dormīt-	dormit-

From the English roots we can, as usual, create English words by adding appropriate prefixes, suffixes, and other elements. To *clamat-* (< L. *clāmāt-*, base of *clāmātus*, past participle of *clāmāre*: to call out, cry out, shout), the first English root in the table above, we can attach the prefix *ex-* (< L. *ex-*: out, out of) and the noun-forming suffix *-ion* (< L. *-iōn-*, base of *-iōnis*, genitive of *-iō*: the act, means, or result of), forming *exclamation*. If we then replace the prefix *ex-* with the prefix *pro-* (< L. *prō-*: before, in front of; forward, forth), we turn *exclamation* into *proclamation*. And by further swapping prefixes we can create *acclamation*, *reclamation*, *disclamation* (the act or process of denying, renouncing, or repudiating), and *declamation* (a formal speech, often pompous or with contrived eloquence).

With regard to *habit-* (< L. *habit-*, base of *habitus*, past participle of *habēre*: to have, to hold), the second English root in the table above, we can simply drop the hyphen, yielding *habit*. If we then add a connecting *-u-* followed by the adjective-forming suffix *-al* (< L. *-āl-*, base of *-ālis*: pertaining to, characterized by), we get *habitual*. And if we replace the *-al* with *-at-* (< L. *-āt-*, base of *-ātus*: past participial suffix with the inflectional meaning: having been or having had) and add a silent final *-e*, we form *habituate* (to accustom to a particular situation, as by frequent repetition or prolonged contact). Likewise, by juggling prefixes and suffixes and using derivatives of the frequentative of Latin *habitus* (see following section), we can produce such words as *inhabit, cohabit, habitat,* and *habitation*.

Similarly, to *script-* (< L. *scrīpt-*, base of *scrīptus*, past participal of *scrībere*: to scratch, to incise, to write), the third English root in the table above, we can add the prefix *sub-* (< L. *sub-*: under, below, beneath) and the noun-forming suffix *-ion* (< L. *-iōn-*, base of *-iōnis*, genitive of *-iō*: the act, means, or result of), forming *subscription*, or "the act, means, or result of (*-ion*) writing (*script-*) below (*sub-*)"—which is generally where you sign your name on a page when you subscribe to a publication. Or if we replace the *sub-* with *pre-* (< L. *prae-*: before, in front of), we get *prescription*, or that which has been written "before" you take any action, i.e., before you go to the drugstore. And if we replace the *pre-* with *pro-* (< L. *prō-*: before, in front of; forward, forth), we derive *proscription* (the act or result of prohibiting, denouncing, or condemning). Originally, in ancient Rome, the state wrote or published the names of those who were outlaws and therefore condemned, or who for other legal reasons were decreed to have their property confiscated. Hence, a *proscription*, etymologically, is "the act, means, or result of (*-ion*) writing (*script-*) before (*pro-*)."

Finally, to *dormit-* (< L. *dormit-*, base of *dormītus*, past participle of *dormīre*: to sleep), the fourth English root in the table above, we can append the noun-forming suffix *-ory* (< L. *-ōrium*: a place for), forming *dormitory* or "a place for (*-ory*) sleeping (*dormit-*)." Or if we replace the *-ory* with the adjective-forming element *-iv-* (< L. *-īvus*: tending to, inclined to) and tack on a silent final *-e*, we derive the rather obscure and slightly comical *dormitive* (dôr´mi·tiv; inducing or promoting sleep). If we then replace the *-ive* with the noun-forming suffix *-ion* (< L. *-iōn-*, base of *-iōnis*, genitive of *-iō*: the act, means, or result of), we derive the equally obscure but slightly more comical *dormition* (the state of sleep or, figuratively, a reference to death, which resembles sleep). And if we add the prefix *ob-* (< L. *ob-*: to, toward, before, against) to *dormition*, we produce the downright tittering *obdormition* (a numbness or tingling feeling in part of the body produced by pressure on a local nerve)—what we commonly refer to as a part of our body being "asleep" or otherwise describe as "pins and needles." In using this word in conversation, I generally preface it with some form of the word "experience," as in the sentences, "Are you experiencing an obdormition?" or "Have you ever experienced a multiple obdormition?" (For a special note about associated words in phrases and sentences, see *collocation* in A CROSS-REFERENCE DICTIONARY.)

Frequentative Verbs

Past participles also furnish us with a small group of derivative words that are amusing to know and sometimes important, too. These are frequentative verbs, which denote, at least in their original form, a repetitive or sustained action of some sort, as we see in our native *babble, twinkle, flutter,* and *clatter*.

In English, frequentative verbs, at least in the examples above, tend to end in *-le* and *-er*, and this pattern is rather well established in our language. Latin, too, has its share of specially formed frequentative verbs, and these are constructed by adding *-āre*, the infinitive ending of first conjugation verbs, to the past participial base of certain verbs—regardless of what conjugation that past participial base may be from. For example, *salīre*, "to jump, to leap," a fourth conjugation verb, has the irregular past participle *saltus*, "having jumped or leaped," which has the resulting base *salt-*. By adding *-āre* to this base, we obtain the frequentative verb *saltāre* with its frequentative meaning, "to jump or leap repeatedly." Similarly, *habēre*, "to have, to hold, " a second conjugation verb, has the past participle *habitus*, "having had or held," which has the base *habit-*. By adding *-āre* to this base, we derive the frequentative verb *habitāre*, which has the meaning, "to have or hold repeatedly or habitually; hence, to remain in a place; hence, to inhabit." These two words are described in the table below.

LATIN FREQUENTATIVE VERBS FROM PAST PARTICIPIAL BASES

Infinitive	Past Participle	PP. Base	Freq. Ending	Freq. Verb
salīre (to jump, leap)	saltus	salt-	-āre	saltāre
habēre (to have, hold)	habitus	habit-	-āre	habitāre

Since *saltāre*, through this process, becomes a first conjugation verb, it will now obey the same linguistic rules and go through the same changes as any other first conjugation verb. Specifically, *saltāre* will now have the base *salt-*, and to this base we can append the first conjugation past participial ending *-ātus*, forming *saltātus*, which then becomes the past participle of *saltāre*. Similarly, *habitāre*, the frequentative of *habēre*, "to have, to hold," has the base *habit-*, and by appending the past participial ending *-ātus* to this base, we create *habitātus*, which is the past participle of *habitāre*. And both of these past participles can now be referred to as "frequentative past participles" since they are derived from the infinitives of frequentative verbs. If all of this seems complicated to you, the table below should clear it up.

LATIN FREQUENTATIVE PAST PARTICIPLES FROM FREQUENTATIVE BASES

Infinitive	Past Participle	Freq. Verb	Freq. Base	PP. Ending	Freq. PP
salīre (to jump, leap)	saltus	saltāre	salt-	-ātus	saltātus
habēre (to have, hold)	habitus	habitāre	habit-	-ātus	habitātus

Thus, Latin *salt-* and *habit-* are frequentative bases that yield, respectively, the English roots *salt-* and *habit-* (not shown in the table). From English *salt-*, we can then form such words as *saltant* (dancing, leaping, or jumping) and *saltigrade* (having legs adapted for jumping or leaping, as certain animals); and from English *habit-*, we can form *habitant* and *inhabitable*. Moreover, Latin *saltātus* (the past participle of *saltāre*, the frequentative of *salīre*) has the past participial base *saltāt-*, which in turn yields the English root *saltat-*; and Latin *habitātus* (the past participle of *habitāre*, the frequentative of *habēre*) has the past participial base *habitāt-*, which yields the English root *habitat-*. And these roots in turn yield additional English words. This process is illustrated in the following table.

ENGLISH ROOTS FROM LATIN FREQUENTATIVE PAST PARTICIPIAL BASES

Freq. Verb	Freq. (Inf.) Base	PP. Ending	Freq. PP.	Freq. (PP.) Base	Eng. Root
saltāre	salt-	-ātus	saltātus	saltāt-	saltat-
habitāre	habit-	-ātus	habitātus	habitāt-	habitat-

To English *saltat-* (< L. *saltāt-*, base of *saltātus*, past participle of *saltāre*, frequentative of *salīre*: to jump, to leap), we can add the noun-forming suffix *-ion* (< L. *-iōn-*, base of *-iōnis*, genitive of *-iō*: the act, means, or result of), forming *saltation* (a jumping, leaping, or dancing movement). If we then append the noun-forming suffix *-ism* (< G. *-ism-*, base of *-ismos*: the act or the result of the act of, but used in this word with the modern meaning: the beliefs, theory, school, or doctrine of), we get *saltationism* (the theory that the evolution of species proceeds in major steps or leaps, as by drastic mutational upheavals rather than by small, gradual changes). Or if we discard this *-ism* and replace the noun-forming suffix *-ion* with the adjective-forming suffix *-ory* (< L. *-ōrius*: pertaining to one who or that which [< *-or*: one who + *-ius*: adjectival suffix]), we wind up with *saltatory* (relating to or adapted for jumping, leaping, or dancing).

Similarly, to *habitat-* (< L. *habtāt-*, base of *habitātus*, past participle of *habitāre*, frequentative of *habēre*: to have, to hold), we can add the noun-forming suffix *-ion* (< L. *-iōn-*, base of *-iōnis*, genitive of *-iō*: the act, means, or result of), yielding *habitation*. And by interchanging prefixes and suffixes, we can produce its relatives, *habitational*, *cohabitation*, and *interhabitation*.

Present Participles

The present participle, after the infinitive and past participle, is our third most important verb form so far as English derivatives are concerned. It may be briefly—and nontechnically—defined as a verb form that serves as an adjective and describes an action that is occurring in the present. In English, we generally form present participles with *-ing*, as in the phrases "the swimming fish" or "the dancing ballerina," but not "dancing is fun," which would make *dancing* a verbal noun or gerund. In Latin, these forms are created by adding one of several specific present participial endings to each of the infinitive bases of the four conjugations. For the sake of comparison and continuity, I have added these endings to the last line of the what is essentially the same table in which I presented the endings of regular infinitives, deponent infinitives, and past participles on page 218.

LATIN INFLECTIONAL ENDINGS OF FOUR VERB FORMS

Verb Form	First Conjugation	Second Conjugation	Third Conjugation	Fourth Conjugation
Infinitive (regular verbs)	-āre	-ēre	-ere	-īre
Infinitive (deponent verbs)	-ārī	-ērī	-ī	-īrī
Past Participle	-ātus	-itus	-tus	-ītus
Present Participle NOM:	-āns	-ēns	-ēns or -iēns	-iēns
GEN:	-antis	-entis	-entis or -ientis	-ientis

You'll notice from this table that both a nominative and a genitive are provided for each of the four conjugations. This is because present participles function, in part, as adjectives, and their bases may be found in the same manner as the bases for Latin third declension nouns and adjectives, which generally requires that you first find their genitives.

To briefly review, when a third declension noun or adjective ends in *-is*, its base can be found simply by dropping that -*is*. However, if the nominative singular does not end in -*is*, then we must look to its genitive singular, which always ends in -*is*, and remove that ending to find its base. Since the nominatives of present participles (words ending in -*āns*, -*ēns*, and -*iēns*) do not end in -*is*, I have provided their respective genitives (-*antis*, -*entis*, and -*ientis*) in the above table, as do English dictionaries in their etymologies. With this information, you can then find their present participial bases, which are always -*ant*-, -*ent*-, or -*ient*-, depending on which conjugation they belong to. For example, the genitive of -*āns* is -*antis*, and its base is -*ant*-. To express this in reverse in a more inclusive manner, we would say: "-*ant*- is the base of -*antis*, which is the genitive of -*āns*, which is the present participial ending of first conjugation verbs ending in -*āre*."

With regard to constructing Latin words, present participles are formed by removing the inflectional ending of an infinitive and appending the corresponding present participial ending, as outlined in the table above, to the base of that infinitive. Thus, Latin *mutāre*, "to change, to alter," a first conjugation verb, has the base *mūt*-. By adding the first conjugation nominative and genitive present participial endings to this base, we derive, respectively, *mūtāns* and *mūtantis*, both of which can be defined, for our purposes, as "changing or altering." In English dictionaries and other language books, these participles are sometimes presented in the format, "*mūtāns, mūtantis*," with only a comma separating the two forms; and in such cases the first term always designates the nominative present participle and the second term the genitive present participle.

Latin *vidēre*, "to see, to look at" is a second conjugation verb and has the base *vid*-. By adding the second conjugation nominative and genitive present participial endings to this base, we derive the present participial forms *vidēns, videntis*, which can be defined as "seeing." In like manner, Latin *crēdere*, "to believe, to trust," a third conjugation verb, has the base *crēd*-, and by attaching the third conjugation nominative and genitive present participial endings to this base, we derive *crēdēns, crēdentis*, "believing, trusting." And Latin *sentīre*, "to feel, perceive," a fourth conjugation verb, has the base *sent*-, from which, by adding the nominative and genitive present participial endings to this base, we obtain *sentiēns, sentientis*, "feeling." This is all summarized in the table below.

LATIN INFINITIVES YIELDING INFINITIVE BASES AND PRESENT PARTICIPLES

Conjug.	Infinitive	Infin. Ending	Infin. Base	Prpl. Ending		Present Participle	
				NOM	GEN	NOM	GEN
First	mūtāre (to change)	-āre	mūt-	-āns	-antis	mūtāns	mūtantis
Second	vidēre (to see)	-ēre	vid-	-ēns	-entis	vidēns	videntis
Third	crēdere (to believe)	-ere	crēd-	-ēns	-entis	crēdēns	crēdentis
Fourth	sentīre (to feel)	-īre	sent-	-iēns	-ientis	sentiēns	sentientis

Just as infinitives have an "infinitive base" that can be found by removing their infinitive endings, and past participles have a "past participial base" that can be found by removing their past participial -*us*, present participles have a "present participial base" that can be found by removing their present participial -*is*. Thus, *mūtantis*, which is the genitive of *mūtāns*, which is the present participle of *mūtāre*, has the present participial base *mūtant*-; *videntis*, the genitive of *vidēns*, the present participle of *vidēre*, has the base *vident*-; *crēdentis*, the genitive of *crēdēns*, present participle of *crēdere*, has the base *crēdent-*; and *sentientis*, the genitive of *sentiēns*, present participle of *sentīre*, has the base *sentient-*. All of these bases, in turn, yield English roots, and in some cases, English words. These Latin forms—and their derivative English roots—are presented below.

LATIN INFINITIVES YIELDING PRESENT PARTICIPIAL BASES AND ENGLISH ROOTS

Conjug.	*Infinitive*	*Infin. Ending*	*Pres. Participle*		*Prpl. Base*	*English Root*
			NOM	GEN		
First	mūtāre (to change)	-āre	mūtāns	mūtantis	mūtant-	mutant-
Second	vidēre (to see)	-ēre	vidēns	videntis	vident-	vident-
Third	crēdere (to believe)	-ere	crēdēns	crēdentis	crēdent-	credent-
Fourth	sentīre (to feel)	-īre	sentiēns	sentientis	sentient-	sentient-

With regard to creating English words, from *mutant-* (< L. *mūtant-*, base of *mūtantis*, genitive of *mūtāns*, present participle of *mūtāre*: to change, to alter), the first English root in the table above, we can simply drop the hyphen and derive English *mutant* (an individual or other organism characterized by severe congenital damage arising from a sudden variation in one or more heritable traits). We can verbalize this process in the following manner: "*mutant* consists of two roots: *mut-* and *-ant*. The *mut-* is derived from Latin *mūt-*, which is the base of *mūtāre*, which means 'to change or alter,' and the *-ant* is derived from Latin *-ant*, which is the base of *-antis*, which is the genitive of *-āns*, which is a present participial suffix of words ending in *-āre* with a meaning essentially equivalent to English *-ing*. So when we put these two elements together we get 'chang- (*mut-*) -ing (*-ant*)' or 'alter- (*mut-*) -ing (*-ant*).'" We can also reconstruct this word as a unit: "*mutant-* is derived from Latin *mutant-*, which is the base of *mutantis*, which is the genitive of *mutāns*, which is the present participle of *mutāre*, which means 'to change or alter.'"

The word *mutant* is interesting in that it is the only common example of *mut-* joining with *-ant*. However, if we remove the *-ant* from *mut-*, we can then attach many other prefixes and suffixes to *mut-*, forming such words as *mutual, mutation, commute, immutable,* and *commutator* (a device for reversing or otherwise altering the direction of an electrical current, usually from A.C. [alternating current] to D.C. [direct current], often found in old direct current motors).

Similarly, to *vident-* (< L. *vident-*, base of *videntis*, genitive of *vidēns*, present participle of *vidēre*: to see), the second English root in the table above, we can add the prefix *pro-* (< L. *prō-*: before, in front of; forward, forth), forming *provident* (providing carefully for future needs or contingencies). The opposite of *provident* is, of course, *improvident*, the prefix *im-*, "not, without," being a derivative of Latin *im-*, which is itself a variant of *in-* used before words beginning with *p* or *b*. As for *credent-* (< L. *crēdent-*, base of *crēdentis*, genitive of *crēdēns*, present participle of *crēdere*: to believe, to trust), the third English root in the table above, we can simply remove the hyphen, deriving the rare and by some standards archaic English word *credent* (krēd´'nt; providing credence; believing). And if we add a connecting *-i-* and the adjective-forming suffix *-al* (< L. *-āl-*, base of *-ālis*: pertaining to, characterized by) to this word and then tack on a final *-s*, we get *credentials* (identification or evidence proving one's identity, status, entitlements, etc.). Finally, to *sentient-* (< L. *sentient-*, base of *sentientis*, genitive of *sentiēns*, present participle of *sentīre*: to feel, to perceive), the fourth English root in the table above, we can add the prefix *con-* (< L. *con-*: with, together), forming *consentient* (agreeing or having a unity of opinions; concordant). Or if we remove the *con-* and replace it with *dis-* (< L. *dis-*: away, from, apart), we obtain *dissentient*, the opposite of *consentient*.

Adjectives that end in *-ant* or *-ent*, such as *dissentient, radiant, elegant*, and *confident*, often have corresponding nouns ending in *-ance* or *-ence*, such as *dissentience, radiance, elegance*, and *confidence*, respectively; and hundreds, if not thousands, of such pairs occur in English. Therefore, it is worthwhile to take a moment to investigate the etymological connection between these pairs.

In Latin, one way of converting an adjective into a noun is by appending the noun-forming suffix *-ia* to the base of the word. Thus, for those words ending in *-ant-* and *-ent-*, by attaching *-ia* to these bases, we can create *-antia* or *-entia*, both meaning "the quality, state, condition; or act, means, result, or process of be<u>ing</u>, hav<u>ing</u>, do<u>ing</u>, perform<u>ing</u>, or manifest<u>ing</u> (that which is designated by the preceding verb base)." Historically, when these forms passed into Old French, the two syllables of *-tia* (the last three letters in *-antia* or *-entia*) gradually elided or slurred together forming *-ce*, and this yielded the Old French noun-forming suffixes *-(an)ce* or *-(en)ce*. Eventually, these suffixes passed unchanged into Middle English and then on to Modern English, thus completing the transformation of the trisyllabic (trī′si·lab′ik; three-syllable) Latin *-antia* and *-entia* into the monosyllabic (one-syllable) English *-ance* and *-ence*.

Gerundives

The gerundive (jə·run′div) is the last of the four verb forms we need to cover in our discussion of Latin verbs. For our purposes, the gerundive may be defined as a verb form that serves as an adjective and expresses such conditions as future obligation, worthiness, duty, and necessity. While not nearly as important as the infinitive, past participle, and present participial forms, gerundives provide English with a number of common and useful words and require some discussion.

Gerundives are passive in meaning, and when analyzing and defining gerundives we can use the formula: "to be or worthy to be (that which is designated by the preceding verb base)." Thus, *amandus*, the gerundive of *amāre*, "to love," can be interpreted, "to be loved or worthy to be loved," and this is exactly what the English name *Amanda* means and whence it derives.

Gerundives—like deponents, past participles, and present participles—are created by adding one of several specific endings to each of the regular infinitive bases of the four conjugations. For the sake of comparison and continuity, I have added these endings to the last line of what is essentially the same table in which I presented the endings of regular infinitives, deponent infinitives, past participles, and present participles on page 222.

Latin Inflectional Endings of Five Verb Forms

Verb Form		First Conjugation	Second Conjugation	Third Conjugation	Fourth Conjugation
Infinitive (regular verbs)		-āre	-ēre	-ere	-īre
Infinitive (deponent verbs)		-ārī	-ērī	-ī	-īrī
Past Participle		-ātus	-itus	-tus	-ītus
Present Participle	NOM:	-āns	-ēns	-ēns or -iēns	-iēns
	GEN:	-antis	-entis	-entis or -ientis	-ientis
Gerundive		-andus	-endus	-endus or -iendus	-iendus

All Latin gerundives end in *-andus*, *-endus*, or *-iendus*, and because of their distinctive "d," it is very difficult to confuse them with anything else. To form Latin gerundives, we simply remove the inflectional ending of a Latin infinitive, which reveals its infinitive base, and affix the corresponding gerundive ending to that base. For example, Latin *memorāre*, "to remember," is a first conjugation infinitive verb because it ends in *-āre*. If we remove the *-āre*, we get its base *memor-*; and by affixing the first conjugation gerundive ending *-andus* to this base, we form *memorandus*, "to be remembered," the gerundive of *memorāre*. Similarly, Latin *verērī*, "to fear," is a second declension deponent verb because it ends in *-ērī* (see table above). By removing this *-ērī*, we reveal its base *ver-*, to which we can add the second conjugation gerundive ending *-endus*, forming *verendus*, "to be revered or worthy to be revered." In like manner, Latin *legere*, "to gather, to choose, to read," is a third conjugation infinitive verb in that it ends in *-ere*, to whose base *leg-* we can append the third conjugation gerundive ending *-endus*, forming *legendus*, "to be gathered, collected, chosen, or read." And Latin *definīre*, "to limit, define," is a fourth conjugation infinitive verb because it ends in *-īre*, to whose base *defin-* we can attach the third conjugation gerundive ending *-iendus*, forming *definiendus*, "to be limited or defined." These forms are illustrated below.

Latin Infinitives Yielding Infinitive Bases, Gerundive Endings, and Gerundives

Conjugation	Infinitive	Inflect. Ending	Infin. Base	Gerundive Ending	Gerundive
First	memorāre (to remember)	-āre	memor-	-andus	memorandus
Second	verērī (to fear)	-ērī	ver-	-endus	verendus
Third	legere (to gather, read)	-ere	leg-	-endus	legendus
Fourth	definīre (to limit, define)	-īre	defin-	-iendus	definiendus

Just as infinitives, past participles, and present participles have their own bases, so, too, do gerundives. The "gerundive base" can be found by simply dropping the *-us* of each gerundive. Thus, *memorandus*, the gerundive of *memorāre*, "to remember," has the base *memorand-*; and *verendus*, the gerundive of *verērī*, "to fear," has the base *ver-*. In like fashion, *legendus*, the gerundive of *legere*, "to gather, to choose, to read," has the base *legend-*; and *definiendus*, the gerundive of *definīre*, "to limit, define," has the base *definiend-*. Conveniently, gerundive bases often become English roots without change. This process is described in the following table.

Conjugation	Infinitive	Infin. Base	Gerundive	Gerundive Base	English Root
First	memorāre (to remember)	memor-	memorandus	memorand-	memorand-
Second	verērī (to fear)	ver-	verendus	verend-	verend-
Third	legere (to gather, read)	leg-	legendus	legend-	legend-
Fourth	definīre (to limit, define)	defin-	definiendus	definiend-	definiend-

Since Latin gerundives are verbal adjectives, they are declined like adjectives and will thus have a total of six masculine, feminine, and neuter endings in their singular and plural forms. But gerundives cannot be declined like just any adjectives; they must be declined like adjectives of the first and second declensions (see pages 208–209).

By way of rapid review: first and second declension adjectives are declined like first and second declension nouns. That is to say, feminine adjectives end in -a in the singular and -ae in the plural; masculine adjectives end in -us in the singular and ī in the plural; and neuter adjectives end in -um in the singular and -a in the plural. These endings, with respect to gerundives, are illustrated below.

LATIN INFLECTIONAL ENDINGS THAT CAN BE ATTACHED TO GERUNDIVE BASES

Number	Masculine	Feminine	Neuter
Singular	-us	-a	-um
Plural	(-ī)	(-ae)	-a

The -ī and -ae are in parentheses because they practically never occur in English words or in dictionary etymologies and need not concern us. By contrast, the masculine singular -us appears regularly in dictionary etymologies, as in Latin *memorandus* (which is provided as the etymon of English *memorandum*) and *reverendus* (which is provided as the etymon of *reverend*). But this masculine -us ending never appears in English words derived from Latin gerundives. Thus, there are only three endings of gerundive bases that occur in English: the neuter singular -um, the neuter plural -a, and, to a much lesser extent, the feminine singular -a.

A few gerundive bases have been adopted into English as both roots and words. Two common examples are *legend-* (< L. *legend-*, base of *legendus*, gerundive of *legere*: to gather, to choose, to read) and *reverend-* (< L. *reverend-*, base of *reverendus*, gerundive of *reverērī*: to fear, greatly respect [< *re-*: back, again, but used in this word as an intensive with the basic meaning: completely, thoroughly, throughout + *verērī*: to fear]). To the root *legend-*, for example, we can affix additional roots, such as the adjective-forming suffix *-ary* (< L. *-ārius*: pertaining to, characterized), resulting in *legendary*. And by adding the prefix *pseud-* (< G. *pseud-*, base of *pseudēs*: false) and a connecting *-o-* to *legendary*, we can create the Greek-Latin hybrid *pseudolegendary*.

More frequently, however, we have borrowed gerundive bases with their inflected endings wholesale from Latin and have not had to create or alter these forms in English as we have done so often with nouns, adjectives, and other verb forms. For example, to form a word meaning "that which is to be done," the ancient Romans took *ag-*, the infinitive base of *agere*, "to do, to act, to drive," and added the gerundive base *-end-* to this infinitive base, to which they then affixed the neuter singular ending *-um*, forming Latin *agendum*, which we have borrowed unchanged into English. To create the plural of *agendum*, they further replaced the neuter singular -*um* with the neuter plural -*a*, forming *agenda*, "things to be done," which we again borrowed wholesale into English and now use as a singular form. Similarly, to develop a word meaning "that which is to be remembered," the ancient Romans took *memor-*, the infinitive base of *memorāre*, "to remember," and added the gerundive base -*and-* to this infinitive base, to which they then affixed the neuter singular -*um*, forming Latin *memorandum*, which we have also borrowed into English. And to form the plural of this word, they, again, replaced the neuter singular -*um* with the neuter plural -*a*, forming *memoranda*, "things to be remembered," which has also become our plural form. Finally, to create a word meaning, "that which is to be propagated," the descendants of the ancient Romans took *propāg-*, the infinitive base of *propāgāre*, "to propagate, breed plants," and added the gerundive base -*and-* to this infinitive base, to which they then affixed the feminine singular -*a* (or, to be precise, the feminine ablative -*ā*), forming *propāganda*, which, after discarding the macron, we have also adopted into English. So in the case of gerundives, the Romans have done most of the work for us.

GREEK

Greek is a highly inflected and complex language—much more so than the younger Latin language. Greek has a dual number (a plural form that refers to only two people or things in addition to the "regular" singular and plural in most languages), middle voice (a form of a verb that is passive in form but active in meaning and normally expresses reflexive or reciprocal action), optative mood (a form of a verb or verb phrase that expresses wishes, desires, or longing), and a staggering array of inflectional endings and variations that makes Greek one of the most difficult languages to learn. It is this complexity and precision that led Samuel Taylor Coleridge to proclaim, "It is hardly possible to conceive a language more perfect than Greek."

Greek and Latin, despite the fact that they use different alphabets and appear different in many ways, are actually closely related. Both languages are descended from the same Indo-European mother tongue in a narrowly divergent line and therefore show many similarities in vocabulary and grammar. For example, Greek *mētēr* and Latin *māter* both mean "mother," and Greek *patēr* and Latin *pater* both mean "father"—the only difference in these pairs being a slight variation in the vowel sounds. These and other vocabulary similarities are illustrated in the table below.

VOCABULARY SIMILARITIES IN LATIN AND GREEK

English Word	Greek Word	Latin Word
mother	mētēr	māter
father	patēr	pater
cow	bous	bōs
field	agros	ager
to gather, to choose	legein	legere

With regard to grammar, Latin has five declensions; Greek has three. But if we compare the characteristics and case endings of Latin and Greek words in these three declensions, the similarities are striking. For example, the first declension of both Latin and Greek consists primarily of feminine nouns, of which the Latin ending is -*a* and the Greek ending is -*a* or -*ē*. The second declension of both Latin and Greek consists of masculine and neuter nouns, of which the regular Latin masculine ending is -*us* and the Greek masculine ending is -*os*, and the Latin neuter ending is -*um* and the Greek neuter ending is -*on*. And the third declension of both Latin and Greek is irregular and complex in the nominative case. However, if we look at the genitives in this declension, we find that Latin nouns characteristically end in -*is*, which we can drop to find their bases, and Greek nouns characteristically end in -*os*, which we can similarly drop to find their bases. These parallels are illustrated below.

PRIMARY DECLENSIONAL SIMILARITIES IN LATIN AND GREEK

Language	First Declension	Second Declension		Third Declension
	FEMININE	MASCULINE	NEUTER	GENITIVE
Latin	-a	-us	-um	-is
Greek	-a, ē	-os	-on	-os

Though this table should not be construed as a summary of these declensions (Greek, for example, has some first declension masculine nouns ending in -*ēs*, and Latin has a number of important second declension masculine nouns ending in -*er*, neither of which is included in this table), it should suggest that learning the fundamentals of Greek grammar may be much easier than you think because of these similarities with Latin. But by far the biggest boon (something to be thankful for; a favor or welcome benefit) in the following presentation of Greek concerns the formulation of its verbs. Ironically, since Greek verbs are so complex and have so many irregular forms and variations, it is not practical to attempt to systematize their regular and irregular infinitives, past participles, present participles, gerundives, and other forms as we have done with Latin. Moreover, English dictionaries seldom if ever provide any information about these forms. Consequently, in this Short Course we shall concentrate on regular infinitives and the bases derived from or closely associated with them. So instead of dealing with five different verb forms as we did in Latin, we will only be considering one verb form in Greek. In short, if you made it through the Latin section, getting through Greek should be a breeze. But for now, let's begin at the beginning—with the Greek alphabet.

The Greek Alphabet

The Greek alphabet, unlike the Latin alphabet, uses characters that are largely foreign to us. While the English alphabet contains twenty-six letters (six of which are vowels—*a, e, i, o, u,* and sometimes *y*), the Greek alphabet contains twenty-four letters (seven of which are vowels—to be discussed shortly). And most of these characters are so strange to us to have given rise to the expression, "It's all Greek to me," meaning, of course, "I don't understand a word of it." This phrase can be traced back to the Medieval Latin quip, *Graecum est; non potest legi,* "It's Greek; it can't be read." The opening lines of the Hippocratic Oath, written in classical Greek almost 2,500 years ago and still sworn to by doctors entering the profession, illustrates this point:

"Ομνυμι 'Απόλλωνα ἰητρὸν καὶ 'Ασκληπιὸν καὶ

I swear by   Apollo   physician   and   Asclepius   and

'Ιγείαν καὶ Πανάκειαν... ἐπιτελέα ποιήσειν

Hygieia   and   Panacea   fulfilled   I will make

κατὰ   δύναμιν   καὶ   κρίσιν   ἐμὴν

according to   my ability   and   my judgment   my

ὅρκον τόνδε

oath   this

Although it may be impossible for us to read these words, the alphabet with which a language represents its words has little or no linguistic significance. For example, the most widely spoken language in India, Hindi (hin´dē), is extremely similar to Urdu, one of the official languages of Pakistan. But while Hindi uses Sanskrit characters to represent its sounds and reads from left to right, Urdu (o͡or´do͡o), for religious and political reasons, uses Persian-Arabic characters for its sounds and reads from right to left. So while speakers of Hindi and Urdu can readily understand each other, it is impossible for them to read each other's language. Similarly, Yiddish (Jewish) is very closely related to German and is actually considered by some to be a dialect of German. But while German is written in Gothic or Roman characters, Yiddish is traditionally written in Hebrew characters, making it *appear* completely unlike German and almost identical to Hebrew, with which, other than having borrowed many words and phrases, it has no linguistic affiliation.

Thus, an alphabet is little more than an arbitrary set of symbols, and owing to this fact any written language can *transliterate* the foreign characters of a different alphabet into the characters of its own alphabet without loss of meaning or, for the student, loss of the ability to dissect, analyze, reconstruct, and define words in those transliterated characters.

On the following page is a chart of the Greek alphabet providing the name and upper- and lower-case form of each letter, its transliterated form in English, and the approximate pronunciation of these letters as used in ancient Greece approximately 2,500 years ago.

THE GREEK ALPHABET

Letter Name	Greek Letter		Transliteration	Pronunciation
	UPPER CASE	LOWER CASE		
alpha	A	α	a	SHORT: ȧ (as in bola)
				LONG: ä (as in bar)
beta	B	β	b	b (as in boy)
gamma	Γ	γ	g	g (as in girl); always hard
delta	Δ	δ	d	d (as in dad)
epsilon	E	ε	e	e (as in bet); always short
zeta	Z	ζ	z	z (as in zebra or adze)
eta	H	η	ē	ā (as in bay); always long
theta	Θ	θ	th	th (as in think); unvoiced
iota	I	ι	i	SHORT: i (as in bit)
				LONG: ē (as in vaccine)
kappa	K	κ	k	k (as in kick)
lambda	Λ	λ	l	l (as in lip)
mu	M	μ	m	m (as in man)
nu	N	ν	n	n (as in night)
xi	Ξ	ξ	x	ks (as in fax)
omicron	O	o	o	ô (as in port); always short
pi	Π	π	p	p (as in pen)
rho	P	ρ	r, rh	r (as in reel); often trilled
sigma	Σ	σ, s	s	s (as in sit)
tau	T	τ	t	t (as in take)
upsilon	Y	υ	y, u	SHORT: ü (as in Fr. *tu*)
				LONG: ü (as in Fr. *rue*)
phi	Φ	φ	ph	f (as in feet)
chi	X	χ	ch, kh	kh (as in chaos, loch); aspir.
psi	Ψ	ψ	ps	ps (as in lips)
omega	Ω	ω	ō	ō (as in slow); always long
rough breathing	'	'	h	h (as in Harry)

Greek, like Latin, is a phonetic language. This means that, unlike English, every letter in Greek (whether in Greek characters or transliterated) is pronounced, and there are no silent letters. As with Latin, however, we do not know for sure how Greek was pronounced. But based on sound philological (an older term designating historical and comparative linguistics) research and supplementary scholarship, we can make some sound educated guesses, and certainly our more plausible guesses involve Greek consonants.

Greek Consonants

Greek consonants, as far as we can tell, are pronounced essentially the same as in English, with the following exceptions and qualifications:

1) The Greeks did not have a character to represent *h*. Instead, they used a "rough breathing" mark that looked like a backwards apostrophe placed over the initial vowel in a word or, if the word began with a diphthong, over the second vowel; and if the word began with a capital letter, the rough breathing mark was placed to the left of that letter. In any case, in English we transliterate these marks as *h*.

> *hydōr* (hü´dōr) "water"
>
> *homos* (hô·môs´) "same"

2) *g* is always hard, as in *get*; never soft, as in *gene*.

> *gignesthai* (gig´nes·thī) "to be born, to become"
>
> *gyros* (gü´rôs) "ring, circle"

3) *th* is always unvoiced, as in *think*; never voiced, as in *them*.

> *thermos* (ther·môs´) "hot"
>
> *thanatos* (thä´nȧ·tôs) "death"

4) *x* is always pronounced like *ks*, as in *fax*; never like *gz*, as in *exonerate*, or *z*, as in *xylophone*.

> *anthrax* (än´thrȧks) "burning coal, charcoal, carbuncle"
>
> *doxa* (dôk´sȧ) "opinion, praise, glory"

5) *r* is often trilled, as in Spanish, Portuguese, Russian, and certain other languages. This is a difficult sound for native speakers of English to make, and if you can't articulate it, simply pronounce an *h* in front of the *r*.

> *rhētōr* (hrā´tōr) "teacher of rhetoric, orator"
>
> *rhis* (hrēs) "nose"

6) *ps*, when occurring at the beginning of a word, is pronounced as though the *p* were quickly inserted just before the *s*. This is also a difficult sound combination for native speakers of English to make, but if you try saying *soup* several times in quick succession and then quickly squeeze in an initial *p*, you may get it. Otherwise, just ignore the *p*.

> *psychē* (psü·khā´) "breath, spirit, soul, mind"
>
> *pseudēs* (pseo͞o·dās´) "false"

7) *ch* is always pronounced like an aspirated (accompanied with a puff of air, as an *h* sound) *k*, as in *loch* (a lake or inlet of the sea) or a heavily breathed *chaos*; never like the "k" in *can* or the "ch" in *charity* or *choo-choo*. In this book, I use the letter combination "kh" to designate this sound.

> *chordē* (khôr·dā´) "catgut, string, cord"
>
> *cholē* (khô·lā´) "bile"

8) *ph* is always pronounced like *f*, as in *feet*; never *p* or *h*, though the ancient Greeks may very well have initially pronounced these two sounds separately, comparable to *ps*.

> *philos* (fi´lôs) "loving, beloved"
>
> *phobos* (fô´bôs) "fear, panic, flight"

Greek Vowels

Greek vowel sounds are the most difficult to assess. Unlike Greek consonants, which are rather limited in their sound possibilities (How many ways, for example, can you pronounce a *b* or a *d*?), vowels have an almost unlimited gradation of sounds. But we do know that the ancient Greeks had seven different vowel characters and, as far as we can establish, ten different vowel sounds. These are presented below.

GREEK VOWELS

SHORT VOWELS			LONG VOWELS		
Greek Letter	*Translit.*	*Pronunciation*	*Greek Letter*	*Translit.*	*Pronunciation*
α alpha (short)	a	à (as in bola)	α alpha (long)	a	ä (as in bar)
ε epsilon	e	e (as in bet)	η eta	ē	ā (as in bate)
ι iota (short)	i	i (as in bit)	ι iota (long)	i	ē (as in bee)
o omicron	o	ô (as in port)	ω omega	ō	ō (as in bowl)
υ upsilon (short)	y, u	ü (as in Fr. *tu*)	υ upsilon (long)	y, u	ü (as in Fr. *rue*)

You may notice from this table that the Greeks had different names and used different characters for short *e* (epsilon) and long *e* (eta), and for short *o* (omicron) and long *o* (omega). Yet for *a*, *i*, and *y*, they used the same characters to represent both short and long sounds. Thus, in reconstructing Greek sounds and spelling, it is easy to determine when they used short and long *e* and short and long *o*, for we need only look at their manuscripts to see which character is recorded; and this explains why English dictionaries always transliterate short *e* as *e* and long *e* as *ē*, and short *o* as *o* and long *o* as *ō*. Yet no one is really sure where the Greeks used short *a*, *i*, or *y* and long *a*, *i*, or *y*; and for this reason English dictionaries rarely provide macrons to distinguish these long vowels from their short counterparts. Accordingly, in this book I have omitted macrons over long *a*, *i*, and *y*.

But even if we did know for sure where the Greeks used these vowels, the question still arises: How did they pronounce them? Research suggests that Greek short *e* (epsilon) and short *i* (iota) were pronounced very much like our short *e* and short *i*, as in *bet* and *bit*, respectively. Short *a* (alpha) was probably pronounced like the *a* in *above* but of slightly longer duration, and I have therefore chosen *bola* to represent this sound, as I have for Latin. Short *o* (omicron) was probably pronounced as an intermediate sound between the *o* of *pot* and the *o* of *port* but probably closer to the to the "ô" sound; and I have therefore used *port* in this book to represent this sound. And long *o* (omega), by contrast, was not only held longer than short *o* (as in the difference in length between our *bowl* and *boat*), but probably was a vowel intermediate in sound between the *o* of *bowl* and the *o* of *born* but most likely a little closer to the "ō" sound; and for this reason, I have used *bowl* to represent this sound.

Long *a* (alpha), *e* (eta), and *i* (iota), as far as we can tell, were pronounced very much like our vowels in *bar*, *bay*, and *bee*, respectively. Short and long *y* (upsilon), however, represent sounds completely foreign to English. While these sounds are very difficult for native English speakers to articulate, we can approximate them by rounding our lips as though we were going to pronounce the "o͞o" in *boot* and then attempting to pronounce the "ē" in *beet*. If we hold the vowel for a relatively short period of time, the sound should closely resemble the vowel in French *tu*, which will approximate short Greek *y*; if we hold it a little longer, it should sound like the vowel in French *rue*, which will approximate long Greek *y*. But because of the difficulty in pronouncing these vowels and our uncertainty as to where the Greeks used each of them, we need not distinguish between short and long *y*, and in this book I use the same pronunciation symbol "ü" to represent both.

Greek Diphthongs

The sounds of Greek diphthongs are a little easier to assess than those of Greek vowels, partly because there are no short and long forms. There are six diphthongs in Greek with which we should be familiar. These are presented in the table below.

GREEK DIPHTHONGS

Diphthong	Translit.	Pronunciation	Greek Word and Pronunciation
αι	ai	ī (as in eye)	*haima* (hī´má) "blood"
ει	ei	ā (as in sleigh)	*glyphein* (glü´fān) "to carve"
αυ	au	ou (as in cow)	*sauros* (sou´rôs) "lizard"
ευ	eu	e‾o‾o (no Eng. equiv.)	*neuron* (ne‾o‾o´rôn) "tendon, cord"
οι	oi	oi (as in boil)	*poiein* (poi·ān´) "to make, to form"
ου	ou	‾o‾o (as in pool)	*bous* (b‾o‾os) "ox, bull, cow"

In learning the sounds of these diphthongs, the first thing to bear in mind is that they are not equivalent to the pronunciation symbols used in this book. For example, I use the pronunciation symbol "ou" to represent the sound in such words as *out*, *lout*, or *about*. But the Greek diphthong *ou* has the sound of "‾o‾o" as in *pool*—an entirely different sound. So you should not confuse pronunciation symbols with Greek letters.

Of the six Greek diphthongs, one of them, *au* (pronounced "ou," as in *out*, not "ô," as in *caught*), is identical to Latin *au*; and two of them, *ai* ("ī," as in *Saigon*) and *oi* ("oi," as in *oil*), are the counterparts, respectively, of Latin *ae* and *oe*. So these diphthongs should not seem entirely "foreign" to you. Greek *ei*, however, may take a little getting used to, but if you note that it is pronounced almost exactly the same as Greek *ē* (eta) and English long *a* (or English *ei*, as in *weigh*, *reign*, *freight*, and *neighbor*), it should be easier to remember. As for *ou*, recall again that it is pronounced like the "‾o‾o" in *pool* (or the *ou* in *coup*, *coupon*, or *Houdini*), not the "ou" in *out* or the "y‾o‾o" in *you*, *pupil*, or *puberty*.

The only diphthong that may pose a real problem is *eu*, for which we have no equivalent in English. Our closest counterpart is the y‾o‾o in *feud* or *few*. But in Greek the *e* was in all likelihood distinctly pronounced before the "‾o‾o" (it is not in *feud* and *few*). In English, however, we can approximate this sound by saying *bet* and *boot* together as fast as we can while omitting the *-t* of *bet* and the *b-* of *boot*. And if we then drop the *b-* of *bet* and the *-t* of *boot*, we will have isolated the *eu* sound.

Latinization and Anglicization

As part of our understanding of Greek-derived letters and spellings, we must also be familiar with two related linguistic developments: Latinization (the adoption of Latin sounds and spelling in words borrowed from other languages—in this case from Greek) and Anglicization (the adoption of English sounds and spelling in words borrowed from other languages—in this case from Latin and Greek).

As you may recall from the beginning of our foray (fôr´ā; a quick and sudden attack or raid; also, an initial venture, especially when outside of one's area of expertise) into bases and roots at the beginning of this Short Course, prior to the English Renaissance of the 16th century, Greek words entering English invariably first passed through Latin. Even before the dawn of English, the Romans, who occupied Britain for over 350 years from A.D. 43 to 410, passed on to the Celtic-speaking Britons a number of Latinized Greek words they had acquired in their earlier conquest of Greece and through other contacts in the area. When the Angles, Saxons, and Jutes began their major invasions of Britain in 449, they also brought with them some Latinized Greek words they had picked up on the continent; and in the course of the systematic Christianization of England after the arrival in 597 of St. Augustine of Rome with his some odd 40 monks who sought to "save" the English, many more Greek words were adopted into English, including *scholē*, "leisure, lecture, school," which had become *schola* in Latin and *scōl* in Old English before eventually becoming Middle English *scole* and Modern English *school*.

Throughout the Middle English period, after the Norman Conquest of 1066 and during the great influx of Parisian French into England in the 13th and 14th centuries, thousands of French (and, hence, slightly altered Latin) words further passed into English. Among these were a substantial number of Latinized and Gallicized (having been made French in sound and form) Greek words, such as *amygdalē*, "almond," which became *amygdala* in Latin and, through a transposition of the *l* in Old French, *almande* in Middle English and *almond* in Modern English. The Latinization and Anglicization of Greek *scholē*, "leisure, lecture, school," and *amygdalē*, "almond," into, respectively, Modern English *school* and *almond*, are outlined below.

LATINIZATION AND ANGLICIZATION OF GREEK *SCHOLĒ* AND *AMYGDALĒ*

Period Borrowed	Greek	Latin	Old English	Middle English	Modern English
Old English	scholē (leisure)	schola	scōl	scole	school
Middle English	amygdalē (almond)	amygdala	———	almande	almond

We can see from these two examples how Greek words ending in -*ē* became Latinized to -*a* before entering Old English or Middle English and eventually dropped their endings in Modern English. Thus, throughout the centuries certain patterns of Latinization and Anglicization became established (of which the foregoing is but one example), and when English began borrowing words wholesale from Greek during and after the Renaissance, it continued to apply these changes.

In other words, a precedent (pres´i·dənt—not prez´i·dent; an act or event that serves as a pattern or guide for subsequent acts or events to follow) was established in Old English and reinforced in Middle English and Modern English in which Greek words entering English, if not already in Latin form, were promptly Latinized, primarily by the alteration of one or more letters in their inflectional endings or diphthongs, or by the change from *k* to *c*. Then they were Anglicized, primarily by the elimination of their inflectional endings, the reduction of a Latin diphthong to one letter, or by the substitution of a silent final -*e* for the Latin or Greek inflectional ending (though occasionally that ending was retained). In fact, in many borrowed words from Latin and Greek two or more of these changes occurred simultaneously. The principles of Latinization and Anglicization of such words are codified (systematically arranged, as of laws, rules, interdictions, etc.) and exemplified (provided or illustrated with an example or examples; also, serving as an example for) below.

PRINCIPLES OF LATINIZATION AND ANGLICIZATION OF GREEK WORDS

1) a Greek word (or ending) passes unchanged into English, such as Greek *chaos*, which becomes English *chaos*, or Greek *drama*, which becomes English *drama*. These are actually examples of the absence of Latinization and Anglicization.

2) a Greek inflectional ending becomes Latinized and then passes unchanged into English, such as the *-os* in Greek *kaktos*, "a prickly plant," which becomes *-us* in Latin *cactus* and then passes unchanged into English as *cactus*.

3) a Greek or Latinized ending drops off completely, such as the *-on* in Greek *eidōlon*, "image," which becomes *-um* in Latin *īdolum* and then drops off in English *idol*.

4) a Greek or Latinized inflectional ending is replaced in English by a silent final *-e*, such as the *-ē* in Greek *zonē*, "belt, girdle," which becomes an *-a* in Latin *zōna* and is then replaced with *-e* in English *zone*.

5) a Greek diphthong becomes a Latin diphthong and then either remains unchanged in English or is reduced to one letter, such as the *-ai* in Greek *aiōn*, "time, age," which becomes *ae* in Latin *aeōn* and is then reduced to *e* in English *eon*.

6) a Greek *k* becomes Latin *c* and passes unchanged into English, such as the *k*'s in Greek *kaktos*, "a prickly plant," which become *c*'s in Latin *cactus* and then pass unchanged into English *cactus*.

These and other examples can be found in the table below, which includes virtually all regular Latinized and Anglicized changes you will encounter in English words derived from Greek.

LATINIZATION AND ANGLICIZATION OF GREEK LETTERS AND WORDS

Gr. Letters	Latinization	Anglicization	Greek Word	Latinized Word	English Word
ai	ae	ae, e (no *a*)	aiōn (time, age)	aeōn	eon
ei	ī, ē	i, e	eidōlon (image)	īdolum	idol
oi	oe	oe, e, o	oikonomia (management)	oeconomia	economy
ou	ū	u	mouseion (home of Muses)	mūsēum	museum
-ē	-a	(dropped), -a, -e	zōnē (belt, girdle)	zōna	zone
-os	-us	(dropped), -e	abyssos (bottomless)	abyssus	abyss
-on	-um	(dropped), -e	eidōlon (image)	īdolum	idol
-os	-is	(dropped), -e	gigantos (huge, fabled beast)	gigantis	giant
k	c	c	kaktos (a prickly plant)	cactus	cactus
-ia	-ia	-y, -ia	oikonomia (management)	oeconomia	economy

These principles and examples will enable you to more intelligently understand and follow dictionary etymologies of Greek words that have become or yielded English words. But you need not memorize this table, for in the remainder of this Short Course and throughout this book you will come across so many examples of these changes that they will become second nature to you. Furthermore, while these changes are important to know, the first step in word-building with Greek elements involves developing a familiarity with Greek bases, prefixes, suffixes, and, to a lesser extent, connecting vowels and combining forms. You will have plenty of opportunity to return to this table later.

Greek Bases

Greek bases, as in Latin, are the most important parts of words—the parts which yield English roots and to which we attach prefixes, suffixes, and other elements to form English words. But, with few exceptions, Greek bases are never Greek words; rather, they are parts of Greek words. Thus, Greek *morphē*, "form, shape," has the base *morph-*, and Greek *phobos*, "fear, panic, flight," has the base *phob-*. In these two examples, the bases are revealed by removing the inflectional endings *-ē* and *-os*, respectively—and determining the bases of Greek nouns and adjectives is generally this simple. (Uncovering the bases of Greek verbs is another matter altogether, which we shall reserve for later.) Below is a list of the most common Greek inflectional endings that can be removed from Greek nouns and adjectives to reveal their bases.

COMMON GREEK INFLECTIONAL ENDINGS THAT CAN BE REMOVED
FROM NOUNS AND ADJECTIVES TO REVEAL THEIR BASES
-a   -ē   -ēs   -os   -on   -is   -ai

Thus, whenever you look up a word in an English dictionary and encounter a Greek noun or adjective in its etymology, you can generally find its base by removing one of these endings; and this base, with the appropriate Latinization and Anglicization (if necessary), will become an English root. Thus, if you look up the word *antarctic,* you will learn that this word is derived from Greek *arktos,* "bear." From the table above, you will note that *-os* is one of the "Common Greek inflectional endings that can be removed from nouns and adjectives to reveal their bases." Therefore, by removing this ending you will expose the Greek base *arkt-,* which, through Latinization, will yield the English root *arct-.* By then adding the prefix *anti-,* "against, opposite of," and the suffix *-ic,* "pertaining to, characterized by," you can re-create *antarctic,* which, etymologically, means "pertaining to (*-ic*) the opposite of (*anti-*) the bear (*arct-*)." The "bear" in this word refers to the Great Bear or Ursa Major, the constellation (containing the Big Dipper) that hovers over the North Pole. Therefore, that which is "opposite of" this bear would be the South Pole, or *antarctic.* In the following pages, you will learn in detail the relationship of Greek case endings to Greek words and English roots.

Greek Prefixes

Greek prefixes, as in Latin, function to modify a base and thereby alter the meaning of a word. But while thousands of Greek bases exist, there are under two dozen common Greek prefixes. In the table on page 240 I have described these common prefixes, which will account for over 95 percent of all Greek-derived prefixes you will encounter in English words.

Phonetically (with regard to speech sounds or their representation in a language), a few Greek-derived prefixes are assimilated, but this occurs far less frequently than in Latin. A much more common occurrence in Greek (but which is also found in Latin) is the dropping of the final vowel in the prefix before the first letter of the following root when that letter is a vowel. Thus, Greek-derived *cata-*, "down, backward, against" drops its final *-a* to become *cat-* before a vowel. Similarly, *apo-*, *ecto-*, *endo-*, and *hypo-* all drop their *o*'s before vowels. These and other examples are shown in the Prefix table.

Also, certain Greek prefixes, as in Latin, occasionally drop their specific meanings and are used instead to intensify the base and other elements of the word, imparting the essential meaning, "completely, thoroughly, throughout, or utterly." Three common Greek prefixes that sometimes double as intensives are *ana-*, *cata-*, and *syn-*.

Greek Suffixes

Greek suffixes, like native and Latin suffixes, determine the part of speech of a word, and this is their most important feature. Therefore, when classifying Greek suffixes, we will categorize them with regard to whether they are adjective-forming, noun-forming, or verb-forming suffixes. Greek adjective-forming suffixes, however, are not very influential in Modern English and have provided us with only five common derivatives. Consequently, most Greek-derived adjectives in English use Latin-derived adjective-forming suffixes, making them linguistic *hybrids* (< L. *hybrid-*, base of *(h)ibrida*: a crossbreed animal, originally a cross between a wild boar and a domesticated sow [sou] or adult female pig).

Greek noun-forming suffixes, however, play a much larger role in English words, and in the table on page 241, I describe 17 of them. Greek verb-forming suffixes, in contrast, do not occur in English with the notable exception of Greek *-izein*, which is Latinized to *-izāre* and Anglicized to *-ize*—a suffix which today is freely attached in English to words of almost any ancestry, forming such misbegotten hybrids as *Canadianize* and *Coca-colonize*.

Greek Connecting Vowels

Greek words, much more so than Latin words, frequently contain two or more bases in addition to other roots. To unite these bases, the Greeks historically used a connecting *-o-*, just as the Romans used a connecting *-i-*; and we have adopted this practice in English when borrowing or coining words from Greek-derived bases. Thus, in the word *monolith* (a large slab of stone, often in the form of a column or monument), a *-o-* is used to join *mon-* (< G. *mon-*, base of *monos*: single, alone) and *lith-* (< G. *lith-*, base of *lithos*: stone). However, if either the final letter of the first base or the initial letter of the second base is a vowel, then that vowel links the two bases and a connecting *-o-* is not necessary. Thus, in *megalith* (a huge stone or boulder, especially one found in ancient ruins or construction work), the *-a-* in *mega-* serves as the connecting vowel, and this word is derived entirely from the two roots *mega-* (< G. *mega-*, base of *megas*: large, great) + *lith-* (< G. *lith-*, base of *lithos*: stone). But it is relatively rare for a Greek base to end in a vowel, and so most of the Greek connecting vowels we observe will be *-o-*.

Greek Combining Forms

The Greeks were particularly fond of the *o*, and, in addition to using it as a connecting vowel, they also employed it in their substantival (noun) and adjectival *-os* and *-on* endings as well as in many other elements. Because of this, the connecting *-o-* in Greek-derived English words is often erroneously (mistakenly or incorrectly) assumed to be part of the base that precedes it, which is collectively referred to as a "combining form" since it can join with other bases. Thus, in *monolith* above, *mono-* (not *mon-*) is generally considered to be the English base, and this is the way English dictionaries generally treat such words. But as we have seen with Latin's connecting *-i-*, this is not a very accurate way to represent a base and a following connecting vowel, which is an unrelated element simply inserted to join two bases. For this reason and to avoid any ambiguity as to what is and what is not a base, in this book I have regularly separated bases from their following *-o-* in my dissections, analyses, and reconstructions.

How to Create English Words from Greek Nouns and Adjectives

With regard to creating English words from Greek nouns and adjectives, we can follow a model similar to that outlined on page 183 for creating English words from Latin words:

1) Note the Greek noun or adjective.

2) Identify its inflectional ending.

3) Remove that inflectional ending to reveal its base.

4) Create an English root from the Greek base, which, in most cases, involves removing any macrons, if present, and Anglicizing any Greek letters.

5) Add one or more prefixes, suffixes, connecting vowels, additional bases, etc., to this root to create an English word.

These steps are outlined below, using the Greek word *ergon*, "work," as an example.

CREATING ENGLISH WORDS FROM GREEK WORDS

Greek Noun	Inflectional Ending	Greek Base	English Root	English Word
ergon (work)	-on	erg-	erg-	en**erg**y

Thus, we begin with the Greek noun *ergon*, "work." We immediately identify and remove its inflectional ending *on*, revealing its base *erg-*. This base, unchanged, becomes the English root *erg-* (there are no letters that need to be Anglicized, such as a Greek *k*, which would typically become an English *c*). And to this root we add the prefix *en-* (< G. *en-*: in, into, within) and the noun-forming suffix *-y* (< G. *-eia*: the act, process, condition, or result of), yielding the English word *energy*.

English Prefix	Etymology	English Derivatives	Compare (cf.) or Contrast (ct.)
a-, an-	< G. *a-, an-*: without, lacking, not	amoral, amorphous, anemia	cf. L. *non-, in-*[2]
amphi-	< G. *amphi-*: around, about	amphitheater, amphibian	cf. L. *ambi-, circum-*
ana-, an-	< G. *ana-*: up, upward, back, again	anagram, analysis, anode	cf. G. *kata-* (E. *cata-*)
anti-, ant-	< G. *anti-*: against, opposite of	antithesis, antonym	ct. L. *ante-*; cf. L. *contrā-*
apo-, ap-	< G. *apo-*: away, from, off	apogee, aphelion	ct. G. *peri-*; cf. L. *ab-, dē-*
cata-, cat-	< G. *kata-*: down, backward, against	cataract, catalepsy, cathode	cf. L. *dē-* (E. *de-*), *dis-*
dia-, di-	< G. *dia-*: through, throughout, across	diagnose, diabetes, diorama	cf. L. *per-, trāns-*; ct. L. *di-*
dys-	< G. *dys-*: bad, difficult	dysfunctional, dyslexia	ct. G. *eu-*; cf. G. *kak-*
ecto-, ect-	< G. *ekto-*: outside	ectoderm, ectoplasm, ectal	ct. G. *endo-, end-*
en-, em- (assim.)	< G. *en-*: in, into, within	endemic, empathy, ellipsis	cf. L. *in-*[1]; E. *a-*[1]
endo-, end-	< G. *endo-*: within	endocrine, endamoebic	cf. G. *ekto-* (E. *ecto-*)
epi-, ep-	< G. *epi-*: over, upon, on	epidermis, eponym	cf. G. *hyper-*; L. *super-*
eu-, ev-	< G. *eu-*: well (in E. well, good)	euthanasia, evangelical	ct. G. *dys-, kak-* (E. *cac-*)
ex-, ec-	< G. *ex-*: out, out of, from	exodus, hysterectomy	cf. L. *ex-*; OE. *out-*
hyper-	< G. *hyper-*: over, above, beyond	hyperactive, hyperbole	ct. G. *hypo-*; cf. L. *super-*
hypo-, hyp-	< G. *hypo-*: under, below, beneath	hypodermic, hyphen	ct. G. *hyper-*; cf. L. *sub-*
meta-, met-	< G. *meta-*: along with, besides, after	metaphor, metempsychosis	cf. L. *trāns-*; G. *para-*
para-, par-	< G. *para-*: besides, alongside	parapsychology, parhelion	cf. G. *meta-*; ct. L. *par-*[2,3,4,5]
peri-	< G. *peri-*: around, about, surrounding	perigee, perihelion	ct. L. *per-*; G. *apo-*
pro-	< G. *pro-*: before, in front of	prologue, prognosis	cf. L. *prō-, prae-* (E. *pre-*)
pros-	< G. *pros-*: to, toward	prosthesis, proselytize	cf. L. *ad-, ob-*
syn-, sy-, sym-	< G. *syn-*: with, together	synthesis, syzygy, symbol	cf. L. *com-*; ME. *with-*

I. Abstract noun-forming suffixes: nouns describing "the quality, state, condition; act, means, result, or process of." Abstract nouns, such as *hysteria, introspection,* and *consternation* (profound dismay or bewilderment), differ from concrete nouns, such as *table, chair,* and *anthropophaginian* (a cannibal), which denote a person or thing.

A. Abstract nouns, particularly those emphasizing "the quality, state, or condition of," but which can also mean "the act, means, result, or process of."

English Suffix	Etymology	English Derivatives	Compare (cf.) or Contrast (ct.)
-ia	< G. *-ia* or sometimes *-eia*	anemia, euphoria, sympathy	cf. L. *-ia* (sometimes < G.*-ia*)
-y	< G. *-ia* or sometimes *-eia*	agony, atrophy, sympathy	cf. L. *-ia*; OE. *-ig* (E. *-y*)

B. Abstract noun-forming suffixes, particularly those generally emphasizing "the act, means, result of process of," but which also can mean "the quality, state, or condition of."

-sis, -se, -sy	< G. *-sis*; or *-s(is)* + E. *-e* or *-y*	thesis, diagnose, hypocrisy	cf. G. adj. *-tikos* (E. *-tic*)
-sia, -sy	< G. *-s(is)* + *-ia*: state or condition of	anesthesia, amnesia, epilepsy	cf. G. adj. *-tikos* (E. *-tic*)
-m	< G. *-m(os)*: the act or result of act of	spasm, sarcasm, pleonasm	cf. G. *-ma, -matos*
-ism	< G. *-is-* (base of *-izein*) + *-m(os)*	hypnotism, somnambulism	cf. G. n. *-istēs* (E. *-ist*)

C. Abstract noun-forming suffixes with the basic meaning: "the result or the result of the act of."

-m, -ma, -me	< G. *-m(a)*: the result of	protoplasm, drama, theme	ct. G. *-mos, -ismos* (E. *-ism*)
-mat-	< G. *-mat(os)* (gen. of *-ma*)	dramatic, problematical	ct. L. *-ātus* (E. *-ate, -at-*)

II. Nouns of agency: "a person or thing connected with," or "one who or that which (performs the action designated by the preceding base or elements)."

-t, -te	< G. *-t(ēs)*: one who or that which	poet, athlete, enthusiast	ct. G. *-t(os)*: verbal suf.
-ter	< G. *-tēr*: one who or that which	character, crater, catheter	ct. OE. *-ere* (E. *-er*)
-ist	< G. *-ist(ēs)*: one who or that which	linguist, socialist, etymologist	cf. G. *-ismos* (E. *-ism*)
-ite	< G. *-it(ēs)*: one from or that which	Sybarite, Israelite, Bronxite	ct. L. pp. *-ītus, -itis*

III. Nouns of place: "a place, dwelling, or abode of (that which is designated by the preceding base or elements)."

-ium	< L. *-ium* < G. *-ion*: a place for	emporium, gymnasium	cf. L. *-ārium, -ōrium,*
-eum	< L. *-eum* < G. *-eion*: a place for	museum, mausoleum, Lyceum	ct. G. *-ion (-ium)*: dim. suf.
-tery	< G. *-tērion*: a place for	monastery, cemetery, phalanstery	ct. ME *-ery*: a place for

IV. Diminutive nouns: nouns denoting that which is "small, little, tiny, or young" with reference to the base noun.

-isk, -iscus	< L. *-iscus* < G. *-iskos*: small, little	asterisk, basilisk, meniscus	cf. L. *-ellus, -ullus,* etc.
-ium	< L. *-ium* < G. *-ion*: small, little	podium, bacterium, pyxidium	ct. G. *-ion*: a place for

241

I. Adjective-forming suffixes having the basic meaning: "pertaining to, characterized by, having the nature of, like, belonging to"; also forming nouns, generally with the meaning: "one who or that which (performs the action designated by the preceding base or elements)."

English Suffix	Etymology	English Derivatives	Comment
-ic	< G. *-ik-*, base of *-ikos*: pert. to	angelic, titanic, epidemic	affixed to n. bases; cf. L. *-ic*
-ac	< L. *-ak-*, base of *-akos*, var. of *-ikos*	cardiac, zodiac, kleptomaniac	used when base ends in *i*
-tic	< L. *-tik-*, base of *-tikos*: pert. to	plastic, cryptic, synthetic	affixed to verb bases

II. Adjective- and noun-forming suffixes having the related meanings: "like, resembling, having the shape or form of."

-oid, -ode	< G. *-o(e)id(ēs)*: shaped like < *eidos*	humanoid, android, nematode	ct. L. *hodos*: way (E. *-ode*)

GREEK-DERIVED VERB-FORMING SUFFIXES

There is only one common Greek-derived verb-forming suffix in English, which has come to us through Latin and is freely attached to words of classical and nonclassical ancestry. It is best defined in relationship to its preceding base or elements but often has one or more of the following meanings: "to become, to cause to become, to make, to form, to render, to engage in, to cause to conform to, to treat or combine with (said of chemical elements, compounds, etc.), etc."

English Suffix	Etymology	English Derivatives	Comment
-ize, -ise, -iz-	< L. *-iz(āre)* (< G. *-izein*) + E. *-e*	criticize, advertise, Anglicization,	cf. L. *-ātus*; ME. *-en*

Greek Nouns

The process of deriving English roots and words from Greek nouns will be considerably easier to understand than was the similar process of deriving English roots and words from Latin. You are now familiar with classical languages and have a basic understanding of nouns, bases, inflectional endings, and their relationship, so none of this material will now be entirely new to you. Moreover, the formation of English words from Greek roots and bases is in itself markedly simpler than that of Latin. But above all, as we have seen, there are a great many parallels between Latin and Greek, so much so that the coverage of Greek—particularly with regard to its untransliterated Greek characters—may, in many ways, appear as a transmogrified (trans·mäg′rə·fīd′ tranz-; a humorous pseudo-Latin term meaning: changed in form or appearance, especially in a strange or grotesque way) version of Latin. Of course, since Greek predates Latin by the better part of a millennium and the direction of borrowing is from Greek to Latin, it should be clear where the transmogrification, if any, lies.

Greek nouns occur in three declensions, of which the first is relatively simple and contains only four case endings we need to learn. The second declension is even simpler and contains three endings of importance to us. And the third declension, while including six case endings and a variety of irregular forms with which we should be familiar, is still quite manageable and relatively easy to understand.

Greek First Declension Nouns

Greek first declension nouns, like those in Latin, are primarily feminine. However, they do include occasional masculine nouns, and we should be familiar with these forms, too.

First declension feminine nouns always end in *-a* or *-ē* in the nominative singular (in Latin, they end in *-a*), and some of these words, such as *plēthōra* (plā´thō·rȧ) "fullness," and *psychē* (psü´khā), "breath, spirit, soul, mind," have been borrowed into English as *plethora* (pleth´ə·rə; an excess or over-abundance) and *psyche* (sī´kē; the mind or soul), respectively. Historically, Greek *plēthōra*, in its original sense of "fullness," passed into Latin where it developed the medical meaning, "an excess of blood or other bodily fluids." This meaning was then adopted in English and remained its primary sense until around 1700, when *plethora* began to develop its secondary and now more common sense of "an excess or overabundance," as in the sentence, "There was a plethora of exhibits at the fair, but a dearth (dûrth; a shortage or scarcity) of concessions and facilities."

But for most Greek words, as in Latin, it is their base that forms the foundation of English words, and the base of first declension feminine nouns can be found by removing their *-a* or *-ē* ending. Thus, Greek *diaita*, "way of life, regimen, diet," has the inflectional ending *-a* and the resulting base *diait-*, which, through Latinization and Anglicization, becomes English *diet*. Similarly, Greek *chordē*, "catgut, string," has the inflectional ending *-ē* and the resulting base *chord-*, which becomes English *chord* and *cord*. These words and bases are illustrated in the following table.

GREEK FIRST DECLENSION FEMININE NOUNS YIELDING ENGLISH WORDS

Nominative Singular	Inflectional Ending	Greek Base	English Word
diaita (way of life, diet)	-a	diait-	diet
chordē (catgut, string)	-ē	chord-	chord, cord

In most cases Greek bases do not form English words, and before we can derive an English word from a Greek base, we must obtain an English root from that base and add prefixes or suffixes (or both) to this root, as we have repeatedly done in Latin. Two common Greek words that provide English roots are *kardia*, "heart," and *morphē*, "form, shape," as illustrated below.

GREEK FIRST DECLENSION FEMININE NOUNS YIELDING ENGLISH ROOTS

Nominative Singular	Inflectional Ending	Greek Base	English Root
kardia (heart)	-a	kardi-	cardi-
morphē (form, shape)	-ē	morph-	morph-

Cardi- and *morph-* are extremely common roots and appear in hundreds of English words. To *cardi-* (< G. *kardi-*, base of *kardia*: heart), we can add the adjective-forming suffix *-ac* (< G. *-ak-*, base of *-akos* [variant of *-ikos* used after *i*]: pertaining to, characterized by), yielding *cardiac*. We can thus verbalize this etymology as follows: "*cardiac* consists of two roots: *cardi-* and *-ac*. The *cardi* is derived from Greek *kardi-*, which is the base of *kardia*, which means 'heart'; and the *-ac* is derived from Greek *-ak-*, which is the base of *-akos*, which is a variant of *-ikos* used after *i* and means 'pertaining to or characterized by.' So when we put these two roots together we get 'pertaining to (-ac) the heart (*cardi-*).'" For over 30 additional *cardi-* words, see chapter CARDI- in the COMMON ROOTS.

Similarly, to the initial side of *morph-* (< G. *morph-*, base of *morphē*: form, shape), the second English root in the table above, we can attach the root *anthrop-* (< G. *anthrop-*, base of *anthrōpos*: human being) and a connecting *-o-*, and to the terminal side of *morph-* we can append the adjective-forming suffix *-ic* (< L. *-ik-*, base of *-ikos*: pertaining to, characterized by), forming *anthropomorphic* (an′thrə‧pə‧môr′fik; having the form or shape of a human being; or attributing human qualities and characteristics to animals, plants, or other inanimate or supernatural beings). If we then remove the *anthrop-* and replace it with the roots *gyn-* (< G. *gyn-*, base of *gynē*: woman, female) and *andr-* (< G. *andr-*, base of *andros*, genitive of *anēr*: man, male), we derive the obscure but entertaining *gynandromorphic* (ji‧nan′drə‧môr′fik, gī-, jī-; of or pertaining to an individual or other organism having both male and female characteristics)—a word almost identical in meaning to the slightly less obscure *androgynous* (an‧dräj′ə‧nəs), which, interestingly, reverses the roots *andr-* and *gyn-* in *gynandromorphic*. Similarly, by swapping prefixes and suffixes, we can create such words as *amorphous* (without shape), *metamorphosis*, *morphology* (the scientific study of form and structure, as in biology, linguistics, etc.), and *morphine*.

When Greek nouns ending in *-ē* become Latinized and Anglicized, they frequently change their *-ē* to *-ā*. Thus, Greek *aortē*, "the great artery," becomes Medieval Latin *aorta*, which then passes unchanged into English as *aorta* (ā‧ôr′tə; the largest artery in the human body, conveying blood from the heart to all parts of the body except the lungs). Similarly, *Athenē*, the Greek goddess of wisdom (identified with the Roman goddess Minerva), becomes *Athena* in Latin and English. And in a slightly more complex manner, Greek *skēnē*, "tent, booth, stage," becomes *scēna* in Latin, of which the Latin base *scēn-* becomes the English root *scen-*, which, with the addition of a final silent *-e*, becomes English *scene*.

Greek plurals of feminine nouns of the first declension also appear in English in their Latinized form. Specifically, these nouns, which end in *-a* and *-ē*, form their plural by adding *-ai* to their base. Thus, Greek *byrs-*, the base of *byrsa*, "skin, hide," after acquiring the plural suffix *-ai*, becomes *byrsai*. But *-ai* is not an acceptable English ending, so Greek *-ai* becomes Latinized to *-ae* before passing into English. Moreover, in this particular word, Greek *y* (which is a transliteration of Greek υ) is, rather surprisingly, changed to *u*, more closely resembling its original Greek character. So with these two changes, Greek *byrsai* becomes English *bursae*, the plural of *bursa*, which has the modern meaning: "a sac or pouchlike chamber, especially one containing a lubricating fluid that reduces friction in or near certain joints." Similarly, Greek *aortē*, "the great artery," has the base *aort-*, which, by acquiring the plural suffix *-ai*, becomes Greek *aortai* and, through Latinization and Anglicization, yields English *aortae*, the plural of *aorta*. These analyses of Greek *byrsa* and *aortē* are summarized below.

GREEK FIRST DECLENSION FEMININE NOUNS YIELDING ENGLISH PLURAL WORDS

Nom. Singular	Greek Base	Gr. Pl. Ending	Gr. Pl. Word	Lat. Pl. Word	Eng. Pl. Word
byrsa (skin, hide)	byrs-	-ai	byrsai	bursae	bursae
aortē (great artery)	aort-	-ai	aortai	aortae	aortae

As you might observe from these examples, both of these words are anatomical or medical terms, for there are no other specialties within English that make such wide use of the Latinized Greek *-ae* plural. But words ending in *-ae* should not automatically be assumed to be from Greek. On the contrary, most of them are derivatives of Latin feminine plurals of first declension nouns ending in *-a* that are *not* derived from Greek (see Latin First Declension Nouns). So whenever you encounter a word ending in *-ae*, always be careful to consider whether it is a Latin word or a Latinized Greek word. To find out, you may have to consult your dictionary.

The Greek first declension, as mentioned, also contains some masculine nouns, and the nominative singular of these nouns characteristically ends in *-ēs*. Their bases, which yield English roots, can be found by dropping this ending. Two examples of first declension masculine nouns are *iōdēs*, "rust-colored, violet," and *despotēs*, "master (of a house), lord." These are described in the table below.

GREEK FIRST DECLENSION MASCULINE NOUNS YIELDING ENGLISH ROOTS

Nominative Singular	Inflectional Ending	Greek Base	English Root
iōdēs (rust-colored, violet)	-ēs	iōd-	iod-
despotēs (master, lord)	-ēs	despot-	despot-

To *iod-* (< G. *iōd-*, base of *iōdēs*: rust-colored, violet), we can append the scientific suffix *-ine*, meaning, in this context, "a chemical element of" (< G. *in-*, base of *inē*: the quality, state, or condition of + E. *-e*: silent final letter), forming *iodine*. If we then remove the *-ine* and replace it with another scientific suffix, *-ide* (abstracted from *(ox)ide*, ultimately < L. *-id-*, base of *-idus*: pertaining to, characterized by + Fr. *-e*: silent final letter), signifying, in this context, the second word or electronegative element or radical in a binary compound, we get *iodide* (a compound of iodine and another element or radical, as *methyl iodide*). Thus, we began with a base over 2,000 years old and have wound up with two modern scientific terms.

Similarly, to *despot-* (< G. *despot-*, base of *despotēs*: master, lord), the second English root in the table above, we can append the adjective-forming suffix *-ic* (< G. *-ik-*, base of *-ikos*: pertaining to, characterized by), forming *despotic*. And if we remove the *-ic* and replace it with the noun-forming suffix *-ism* (< G. *-ism-*, base of *-ismos*: the act or the result of the act of), we get *despotism*, a practice which, unfortunately, is probably considerably older than its name.

Greek Second Declension Nouns

Greek second declension nouns are either masculine or neuter, and these are in many ways the exact counterparts of their Latin cousins.

While Latin second declension masculine nouns end in *-us*, Greek second declension masculine nouns end in *-os*; and, as in Latin, some of these words have come down to us unchanged or essentially unchanged. For example, Greek *kosmos*, "order, form, harmony, universe," has become English *cosmos*, and Greek *kudos*, "honor, praise, acclaim," has become English *kudos*, with the same meaning. In other Greek-derived words, the masculine *-os* ending has been Latinized by changing it to the corresponding Latin *-us*, as in *thesaurus* (< G. *thēsauros*: a treasury, storehouse) and *Helianthus* (the generic name for the sunflower < G. *hēli-* [base of *hēlios*]: sun + *anthos*: flower). And in still other words, the Greek ending has just dropped off, as in *myth* (< G. *mythos*: word, speech, story) and *hymn* (< G. *hymnos*: a song in praise of the gods or heroes).

But as usual, before we can derive an English word from a Greek word, we must generally derive a Greek base from that word, which in turn yields an English root to which we can add prefixes, suffixes, and other roots. In second declension masculine nouns, the base can always be found by dropping its inflectional *-os*, which then yields an English root. Two common Greek nouns that provide Greek bases and English roots along with many colorful derivatives are *bios*, "life," and *hippos*, "horse," as outlined below.

GREEK SECOND DECLENSION MASCULINE NOUNS YIELDING ENGLISH ROOTS

Nominative Sing.	Inflectional Ending	Latin Base	English Root
bios (life)	-os	bi-	bi-
hippos (horse)	-os	hipp-	hipp-

To *bi-* (< G. *bi-*, base of *bios*: life), we can add a connecting *-o-* and the combining form *-logy*, "the science, study, theory, or doctrine of" (< G. *-log-* [base of *logos*]: word, thought, reason, reckoning, discourse + *-ia*: the act, process, condition, or result of), forming *biology*. If we then remove the *-logy* and replace it with *-graphy* (< G. *graph-* [base of *graphos*]: written, drawn [< *graphein*: to write, to draw] + *-ia*: the act, process, condition, or result of), we get *biography*. Similarly, by removing *-graphy* and appending the appropriate endings, we can create, respectively, the Greek-Old English, Greek-Arabic, Greek-Latin, and Greek-Scandinavian hybrids *biofeedback* (a technique for learning to control certain normally involuntary bodily functions, such as blood pressure or heart rate, initially with the help of monitoring devices), *biohazard* (a health risk created by the release or potential release of disease-producing agents into the environment, especially those genetically engineered or cultured in a laboratory), *bioluminescence* (the light or glow emitted by certain living organisms, such as fireflies or glowworms), and *biofog* (a fog emanating from the body of a person or animal, produced by the condensation of warm water vapor in cold air). Have you ever seen your breath on a cold day?

Likewise, to *hipp-* (< G. *hipp-*, base of *hippos*: horse), the second English root in the table above, we can add a connecting *-o-*, the root *potam-* (< G. *potam-*, base of *potamos*: river), and the Latin second declension masculine ending *-us* (Latinizing Greek *-os*), yielding *hippopotamus*, or "river horse." And if we Latinize Greek *hippos* to *hippus* and prefix *eo-* (< G. *ēo-*, base of *ēoos*, genitive of *ēōs*: dawn) to this form, we get *eohippus* or "dawn horse" (an extinct forebear of the modern horse about the size of a small coyote that flourished approximately 50 million years ago). If we then replace the *eo-* with *mes-* (< G. *mes-*, base of *mesos*: middle) and add a connecting *-o-*, we derive *mesohippus* (a somewhat larger extinct horse about the size of a German shepherd or Great Dane that flourished approximately 40 million years ago); and if we replace the *mes-* with *prot-* (< G. *prot-*, base of *protos*: first), we wind up with *protohippus* (an even larger extinct horse about the size of a donkey that flourished approximately 25 million years ago). So as the horse has grown over the years so too will your vocabulary. For additional *hipp-* words, see "Words with Animals in Them" in the SUBJECTS.

Greek second declension nouns, as in Latin, also have neuter forms, and while the Latin form usually ends in *-um*, the Greek form ends in *-on*. As usual, some of these Greek words have come down to us essentially unchanged, such as *rhododendron* (a genus of predominantly evergreen shrubs and trees having attractive pink, white, or purple flowers < G. *rhod-* [base of *rhodon*]: rose + *-o-*: connecting vowel + *dendron*: tree; hence, a "rose tree") and *moron* (< G. *mōron*, neuter of *mōros*: foolish, dull, stupid; see *sophomore* in chapter BIBLI- in the COMMON ROOTS). Other second declension nouns have been borrowed after abandoning their inflectional *-on*, such as *polygon* (a closed geometrical figure with three or more sides < G. *polygōn-*, base of *polygōnon*, neuter of *polygōnos*: many-angled [< *poly-*: much, many + *-gōnos*: angled < *gōnia*: angle]) and *petal* (< G. *petalon*: leaf). And some of these nouns have passed to us after Latinization of the Greek *-on*, such as *phylum* (the primary division in the scientific classification of animals and other living creatures, ranking below a "kingdom" and above a "class" < G. *phylon*: tribe, stock, race) and *geranium* (any of a number of plants within the genus *Geranium*, having deeply lobed leaves and attractive pink-purple flowers < G. *geranion*: any of various plants whose seed pod was fancied to resemble a crane's bill < *geran-* [base of *geranos*]: crane + *-ion*: a diminutive suffix having the basic meaning: small, little, tiny).

But most Greek neuter nouns of the second declension have become English words by first dropping their *-on* ending to yield Greek bases, which then become English roots. Two typical second declension neuter nouns are *kentron*, "the stationary point on a drawing compass; center," and *phyton*, "plant," as illustrated below.

GREEK SECOND DECLENSION NEUTER NOUNS YIELDING ENGLISH ROOTS

Nominative Singular	Inflectional Ending	Greek Base	English Root
kentron (center)	-on	kentr-	centr-
phyton (plant)	-on	phyt-	phyt-

To *centr-* (< G. *kentr-*, base of *kentron*: the stationary point on a drawing compass; hence, center), we can append the adjective-forming suffix *-al* (< L. *-āl-*, base of *-ālis*: pertaining to, characterized by), forming *central*. If we then replace the *-al* with another adjective-forming suffix, *-ic* (< G. *-ik-*, base of *-ikos*: pertaining to, characterized by), we get *centric*, a close but seldom used synonym of *central*. If we further attach the prefix *ec-* (< G. *ek-*, variant and assimilated form of *ex-*: out, out of) to this word, we derive *eccentric*, or, etymologically, "pertaining to (*-ic*) out of (*ec-*) the center (*centr-*)." And if we then remove the *ec-* and insert *heli-* (< G. *hēli-*, base of *hēlios*: sun) and a connecting *-o-*, we produce *heliocentric* (hē´lē·ō·sen´trik; having or regarding the sun as the center of the solar system or of some other physical or spiritual realm). Finally, if we discard the *heli-* and replace it with *ego* (< L. *ego*: I), we transform *heliocentric* in *egocentric*.

Similarly, to *phyt-* (< G. *phyt-*, base of *phyton*: plant), the second English root in the table above, we can add a connecting *-o-* and *-logy*, "the science, study, theory, or doctrine of" (< G. *-log-* [base of *logos*]: word, thought, reason, reckoning, discourse + *-ia*: the act, process, condition, or result of), yielding *phytology*, a highfalutin (pretentious and grandiloquent) synonym for *botany*. Or if we clip the *-log-* and replace it with *-phag-* (< G. *-phag-*, base of *-phagos*: eating, devouring [< *phagein*: to eat, to devour]), we get *phytophagy* (fī·täf´ə·jē), which, as any one at the local plant will tell you, is "the quality, state, or condition of being *phytophagous* (fī·täf´ə·gəs)," which is a Greek-derived synonym for the Latin-derived *herbivorous* (< L. *herb-* [base of *herba*]: grass, plant, herb + *-i-*: connecting vowel + *-vor-* [base of *-vorus*]: eating, devouring [< *vorāre*: to eat, to devour] + E. *-ous*: full of, abounding in, characterized by, like [< L. *-ō(s)us* in most E. words, but in this derivative an Anglicization of L. *-us*: adjectival suffix]). Thus, Latin *-vorous* and Greek *-phagous* are exact counterparts, and we see this duality in such English pairs as *carnivorous/creophagous* (feeding on flesh, as lions, tigers, and most humans), *insectivorous/entomophagous* (feeding on insects, as the Venus's-flytrap), *sanguivorous/hematophagous* (feeding on blood, as the vampire bat), and *frugivorous/carpophagous* (feeding on fruit, as some of our less hematophagous bats).

Greek second declension neuter nouns also have plural forms that sometimes show up in English. Just as Latin second declension neuter nouns ending in *-um* have a plural ending *-a* that is attached to the base of the Latin noun, Greek neuter nouns ending in *-on* have a plural ending *-a* that is attached to the base of the Greek noun. Thus, Greek *kritērion*, "a standard," has the base *kritēri-*, and by adding the Greek plural *-a* to this base, we get the Greek plural *kritēria*, which is Latinized to *criteria* and becomes English *criteria*. Similarly, Greek *phainomenon*, "appearance," has the base *phainomen-*, and by attaching the Greek plural *-a* to this base, we obtain the Greek plural *phainomena*, which in Late Latin becomes *phaenomena* before becoming English *phenomena*. This is all summarized in the table below.

GREEK SECOND DECLENSION NEUTER NOUNS YIELDING ENGLISH PLURAL WORDS

Nom. Singular	Greek Base	Pl. Ending	Greek Pl. Word	Latin(ized) Pl. Word	Eng. Pl. Word
kritērion	kritēri-	-a	kritēria	criteria	criteria
phainomenon	phainomen-	-a	phainomena	phaenomena	phenomena

With regard to the Latinization and Anglicization of Greek *phainomena*, it is interesting to note how the Greek diphthong *-ai-* first changed to the Late Latin diphthong *-ae-* and then to the English single letter *-e-*. However, what is a little surprising is that when the *-ai-* in this word changed to *-ae-*, its Greek singular ending *-on* did not also change to its Latinized equivalent *-um* (not shown in the table). Thus, Greek *phainomenon* became Late Latin *phaenomenon* rather than the expected **phaenomenum*. But such are the vicissitudes (vi·sis´i·tōōdz´, -tyōōdz´; the normal but unpredictable changes, shifts, or ups and downs in life or other natural processes) of language.

Greek Third Declension Nouns

Greek third declension nouns are the most complex nouns in Greek because they include a multitude of endings with a variety of differently formulated bases.

As with Latin third declension nouns, because of this richness and variation in form, it is frequently difficult if not impossible to determine the bases of third declension nouns from their nominative singular form. However, in some cases the nominative singular will constitute the base and, with slight change, may even yield an English word. Thus, Greek *axōn*, "an axil or axis," has the base *axōn-*, which yields the English word *axon* (the part of a nerve cell that conducts a nerve impulse away from the cell body). Similarly, Greek *astēr*, "star," has the base *astēr-*, which yields English *aster*, the flower—so named because of its colorful daisy-like ray flowers surrounding a disk of tiny yellow tube flowers. And, of course, if we append to *aster-* the adjective- and noun-forming suffix *-oid*, "resembling, like" (< G. *-o(e)id(ēs)*: shaped-like < *eidos*: form, shape), we get *asteroid*, which, etymologically, is "that which resembles a star."

But with most third declension nouns we cannot determine their bases and, hence, their English derivative roots from their nominative forms and will have to look to their genitives. These end in *-os* (just as Latin third declension genitives end in *-is*), and by dropping this ending we can uncover their bases and the resulting English roots. For example, the nominative singular *ornis*, "bird," has the genitive *ornithos*, and by dropping the *-os*, we uncover the base *ornith-*, which passes unchanged into English. Similarly, Greek *phylax*, "a guard," has the genitive *phylakos*, which, in dropping the *-os*, reveals the base *phylak-*, which becomes English *phylac-*. And Greek *pais*, "boy, child," has the genitive *paidos* and hence the base *paid-*, which yields English *ped-*. These are all represented in the table below.

GREEK THIRD DECLENSION NOUNS YIELDING GREEK BASES AND ENGLISH ROOTS

Nominative Singular	Genitive Singular	Inflect. Ending	Greek Base	English Root
ornis (bird)	ornithos	-os	ornith-	ornith-
phylax (a guard)	phylakos	-os	phylak-	phylac-
pais (boy, child)	paidos	-os	paid-	ped- (child)

To English *ornith-* (< G. *ornith-*, base of *ornithos*: bird), we can attach a connecting *-o-* and the English combining-form *-logy*, "the science, study, theory, or doctrine of" (< G. *-log-* [base of *logos*]: word, thought, reason, reckoning, discourse + *-ia*: the act, process, condition, or result of), forming *ornithology* (the branch of zoology dealing with the study of birds). Or if we replace the *-logy* with *-osis*, a scientific and medical suffix, having, in this word, the modern medical meaning, "a diseased or abnormal state or condition of" (< G. *-o-*: connecting vowel + *-sis*: the act, process, condition, or result of), we derive *ornithosis* (an infectious disease of birds, similar to parrot fever or psittacosis [sit´ə· kō´sis; < G. *psittak-* [base of *psittakos*]: parrot + *-osis*). And if we replace the *-sis* in *ornithosis* with the English combining form *-mancy*, "divination or prophecy by" (< G. *mant-* [base of *mantis*]: prophet, seer, soothsayer + *-eia*: the act, process, condition, or result of), we derive the obscure but colorful *ornithomancy* (ôr´nə·thə·man´sē; divination or prophecy by observing the flight of birds).

Similarly, to *phylac-* (< G. *phylak-*, base of *phylakos*: a guard), the second English root in the table above, we can add the prefix *pro-* (< G. *pro-*: before, in front of) and the adjective-forming suffix *-tic* (< G. *-tik-*, base of *-tikos*: pertaining to, characterized by), creating the English word *prophylactic* (preventing or protecting, or that which prevents or protects, especially against disease or infection), a word we hear much about in dentistry and certain more delicate areas. And if we remove the *pro-* and replace it with *tachy-* (< G. *tachy-*, base of *tachys*: fast, swift, rapid), we turn up the unusual and complex *tachyphylactic* (tak´ē·fī·lak´tik; having or characterized by a decreased sensitivity to a substance, as a drug or toxin, achieved by prior ingestion or injection of small dosages of that substance). A very similar word to *tachyphylactic* but with its emphasis on the "toxin" rather than the "drug" is *mithridatic* (mith´ri·dat´ik; of or characterized by having developed an immunity to a poison by taking gradually increasing dosages of that poison), a word named after "Mithridates the Great," king of Pontus (an ancient kingdom south of the Black Sea) from 120 B.C. to 63 B.C., who presumably immunized himself against being poisoned by his rivals by using this method. However, what his rivals could not accomplish he himself had by committing suicide in 63 B.C. Yet in a sense he never died: his name lives on as an English eponym (the name of a real or imaginary person from which a word or name derives, or the word itself).

Finally, to the initial side of *ped-*, "child," (< G. *pais-*, base of *paidos*: boy, child), the third English root in the table above, we can insert the root *orth-* (< G. *orth-*, base of *orthos*: straight, correct) followed by a connecting *-o-*, and to the terminal side of *ped-* we can append the noun-forming suffix *-ics*, meaning, in this context, "the art, science, study, or discipline of" (< L. *-ic-*, base of *-ica-*, neuter plural of *-icus*: pertaining to, characterized by [< G. *-ika*, neuter plural of *-ikos*] + E. *-s*: plural suffix]), forming *orthopedics* (the branch of medicine that deals with the treatment and care of injuries and impairments of the musculoskeletal system), which originally, in ancient Greece, focused primarily on ensuring the proper bone development of children and, in particular, of little boys. In the word *orthopedics*, if we discard the *orth-* and replace it with *log-* (< G. *log-*, base of *logos*: word, speech), we come up with *logopedics* (the scientific study and treatment of speech defects). And by removing the *log-* and *-o-* and adding a variety of prefixes and suffixes, we can create such *ped-*, "child," words as *pedagogue, pediatrics, pedodontics* (pē′də·dän′tiks; the branch of dentistry specializing in the care and treatment of children's teeth), and *encyclopedia*.

A special group of third declension nouns that provide English with a relatively large group of derivatives ends in *-ma* in the nominative and *-matos* in the genitive. These endings are unusual in that each one forms a separate word from which a Greek base and, hence, an English root may be formed. Thus, unlike most Latin and Greek words in which a base is derived either from the nominative or genitive, in these forms, a base is derived from both the nominative and genitive.

The nominative base is obtained by dropping the *-a* from its *-ma* ending, and the genitive base is obtained by dropping the *-os* from its *-matos* ending. For example, *sōma*, "body," has the genitive *sōmatos*. By removing the *-a* from *sōma*, the Greek base *sōm-* is derived, which becomes the English root *som-*; and by removing the *-os* from *sōmatos*, the Greek base *sōmat-* is derived, which becomes the English root *somat-*. Similarly, *haima*, "blood," has the genitive *haimatos*. By dropping the *-a* from *haima*, the Greek base *haim-* is obtained, which, through Latinization and Anglicization, becomes English *hem-*; and by dropping the *-os* from *haimatos*, the Greek base *haimat-* is obtained, which, through the same linguistic processes, becomes English *hemat-*. This is all illustrated in the table below.

GREEK THIRD DECLENSION *-MA, -MATOS* NOUNS YIELDING ENGLISH ROOTS

Nom. Sing.	Genitive Sing.	Inflect. Endings		Greek Bases		English Roots
		NOM	GEN	NOM	GEN	
sōma (body)	sōmatos	-a	-os	sōm-	sōmat-	som-, somat-
haima (blood)	haimatos	-a	-os	haim-	haimat-	hem-, hemat-

We can create English words from these roots as we do with any other roots. For example, to the initial side of English *som-* (< G. *sōm-*, base of *sōma*: body), we can attach *chrom-* (< G. *chrōm-*, base of *chrōma*: color) and a connecting *-o-*, and to the terminal side of *som-* we can append a silent final *-e*, forming *chromosome*. If we then replace the *chrom-* with *mon-* (< G. *mon-*, base of *monos*: single, alone), we get *monosome* (a chromosome having no paired counterpart, especially an unpaired X [female] chromosome). And if we replace the *mon-* with *acr-* (< G. *akr-*, base of *akros*: top, tip, high point), we derive *acrosome* (a delicate sac or body at the tip of a sperm which contains enzymes that dissolve the protective coating of the female egg, allowing the sperm to enter). We can then discard the *-o-* and *-some* and tack on an *-onym* (< G. *onym-*, base of *onyma*: name), producing *acronym* (a word formed from the first or first few letters of two or more words). And if we replace the *acro-* with *epi-* (< G. *epi-*: over, upon, on), we derive *eponym*, a word we recently encountered in relation to Mithridates the Great. Other *-onym* words include *synonym, antonym, pseudonym* (a fictitious name, especially one used by an author; pen name), *anonym* (an anonymous person), *ananym* (a name spelled backward), *caconym* (an erroneous or linguistically undesirable name, especially in taxonomic classifications), and *anthroponym* (an·thräp´ə·nim; a personal name).

Similarly, to English *somat-* (< G. *sōmat-*, base of *sōmatos*, genitive of *sōma*: body), the second English root in the table above, we can add the adjective-forming suffix *-ic* (< G. *-ik-*, base of *-ikos*: pertaining to, characterized by), creating *somatic* (of or relating to the body, particularly as distinguished from the mind). If we then prefix the *somat-* with *psych-* (< G. *psychē*: breath, spirit, soul, mind) and insert a connecting *-o-* between these roots, we derive *psychosomatic* (of or relating to a disease or physical condition that originates in the mind or is aggravated by psychological or emotional factors). And if we then switch the *psych-* with *somat-*, we get its opposite, *somatopsychic* (sə·mat´ə· sī´kik, sō´mə·tə·sī´kik; of or relating to a psychological condition or state that originates in or is aggravated by a physical disorder or disease).

To English *hem-* (< G. *haim-*, base of *haima*: blood), the third English root in the table above, we can append the adjective-forming suffix *-al* (< L. *-āl-*, base of *-ālis*: pertaining to, characterized by), forming *hemal* (of or pertaining to the blood). If we then remove the *-al* and affix a connecting *-o-* and *-rrhag-* (< G. *-rrhag-* < *rhēgnynai*: to break, to burst) and tack on a silent final *-e*, we get *hemorrhage*. Or if we replace the *-rrhag-* with *cyt-* (< G. *kyt-*, base of *kytos*: a hollow vessel, receptacle, cell), we derive *hemocyte* (a blood cell). And if you really like technical terms, we can remove the final *-e* and add another connecting *-o-*, the root *poie-* (< G. *poie-*, base of *poiein*: to make, to form), and the noun-forming suffix *-sis* (< G. *-sis*: the act, process, condition, or result of), creating *hemocytopoiesis* (hē´mō· sī´tō·poi·ē´sis; the formation and development of blood cells, usually in the bone marrow), which, being such a mouthful, is usually represented by its shortened form, *hemopoiesis*.

To English *hemat-* (< G. *haimat-*, base of *haimatos*, genitive of *haima*: blood), the fourth English root in the table above, we can append the adjective-forming suffix *-ic* (< G. *-ik-*, base of *-ikos*: pertaining to, characterized by), forming *hematic* (of or pertaining to the blood). Thus, *hemal* and *hematic* are synonyms, and this illustrates how two words, one derived from the Greek nominative base *haim-* and the other derived from the Greek genitive base *haimat-*, have come to coexist in English. Similarly, we have the pairs *hemopoiesis* (the formation and development of bloods cells—described above) and *hematopoiesis* (hē´mə·tō·poi·ē´sis); and *hemorrhea* (hem´ə·rē´ə, hē´mə-) and *hematorrhea* (hē´mə·tə· rē´ə, hem-´; a copious flowing of blood from a ruptured blood vessel or hemorrhage < G. *haim-* and *haimat-*, respectively + *-o-*: connecting vowel + *-rrhoia*: a flowing [< *rhoia*: a flow < *rho-* (base of *rhein*: to flow) + *-ia*: the act, process, condition, or result of]).

But not all words derived from *hem-* and *hemat-* form corresponding pairs or synonyms. *Hemophilia* and *hemorrhoid*, words derived from the nominative base *haim-*, do not have corresponding forms derived from the genitive base *haimat-*. Conversely, *hematoma* (hē´mə·tō´mə; a localized mass of blood, usually clotted, beneath the skin or in an organ or tissue, caused by a break in the wall of one or more blood vessels; cf. CIRCUMORBITAL HEMATOMA), a word derived from the genitive base *haimat-*, does not have a corresponding form derived from the nominative base *haim-*. So do not get carried away by "creating" words that do not exist.

In addition to providing us with many interesting words, Greek nouns ending in -*ma* have furnished English with an alternative plural form to our more mundane (common, ordinary) native -*s*.

To create a plural of a Greek third declension noun ending in -*ma*, we must start with the genitive of that word, which ends in -*matos*. We then remove the -*os*, revealing the base -*mat*-, and to this base we add the Greek plural suffix -*a*. This then results in a word ending in -*mata*, which serves as the plural ending for both the genitive and the nominative and passes unchanged into English.

For example, Greek *sōma*, "body," has the genitive *sōmatos* and the resulting base *sōmat*-. By adding an -*a* to this base, we form the Greek plural form *sōmata*, which yields the alternative English plural *somata* (sō′mə·tə) for the English word *soma* (sō′mə; the body of an animal or plant as distinguished from its germ or sex cells). Thus, in English we can use either *somas* or *somata* as the plural of *soma*, as in the sentence, "The somas [or somata] of these insects are not affected by the radiation though their germ cells are." Similarly, Greek *karkinōma*, "cancer," has the genitive *karkinōmatos* and the resulting base *karkinōmat*-. By adding an -*a* to this base, we derive the Greek plural form *karkinō-mata*, which yields the alternative English plural *carcinomata* (kär′sə·nō′mə·tə) to the more common *carcinomas*. The construction of these alternative plural endings is summarized below.

GREEK THIRD DECLENSION PLURALS OF WORDS ENDING IN -*MA*

Nominative Singular	Genitive Singular	Greek Base	Plural Ending	Greek Plural	English Plural
sōma (body)	sōmatos	sōmat-	-a	sōmata	somata
karkinōma (body)	karkinōmatos	karkinōmat-	-a	karkinōmata	carcinomata

Greek *karkinōma*, incidentally, is composed of two Greek elements: *karkin*-, the base of *karkinos*: crab, cancer + -*ōma*: the result of (which is itself composed of two elements: -*ō*-, the base of verbs ending in -*oun*, and -*ma*: the result of). In English, however, -*oma* has developed the specialized medical meaning,"a tumor or swelling of (that which is designated by the preceding base or elements)." Hence, English *carcinoma* means "a crab (*carcin*-) tumor (-*oma*)"—the ancient Greeks having associated cancer with crabs with regard to the crablike pattern of distended blood vessels radiating from the site of certain cancers. And the ancient Romans, either impressed by this observation or simply following without thinking, translated Greek *karkinos* into *cancer*, which therefore also means "crab."

In addition to Greek nouns ending in -*matos*, those ending in -*sis* have not only furnished us with a large number of derivatives—such as *diagnosis*, *prognosis*, *crisis*, *analysis*, *emphasis*, and *psycho-analysis*—but have provided us with another plural ending, -*ses*, or more accurately, -*es*.

The etymology of this plural is as follows: Greek words ending in -*sis* have a base that can be found by dropping the final -*is*. To this base the Greek plural suffix -*eis* is attached, creating a plural form which, through the reduction of the Greek diphthong *ei* to English *e*, yields our Greek-derived plural -*es* (not to be confused with our native plural -*es*). Since the end of the Greek base is always -*s* (the remaining letter after the inflectional -*is* is dropped), the affixation of -*eis* to this -*s* forms the Greek plural ending -*seis*, which then becomes English -*ses*. Thus, the Greek singular and plural endings appear as -*sis* and -*seis*, respectively, which in turn become English -*sis* and -*ses*.

For example, Greek *diagnōsis*, "a discerning or distinguishing," is a third declension noun that ends in *-sis*. By dropping its final *-is*, we disclose its base *diagnōs-*, which, by the addition of the Greek plural *-eis*, forms *diagnōseis*, which then passes into English as *diagnoses*. Similarly, Greek *prognōsis*, "a knowing beforehand or foreknowledge," is a third declension noun having the base *prognōs-*. By attaching the Greek plural ending *-eis* to this base we get *prognōseis*, which passes into English as *prognoses*. These examples are shown below.

GREEK THIRD DECLENSION PLURALS OF WORDS ENDING IN *-SIS*

Nominative Singular	Greek Base	Plural Ending	Plural Word	English Word
diagnōsis (a discerning)	diagnōs-	-eis	diagnōseis	diagnoses
prognōsis (foreknowledge)	prognōs-	-eis	prognōseis	prognoses

Greek *diagnōsis*, incidentally, is composed of three Greek roots: *dia-*: through, throughout, across + *gnō-* (the base of *gignōskein*): to know + *-sis*: the act, process, condition, or result of. *Prognōsis* is also composed of three roots: *pro-*: before, in front of + *gnō-* (the base of *gignōskein*): to know + *-sis*: the act, process, condition, or result of. Thus, *diagnōsis* and *prognōsis* are distinguished only by their prefixes, and in English a *diagnosis* commonly refers to the act or process of identifying, through medical examination, the nature and cause of a disease or injury, whereas *prognosis* refers to the prediction (i.e., the foreknowledge), usually by a physician, of the course and outcome of that disease or injury and the patient's chances of recovery. A *diagnosis*, therefore, always precedes a *prognosis*, and a physician must *diagnose* before he or she can *prognosticate*. (Interestingly, *prognose*, as a counterpart to *diagnose*, has never become popular in English, and medical personnel generally use *prognosticate* to express this sense. But *prognosticate*, unlike *diagnose*, is much more common in nonmedical usage, where it means, "to predict, foretell, or prophesy.")

To return to plurals. Certain other third declension Greek nouns form plurals by attaching *-es* (rather than *-eis*) to the base of their *genitive*. With regard to English derivatives, this is most notable in those words ending in *-x*. For example, Greek *larynx*, "the upper end of the windpipe or trachea," has the genitive *laryngos* with the resulting base *laryng-*. By attaching *-es* to this base, we form the Greek plural *larynges*, which then passes into English as *larynges* (lə‧rin´jēz), the plural of English *larynx* (the muscular upper end of the trachea, containing the vocal cords). Similarly, Greek *mēninx*, "membrane," has the genitive *mēningos* with the resulting base *mēning-*. And by attaching *-es* to this base, we produce the Greek plural *mēninges* and, hence, English *meninges* (mə‧nin´jēz; the three membranes that surround and protect the brain and spinal cord), the plural of the seldom heard *meninx* (mē´ningks). These are illustrated in the table below.

GREEK THIRD DECLENSION PLURALS OF WORDS ENDING IN *-X*

Nominative Singular	Genitive Singular	Greek Base	Plural Ending	Greek Plural	English Plural
larynx (upper windpipe)	laryngos	laryng-	-es	larynges	larynges
mēninx (membrane)	mēningos	mēning-	-es	mēninges	meninges

Of course, in place of the Greek-derived, English plural *-es* (not isolated in the table above, but see columns four and six), we could just as easily attach other English suffixes to the English roots derived from the Greek bases *laryng-* and *mēning-* (see column three). For example, to English *laryng-* (< G.

laryng-, base of *laryngos*, genitive of *larynx*: upper windpipe), we could add the noun-forming suffix *-itis*, "the inflammation of" (< G. *-itis*, feminine form of the adjective-forming suffix *-itēs*: of, relating to, belonging to, or having the characteristics of—but understood in this context to mean "the disease of"), forming *laryngitis*. And if we attach this suffix to *mening-* (< G. *mēning-*, base of *mēningos*, genitive of *mēninx*: membrane), we get *meningitis* (the inflammation of the meninges, generally caused by a bacterial or viral infection and characterized by high fever, intense headache, loss of appetite, and other symptoms). By adding other appropriate suffixes and combining forms to *laryng-*, we can form such words as *laryngeal*, *laryngology*, *laryngologist*, *laryngoscopy*, and *laryngopharyngeal*. And by affixing these and similar suffixes and combining forms to *mening-*, we can create such words as *meningeal*, *meningitic*, *meningioma*, *meningococcus*.

One final caveat (a caution or warning) with regard to identifying third declension nouns: certain nouns in this declension end in *-os* in the nominative singular, which is identical to the nominative singular ending of most second declension masculine nouns. Moreover, the bases of both of these forms can be found by dropping this *-os*. For example, Greek *hēlios*, "sun," *hippos*, "horse," and *polemos*, "war," are second declension nouns and have the respective bases, *hēli-*, *hipp-*, and *polem-*. On the other hand, Greek *anthos*, "flower," *ethnos*, "people, nation," and *kallos*, "beauty," are third declension nouns and have the respective bases, *anth-*, *ethn-*, and *kall-*. So how can you tell to which declension a nominative Greek noun ending in *-os* belongs? Well, in the first place—and please don't quote me on this—since there are substantially more second declension nouns that end in *-os* than third declension nouns, if really pressed for an answer you can conjecture (that's a fancy word for *guess*) that the word is a second declension noun, and most of the time you'll be right. Then again, you may be rolling snake eyes (a cast of two in craps, which means you lose). The real answer—which is no answer—is that unless you study Greek you can't know. But for our purposes it doesn't really matter, for we will dissect, analyze, and reconstruct *all* nominative singular nouns ending in *-os* in the same exact way, regardless of declension. But don't always assume that what you think is a second (or third) declension neuter noun is necessarily a second (or third) declension neuter noun.

Greek Adjectives

Greek adjectives are classified in two groups: those adopted from the inflectional endings of first and second declension nouns (which are usually classified together, as they are in Latin) and those adopted from the inflectional endings of first and third declension nouns (which are also usually classified together). In Latin, as you may recall, third declension adjectives stand alone.

In forming adjectives, Greek words change their inflectional endings to agree with the case (nominative, genitive, etc.), gender (masculine, feminine, or neuter), and number (singular or plural) of the noun they are modifying. Thus, an adjective that modifies a genitive neuter plural noun must use a genitive neuter plural ending, and an adjective that modifies an ablative feminine singular noun must use an ablative feminine singular ending. But, again, since we are not attempting to learn Greek or to construct Greek phrases or sentences, we need only be aware of a few of these endings, and most of them we already know from our discussion of Greek nouns.

Greek First and Second Declension Adjectives

Greek first and second declension adjectives are classified together because, as with Latin, they utilize the feminine endings of the first declension and the masculine and neuter adjectives of the second declension. So together these two declensions supply the endings for all three genders.

Greek first declension *feminine* nouns, you'll recall, always end in *-a* or *-ē*. Second declension *masculine* nouns end in *-os*, and second declension *neuter* nouns end in *-on*. Together, these constitute four singular forms we should be familiar with, and any Greek adjective that falls within the category we call "first and second declension Greek adjectives" must attach one of these endings to its base to enable it to agree with the noun it is modifying. In the following table, the masculine, feminine, or neuter forms of *kakos*, "bad, evil," and *heteros*, "other," are shown in their singular forms to illustrate how these endings look in actual words.

GREEK FIRST AND SECOND DECLENSION ADJECTIVES YIELDING ENGLISH ROOTS

Masculine	Feminine	Neuter	Greek Base	English Root
kakos (bad, evil)	(kakē)	(kakon)	kak-	cac-
heteros (other)	(hetera)	(heteron)	heter-	heter-

The first thing to note here is that these bases remain constant regardless of gender. Thus *kakos*, *kakē*, and *kakon* all have the base *kak-*, and *heteros*, *hetera*, and *heteron* all have the base *heter-*. The feminine and neuter forms are in parentheses because, as with Latin, English dictionaries provide only the masculine adjectival forms and, with few exceptions, this is the only form you need to know. Thus, when analyzing and reconstructing English adjectives based upon *cac-*, the Anglicized form of Greek *kak-*, you will trace these to masculine *kakos*, which is the only form you will see in dictionaries. Since it is not necessary to distinguish the gender or number of Greek adjectives—or to attach the appropriate endings so that they agree with any particular noun—the process of dissecting, analyzing, and reconstructing adjectives will be the same as that used for nouns; and unless you happen to be aware that a particular Greek word is an adjective, you would not know the difference.

For example, to English *cac-* (< G. *kak-*, base of *kakos*: bad, evil), we can add a connecting *-o-*, the root *phon-* (< G. *phōn-*, base of *phōnē*: sound, voice), and the adjective-forming suffix *-ous* (in most words < L. *-ōsus*: full of, abounding in, characterized by, like; but in this word an Anglicization of G. *-os*: adjectival suffix), forming *cacophonous* (having or emitting a harsh, grating sound or sounds). And we might verbalize this etymology: "*cacophonous* consists of four elements: *cac-*, *-o-*, *phon-*, and *-ous*. The *cac-* is derived from Greek *kak-*, which is the base of *kakos*, which means 'bad or evil.' The *-o-* is derived from Greek *-o-*, which is a connecting vowel used to link different elements in primarily Greek-derived words. The *phon-* is derived from Greek *phōn-*, which is the base of *phōnē*, which means 'sound or voice,' and the *-ous* is an Anglicization of the Greek adjective-forming suffix *-os*, which in this word can be said to mean 'full of, abounding in, characterized by, or like.' So when we put all of these elements together we get 'full of or abounding in (*-ous*) bad (*cac-*) sound (*phon-*).'"

Similarly, to *heter-* (< G. *heter-*, base of *heteros*: other), the second English root in the table above, we can add the connecting vowel *-o-*, the root *sex-* (< L. *sex-*, base of *sexus*: sex), a connecting *-u-*, and the adjective-forming suffix *-al* (< L. *-āl-*, base of *-ālis*: pertaining to, characterized by), forming *het-*

erosexual. And if we replace the *heter-* with *hom-* (< G. *hom-*, base of *homos*: same), we transform *heterosexual* into *homosexual*. But the *homo-* in *homosexual* (which actually comprises two elements: *hom-*: same + *-o-*: connecting vowel) should not be confused with the *Homo* in *Homo sapiens*, which, as we have seen, derives from Latin *homō*, "human being" (and comprises but one root). Other *heter-* words you might try to work into conversation include *heterogeneous* (het´ər·ə·jē´nē·əs; composed or made up of dissimilar or unrelated parts, elements, types, etc.), *heterodox* (opposed or departing from established or accepted doctrines or beliefs; unorthodox), and *heteronym* (a word with the same spelling as another but having a different meaning and pronunciation, as bass [bās; a deep, low-pitched sound or tone, or an instrument or male singing voice having such sound or tones]; and bass [bas; any of two families of fish, one of freshwater and the other marine]). You might also wish to check your dictionary for the related but confusable terms, *homonym*, *homophone*, and *homograph*, but you should first try to figure out their meanings based on the two defining roots in each word.

A useful observation about Greek-derived compound adjectives is that, as with English adjectival phrases (e.g., *a small car*; *the highest mountain*; *circumorbital hematoma*), the adjectival element often comes first and is followed by or joined to the substantival (noun) element it modifies. Thus, in *cacophonous*, the adjectival element *cac-* (< G. *kak-*, base of *kakos*: bad, evil) occurs in the beginning of the word and is then joined via a connecting *-o-* to the substantival element *phon-* (< G. *phōn-*, base of *phōnē*: sound, voice); and in *heterosexual*, the adjectival element *heter-* (< G. *heter-*, base of *heteros*: other) occurs first and is also joined via a connecting *-o-* to the substantival element *sex* (< L. *sex-*, base of *sexus*: sex). We will see this pattern repeated, with or without connecting *-o-*'s, throughout this book.

Greek First and Third Declension Adjectives

Greek first and third declension adjectives are classified together because they use the feminine endings of the first declension and the masculine and neuter adjectives of the third declension. So together these two declensions supply the endings for all three genders.

The endings in first and third declension adjectives, unlike those of first and second declension adjectives, will be new to you. Generally, the masculine form has the ending *-ys*, of which its base can be found by dropping the *-s* or, less frequently, the *-ys*; the feminine form has the ending *-eia*, and its base can be found by dropping this *-eia* (note that this form still ends in the characterictic feminine *-a*); and the neuter form has the ending *-y*, and its base can likewise be found by dropping this *-y*. These adjectival endings in the Greek words *bradys*, "slow, heavy," and *tachys*, "fast, swift, rapid," are evident in the table below.

GREEK FIRST AND THIRD DECLENSION ADJECTIVES YIELDING ENGLISH ROOTS

Masculine	Feminine	Neuter	Greek Base	English Root
bradys (slow, heavy)	(bradeia)	(brady)	brady-	brady-
tachys (fast, swift, rapid)	(tachyeia)	(tachy)	tachy-	tachy-

Again, the feminine and neuter forms are in parentheses because, as with first and third declension adjectives, English dictionaries generally provide only the masculine form, and these are the ones we must know. Thus, to English *brady-* (< G. *brady-*, base of *bradys*: slow, heavy), we can add *cardi-* (<

G. *kardi-*, base of *kardia*: heart) and the noun-forming suffix *-ia* (< G. *-ia*: the state, condition, or result of), yielding the medical term *bradycardia* (an abnormally slow heartbeat, generally below 60 beats per minute in adults who do not engage in regular physical activity). If we then remove the *cardi-* and replace it with *lex-* (< G. *lex-*, base of *lexis*: word, speech, text), we get *bradylexia* (abnormally slow reading), not to be confused with *dyslexia* (an impairment in the ability to read < G. *dys-*: bad, difficult [in E., also meaning: abnormal, dysfunctional, impaired] + *lex-* [base of *lexis*]: word, speech, text + *-ia*: the state, condition, or result of). Similarly, by switching suffixes, we can form *bradylalia* (brad´i·lā´ lē·ə; abnormally slow or labored speech < G. *brady-* [base of *bradys*]: slow, heavy + *lal-* [base of *lalein*]: to speak, babble, chatter + *-ia*: the state, condition, or result of), *bradyphagia* (brad´i·fā´jē·ə; abnormally slow eating < G. *brady-* [base of *bradys*]: slow, heavy + *-phag-* [base of *-phagos*]: eating, devouring + *-ia*: the state, condition, or result of), and *bradytocia* (brad´i·tō´sē·ə; abnormally slow or lingering childbirth < G. *brady-* [base of *bradys*]: slow, heavy + *tok-* [base of *tokos*]: childbirth + *-ia*: the state, condition, or result of).

Similarly, to English *tachy-* (< G. *tachy-*, base of *tachys*: fast, swift, rapid), the second English root on the table above, we can add *cardi-* (< G. *kardi-*, base of *kardia*: heart) plus the noun-forming suffix *-ia* (< G. *-ia*: the state, condition, or result of), yielding the medical term *tachycardia* (an abnormally fast heartbeat, generally above 100 beats per minute in adults at rest). Or if we remove the *cardi-* and replace it with *phylac-* (< G. *phylak-*, base of *phylakos*: a guard) and append the adjective-forming suffix *-tic* (< G. *-tik-*, base of *-tikos*: pertaining to, characterized by), we get *tachyphylactic* (tak´ē·fī·lak´tik), a word we have already met in connection with *prophylactic*. Other *tachy-* words of some interest include *tachypnea* (tak´i(p)·nē´ə; abnormally fast breathing < G. *tachy-* [base of *tachys*]: fast, swift, rapid + ?*pn(o)ē*: a breathing [< *pn(ein)*: to breathe] + *-(i)a*: the state, condition, or result off), *tachyphagia* (abnormally fast eating < G. *tachy-* [base of *tachys*]: fast, swift, rapid + *-phag-* [base of *-phagos*]: eating, devouring + *-ia*: the state, condition, or result of), and *tachymeter* (ta·kim´i·tər, tə-; any of several types of surveying instruments designed for rapidly determining elevations, directions, and distances < G. *tachy-* [base of *tachys*]: fast, swift, rapid + E. *-meter* [< G. *metron*: a measure]). Incidentally, the first element *tachy-* in *tachymeter* is derived from the base of the Greek adjective *tachys*, "fast, swift, rapid," and should not be confused with the first element *tach-* in *tachometer* (ta·käm´i·tər, tə-; an instrument for measuring revolutions per unit of time, as that found in certain non-American automobiles), which is derived from the base of the Greek noun *tachos*, "speed."

Greek Verbs

Whereas most English derivatives from Latin verbs can be traced to the bases of infinitives, past participles, or present participles (with gerundives running a distant fourth), English derivatives from Greek verbs can be traced to an infinitive or one or more of six different verb forms derived from an infinitive, called *principal parts*. For the common verb *graphein*, "to write, to draw," the six principal parts are shown below.

GREEK PRINCIPAL PARTS OF THE VERB GRAPHEIN

Present	Future	Aorist	Perfect	Perf. Middle/Passive	Aorist Passive
graphō	grapsō	egrapsa	gegrapha	gegrammai	eigraphēn

Don't let that table scare you. There is no reason to learn the names or meanings of these parts (unless you intend to study Greek), and I include them only to give you a sense of where our Greek-derived verbal roots originate. In this paradigm, two Greek bases, *graph-* and *gram-*, derive from four of these six parts and ultimately from the infinitive *graphein*; and these bases, in turn, yield English roots which then join with other English roots to form English words. For other Greek words using other paradigms, the number and combination of principal parts, bases, and hence English roots vary.

In English dictionaries, the principal parts are *never* cited, regardless of the size of the dictionary or the origin of a word. This is unfortunate because with Latin, the infinitive, past participial, present participial, and gerundive forms are always provided in college and unabridged dictionaries. But with Greek verbs, only the infinitive and the specific base from which a particular English root derives is given, and English dictionaries invariably state or imply that the base is derived from or akin to the infinitive, completely bypassing the six principal parts. This then explains why Greek bases often have letters that are not reflected in the infinitive, and unless you study Greek you will have no way of knowing from which principal part, if any, a particular base derives.

Because of this limitation in English dictionaries, when we are considering the etymology of a Greek-derived English word, we will focus on two verb forms: the Greek infinitive, which forms the foundation of the six principal parts, and the particular Greek base, which is derived either directly or indirectly from the infinitive and yields an English root that forms the basis of the word. In this regard, the infinitive is clearly the fundamental and most important verb form to understand.

Most Greek infinitives end in *-ein*, or, to a lesser extent, *-nai*, *-an*, *-oun*, or, for deponents (verbs that have a passive form but active voice), *-thai*, as in *-asthai*, *-esthai*, *-eisthai*, and *-ousthai*. Indeed, it would be a great convenience if, as with Latin words, we could simply remove these inflectional endings to reveal the base of a Greek verb. But with the exception of certain verbs ending in *-ein*, such as *ballein*, "to throw," and *pherein*, "to bear, to carry," this will generally not work. And even for these verbs it will only work in certain situations.

To return to our example of *graphein* with its six principal parts, if you look up a word in a college or unabridged dictionary that is derived from the base of one of these six parts, such as *biography*, you will ultimately be informed of the Greek infinitive and base forming the foundation of this word, though you may have to do a certain amount of cross referencing (i.e., jumping around) between dictionary entries and apply a little inductive reasoning to turn up this information.

Specifically, you will first be informed, depending on which dictionary you consult, that the first element *bio-* (English dictionaries love to join combining forms with connecting vowels as though they were one root) is derived from Greek *bios*, which means "life," and that the second element, *-graphy* (which you will probably be directed to look up in another part of the dictionary) is derived from Greek *-graphia*, "a drawing" (with possibly some other roots or combining forms, such as *-graphos*, "written, drawn," cited as sources or intermediate forms). In any case, once you remove the obvious noun-forming suffix *-ia* from *-graphia* (or the *-os* from *-graphos*), this will reveal the base *graph-*, which most dictionaries will then inform you, either directly or indirectly, is derived from *graphein*, which they will variously define as "to write," "to draw," "to scratch," "to incise," or some combination of these. So with a modicum of patience and investigation you can determine that the *-graphy* in *biography* is derived from Greek -*graphia*, which is constructed upon the base *graph-*, which in turn is derived from the infinitive *graphein*.

Similarly, if you look up *program*, you will learn that this word is derived from Greek *programma*, which most dictionaries will indicate (without informing you that *programma* means "a written public notice") is derived from *prographein*, "to write in public," which in turn comes from the two elements *pro-*, "before, in front of," and *graphein*, "to write, to draw," etc. And other dictionaries, after citing *programma*, will send you to the headwords *pro-* and -*gram* (or some other word or root), where they will inform you that English -*gram* is derived from Greek -*gramma*, which means "that which is written or drawn." At some point, however, most dictionaries will state or imply that -*gramma*, or one of its related forms, is derived from *graphein*. With this information, then, after you remove the noun-forming suffix -*ma* from Greek -*gramma* or the prefix *pro-* and the suffix -*ma* from Greek *programma* (depending on which dictionary you are using), you will see that *gram-* is the base of *program* and is either derived from or akin to the Greek infinitive *graphein*.

Another common—and regular—Greek verb is *lyein*, "to loosen, break up, separate," which has the following six principal parts:

GREEK PRINCIPAL PARTS OF THE VERB LYEIN

Present	Future	Aorist	Perfect	Perf. Middle/Passive	Aorist Passive
lyō	lysō	elysa	lelyka	lelymai	elythēn

A glance at this table will reveal that the common base must be *ly-* since this is the only combination of letters found in all six principal parts as well as in the infinitive *lyein*. And if an English root is derived from this verb, it too should logically be *ly-*. This is indeed the case, and in dictionary etymologies of English words derived from these principal parts, both the infinitive *lyein* and the common base *ly-* will always be cited. With this information, we can now construct some derivative English words.

To begin, if we prefix *hydr-* (< G. *hydr-*, base of *hydōr*: water) and a connecting -*o-* to *ly-* (< G. *ly-*, base of *lyein*: to loosen, break up, separate) and append the noun-forming suffix -*sis* (< G. -*sis*: the act, process, condition, or result of) to the end of this formation, we derive *hydrolysis* (hy·drăl´i·sis; a chemical reaction in which a compound splits or decomposes into two or more other compounds as a result of combining with water). If we then replace the *hydr-* with *electr-*, "electric" (< G. *ēlektr-*, base of *ēlektron*: amber [a hard, translucent, brownish-yellow fossil resin derived from certain evergreen trees and sometimes found along seacoasts], which fascinated the ancients by its ability to generate static electricity when rubbed), we derive *electrolysis* (i·lek·trăl´i·sis; the destruction or decomposition of a chemical compound or other substance, as human hair roots, by the application of an electric current). And if we replace the *electr-* with *onych-* (< G. *onych-*, base of *onychos*, genitive of *onyx*: nail, claw, hoof), we derive *onycholysis* (ăn´i·kăl´i·sis; the loosening and detachment of a fingernail or toenail from its nail bed—often occurring after unceremoniously striking one's finger with a hammer). Finally, if we substitute -*phag* (< G. *phag-*, base of *phagos*: eating, devouring [< *phagein*: to eat, to devour]) for -*lysis* and append a final -*ist* (< G. -*ist-*, the base of -*istēs*: one who), we wind up with the very practical and rather amusing *onychophagist* (ăn´ə·kăf´ə·jist; a nail-biter), a word you should have no difficulty working into conversation, especially if you're a parent.

Ablaut and Reduplication

Many Greek bases with derivative roots in English exhibit a process known as *ablaut* (äb´lout, ab´-; < Ger. *ab*: off, from + *Laut*: sound) or *apophony* (ə·päf´ə·nē; < G. *apo-*: away, from, off + *phōn-* [base of *phōnē*]: sound, voice + *-ia*: the act, process, condition, or result of). In this process, a word changes its internal vowel rather than or in addition to its inflectional ending to alter its tense or part of speech. For example, in English we normally add a *-d* or *-ed* to a verb to convert it from the present tense to the past tense, as in *talk* and *talked*. But in some words, we instead change an internal vowel to represent the same shift in tense, as in *drink, drank, drunk*; and *sing, sang, sung* (which, by making one more change, we can convert into the noun *song*). And in still other words, we shift one or more consonants as well as the vowel to effect this change, as in *fly, flew, flown*. (In our discussion of declensions on page 189, we cited the nouns *goose, mouse, tooth, foot, louse, man*, and *woman* as examples of words that form their plurals primarily by changing an internal vowel rather than appending an inflectional ending. While this process is similar to ablaut as described here, historically it is derived from a different process, one technically known as *umlaut*, which, involving Old English phonology, is beyond the scope of this book.)

Similarly, the Greek verb *legein*, "to gather, to choose, to speak," has the *apophonic* bases *log-* and *lek*; the verb *pherein*, "to bear, to carry," has the apophonic bases *pher-* and *phor-*; and *ballein*, "to throw," has the apophonic bases *ball-* and *bol-* as well as a third base, *blē-*, in which the internal vowel has gone one step beyond changing its sound: it's disappeared!

But the complications in determining verb bases do not end here. In many Greek verbs, a process know as reduplication occurs, in which a derivative or special tense of a verb is created by doubling or partially doubling a specific syllable. Unfortunately, this reduplicated syllable is not reflected in the verb's base. So when looking at an infinitive, unless you are aware of this process, it will be difficult if not impossible to determine the verb's base. But if you think in terms of reduplication you can frequently come up with or approximate the base.

For example, in the verb *tithenai*, "to put, to place," the initial *ti-* appears to be a partial reduplication of the following three letters, *-the-*. If we therefore discard the *-ti-* as well the final verb ending *-nai*, we are left with the base *the-*, which becomes the English root *the-* and appears in such words as *thesis, parenthesis*, and *hypothesis* (a proposition, or set of propositions, set forth to explain certain phenomena but which lacks the acceptability of a theory and must be further tested or investigated). Similarly, in the Greek verb *didonai*, "to give," if we discard the initial *di-* and the final *-nai*, we are left with the base *do-*, which becomes the English root *do-* and turns up in such words as *dose, antidote*, and *anecdote*.

Thus, ablaut and reduplication—among many other factors—make classification and systemization of Greek verbs and verb bases very difficult. So for the most part you will just have to learn which bases are derived from which infinitives. But with the clues so far provided and the fact that Greek verb bases often begin with the same letter or letters as their infinitives, you should have little difficulty recognizing and remembering Greek bases.

Three-Root Infinitives

Greek verbs generally yield one, two, or three Greek bases per infinitive that become English roots. Thus, *gignesthai,* "to be born, to become," has three Greek bases, *gen-, genē-,* and *gon-,* that yield, respectively, the English roots *gen-, gene-,* and *gon-.* And Greek *ballein,* "to throw," also has, as we have seen, the three Greek bases *ball-, bol-,* and *blē-* that yield, respectively, the English roots *ball-, bol-,* and *ble-* (of which the final *-e* should not be confused with the native silent final *-e*). This information is summarized in the table below.

GREEK INFINITIVES YIELDING THREE ENGLISH ROOTS PER INFINITIVE

Greek Infinitive	*Greek Bases*	*English Roots*
gignesthai (to be born)	gen-, genē-, gon-	gen-, gene-, gon-
ballein (to throw)	ball-, bol-, blē-	ball-, bol-, ble-

From these Greek infinitives, we can create an especially large number of English derivatives since we now have three roots per infinitive to work with. For example, if we prefix *phyl-* (< G. *phyl-,* base of *phylon*: tribe) and a connecting *-o-* to English *gen-* (< G. *gen-,* base of *gignesthai*: to be born, to become), the first English root in the table above, and append the noun-forming suffix *-y* (< G. *-ia*: the act, process, condition, or result of) to the end of this formation, we get *phylogeny* (fī·läj´ə·nē; the evolution or line of descent of an animal or plant species). If we then replace the *phyl-* with *ont-* (< G. *ont-,* base of *ontos,* genitive of *ōn,* neuter present participle of *einai*: to be), we derive *ontogeny* (än·täj´ə·nē; the life and development of an individual organism as distinguished from that of the species). Biology provides the maxim, "ontogeny recapitulates phylogeny," which means that an individual manifests or "repeats" certain evolutionary characteristics in its own specific (used in the sense of "pertaining to or characteristic of a species") development. For example, a human embryo exhibits some of the features of lower species of animals, such as rudimentary gill slits, attesting to our descent along the evolutionary timeline.

Similarly, to *gene-* (< G. *genē-,* base of *gignesthai*: to be born, to become), the second English root in the table above, we can add the noun-forming suffix *-sis* (< G. *-sis*: the act, process, condition, or result of), forming *genesis* (the origin or creation of something, or the manner in which it is created or formed—giving rise, with a capital *G,* to the first book of the Bible). And to *gon-* (< G. *gon-,* base of *gignesthai*: to be born, to become), the third English root in the table above, we can add the prefix *epi-* (< G. *epi-*: over, upon, on, besides, in addition to) and a silent final *-e,* creating *epigone* ("the afterborn," or any less distinguished follower or descendant, as the unexceptional adult child of a famous and important person).

To English *ball-* (< G. *ball-,* base of *ballein*: to throw), the fourth English root in the table above, we can affix *-ist-* (< G. *-ist-,* base of *-istās,* variant of *-istēs*: one who, that which) and the noun-forming suffix *-ics,* meaning, in this context, "the art, science, study, or discipline of" (< L. *-ic-,* base of *-ica-,* neuter plural of *-icus*: pertaining to, characterized by [< G. *-ika,* neut. pl. of *-ikos*] + E. *-s*: plural suffix]), forming *ballistics* (the scientific study of the motion, characteristics, and identification of projectiles, as bullets, torpedoes, and mortar shells). Or if we replace the *-ics* with *-a* (< G. *-ā-,* which is technically part of the inflectional ending of *-istās*; see -IST- above), we derive *ballista* (a military contraption resembling a large crossbow, used by the Greek, Roman, and other armies to hurl heavy stones and other objects at their enemies).

Similarly, to *bol-* (< G. *bol-*, base of *ballein*: to throw), the fifth English root in the table above, we can attach the prefix *sym-* (< G. *sym-*, a variant and assimilated form of *syn-*: with, together), forming *symbol*, or, etymologically, that which is "thrown (*bol-*) together (*sym-*)," a sense that led to a comparison of that which was thrown together and eventually to a representation or "symbol" of that which was compared. If we then replace the *sym-* with *hyper-* (< G. *hyper-*: over, above, beyond, excessively) and append a final *-e* (not a silent final *-e*, but a derivative of G. *-ē*: the first declension feminine ending, used in this word to create a noun from a verb), we derive *hyperbole* (a word or figure of speech containing an absurd exaggeration, as "He's as strong as an ox" or "She has looks that could kill." For additional examples, see *hyperbole* in chapter HYPER- in the COMMON ROOTS).

Finally, to *ble-* (< G. *blē-*, base of *ballein*: to throw), the sixth English root in the table above, we can add the prefix *em-* (< G. *em-*, variant of *en-*: in, into, within) and the noun-forming suffix *-m* (< G. *-ma*: the result of), forming *emblem*, or, etymologically, "the result of (*-ma*) throwing (*ble-*) in (*em-*)," a word which, in Latin, came to refer to inlaid ornamental work, such as wood or ivory, and, later, embossed ornamental work—a sense which, in English, grew to designate a design or symbol of that which represents something else. And if we then replace the *em-* in *emblem* with *pro-* (< G. *pro-*: before, in front of; forward, forth), we get *problem* or "the result of (*-m*) throwing (*ble-*) in front of or forward (*pro-*)," a word that originally designated an obstacle or something thrown in the way of someone, which created, as it were, a problem.

Two-Root Infinitives

Greek infinitives, such as *gignesthai*, "to be born, to become," and *ballein*, "to throw," which ultimately furnish English with three roots each, are actually quite rare. A much larger number of Greek infinitives provide English with two roots each. Examples of these are *pherein*, "to bear, to carry," which has the Greek bases *pher-* and *phor-* and yield English roots with the same spellings, and *prassein*, "to do, to perform," which has the Greek bases *prak-* and *prag-* and yield the English roots *prac-* and *prag-*. These are presented in the following table.

GREEK INFINITIVES YIELDING TWO ENGLISH ROOTS PER INFINITIVE

Greek Infinitive	Greek Bases	English Roots
pherein (to bear, to carry)	pher-, phor-	pher-, phor-
prassein (to do, to perform)	prak-, prag-	prac-, prag-

To English *pher-* (< G. *pher-*, base of *pherein*: to bear, to carry), we can add the prefix *peri-* (< G. *peri-*: around, about, surrounding, near) and the noun-forming suffix *-y* (< G. *-ia*: the act, process, condition, or result of), forming *periphery* (the perimeter or external boundary of any area or surface). If we then swap the *peri-* for *Christ* (< G. *christ-*, base of *christos*: anointed [< *chriein*: to anoint; a translation of Hebrew *māshīaḥ*: to anoint > E. *messiah*]; Jesus Christ was originally "Jesus the Christ," or "Jesus the Anointed," *Christ* being erroneously assumed to be Jesus' last name), delete the *-y*, and insert a connecting *-o-* between *Christ* and *pher-*, we derive *Christopher*, which, etymologically, means "to bear (*pher-*) Christ (*Christ*)," a word applied by early Christians to themselves, who believed that they bore Christ in their hearts. Other *Christ* names include *Chris, Christine, Christiana, Chrissie, Christabel* and a whole slew of foreign forms, including German *Christa*, Swedish *Kristina*, and Polish *Krystyna*.

Similarly, to *phor-* (< G. *phor-*, base of *pherein*: to bear, to carry), the second English root in the table above, we can add the prefix *meta-* (< G. *meta-*: along with, beside, after, beyond), creating *metaphor* (a figure of speech in which a word or phrase normally associated with one thing is applied to or identified with another, as in Shakespeare's, "How sweet the moonlight sleeps upon this bank"; or, more broadly, anything that symbolizes or conceptualizes something else, especially that which is reflective or philosophical, as "Illness is a metaphor for discontent"). If we then replace *meta-* with *eu-* (< G. *eu-*: well) and append the noun-forming suffix *-ia* (< G. *-ia*: the act, process, condition, or result of) to this formation, we produce *euphoria* (a feeling of great happiness and exhilaration, especially when not justified by external reality).

To *prac-* (< G. *prak-*, base of *prassein*: to do, to perform), the third English root in the table above, we can append *-tic-* (< G. *-tik-*, base of *-tikos*: pertaining to, characterized by) and the adjective-forming suffix *-al* (< L. *-āl-*, base of *-ālis*: pertaining to, characterized by), forming *practical*. And if we drop the *-al* and add *chir-* (< G. *ch(e)ir*: hand) and a connecting *-o-* to the beginning of this formation, we get *chiropractic* (a system for treating certain diseases and ailments based on the belief that ill health is often the result of faulty transmission of nerve impulses, which manipulation of the spinal column and other body structures can help correct).

Finally, if we affix *-mat-* (< G. *-mat-*, base of *-matos*, genitive of *-ma*: the result of) and the adjective-forming suffix *-ic* (< G. *-ik-*, base of *-ikos*: pertaining to, characterized by) to *prag-* (< G. *prag-*, base of *prassein*: to do, to perform), the fourth English root in the table above, we get *pragmatic* (practical in thought and action, especially as distinguished from theory or speculation). And if we exchange the *prag-* for *brady-* (< G. *brady-*, base of *bradys*: slow, heavy), we derive the obscure medical term *bradypragia* (brad´i·prā´jē·ə; abnormally slow movement or activity)—which, interestingly, does not have a counterpart in **tachypragia*. Evidently, "abnormally fast movement or activity" is either more common or considered more desirable in our society than "abnormally slow movement or activity" and does not qualify for an esoteric (known only to a few; secret, obscure) medical label. Thus, our common terms *hyper* and *hyperactivity* (see these in A CROSS-REFERENCE DICTIONARY) provide the lay and medical counterparts to *bradypragia*.

One-Root Infinitives

The great majority of Greek infinitives, however, do not furnish bases that yield three or even two English roots per infinitive but merely provide one—which, of course, makes associating bases with their infinitives easier for us. Two common examples are *histanai*, "to set, to stand," which has the Greek base *sta-* and yields the English root *sta-*, and *plassein*, "to form, to mold," which has the Greek base *plas-* and yields English *plas-*. These are shown below.

Greek Infinitive	Greek Base	English Root
histanai (to set, to stand)	sta-	sta-
plassein (to form, to mold)	plas-	plas-

To *sta-* (< G. *sta-*, base of *histanai*: to set, to stand), we can add the prefix *ec-* (< G. *ek-*, variant of *ex-*: out of, from, forth) and the noun-forming suffix *-sy* (< G. *-sis*: the act, process, condition, or result of), forming *ecstasy* (intense delight or joy) or, etymologically, "the condition of (*-sis*) standing (*sta-*) out of (*ec-*) [one's mind]," as in a trance. If we then replace the *ec-* with *pro-* (< G. *pro-*: before, in front of) and append a *-t-* (< G. *-tēs*: one who or that which) and silent final *-e* to *sta-*, we derive *prostate* (a round, walnut-sized gland in males that surrounds the urethra at the base of the bladder and secretes a slightly alkaline fluid that constitutes the bulk of the semen), which, etymologically, is "that which (*-t-*) stands (*sta-*) before (*pro-*) [the bladder]." But *prostate* should not be confused with *prostrate* (lying face down on the ground, as in humility or from disease), which is derived from Latin *prōstrātus* and has no relationship to *prostate*.

Finally, to *plas-* (< G. *plas-*, base of *plassein*: to form, to mold), the second English root in the table above, we can affix a *-t-* (< G. *-tos*: a verbal suffix with the inflectional meaning: having been or having had—not to be confused with the *-t-* in *prostate*; see preceding paragraph) and the adjective-forming suffix *-ic* (< G. *-ik-*, base of *-ikos*: pertaining to, characterized by), forming *plastic*. Or if we substitute the noun-forming suffix *-y* (< G. *-ia*: the act, process, condition, or result of) for the adjective-forming suffix *-ic*, we get **plasty*, which is not a word but with the addition of an initial hyphen becomes the combining form *-plasty*, which has the modern scientific meaning: "plastic surgery of or relating to (that part or parts of the body specified by the preceding base or elements)." Then, by prefixing the appropriate elements, we can create such words as *rhinoplasty* (rī′nō·plas′tē, rī′nə-; plastic surgery of the nose, i.e., a "nose job" < G. *rhin-*, base of *rhinos*, genitive of *rhis*: nose; this is the same *rhin-* as in *rhinoceros*); *blepharoplasty* (blef′ə·rō·plas′tē, blef′ə·rə-; plastic surgery of the eyelid, usually to correct drooping eyelids < G. *blephar-*, base of *blepharon*: eyelid); *mammoplasty* (reconstructive surgery of the breasts, generally to increase or decrease their size or to alter their shape < L. *mamm-*, base of *mamma*: breast); *angioplasty* (an′jē·ə·plas′tē; a surgical treatment for removing or reducing an obstruction in a blood vessel by inserting a balloon-tipped catheter [kath′i·tər] or extremely thin tube into the vessel and inflating the balloon at the point of obstruction, compressing or redistributing the debris < G. *ang(e)i-*, base of *angeion*: little vessel, blood vessel, diminutive of *angos*: vessel, chest, box).

OTHER TYPES OF WORD-BUILDING

In addition to the systematic construction of English words from Latin, Greek, and native elements, there are other ways to create words with which we should be familiar. We have seen some of these in the SUBJECTS. A few of the more colorful types include: ACRONYMS (words constructed from the first or first few letters of two or more words), such as *scuba*, which derives from *s(elf)-c(ontained) u(nderwater) b(reathing) a(pparatus)* and NORAD, which derives from *Nor(th American) A(ir) D(efense Command)*; PORTMANTEAU WORDS (words blended from the letters of two or more words), such as *brunch*, which is a blend of *br(eakfast)* and *(l)unch*, and *subtopia*, which is a fanciful blend of *sub(urban)* and *(u)topia*; CLIPPED FORMS (short abbreviated words formed by dropping one or more syllables from a longer word or phrase, sometimes with a slight alteration in spelling), such as *lab* from *laboratory*, or *fridge* from *refrigerator*; PROPRIETARY TERMS (company trademarks that have become words), such as *Band-Aid* and *Kleenex*; EPONYMS (words derived from real or imaginary persons' names, or the person after whom these words are named), such as *derringer* (named after Henry Deringer—note the insertion of a second *r* in *derringer*) and *Peeping Tom* (named after the only person who peeped at Lady Godiva as she rode naked through Coventry, a city in central England); and TOPONYMS (words derived from place-names), such as *palace* (named after a hill in Rome, the *Palātium*, upon which the emperor's palace was built) and *Neanderthal* (named after a valley in Germany where the first skeletal remains of this late Paleolithic human being were exhumed).

PART V
A CROSS-REFERENCE DICTIONARY

A-, AN-, 69–71

*a-*¹ < OE. *a-*, a reduced form of *on, an*: on, in, into; in the state of; at, to, toward, in the direction of: ASLEEP, ASTERN, *afoot, afar*, 69, 172

*a-*² < OE. *a-*, a reduced form of *of-*: of, off, away, from: AKIN, *anew, afresh*, 69, 172

*a-*³ < OE. *ā-*: out, up (indicating the beginning or end of an action): ARISE, *awake, ashamed*, 69, 172

*a-*⁴ < G. *a-*: without, lacking, not: AGNOSTIC, AMORAL, *amenorrhea* (ā·men´ə·rē´ə; the lack or absence of a menstrual flow < G. *a-*: without + *mēn*: month + *-o-*: conn. vowel + *-rrhoia*: a flowing; hence, "without a monthly flowing"; cf. DYSMENORRHEA), *69*, 69, 70, 133, 240, see also under AN-¹

*a-*⁵ < L. *a-*, var. of AD- (used before *sc, sp, st*, and *gn*): to, toward, near, in addition to: *ascend, aspect, astringent*, AGNATE, 184

*a-*⁶ < L. *ā-*, var. of AB-¹ (used before *v* and *p*): away, from, away from: *avert*, AVOCATION, APERIENT, 184

*a-*⁷ (L. and G. nonprefixes), 69

*a-*⁸ (native and nonclassical prefixes), 69, see also A-¹, A-², A-³

*-a*¹ < L. *-a*: first decl. fem. ending, 191-92

*-a*² < G. *-a*: first decl. fem. ending, 243-44

*-a*³ (in *influenza*) < Ital. *-a* < L. *-(i)a*: the act, process, condition, or result of. For an explanation of how the *-i-* in L. *-(i)a* ultimately became, in conjunction with the preceding *t* in *-(en)t(ia)*, the *z* in E. *influenza*, see -ENZ-; *132*

*-a-*¹ < L. *-ā-*: conn. vowel (tech., the "thematic" or stem-ending *ā* of first conjugation verbs ending in *-āre* or *-ārī*), *119, 216*, see also under EDUCABLE and FUNDAMENT, and cf. -AT- and -ATE

*-a-*² (abstracted from G. *-agog-*), 45

ab-¹ (ab, əb) a L-derived prefix having the related meanings: away, from, away from: ABDUCT, *abjure* (to renounce or repudiate; cf. *adjure* under AD-), *abdicate*. **Note:** *ab-* becomes *abs-* before *c* and *t*: *abscond, abstract, abstruse* (hard to understand; obscure; recondite); and *ab-* becomes *a-* before *v* and *p*: *avert, avocation* (a secondary job or activity, engaged in primarily for pleasure; hobby), *aperient* (a mild laxative). But do not confuse *ā-*, var. of *ab-*, with A-¹, A-², A-³, A-⁴, A-⁵, and A-⁷. **[ab-]** < L. *ab-* (a prefixal form of the prep. *ab*): away, from, away from. For semantically similar prefixes, see L. *dē-* and *dis-*, and G. *apo-*; *76, 89*, **106**, *106*

ab-² < L. *ab-*, assim. form of AD- (used before *b*): to, toward, near, in addition to: *abbreviate, abbreviated, abbreviation* (see note under AD-)

abbreviate, see under AD- and AB-²

abbreviation, see under AD- and AB-²

abdicate, see under AB-¹

ABDUCT (ab·dukt´, əb-) *v.* to forcefully or deceptively carry off or lead away (a person); kidnap. **[ab- + duct-]** < L. *ab-*: away, from, away from + *duct(us)* (pp. of *dūcere*: to lead, to bring). RECON: *to lead or bring* (**duct-**) *away from* (**ab-**), 89, see also under AB-¹

abduction, 76

ab**duct**or, *77*, **106**

abhorrence, see under -ENCE

abjuration, 122

abjure, see under AB-¹

ablative, 189-90, 194

Ablaut and Reduplication, 260

able, see under EDUCABLE, AFFABLE, and INELIGIBLE

-able, see under EDUCABLE, AFFABLE, and INELIGIBLE

ablutomania, 144

ab**ortifacient**, *98*, **109**

abortive, see under -IVE

abrade, see under ERODE

abreaction, *89*, 91

abrogation, 122

abs-, see under AB-¹

abscond, see under AB-¹

ab**stergent**, see under -ENT

abstract, see under AB-¹

abstruse, see under AB-¹

absurdity, see under -TY

abyss (Anglicization of L. *abyssus*), 236, see following entry

abyssus (Latinization of G. *abyssos*), 236, see preceding entry

~*ac* < G. *-ak-*, base of *-akos* (var. of *-ikos* used after *i*): pert. to, charact. by, *52*, see also -IC

ac-, see under AD-

a can of worms, 151

a**cardio**hemia, *53*, **102**

ACAROPHOBIA (ak´ər·ə·fō´bē·ə) *n.* an irrational or intense dread of mites or other small creatures, often with the belief that such creatures are crawling beneath one's skin. [< G. *akar(i)*: mite, lit., too small to cut (< *a-*: without, lacking, not + *keirein*: to cut + *-o-*: conn. vowel + -PHOBIA], 143

acatalectic, see under LEC-²

Accentuation, English, xxiv

accident (ak´si·dənt) *n.* **1.** an unplanned and discomforting occurrence, often resulting in bodily harm, damage, loss of property, etc.; mishap. **2.** any occurrence that is not expected or intended: *Our encounter in the nightclub was purely an accident.* **3.** fortune; fate; luck: *Her wealth and empire were accidents of birth.* **[ac- + -cid- + -ent]** < L. *ac-* (assim. form of AD-): to, toward + *-cid(ere)* (comb. form of *cadere*): to fall + *-ent(is)* (gen. of *-ēns*): prpl. suffix having the SUBSTANTIVE meaning: one who or that which (performs the action designated by the preceding base or elements; see -ENT for further information). RECON: *that which* (**-ent**) *falls* (**-cid-**) *to or toward* (**ac-**). An accident, by definition, is not intentional. It is rather a "falling" of circumstances "to or toward" some indeterminate fate. For a more extensive etymological discussion, see INCIDENT; *54*, see also under AD- and -CID-²

acclamation 219

accordionist, see under -IST

accusative, 57, 189-90, 194

Aceldama, 137

a**cephalo**cardia, *53*, **102**

a**cephal**ous, *71*, **105**

acēre, 109

acetic acid, see under VINEGAR

a(cetyl), 133

a(cetylirte), 133

acetylsalicylic acid, 133, *133*

achalasia, see under CARDIOSPASM

Acherontic, 136

Achilles, see under ARISTOTLE

"Achilles' heel," see under ARISTOTLE

acid-, **109**, see also under BELLADONNA

acidify, *98*, **109**

acid(us), 109

aciform, 149

acinaciform, 149

aciniform, 149

-acious, **107**, *107*

ACKNOWLEDGMENTS, 39-40

a close call, 152

a cover-up, 153

acquire, see under AD-

acrimonious, 210

ACRONYMS, 14, **130**, *250*

acrophobia, 142, see also under -PHOBIA

acrosome, 250

A CROSS-REFERENCE DICTIONARY, 267–326. Explanation of features (numbered by section): 3-4, **19-20**, *22-25, 25*, 26-27, 27-30, *30-31*, 32, 33-34, **34-36**, *36-37*

ACT- (AG-, IG-), 87–89

act-, *87, 87, 88, 89*

actor, 88

ac**tress**, *89*, **108**, see also under -ESS

actual, *89*, **108**

āctus, 87

acupuncture, 166

ad- (ad, əd) an extremely productive L-derived prefix having the associated meanings: to, toward, near, in addition to: *advocate, adrenal, adjure* (to command or solemnly request; cf. *abjure* under AB-). **Note:** *ad-* is ASSIMILATED in the following manner: *ad-* becomes *ab-* before *b*: *abbreviate; abbreviated, abbreviation*, etc. (the only common examples; but do not confuse *ab-*, assim. form of *ad-*, with AB-¹); *ad-* becomes *ac-* before *c* and *q*: ACCIDENT, *acquire*; *af-* before *f*: *affluent, affliction*; *ag-* before *g*: AGGRESSION, AGGRAVATION (see AG-², but do not confuse with AG-¹); *al-* before *l*: *allocate, alliteration*; *an-* before *n*: *annotate, annihilate* (see AN-², but do not confuse with AN-¹ and AN-³); *ap-* before *p*: *appear, appose* (to place side by side; JUXTAPOSE; cf. *oppose* under OB-); *ar-* before *r*: *arrest, arrive*; *as-* before *s*: *assert, assent*; and *at-* before *t*: *attend, attrition*. Also, *ad-* becomes *a-* before *sc, sp, st*, and *gn*: *ascribe, aspire, astringent, agnate* (related through the father's side of the family; cf. *enate* under EX-¹). But do not confuse *a-*, var. of *ad-*, with A-¹, A-², A-³, A-⁴, A-⁶, and A-⁷. **[ad-]** < L. *ad-* (a prefixal form of the prep. *ad*): to, toward, at. For a Greek prefix with a similar meaning, see *pros-*; *78*, **106**, *106, 107*

adamantine, see under -INE¹

Adam's ale, 137

alchemy, see under AL

alcohol (al´kə·hôl´, -həl´) *n.* **1.** a clear, colorless liquid produced by the fermentation or distillation of certain carbohydrates, constituting the intoxicating agent in spirituous beverages and used in medicine and industry as well as for self-indulgence; grain alcohol. **2.** gin, vodka, rye, bourbon, or any other intoxicating liquor containing this liquid. **3.** any of a class of chemical compounds in which a hydroxyl group is bound to a hydrocarbon group, including ethanol (grain alcohol) and methanol (wood alcohol). **[al +** **-cohol]** < Arabic *al:* the (the Arabic definite article; see AL) + ML. *-cohol,* a rendering of Arabic *kuhl:* powder of antimony; (cf. BENZALDEHYDE). **RECON:** *the* (al) *powder of antimony* (-cohol). But how did "the powder of antimony" evolve into our modern definitions of alcohol? For millennia (thousands of years), powdered antimony was used as a cosmetic to darken and stain the eyelids of women. Around A.D. 1000, however, Arabian alchemists discovered that by sublimating this powder (heating it to a vapor and then condensing it to a solid without changing it into a liquid), the quality of the cosmetic could be markedly improved. As this practice spread—and because of the medieval tradition of translating scientific terms into Latin—Arabic *al-kuhl* became Medieval Latin *alcohol,* which passed unchanged into Early Modern English. But by the mid-16th century the meaning of alcohol had "generalized" or broadened from "the powder of antimony" to *any* powder obtained through sublimation, and by the late 17th century it encompassed any liquid or solid obtained through such a process. From this reference to a liquid, its meaning then "specialized" or narrowed to denote the quintessence or concentrated essence of a liquid, and by the late 18th century its meaning had further narrowed to denote the intoxicating principle of wine, then referred to as "alcohol of wine"—a phrase which by the late 19th century had shortened to its earlier "alcohol." Since, chemically, the intoxicating agent in wine is the same as that in any other intoxicating beverage, the meaning of alcohol again broadened to include all fermented and distilled liquors, both potable (pō´tə·b'l; drinkable) and poisonous. But as modern science increasingly unraveled and codified the principles of organic chemistry, its meaning once again narrowed to the point of denoting only those chemical compounds consisting of a hydroxyl group bound to a hydrocarbon group. Notwithstanding this restriction, the scientific definition of alcohol encompasses a vast number of substances in addition to ethanol and methanol, and the net effect of this specialization of meaning has been a generalization of referents that *alcohol* denotes, including, for example, certain sedatives and sleeping pills. In short, *alcohol* has ridden a linguistic roller coaster of narrowing and broadening or, if you will, contraction and expansion—poetically mirroring that wretched feeling an overindulgence of the potable variety has on one's brain . . . *the day after.*

alcoholism, see under -ISM

Aldebaran, see under AL

Alexander the Great, see under ARISTOTLE

a̲lexia, 71, **105**

al fresco, 138

alg- < G. *alg-,* base of *algos:* pain, grief, distress, suffering (< *algein:* to feel pain, grief, or distress; suffer), 52, **105**

ALGOPHOBIA *n.* an abnormal fear or dread of pain; ODYNOPHOBIA [< ALG- (see preceding entry) + -*o*-: conn. vowel + -PHOBIA], 143

algorithm, see under AL

alg(os), 105

alienate, see under -ATE

-ālis, 90

-āl(is), 105, 108

alkaloid, see under BELLADONNA (MORPHINE, PTOMAINE, -INE²)

Allen, Woody, 71

alliteration, 123, see also under AD-

allocate, see under AD-

allo̲cution, 83, **107**

almond, 234

alnico, 130

aloha, 138

alumnus. 198

alveolus, see under BRONCHIAL

Amanda, 225

amaranthine, 115

a̲masti̲a, 71, **105**

AMATHOPHOBIA (am´ə·thə·fō´bē·ə) *n.* an abnormal dislike or aversion to dust, as on one's clothing or furniture; KONIOPHOBIA. [< G. *amath(os):* sand + -*o*-: conn. vowel + -PHOBIA], 143

amazon, 136

Amazons, queen of the, 148

ambassador, see under -ATE

ambi-, 57, 108, 108

ambidextrous (am´bə·dek´strəs) *adj.* **1.** able to use both hands with equal dexterity; neither right-handed nor left-handed. **2.** unusually skillful; FACILE; adroit: *an ambidextrous magician.* **3.** deceitful or double-dealing; duplicitous: *In business affairs, he's sly, cunning, and ambidextrous.* **[ambi- +** **dextr- + -ous]** < L. *ambi-:* both, around, about (akin to G. *amphi-*) + *dextr(e)r:* right, right-handed, on the right side + E. *-ous:* full of, abounding in, charact. by, like (< L. *-ōsus*). **RECON:** *charact. by* (-ous) *both* (ambi-) *right-handed* (dextr-). The ambidextrous person, equally coordinated using the left as well as the normally more adept right hand, possesses, in a manner of speaking, two right hands, 57, 90

ambi̲guous, 89, **108**

ambivalent (am·biv´ə·lənt) *adj.* having conflicting positive and negative feelings toward a person, object, or idea: *I was ambivalent about going to Europe.* **[ambi- + val- + -ent]** < L. *ambi-:* both, around, about + *val(ēre):* to be strong, to be worth, to be of value + -*ent(is)* (gen. of -*ēns*): prpl. suffix having the inflectional meaning: be̲ing, hav̲ing, do̲ing, perform̲ing, or manifest̲ing (that which is designated by the preceding verb base), equivalent in meaning to E. participles ending in -*ing;* see -ENT for further information. **RECON:** *valu-* (val-) *-ing* (-ent) *both* (ambi-). **SEC. DISS:** [ambi- + **valent**] **Note:** L. *val(ēre):* to be strong, to be worth, to be of value + -*ent(is)* (gen. of -*ēns*): prpl. suffix having an inflectional meaning equivalent to E. participles ending in -*ing* > L. *valent(is):* valuing > E. *valent* (vā´lənt), having the modern psychological meaning: attracted to or averse to a specific object or event. **SEC. RECON:** *both* (ambi-) *attracted to* [and] *averse to a specific object or event* (valent). A hidden problem with this secondary reconstruction is that *ambivalent,* first recorded in 1916, in all likelihood predates *valence* (the SUBSTANTIVE form of *valent,* which is not recorded) by at least 19 years—*valent* thus being a *back formation* (a derivative of rather than what one would normally expect to be the base or parent form of a longer word; cf. *typewrite* < *typewriter; enthuse* < *enthusiasm; burgle* < *burglar;* and *swindle* < *swindler*) of *ambivalent.* But for one not privy to this etymological esoterica (obscure information known only to a few), this secondary reconstruction, though historically inaccurate, nevertheless illustrates how one can combine DISPARATE English roots as a tool for ascertaining the approximate meanings of E. words. But if *ambivalent* does indeed predate *valent,* does any other English word provide a clue as to the origin of *ambivalent*? Historically, *ambivalent* was coined on analogy with *equivalent,* which etymologically means "even in strength, worth, or value" (< L. *(a)equ(us):* even, level, just + -*i-:* conn. vowel + *val(ēre):* to be strong, to be worth, to be of value + -*ent(is)* [gen. of -*ēns*]: -ing). On this basis, *ambivalent* was conceived and understood to mean "both [even] in strength, worth, or value"—an apt construction for a person emotionally pulled in opposite (and conflicting) positive and negative directions, 57, 85

ambulance (am´byə·ləns) *n.* a specially equipped vehicle for transporting the injured or sick, usu. to a hospital. **[ambul- + -ance]** < L. *ambul(āre):* to walk, to travel, to go about + E. -*ance:* the quality, state, condition; act, means, result, or process of ___ing (ult. < L. -*antia* < -*ant(is)* [gen. of -*āns*]: prpl. suffix having the inflectional meaning: be̲ing, hav̲ing, do̲ing, perform̲ing, or manifest̲ing [that which is designated by the preceding verb base; see -ANT for further information] + -*ia:* the quality, state, condition; act, means, result, or process of. For a brief analysis of how Latin -*ant-* + -*ia* evolved into English -*ance,* see -ANCE. **RECON:** *the act, condition, or result of* (-ance) *walk-* (ambul-) *-ing* (-ance). **Note:** Because Latin -*ance* combines two meanings derived from two distinct Latin roots (-*ant(is)* + -*ia*), this reconstruction must cite -*ance* twice and is slightly confusing. However, if we reconstruct *ambulance* based entirely upon its Latin roots, we can eliminate this repetition and at the same time be more precise in our isolation and definition of each root. Hence, our **ALT. DISS:** [ambul- + **-ant- + -ia**] < L. -*ant(is)* (gen. of -*āns*): prpl. suffix having the inflectional meaning: be̲ing, hav̲ing, do̲ing, perform̲ing, or manifest̲ing (that which is designated by the preceding verb base), equivalent in meaning to E. participles ending in -*ing* + -*ia:* the quality, state, condition; act, means, result, or process of. **ALT. RECON:** *the act or result of* (-ia) *walk-* (ambul-) *-ing* (-ant-). But how did "the act or result of walking" evolve into our modern definition of *ambulance*? The evolution of this word becomes clear when we recognize that *ambulance* is a slightly altered abstraction of the French phrase *hôpital ambulant* or "walking hospital," a phrase first recorded in English in 1809 to denote a small mobile hospital designed to "walk with" an army from battlefield to battlefield but which in 1854 (during the Crimean War) shifted its referent from a battlefield hospital to a vehicle (in those days, a crude wagon or cart) for transporting the wounded from the battlefield to a hospital. Interestingly, a similar development that occurred in the United States at about the same time—a development that does not factor into our modern definition of *ambulance*—was the "transference" in meaning of *ambulance* from a "walking hospital" to "a large, cumbersome covered wagon," a conveyance poetically referred to by early settlers as a *prairie schooner,* 78

ambulatory (am´byə·lə·tôr´ē) *adj.* **1.** of, relating to, or capable of walking: *an ambulatory patient.* **2.** moving from place to place: *an ambulatory lecturer.* **[ambul- + -at- + -ory]** < L. *ambul(āre):* to walk, to travel, to go about + -*āt* (base of -*ātus*): ppl. suffix with the inflectional meaning: having been or having had; in E. (without the MACRON), also meaning: having, possessing, charact. by + E. -*ory:* relating to, tending to, inclined to, charact. by (< L. -*ōrius:* pert. to one who or that which [< -*or:* one who + -*ius:* adj. suffix with the basic meaning: of or pert. to]). **RECON:** *charact. by* (-at-) *tending to* (-ory) *walk, travel, or go about* (ambul-), 78, see also under -ORY¹

ameliorate, see under SOPHISTICATED

amenities, see under VINEGAR

AMENOMANIA (ə·men´ə·mā´nē·ə) *n.* an abnormal state of elation or gaiety; the manic phase in manic-depressive psychoses; CHEROMANIA. [< L. *am(o)en(us):* pleasing [cf. *amenities*] + G. -*o*-: conn. vowel + -MANIA], 145

amenorrhea, see under A-¹

a̲menti̲a, 71, **105**

Amharic, see under SEMITIC

amiable, see under AFFABLE and CORDIAL

a mismatch, 153

a̲mnesia, 71, **105**

amniomancy, 150

amoeba, see under -CUL-¹

amoral, 71, **105**
amorphous, 71, **105**
amorphous, 244
amphi-, 57
amphibian (am·fib´ē·ən) *n.* **1.** any of a class of scaleless, cold-blooded vertebrates, as frogs, toads, and salamanders, that typically begin life in the water,
breathing by gills, but with maturity develop lungs or other breathing apparatus and move to land. **2.** any animal or plant that characteristically lives
both on land and in water: *The alligator is quite the amphibian* [though technically it is a reptile]. **3.** any aircraft capable of taking off from and landing
on water and land. —*adj.* **4.** of or relating to an amphibian or amphibians
(defs. 1-3). **5.** living, capable of living, or functioning on both land and
water. **[amphi- + bi- + -an]** < G. *amphi-:* around, about, both, on both
sides, of both kinds (akin to L. *ambi-*) + *bi(os):* life + L. *ān(us):* of, pert. to,
charact. by, or belonging to or one who or that which (performs the action
designated by the preceding base or elements). RECON: *pert. to or charact.
by* (-**an**) *life* (**bi-**) *of both kinds* (**amphi-**) OR *one who or that which* (-**an**) *has
life* (**bi-**) *of both kinds* (**amphi-**), *57*
amphitheater (am´fə·thēə´tər) *n.* **1.** a round or oblong building with tiers of
seats surrounding an open arena (a round or oval central area within a building or stadium), formerly used in ancient Rome for chariot races, gladiatorial
contests, and other exhibitions; cf. CIRCUS. **2.** any place or structure resembling this, as a stadium, an enclosed building with an arena for conducting
sports and other events, a circular lecture hall with tiered seating, etc. **3.** the
locale or vehicle for any competition or other action: *Presidential debates
are an amphitheater for promises and disclosures.* **[amphi- + thea- + -ter]**
< G. *amphi-:* around, about, both, on both sides, of both kinds (akin to L.
ambi-) + *thea(sthai):* to view, behold (< *thea:* a viewing) + E. *-ter:* the
means, instrument, or place of (< G. *-tron*). But note: G. *-tron* > L. *-trum* >
OF. *-tre* > ME. *-ter* > E. *-ter.* Hence, the *-er* in *amphitheater* is not the E.
agential suffix *-er,* "one who or that which," but is rather a ME. METATHE-
SIS of OF. *-(t)re,* ult. > E. *-(t)er.* RECON: *a place for* (-**ter**) *viewing* (**thea-**)
around (**amphi-**), *57*
amygdalē, 234
AN- (A-), 69–71
an-¹ < G. *an-,* var. of A-⁴ (used before a vowel or sometimes *h*): without, lacking, not: ANEMIA, ANHYDROUS, anodontia (an´ə·dän´shə, -shē·ə; the lack or
absence of teeth, esp. when congenital), *69, 69, 70, 71*
an-² < L. *an-,* assim. form of AD- (used before *n*): to, toward, near: *announce,
annotation, annexation*
an-³ < G. *an-,* var. of ANA- (used before a vowel): up, upward; back, backward;
anew, again; thoroughly: *anode* (the negative electrode in a battery, from
which current flows; also, the positively charged electrode in an electrolytic
cell or electron tube), ANAGOGY, *aneurysm* (a dilatation or "ballooning" of
the inner wall of an artery or other blood vessel due to a weakening of that
vessel), *101*
an-⁴ (nonprefix letter combinations in L. and G.), *69*
-an (ən, in, ´n, ān) a L-derived suffix (often appearing as an "infix") having adjectival and SUBSTANTIVAL meanings: *adj.* **1.** of, pertaining to, characterized
by, having the nature of, like, relating to, belonging to: AGRARIAN, *inhuman,*
CIRCUMFORANEOUS. —*n.* **2.** one who or that which (performs the action designated by the preceding base or elements): OPTICIAN, *musician, vegetarian.*
[-an] < L. *-an-,* base of *-ānus:* of, pert. to, charact. by, having the nature of,
like, belonging to, *59, 65*
Ana-, 102
ana- (an´ə) a G-derived prefix having four general meanings: **1.** up, upward:
anabolism (ə·nab´ə·liz´m; the constructive phase in metabolism, during
which complex substances are synthesized from simpler substances; cf.
CATABOLISM), *anadromous* (ə·nad´rə·məs; designating those fish, as salmon,
that live in the sea but swim upstream to spawn; cf. CATADROMOUS). **2.** back,
backward: *anagram, ananym* (a name spelled backwards; cf. *synonym,
antonym*). **3.** anew, again: *anabiosis* (an´ə·bī·ō´sis; the resuscitation or
renewal of life after near or apparent death), *Anabaptist* (a member of any of
various Protestant sects formed in the 16th century that believed in adult, not
infant, baptizism). **4.** completely, thoroughly, throughout, utterly: *analysis,
anaphylaxis* (an´ə·fə·lak´sis; a severe allergic reaction to a substance after
an initial sensitizing exposure to it). **Note:** *ana-* becomes *an-* before vowels
(particularly *e, i,* and *o*): ANODE, ANEURYSM, and *anagogy* (a spiritual interpretation of words and passages in the Scriptures that seek to reveal hidden
meanings about an afterlife). However, Greek *an-,* variant of *ana-,* should
not be confused with the far more prevalent G. *an-,* variant of A-⁴, "without,
lacking, not," used before vowels and *h* in such words as ANEMIA, ANHY-
DROUS, and *anonym* (an anonymous person; cf. *ananym* in def. 2). And
Greek *an-,* variant of *ana-,* and Greek *an-,* variant of A-⁴ should not be confused with Latin *an-,* assimilated form of *ad-,* "to, toward, near," which
occurs in such words as *announce, annotate,* and *annunciate.* **[ana-]** < G.
ana-: up, back, again, thoroughly, *102*
an(a)-, 101
Anabaptist, see under ANA-
anabiosis, see under ANA-
anabolism, 125, see also under ANA-
Anacardium occidentale, 53, **102**
anadiplosis, 123
anadromous, see under ANA-
anagogy, 47, **101**, *see also under* ANA *and* AN-³
anagram, see under ANA-
analects (an´ə·lekts´) *pl. n.* selected literary excerpts or passages from the writ-

ings of one or more authors. **[ana- + lec- + -t- + -s]** < G. *ana-:* up, upward;
back, backward; anew, again; thoroughly + *lek-* (base of *legein*): to gather, to
choose, to speak + *-t(os):* verbal adj. suffix with the inflectional meaning:
having been or having had (that which is designated by the preceding verb
base) + E. *-s:* pl. suffix with the inflectional meaning: more than one; hence,
those, they, them, etc. (< OE. *-as,* masc. pl. suffix of certain nouns; but in
this word, E. *-s* is a LOAN TRANSLATION of G. *-a* in *(analekt)a,* neut. pl. of
(analekt)os). RECON: *those* (-**s**) *having been* (-**t-**) *gathered* (**lec-**) *up* (**ana-**).
The Analects of Confucius, a collections of anecdotes, maxims, and dia-
logues of Confucius compiled in the 4th century B.C., is probably the best-
known usage of the word *analects, 81*
Analects of Confucius, The, see under ANALECTS (preceding entry)
analgesic, 71, **105**, 133
Analysis, 8-9 (of Detailed Example within the COMMON ROOTS), 23 (of A
CROSS-REFERENCE DICTIONARY entry *cadaverine*)
analysis, see under ANA-
analytic (language), *187*
ananym, 251, see also under ANA-
anaphora, 123
anaphrodit**ous,** 71, **105**
anaphylaxis, see under ANA-
anarch**y,** 71, **105**
anatomy, see under -TOMY
-ance (əns, ´ns, ənts) a L-derived *n*-forming suffix having two classes of
closely associated meanings: **1.** the quality, state, or condition of being, having, or manifesting (that which is designated by the preceding base or elements): *ignorance, brilliance, fragrance.* **2.** the act, means, result, or process of doing or performing (that which is designated by the preceding base
or elements): *resistance, remittance, observance* (see also *endurance* for a
melding of defs. 1 and 2). **[-ance]** < L. *-antia:* the quality, state, condition;
act, means, result, or process of being, having, doing, performing, or manifesting (that which is designated by the preceding verb base) < *-ant-* (base of
-antis, gen. of *-āns):* prpl. suffix having an inflectional meaning equivalent
to E. participles ending in *-ing* (see -ANT for further information) + *-ia:* the
quality, state, condition; act, means, result, or process of. But how did Latin
-ant- + -ia evolve into English *-ance*? First, as we have seen, these two Latin
roots coalesced to form Latin *-antia.* From here, this compound entered Old
French in which the two syllables of *-tia* gradually ELIDED to form *-ce,* yielding the Old French *n*-forming suffix *-(an)ce.* And this suffix then passed unchanged into Middle English and Modern English, thus completing the
transformation of the trisyllabic Latin *-antia* (formed from its constituent
roots *-ant- + -ia*) into the monosyllabic English *-ance.* For a virtually identical suffix, see -ENCE; **106**
ancillary (an´sə·ler´ē) *adj.* helping or assisting; auxiliary, subordinate. **[anc- +
-ill- + -ary]** < L. *anc(ula):* female slave, handmaid (< *ambi-:* both, around +
?*colere:* to cultivate OR **-quola:* a turning about) + *-ill(a):* small, little + E.
-ary: pert. to, charact. by (< L. *-āris*). RECON: *pert. to* (-**ary**) *a little* (-**ill-**) *female slave* (**anc-**). Female slaves assisted and were subservient to their masters, *69*
andr- < G. *andr-,* base of *andros,* gen. of *anēr:* man, male, *62*
androcracy, 62
androgynous, 244
androphobia, 142
anecdot**e,** 71, **105**
anemia, 10, 52, 69, 69, *see also under* AN-¹ *and* -EMIA
ANEMOPHOBIA (an´ə·mə·fō´bē·ə) *n.* an irrational or intense fear of drafts or
wind, as during a thunderstorm. [< G. *anem(os):* wind + *-o-:* conn. vowel +
-PHOBIA], 143
anesthe**sia,** 71, **105**
aneurysm, see under ANA- *and* AN-³
ANGELIC (an·jel´ik) *adj.* of or like an angel, esp. in appearance or characteristics. **[angel- + -ic]** < G. *angel(os):* messenger (a transl. of Heb. *mal´akh*) +
-ik(os): pert. to, charact. by. RECON: *pert. to* (-**ic**) *a messenger* (**angel-**). In
early Judaic writings, an angel was a messenger of Jehovah, or *mal´akh-
yehowāh,* 47, *see also under* -IC
angels, see under HIERARCHY
ANGINOPHOBIA (an´ji·nə·fō´bē·ə) *n.* an irrational or intense fear or dread of
choking. [< L. *angin(a):* an inflammation of the throat accompanied by choking (< G. *anchonē:* strangulation, hanging < or akin to *anchein:* to squeeze,
constrict) + G. *-o-:* conn. vowel + -PHOBIA], 143
angioplasty, 264
angiosperm, 117
Anglophile, see under -PHILE
Anglophobe, see under -PHOBE
angust-, xviii
anhedonia, 71
anhydrous, 27 (as a guide to understanding the Brief Analyses), 71, *see also
under* AN-¹
animal magnetism, see under MESMEROMANIA
animalcule, see under -CUL-¹
ANIMALS, WORDS WITH, 148, *see also* ACAROPHOBIA, AILUROPHOBIA, API-
PHOBIA, BATRACHOPHOBIA, CYNOPHOBIA, DORAMANIA, ENTOMOMANIA, EQUINO-
MANIA, EQUINOPHOBIA, GALEOPHOBIA, HELMINTHOPHOBIA, HIPPOPHOBIA, HIPPO-
MANIA, ICHTHYOPHOBIA, MELISSOPHOBIA, MUSOPHOBIA, MYRMECOPHOBIA,
ORNITHOPHOBIA, PEDICULOPHOBIA, VERMIPHOBIA
animation, 120
animosity, see under IN-²

annexation, see under AN-²
Annie Hall, 71
annihilate, see under AD-
annotate, see under AD- and ANA-
annotation, see under AN-²
announce, see under AN-² and ANA-
annual, see under SPHINCTER
annular, see under SPHINCTER
annunciate, see under ANA-
ann(us), 90
anode, see under ANA- and AN-³
anodontia, see under AN-¹
<u>anomie</u>, <u>71</u>, **105**
<u>anonychia</u>, <u>71</u>, **105**
<u>anonym</u>, <u>71</u>, **105**, see also under ANA-
anonymous, see under -OUS
anopheles, 86
<u>anorchia</u>, <u>71</u>, **105**
<u>anorexia</u>, <u>71</u>, **105**

A NOTE TO THE PROFESSIONAL, 38-39
<u>anotia</u>, <u>71</u>, **105**
answer the bell, 153
~ant (ənt, 'nt) a L-derived suffix having adjectival and SUBSTANTIVAL meanings: *adj.* **1.** being, having, doing, performing, or manifesting (that which is designated by the preceding base or elements), equivalent in meaning to *-ing* when forming participles (not gerunds): *radiant, insignificant,* DEVIANT. —*n.* **2.** one who or that which (performs the action designated by the preceding base or elements): *fumigant,* DEVIANT, *intendant* (but compare the *-ant* in *intendant* with the *-ent* in its synonym SUPERINTENDENT). **[-ant]** < L. *-ant-,* base of *-antis,* gen. of *-āns:* prpl. suffix of verbs ending in *-āre* and *-ārī,* having the inflectional meaning: being, having, doing, performing, or manifesting (that which is designated by the preceding verb base), equivalent in meaning to E. *-ing* when forming PARTICIPLES, not GERUNDS, as in "the dancing troupe," not "dancing is fun." For a virtually identical suffix, see -ENT; *106*
antarctic, 237
Antarctica, *148*
antebellum 197
antenna, *191, 192*
antepenult, *179*, *213*
anterior, *213*
anth-, xvii, xviii
anthelion, *116*
anthem- < G. *anthem-,* base of *anthemon:* flower (akin to *anthos:* flower), *147*
anther, xvii
anthology (an·thäl´ə·jē) *n.* a collection of writings by one or various authors. **[anth- + -o- + log- + -y]** < G. *anth(os):* flower + *-o-:* conn. vowel + *log-* (base of *legein):* to gather, to choose, to speak) + E. *-y:* the act, process, condition, or result of (< G. *-ia).* RECON: *the act or process of* (**-y**) *gathering* (**log-**) *flowers* (**anth-**). Originally, an anthology was a collection of choice short poems, rendered metaphorically as "flowers of verse," *xvii, 69*
ANTHOMANIA *n.* an extreme enthusiasm for or preoccupation with flowers or plants. [< G. *anth(os):* flower + *-o-:* conn. vowel + -MANIA], *145*
ANTHOPHOBIA *n.* an abnormal dislike or aversion to flowers or plants. [< G. *anth(os):* flower + *-o-:* conn. vowel + -PHOBIA], *143*
anthropology (an´thrə·päl´ə·jē) *n.* the scientific study of the origins, physical characteristics, social organization, and customs of peoples throughout the world. **[anthrop- + -o- + log- + -y]** < G. *anthrōp(os):* human being + *-o-:* conn. vowel + *log(os):* word, thought, reason, reckoning, discourse (< *legein:* to gather, to choose, to speak) + E. *-y:* the act, process, condition, or result of (< G. *-ia).* RECON: *the act, process, or result of* (**-y**) *thought* (**log-**) *about human beings* (**anthrop-**). SEC. DISS: [anthrop- + -o- + **-logy**] Note: G. *log(os):* word, thought, reason, reckoning, discourse + *-ia:* the act, process, condition, or result of > G. *-logia* > the E. *n*-forming comb. form -LOGY, having, in this entry, the scientific and literary meaning: the science, study, theory, or doctrine of. SEC. RECON: *the science or study of* (**-logy**) *human beings* (**anthrop-**), *69,* see also under -O-¹
anthropomorphic, 244
anthroponym, 251
anthropophagous, 117
anthrōpos, 117
anti-, **hyper-1**, *hyper-1*, **107**, *107*
antidisestablishmentarianism (an´tī·dis´ə·stab´lish·mən·te r´ē·ə·niz´´m, an´tē-) *n.* opposition to the disestablishment of or withdrawal of state support from an established church. **[anti- + dis- + e- + sta- + -bl- + -ish + -ment + -ari- + -an + -ism]** < G. *anti-:* against, opposed to, the opposite of + L. *dis-:* not, without, the reverse or undoing of + OF. *e-:* prothetic (of or relating to a sound or syllable added to the beginning of a word) vowel + L. *stā(re):* to set, to stand + *-b(i)l(is):* tending to (be), inclined to (be) + E. *-ish:* a *v*-forming suffix with the inflectional meanings: to make, to do, to become, to form, etc. (< OF. *-iss-,* base of verbs ending in *-ir* < L. *-isc(ere):* inchoative verb ending; cf. -SC-, but do not confuse Fr-derived *-ish* with native -ISH) + L. *-ment(um):* the act, means, or result of + *-āri(us):* pert. to, charact. by + *-ān(us):* of, pert. to, charact. by, or belonging to OR one who or that which + E. -ISM: a *n*-forming suffix having, in this entry, the related meanings: the beliefs, school, or doctrine of (< G. *-ism(os):* the act or the result of the act of [< *-is-:* denom. base of verbs ending in *-izein* + *-m(os):* the act or result of

the act of]). RECON: *the doctrine of* (**-ism**) *one who* (**-an**) *is charact. by* (**-ari-**) *against* (**anti-**) *the act of* (**-ment**) *tending to* (**-bl-**) *not* (**dis-**) *make* (**-ish**) *stand* (**sta-**). In reality, however, this word was not constructed from these nine disparate (dis´pər·it, di·spar´it; distinct in kind or form; diverse) elements but rather was formed by combining four generally more complex roots and words, which had been previously culled and, in part, assembled from this group. Hence, our SEC. DISS: [anti- + **disestablishment** + **-arian** + -ism] Note: L. *dis-:* not, without, the reverse or undoing of + OF. *e-:* prothetic vowel + L. *stā(re):* to set, to stand + *-b(i)l(is):* tending to (be), inclined to (be) + E. *-ish:* to make, to do, to become, to form + L. *-ment(um):* the act, means, or result of > E. *disestablishment.* Also note: L. *-āri(us):* pert. to, charact. by + *-ān(us):* of, pert. to, charact. by, or belonging to OR one who or that which > L. *-āriān(us)* > the E. *adj-* and *n*-forming suffix *-arian,* having, in this entry, the associated SUBSTANTIVE meanings: one who believes in, advocates, or supports (that which is designated by the preceding base or elements). SEC. RECON: *the beliefs or doctrine of* (**-ism**) *one who advocates* (**-arian**) *the opposite of* (**anti-**) *disestablishment* (**disestablishment**). In 1869, William Gladstone, prime minister of Britain, disestablished the Irish Protestant Church to which all inhabitants of Ireland, including Roman Catholics, had been compelled to pay tithes (tīthz; a tax, levy, or regular contribution to support a church or religious institution, esp. when one-tenth of one's annual income or wages). This greatly angered many Protestants and others who favored the status quo (stat´əs kwō, stā´təs kwō; the existing state of affairs) and catapulted antidisestablishmentarianism into British politics, *171,* but see also the compound suffix *-arian* in AGRARIAN and the partially coincidental letter combination *-arian* in CAESARIAN SECTION
antifeminist, 192
antihypertensive, **63**, *64*
antimacassar, *121, 135*
anti<u>malarial</u>, <u>86</u>, **107**
antipyretic, *133*
-antis (-āns), 106
antisocial, 194
antithesis, see under DIS-
ANTLOPHOBIA *n.* an irrational or intense fear of floods. [< G. *antl(os):* hold of a ship, bilge water (water seepage accumulated in the hull of a boat or ship), flood + *-o-:* conn. vowel + -PHOBIA], *143*
antonym, *251,* see also under ANA-
antonymous, see under NOCENT
antonyms, see under NOCENT
antonymy, see under NOCENT
-ān(us), 86
anxiety, see under -TY
Anzac, *130*
aorta, *244*
ap-, see under AD-
apartheid, *138*
<u>apath</u>y, <u>71</u>, **105**, see also under AFFABLE
aperient, see under AB-¹ and A-⁶
<u>aphalang</u>ia, <u>71</u>, **105**
aphasia (ə·fā´zhə) *n.* a partial or total loss of the ability to speak or understand spoken or written words, resulting from a head injury or disease of the brain, esp. a stroke. **[a- + pha- + -s- + -ia]** < G. *a-:* without, not + *pha(nai):* to speak + *-s(is):* the act, process, or result of + *-ia:* the act, process, or condition of. RECON: *the condition of* (**-ia**) *the act of* (**-s-**) *not* (**a-**) *speaking* (**pha-**), *81*
aphelion, *116*
aphrodisiac, *136*
APHRODISIOMANIA *n.* abnormally exaggerated or uncontrollable sexual desire; EROTOMANIA. [< G. *aphrodisi(os):* of Aphrodite (af´rə·dī´tē; goddess of love and beauty; Venus) + *-o-:* conn. vowel + -MANIA], *145*
aphrodit-, **105**
Aphrodite, *58,* see also under APHRODISIOMANIA
Aphrodit(ē), 105
a pig in a poke, *151*
APIPHOBIA *n.* an intense and sometimes irrational fear or dread of bees, as by one who is allergic to bee stings; MELISSOPHOBIA. [< L. *api(s):* bee + -PHOBIA], *143*
apo-, 240, see also under APOLUNE
apogee, *116*
apolune (ap´ə·lōōn´) *n.* the point in a lunar orbit of a satellite or any other object that is farthest from the moon; PERILUNE. **[apo- + lun- + -e]** < G. *apo-:* away, from, away from, off + *lūn(a):* moon + E. *-e:* silent final letter. RECON: *away from* (**apo-**) *the moon* (**lun-**)
apophasis, *123*
apophony, 260
a posteriori, *126*
apparatus, see under PAR-³
apparent, see under PAR-⁴
apparition, see under PAR-⁴
appear, see under AD-
appellant, *122*
appellation, see under DENOMINATIVE
appendectomy, see under -TOMY, -ECTOMY, and -STOMY
append<u>icitis</u>, <u>68</u>, **104**
appendix (human), *149, 202,* see also under -ECTOMY
appose, see under AD-

approachable, see under AFFABLE
approval, see under -AL
aquamarine, 115
aqueduct, 76
-ar, *51*, 92,
ar-, see under AD-
Arabian Sea, see under INDO-EUROPEAN
Arabic, see under SEMITIC
arachnophobia, 142
Aramaic, see under SEMITIC
Arawak, see under IGUANA
arch-, **105**
archangels, see under HIERARCHY, and for ety., cf. ANGEL
archegonium, 117
ARCHITECTURE, 114
architrave, 114
arch(os), *105*
-archy (är′·kē) a G-derived *n*-forming comb. form having the essential meaning: rule by or government of (that group, body, or individual designated by
the preceding base or elements): PATRIARCHY, MATRIARCHY, *oligarchy* (äl′i·
gär′kē; a form of government in which power is held by a few individuals or
a ruling clique; cf. OLIGEMIA). **[arch-** + **-y]** < G. *-archos* or *-archēs* (comb.
forms of *archos*): first, chief, ruler (< *archein*: to rule, orig., to be first, to
begin, to take the lead) + E. *-y*: the act, process, condition, or result of (< G.
-ia). RECON: *the act, process, or result of* (-y) rule (**arch-**) by [*that group,
body, or individual designated by the preceding base or elements*] OR *the
act, process, or result of* (-y) ____( ) *ruler* (**arch-**) [the parentheses to be
filled in with the base preceding **-arch**, and its definition to be placed on the
line], 60
ARDUOUS (är′jŌŌ·əs) *adj.* **1.** requiring great energy or exertion; strenuous; la-
borious. **2.** hard to climb or ascend; steep; precipitous: *an arduous mountain
trail.* **[ardu-** + **-ous]** < L. *ardu(us)*: high, steep, difficult + E. *-ous*: full of,
abounding in, charact. by, like (< L. *-ō(s)us* in most E. words, but in this
derivative an Anglicization of L. *-us*: adj. suffix; see -OUS for further information). RECON: *full of, charact. by, or like* (**ous-**) *that which is steep or
difficult* (**ardu-**), 59
-āre, *96*
arena, see under AMPHITHEATER and CIRCUS
Argentina, 147
ARIA (är′ē·ə) *n.* an often elaborate musical composition for solo voice with
instrumental accompaniment, as in an opera, oratorio (a long, dramatic lyric
production, usually based on a religious theme, but performed without stage
action, costumes, or scenery), or cantata (kən·tä′tə; a choral composition,
often resembling a short oratorio, that tells a story which is sung but not
acted). **[aria]** < Ital. *aria*: air, melody, song < L. *āer(a)* (var. accus. of *āēr*):
air < G. *āer(a)* (accus. of *āēr*): air. RECON: *air, melody, song* (**aria**). **Note:**
The *-ia* in Italian *aria* is an alteration of the Latin and Greek case ending *-a*
and should not be confused with the suffix *-ia*, "the quality, state, condition; act, means, result, or process of," which we see in hundreds of
English words, including INSOMNIA, EUPHORIA, and TRYPANOSOMIASIS,
85
aria < Ital. *aria*: air, melody, song < L. *āera* (< *āer-*, base of *āēr*: air + *-a*: accus. case ending): air < G. *aera*, accus. of *āēr*: air, *85*
-arian, see under AGRARIAN and ANTIDISESTABLISHMENTARIANISM
-āris, *51*, see also under -ARY
arise (ə·rīz′) *v.* to get up or awaken. **[a-** + **ris-** + **-e]** < OE. *ā-*: out, up (indicating the beginning or end of an action; see A-¹) + *rīs(an)*: to rise + E. *-e*: silent
final letter. RECON: *rising* (**ris-**) *up* (**a-**), 69
arist- < G. *arist-*, base of *aristos*: best, *61*, see also under ARISTOTLE
aristate, 117
Aristocles, see under ARISTOTLE
aristocracy, *60*, **61**, *61*
aristocratie, *61*
aristokratia, *61*
ARISTOTLE (ar′is·tät′l) a 4th century B.C. Greek philosopher, the pupil of Plato
and tutor of Alexander the Great, who, in contrast to Plato, emphasized the
logical and analytical rather than idealistic and theoretical, pursuit of human
knowledge. **[arist-** + **-o-** + **-tl-** + **-e]** < G. *arist(os)*: best (superl. of *ar(i)*:
?upperclass + *-istos*: superl. suffix; cf. KAKISTOCRACY) + *-o-*: conn. vowel +
-t(e)l(ēs): perfected OR fulfilled (either < *teleios, teleos*: perfected, completed
OR *telein*: to fulfill, complete—both < *telos*: an end, completion) + E. *-e*:
silent final letter. RECON: *perfected* (**-tl-**) *the best* (**arist-**) OR *fulfilled*
(**-tl-**)*the best* (**arist-**). Interestingly, Plato's original name was *Aristocles* or
"best fame" (< G. *arist(os)*: best + *-o-*: conn. vowel + *kle(o)s*: fame, glory);
and *Cleopatra*, containing the same *cle-*, means "fame of father" (< G.
kle(os): fame, glory + *-o-*: conn. vowel + *patr(os)*: father + *-a*: fem. suffix; cf.
PATRIARCHY). *Patroclus* (the best friend of Achilles, whose death in the Tro-
jan War incited Achilles to reenter that war, in which he, Achilles, was in
turn killed by an arrow to his "Achilles' heel," the only vulnerable spot on
his body; hence, a phrase that has come to designate one's weak spot or fatal
flaw) is an etymological reversal of the two bases in *Cleopatra*—as is
Theodore of *Dorothy* (< G. *dōr(on)*: gift + *the(os)*: god; hence, "gift of god").
For a more intricate Germanic reversal, consider the etymologies of Harold
and Walter (not included in this dictionary); 61, 146, see also under PERI-
PATETIC
arithm-, **103**
arithmo**cracy**, *62*, **103**

arithm(os), *103*
-ārius, *48*, *88*, *105*, *107*, *108*, *passim*
Armenian, see under INDO-EUROPEAN
army, 154
AROUND, ABOUT, SURROUNDING (CIRCUM-), 57–59
arrest, see under AD-
arrival, see under -AL
arrive, see under AD-
ART, **115**
art-, **109**
arthritis, itis-1, 67
arthr(on), itis-1
art**ifact**, *98*, **109**
art**ifice**, *98*, **109**
art(is) (ars), *109*
-ary (er·ē) a L-derived suffix having adjectival and SUBSTANTIVAL meanings:
adj. **1.** pertaining to, characterized by, having the nature of, like, relating to,
belonging to: *literary, monetary, lapidary* (of or relating to the art of cutting
and engraving precious stones < L. *lapid(is)* [gen. of *lapis*]: stone + *-ār(ius)*:
pert. to, charact. by; also, one who or that which). —*n.* **2.** a person or thing
associated or connected with; specifically, one who or that which belongs to,
works with, is skilled in, or is otherwise characterized by (that which is
designated by the preceding base or elements): DICTIONARY, *lapidary* (a person who cuts and polishes precious stones). **3.** the quality, state, condition;
act, means, result, or process of: *lapidary* (the art of cutting and polishing
precious stones). **3.** a place for: *aviary* (ā′vē·er·ē; a large cage, building, or
other enclosure for housing birds, as in a zoo < L. *av(is)*: bird + *-i-*: conn.
vowel + *-āri(um)*: a place for). **[-ary]** < L. *-ārius*: pert. to, charact. by, having the nature of, like (for most adjectives and nouns; see *literary* and *lapidary* above); or < *-ārium*: a thing which pertains to (see DICTIONARY) or a
place for (see *aviary* above), both < *-ārius*; or for certain other adjectives
and nouns, independently < *-āris*: pert. to, charact. by, having the nature of,
like (see *military* and ANCILLARY), *88*, *88*, *105*, *107*, *108*
as-, see under AD-
ascend, *126*, see also under A-⁵
ascension, *126*
as cool as a cucumber, 151
ascribe, see under AD-
asleep (ə·slēp′) *adv.* in a state of sleep or that which resembles sleep; dormant;
dead. **[a-** + **sleep]** < OE. *a-*, a reduced form of *on, an*: on, in, into; in the
state of; at, to; see A-¹) + *slǣp(e)*: sleep. RECON: *in the state of* (**a-**) *sleep*
(**sleep**), *45*, 69
aspect, see under A-⁵
a**sphyx**ia, *71*, **105**
aspire, see under AD-
aspirin, **133**, *133*
a spitting image, 151
a split decision, 153
assent, see under AD-
assert, see under AD-
assimilated, see ASSIMILATION (following entry) for an understanding of the
process, and cf. AD-, COM-, DIS-, EN-, EX-, IN-¹, IN-², OB-, SUB-, SYN- for examples of the process
assimilation (the process), *181*
association, *194*
assonance, 123
aster-, *18*
astern (ə·stûrn′) *adv.* behind, at, or toward the back of a ship or other vessel.
[a- + **stern]** < OE. *a-*, a reduced form of *on*: on, in, into; to, toward, in the
direction of + ON. *stjōrn*: steering (> E. *stern*: the back of a boat or ship).
RECON: *in the direction of* (**a-**) *the steering* (**stern**). The steering apparatus of
a boat or ship is always at the back of the craft, 69
asteroid, *18*, *248*
a**stomi**a, *71*, **105**
astragalomancy, 150
astraphobia, see under BRONTOPHOBIA
astringent, see under AD- and A-⁵
ASTRONOMY, 116
astrophobia, see under BRONTOPHOBIA
asymmetrical, see under SYN-
a**symm**etry, *71*, **105**
asynchronous, 120
asyndeton, 123
at-, see under AD-
-at- < L. *-āt-*, base of *-ātus*, ppl. suffix of first conjugation verbs ending in *-āre*
or *-ārī* with the inflectional meaning: having been or having had; in English,
the base *-at-* (without the MACRON) also means: having, possessing, characterized by; and it is often used as a verb with the associated meanings: to
cause, to become, to cause to become, to make, to do, to act, to form, etc.
Note: L. *-at-*, base of *-ātus*: having been, having had + E. *-e*: silent final letter > the E. suffix -ATE, having a wide variety of adjectival, SUBSTANTIVAL,
and verbal meanings (see following entry), *57*, *57*, *79*, *88*, *94*, *105*, *108*, *passim*
-ate (āt, it) a highly productive L-derived suffix having adjectival, SUB-
STANTIVAL, and verbal meanings: *adj.* **1.** having, having been, possessing, or
charact. by (that which is designated by the preceding base or elements):
vertebrate, craniate (having a cranium or skull). **2.** resembling, having the

form of, shaped (like): CORDATE, ovate (egg-shaped), *pinnate* (feather-shaped). —*n.* **3.** the rank or office of: *senate*, *consulate* (kän′s′l·it; the office or residence of a consul: a dignitary living in a foreign country for the purpose of protecting the interests of his or her country's citizens residing in that land; cf. *ambassador*). **4.** the holder of the office of: *primate* (prī′mit, -māt; an archbishop or highest ranking bishop of a country or province—not to be confused with the mammalian primate; cf. also *prelate* under -URE). **5.** a group or body characterized by common goals, interests, status, etc: *electorate*, *professoriate*. **6.** a person or thing that is the result of an action: *mandate*, *retardate* (ri·tär′dāt; a retarded person). —*v.* **7.** an action suffix having an almost unrestricted variety of meanings, best defined in relationship to its preceding base but often having one or more of the following meanings: to cause, to become, to cause to become, to make, to do, to act, to form, to produce, to provide, to function, to manage, to arrange, to combine with, etc.: NAVIGATE, *alienate*, *salivate*. **[-at- + -e]** < L. -*āt(us)*, ppl. suffix of first conjugation verbs ending in -*āre* and -*ārī* with the inflectional meaning: having been or having had (that which is designated by the preceding verb base, equivalent in meaning to E. -*en*, as in *spoken* or *broken*, or -*ed*, as in SOPHISTICATED or UNDAUNTED; cf. also G. -*t(os)* under ANALECTS and MONOZYGOTIC) + E. -*e*: silent final letter. However, many English nouns ending in -*ate* are derived directly from the Latin SUBSTANTIVE ending -*ātus* (gen: -*ātūs*): the office or the holder of the office of (ult. < the verbal ending -*āt(us)* [pp. of -*āre*]: having been, having had) + -*us*: fem. substantive suffix of the fourth declension, **57, 88, 94, 108,** *passim*

"atheist" (ā′thē·ist) *n.* a person who does not believe in the existence of a supernatural being or God; cf. AGNOSTIC. **[a- + the- + -ist]** < G. *a-*: without, not + *the(os)*: god + -*ist(ēs)*: one who (< -is-: final letter of the base of denom. verbs ending in -*izein* + -*t(ēs)*: one who or that which). RECON: *one who* (**-ist**) *is without* (**a-**) *god* (**the-**), 69, see also under THE-¹
athletics, see under -ICS
atoll, see under BIKINI
atom, 70, *45*
atomic number, see under TRANS-
atomos, 70
atrophy, 67, 70
atropine, 136, see also under BELLADONNA
attend, see under AD-
attendant, see under -ANT, -ENT, and SUPERINTENDENT
attention-deficit hyperactivity disorder, see under HYPERACTIVITY
attention-deficit syndrome, see under HYPERACTIVITY
at the drop of a hat, 153
attrition, see under AD-
-*ātus, 57,* see also under -A¹- and -ATE
-*āt(us), 108*
a̲typ̲ical, 71, 105
audible, 215
auditory tube, see under EUSTACHIAN TUBE
auger, see under TRYPANOSOMIASIS
august-, xviii
aur-, 108
aur(is), 108

AURORA AUSTRALIS (ə·rôr′ə ô·strā′lis, ô·rôr′ə) the scientific name of the *southern lights*, a luminous display of mutating (changing) rays, arcs, bands, streamers, and "curtains" of various colors in the night sky of southern regions, resulting primarily from the bombardment of atoms in the upper atmosphere by charged solar particles attracted to the earth's south magnetic pole; cf. AURORA BOREALIS. **[aurora** (+) **austr-** + **-alis]** < L. *aurōra*: dawn (+) *austr(ī)* (gen. of *auster*): south wind, south + -*alis*: pert. to, charact. by, having the nature of, like. RECON: *like or having the nature of* (**-alis**) *dawn* (**aurora**) *of the south* (**austr-**). While exploring the southern hemisphere in 1773, Captain James Cook observed and later chronicled (and thus helped popularize) *aurora australis* or "southern dawn," a term actually coined decades earlier on analogy with *aurora borealis*, 65
AURORA BOREALIS (ə·rôr′ə bôr′ē·al′is, ô·rôr′ə) the scientific name of the *northern lights*, a luminous display of mutating (changing) rays, arcs, bands, streamers, and "curtains" of various colors in the night sky of northern regions, resulting primarily from the bombardment of atoms in the upper atmosphere by charged solar particles attracted to the earth's north magnetic pole; cf. AURORA AUSTRALIS above. **[aurora** (+) **bore-** + **-alis]** < L. *aurōra*: dawn (+) G. *bore(ās)*: north wind, north + L. -*alis*: pert. to, charact. by, having the nature of, like. RECON: *like or having the nature of* (**-alis**) *dawn* (**aurora**) *of the north* (**bore-**). Pierre Gassendi, the French astronomer who coined *aurora borealis* in 1621, fancied these lights to be a second coming of dawn from the northern (*boreālis*) horizon—hence, the poetic translation: "northern dawn," 65
aust(e)r, 103
austr-, 103
aut- < G. *aut-*, base of *autos*: self, oneself, *49*, **103**
auteur, 120
autism, see under -ISM
autobiographer (ô′tō·bī·ä′grə·fər) *n.* a person who writes the history or story of his or her own life. **[aut- + -o- + bi- + -o- + graph- + -er]** < G. *aut(os)*: self, oneself + -*o-*: conn. vowel + *bi(os)*: life + -*o-*: conn. vowel + *graph(os)*: drawn, written (< *graphein*: to write, to draw) + E. -*er*: one who or that which (performs the action designated by the preceding base or elements) (< OE. -*er(e)* < or akin to L. -*ārius*; see -ARY). RECON: *one who* (**-er**) *writes or has written* (**graph-**) *about the life* (**bi-**) *of oneself* (**aut-**), *48, 90,* see also under BI-²
aut̲ocracy̲, 62, **103**
auto da fe, 138
automation, 196
aut(os), 103
av-, 102, 103
avert, see under AB-¹ and A-⁶
avian, 139, *199*
aviary, 199, see also under -ARY and DICTIONARY
aviator. 200
aviatrix, 200
av̲icide, 56, **102**
avine, 139
av(is), 102, 103
avocation, see under AB-¹ and A-⁶

B

ba-, 104
babushka, 138
Bacchic, see under PHALLIC
back, 91
"backboned" (animals), see under OVARY
back formation, see under AMBIVALENT
bacter-, 102
bacte̲ricide̲, 56, **102**
baculiform, see under CHROMOSOME
BAD, BADLY, ILL (DISEASE, SICKNESS) (**MAL-, MALE-** [MAL, MALUM]), **84–86**
"bad air," 86
badly, see under -LY²
bain-marie, 137
ba(inein), 104
baktēr(ion), 102
baldachin, 119
balletomania, 144
ballista, 261
ballistics, 261
ballpark figure, 152
Balto-Slavic, see under INDO-EUROPEAN
Band-Aid, 133, 265
Barnum, P. T., 139
baron, see under DUKE
baronet, see under DUKE
base (in chemistry), see under BELLADONNA

BASEBALL, COMMON EXPRESSIONS DERIVED FROM, 152
basic (in chemistry), see under BELLADONNA
BASIPHOBIA *n.* an irrational fear or dread of walking. [< G. *ba(inein)*: to step, to walk, to go + *si(s)*: + -PHOBIA], 143
BATHOPHOBIA *n.* an irrational or intense fear or dread of depths, as while swimming in deep water or when walking into a dark room. [< G. *bath(os)*: depth + -*o-*: conn. vowel + -PHOBIA], 143
bathysiderodromophobia, see under SUBWAY
batik, 138
BATRACHOPHOBIA *n.* an abnormal fear or dread of frogs. [< G. *batrach(os)*: frog + -*o-*: conn. vowel + -PHOBIA], 143, see also under RHABDOPHOBIA
batting average, 152
bayonet, 135
bdellatomy, 155
bear, 139
beat around the bush, 151
beaten, see under -ATE
Beatlemania, 144
beat the count, 153
because, 192
beefalo, 131
befall, see under INCIDENT
beget, see under PHALLIC and GENERATE
Begonia c̲ircuml̲obata, 59, **103**
BELDAM (bel′dəm, -dam) *n.* an old woman, esp. an ugly or hideous one; hag. **[bel- + dam-]** < OF. *bel(le)*: beautiful; later used as a title of respect (< L. *bella*, fem. of *bellus*: beautiful, handsome) + *dam(e)*: lady (< L. *domina*, fem.

of *dominus*: lord, master < or akin to *domus*: house; cf. BELLADONNA and DANGER). RECON: *beautiful* (**bel-**) lady (**dam-**). But how did "beautiful lady" degenerate into "old woman"? After its formation in Middle English from the late Old French words *belle*, "beautiful," and *dame*, "lady," *beldam* evolved into a polite and respectful term for a grand- (*bel-*) -mother (*-dam*), later extended to a *great* grandmother and then generalized to any very old woman. But because of the association of extreme age with the loss of physical beauty, what was formerly a reverential term for the matriarch of the family deteriorated into a depiction of an old woman's most visible but least flattering feature—her wizened (withered and wrinkled) appearance, 72

BELLADONNA (bel´ə·dän´ə) *n*. **1.** a poisonous European plant, *Atropa belladonna*, of the nightshade family, having purplish, campanulate (bell-shaped) flowers and shiny black berries; deadly nightshade. **2.** an alkaloid (a nitrogen-containing organic compound having basic [of or pertaining to a chemical base, as distinguished from an acid] chemical properties, such as caffeine, nicotine, MORPHINE, and cocaine) derived from the leaves and roots of this plant, used in medicine to treat spasm, gastrointestinal disorders, and to dilate the pupil of the eyes; atropine. [**bella** + **donna**] < Ital. *bella*: beautiful (< or infl. by L. *bella*, fem. of *bellus*: beautiful, handsome) + *donna*: lady (< or infl. by L. *domina*, fem. of *dominus*: lord, master < or akin to *domus*: house; cf. BELDAM and DANGER). RECON: *beautiful* (**bella**) *lady* (**donna**). The belladonna was so named not because it is a beautiful plant but because its extract was purportedly used by Italian Renaissance women to dilate their pupils to give their eyes a beautiful sloe (large and dark, like the purplish-black fruit of the blackthorn bush) appearance. Or as an alternative explanation, the belladonna may have been named after its reputed use by Leucota, a famous Italian poisoner, to dispose of beautiful women, perhaps as a service to less attractive but more influential women who did not relish the competition. In either case, *belladonna* may, in fact, not even derive from L. *bellus* + *dominus* but be a corruption of an earlier Celtic form, 72, 197

bellicose, 197
bellicosity 197
bellum (war), 197
bellus, 72
bellybutton, 58
"belly-speaker," 82
BELONEPHOBIA (bel´ə·nə·fō´bē·ə) *n*. an irrational fear or dread of needles and pins.[< G. *belonē*: needle + -PHOBIA], 143
ben-, *72, 72*
bene, 72, 85
BENE-, BEN-, 30 (as a guide to understanding the Technical Information within the COMMON ROOTS): **72–74**
bene-, *72, 72, 73, 74*
beneath (bi·nēth´) *adv*. **1.** in or to a lower place, position, rank, state, etc.; below; underneath: *to walk beneath a bridge.* —*prep.* **2.** lower in place, position, rank, state, etc.; below; under: *In presidential succession, the president pro tempore* (tem´pə·rē) *is beneath the Speaker of the House.* [**be-** + **-neath**] < OE. *be-* (an unstressed form of *bī*): by, about, near, at + *neothan*: below. RECON: *by or near* (**be-**) *below* (**-neath**), 72
bene**cept**or, 74, **105**
bene**dic**ence, 74, **105**
Benedick, 74
benedict, 73, *74*
Benedictine, 74
benediction, 73, *73, 81, 85*
bene**dict**ional, 74, **105**
bene**dict**ionale, 74, **105**
benedictionary, 74, **105**
benedictory, 74, **105**
bene**fac**tion, 74, **105**
benefactive, 74, **105**
benefactor, *72, 73, 85*
bene**factrices**, 74, **105**
benefic, *72, 73, 85*
bene**fice**, 74, **105**
bene**fic**ence, 74, **105**
bene**fic**ent, 74, **105**
bene**fic**ential, 74, **105**
bene**fic**ial, 74, **105**
beneficially, 74, **105**
bene**fic**iary, 74, **105**
bene**fic**iate, 74, **105**
benefit, 74, **105**
benefiter, 74, **105**
benefiting, 74, **105**
Benelux (ben´ə·luks´) *n*. **1.** an economic union of Belgium, the Netherlands, and Luxembourg, established in 1948. **2.** Belgium, the Netherlands, and Luxembourg considered collectively. [**Be-** + **ne-** + **lux-**] < *Be(lgium)* + *Ne(therlands)* + *Lux(embourg)*. RECON: *Belgium* (**Bel-**), *the Netherlands* (**ne-**), *and Luxembourg* (**lux-**), 72
benevolent, *72, 73, 85*, see also under VOL-¹
bene**vol**ist, 74, **105**
benign, 74, **105**
benignity, 74, **105**
benignly, 74, **105**
benison, *72, 73, 85*
Benito, 74

Benjamin (ben´jə·min) a masculine name. Nicknames and diminutives: *Ben, Benny, Bennie, Benjy,* etc. [**Ben-** + *-jamin*] < Heb. *bin-*: son of + *-yāmīn*: the right hand (orig., south). RECON: *son of* (**Ben-**) *the right hand* (*-jamin*). In the Old Testament, Rachel, parturient (in the process of giving birth) and aware that she would soon die from her travail (trə·vāl´; childbirth), called her unborn child Benoni, or "son of my sorrow." But Jacob, the father, having prescience (presh´(ē)əns; foreknowledge) that this child would be his "son of the right hand" or favorite son, called him Benjamin; *30-31* (explanation of features in this entry), 72
Benkovich, 74
Benkowski, 74
Bennett, 74
Benoit, 74
Benson, 74
benzaldehyde (ben·zal´də·hīd´) *n*. a clear, volatile oil having the odor of bitter almonds, used in the manufacture of dyes, perfumes, solvents, flavorings, etc. [**benz-** + **al-** + **de-** + **hyd-** + **-e**] < E. *benz(oic)* (of *benzoin* [ben´zō·in, ben·zō´-], an aromatic resin obtained from trees of the genus *Styrax*, found in Java, Sumatra, and other areas) + NL. *al(cohol)* (ult. < Arabic *al-kuḥl*: the powder of antimony; cf. ALCOHOL) + *de-*: without, not (< L. *dē-*: away from, off, down, the reversal of) + *hyd(rogenātum)*: hydrogenated (ult. < G. *hydr-*, base of *hydōr*: water) + E. *-e*: silent final letter. RECON: *benzoic* (**benz-**) *alcohol* (**al-**) *which is not* (**de-**) *hydrogenated* (**hyd-**), 72
benzoin, see under BENZALDEHYDE
bescuit, 91
besti-, 103
bēsti(a), 103
bestiocracy, *62*, **103**
Beverly, 148
bevy (bev´ē) *n*. **1.** a group or flock, as of quail or larks; see COLLECTIVE NOUNS OF VENERY. **2.** any collection or assemblage, esp. of girls or young women: *a bevy of beauties*. [**bevy**] < ME. *bevey*: quail, ladies < NormFr. *bevée*: a hunting noun of assemblage, perhaps < L. *bibere*: to drink, to imbibe, as in its Ital. derivative *bevuta*: a drinking group or party. RECON: *quail, ladies* (**bevy**), 154, see also under BIKINI
bhakti, 138
BI-, BIN-, BIS-, *90–92*
bi-¹ < L. *bi-*, comb. form of *bis*, two, twice, double (akin to G. *dis*; cf. DI-²): BICENTENNIAL, BILINGUAL, *bisexual*, **90**, 91
bi-² < G. *bi-*, base of *bios*: life: BIOLOGY, AUTOBIOGRAPHER, BIODEGRADABLE, *48*, **90**, *106*, *108*
bi-³ (abstracted from *bibli-*: book, books, bible), *90*
-bi- (misc. letter combination), *90*
BIBLE, WORDS AND PHRASES DERIVED FROM, 137
BIBLI-, 48–50
bibli-, *48, 48, 49, 50, 144*
biblia, 48
biblia sacra, 48
biblical, *49, 90*
biblicality, 50, **101**
biblically, 50, **101**
biblicism, 50, **101**
biblic**liter**acy, 50, **101**
biblio**clast**, 50, **101**
bibliofilm, 50, **101**
bibliogenesis, 50, **101**
biblio**gnost**, 50, **101**
bibliogony, 50, **101**
bibliographer, *36, 48, 90,*
bibliographically, 50, **101**
bibliography, 50, **101**
biblio**klept**, *xiii, 36, 49*
biblio**klept**omania, 36, *171*, **144**, see also under MAN-²
biblio**latr**ist, 50, **101**
bibli**ology**, 50, **101**
bibliomancy, 150
biblio**mane**, 50, **101**
biblio**mania**, 50, **101**
biblion, 48
biblio**pegist**, 50, **101**
biblio**phagist**, 50, **101**
bibliophagist, 155
bibliophile, *49*, see also under -PHILE
bibliophilistic, 50, **101**
bibliophobe, 49
bibliopole, 50, **101**
bibliosoph, 49
biblio**taph**, 50, **101**
biblio**theca**, 50, **101**
bibliotherapy, 50, **101**
biblio**tics**, 50, **101**
biblio**tist**, 50, **101**
biblos, 48
bi**camer**al, *92*, **108**
bi**caud**al, *92*, **108**
bicentennial < L. *bi-*, comb. form of *bis*: two, twice, double + CENTENNIAL, **90**, *90*, see also under BI-¹

brontosaurus, see under BRONTOPHOBIA
Bronx cheer, 152
brother, 139
brotherly, see under -LY¹
brunch, 131
brusquerie, see under AFFABLE
bruxism, see under BRUXOMANIA
BRUXOMANIA *n.* a psychoneurotic compulsion for gritting or grinding the teeth. This is distinguished from *bruxism*, also called *odontoprisis* (ō·dän´tō·prī´sis, ō´dän·täp´ri·sis), which is not as pronounced and often performed with little or no awareness. [< G. *bryx(is)*: a gnashing or grinding of the teeth (< *brychein* or *brykein*: to gnash or grind teeth) + -o-: conn. vowel + -MANIA], 145
bryology, 117
bulimia, see under SITOMANIA
bureau-, 103, *103*
bureau<u>cracy</u>, **62, 103**
burglar, see under AMBIVALENT
burgle, see under AMBIVALENT

burs- < ML. *burs*-, base of *bursa*: a bag, pouch, purse (< G. *byrsa*: a skin, hide, wineskin), *67*
bursa, 244
BURSAR (bûr´sər) *n.* a treasurer or administrator in charge of funds, esp. at a college or university. [**burs-** + **-ar**] < ML. *burs(a)*: a bag, pouch, purse (< G. *byrsa*: a skin, hide, wineskin) + -*ār(ius)*: pert. to, charact. by OR one who or that which (performs the action designated by the preceding base or elements). RECON: *pert. to or charact. by* (**-ar**) *a purse* (**burs-**) OR *one who* (**-ar**) [keeps] *a purse* (**burs-**). In Middle English and Old French, this word was spelled, respectively, *bouser* and *boursier*—both forms ending in -*er* (< OF. -*er*, -*ier* < L. -*ārius*). But in Modern English, the -*er* was changed to -*ar*, evidently in imitation of the -*ārius*) in Medieval Latin *bursārius*, "purse-keeper," the ETYMON of English *bursar*, *67*
bursiform, 149
bursitis, 67
bush-league, 152
buzzword, see under -WORD
Byblos, 48
byblos, 48

C

cabriole, 121
cac-, 84
CACODEMONOMANIA (kak´ō·dē´mə·nə·mā´nē·ə) *n.* a psychotic condition in which a person believes he or she is possessed by an evil spirit; also, the experience of demonic possession. [< G. *kak(os)*: bad + -o-: conn. vowel + *daimōn*: deity, lesser god, spirit, fate + -o-: conn. vowel + -MANIA], 145
caconym, 251
cacophonous (kə·käf´ə·nəs) *adj.* emitting or having a harsh, grating sound or sounds; discordant, dissonant: *the cacophonous clatter of children in the schoolyard.* [**cac-** + **-o-** + **phon-** + **-ous**] < G. *kak(os)*: bad + -o-: conn. vowel + *phon(ē)*: sound, voice + E. -*ous*: full of, abounding in, charact. by, like (< L. -*ō(s)us* in most E. words, but in this derivative an Anglicization of G. -*os*: adj. suffix; see -OUS for further information). RECON: *full of* (**-ous**) *bad* (**cac-**) *sound* (**phon-**), *84, 255*, see also under -OUS
cactus (Anglicization and Latinization of G. *kaktos*), 236
cadaver (kə·dav´er) *n.* a dead body, esp. a human corpse used in medical schools for dissection and study. [**cadaver**] < L. *cadāver*: dead body, corpse (< or akin to *cadere*: to fall; cf. INCIDENT. RECON: *dead body* (**cadaver**). A cadaver, etymologically, is the remains of one who has fallen and died, *93*
cadāver, 93
cadaverine (kə·dav´ə·rēn´, -ər·in) *n.* a colorless, syrupy, toxic PTOMAINE present in decomposing flesh and other substances. [**cadaver** + **-in-** + **-e**] < L. *cadāver*: dead body, corpse (< or akin to *cadere*: to fall; cf. INCIDENT) + -*īn(a)* (fem. of -*īnus*): pert. to, charact. by; also, a fem. abstract *n*-forming suffix having the basic meaning: the quality, state, or condition of + -*e*: silent final letter. RECON: *the quality, state, or condition of* (**-in-**) *a dead body* (**cadaver**). SEC. DISS: [cadaver + **-ine**] Note: L. -*īn(a)*: the quality, state, or condition of + E. -*e*: silent final letter > the E. *n*-forming suffix -INE², having, in this entry, the medical and scientific meaning: an ALKALOID or nitrogenous base of (that which is designated by the preceding base or elements). SEC. RECON: *an alkaloid of* (**-ine**) *a dead body* (**cadaver**); cf. PTOMAINE for a parallel but primarily Greek-derived secondary reconstruction, *22-25* (explanation of features in this entry), *93*
cadaverous (kə·dav´er·əs) *adj.* **1.** of, resembling, or suggestive of a CADAVER; corpselike. **2.** haggard, emaciated (i·mā´shē·ā´tid, -sē-; abnormally thin due to starvation or disease). **3.** pale, wan (wän; sickly pale, as from an emaciating disease). [**cadaver** + **-ous**] < L. *cadāver*: dead body, corpse (< or akin to *cadere*: to fall; cf. INCIDENT) + E. -*ous*: full of, abounding in, charact. by, like (< L. -*ōsus*). RECON: *like* (**-ous**) *a dead body* (**cadaver**), *93*
caduceus (kə·dōō´sē·əs) *n.* **1.** in classical mythology, the magic wand or staff of Hermes (hûr´mēz; the Greek messenger of the gods, identified with the Roman god Mercury), having two snakes coiled around it and two outspread wings at its top. **2.** a picture or representation of this staff, used as a symbol of the medical profession and as the insignia of the United States Army Medical Corps. [**caduc-** + **-eus**] < L. *cādūc-* (an alter. of G. *karyk-*, base of *karyx*): herald (an imperial or official messenger and proclaimer) + -*eus* (< G. -*eios*): pert. to, charact. by; but used here as a var. of -*eum* (< G. -*eion*): that which pertains to; hence, a thing connected with (< L. -*eus* < G. -*eios*). RECON: *a thing connected with* (**-eus**) *a herald* (**caduc-**). In addition to his internuncial (in´tər·nun´shəl, -shē-əl, -sē-əl; serving in the capacity of a messenger) responsibilities, Hermes served, under the identity of the Egyptian-influenced Hermes Trismegistus (tris´mə·jis´təs; thrice or three times greatest), as a god of alchemy and, hence, medicine—the two snakes coiled around his staff being a symbol of the medical renewal of life. However, his staff, the caduceus, is often confused with another medical staff, the *staff of Aesculapius* (es´kyoo·lā´pē·əs, -kyə-), named after the Roman god of medicine, whose name, in turn, is a rendering of that of the Greek god of medicine, *Asclepius* (as·klē´pē·əs, ə·sklē´-). But the staff of Aesculapius differs

from the caduceus in having one, rather than two, snakes coiled around it and two short ramifications (branches forking off from a larger branch or trunk; hence, developments or consequences growing out of something else), rather than two outspread wings, at its top. It is also a symbol of the medical profession and is the insignia of the American Medical Association, *75*
caedere, 54
caes-, 54
Caesar, Julius, *54*, see also under CAESARIAN SECTION immediately below
Caesarian section (si·zer´ē·ən sek´shən) [also **c-**] a surgical operation for delivering a baby through an incision in the abdominal and uterine walls of the mother. Also spelled *Caesarean, Cesarean, Cesarian.* [**Caesar** + **-i-** + **-an** + SECTION] < L. *Caesar*: Julius Caesar + -*i*-: conn. vowel + -*ān(us)*: of, pert. to, charact. by + E. *section*: surgical incision. RECON: *the surgical incision* (SECTION) *of* (**-an**) *Julius Caesar* (**Caesar**). Legend has it that Julius Caesar was born *ā caesō mātris ūterē*, "from the cut womb of his mother," and that his last name therefore derives from Latin *caes-* (base of *caesus*, pp. of *caedere*: to cut, to kill) + -*ār(ia)* (fem. of -*ārius*): pert. to, charact. by. But in 100 B.C. (the approximate date of Caesar's birth), what we now call a Caesarian section was performed only on women who had died in parturition (childbirth) since the medical practice of suturing (sōō´chə·ring; the stitching together of the two edges of an incision or wound) had not yet developed, and no woman could survive the bleeding— live Caesarians being first performed around 1500. Yet Caesar's mother, Julia, was not only alive when Caesar wrote *De bello Gallico*, "The Gallic War," but actually outlived her son, who was assassinated in 44 B.C. Moreover, the family name Caesar was already well established long before Julius Caesar's birth and was, in fact, a prestigious name in ancient Rome. So it is not plausible that Julius Caesar was born *ā caesō mātris ūterē*, nor is it possible that his family name was coined as a consequence of his alleged surgical delivery (though it is conceivable that some remote ancestor of Julius Caesar, whose mother did die in childbirth, was delivered in this manner, yielding the name *Caesar*). More likely, however, *Caesar* is a corruption of a foreign term, perhaps of Etruscan (an extinct language spoken in what is now west-central Italy) origin, that was later influenced and altered by Latin *caesus*, "cut"— spawning the myth of Julius Caesar's birth and *Caesarian section, 54*, see also the compound suffix -*arian* under AGRARIAN and ANTIDISESTABLISHMENTARIANISM, which, partially by coincidence, matches the last five letters in *Caesarian*
caesus, 54
caffeine, see under -INE²
calciferol, 125
calcification (kal´sə·fi·kā´shən) *n.* **1.** the formation of or conversion into calcium oxide (the chemical name of lime, a white caustic substance produced by calcining [kal´si·ning, kal·sī´-; heating or burning until it becomes a powder] calcium carbonate, the major constituent of limestone, marble, oyster shell, coral, and related substances). **2.** the abnormal deposition of calcium compounds in soft body tissues and organs, as arteries, joints, bladders, and heart valves, resulting in hard stony concretions (solidified masses) with potentially severe or catastrophic medical consequences. **3.** hardening, solidification, or inflexibility: *Twenty years of conditioning resulted in the calcification of his attitudes towards women*; cf. PETRIFY. [**calc-** + **-i-** + **-fic-** + **-at-** + **-ion**] < L. *calc(is)* (gen. of *calx*): lime, limestone, pebble (< G. *chalix*: small stone, pebble) + -*i*-: conn. vowel + -*fic(āre)*: to make or do repeatedly (< -*fic(us)*: making, doing, causing, producing [< -*ficere*, comb. form of *facere*: to make, to do] + -*āre*: verbal suffix) + -*āt*- (base of -*ātus*), ppl. suffix with the inflectional meaning: having been or having had; in E. (without the MACRON), also meaning: having, possessing, or charact. by + -*iōn(is)* (gen. of -*iō*): the act, means, or result of. RECON: *the act, means, or result of* (**-ion**)

having (**-at-**) *repeatedly made* (**-fic-**) *lime or limestone* (**calc-**). SEC. DISS: [calc- + -i- + **-fication**] Note: L. *-fic(āre)*: to make or do repeatedly (ult. < *facere*: to make, to do) + *-āt-* (base of *-ātus*): having been, having had + E. *-iōn(is)* (gen. of *-iō*): the act, means, or result of > the E. *n*-forming suffix *-fication*, having the related meanings: the making, making of, doing, causing, or production of. SEC. RECON: *the making or production of* (**-fication**) *lime or limestone* (**calc-**), 96
calcining, see under CALCIFICATION
calcium carbonate, see under CALCIFICATION
calcium oxide, see under CALCIFICATION
calculi, see under -IASIS
call-, 109
callipygian, 155
call(um), 109
calvary, 137
cambion, see under RECUMBENT
camcorder, 131
camer-, 108
campanulate, see under BELLADONNA
Canadianica, 238
canary, 148
cancer, 148
candelabrum, 121
candidate, 147
canicide, 56
canine, 199, see also under -INE¹
canis, 56
canon, 109
canōn, 109
cantaloupe, 135
cantata, see under ARIA
capelline, see under VERMICELLI
capital, 114
capnomancy, 150, see also under RHABDOPHOBIA
capsule, see under -UL-¹
carbolic acid, see under -OL
carbon dioxide, see under DI-²
carcinoma, 124
CARCINOPHOBIA (kär´sə·nə·fō´bē·ə) *n.* an abnormal and often persistent fear or dread of cancer. [< G. *karkin(os)*: crab, cancer + *-o-*: conn. vowel + -PHOBIA], 143
card, 51
carde, 51
CARDI-, 51–53
cardi-, 10, *51*, 51, 104
cardia (kär´dē·ə) *n., pl.* cardiae (kär´dē·ē´) *or* cardias (kär´dē·əz). **1.** the SPHINCTER between the outlet of the ESOPHAGUS and the inlet to the stomach; cardiac ORIFICE; cf. PYLORUS. **2.** the upper portion of the stomach. [**cardia**] < G. *kardia*: heart, cardia (def. 1). The cardiae (def. 1 and 2) were presumably named because they are on the heart or cardiac side of the stomach and not because they have any structural or functional relationship to the heart, *52*, see also CARDIOPYLORIC
cardiac, 52, *243*
cardiac arrest, 51
cardiac orifice, see under CARDIA
cardialgia, 10-11 (as a guide to understanding the Brief Analyses), 52
cardinal (kär´di·n´l) *adj.* **1.** of paramount importance; chief; principal: *the four cardinal virtues.* **2.** bright red. —*n.* **3.** a Roman Catholic ecclesiastic (i·klē´zē·as´tik; a member of the clergy), appointed by and ranking immediately below the pope. **4.** a bright red color. **5.** a crested American songbird, *Cardinalis cardinalis*, the male of which has bright red feathers and a bright red beak. [**cardin-** + **-al**] < L. *cardin(is)* (gen. of *cardō*): door hinge, hinge, pivot, that upon which something turns or depends + *-āl(is)*: pert. to, charact. by. RECON: *pert. to* (**-al**) *that upon which something turns or depends* (**cardin-**). The Roman Catholic cardinal, second in line to the pope, was formerly a very powerful personage upon whom many people's lives and livelihoods depended. Indeed, his influence was so extensive that his scarlet robe gave rise to "bright red" meaning of cardinal, which in turn became the name of a red-colored bird, fish, flower, and woman's garment. As for the cardinal virtues—prudence, justice, temperance, and fortitude—they have nothing to do with red but arose from the notion that attainment of the good life "hinged" on properly observing them, *51*
cardinal numbers, see under QUINT-
cardinalate (kär´din´l·āt´) *n.* **1.** the council of cardinals, responsible for electing and advising the pope; College of Cardinals. **2.** the rank, office, or term of a cardinal. [**cardin-** + **-al** + **-at-** + **-e**] < L. *cardin(is)* (gen. of *cardō*): door hinge, hinge, pivot, that upon which something turns or depends + *-āl(is)*: pert. to, charact. by + *-āt(us)*: the office or holder of the office of; orig., a ppl. suffix with the inflectional meaning, "having been or having had," but in this word derived from a fem. SUBSTANTIVE derivative of this suffix (see -ATE for further information) + E. *-e*: silent final letter. RECON: *the office* (**-at-**) *charact. by* (**-al**) *that upon which something turns or depends* (**cardin-**). SEC. DISS: [**cardinal** + **-ate**] Note: L. *cardin(is)* (gen. of *cardō*): door hinge, hinge, pivot, that upon which something turns or depends + *-ālis*: pert. to, charact. by > L. *cardinālis* > E. CARDINAL: a Roman Catholic ECCLESIASTIC ranking immediately below the pope. Also note: L. *-āt(us)*: the office or

holder of the office of + E. *-e*: silent final letter > E. -ATE, having, in this entry, two separate but closely related meanings: a body or group charact. by common goals, interests, status, etc.; and the rank or office of that person, group, or body (designated by the preceding base or elements). SEC. RECON: *a body of* (**-ate**) *cardinals* (**cardinal**) OR *the rank or office of* (**-ate**) *a cardinal* (**cardinal**), *51*
cardio**hepat**ic, 53, **102**
cardi**oid**, 53, **102**
cardiologist, 51
cardiology, 52
cardio**myo**pathy, 13-14 (as a guide to understanding the HELPFUL HINTS), 53, **102**
cardio**nephr**ic, 53, **102**
cardio**path**y, 53, **102**
cardio**phob**ia, 53, **102**
cardioplasty (kär´dē·ə·plas´tē, kär´dē·ō-) *n.* plastic surgery of the CARDIA (def. 1) or surrounding tissue. [**cardi-** + **-o-** + **plast-** + **-y**] < G. *kardi(a)*: heart, CARDIA (def. 1) + *-o-*: conn. vowel + *plast(os)*: formed, molded (< *plas(sein)*: to form, to mold + *-tos*: verbal suffix with the inflectional meaning: having been or having had) + E. *-y*: the act, process, condition, or result of (< G. *-ia*). RECON: *the process of* (**-y**) *molding* (**plast-**) *the cardia* (**cardi-**). SEC. DISS: [**cardio-** + **-plasty**] Note: G. *kardi(a)*: heart, cardia + *-o-*: conn. vowel > G. *kardio-* > the E. comb. form *cardio-*: heart, cardia. Also note: G. *plast(os)*: formed, molded + *-ia*: the act, process, condition, or result of > G. *plastia-* > the E. *n*-forming comb. form *-plasty*, having, in this entry, the modern medical meaning: plastic surgery of (that anatomical structure or part of the body specified by the preceding base or elements). SEC. RECON: *plastic surgery of* (**-plasty**) *the cardia* (**cardi-**), *52*
cardio**pleg**ia, 53, **102**
cardio**pulmon**ary, 53, **102**
cardiopyloric (kär´dē·ō·pī·lôr´ik, kär´dē·ə-, -pi-) *adj.* **1.** pertaining to the CARDIA (def. 1) and the PYLORUS. **2.** pertaining to the cardiac and pyloric regions of the stomach. [**cardi-** + **-o-** + **pyl-** + **-or-** + **-ic**] < G. *kardi(a)*: heart, CARDIA (def. 1) + *-o-*: conn. vowel (in this context rep. "and") + *pyl(ē)*: gate + *o(u)r(os)*: guard, watcher (< *or* akin to *horan*: to see, view) + *-ik(os)*: pert. to, charact. by. RECON: *pert. to* (**-ic**) *the cardia* (**cardi-**) (**-o-**) *and gate* (**pyl-**) *watcher* (**-or-**) OR (when attributing "and" to *-o-*) *pert. to* (**-ic**) *the cardia* (**cardi-**) *and* (**-o-**) *gate* (**pyl-**) *watcher* (**-or-**). SEC. DISS: [cardi- + **-o-** + **pyloric**] Note: G. *pyl(ē)*: gate + *o(u)ros*: guard, watcher > G. *pylōros*: gatekeeper, pylorus > E. *pylor(us)* + *-ic*: pert. to, charact. by (< G. *-ikos*) > *pyloric*: pert. to the pylorus or the region of the pylorus. SEC. RECON: *pert. to the pylorus* (**pyloric**) *and* (**-o-**) *cardia* (**cardi-**), *52*
cardio**ren**al, 53, **102**
cardiospasm (kär´dē·ə·spaz´əm, kär´dē·ō-) *n.* the failure or inability of the CARDIA (def. 1) to properly relax and open after swallowing, resulting in the retention of food in the esophagus. [**cardi-** + **-o-** + **spas-** + **-m**] < G. *kardi(a)*: heart, CARDIA (def. 1) + *-o-*: conn. vowel + *spas* (base of *span*): to draw, pull, violently contract + *-m(os)*: the act or the result of the act of. RECON: *the act of* (**-m**) *the cardia* (**cardi-**) *violently contracting* (**spas-**). Medically, this term is a misnomer. A spasm, which is an involuntary contraction of a muscle normally in a relaxed state, is not a factor in cardiospasm. Rather, the dysfunction present is the failure of a muscle normally in a contracted state to relax. The medical term for this essentially opposite condition is *achalasia* (ak´ə·lā´zha) < G. *a-*: without, lacking, not + *chala(n)*: to loosen + *-s(is)*: the act, process, or result of + *-ia*: the state or condition of. Hence, *the condition of* (**-ia**) *the result of* (**-s-**) *not* (**a**) *loosening* (**chala-**), *52*
cardio**tach**ometer, 53, **102**
cardio**therap**y, 53, **102**
cardiovascular, 51, *51*, see also under -O-² and -CUL-¹
carditis, 68, **104**
Carduus benedictus, 74
carn(is), 94, *117*
carnivorous, 117, see also under -OUS
Caroline Islands, see under MICRONESIA
carpophagous, 117
cast, 154
cast-, 108
castaneous, 115
castigate, 89, **108**
cast(us), 108
casuistry, 126
cat, 139
cat- see under CATA- immediately below
cata- (kat´ə) a G-derived prefix having four often overlapping meanings: **1.** down, downward: *catabolism* (kə·tab´ə·liz´m; the destructive phase of metabolism, during which complex substances are broken down into simpler substances, with the release of energy; cf. ANABOLISM), *catadromous* (kə·tad´rə·məs; designating those fish that live in fresh water but migrate to the sea to spawn, as certain eels; cf. ANADROMOUS). **2.** back, backward, often connoting (signifying or suggesting as an attendant meaning or condition; cf. CONNOTATION) the degeneration or regression of: *catalepsy* (a physical condition, often associated with SCHIZOPHRENIA, characterized by immobility, muscular rigidity, and loss of response to stimuli), *cataplasia* (kat´ə·plā´zhə, -zhē·ə; a reversion or degeneration of body cells or tissues to a more primitive, less differentiated form). **3.** against, contrary; wrong, amiss: *catapult* (an ancient military contraption for hurling stones, spears, arrows, and other objects; cf. BALLISTA), *catachresis* (kat´ə·krē´sis; an improper or strained use

of a word or phrase, either through error or for rhetorical effect. Example: *He planted the seeds of his creation on a back burner).* **4.** completely, thoroughly, throughout: *catalyst* (a substance that produces or accelerates a chemical reaction without itself being consumed or permanently altered in the process), *catalog* (etymologically, a complete counting, reckoning, or speaking for; see -LOGY for the sense development of the second element *-log*). **Note:** *cata-* becomes *cat-* before vowels and *h*: *category, cathode* (the positive electrode in a battery, to which current flows; also, the negatively charged electrode in an electrolytic cell or electron tube), *cathedral* (the principal church in a district under a bishop's jurisdiction). **[cata-]** < G. *kata-*: down, back, against, thoroughly; cf. ANA-, and for a Latin prefix with a similar meaning, see DE-cle of power. —v. **6.** to surround or enclose with a single, curved line: *Circle the correct answer.* **7.** to move around or about: *To survive, you must carefully circle the mine fields.* [**circ-** + **-l-** + **-e**] < L. *circ(us)*: circle, ring, racecourse (< or akin to G. *kirkos*, METATHESIS of *krikos*: circle, ring) + *-(u)l(us)*: a dim. suffix having the basic meaning: small, little, tiny + E. *-e*: silent final letter. RECON: *small* (**-l-**) *ring* (**circ-**), 57

circulate (sûr´kyə·lāt´) *v.* **1.** to move in a circle or circular course; cycle: *Water circulates throughout the engine of a car.* **2.** to pass freely throughout: *Air circulates throughout a room.* **3.** to pass from person to person or place to place: *Rumors circulate quickly; She circulates in high society.* [**circ-** + **-ul-** + **-at-** + **-e**] < L. *circ(us)*: circle, ring, racecourse (< or akin to G. *kirkos*, METATHESIS of *krikos*: circle, ring) + *-ul(us)*: a dim. suffix having the basic meaning: small, little, tiny + *-āt-* (base of *-ātus*), ppl. suffix with the inflectional meaning: having been or having had; in E. (without the macron), also meaning: having, possessing, or charact. by, but used in this entry as a verbal suffix with the senses described under "NOTE" below + E. *-e*: silent final letter. RECON: *having been* (**-at-**) *a little* (**-ul-**) *circle* (**circ-**), 57. SEC. DISS: [circ- + -ul- + **-ate**] Note: L. *-āt-* (base of *-ātus*): having been, having had + E. *-e*: silent final letter > E. -ATE, used in this entry as a *v*-forming suffix, having the related meanings: to cause, to become, to cause to become, to make, to do, to form. SEC. RECON: *to make* (**-ate**) *a little* (**-ul-**) *circle* (**circ-**), 57, see also under -UL-¹

CIRCUM-, 57–59
circum-, *57*, *57*, *58*, **106**, *106*, **107**, *107*, *123*
circumambulation (sûr´kəm·am´byə·lā´shən) *n.* **1.** the act of walking around: *Her slow and deliberate circumambulation of the statue suggests she is an artist.* **2.** the act of walking or wandering about, often aimlessly and without purpose: *a leisurely circumambulation of the countryside.* [**circum-** + **ambul-** + **-at-** + **-ion**] < L. *circum-*: around, about, surrounding (< or akin to G. *kirkos*, METATHESIS of *krikos*: circle, ring) + *ambul(āre)*: to walk, to travel, to go about + *-āt-* (base of *-ātus*), ppl. suffix with the inflectional meaning: having been or having had; in E. (without the macron), also meaning: having, possessing, or charact. by + L. *-iōn(is)* (gen. of *-iō*): the act, means, or result of. RECON: *the act or result of* (**-ion**) *having been* (**-at-**) *walking* (**ambul-**) *around or about* (**circum-**), 57, 78
circumarticular, 58
circum**austral**, 59, **103**
circum**a**viate, 59, **103**
circum**bore**al, 59, **103**
circumcision, 54, 57, **58**
circum(cision), 58
circum-Cytherean, 58
circum**duct**ion, 59, **103**, see also following entry
circumduction, *77*, **106**, see also preceding entry
circumference, 58, *57*, see also under -ENCE
circum**flex**, 59, **103**
circum**fluent**, 59, **103**
circumforaneal, 59
circumforanean, 59
circumforaneous, *57*, 59, see also under FOR-²
circum**fuse**, 59, **103**
circumgyral, 59
circum**jacent**, 59, **103**
circum-Jovian, 58
circum**littor**al, 59, **103**
circum**locut**ion, *83*, **107**, see also preceding entry
circum**locu**tion, *xii*, 59, **103**, *123* see also following entry
circumlocutory, *83*, **107**
circumlunar, 58
circum-Mercurial, 58
circum**nat**ant, 13 (as a guide to understanding the HELPFUL HINTS), 59, **103**
circumnavigate, *57*, 58
circumnebulous, 59
circum**neutro**philous, 59, **103**
circum**nutate**, 59, **103**
circumorbital, 58
circumorbital hematoma, 58, 251, 256, see also under HEMATOMA
circumplanetary, 58
circum-Saturnian, 58
circum**scissle**, 59, **103**
circumscribe, *57*, **58**
circum**script**ion, 59, **103**
circumsept, 58
circumsolar, 58
circum**spect**, 59, **103**
circum**stance**, 59, **103**
circum**stantial**, 59, **103**
circumstellar, 58
Circumstraint, 58
circumterraneous, 58
circumterrestrial, *xiii*, 58
circumumbilical, 58
circum**und**ulation, 59, **103**
circum**vall**ate, 59, **103**
circumvascular, 58
circum**vent**, 13 (as a guide to understanding the HELPFUL HINTS), 57, 59, **103**

circumvestite, 59
circum**vol**ant, 59, **103**, see also under VOL-¹
circumvolitate, 59
circum**volu**tion, 59, **103**
Circus Maximus, see under CIRCUS
circus (L.), 57
circus (sûr´kəs) *n.* **1.** a form of public entertainment featuring acrobats, dancing animals, clowns, jugglers, stilt walkers, and other unusual and often bizarre performers, generally held in a circular or oblong arena within a building or large tent. **2.** *Colloq.* anything suggestive of the apparent disorder, commotion, and farcicality (the quality or state of being a farce) of such an entertainment: *With everyone yelling at the same time, the news conference turned into a circus.* [**circus**] < L. *circus*: circle, ring, racecourse (< or akin to G. *kirkos*, METATHESIS of *krikos*: circle, ring). The early circuses of ancient Rome, exemplified by the *Circus Maximus* ("Largest Racecourse"), featured chariot races, fierce gladiatorial contests, and other, often brutal exhibitions, all held within the circular, central area of a large AMPHITHEATER, 57
cirrhosis, see under -OSIS
-cis- < L. *-cīs-*, base of *-cīsus*, pp. of *-cidere*, comb. form of *caedere*: to cut, to kill, 58
-cīs-, *54*
-cīsus, *54*
cisvestite, 155
cit-, **104**
cit(āre), *104*
city, *18*, *162*
civ-, **109**
civil disobedience, 200
civil liberties, 200
civil rights, 200
civil, 200
civilian, 200
civilization, 200
civilize, 200
cīvis, *18*
cīvitās, *18*
-cl-, **93**, *93*
clamorous, 215
CLASSICAL MYTHOLOGY, WORDS DERIVED FROM, 136
clast-, **101**
claustrophobia, 142
claviform, 149
Cleopatra, see under ARISTOTLE
cleptobiosis, 144
CLINOMANIA (klī´nō·mā´nē·ə) *n.* a morbid preoccupation with or constant desire for bed rest; cf. KATHISOMANIA. [< G. *klin(ē)*: bed, couch (< or akin to *klinein*: to lean) + *-o-*: conn. vowel + -MANIA], 145
CLIPPED FORMS, 132
cloning, see under SUPERMAN
clowder, 154
clus-, **107**
-clūs(us) (*claudere*), **107**
co- < L. *co-*, var. of COM- (used before *gn*, *h*, or a vowel): with, together, (sometimes used intensively, i.e., completely, thoroughly, throughout, utterly): *cognition* (the process or condition of knowing or perceiving), CO-HABIT, *coarctation* (the narrowing or constriction of a blood vessel, often seen in heart attack and stroke patients), see also under COM-
coarctation, see under CO-
Coca-colonize, 238
coefficient, 118
coenzyme, 125
cognate (käg´nāt) *adj.* **1.** related by blood or through a common ancestor; kindred; AKIN. **2.** descended or derived from a common ancestral language: *French and Italian are cognate languages, both having descended from Latin.* **3.** similar in nature or quality; consimilar. —*n.* **5.** a person related to another through a common ancestor. **6.** a word or root in one language that is derived from the same ancestral form as a word or root in another language: *English "fish" and Latin "piscis" are cognates because they are both derived from the prehistoric Indo-European root *peisk-.* [**co-** + **gn-** + **-at-** + **-e**] < L. *co-* (var. of *com-*): with, together + *gn(āscī)*: to be born + *-āt-* (base of *-ātus*), ppl. suffix with the inflectional meaning: having been or having had; in E. (without the macron), also meaning: having, possessing, or charact. by + E. *-e*: silent final letter. RECON: *having been* (**-at-**) *born* (**gn-**) *together* (**co-**). SEC. DISS: [co- + gn- + **-ate**] Note: L. *-āt-* (base of *-ātus*): having been, having had + E. *-e*: silent final letter > the E. *adj*-forming suffix -ATE, having, in this entry, the basic meaning: having, having been, possessing, or charact. by. SEC. RECON: *having been* (**-ate**) *born* (**gn-**) *together* (**co-**), 51, see also under COM-, and cf. AGNATE and ENATE
cognition, see under CO-
cohabit, *94*, see also under CO-
cohabit, 220
cohabitation, 222
cohere, see under COM-
coition (kō·ish´ən) *n.* sexual intercourse. [**co-** + **-it-** + **-ion**] < L. *co-* (var. of *com-*): with, together + *-it(us)* (pp. of *īre*: to go) + *-iōn(is)* (gen. of *-iō*): the

act, means, or result of. RECON: *the act of* (**-ion**) *going* (**-it-**) *together* (**co-**); cf. COITUS, and see also under VOLITION

COITOPHOBIA (kō´i·tə·fō´bē·ə) *n.* an irrational, intense, and persistent fear or dread of sexual intercourse. [< L. *coit(us)* (see COITION in preceding entry) + G. *-o-*: conn. vowel + -PHOBIA], 143

coitus, see under VOLITIVE

Coke, 133

col- < L. *col-*, assim. form of COM- (used before *l*): with, together (sometimes used intensively, i.e., completely, thoroughly, throughout, utterly): *collide, colleague,* COLLOCATE, *82,* **107***, 107*

colere, 17

COLLATERAL ADJECTIVES, COMMON NOUNS AND THEIR, 139

colleague, see under COL-

collect, see under COM-

COLLECTIVE NOUNS OF VENERY, 154

College of Cardinals, see under CARDINALATE

collide, see under COL-

COLLINEAR (kō·lin´ē·ər, kə-) *adj.* lying in or appearing on a straight line: *Are the rows of seats in the theater semicircular or collinear?* [**col-** + **line-** + **-ar**] < L. *col-* (assim. form of COM-): with, together (sometimes used intensively, i.e., completely, thoroughly, throughout, utterly) + *line(a)*: linen thread, string, line (< *līnea,* fem. of *līneus*: of string, flax < *līnum*: flax [linen is manufactured from the slender fibers of the flax plant]) + *-ār(is)*: pert. to, charact. by. RECON: *pert. to or charact. by* (**-ar**) *a line* (**line-**) *throughout* (**col-**)*,* 82, see also under COL-

collocate (käl´ə·kāt´) *v.* **1.** to place or position together, esp. side by side or in some specified arrangement: *Electromagnetic forces collocate atoms within molecules.* **2.** to arrange or place in order: *Collocate your ideas before speaking.* **3.** to combine or juxtapose (place side by side) two or more words in a sentence or phrase to form a COLLOCATION (see following entry). [**col-** + **loc-** + **-at-** + **-e**] < L. *col-* (assim. form of *com-*): with, together + *loc(āre)*: to place (< *locus*: a place, site) + *-āt-* (base of *-ātus*), ppl. suffix with the inflectional meaning: having been or having had; in E. (without the MACRON), also meaning: having, possessing, or charact. by + E. *-e*: silent final letter. RECON: *having been* (**-at-**) *placed* (**loc-**) *together* (**col-**). SEC. DISS: [**col-** + loc- + **-ate**] Note: L. *-āt-* (base of *-ātus*): having been, having had + E. *-e*: silent final letter > the E. *adj*-forming suffix -ATE, having, in this entry, the basic meaning: having, having been, possessing, or charact. by. SEC. RECON: *having or having been* (**-ate**) *placed* (**loc-**) *together* (**col-**)*,* 81, see also under COL-

collocation (käl´ə·kā´shən) *n.* **1.** the act or result of placing or positioning together, esp. side by side or in some specified arrangement: *The collocation of buildings in the development were attractive but unimaginative.* **2.** the act or result of arranging or placing in order: *The collocation of files by date of purchase enabled us to keep track of our expenses.* **3.** the combining or juxtaposition (the act of placing side by side) of two or more words in a phrase or sentence to reproduce an established and familiar pattern of usage, deviation from which strikes native speakers as contrived, bizarre, or an indication that one has not mastered the language. Examples: *in the first place* (not *in the first spot*), *to perform an operation* (not *execute an operation*), *to crack a smile* (not *break a smile*), *to run for office* (not *stand for office*—though *stand for election* is the preferred LOCUTION in Britain), *under partly cloudy skies* (not *below partly cloudy skies* or *under partially cloudy skies* or *beneath partially cloudy skies*—Hold on! How many skies do we have?). There are tens of thousands of collocations in the English language, and this is one reason why mastering English is so difficult for foreign speakers. [**col-** + **loc-** + **-at-** + **-ion**] < L. *col-* (assim. form of *com-*): with, together + *loc(āre)*: to place (< *locus*: a place) + *-āt-* (base of *-ātus*), ppl. suffix with the inflectional meaning: having been or having had; in E. (without the MACRON), also meaning: having, possessing, or charact. by + *-iōn(is)* (gen. of *-iō*): the act, means, or result of. RECON: *charact. by* (**-at-**) *the act or result of* (**-ion**) *placing* (**loc-**) *together* (**col-**)*,* 220

collodion, 127

colloquia, *83,* **107**

colloquial, 82

colloquium, *83,* **107**

colloquy, *83,* **107**

colocolostomy, see under -STOMY, -TOMY, and -ECTOMY

colonnade, 114

Colorado, 147

COLORFUL EXPRESSIONS IN THE ENGLISH LANGUAGE, 151

COLORS, WORDS WITH, 147

colostomy (kə·läs´tə·mē) *n.* **1.** the surgical construction of an artificial passageway from the colon to the outside of the body, serving as a substitute anal opening to the lower abdomen, as for a person whose colon has been partially removed due to cancer; cf. COLOCOLOSTOMY. **2.** the passageway or opening so constructed. [**col-** + **-o-** + **stom-** + **-y**] < G. *kol(on)*: large intestine + *-o-*: conn. vowel + *stom(a)*: mouth + E. *-y*: the act, process, condition, or result of (< G. *-ia*). RECON: *the act, process, or result of* (**-y**) *[forming] a mouth* (**stom-**)*for the large intestine* (**col-**). SEC. DISS: [**colo-** + **-stomy**] Note: G. *kol(on)*: large intestine + *-o-*: conn. vowel > the E. comb. form *colo-*: colon. Also note: G. *stom(a)*: mouth + *-ia*: the act, process, condition, or result of > G. *-stomia* > the E. *n*-forming comb. form *-stomy*, having, in this entry, the modern medical meaning: the surgical construction of an artificial "mouthlike" opening or channel passing to the outside of the body from (that anatomical structure or part specified by the preceding base or elements). SEC. RECON: *the surgical construction of an artificial channel*

passing to the outside of the body from (**-stomy**) *the colon* (**colo-**), see under -TOMY, -STOMY, and -ECTOMY

colp-, 104

colpitis, 68, **104**

com- (käm, kəm) a L-derived prefix having the basic meaning: with, together (sometimes used intensively, i.e., completely, thoroughly, throughout, utterly): *complex, compact, complete, uncomfortable.* **Note:** *com-* IS ASSIMILATED in the following manner: *com-* becomes *col-* before *l*: *collect,* COLLINEAR; *cor-* before *r*: *correct, correspond*; and *con-* before *n*: CONNOTATION, *connection, connubial* (kə·nōō´bē·əl; of marriage; conjugal). But in addition to preceding *n, com-* becomes *con-* before *v, d, t,* and most other consonants: *convene, condign* (deserved, said esp. of punishment), *incontinent* (unable to restrain the discharge of urine from the body), *conceal*; and *com-* becomes *co-* before *gn, h,* or a vowel: COGNATE, *cohere* (to stick together), *co-opt* (to appoint, persuade, pre-empt, take the place of). [**com-**] < L. *com-* (a prefixal form of the prep. *cum*): with, together. For a Greek prefix with an almost identical meaning, see syn-; *106, 107,* **108***, 108, 109,* see also under CON-, and cf. DIS-

combination, *92,* **108**

come off the bench, 152

come out swinging, 153

commendatory, see under OFFICIOUS

Commentary (of Detailed Example within the COMMON ROOTS), 8, 10

commodity, 6

COMMOM ROOTS, 4-12 (explanation of features), **43-98**

COMMON EXPRESSIONS DERIVED FROM BASEBALL, 152

COMMON EXPRESSIONS DERIVED FROM BOXING, 153

COMMON GREEK INFLECTIONAL ENDINGS THAT CAN BE REMOVED FROM NOUNS AND ADJECTIVES TO REVEAL THEIR BASES (table), 237

COMMON NOUNS AND THEIR COLLATERAL ADJECTIVES, 139

commutator, 118, *224*

commute, 224

compact, see under COM-

comparative, 211

Comparison of Adjectives, 211-14

comparison, 211, see also under PAR-⁵

compatible, see under NOCENT

complete, see under COM-

complex, see under COM-

con- < L. *con-*, assim. form and var. of COM- (used before *v, d, t,* and most other consonants): with, together (sometimes used intensively, i.e., completely, thoroughly, throughout, utterly): CONNOTATION, *contact, constellation, confuse, 76, 88,* **106***, 106,* **109***, 109, 122,* see also under COM-

conceal, see under COM-

conceptive, see under PHALLIC

concise, see under -CIS-

concord, see under DIS-

concretion, see under CALCIFICATION

condescend, 126

condign, see under COM-

condom, see allusion to under EPI-

conducive, 77, **106**

conduct, 76

conductance, 77, **106**

conduction, 76

conductivity, 77, **106**

conductor, 77, **106**

Condum, Colonel, see under EPI-

confection, 98, **109**

confidence, 225, see also under -ENCE

confident, 206, see also under -ENT

confluence, see under EX-¹

Confucius, see under ANALECTS

confuse, see under CON-

congressional, 80, **106**

conjugal, see under COM-

conjunction, see under DIS-

connection, see under COM-

connotation (kän´ə·tā´shən) *n.* the secondary, often subjective, meaning of a word in addition to its primary, objective meaning: *The connotation of "mother" is, for many people, that of a warm, loving parent caring for and looking after her children*; cf. DENOTATION. [**con-** + **not-** + **-at-** + **-ion**] < L. *con-* (assim. form of COM-): with, together (also used intensively, i.e., completely, thoroughly, throughout, utterly) + *not(a)*: mark, sign + *-āt-* (base of *-ātus*), ppl. suffix with the inflectional meaning: having been or having had; in E. (without the MACRON), also meaning: having, possessing, or charact. by + *-iōn(is)* (gen. of *-iō*): the act, means, or result of. RECON: *the act or result of* (**-ion**) *having been* (**-at-**) *thoroughly* (**con-**) *marked* (**not-**). In this word, the *con-* is used as an intensive to indicate that, in distinction to the *de-* in DENOTATION, this word encompasses more than the literal definition of a word, 8, 46

connoting, see under CATA-

connubial, see under COM-

conoid, see under FORESKIN

consentient, 225

conservative (kən·sûr´və·tiv) *adj.* **1.** favoring social or political institutions as they currently exist or the return to more traditional values and institutions as they have existed in the recent past. **2.** [sometimes c-] of or pertaining to a member of the Conservative party. **3.** traditional in manner or style: *conservative business attire.* **4.** purposely low or moderate, as in price, value, estimation, etc.: *a conservative assessment of the damage.* —*n.* **5.** a person who espouses or advocates conservative principles or beliefs (see defs. 1 and 2); cf. LIBERAL and PROGRESSIVE. [**con-** + **serv-** + **-at-** + **-iv-** + **-e**] < L. *con-* (assim. form and var. of COM- used before most consonants): with, together (also used intensively, i.e., completely, thoroughly, throughout, utterly) + *servāre*): to watch over, guard, keep, preserve + *-āt-* (base of *-ātus*), ppl. suffix with the inflectional meaning: having been or having had; in E. (without the macron), also meaning: having, possessing, or charact. by + L. *-īv(us)*: tending to (be), inclined to (be) + E. *-e*: silent final letter. RECON: *having been (-at-) inclined to (-iv) thoroughly (con-) preserve (serv-).* SEC. DISS: [con- + serv- + -at- + -ive] **Note:** L. *-īv(us)*: tending to (be), inclined to (be) + E. *-e*: silent final letter > the E. *adj*-forming suffix -IVE, having the associated meanings: tending to (be), inclined to (be), charact. by, having the nature of. SEC. RECON: *charact. by (-at-) tending to (-ive-) thoroughly (con-) preserve (serv-),* 88

consimilar, see under AKIN and COGNATE
consonants, see under LATIN CONSONANTS and GREEK CONSONANTS
constellation, see under CON-
(con)straint, circumm-2
consul, see under -ATE
consulate, see under -ATE
contact, see under CON-
continental, see under -AL
contra- < L. *contrā-* (a prefixal form of the adv. and prep. *contrā*): against, opposite to, on the contrary of, *122*
contrail, 131
contravention, 122
contre-, 108
contribution, 204
convalescence, see under -SC-
convection, 118
convene, see under COM-
convenient, see under NOCENT
convention, 122, see also under VENT-¹
conversational, 82
cooperate, 16, 201
cooperative, 16, 201
co-opt, see under COM-
coplanarity, 114
copper, 135
coprolalomania, 144
coprophagous, 155
COPROPHOBIA *n.* a morbid and often persistent fear or dread of feces or fecal matter. [< G. *kopr(os)*: dung, excrement, feces + *-o-*: conn. vowel + -PHOBIA], 143
cor, 51, 93
cor-, see under COM-
corbel, 114
cordate (kôr´dāt) *adj.* heart-shaped: *I have three cordate and two* SAGITTATE *leaves in my herbarium* (dried plant collection); cf. also OBCORDATE, OVATE, and PINNATE. [**cord-** + **-at-** + **-e**] < L. *cord(is)* (gen. of *cor*): heart + *-āt-* (base of *-ātus*), ppl. suffix with the inflectional meaning: having been or having had; in E. (without the macron), also meaning: having, possessing, or charact. by + E. *-e*: silent final letter. RECON: *having been or having had (-at-) a heart (cord-).* SEC. DISS: [cord- + -ate] **Note:** L. *-āt-* (base of *-ātus*): having been, having had + E. *-e*: silent final letter > the E. *adj*-forming suffix -ATE, having, in this entry, the associated meanings: possessing, charact. by, resembling, shaped (like). SEC. RECON: *resembling (-ate) a heart (cord-)* OR *heart (cord-) shaped (-ate),* 51, 93, see also under -ATE
cordial (kôr´jəl) *adj.* **1.** warm and friendly; amiable (ā´mē·ə·b'l); genial (jēn´yəl), (jē´nē·əl). **2.** deeply felt; sincere: *I offer you my cordial apologies.* —*n.* **3.** a sweet, syrupy, alcoholic liquor; liqueur. [**cord-** + **-i-** + **-al**] < L. *cord(is)* (gen. of *cor*): heart + *-i-*: conn. vowel + *-āl(is)*: pert. to, charact. by. RECON: *pert. to (-al) the heart (cord-).* A former meaning of *cordial* was "of or pertaining to the heart." This evolved into "that which warms the heart," which both a cordial and a warm, friendly person appear to accomplish, 51, 93
cordis, 51, 93
corn-, 109
cornet, 204
corn<u>ification</u>, <u>98</u>, **109**
corn(ū), 109
cornū, 204
cornucopia, 205
corona discharge, 95
coronet, 204
CORP-, CORPUS, CORPOR-, 22 (as a guide to understanding the Technical Information within the COMMON ROOTS), **93–95**
corp-, 93, 94, 95,
corpor- *93, 94,* **108**
corpor<u>ality</u>, <u>95</u>, **109**
corpor<u>ation</u>, <u>95</u>, **109**
corpor<u>atism</u>, <u>95</u>, **109**
corpor<u>ative</u>, <u>95</u>, **109**
corpor<u>eity</u>, <u>95</u>, **109**

corpor<u>ification</u>, <u>95</u>, **109**
corporis, 93
corpori)s (corpus), 108
corposant, 95
corp<u>s</u>, <u>95</u>, **109**
corp<u>se</u>, <u>95</u>, **109**
corpulent, <u>95</u>, **109**
CORPUS, (CORP-, CORPOR-), 93–95
corpus, *93, 93, 93*
corpus callosum, <u>95</u>, **109**
corpus cavern<u>osum</u>, <u>95</u>, **109**
corpuscle, 93
corpus<u>cularity</u>, <u>95</u>, **109**
corpus<u>culiferous</u>, <u>95</u>, **109**
corpus de<u>licti</u>, <u>95</u>, **109**
corpus juris **canonici**, <u>95</u>, **109**
corpus <u>juris</u>, <u>95</u>, **109**
corpus juris **civilis**, <u>95</u>, **109**
corpus luteum, <u>95</u>, **109**
corpus stri<u>atum</u>, <u>95</u>, **109**
correct, see under COM-
correspond, see under COM-
correspondent, see under -ENT
cortex, 202
corticis, 202
cosm-, *xx,* **103**
cosm<u>ocracy</u>, *xix,* <u>62</u>, **103**
cosmogony, xix
cosmography, xix
cosmolatry, xix
cosmology, xix
cosmos, 245
cosmosophy, xix
coterie, see under CIRCLE
cotto, 91
count, see under DUKE
counter-, 108
counter<u>active</u>, **89,** **108**
countess, see under DUKE
coup de grâce, see under MISERICORD
courage (kûr´ij) *n.* a mental posture or state of mind that enables a person to face adversity with confidence and resolution rather than with fear and timidity (a lack of self-assurance); bravery; boldness. [**cour-** + **-age**] < OF. *cuer*: heart (< L. *cor*: heart) + *-age*: the quality, state, condition; act, means, result, or process of (< L. *-āticum*, neut. of *-āticus*: pert. to, charact. by, charact. by having [< either *-āt(us)*: having been, having had + *-icus*: pert. to, charact. by OR < L. words ending in *-ā* [see -A¹ and -A²] + *-ticus*: pert. to, charact. by]). RECON: *the quality, state, or condition of (-age) heart (cour-).* The heart was formerly (and metaphorically still is) believed to be the source of human emotions, particularly the more exalted (elevated or raised, as in honor or power; noble; elated) emotions of love and courage. Hence, *take heart, have a heart, heartbroken, halfhearted, cross your heart, eat your heart out,* etc., *51*
couturier, 119
cove all the bases, 152
covey, 154
cox-, 104, **107**
cox(a), 104, 107
cox<u>itis</u>, <u>68</u>, **104**
crabs (pubic lice), see under PEDICULOPHOBIA; and for two related medical terms, see PED-³
-crac-, 60
-CRACY, 60–62
-cracy, 60, 60, 61, 62, see also under KAKISTOCRACY
crag, see under CREMNOPHOBIA
craniate, see under -ATE
Crapper, Thomas, see under EPI-
crash, 154
creat-, 104
CREATING ENGLISH WORDS FROM GREEK WORDS (outline), 239
CREATING ENGLISH WORDS FROM LATIN WORDS (outline), 184
CREATOR (krē·ā´tər) *n.* **1.** a person or thing that creates. **2.** in monotheistic and other religions, a supreme being generally regarded as omnipotent (all-powerful) and omniscient (all-knowing); God. [**creat-** + **-or**] < L. *creāt(us)* (pp. of *creāre*: to make, create) + *-or*: one who or that which. RECON: *one who (-or) makes or creates (creat-),* 88
credentials, 224
credenza, 121
CREMNOPHOBIA *n.* an irrational or intense fear or dread of cliffs. [< G. *krēmn(os)*: cliff, crag (krag; a sharply projecting mass of jagged rock forming part of a cliff or bluff); precipice (< *kremannynai*: to hang) + *-o-*: conn. vowel + -PHOBIA], 143
crenellation, 114
creophagous, 117
crescent, see under -SC-
Crete, see under INDO-EUROPEAN
cri-, 104

D

defector (di·fek´tər) *n.* **1.** a person who disavows allegiance to his or her country and establishes residence in another country. **2.** a person who abandons any cause, organization, affiliation, etc., usu. for the purpose of joining or adopting a different and often opposing one. **[de- + -fect- + -or]** < L. *dē-*: away from, off, down, the reversal or undoing of + *-fect(us)* (pp. of *-ficere*, comb. form of *facere*: to make, to do) + *-or*: one who or that which. RECON: *one who* (**-or**) *makes or does* (**-fect-**) *away with* (**de-**), 85, 96

defeminize, 192

defenestration, 114

Defenestration of Prague, 114

Definition (of Detailed Example within the COMMON ROOTS), 8-9

definitions within definitions (rationale), 31

degradation, 79

dem-, 46, **60**, *60*, 61

dēmagōgos, 46

demagogue, 6, **46**

demago*guery*, 47, **101**

dema*goguism*, 47, **101**

dema*gogy*, 47, **101**

DEMENTIA (di·men´shə, -shē·ə) *n.* severe deterioration or impairment of mental abilities resulting from a structural disorder in the brain. **[de- + ment- + -ia]** < L. *dē-*: away from, off, down, out of + *ment(is)* (gen. of *mēns*): mind + *-ia*: the state, condition, or result of. RECON: *the state, condition, or result of* (**-ia**) *out of* (**de-**) *mind* (**ment-**). Dementia originally meant craziness or madness, 53

democracy, 46, **60**, *60*

Democritus, 70

demon-, 103

demonocracy, 62, **103**

demophobia, 142

dēm(os), 61

DENDROPHOBIA *n.* an irrational fear or dread of trees or forests; cf. HYLOPHOBIA. [< G. *dendr(on)*: tree + *-o-*: conn. vowel + -PHOBIA], 143

denigrate, 147

denims, 135

denominative (di·näm´ə·nə·tiv, -nā´tiv) *adj.* **1.** bestowing or conferring a distinctive appellation (a name, title, or designation); naming: *Tomorrow we begin the denominative process of classifying the new species.* **2.** designating a word, base, or phrase formed from a noun or adjective, especially one that is verbal. In English, *to house* is a denominative verb derived from the noun *house*; in Greek, *-izein* is a denominative verb-ending affixed to a variety of noun and adjective bases to form verbs from nouns and adjectives. — *n.* **3.** a word, base, or phrase formed from a noun or adjective. **[de- + nomin- + -at- + -iv- + -e]** < L. *dē-*: away from, off, down + *nōmin(is)* (gen. of *nōmen*): name, noun + *-āt-* (base of *-ātus*), ppl. suffix with the inflectional meaning: having been or having had; in E. (without the MACRON), also meaning: having, possessing, or charact. by + L. *-īv(us)*: tending to (be), inclined to (be) + E. *-e*: silent final letter. RECON: *having been* (**-at-**) *tending to* (**-ive**) *name or noun* (**nomin-**) *down* (**de-**). SEC. DISS: [de- + nomin- + -at- + -ive] Note: L. *-īv(us)*: tending to (be), inclined to (be) + E. *-e*: silent final letter > the E. *adj*-forming suffix -IVE, having the associated meanings: tending to (be), inclined to (be), charact. by, or having the nature of. SEC. RECON: *charact. by* (**-at-**) *tending to* (**-ive**) [form] *down* (**de-**) [from a] *noun* (**nomin-**),81, *passim*

denotation (dē´nō·tā´shən) *n.* the primary, explicit meaning of a word without reference to its subjective implications or associated meanings: *The denotation of "mother" is that of a female parent of a human or animal*; cf. CONNOTATION. **[de- + not- + -at- + -ion]** < L. *dē-*: away from, off, down + *not(a)*: mark, sign + *-āt-* (base of *-ātus*), ppl. suffix with the inflectional meaning: having been or having had; in E. (without the MACRON), also meaning: having, possessing, or charact. by + *-iōn(is)* (gen. of *-iō*): the act, means, or result of. RECON: *the act or result of* (**-ion**) *having been* (**-at-**) *marked* (**not-**) *down* (**de-**); see under DESPONDENT

dentil, 114

dentition, see under -ISIS

depend, see under DE-

deponent verbs, 215

depopulate, see under DE-

depress, see under DE-

der Führer, see under IL DUCE

Deringer, Henry, see under EPI-

dermat-, 104

dermatitis, 68, **104**

dermat^os) (derma), 104

derringer, 265, see also DERINGER, HENRY

descend, 126

descendant, 126

DESPONDENT (di·spän´dənt) *adj.* very disheartened or dejected. **[de- + spond- + -ent]** < L. *dē-*: away from, away from, off, down + *spond(ēre)*: to promise + *-ent(is)* (gen. of *-ens*): prpl. suffix having the inflectional meaning: being, having, doing, performing, or manifesting (that which is designated by the preceding verb base), equivalent in meaning to E. participles ending in *-ing*; see -ENT for further information. RECON: *promis-* (**spond-**) *-ing* (**-ent**) *away* (**de-**). Parents who in yesteryear (and still, in some cases, today) "promised away" their daughters in marriage often became disheartened and dejected—hence, the negative DENOTATION of this word, 89, **108**

despotism, 245

Detailed Example of COMMON ROOTS (explanation of features), **8-10**

DETENTION (di·ten´shen) *n.* **1.** temporary confinement, as in a jail or other government building. **2.** any restraint or forced delay, esp. one that impedes physical progress or movement: *Our detention at the weigh station lasted two hours.* **[de- + tent- + -ion]** < L. *dē-*: away from, off, down + *tent(us)* (pp. of *tenēre*: to have, to hold) + *-iōn(is)* (gen. of *-iō*): the act, means, or result of. RECON: *the result of* (**-ion**) *holding* (**tent-**) *down* (**de-**), 58, 89, deuterogamy, 146

Deutsche mark, see under DUCHESS

Deutschland, see under DUCHESS

DEVIANT (dē´vē·ənt) *adj.* **1.** straying or departing from what is considered normal in a group or society: *deviant behavior.* —*n.* **2.** a person whose behavior is markedly and habitually deviant (see def. 1). **[de- + vi- + -ant]** < L. *dē-*: away from, off, down + *-vi(āre)*: to march, to journey (< *via*: a way, road; march, journey) + *-ant(is)* (gen. of *-āns*): prpl. suffix having the inflectional meaning: being, having, doing, performing, or manifesting (that which is designated by the preceding verb base), equivalent in meaning to E. participles ending in *-ing* but also having the SUBSTANTIVE meaning: one who or that which (performs the action designated by the preceding verb base); see -ANT for further information. RECON: *march-* (**vi-**) *-ing* (**-ant**) *away from* (**de-**) OR *one who* (**-ant**) *marches* (**vi-**) *away from* (**de-**), 76

devilish, see under -ISH

de**vitri**fication, 98, **109**

devotees, see under PHALLIC

dexter, 102

dextr-, 102, *102*

dextrocardial, 53, **102**

dextrose, 125

di-¹ < L. *di-*, var. of *dis-* (used before various consonants): away from; apart, without; the reverse or undoing of (also used intensively, i.e., completely, thoroughly, throughout, utterly): DIGRESSION, *divulge, diversion.* For semantically similar prefixes, see L. *dē-* and G. *apo-*, 106, *106*, see also under DE-

di-² < G. *di-*, comb. form of *dis*: two, twice, double (akin to L. *bis*): dilemma, *carbon dioxide, diglot* (a book, periodical, newspaper, etc., written in two languages)

diagnose, 253

diagnosis, 253

dial, 206

dialect, see under LEC-¹

diaphanous, 119

diary, 206

dīcere, 72, 81, 84

dichotomy, see under -TOMY

dict-, 72, *72*, 73, 81, **84**, *84*, **105**

-**diction**, 73

DICTIONARY (dik´shə·ner´ē) *adj.* **1.** a book or reference containing a general or specialized selection of words, usu. listed alphabetically and providing such information as definitions, pronunciations, etymologies, inflected forms, etc. **2.** a book or reference providing information on any subject or branch of knowledge: *a dictionary of butterflies and moths.* **[dict- + -ion + -ary]** < L. *dict(us)* (pp. of *dīcere*: to say, to speak) + *-iōn(is)* (gen. of *-iō*): the act, means, or result of + E. *-ary*: one who or that which (performs the action designated by the preceding base or elements) (< L. *-ārium*: a thing which pertains to, neut. of *-ārius*: pert. to, charact. by, having the nature of, like). RECON: *the act, means, or result of* (**-ion**) *that which* (**-ary**) *says or speaks* (**dict-**). But do not confuse E. *-ary* when used as a SUBSTANTIVE suffix (esp. with < L. *-ārium*; see AVIARY) with E. *-ary* when used as an adjective suffix (< L. *-ārius* or *-āris*; see LAPIDARY and ANCILLARY); 73, *81*, see also DICTIONARIES, HOW TO USE(following entry)

DICTIONARIES, HOW TO USE, 165-66, 168, 258-59

dictus, 72, 74, 81, 84

dict(us) (*dīcere*), 105

(di)do(nai), 105

Didymus, 137

dielectric, 118

diēs, 107

dif-, see under DIS-

different, see under DIS-

di**fficul**ty, 98, **109**, see also under DIS-, -UL-¹, and -TY

diffident, 206

diffusion, see under DIS-

digestion, see under DIS-

digit- < L. *digit-*, base of *digitus*: finger, toe, 79, *digit-3*

DIGITAL (dij´i·t'l) *adj.* **1.** of, resembling, or manipulated by a finger or toe. **2.** displaying specific numbers, as on a screen, rather than pointing to one of a series of numbers or symbols, as on a dial. **[digit- + -al]** < L. *digit(us)*: finger, toe + *-al*: pert. to, charact. by. RECON: *charact. by* (**-al**) *a finger or toe* (**digit-**), 79, 94, *193*

digitigrade, 79, *80*

diglot, see under DI-²

di**gression**, 80, *106*, see also under DI-¹

dilatation, see under DYSMENORRHEA

dilation, see under DYSMENORRHEA

dilemma, see under DI-²

diligence, see under -ENCE

diligent, see under DIS- and -ENT

dilution, see under DIS-

Dionysian, see under PHALLIC

Dionysius, 119

Dionysus, see under PHALLIC

dioxide, carbon, see under DI-²

diphthongs, see under LATIN DIPHTHONGS and GREEK DIPHTHONGS

diplo-, **102**

diplocardiac, *53*, **102**

diplo(os), 102

dipsomania, 144

DIPSOPHOBIA *n.* an abnormal or intense fear or dread of drinking, esp. alcoholic beverages. [< G. *dips(a)*: thirst + *-o-*: conn. vowel + -PHOBIA], 143

dis (days), **107**, *107*

dis- (dis) a L-derived prefix having three broad meanings, the first two similar and often overlapping and the third the effective antithesis (an·tith´ə·sis; the direct opposite) of the first two: **1.** away, from, apart: *discard, dissolve, dis-associate,* DISSOCIATE. **2.** not, without; the reverse or undoing of; the expulsion or removal of: *disown, disintegrate, disbelief, disbar.* **3.** completely, thoroughly, throughout, utterly: *disannul* (to annul completely), *dissever* (to sever or divide, as into pieces or parts), *disturb* (< L. *disturb(āre)*: to drive asunder, demolish < *dis-*: completely, thoroughly, throughout + *turb(āre)*: to confuse, throw into disorder; hence, "to thoroughly throw into disorder"). **Note:** *dis-* is often substituted for *con-* in English words to form new words opposite in meaning to those in which the substitution occurs, e.g., *concord/discord, conjunction/disjunction,* and CONSENTIENT/DISSENTIENT. Also note: *dis-* is assimilated to *dif-* in words beginning with *f: different, diffusion, difficulty,* DIFFIDENT; and *dis-* becomes *di-* before a variety of consonants, particularly those that are voiced: *division, digestion, diligent, dilution.* However, Latin *di-,* var. of *dis-,* should not be confused with Greek *di-,* combining form of *dis-:* two, twice, double. For further information, see DI-¹ and DI-². **[dis-]** < L. *dis-:* away, from, apart, asunder, in two. For semantically similar prefixes, see also L. *ab-* and *sē-,* G. *apo-,* and OE. *for-;* *106,* see also under DI-¹

disaccharide, 125

disannul, see under DIS-

disassociate, see under DIS-

disbar, see under DIS-

disbelief, see under DIS-

discard, see under DIS-

disclamation 219

disco, 132

discomfort, 210

DISCOPHILE (dis´kō·fīl´, dis´kə-) *n.* a collector of or expert in phonograph records, esp. rare records. [**disc-** + **-o-** + **phil-** + **-e**] < G. *disk(os)*: discus, platter, quoit (a ring of rope or flattened metal) (< *dikein*: to throw, cast) + *-o-*: conn. vowel + *phil(os)*: loving, beloved (< *philein*: to love) + E. *-e*: silent final letter. **RECON:** *loving* (**phil-**) *discuses or platters* (**disc-**). **SEC. RECON: [disco-** + **-phile] Note:** G. *disk(os)*: discus, platter, quoit + *-o-*: conn. vowel > the E. comb. form *disco-*: phonograph record. Also note: G. *phil(os)*: loving, beloved + E. *-e*: silent final letter > the E. *n*-forming comb. form -PHILE, having the modern meaning: one who is fond of, likes, loves, or has an abnormal attraction for. **SEC. RECON:** *one who loves* (**-phile**) *records* (**disco-**), 49

discord, see under DIS-

disestablishment, see under ANTIDISESTABLISHMENTARIANISM

disintegrate, see under DIS-

disjunction, see under DIS-

dismally, *86,* **107**

disown, see under DIS-

disparage, see under PAR-⁵

disparate, see under ANTIDISESTABLISHMENTARIANISM

disruptive, see under -IVE

Dissection, 8-9 (of Detailed Example within the COMMON ROOTS), 23 (of A CROSS-REFERENCE DICTIONARY entry *cadaverine*)

dissentience, 225

dissentient, 225

dissever, see under DIS-

dissociate, *194*

dissolve, see under DIS-

distaff, see under DUKE

distinctive, see under -IVE

distribution, *204*

disturb, see under DIS-

disyllabic, 76

diurnal, 206

diversion, see under DI-¹

diverti**cul**itis, *68,* **104**

diverticulum, see under -CUL-²

divination, see under RHABDOPHOBIA

division, see under DIS-

divulge, see under DI-¹

dizygotic (dī´zī·gät´ik) *adj.* developed from two separately fertilized ova (ō´va; plural of *ovum:* egg cell), as fraternal twins; cf. MONOZYGOTIC. **[di-** + **zyg-** + **-o-** + **-t-** + **-ic]** < G. *di-* (comb. form of *dis-*): two, twice, double + *zyg(oun)*: to join together, to yoke (< *zygon*: a yoke) + *-o-*: conn. vowel + *-t(os)*: verbal suffix with the inflectional meaning: having been or having had (that which is designated by the preceding verb base) + *-ik(os)*: pert. to, charact. by. **RECON:** *two* (**di-**) *charact. by* (**-ic**) *having been* (**-t-**) *joined* (**zyg-**).

The "joining" is of two spermatozoa (sperm cells, the plural of *spermatozoon*) with two respective ova, resulting in two fertilized eggs and two potential individuals, *37, 37, 116,* see also under ZYG-

TO DO, TO ACT, TO DRIVE (AG-, ACT-, -IG-), 87–89

Doberman, 134

DOCILE (däs´´l) *adj.* of or characteristic of a person or animal who is relatively submissive and passively follows orders with little or no resistance; easily led, managed, or controlled: *a docile co-worker; docile livestock being led to slaughter.* **[doc-** + **-il-** + **-e]** < L. *doc(ēre)*: to teach + *-il(is)*: tending to (be), inclined to (be) + E. *-e*: silent final letter. **RECON:** *inclined to be* (**-il-**) *taught* (**doc-**). **SEC. DISS:** [doc- + **-ile** Note: L. *-il(is)* + E. *-e*: silent final letter > the E. *adj*-forming suffix -ILE, having the slightly expanded meanings: tending to (be), inclined to (be), able to (be), capable of (being); cf. -ABLE for a similar etymological development. **SEC. RECON:** *capable of being* (**-ile**) *taught* (**doc-**). Originally, *docile* meant easy to teach or train, as of a farm hand or child in school. Hence, *docile,* in this context, was a positive term denoting a person who was willing to learn and be instructed; hence, the subtle but significant shift in meaning from a person willing to be led and supervised in a learning situation to one who is by nature or conditioning easily led, managed, or controlled, 98, see also under -ILE

doctrine, see under -INE²

docudrama, 120

document, 197

documentary, 120

documentum, 197

dog, 139

dog days, 151

dog French, see under DOGGEREL

doggerel (dô´gər·əl, däg´ər-) *n.* **1.** crude, poorly constructed, and often jerky poetry, usually the result of ineptitude on the part of the poet, but sometimes employed for comic or burlesque effect. —*adj.* **2.** of or pertaining to such poetry. **[dogg-** + **-erel]** < ME. *dogge(r)*: dog (< OE. *docga*: a powerful breed of dog + OF. *-erel* (a shortened form of *-erelle*): a dim. or, in this word, PEJORATIVE suffix, having the associated meanings: unimportant, insignificant, inferior, worthless, wretched, despicable, etc. **RECON:** *inferior or wretched* (**-erel**) *dog* (**dogg-**). As an adjective, *dogerel* (with one *g*) first appeared in 1386 in Geoffrey Chaucer's *The Tale of Melibee,* though recent scholarship has turned up a SUBSTANTIVE form used in 1277. While *doggerel* originally denoted verse of irregular and loose measure (rather than poorly constructed or necessarily bad verse), it was no doubt influenced by the PEJORATIVE sense of *dog,* which we see in such phrases as *dog Latin* (barbarous or ungrammatical Latin, or a word or locution imitating or spoofing Latin), *dog French,* and the archaic *dog rime* (an inferior or poorly contrived rhyme) and *dog's logic* (illogic), *81*

dog Latin, see under DOGGEREL

dogmas, see under LIBERAL

dog rime, see under DOGGEREL

dog's logic, see under DOGGEREL

dolabriform, 149

dolioform, 149

dominions, see under HIERARCHY

don't count me out, 153

DORAMANIA *n.* an extreme attraction to or compulsion to touch an animal's fur; also, a preoccupation with and compulsion to buy furs. [< G. *dor(a)*: skin, hide + *-o-*: conn. vowel + -PHOBIA], 145

dormition, 220

dormitive, 220

dormitory, 220, see also under -ORY²

DOROMANIA *n.* a morbid sense of obligation or compulsion to give gifts, sometimes accompanied by joy, at other times by distress. [< G. *dōr(on)*: gift + *-o-*: conn. vowel + -PHOBIA], 145

Dorothy, see under ARISTOTLE

dors-, **106**

dorsigrade, *80,* **106**

dors(um), 106

doubleheader, 152

doubting Thomas, 137

d(o)ul(os), 103

down and out, 153

down but not out, 153

down for the count, 153

down the tubes, 151

Dreser, Hermann, 133

droit, 107, *107*

DROMOMANIA *n.* an extreme enthusiasm for or compulsion for traveling or, in the case of more seriously disturbed persons, for wandering from home; cf. ECDEMOMANIA, HODOMANIA, and PORIOMANIA. [< G. *drom(os)*: a running, race, course (< *dramein*: to run) + *-o-*: conn. vowel + -MANIA], 145

DROMOPHOBIA *n.* an irrational fear of crossing streets or wandering about. [< G. *drom(os)*: a running, race, course (< *dramein*: to run) + *-o-*: conn. vowel + -PHOBIA], 143

dubious, 169

DUC-, DUCT-, 75–77

duc-, 75, *75*

dūc-, 75

-duc- (misc. letter combination), 75

-ducāre, 75

dūcere, 75

duchess (duch´is) *n.* **1.** the wife or widow of a DUKE. **2.** a woman equivalent in status to a duke, possessing and ruling a DUCHY. **[duch- + -ess]** < OF. *duc*: duke (< L. *dux* [gen: *ducis*]: leader, commander, ruler [< L. *dūcere*: to lead, to bring]) + *-ess(e)* (< LL. *-issa* < G. *-issa*): a fem. *n*-forming suffix having the basic meaning: a female (of), or she who (performs the action designated by the preceding base or elements). **RECON:** *a female* (**-ess**) *duke* (**duch-**). The *duch-* in *duchess* (or *duchy*) is neither the source of nor in any way related to English *Dutch*, which, of course, designates the people living in or descended from those living in, or once living in, the Netherlands — their language. So while the *duch-* in *duchess* is derived, through Old French *duc*, from Latin *dūcere*, "to lead, to bring," its homophone (a word or element pronounced the same as another but differing in meaning and often spelling and origin) *Dutch* is derived from Middle Dutch *duutsch*, "Dutch, German," which is closely related to German *Deutsch*, "German," which we see in such words and phrases as *Deutschland*, the German name for Germany, and *Deutsche mark*, the monetary unit of Germany. Indeed, because Middle Dutch *duutsch* meant German as well as Dutch, and because its modern Dutch derivative *Duits* means only German, the Dutch today never call themselves "Dutch" but instead refer to themselves as *Nederlanders* (nā´dər·län´tərs) and to their language as *Nederlands* (nā´dər·länts´; formerly spelled *Nederlandsch*) or sometimes, particularly in the two major provinces of North Holland and South Holland, as *Hollands* (hu´länts; formerly spelled *Hollandsch*), 75, see also under DUKE

duchy, see under DUKE

duckling (duk´ling) *n.* a young duck. **[duck + -ling]** < OE. *dūc(e)*: diver, ducker, duck + *-ling*: a person or other living organism belonging to, descended from, having the qualities of, or otherwise associated with (that which is designated by the preceding base or elements), but also used as a dim. suffix with the related meanings: small, little, tiny; young; unimportant (prob. < a combination of the *n*-forming and, in some applications, dim. suffixes *-(o)l*, *-(u)l*, or *-(e)l* + *-ing*: verbal noun; cf. GERUND). **RECON:** *a small* (**-ling**) *duck* (**duck**), 75

DUCT-, (DUC-), 75–77

duct-, *xix*, 75, 75, 76, 103

duct*ile*, 77, **106**

duct*ule*, 77, **106**

ductus, 75

duct(us) (*dūcere*), 103*

duke (dook) *n.* **1.** in Great Britain and certain other countries, the highest titled nobleman, ranking immediately below a prince. **2.** in most countries of continental Europe, a powerful male ruler of a large and prestigious territory, called a *duchy*; cf. DUCHESS. **[duk- + -e]** < OF. *duc*: duke (< L. *dux* [gen: *ducis*]: leader, commander, ruler [< L. *dūcere*: to lead, to bring]) + E. *-e*: silent final letter. **RECON:** *duke* (**duk-**). In British peerage (the peers or nobles collectively of a country, state, or other geopolitical area), there are five degrees of nobility, represented, in descending order, by the *duke*, *marquess* (mär´kwis), *earl*, *viscount* (vī´kount´), and *baron*. Immediately above the duke are the *prince* and *king*, who are not peers but members of the royal family, and below the baron are the *baronet* (a male commoner holding a hereditary title of honor) and *knight* (a male commoner granted a nonheredi-

tary title of honor). At the lower end of the hierarchy are the *thane* (a male commoner ranking above an ordinary freeman but generally below a nobleman), *ceorl* (chä´ôrl, cheôrl, cherl; a freeman of the lowest class, but now more commonly spelled *churl*, which further depicts any rude, crude, or boorish person, regardless of background), *serf* (a person owned by another, but not able to be sold apart from the land), and *slave* (a person owned by another, but able to be sold apart from the land). On the European continent, the nomenclature is somewhat different: an earl is a *count*, and a marquess is a *marquis* (generally pronounced mär·kē´)—not to be confused with *marquee* (mär·kē´), the awning above the entrance to a movie theater, hotel, or other establishment, a word derived from an assumed (but nonexistent) singular of *marquise* (mär·kēz´), the wife, widow, or female equivalent of a marquis, which itself should not be confused with *marchioness* (mär´shə·nis), the wife, widow, or female equivalent of a marquess; and *marchioness*, in turn, should not be confused with *marquisette* (mär´ki·zet´, -kwi-), a thin, tightly woven meshlike fabric of silk, nylon, cotton, or rayon, which, in turn, should not be confused with *marquisate* (mär´kwi·zit), the territory ruled by a marquis or margrave. And what is a *margrave*? The former military governor of a German *mark*, of course—which is a frontier or borderland, historically between warring or hostile German provinces, which has its equivalent in the English *march* . . . . But to return to the distaff (female—named after the staff that holds raw flax, wool, etc., used in spinning) side of the five degrees of British peerage, the wife, widow, or female equivalent of a duke is a DUCHESS, that of a marquess is (as we have already seen) a *marchioness*, that of an earl is a *countess*, that of a viscount is a *viscountess* (vī´koun´tis), and that of a baron is a *baroness*, 75

dul-, 103

dulc-, **109**

dulc*ification*, 98, **109**

dulc(is), 109

dul*ocracy*, 62, **103**

dungarees, 135

duodenum, see under PYLORUS

duplicitous, see under AMBIDEXTROUS

Dutch, see under DUCHESS

dux, 75

dynamics, see under KINETICS

dynamometer, 118

dys-, 84

dyslexia, 257

dysmenorrhea (dis´men·ə·rē´ə) *n.* painful or difficult menstruation, caused by dilatation (an abnormal enlargement or stretching of a body cavity or opening; dilation) of the CERVIX, intense uterine contractions, pelvic inflammation, or other abnormal conditions; cf. AMENORRHEA. **[dys- + men- + -o- + -rrhea]** < G. *dys-*: bad, difficult (in E., also meaning: abnormal, dysfunctional, impaired) + *mēn(os)* (gen. of *mēn*): month + *-o-*: conn. vowel + *-rrhoia*: a flowing (< *rhoia*: a flow [< *rho-*, base of *rhein*: to flow + *-ia*: the act, process, condition, or result of]). **RECON:** *a difficult* (**dys-**) *monthly* (**men-**) *flowing* (**-rrhea**), 84

dysteleology, 126

DYSTROPHY, MUSCULAR, see MUSCULAR DYSTROPHY, 70

E

e- < L. *ē-*, var. of EX-¹ (used before most consonants): out, out of, from, forth, without, former: EJECT, EGRESS, *elect*, 79, 82, 83, **106**, see also under EX-¹

ē- (var. of EX-¹), *106*

-e (silent final letter), 49, 54, 79, 88, *passim**

-e-¹ < L. *-e-*: conn. vowel: ANXIETY, INEBRIETY, SATIETY

-e-² (reduced form of L. *-ae-*), 46, 69, see also explanation under ANGLICIZATION

-e-³ (abstracted from L. *-eus*), see under MENINGEAL and LARYNGOPHARYNGEAL

earth, 139

Easter Island, see under POLYNESIA

eat crow, 151

eat your heart out, see under COURAGE

ec- < G. *ek-*, var. and assim. form of EX-² (used before a consonant): out, out of, from: *eclipse*, ECLIPTIC, *hysterectomy*, 124

ecclesiastic, see under CARDINAL

ECDEMOMANIA (ek·dem´ō-mā´nē-ə, -dē·mō-) *n.* an abnormal desire or compulsion for wandering; wanderlust; cf. DROMOMANIA, HODOMANIA, and PORIOMANIA. **[**< G. *ekdēm(os)*: away from home (< G. *ek-* [var. of EX-² used before a consonant]: out of, from, forth + *dēm(os)*: people, populace, district) + *-o-*: conn. vowel + *-MANIA*], 145

ecdysiast, see under EX-²

echogram, see under SONOGRAM

eclectic, see under LEC-¹

eclipse, see under EX-²

ecliptic, 116, see also under ZODIAC

ecstasy, see under EX-² and STA-²

ectomorph, 117

-ECTOMY (ek´tə·mē) a G-derived *n*-forming comb. form having the modern

medical meaning: the surgical removal or EXCISION of (that anatomical structure or part specified by the preceding base or elements): TONSILLECTOMY, *appendectomy* (the surgical removal of the appendix), *cholecystectomy* (kō´lə·si·stek´tə·mē; the surgical removal of the gall bladder; lit., the process of cutting out the bile sac; cf. HEPATOCYSTIC). **[ec- + tom- + -y]** < G. *ek-* (var. of EX-² used before a consonant): out of, from, forth + *tom(ē)*: a cutting (< *temnein*: to cut) + E. *-y*: the act, process, condition, or result of (< G. *-ia*). **RECON:** *the act, process, or result of* (**-y**) *cutting* (**tom-**) *out* (**ec-**) [*that anatomical structure or part specified by the preceding base or elements*]. But do not confuse *-ectomy*, "the surgical excision of," with *-(o)tomy*, "the surgical incision of": LOBOTOMY, PHLEBOTOMY, TRACHEOTOMY. And do not mistake *-ectomy* or *-(o)tomy* for *-(o)stomy*, "the surgical construction of a 'mouthlike' opening of": COLOSTOMY, TRACHEOSTOMY, COLOCOLOSTOMY; see under -TOMY and -STOMY

ed-, **109**

edelweiss, 147

Edersheim, Alfred, 62

edi*fy*, 98, **109**

editorial, see under -AL

educable (ej´oo·kə·b´l, ej´ə-) *adj.* capable of being taught, trained, instructed, or schooled. **[e- + duc- + -a- + -bl- + -e]** < L. *ē-* (var. of EX-¹ used before most consonants): out, out of, from, forth + *-duc(āre)*: to continue to lead or bring (< *dūcere*: to lead, to bring) + *-ā-*: conn. vowel (tech., the "thematic" or stem-ending *ā* of first conjugation verbs ending in *-āre* or *-ārī*; see -A-¹ and -AT-) + *-b(i)l(is)*: tending to (be), inclined to (be) + E. *-e*: silent final letter. **RECON:** *tending or inclined* (**-bl-**) *to continue to lead or bring* (**duc-**) *out of* (**e-**). **SEC. DISS:** [e- + duc- + -able] **Note:** L. *-ā-*: conn. vowel + *-b(i)l(is)*:

tending to (be), inclined to (be) + E. *-e*: silent final letter > the E. *adj*-forming suffix *-able*, having the expanded meaning (partly in confusion with E. *able* < L. *(h)abilis*: easy to hold or handle; skillful [< *habēre*: to have, to hold]—a word completely unrelated to L. *-bilis*): able to (be), capable of (being), tending to (be), inclined to (be). SEC. RECON: *able to* (**-able**) *continue to lead or bring* (**duc-**) *out of* (**e-**). Though its elements derive from Latin, *educable* was "constructed" in English during the first half of the 19th century from the components *educ(ate)* + *-able*. Thus, for the sense development of this word, see EDUCATE in the following entry, *75*

educate (ej´ŏŏ·kāt´, ej´ə-) *v.* **1.** to train or develop the knowledge, ability, or skills of, esp. through schooling or formal instruction. **2.** to pay or provide for such schooling or instruction: *In his will, he promised to educate his children.* **3.** to inform or enlighten: *to educate the public about the dangers of genetic engineering.* **4.** to cultivate an appreciation or taste for: *to educate one's ear to fine music.* [**e- + duc- + -at- + -e**] < L. *ē-* (var. of EX-¹ used before most consonants): out, out of, from, forth + *-duc(āre)*: to continue to lead or bring (< *dūcere*: to lead, to bring) + *-āt-* (base of *-ātus*), ppl. suffix with the inflectional meaning: having been or having had; in E. (without the MACRON) also meaning: having, possessing, or charact. by, and often used as a verbal suffix with the senses described under "NOTE" below) + E. *-e*: silent final letter. RECON: *having* (**-at-**) *continued to lead or bring* (**duc-**) *out of* (**e-**). SEC. DISS: [e- + duc- + -ate] Note: L. *-āt-* (base of *-ātus*): having been, having had + E. *-e*: silent final letter > E. -ATE, used in this entry as a *v*-forming suffix, having the related meanings: to cause, to become, to cause to become, to make, to do, to form, to function, to manage, etc. SEC. RECON: *to function or manage* (**-ate**) *to continue to lead or bring* (**duc-**) *out of* (**e-**). Originally, Latin *ēducātus* meant "having brought up (children) out of (ignorance)—a word that quickly broadened in meaning to simply "having raised (children)," but today is used in its more restricted sense of "having provided training or knowledge for," *75*

educible, *77*, **106**
eduction, *77*, **106**
effective, see under EX-¹
effeminate, *192*
effluence, see under EX-¹
effort, see under EX-¹
effortless, *210*
egomania, *144*
egregious, *213*, see also under EX-¹
egress, *79*, see also under E-¹
EGRET (ē´gret, -grit) *n.* any of various herons, usually having long white feathers and a yellowish or sometimes black bill. [**egr- + -et**] < OF. *aigr(on)*: heron + *-ett(e)*: a dim. suffix having the basic meaning: small, little, tiny). RECON: *little* (**-et**) *heron* (**egr-**), *79*
eidos, *18*
(e)is-, *101*
ejaculate, see under JAC-¹
EJECT (ē·jekt´ i-) *v.* to expel or throw out. [**e- + -ject**] < L. *ē-* (var. of EX-¹ used before most consonants): out, out of, from, forth + *ject(us)* (pp. of *jacere*: to throw). RECON: *to throw* (**-ject**) *out* (**e-**), *79*, *82*, see also under E-
elect, see under E-
electorate, see under -ATE
"electrical glow," *95*
electrolysis, *259*
elegance, *225*
elements (fire, earth, air, and water), *146*
elephantiasis, see under -IASIS
ELEUTHEROMANIA (i·lŏŏ´thər·ə·mā´nē·ə) *n.* a preoccupation with or compulsion for freedom. [< G. *eleuther(os)*: free + *-o-*: conn. vowel + -MANIA], *145*
elided, see under -ENCE
elision, see under -ENZ-
elocution, *xii*, *81*, **83**
eloquence, see under -ENCE
eloquent, *82*, see also under EX-¹
elucidating, see under OLIGEMIA
-em-, *69*, *69*, *70*, **104**
emaciated, see under CADAVER
Emancipation Proclamation, *204*, see also under MAN-¹
emblem, *262*
EMETOPHOBIA (em´ə·tə·fō´bē·ə) *n.* a morbid fear or dread of vomiting. [< G. *emet(os)*: vomiting (< *emein*: to vomit) + *-o-*: conn. vowel + -PHOBIA], *143*
-emia (ē´mē·ə) a G-derived *n*-forming suffix having the modern medical meaning: a disordered or diseased condition of the blood caused or characterized by (that which is designated by the preceding base or elements): ANEMIA, LEUKEMIA, *uremia* (yŏŏ·rē´mē·ə; an abnormal condition caused by the retention of urinary products in the blood): [**-em + -ia**] < G. *(h)aim(a)*: blood + *-ia*: the state, condition, or result of > E. *-ia*, having, in this entry, the specialized medical meaning: a disordered or diseased condition of. RECON: *a disordered or diseased condition of* (**-ia**) ___( ) *blood* (**-em-**) [the parentheses to be filled in with the base or elements preceding **-emia**, and its definition to be placed on the line]. For an example and a slightly different approach to the same reconstruction, see OLIGEMIA; and for a step-by-step analysis of how Greek *haima* evolved into English *-em-*, see ANEMIA; *70*
emmen-, **101**
emmēn(a), 101
emmenagogue, *47*, **101**
Empedocles, *146*

emulsion, *127*
en-¹ < OF. *en-* < L. *in-*: in, into, within: *encourage, encircle, endanger, xviii,* **108**, *108*, see also under IN-¹
en-² < G. *en-*: in, into, within: *enthusiasm, encyclopedia,* ENDEMIC, ENGASTRILOQUE, *82*, *142*
en**act**ment, *89*, **108**
enamored, see under IN-¹
enate, see under EX-¹
-ence (əns, 'ns) a L-derived *n*-forming suffix having two classes of closely associated meanings: **1.** the quality, state, or condition of be**ing**, hav**ing**, or manifest**ing** (that which is designated by the preceding base or elements): *existence, confidence, eloquence.* **2.** the act, means, result, or process of do**ing** or perform**ing** (that which is designated by the preceding base or elements): *convalescence, abhorrence, diligence* (see also PERSISTENCE for a melding of defs. 1 and 2). [**-ence**] < L. *-entia* (or sometimes an alter. of OF *-ance*): the quality, state, condition; act, means, result, or process of be**ing**, hav**ing**, do**ing**, perform**ing**, or manifest**ing** (that which is designated by the preceding verb base) < *-ent-* (base of *-entis*, gen. of *-ēns*): prpl. suffix having an inflectional meaning equivalent to E. participles ending in *-ing* (see -ENT for further information) + *-ia*: the quality, state, condition; act, means, result, or process of. But how did Latin *-ent* + *-ia* evolve into English *-ence*? First, as we have seen, these two Latin roots coalesced to form Latin *-entia*. From here this compound entered Old French in which the two syllables of *-tia* gradually elided (slurred together, resulting in the omission and often the alteration of one or more letters or syllables in a word or adjacent words; cf. ELISION) to form *-ce*, yielding the Old French *n*-forming suffix *-(en)ce*. And this suffix then passed unchanged into Middle English and Modern English, thus completing the transformation of the trisyllabic Latin *-entia* (formed from its constituent roots *-ent-* + *-ia*) into the monosyllabic English *-ence*. For a virtually identical suffix, see -ANCE; *58*, *58*, **105**, **109**, *146*, *passim*
encephalitis (en·sef´ə·lī´tis) *n.* inflammation of the brain, caused by an injury, virus, poison, or other agent, or as a sequela (si·kwel´ə, -kwē´lə; a disease or condition following and usually resulting from a prior disease or condition) of the flu, measles, chickenpox, or other illness. [**en- + cephal- + -itis**] < G. *en-*: in, into, within + *kephal(ē)*: head + E. *-itis*: the inflammation of (< G. *-itis*: [understood to mean] the disease of [orig., abstracted from the phrase, *hē arthritis nosos*: the disease of the joint], fem. of the *adj*-forming suffix *-itēs*: of, relating to, belonging to, or having the characteristics of). RECON: *the inflammation of* (**-itis**) *within* (**en-**) *the head* (**cephal-**). SEC. DISS: [encephal- + -itis] Note: G. *en-*: in, into, within + *kephal(ē)*: head + *-os*: masc. suffix > G. *enkephal(os)*: that which is within the head; hence, the brain > the E. comb. form *encephal-*: brain. SEC. RECON: *the inflammation of* (**-itis**) *the brain* (**encephal-**), *xviii*, *67*
enchant, see under IN-¹
encircle, see under EN-¹
enclose, see under IN-¹
encourage, see under EN-¹
-ency, **108**
encyclopedia, *36*, *250*, see also under EN-² and PED-²
end-, **102**, *104*
endanger, see under EN-¹
-ende, *105*
endemic (en·dem´ik) *adj.* **1.** native to or prevalent in a particular country, region, or people; indigenous: *an endemic disease.* —*n.* **2.** an animal or plant native to or prevalent in a particular country or region. **3.** a disease found primarily in a certain country, region, culture, etc.; cf. EPIDEMIC. [**en- + dem- + -ic**] < G. *en-*: in, into, within + *dēm(os)*: people + *-ik(os)*: pert. to, charact. by. RECON: *charact. by* (**-ic**) *within* (**en-**) *the people* (**dem-**); see also under EN-²
endo**cardi**um, *53*, **102**
endometriosis, see under METR-²
endo**metr**itis, *68*, **104**
endomorph, *117*
end(on), *102*, *104*
-ene (chemical suffix), see under -INE²
enemy, see under IN-²
ener**g**y, *239*
engastriloque, *82*
ENGINEERING, 118
English Accentuation, xxiv
ENGLISH TABLES (in addition to the following tables, see entries beginning with "NATIVE")
ENGLISH DECLENSIONS OF *DOG* (table), *189*
ENGLISH DECLENSIONS OF *GOOSE* (table), *189*
ENGLISH DECLENSIONS OF *I* (table), *189*
ENGLISH LANGUAGE, THE THREE PERIODS OF THE (diagram), *165*
ENGLISH ROOTS FROM LATIN FREQUENTATIVE PAST PARTICIPIAL BASES (table), *221*
ENGLISH WORDS, CREATING FROM GREEK WORDS (outline), *239*
ENGLISH WORDS, CREATING FROM LATIN WORDS (outline), *184*
enmity, see under AFFABLE, IN-², and -TY
-enn-, *90*, *90*
enology, see under OINOMANIA
-ēns (*-iēns*), *97*
ensiform, *149*
-ent (ənt, 'nt) a L-derived suffix having adjectival and SUBSTANTIVAL meanings: *adj.* **1.** being, hav**ing**, do**ing**, perform**ing**, or manifest**ing** (that which is

designated by the preceding base or elements), equivalent in meaning to *-ing* when forming participles (not gerunds): *confident, diligent, abstergent* (cleansing). —*n.* **2.** one who or that which (performs the action designated by the preceding base or elements): AGENT, *student, correspondent,* SUPERINTENDENT (but compare the *-ent* in SUPERINTENDENT with the *-ant* in its synonym *intendant*). **[-ent]** < L. *-ent-*, base of *-entis,* gen. of *-ēns*: prpl. suffix of verbs ending in *-ēre, -ere,* or *īre* (or sometimes an alteration of OF *-ant*), having the inflectional meaning: be<u>ing</u>, hav<u>ing</u>, do<u>ing</u>, perform<u>ing</u>, or manifest<u>ing</u> (that which is designated by the preceding verb base), equivalent in meaning to E. *-ing* when forming PARTICIPLES, not GERUNDS, as in "the running quarterback," not "running is good exercise." For a virtually identical suffix, see -ANT; *55, 73, 82, 85, 89,* **105, 108, 109,** *121, 126, 155, passim*

-(en)t + -ia, 108
entablature, 114
entasis, 114
enthalpy, 118
ENTHEOMANIA *n.* a preoccupation with religion, specif., a psychotic condition in which a person believes himself or herself to be specially selected to do God's work. [< G. *en-*: in, into, within + *the(os)*: god + *-o-*: conn. vowel + -MANIA], 145
enthuse, see under AMBIVALENT
enthusiasm, see under AMBIVALENT and EN-²
-ent(is) (-ēns), 105, 108, 109
-ent(is) + -ia, 105, 108, see also under -ENCE
entom- < G. *entom-*, base of *entoma*: insects, orig., cut in or notched, short for *entoma zōa*: cut in or notched animals < *entom-* (base of *entomon,* neut. of *entomos*: cut in < *en-*: in, into, within + *tom-* [base of *temnein*]: to cut + *-os*: masc. sing. suffix) + *-a*: neut. plural suffix (+) *zō(ion)*: animal, living being (< or akin to *zoē*: life) + *-a*: neut. plural suffix. In *entoma zōa,* the *zōa* dropped off in early Greek, and the meaning of the phrase became concentrated in the first word, *entoma.* Similarly, in Latin *insectum animale,* a translation of the singular of Greek *entoma zōa* (see ZODIAC), the *animale* dropped off, leaving *insectum,* which eventually became English *insect, 142*
entom(a) (zōa), 142
ENTOMOMANIA *n.* an extreme enthusiasm for or preoccupation with insects. [< ENTOM- + -O-¹ + -MANIA], 145
entomophobia, *xiii,* **142**
entropy, 118
-enz- (in *influenza*) < Ital. *-enz-* < L. *-ent-,* base of *-entis,* gen. of *-ēns*: prpl. suffix having the inflectional meaning: be<u>ing</u>, hav<u>ing</u>, do<u>ing</u>, perform<u>ing</u>, or manifest<u>ing</u> (that which is designated by the preceding verb base), equivalent in meaning to E. participles ending in *-ing.* Technically, the *-z-* in *influenza* is an elision (i·lizh´ən; the slurring together of speech sounds, resulting in the omission and often the alteration of one or more letters or syllables in a word or adjacent words or elements; cf. ELIDED) of the *t* and *i* in Latin *-(en)ti(a),* forming Italian *-(en)z(a).* For more information, see -A³ and -ENCE; *132*
eohippus, 16, 246
eon (Anglicization of L. *aeōn*), 236
EOSOPHOBIA (ē·äs´ə·fō´bē·ə) *n.* an irrational fear or dread of dawn. Certain agoraphobics (AGORAPHOBIA) roam the streets at night and experience eosophobia if they cannot get back home by dawn. Vampires are cinematographically also afflicted with this ailment. [< G. *ēōs*: dawn (cf. EOHIPPUS) + *-o-*: conn. vowel + -PHOBIA], 143
ep- < G. *ep-,* var. of *epi-* (used before a vowel or *h*): over, upon, on, beside, after: EPONYM, EPHEMERAL, **101,** see also under EPI-
ep<u>agoge</u>, *47,* **101**
ephemeral, see under EPI-
epi- (ep´ə, ep´i) a G-derived prefix having two basic meanings: **1.** over, upon, on: *epicenter* (the point on the earth's surface directly above an earthquake's center or focus), *epidermis* (the outer layer of the skin, directly above the dermis). **2.** besides, in addition to, after: *epilogue* (a concluding section added to a play, novel, poem, etc.), *epigone* (ep´i·gōn´; a less distinguished follower or descendant, as the unexceptional adult child of a famous person). **Note:** *epi-* becomes *ep-* before *h* or a vowel: *ephemeral* (short-lived; lit., lasting one day), *eponym* (the name of a real or imaginary person from which a word or name derives, or the word itself, e.g., William Lynch, Joseph Guillotin, Henry Deringer, the Fourth Earl of Sandwich, and the legendary Colonel Condum and Thomas Crapper. Mr. Crapper's biography is entitled, appropriately enough, *Flushed With Pride*). **[epi-]** < G. *epi-* (a prefixal form of the prep. and adverb *epi*): on, over, upon, besides. For a Latin prefix with certain meanings in common, see *ob-*; *61,* **102,** *102*
ep(i)-, 101
epi<u>cardium</u>, **53, 102**
epicenter, see under EPI-
epidemic, 61
epidermis, see under EPI-
epigone, see under EPI-
epilogue, see under EPI-
epiphytotic, 61
epistemology, 126
epithalamion, 123
epithelioma, 124
epizootic, 61
EPONYMS, **134,** 265, see also under EPI-
equinophobia, see under HIPPOPHOBIA
-er, 48, 48, **105**

-ere, 48
-er(e), 105
EREMIOMANIA (ə·rē´mē·ō·mā´nē·ə) *n.* a preoccupation with or overbearing need for quietude or stillness. [< G. *erēmi(a)*: a desert, solitude (*erēm(os)*: solitary, alone, empty + *-ia*: the act, state, condition, or result of) + *-o-*: conn. vowel + -MANIA], 145
ERGASIOMANIA (ûr·gā´zhē·ə·mā´nē·ə; an extreme enthusiasm for, preoccupation with, or compulsion for work or activity. The ergasiomaniac always has to stay busy; cf. ERGOMANIA. [< G. *ergas-* (base of *ergazesthai*): to work (< *ergon*: work) + *-i(a)*: the act, state, condition, or result of + *-o-*: conn. vowel + -MANIA], 145
ERGASIOPHOBIA (ûr·gā´zhē·ə·fō´bē·ə) *n.* an abnormal fear or dread of work or activity. [< G. *ergas-* (base of *ergazesthai*): to work (< *ergon*: work) + *-i(a)*: the act, state, condition, or result of + *-o-*: conn. vowel + -PHOBIA], 143
ERGOMANIA *n.* an extreme enthusiasm for, preoccupation with, or compulsion for work; cf. ERGASIOMANIA. [< G. < *erg(on)*: work + *-o-*: conn. vowel + -MANIA], 145
ergosterol, 125
-(e)rie, 101
ERODE (i·rōd´) *v.* **1.** to wear away; eat into; abrade: *The stream eroded the rocks.* **2.** to form or create as the result of wearing away: *The stream eroded a gully.* **3.** to diminish or gradually destroy: *Inflation erodes the dollar.* **[e- + rod- + -e]** < L. *ē-* (var. of EX-¹ used before most consonants): out, out of, from, forth + *rōd(ere)* to gnaw + E. *-e*: silent final letter. RECON: *to gnaw* (**rod-**) *out* (**e-**), 55, 82
EROTOMANIA (i·rō´tə·mā´nē·ə, -ə, er´ə·tə´mā´nē·ə) *n.* abnormally exaggerated or uncontrollable sexual desire; APHRODISIOMANIA. [< G. *erōt(os)* (gen. of *erōs*): sexual love + *-o-*: conn. vowel + -MANIA], 145
EROTOPHOBIA (i·rō´tə·fō´bē·ə, -rät´ə-, er´ə·tə´fō´bē·ə) *n.* an irrational and often unremitting fear or dread of sexual arousal. [< G. *erōt(os)* (gen. of *erōs*): sexual love + *-o-*: conn. vowel + -PHOBIA], 143
erstwhile, see under SUBWAY
eruciform, 149
erythr-, 93
erythrocyte, 52, 93
ERYTHROMANIA (i·rith´rə·mā´nē·ə) *n.* an extreme attraction to or preoccupation with the color red; also, uncontrollable blushing. [< G. *erythr(os)*: red + *-o-*: conn. vowel + -MANIA], 145
erythrophobia, 93
erythr(os), 93
escalator, 133
escalier (Fr.): staircase < OF. *e-*: prothetic vowel (see under ANTIDISESTABLISHMENTARIANISM) + LL. *scāl(a)*: stair, slope (< L. *scālae*: ladder, steps < *scandere*: to climb; cf. TRANSCENDENTALISM) + OF. *-ier*: one who or that which (< L. *-ārius), 138*
escape, see under EX-¹
escort, see under EX-¹
esophagus (i·säf´ə·gəs, ē-) *n.* the muscular passageway or tube through which food passes from the throat to the stomach; gullet. **[es- + -o- + -phagus]** < G. *(o)is(ein)*: shall carry (tech., the fut. infin. of *pherein*: to bear, to carry) + *-o-*: conn. vowel + *-phagos*: eating, devouring; that which is eaten, hence food (< *phagein*: to eat, to devour). RECON: *shall carry* (**es-**) *food* (**-phagus**). The only function of the esophagus is to transport or "carry" food from the throat to the stomach and sometimes vice versa, 52
esoterica, see under AMBIVALENT
esplanade, see under EX-¹
esprit (Fr.): spirit, wit < OF. *e-*: prothetic vowel (see under ANTIDISESTABLISHMENTARIANISM) + L. *sp(ī)rit(us)*: breath, soul, life (< *spīrāre*: to breathe, to blow), *138*
esprit de l'escalier, 138
~**ess** (es, is) a native *n*-forming suffix designating a female (of) or she who (performs the action designated by the preceding base or elements), often corresponding to agential nouns ending in *-or* or *-er,* or suffixed to existing words to create fem. forms: ACTRESS, *sorceress, shepherdess, ogress* (ō´gris; a female ogre [ō´gər; in fairy tales, an ugly giant who feeds on human beings]; cf. EGRESS); cf. -TRIX. **[-ess]** < OF. *-ess(e)* (< L. *-issa* < G. *-issa), 108*
ess- < L. *ess-,* base of *esse*: to be, *146*
-ess(e), 108
essential hypertension, 64
esthe-, 105
estrogen, see under OVARY
ethanol, see under ALCOHOL
ethics, see under -ICS
ethn-, 103
ethno<u>cracy</u>, *62,* **103**
ethn(os), 103
Etruscan, see under CAESARIAN SECTION
-ety (i·tē, ə·tē) a L-derived *n*-forming suffix having the closely related abstract meanings: the quality, state, or condition of: *sobriety* (sə·brī´i·tē, sō-; the state of being or remaining sober, esp. for an alcoholic or one who tends toward alcoholism), *inebriety* (in´i·brī´i·tē; the state or condition of being or becoming intoxicated, esp. habitually; drunkenness; intoxication), *moiety* (moi´ə·tē; a half or an approximate half; also, an indefinite part or portion). **[-e- + -ty]** < L. *-e-*: conn. vowel + *-tās*: the quality, state, or condition of. For further information and examples, see -TY and -ITY.
ETYMOLOGY (et´ə ·mäl´ə·jē) *n.* the study of the origin and development of

words, word roots, and related linguistic forms, with emphasis on how their structure, pronunciation, and meaning have evolved over time, usually centuries and MILLENNIA; cf. *entomology* (see ENTOMOPHOBIA). **[etym-** + **-o-** + **log-** + **-y]** < G. *etym(on)*: the true or literal sense of a word (neut. of *etymos*: true) + *-o-*: conn. vowel + *log(os)*: word, thought, reason, reckoning, discourse (< *legein*: to gather, to choose, to speak) + E. *-y*: the act, process, condition, or result of (< G. *-ia*). RECON: *the act, process, or result of* (**-y**) *thought* (**log-**) *about the true or literal sense of a word* (**etym-**). SEC. DISS: [etym- + -o- + -logy] Note: G. *log(os)*: word, thought, reason, reckoning, discourse + *-ia*: the act, process, condition, or result of > G. *-logia* > the E. *n*-forming comb. form -LOGY, having, in this context, the scientific and literary meaning: the science, study, theory, or doctrine of. SEC. RECON: *the scientific study of* (**-logy**) *the true or literal sense of a word* (**etym-**), 10, 11, 14, 20, 166, *passim*

eu-, 72

EULOGY (yōō′lə·jē) *n.* a speech or writing praising a person, esp. one who has recently died. **[eu-** + **log-** + **-y]** < G. *eu-*: well + *log(os)*: word, thought, reason, reckoning, speech, discourse (< *legein*: to gather, to choose, to speak) + E. *-y*: the act, process, condition, or result of (< G. *-ia*). RECON: *the act, process, or result of* (**-y**) *discoursing* (**log-**) *well* (**eu-**). SEC. DISS: [eu- + -logy] Note: G. *log(os)*: word, thought, reason, reckoning, speech, discourse + *-ia*: the act, process, condition, or result of > G. *-logia* > the E. *n*-forming comb. form -LOGY, having, in this entry, the literary meaning: a writing or speaking (in the manner specified by the preceding base or elements). SEC. RECON: *a speaking* (**-logy**) *well* (**eu-**), 11, 70, 72, 83, see also under -Y

EUPHORIA (yōō·fôr′ē·ə) *n.* **1.** a feeling of great happiness and exhilaration, esp. when not justified by external circumstances: *His euphoria upon getting a date seemed a little sad to us.* **2.** a similar state or condition induced by drugs, alcohol, meditation, or other special circumstances. **[eu-** + **phor-** + **-ia]** < G. *eu-*: well, good + *phor(os)*: bearing, carrying (< *pherein*: to bear, to carry) + *-ia*: the state or condition of. RECON: *the state or condition of* (**-ia**) *bearing* (**phor-**) *well* (**eu-**), 68

Europe, see under INDO-EUROPEAN

eustachian tube (yōō·stā′shən tōōb′; yōō·stā′kē·ən) *n.* an extremely slender tube connecting the space immediately behind the eardrum to the nasal passageway in the upper throat, which serves to equalize the air pressure on the inner side of the eardrum with that on the outer side; auditory tube. **[eustachi-** + **-an** (+) **tub-** + **-e]** < *Eustachi(us)*: Latinized surname of *Bartolommeo Eustachio*, a 16th-century Italian doctor and anatomist who first described this structure in 1563 + L. *ān(us)*: of, pert. to, charact. by, or belonging to (-an) + *tub(us)*: a pipe, tube + E. *-e*: silent final letter. RECON: *of or pert. to* (**-an**) *the tube* (**tub-**) *of Eustachius* (**eustachi-**) OR *of or pert. to* (**-an**) *Eustachius's* (**eustachi-**) *tube* (**tub-**). If you've ever been in an airplane as it begins its descent into an airport (or if you've been in a car as it zooms down a steep hill or an elevator as it quickly descends from a high floor), then you know that uncomfortable pressure that can build in your ears when your eustachian tubes do not open fast enough or wide enough to allow the air pressure behind your eardrums to equal the greater atmospheric pressure on the outer side of your eardrums. (The atmospheric pressure is always greater at lower altitudes because there is a greater quantity of air and, hence, more air weight or "pressure" remaining above.) However, swallowing or yawning will help open and distend your eustachian tubes. But if you have a bad cold and your eustachian tubes are swollen closed, this will probably not work for you, and there is little you can do to keep your delicate eardrums from bulging inward in response to the greater atmospheric pressure—and this can become quite unpleasant and even painful. . . . Question: Since commercial airliners provide "pressurized cabins," why should you experience *any* pressure change as the plane descends?

EUTHANASIA (yōō′thə·nā′zhə) *n.* the painless and benevolent killing of a person or animal suffering from an incurable and often painful disease or condition; mercy killing. **[eu-** + **thanas-** + **-ia]** < G. *eu-*: well + *thanat(os)*: death + *-ia*: the act, process, condition, or result of. RECON: *the process or condition of* (**-ia**) *a well* (**eu-**) *death* (**thanas-**), 25, 47, *72*, see also under -IA

evenly matched, 153

event, see under VENT-¹

evergreen, see under DECIDUOUS

evitable, see under NOCENT

*ex-*¹ (eks, iks, igz, egz) a L-derived prefix having a variety of substantially different meanings: **1.** out, out of; from, forth: *export, exhale, inexorable* (pertaining to that which cannot be altered or stopped; relentless; unyielding). **2.** without, lacking, not: *excoriate* (to strip or rub off the skin; figuratively, to scold, berate, or denounce), *excorticate* (to remove the husk, bark, or peel

from; decorticate), *excaudate* (tailless). **3.** completely, thoroughly, throughout, beyond: *exterminate, excruciating, exasperate.* **4.** former: *ex-convict, ex-husband, ex-president.* **Note:** *ex-* generally becomes *e-* before most consonants, particularly those that are voiced: ELOCUTION, EGREGIOUS, *enate* (ē′nāt; related through the mother's side of the family; cf. *agnate* under AD-); and *ex-* is also assimilated to *ef-* before *f*: *effort, effective, effluence* (that which flows out, as a vapor or emanation; cf. *affluence* and *confluence*). Moreover, when *ex-* passes through French, it often becomes *es-*: *escape, escort, esplanade* (an open and usually long, level walkway; promenade). Finally, when *ex-* is affixed to a word beginning with *s*, that *s* is usually dropped: *execute, expectation, execrate* (to damn, denounce; abhor, abominate; curse, imprecate). **[ex-]** < L. *ex-* (a prefixal form of the prep. *ex*): out, out of, from, beyond, 106

*ex-*² (eks, iks, igz, egz) a G-derived prefix having the basic meaning: out, out of; from, forth: *exodus, exorcise* (to expel or seek to expel evil spirits, as by religious incantation—not to be confused with *exercise*), *exergue* (eg·zûrg′, ig′zûrg, ek′sûrg; the space on a coin below the design or picture, where the date is usually stamped). **Note:** *ex-* generally becomes *ec-* before consonants: *eclipse, ecstasy, ecdysiast* (ek·diz′ē·ast′, -ist; the "respectable" term for a stripteaser, an actual word coined by H. L. Mencken in 1940). **[ex-]** < G. *ex-* (a prefixal form of *ex*): out, out of, from, beyond

exacerbated, see under PSYCHOSOMATIC

exaltation, 154

exalted, see under COURAGE

exam, 132

Example (within SUBJECTS), 26

exasperate, see under EX-¹

excaudate, see under EX-¹

excise, see under -CIS-

excision (ek·sizh′ən, ik-) *n.* **1.** the act of removing, expunging (eradicating or blotting out), or cutting out: *the excision of an offensive chapter in a book.* **2.** the surgical removal of: *the excision of a cancerous tumor.* **[ex-** + **-cis-** + **-ion]** < L. *ex-*: out, out of + *-cis(us)* (pp. of *-cīdere*, comb. form of *caedere*: to cut, to kill) + *-iōn(is)* (gen. of *-iō*): the act, means, or result of. RECON: *the act, means, or result of* (**-ion**) *cutting* (**-cis-**) *out* (**ex-**), 54

exclamation, 219

ex-convict, see under EX-¹

excoriate, see under EX-¹

excorticate, see under EX-¹

excruciating, see under EX-¹

execrate, see under EX-¹

execration, 84

execute, see under EX-¹

exercise, see under EX-²

Exercise-Helpful Hints entries (guide to understanding their page references in A CROSS-REFERENCE DICTIONARY), 36

Exercises (how to do), **11-12**

exergue, see under EX-²

exhale, see under EX-¹

ex-husband, see under EX-¹

exi**g**ency, 89, **108**

exi**g**uous, 89, **108**

existence, see under -ENCE

exit, see under VOLITIVE

exodus, see under EX-²

exorcise, see under EX-²

expectation, see under EX-¹

EXPLOSION (ek·splō′zhən, ik-) *n.* a violent blowing up or apart, usually accompanied by a loud noise. **[ex-** + **-plos-** + **-ion]** < L. *ex-*: out, out of, from, forth + *-plōs(us)*: clapped, applauded (< *-plōdere*, comb. form of *plaudere*: to clap) + *-iōn(is)* (gen. of *-iō*): the act, means, or result of. RECON: *the act of* (**-ion**) *clapping* (**-plos-**) *out* (**ex-**). *Explosion* was originally an expression of contempt and rejection, used especially to describe the practice of driving an incompetent actor off the stage with boos, hisses, and clapping, 79, 82

export, see under EX-¹

exposure, 127

ex-president, see under EX-¹

expunging, see under EXCISION

extant, see under INDO-EUROPEAN

exterminate, see under EX-¹

extolling, see under OFFICIOUS

extra innings, 152

F

fa-, 81

fable, see under PARABLE

FAC- (FACT-, -FECT-, -FIC-, -FY), 96–98

fac-, **96**, *96, 98*

-face < L. *-fātiō*: a speaking < *fāt-* (base of *fātus*, pp. of *fārī*: to speak) + *-iō*: the act, means, or result of (cf. -ION). In Old French, the two syllables of *-tiō* in

-fātiō gradually ELIDED, forming *-ce* and, hence, *-face*, which appears in English *preface*. However, this *-face* has no relationship with English *face*, which is derived from Latin *faciēs*, "form, figure, face" (a word closely related to Latin *facere*, "to make, to do," and appears in such English words and compounds as *lightface*, *boldface*, and *deface*, *xv*, *xv*

face, see under -FACE (preceding entry)

facere, 96, 97, 107

facile, 96, **98,** see also under AMBIDEXTROUS

facility, 98, **109**

facsimile, 98, **109**

FACT-, -FECT-, FAC-, -FIC-, -FY, 96–98

fact-, 73, 85, **fact-1**, 96, **105**

FACTORY (fak´tə·rē) *n.* **1.** a building or other facility in which products are manufactured; manufacturing plant. **2.** any place, person, or thing that churns out uniform products, purportedly without regard for the quality or individuality of that product: *a diploma factory*; *a baby factory*. **[fact- + -ory]** < L. *fact(us)* (pp. of *facere*: to make, to do) + *-ōrium*: a place for (neut. of *-ōrius*: pert. to one who or that which [< *-ōr*: one who + *-ius*: adj. suffix with the basic meaning: of or pert. to]). RECON: *a place for* **(-ory)** *making* **(fact-)**. ALT. DISS: **[fact- + -or + -y]** < L. *fact(us)* (pp. of *facere*: to make, to do) + *-or*: one who or that which + E. *-y*: the act, process, or result of (< L. *-ia*). RECON: *the act, process, or result of* **(-y)** *one who or that which* **(-or)** *makes* **(fact-)**. The reason for the discrepancy between these etymologies is that in Medieval Latin the term *factōria*, "establishment for factors or agents," arose, suggesting a clear derivation of English *-y* in *factory* from Latin *-ia*, which tends to support the latter hypothesis (and is, in fact, the etymology most frequently cited for *factory*). However, in Late Latin, hundreds of years earlier, the term *factōrium*, "oil mill, oil press" was EXTANT, which suggests a derivation of English *-ory* in *factory* from Latin *-ōrium* and tends to support the first hypothesis. It is therefore my contention that two parallel developments of *factory* occurred, and the meanings that we generally attribute to *factory* (see definitions above) are either derivatives from or influenced by the older Late Latin form, *factōrium*; 73, see also under -ORY²

-factum, 105

factus, 96

fact(us) (*facere*), 105

faculty, see under -UL-²

Fahrenheit, 134

fais-, 107

-fi(a)it, 105

Fall, the, see under INCIDENT

fall, 139, see also under INCIDENT

fall apart, see under INCIDENT

fall asleep, see under INCIDENT

fall behind, see under INCIDENT

fall down, see under INCIDENT

fall for, see under INCIDENT

fall in, see under INCIDENT

fallopian tube, 76

fallout, see under INCIDENT

fall out, see under INCIDENT

fant-, 102

fant(is) (*fāns*) (*fārī*), 102

fārī, 81

farm out, 152

farsicality, see under CIRCUS

fascist, see under -IST

FASHION AND FABRICS, 119

father, 139

faux pas, 138

"fear of flying," see under AEROPHOBIA

feas-, 107

FEBRIPHOBIA *n.* an abnormal or irrational fear or dread of fever; PYREXIOPHOBIA. [< L. *febr(is)*: fever + *-i-*: conn. vowel + -PHOBIA), 143

(febris) acū(ta), 86

-FECT- (FACT-, -FEC-, FAC-, -FIC-, -FY), 96–98

-fect-, *96*, 96, 97

-fectus, 96

fecund, see under PROLIFIC

feet of clay, 151

fem-, 102

femicide, 56, **102**

fēm(ina), 102

feminine, 192, see also under -INE¹

femininity, 192

feminism, 192

fenestr- < L. *fenestr-*, base of *fenestra*: a hole in a wall, orig. to admit light; window, *114*

fenestration, 114

fer- < L. *fer-*, base of *ferre*: to bear, to carry, *58*, **109**

fer(re), 109

ferruginous, 115

fetid, see under PTOMAINE

fettuccine, see under VERMICELLI

f(e)u, 95

-fic, 73, 85, 96, 97

-FIC- (FACT-, -FECT-, FAC-, -FY), 96–98

-fic-, *96*, 96

-ficāre, 96

-fication, 96, see also under CALCIFICATION

-ficere, 96

-fic(ere), 96

-ficus, 96

-fic(us), 96, 105

fidelity, 206

fiduciary, 206

fifth being, 146

fiftyish, see under -ISH

fil- < L. *fil-*, base of *fīlāre*: to draw out thread, to spin (< *filum*: thread, string); or directly < *fil-*, base of *filum*: thread, string, *119*

filia, 55

filicide, 55, see also under -CID-¹

filiform, 149

filipendulous, 119, see also under -UL-²

filius, 55

FILM AND FILMMAKING, 120

film-, 101

film(en), 101

film noir, 120

fil(um), 119

final draft, 50

fire, earth, air, and water, 146

firmus, 208

firstly, see under -LY²

-fit, 105

fixative, 127

flaccid, see under IL DUCE

flagellate (*adj.* flaj´ə·lit, -lät; *v.* flaj´ə·lät´) *adj.* **1.** having a whiplike appendage used for locomotion, as on sperm cells, certain protozoa and bacteria, etc. —*v.* **2.** to whip; flog; lash. **[flag- + ell- + -at- + -e]** < L. *flag(rum)*: a whip + *-ell(um)*: a dim. suffix having the basic meaning: small, little, tiny + *-āt-* (base of *-ātus*), ppl. suffix with the inflectional meaning: having been or having had; in E. (without the macron), also meaning: having, possessing, or charact. by + E. *-e*: silent final letter. RECON: *having had* **(-at-)** *a little* **(ell-)** *whip* **(flag-)**. SEC. DISS: **[flag- + ell- + -ate]** Note: L. *-āt-* (base of *-ātus*): having been, having had + E. *-e*: silent final letter > the E. *adj*-forming suffix -ATE, having, in this entry, the basic meaning: having, having been, possessing, or charact. by. SEC. RECON: *possessing* **(-ate)** *a little* **(ell-)** *whip* **(flag-)**, see under TRYPANOSOMIASIS

flax, see under COLLINEAR and PATRILINEAL

flex-, 103

flex(us) [*flectere*], 103

flu, 132, *132*, 132

flu- < L. *flu-*, base of *fluere*: to flow, **103**, *132*

flu(ere), 103

fly in the ointment, 151

foci, 198

focus (E.), 198

focus (L.), *198*

focuses, 198

foli-, *xviii,* **108**

foli(um), 108

foot, 139

for-¹ < OE. *for-, fær-*: away, apart, off: *forget, forgive, forgo*, 172

for-² < L. *for-*, base of *forum*: marketplace, public square; orig., any outdoor area: FORUM, CIRCUMFORANEOUS, *forensic* (of, relating to, or appropriate to courts of law or formal debate; also, concerning the application of scientific research to matters of law, esp. in the investigation of crime), 59

foray, 234

fore- < OE. *fore-* (a prefixal form of the adv. and prep. *fore*): before in time or space, in front of: *forefather, forearm,* FORESKIN; cf. FOR-¹, *xi,* xi, *xv, xvi,* 1

forearm, see under FORE-

forefather, see under FORE-

FOREIGN WORDS AND PHRASES IN THE ENGLISH LANGUAGE, 138

forensic, see under FOR-²

foreskin (fôr´skin´) *n.* the loose, conoid (kō´noid; cone-shaped) flap of skin that surrounds and encloses the glans or head of the penis; prepuce (prē´pyōōs). **[fore- + skin]** < OE. *fore*: before in time or space, in front of (akin to L. *prō-* and G. *pro-*) + ON. *skinn*: hide, pelt, skin. RECON: *the skin* **(skin)** *in front of* **(fore-)**. The foreskin often extends beyond and partially covers the meatus (mē·ā´təs; opening) of the penis, 57, 58

FOREWORD, XI–XIII

Foreword, xv, 1

foreword, xi, xv, xvi, 1, see also under -WORD

forgive, see under FOR-¹

-form < L. *-fōrm-*, base of *-fōrmis*: having the form or shape of < *fōrma*: form, shape, *shap-1*

formication, 148

fort-, 210

forte, 210

fortification, 209-10

fortis, 209, 210

fortis me fieri fecit, **135**

fortissimo, 210

fortitude, 210

fortress, 210

FORUM (fôr´əm) *n.* **1.** any meeting hall, assembly, radio or television program, etc., in which issues of public concern are discussed. **2.** a court or tribunal. **[forum]** < L. *forum*: marketplace, public square; orig., any outdoor area; cf.

agora under AGORAMANIA. RECON: *marketplace, public square* (**forum**) In ancient Roman cities, a forum was any public place where people shopped, assembled, and conducted political and judicial affairs, 59

forum , 197

Fowler, Henry, xv

Frankish, see under -ISH

fräter, 55

fratricide, 55

Free States, see under SUBWAY

French, 163-64, see also under NATIVE / FRENCH-DERIVED SYNONYMS and INDO-EUROPEAN

Frequentative Verbs (Latin), **220-22**

fridge. 265

Frisbee, 133

fructivorous, 117

frugivorous, 117

fug- < L. *fug-*, base of *fugere*: to run away, flee, *118*

Führer, der, see under IL DUCE

fulvous, 115

fum- < L. *fūm-*, base of *fūmus*: smoke, steam, vapor, fume, *88*

fumarole, 194

fumatorium, 194

fumigant, 194

fumigate, **32-33** (as a guide to understanding the Brief Analyses), **88**, *194*, see also under -IG-

funct-, **107**

functional shift, 182

funct(us) (*fungī*), 107

fundament (fun´də·mənt) *n.* **1.** a base or foundation. **2.** a basic or underlying principle. **3.** the part of the body upon which a person sits; buttocks. **4.** the ORIFICE near the base of the buttocks; anus. [**fund-** + **-a-** + **-ment**] < L. *fund(āre)*: to lay the bottom or foundation of (< *fundus*: bottom, foundation) + *-ā-*: conn. vowel (tech., the "thematic" or stem-ending *ā* of first conjugation verbs ending in *-āre* or *-ārī*; see -A-¹ and -AT-) + *-ment(um)*: the act, means, or result of. RECON: *the result of* (**-ment**) *laying the bottom or foundation of* (**fund-**). Note: the *e* in *fundament* is pronounced like the *e* in *judgment* or *instrument*, not the *e* in *fundamental*, 66

fung-, **102**

fungi. 198

fungicide, <u>56</u>. **102**

fung(us), *102*

fungus, 193. 198, 198

funguses. 198

furc-, **108**

furc(a), *108*

furole, 95

fus-, **103**

fuscous, 115

fust-, **108**

fustigate, <u>89</u>, **108**

fūst(us), *108*

fūs(us) (*fundere*), *103*

-FY (FACT-, -FECT-, FAC-, -FIC-), **96–98**

-fy, **96**, *96*, *98*

G

gaffer, 120

gaggle, 154

galact- < G. *galakt-*, base of *galaktos*, gen. of *gala*: milk, *47*

galactagogue, **47**

GALACTIC (gə·lak´tik) *adj.* **1.** of or pertaining to a galaxy or the Milky Way (the galaxy containing our solar system, visible as a faintly luminous band of stars overarching the night sky). **2.** extremely large; immense. **3.** of, derived from, or relating to milk, esp. the secretion or flow of milk. [**galact-** + **-ic**] < G. *galakt(os)* (gen. of *gala*): milk + *-ik(os)*: pert. to, charact. by. RECON: *pert. to* (**-ic**) *milk* (**galact-**). *Galaxy* was formerly the specific name for the Milky Way, which the ancients fancied to be a cosmic road or way of milk encircling the earth. And *Milky Way*, in turn, was a LOAN TRANSLATION (via Middle English *melky waye*) of Latin *via lactea*, which was itself a partial translation of Greek *kyklos galaxias*, "circle of milk," which may be the source of our obsolete *lacteous circle*, a synonym for *Milky Way*, 47

GALEOPHOBIA (gal´ē·ə·fō̄́bē·ə, gā́lē-) *n.* an irrational dislike or fear of cats; AILUROPHOBIA. [< G. *gale(ē)*: weasel, a weasel-like animal; hence, a cat (but do not confuse G. *gale(ē)* with G. *gale(os)*: dogfish, shark) + *-o-*: conn. vowel + -PHOBIA], 143

gametophobia, 142

GAMOMANIA *n.* an extreme preoccupation with or compulsion to be married. [< G. *gam(os)*: marriage + *-o-*: conn. vowel + -MANIA], 145

garrulous, see under -UL-²

gasoline, see under -INE²

gastr-, **104**

gastri, 82

gastritis, <u>68</u>, **104**

gastromancy, 150

gastr(os) (*gastēr*), 82, *104*

GATT, 130

Gehenna, 137

gen-, **102**

gene-, **101**

genē-, *101*

generally, see under -LY²

GENERATE (jen´ə·rāt´) *v.* **1.** to bring into being; create; produce. **2.** to reproduce; procreate (to bring forth offspring; beget. [**gener-** + **-at-** + **-e**] < L. *gener(āre)*: to bring into being, create, produce, beget (< *generis*, gen. of *genus*: birth, origin, race, kind, species) + *-āt-* (base of *-ātus*), ppl. suffix with the inflectional meaning: having been or having had; in E. (without the macron), also meaning: having, possessing, or charact. by, and often used as a verbal suffix with the senses described under "NOTE" below + E. *-e*: silent final letter. RECON: *having been* (**-at-**) *brought into being* (**gener-**). SEC. DISS: [**gener-** + **-ate**] Note: L. *-āt-* (base of *-ātus*): having been, having had + E. *-e*: silent final letter > E. -ATE, used in this entry as a *v*-forming suffix, having the related meanings: to cause, to become, to cause to become, to make, to do, to form, to function, to manage, etc. SEC. RECON: *to cause* (**-ate**) *to bring into being* (**gener-**), 88

generative, see under PHALLIC

genes, see under CHROMOSOME

genesis, 261, see also under -SIS

gene splicing, see under SUPERMAN

genetic engineering, see under SUPERMAN

genetics, see under -ICS

genial, see under AFFABLE and CORDIAL

geniculate, 205

geniculation, 205

genitive, 189-90, 194

genocide, <u>56</u>, **102**

gen(os), *102*

genuflection, 205

genuflectory, 205

genus, 202, *203* (in scientific terminology)

geoduck, see under GWEDUC

geranium, 247

gerascophobia, see under GERONTOPHOBIA

German, see under INDO-EUROPEAN

Germanic, see also under INDO-EUROPEAN

geront-, **103**

gerontocracy, <u>62</u>, **103**

GERONTOPHOBIA (jə·rän´tō·fō̄́bē·ə) *n.* an unusual fear or dislike of old people—not to be confused with *gerascophobia* (jə·ras´kə·fō̄́bē·ə), fear of growing old. [< G. *geront(os)* (gen. of *gerōn*): old man + *-o-*: conn. vowel + -PHOBIA], 143

geront(os) (*gerōn*), *103*

gerund (jer´ənd) *n.* a verb form ending in *-ing* that functions as a noun but has characteristics of a verb, as in "*Dancing* is fun," but *not* "the dancing troupe" (in which *dancing* is a participle); verbal noun; cf. PRESENT PARTICIPLE and PAST PARTICIPLE. [**ger-** + **-und**] < L. *ger(ere)*: to bear, to carry + *-und(um)* (var. of *-endum*): neut. GERUNDIVE suffix having the basic meaning: to be or worthy to be (that which is designated by the preceding verb base). RECON: *to be or worthy to be* (**-und**) *borne or carried* (**ger-**), 222

gerundives (Latin), **225-28**

gethsemane, 137

get to first base, 152

Geum urbanum, see under HERB BENNET

giant (Anglicization of L. *gigantis*), 236

gigant-, **102**

giganticide, <u>56</u>, **102**

gigantis (Latinization of G. *gigantos*), 236

gigant(is) (*gigās*), *102*

gignere, 105, 107

gignesthai, 261

(gi)gnōs(kein), *101*

Gilbert Islands, see under MICRONESIA

gingiv-, **104**

gingiv(a), *104*

gingivitis, <u>68</u>, **104**

gladly, see under -LY²

Gladstone, William, see under ANTIDISESTABLISHMENTARIANISM

glans, 58, see also under FORESKIN

glasphalt, 131

comb. form -LOGY, having, in this context, the scientific and literary meaning: the science, study, theory, or doctrine of. SEC. RECON: *the science or study of* (**-logy**) *women* (**gynec-**), 61, *81*
GYNECOMANIA *n.* an abnormally strong and often uncontrollable sexual desire

for women, traditionally said of men; SATYRIASIS. [< G. *gynaik(os)* (gen. of *gynē*): woman, female + *-o-*: conn. vowel + -MANIA], 145
gynecomastia, 155
gynephobia, 142

-*h*- (rough breathing), 69
habeas corpus, 94
habēre, 94, 221
habitant, 94, 221
habitāre, 94
habitat, 220
habitation, 220, 222
habitational, 222
habituate, 220
habitus, 94
hadephobia, see under STYGIOPHOBIA
Hades, see under STYGIOPHOBIA
hag, see under BELDAM
hagi- < G. *hagi,* base of *hagios:* holy, sacred, 49, **103**
hagiocracy, 62, **103**
hagiographer (hag´ē·äg´rə·fər, hā´jē-) *n.* a person who writes about the lives of the saints. [**hagi-** + **-o-** + **graph-** + **-er**] < G. *hagi(os):* holy, sacred + *-o-*: conn. vowel + *graph(os):* drawn, written (< *graphein:* to write, to draw) + E. *-er*: one who or that which (performs the action designated by the preceding base or elements) (< OE. *-er(e),* akin to or perhaps < L. *-ārius*). RECON: *one who* (**-er**) *writes* (**graph-**) *about those who are holy* (**hagi-**), 49
hagi(os), 103
haim-, 69, 251
haima, xviii, 69, 251
haim(a) 102
(h)aim(a), 104
haimat-, 251
halfhearted, see under COURAGE
halibut, 148
HAMARTOMANIA (hä·mär´tə·mā´nē·ə) *n.* a tendency or compulsion to sin or err. [< G. *hamart(ia):* a fault, failure, sin (< *hamart(anein):* to err, to fail, to sin) + *-o-*: conn. vowel + -MANIA], 145
HAMARTOPHOBIA (hä·mär´tə·fō´bē·ə) *n.* an abnormal fear or dread of erring or sinning. [< G. *hamart(ia):* a fault, failure, sin (< *hamart(anein):* to err, to fail, to sin) + *-o-*: conn. vowel + -PHOBIA), 143
Hamito-Semitic, see under SEMITIC
hand, 139
handle with kid gloves, 151
hang in there, 153
haptophobia, 142
hard-nosed, 153
hardtack (härd´tak´) *n.* hard, unleavened (un·lev´ənd; not provided with a fermenting agent, as yeast, and therefore not rising during cooking or processing) bread, formerly eaten primarily aboard ship and in the military. [**hard** + **tack**] < OE. *heard:* hard, solid, firm + E. *tack:* food, foodstuff (< ?). RECON: *hard* (**hard**) *food* (**tack**), 91
hard up, 151
harmless drudge, 49
Harold, see under ARISTOTLE
HARPAXOPHOBIA *n.* an intense or persistent fear or dread of robbers, esp. of becoming a victim of robbers. [< G. *harpax:* robber (< or akin to *harpazein:* to snatch, to seize) + *-o-*: conn. vowel + -PHOBIA], 143
harp on, 151
hassock, 121
hateful love, 50
have a heart, see under COURAGE
have a jag on, 151
Hawaii, see under POLYNESIA
hē, 66, 67
HEART (**CARDI-**), 51–53
heart, 51, see also expressions under COURAGE
heartbroken, see under COURAGE
hē arthritis nosos, 66, 67
heavenly, see under -LY¹
heavens, see under TRANSATLANTIC
Hebrew, see under SAC and SEMITIC
hedon- < G. *hēdon-,* base of *hēdonē:* pleasure, delight (< or akin to *hēdys:* sweet), 71
HEDONIST (hēd´n·ist) *n.* a person who pursues or believes in pursuing a life of pleasure and self-gratification. [**hedon-** + **-ist**] < G. *hēdon(ē):* pleasure, delight (< or akin to *hēdys:* sweet) + *-ist-*: final letter of the base of denom. verbs ending in *-izein* + *-t(ēs):* one who or that which). RECON: *one who* (**-ist**) *pleasures* (**hedon-**), 71
HEDONOMANIA (hē´də·nō·mā´nē·ə) *n.* a preoccupation with or compulsion for

pleasure. [< G. *hēdon(ē):* pleasure, delight (< or akin to *hēdys:* sweet) + *-o-*: conn. vowel + -MANIA], 145
(he)ingre, 107
Heli-, *xviii*
heli-, *xvii*
*Hēlianthos mikrokephalos, 169
Helianthus angustifolius, xvii, xviii, passim
Helianthus decapetalus, xvii, xviii, passim
Helianthus giganteus, xvii, xviii, passim
Helianthus microcephalus, xvii, xviii, 2, passim
Helianthus tuberosus, xvii, xviii, passim
Helianthus, xvii, passim
heliocentric, xvii
heliograph, 127
heliolatry, see under HELIOMANIA
HELIOMANIA (hē´lē·ō·mā´nē·ə) *n.* an extreme attraction to and desire to be in the sun—not to be confused with *heliolatry* (hē´lē·äl´ə·trē), worship of the sun; cf. COSMOLATRY. [< G. *hēli(os):* sun + *-o-*: conn. vowel + -MANIA], 145
HELIOPHOBIA (hē´lē·ə·fō´bē·ə) *n.* an irrational fear or dread of sunlight; cf. PHOTOPHOBIA and PHENGOPHOBIA. [< G. *hēli(os):* sun + *-o-*: conn. vowel + -PHOBIA], 143
Helios, xvii
Hellenic, see under INDO-EUROPEAN
helminth-, 101
helminthagogue, 46, 101
helminthicide, 56
HELMINTHOPHOBIA *n.* an irrational and often intense fear or dread of infestation by worms. Some people become temporary *helminthophobics* after eating pork. However, if the worms are visible and outside the body (with no likelihood of being ingested), the fear of them is *vermiphobia.* [< G. *helminth(os)* (gen. of *helmins*): worm, esp. an intestinal worm + *-o-*: conn. vowel + -PHOBIA], 143
helminth(os), 101
HELPFUL HINTS, 12-14 (explanation of features), **99-109**
hem-, *xviii, xviii, xix,* **102**
hemagogue, xviii, xix, 170
hemal, 170, 251
hemangioma, 170
hemapoiesis, 170
hematic, 170, 251
hematoma (hē´mə·tō´mə) *n.* a localized mass of blood, usually clotted, beneath the skin or in an organ or tissue, caused by a break in the wall of one or more blood vessels. [**hemat-** + **-oma**] < G. *haimat(os)* (gen. of *haima*): blood + E. *-oma*: a tumor or swelling of (< G. *-ō-*: conn. vowel [tech., the final letter of the base of denom. verbs ending in *-oun*] + *-ma*: the result of). RECON: *a swelling of* (**-oma**) *blood* (**hemat-**). For a step-by-step analysis of how Greek *-ai-* evolved into English *-e-*, see ANEMIA and ANGLICIZATION; 58, see also under *-o-³* and CIRCUMORBITAL HEMATOMA
hematomyelitis, xviii, xix, 170
hematophagia, xviii, xix, 170
HEMATOPHOBIA (hē´mə·tə·fō´bē·ə, hem´ə-) *n.* an irrational fear of or aversion to blood. [< G. *haimat(os)* (gen. of *haima*): blood + *-o-*: conn. vowel + -PHOBIA], 143
hematopoiesis, 251
hematorrhea, xviii, 170, 251
hemocytometer, xviii, 170
hemocytopoiesis, xviii, xix, 2, 251
hemopoiesis, 251
hemorrhea, 251
hendecagon, 146
hepat-, **102,** *104*
hepatitis, 68, **104**
*hepatocholecystic, see HEPATOCYSTIC (following entry)
hepatocystic (hep´ə·tō·sis´tik) *adj.* pertaining to the liver and gallbladder. [**hepat-** + **-o-** + **cyst-** + **-ic**] < G. *hēpat(os)* (gen. of *hēpar*): liver + *-o-*: conn. vowel (in this context rep. "and") + *kyst(is):* bag, pouch, sac, bladder + *-ik(os):* pert. to, charact. by. RECON: *pert. to* (**-ic**) *the bladder* (**cyst-**) *and liver* (**hepat-**) OR (when attributing "and" to *-o-*) *pert. to* (**-ic**) *the bladder* (**cyst-**) *and* (**-o-**) *liver* (**hepat-**). **Note:** In medical terminology, *cyst-* usually refers to the urinary bladder, and *cholecyst-* to the gallbladder or "bile sac" (< G. *cholē:* bile + *kyst(is):* sac, bladder; cf. CHOLECYSTECTOMY). However, because of the intimate relationship between the liver and gallbladder, it is generally understood in *hepatocystic* which bladder is being referred to. Nevertheless, the etymologically correct and medically unambiguous term

would have been *hepatocholecystic*; cf. CERVICOFACIAL, LARYN-
GOPHARYNGEAL, and OCULOGASTRIC, *52*

hēpat(os) (*hēpar*), *102, 104*

herald, see under CADUCEUS

herbarium, see under CORDATE

herb bennet (ûrb´ ben´it, hûrb´) a common European plant, *Geum urbanum*,
of the rose family, having small yellow flowers, lobed leaves, and an aromatic root, formerly believed to have remarkable medicinal and PROPHYLAC-
TIC properties. **[herb + bennet]** < L. *herb(a)*: plant, plant stalk, herb, weed
+ OF. *beneit(e)*: blessed (< L. *benedicta*: blessed < *bene*: well + *dicta* [fem.
of *dictus*, pp. of *dīcere*: to say, to speak]). **RECON:** *the blessed* (**bennet**) *herb*
(**herb**). Of herb bennet, Platearius wrote in 1486: "Where the root is in the
house the devil can do nothing, and flies from it; wherefore it is blessed
above all other herbs." The only problem is that we do not know if Platearius
was referring to the same herb bennet, i.e., *Geum urbanum*, *74, 191*

heret-, *102*

heret(ic), *102*

hereticide, *56*, *102*

hermaphrodite, *136*

hermeneutic, *126*

Hermes, see under CADUCEUS

Hermes Trismegistos, see under CADUCEUS

hermetic, *136*

He's as large as a mountain, *64*

He's not a bad athlete, *64*

hetaer-, *103*

hetaerocracy, *62*, *103*

hetair(a), *103*

heterodox, *256*

heterogeneous, *256*

heteronym, *256*

heterosexual, *255-56*

hexagynous, *117*

hibernaculum, see under -CUL-²

hibernates, see under -CUL-²

hier-, *103*

hierarchy (hī´ə·rär´kē) *n.* **1.** any group of persons or things ranked in order of
importance, superiority, excellence, power, etc. **2.** the rulers or ruling body
within any government, organization, business, club, etc. **3.** a church
government consisting of clergy and other officials in successive ranks or
grades. **[hier- + arch- + -y]** < G. *hier(os)*: holy, sacred + *-arch(ēs)* (comb.
form of *archos*): first, chief, ruler (< *archein*: to rule, orig., to be first, to
begin, to take the lead) + E. *-y*: the act, process, condition, or result of (< G.
-ia). **RECON:** *the act, condition, or result of* (**-y**) *the* holy (**hier-**) *ruler*
(**arch-**). **SEC. DISS:** [hier- + **-archy**]. Note: G. *arch(os)*: first, chief, ruler (<
archein: to rule) + *-ia*: the act, process, condition, or result of > G. *-archia*:
the act of ruling; hence, a ruling, government > the E. *n*-forming comb. form
-ARCHY: rule by or government of. **SEC. RECON:** *rule by or government of*
(*-archy*) *the holy* (**hier-**). In 14th century medieval angelology, *hierarchy*
denoted any one of the three divisions of the nine "choirs" of angels, i.e.,
angels, archangels, principalities; powers, virtues, dominions; thrones,
cherubim, seraphim. Then within the century, *hierarchy* expanded to include the
ranks and grades of the clergy, and by the 17th century it included the
gradation of ranks for any group of people and, finally, of any series of
things, *60*

hierocracy, *62*, **103**

hier(os), *103*

Hindi, see also under INDO-EUROPEAN

hipp- < G. *hipp-*, base of *hippos*: horse, *148*

hippocampus, *148*

Hippocratic Oath, *229*

Hippocrene, *148*

hippodrome, *148*, see also under -MANIA

Hippolyta, *148*

hippomancy, *150*, see also under RHABDOPHOBIA

HIPPOMANIA *n.* an extreme enthusiasm for, love of, or preoccupation with
horses; equinomania (ə·kwī´nō·mā´nē·ə). [< G. *hipp(os)*: horse + *-o-*: conn.
vowel + -MANIA], *145*, see also under -MANIA

HIPPOPHOBIA *n.* an abnormal fear or dread of horses; equinophobia (ə·kwī´nə·
fō´bē·ə). [< G. *hipp(os)*: horse + *-o-*: conn. vowel + -PHOBIA], *143*

hippopotamus, *16*, **148**, *148*, *246*

Hiroshima, *70*

(hi)sta(nai), *104*

histor-, *105*

histor(ia), *105*

HISTORIC (hi·stôr´ik) *adj.* **1.** important, famous, or well-known in history: *a
historic event*. **2.** historical. **[histor- + -ic]** < G. *histor(ia)*: a learning or
knowing by inquiry, narrative, or record (< *historein*: to inquire < *histōr*:
wise man, judge) + *-ik(os)*: pert. to, charact. by. **RECON:** *pert. to* (**-ic**) *knowing by inquiry* (**histor-**), *49, 64*

HISTORICAL (hi·stôr´i·kəl) *adj.* **1.** of or pertaining to history. **2.** depending
upon, substantiated by, or suggestive of the trends or facts of history: *a historical novel*. **3.** historic. **[histor- + -ic + -al]** < G. *histor(ia)*: a learning or
knowing by inquiry, narrative, or record (< *historein*: to inquire < *histōr*:
wise man, judge) + *-ik(os)*: pert. to, charact. by + L. *-āl(is)*: pert. to, charact.
by. **RECON:** *charact. by* (**-al**) *pert. to* (**-ic**) *knowing by inquiry* (**histor-**),
49

History of the christian [sic] *church*, *62*

hit-and-run, *152*

Hitler, Adolf, see under IL DUCE

HODOMANIA *n.* an extreme enthusiasm for, preoccupation with, or compulsion
to travel; cf. ECDEMOMANIA, DROMOMANIA, and PORIOMANIA. [< G. *hod(os)*:
way, path + *-o-*: conn. vowel + -MANIA], *145*

HODOPHOBIA *n.* an irrational fear or dread of travel. [< G. *hod(os)*: way, path +
-o-: conn. vowel + -PHOBIA], *143*

hoi polloi, *138*

hold (of a ship), see under ANTLOPHOBIA

Hollands, see under DUCHESS

hologram, *127*

holograph, *122*

homeless, see under -LESS

HOMICHLOPHOBIA (hō·mik´lə·fō´bē·ə, häm´i·klə-) *n.* an irrational or intense
fear or dread of fog. [< G. *homichl(ē)*: mist, fog, steam + *-o-*: conn. vowel +
-o-: conn. vowel + -PHOBIA], *143*

homicide, *54, 55*

HOMICIDOMANIA (häm´ə·sī´dō·mā´nē·ə) *n.* a morbid preoccupation with or
compulsion to murder. [< L. *hom(o)*: person + *-i-*: conn. vowel + *cīd(ium)*:
the killing of [< *-cīdere*, comb. form of *caedere*: to kill, to cut] + G. *-o-*:
conn. vowel + -MANIA], *145*

HOMILOPHOBIA (häm´ə·lə·fō´bē·ə) *n.* an intense dislike or aversion to sermons.
If you're a teenager, you should teach this word to your parents. [< G.
homil(ia): sermon, assembly (*homil(os)*: crowd, assembly + *-ia*: the act, state,
condition, or result of) + *-o-*: conn. vowel + -PHOBIA], *143*

Homo sapiens neanderthalensis, *xvii*

Homo sapiens sapiens, *xvii*

hom(ō), *54*

homograph, *256*

homographs (overview of treatment in A CROSS-REFERENCE DICTIONARY), *34-36*

homonym, *256*

homophone, *256*, see also under DUCHESS

Homo sapiens, *203*, *256*

homosexual, *256*

hopped, see under UNDAUNTED

horn of plenty, *205*

horr-, *109*

horr(ēre), *109*

HORRIFIC (hô·rif´ik, hə-) *adj.* causing horror; horrifying; horrible. **[horr- + -i-
+ -fic]** < L. *horr(ēre)*: to bristle with fear; tremble, shake + *-i-*: conn. vowel
+ *-fic(us)*: making, doing, causing, producing (< *-fic(ere)* [comb. form of
facere: to make, to do + *-us*: adj. suffix). **RECON:** *causing* (**-fic**) *to bristle
with fear* (**horr-**), *73, 96, 97*

horrify, *98*, **109**

horripilation, *124*

hostile, see under -ILE

hostility, see under -ITY

HOW TO USE THIS BOOK, 21-36, see also ORGANIZATION OF THE TEXT

HOW ENGLISH WORDS ARE CREATED: A SHORT COURSE,
157-265; (how to read and understand this material) 15-19

How To Create English Words From Greek Nouns and Adjectives (outline), **239**

How to Create English Words From Latin Words (outline), **183-84**

"How's it going?" see under PHATIC

"How ya doing?" see under PHATIC

HUNTING TERMS, 154

Hutchinson, Bishop Francis, *82*

HYALOPHOBIA (hī´ə·lō·fō´bē·ə) *n.* an irrational fear of handling or being around
glass, generally because of the ease at which it breaks. [< G. *hyal(os)*: glass +
-o-: conn. vowel + -PHOBIA], *143*

hydōr, *101, 102*, see also HYDR- (following entry)

hydr- < G. *hydr-*, base of *hydōr*: water > E. *hydr-*: water, hydrogen: HYDRO-
PHOBIA, *hydrocarbon* (any compound consisting solely of hydrogen and carbon), *28, 71*, **101**, *101*, **102**, *102*

hydrocarbon , see under HYDR-

HYDRODIPSOMANIA *n.* a compulsion for drinking water, sometimes seen in bouts
of uncontrollable thirst; cf. HYDROMANIA (following entry). [< G. *hydr-* (base
of *hydōr*): water + *-o-*: conn. vowel + *dips(a)*: thirst + *-o-*: conn. vowel +
-MANIA], *145*

hydrolysis, *259*

HYDROMANIA *n.* a compulsion for drinking water, often caused by an abnormal
thirst; also, a desire to commit suicide by drowning; cf. HYDRODIPSOMANIA
(preceding entry). [< G. *hydr-* (base of *hydōr*): water + *-o-*: conn. vowel +
-MANIA], *145*

hydropericarditis, *14* (as a guide to understanding the HELPFUL HINTS), *53*, **102**

HYDROPHOBIA (hī´drə·fō´bē·ə) *n.* **1.** an abnormal fear or dread of water. **2.**
rabies. **[hydr- + -o- + phob- + -ia]** < G. *hydr-* (base of *hydōr*): water + *-o-*:
conn. vowel + *phob(os)*: fear, panic, flight (< *phobein* or *phebesthai*: to flee
in fright) + *-ia*: the act, process, condition, or result of. **RECON:** *the condition
of* (**-ia**) *fearing* (**phob-**) *water* (**hydr-**). **SEC. DISS:** [hydro- + **-phobia**]
Note: G. *hydr-* (base of *hydōr*): water + *-o-*: conn. vowel > G. *hydro-* > the
E. comb. form *hydro-*: water. Also note: G. *phob(os)*: fear, panic, flight + *-ia*:
the act, process, condition, or result of > G. *-phobia* > the E. *n*-forming
comb. form -PHOBIA, having the modern medical meaning: an irrational or
intense fear or dread of. **SEC. RECON:** *an irrational fear or dread of*
(**-phobia**) *water* (**hydro-**). An extraordinary symptom of advanced rabies is

ig- (Latin and nonclassical initial letter combination), *87*

-IG- (AG-, ACT-), *87–89*

-ig- < L. *-ig-,* base of *-igere-,* comb. form of *agere:* to do, to act, to drive: FU-MIGATE, INTRANSIGENT, SUFFUMIGATE; *57, 57, 87, 87, 88, 89*

-igere, 57, 87

igloo (ig´lōō) *n.* a dome-shaped Eskimo hut, usually built out of blocks of packed snow. **[igloo]** < Inuit (in´yōō·it; a synonym and more acceptable term for *Eskimo,* which outsiders historically but erroneously reconstructed as "eaters of raw flesh," and which the Inuit therefore find offensive; *Inuit* means "people" in Inuit) *iglu:* house, snow house, *87*

ignivomous, *155*

ignoble, see under IN-²

ignore (ig·nôr´) *v.* to deliberately disregard or refuse to consider. **[ignor- + -e]** < L. *ignōrāre):* to have no knowledge of, disregard (< L. *i-* [var. of *in-* used before *gn*]: not + *gnārus:* knowing, aware, acquainted with; hence, *i-* + *gnārus* = not aware) + E. *-e:* silent final letter. RECON: *to have no knowledge of* (**ignor-**), *87,* see also under IN-²

iguana (i·gwä´nə) *n.* any of a genus of harmless, tropical American lizards. **[iguana]** < Arawak (an American Indian language formerly spoken in the West Indies, but now confined to northeast South America) *iwana:* iguana, *87*

-ik(a), 101

-ik(os), 61, see also under -IC

Il Duce (ēl dōō´che, -chā) *Ital.* "The Leader." The title assumed by Benito Mussolini as leader of fascist Italy from 1922 till his death in 1945. **[il (+) duc- + -e]** < Ital. *il:* the (< L. *ille:* that) (+) *duc-:* leader (< L. *dux* [gen: *ducis*]: leader, commander, ruler [< L. *dūcere:* to lead, to bring]) + *-e:* SUB-STANTIVE suffix. RECON: *the* (**il**) *leader* (**duc-**). Interestingly, Italian has another word for "leader," *duca,* that Mussolini might have have chosen for his title. But this word connotes an aristocratic leader or DUKE, and Mussolini evidently preferred the more militant *duce.* Similarly, Mussolini's wartime ally, Adolf Hitler, who also styled himself "The Leader," chose the more emphatic *der Führer* (der fyür´ər) over the relatively flaccid (flak´sid, but now increasingly flas´id; weak, limp) *der Leiter* (der lī´tər). . . . He too died in 1945, *75*

-il < L. *-il-,* base of *-ilis:* able to (be), capable of (being), tending to (be), in-clined to (be); or *-īl(is):* pert. to, charact. by. Note: L. *-il(is)* or *-īl(is)* + E. *-e:* silent final letter > the E. *adj-*forming suffix -ILE (see following entry), *88, 98,* **106**

-ile (il, ´l, īl) a L-derived *adj-*forming suffix having two common meanings: **1.** able to (be), capable of (being), tending to (be), inclined to (be): *agile,* DOCILE, PROTRUSILE. **2.** pertaining to, characterized by, having the nature of, like: *hostile,* JUVENILE, SENILE. **[-il + -e]** < L. *-il(is):* tending to (be), inclined to (be) (attached to infinitive and ppl. bases) or *-īl(is):* pert. to, charact. by (attached to noun and adj. bases) + E. *-e:* silent final letter. Note: Latin *-ilis* and Latin *-bilis* are almost identical in meaning, *-bilis* being an extended form of *-ilis.* Therefore, their English derivatives, *-ile* and *-bile,* are also al-most identical in meaning. For more information, see *-b(i)l(is)* under EDUCA-BLE

-il(is), 106, 109

illegal, 200

illegality, 201

illegible, see under IN-²

illegitimate, 201

illiterate, see under IN-² and NOCENT

illusion, see under IN-¹

illustration, see under IN-¹

I'm so hungry I could eat a horse, 64

im- < L. *im-,* var. of IN-² (used before *p* or *b*): not, without, *97*

imbecile, see under IN-²

imbibe, see under IN-¹

immaculate, see under IN-²

immerse, see under IN-²

immoral, see under IN-²

IMMORTAL (i·môr´t'l) *adj.* **1.** living or lasting forever; undying; everlasting. — *n.* **2.** a god, person, or other being conceived of as living forever or of having eternal fame; cf. OMNIPOTENT and OMNISCIENT. **[im- + mort- + -al]** < L. *im-* (assim. form of IN-²): not, without + *mort(is)* (gen. of *mors*): death, dying + *-āl(is):* pert. to, charact. by. RECON: *charact. by* (**-al**) *not* (**im-**) *dying* (**mort-**), *91, 97,* see also under IN-²

immure, see under IN-¹

immutable, 224

impeccable, see under NOCENT

impecunious, see under IN-²

impel, see under IN-¹

imperfect, *96,* **97**

imprecate, see under EX-¹

imprecation, *84*

improvident, *224*

impute, *166*

-in, 125, 133, see also under -IN- (following entry) and -INE²

-in- < L. *-īn-,* base of *-īnus* (or *-in-,* base of *-inus* < G. *-inos*), pert. to, charact. by, having the nature of, like. For a more in-depth discussion, see -INE¹ and -INE²; **106,** *115*

in-¹ (in) a L-derived prefix having the associated meanings: in, into, within, to, toward (also used intensively, i.e., completely, thoroughly, throughout, utterly): INDUCTION, *include, incarcerate* (imprison); cf. EN-¹ and EN-². **Note:**

in- is ASSIMILATED in the following manner: *in-* becomes *il-* before *l: illusion, illustration; im-* before *m: immerse, immure* (to imprison or confine, esp. within a wall); and *ir-* before *r: irruption, irrigation.* Also, *in-* becomes *im-* before *p* and *b: impel, imbibe;* and in OF. *in-* became *en-,* supplying the prefix for *enclose, enchant,* and *enamored* (i·nam´ərd; filled with love; charmed; captivated; cf. PARAMOUR). **[in-]** < L. *in-* (a prefixal form of or akin to the prep. *in*): in, into, to, toward, *75, 75, 94,* **106,** *106, 108,* **109,** *109, 132,* see also under EN-¹

in-² (in) a L-derived prefix having the common meaning: not, without: *inactive, inadequate, incapacity;* cf. A-⁴, UN-, and NON-. **Note:** *in-* is ASSIMILATED in the following manner: *in-* becomes *il-* before *l: illiterate, illegible; im-* be-fore *m:* IMMORTAL, *immoral;* and *ir-* before *r: irrational, irreversible.* Also, *in-* becomes *im-* before *p* and *b:* IMPERFECT, *impecunious* (poor or penniless), *imbecile; i-* before *gn:* IGNORE, ignoble; and *en-* in two words borrowed from Old French: *enemy* and *enmity* (ill will; hostility; animosity). **[in-]** < L. *in-:* without, not, *69,* 89, *94,* **108,** *108,* **109,** *109,* see also under NOCENT

inactive, 89, **108,** see also under IN-²

inadequate, see under IN-²

inadvertent, see under NOCENT

in a pig's eye, 151

in a slump, 152

inaudible, 215

incapacity, see under IN-²

incarcerate, 94, see also under IN-¹

incarnadine, 115

incarnate, 94

incense, 76

inceptive, see under -SC-

inchoative, see under -SC-

incident (in´si·dənt) *n.* **1.** anything that happens or occurs; happening; occur-rence. **2.** a relatively minor episode, often related to or occurring as a result of something more important: *The incident occurred on our way to the theater.* **3.** a relatively minor distur-bance or conflict, as between hostile nations or factions, that can precipitate a major crisis: *The border incident led to war.* —*adj.* **4.** likely or inclined to happen, esp. as a consequence of some other occurrence or event (followed by *to*): *the hardships incident to motherhood.* **5.** falling upon or striking: *incident cosmic rays.* **[in- + -cid- + -ent]** < L. *in-:* in, into, within, on + *-cid(ere)* (comb. form of *cadere*): to fall + *-ent(is)* (gen. of *-ēns*): prpl. suffix having the SUBSTANTIVE meaning: one who or that which (performs the action designated by the preceding base or elements); see -ENT for further in-formation. RECON: *that which* (**-ent**) *falls* (**-cid-**) *in, into, or within* (**in-**). An incident, etymologically, is anything that falls in or within a larger context. Unlike an ACCIDENT, which, etymologically, is a falling "to or toward" some indeterminate fate, an *incident* is more a part of something that already exists. OCCIDENT, like *accident,* is also a falling "to or toward," but in its original sense of depicting the setting sun, reflects a more literal meaning of "fall" (as in *fall down*) than does *incident,* in which the "fall" has become increasingly figurative (as in *fall in*). This "metaphorical shift" in which a word meaning "that which falls in or within" becomes an "occurrence" or "happening" (or develops some other linguistic extension) is a common and predictable PHENOMENON observed in many languages. In English, for exam-ple, *fall* variously exhibits literal and figurative meanings in such words and expressions as *befall, fall behind, fall asleep, fall apart, fall out, fallout, fall for, The Fall,* and the season *fall* (which falls after the culmination of sum-mer); and in Latin, *cadere,* "to fall," obeys these same linguistic rules, as ev-idenced by its English derivatives ACCIDENT, OCCIDENT, INCIDENT, and DE-CIDUOUS, *54*

incise (in·sīz´) *v.* to carve or cut into, esp. for the purpose of making designs or inscriptions; engrave. **[in- + -cis- + -e]** < L. *in-:* in, into, within + *-cis(us)* (pp. of *-cīdere,* comb. form of *caedere:* to cut, to kill) + E. *-e:* silent final let-ter. RECON: *to cut* (**-cis-**) *into* (**in-**), 58

incision (in·sizh´ən) *n.* **1.** a cut, notch, or gash: *Most leaves have natural inci-sions on their edges.* **2.** a sharp, penetrating, or trenchant (cutting and hard-hitting) comment or personality trait; incisiveness: *Her wit and incision were not appreciated in the public relations firm.* **3.** a surgical cut or cutting into. **4.** the cicatrix (sik´ə·triks´, si·kā´triks; scar) resulting from such a cut or wound. **[in- + -cis- + -ion]** < L. *in-:* in, into, within + *-cis(us)* (pp. of *-cīdere,* comb. form of *caedere:* to cut, to kill) + *-iōn(is)* (gen. of *-iō*): the act, means, or result of. RECON: *the act, means, or result of* (**-ion**) *cutting* (**-cis-**) *into* (**in-**), *54, 58*

include, see under IN-¹

incompatible, see under NOCENT

incompetent, 94

incontinent, see under COM-

inconvenient, see under NOCENT

in**corpora**ble, 95, **109**

in**corpora**te, 95, **109**

incorporeal, 94

in**corpore**ity, 95, **109**

incubus, see under RECUMBENT

incumbent, 94

incurable, 94

index, 202

Indic, see under INDO-EUROPEAN

indices, 202

indifference, see under AFFABLE
indigenous, see under ENDEMIC
Indo-European (in´dō·yo͝or´ə·pē´ən) n. **1.** a large family of extinct and extant
(ek´stənt, ek·stant´; still existing; not extinct, lost, or destroyed) languages
spoken today by approximately half of the world's population and including
almost every modern European language and most of those in Russia, south-
west Asia (including Iran, Afghanistan, and Pakistan), and northern India.
This family comprises eight surviving branches: Hellenic (Greek), Italic,
Germanic, Celtic, Armenian, Albanian, Balto-Slavic (comprising the Baltic
and Slavic subgroups), and Indo-Iranian (comprising the Indic [of India and
most of its languages] and Iranian subgroups); and it includes hundreds of
different languages and dialects within these branches, including Greek,
Latin, French, English, German, Russian, Swedish, Yiddish (Jewish), Welsh
(the Celtic language of Wales), Hindi (hin´dē; the most widely spoken language of India), and Sanskrit; cf. AFRO-ASIATIC. **2.** the prehistoric parent language of the Indo-European family of languages, hypothesized to have
flourished CIRCA 5,000 B.C. somewhere north of the Black Sea (a huge, lake-
like sea north of Turkey, over twice the size of Lake Superior). This language is also called *Proto-Indo-European*, which is useful in distinguishing
it from *Indo-European* in def. 1. **3.** a member of any of the peoples or cultures speaking an Indo-European language. —*adj.* **4.** of or designating the
Indo-European family of languages or any of the peoples speaking one or
more of its languages as their native tongue. **[Ind- + -o- + Europ- + -e- +
-an]** < E. *Ind(ia)*: India < G. *Ind(os)*: the Indus River [a 1,900-mile river
flowing from Tibet, through India and Pakistan, to the Arabian Sea, west of
India] < Old Persian *Hindu*: the Indus, ult. < Sanskrit *sindhu*) + -*o*-: conn.
vowel + *Europ(e)*: Europe (< G. *Eurōpē*: in Greek mythology, a Phoenician
[of or relating to Phoenicia, an ancient kingdom in the region of present-day
Lebanon and Syria] princess abducted by Zeus in the form of a white bull
and carried off to Crete [an island in the Mediterranean, southeast of
Greece], where she became the first mortal to walk in that part of the
world—later named *Europe* in her honor) + -*e*-: conn. vowel (tech., a derivative of Fr. *(Europ)é(en)* < L. *(Europ)ae(us)*, ult. < G. *(Eurōp)a*) + *ān(us)*: of,
pert. to, charact. by, or belonging to. RECON: *belonging to* (**-an**) *India* (**Ind-**)
and Europe (**Europ-**). Proto-Indo-European and its early derivative languages, spoken in various forms and dialects from northern India to the tip
of western Europe (including Iceland), became extinct thousands of years
before the dawn of written language. Therefore, we have no records of these
languages, either directly or indirectly, and no native speaker has uttered a
sound in Proto-Indo-European for over 6,000 years. Nevertheless, philologists (an older term for historical and comparative linguists) have miracu-
lously succeeded in reconstructing thousands of Indo-European roots and
words and a significant part of its grammar based upon analyses of cognates
in daughter languages; and almost every word and root in this book can be
specifically shown to have derived from one of these Indo-European roots.
For several examples of Indo-European roots and derivatives, see AKIN and
COGNATE, 228
Indo-Iranian, see under INDO-EUROPEAN
induce, 75
indu**cement**, *77*, **106**
indu**ctance**, *77*, **106**
induction, *94*, *75*, *75*, see also under IN-¹ and DEDUCTION
Indus, see under INDO-EUROPEAN
-ine¹ (īn, in, ēn) a L- or occasionally G-derived *adj*-forming suffix having the
associated meanings: pertaining to, characterized by, having the nature of,
like, relating to, belonging to: *canine* (L.), *feminine* (L.), ULTRAMARINE (L.),
adamantine (G.; ad´ə·man´tēn, -tin, -tīn; hard and unyielding, either literally,
as a diamond, or figuratively, as one's temperament). **[-in- + -e]** < L. -*īn(us)*
(or -*in(us)* < G. -*inos*): pert. to, charact. by, having the nature of, like, belonging to + E. -*e*: silent final letter
-ine² (in, īn, ēn, 'n) a L- or occasionally G-derived *n*-forming suffix having a
wide variety of sometimes arbitrary meanings: **1.** the quality, state, condition; act, means, result, or process of: *doctrine*, *medicine*. **2.** a female _____:
chorine (kôr´ēn; a chorus girl, i.e., a female chorus singer or dancer), *undine*
(un·dēn´, un´dēn; a female water spirit). **3.** a commercial product of: *Vase-
line*, *Visine*. **4.** an ALKALOID or nitrogenous base of: *caffeine*, MORPHINE,
PTOMAINE. **5.** a chemical element of: IODINE, *chlorine*. **6.** a HYDROCARBON or
mixture of hydrocarbons of: *gasoline*, *kerosine* (also spelled *kerosene*, the
-*ene* denoting an unsaturated hydrocarbon of various configurations; cf.
-OL). **[-in- + -e]** < L. -*īn(a)* or -*in(a)*, fem. abstract *n*-forming suffixes having
the basic meanings: the quality, state, condition; act, means, result, or
process of (< -*īnus* or -*inus*: pert. to, charact. by; see -INE¹) + E. -*e*: silent
final letter; or < G. -*in(ē)*: fem. abstract *n*-forming suffix + E. -*e*: silent final
letter, *125*
inebriety, see under -ETY
ineffi**cient**, *98*, **109**
INELIGIBLE (in·el´i·jə·bəl) *adj.* not qualified to run for office, enter a contest,
apply for a scholarship, etc. **[in- + e- + -lig- + -i- + -bl- + -e]** < L. *in-*: not,
without + *ē-* (var. of EX-¹ used before most consonants): out of, from, forth +
-*lig(ere)* (comb. form of *legere*): to gather, to choose, to read + -*i*-: conn.
vowel + -*b(i)l(is)*: tending to (be), inclined to (be) + E. -*e*: silent final letter.
RECON: *not* (**in-**) *inclined to* (**-bl-**) *choose* (**-lig-**) *out of* (**e-**). SEC. DISS: [in-
+ e- + -lig- + -**ible**] Note: L. -*i*-: conn. vowel + -*b(i)l(is)*: tending to (be),
inclined to (be) + E. -*e*: silent final letter > the E. *adj*-forming suffix -IBLE,
having the expanded meaning (influenced, in part, by confusion with E. *able*
< L. *(h)abilis*: easy to hold or handle; skillful [< *habēre*: to have, to hold]—a
word completely unrelated to L. -*bilis*): able to (be), capable of (being),

tending to (be), inclined to (be). SEC. RECON: *not* (**in-**) *able* (**-ible**) *to choose*
(**-lig-**) *out of* (**e-**), 89, 94
ineluctable, 216
inertia, see under -IA
inevitable, see under NOCENT
inexorable, see under EX-¹
inf**ant**icide, 14 (as a guide to understanding the HELPFUL HINTS), **56**, **102**
infantile paralysis, 67
infantry (in´fən·trē) n. **1.** soldiers or other military forces that fight on or are
trained and equipped to fight on foot, as with rifles, machine guns,
flamethrowers, bazookas, etc. **2.** (*I-*) a military unit of such soldiers: *the 59th
Infantry*. **[in- + f- + -ant- + -ry]** < L *in-*: not, without + *f(ārī)*: to speak +
-*ant(is)* (gen. of -*āns*): prpl. suffix having the inflectional meaning: being,
having, doing, performing, or manifesting (that which is designated by the
preceding verb base), equivalent in meaning to E. participles ending in -*ing*
(see -ANT for further information) + E. -*ry*: a *n*-forming suffix having, in this
context, the restricted meaning: a group or body of (those who are designated by the preceding base or elements) (< OF. -*erie*, ult. < L. -*ārius*: pert.
to, charact. by). RECON: *a group or body of those* (**-ry**) *not* (**in-**) *speak-* (**f-**)
-*ing* (**-ant-**). But how did this rather odd etymological meaning evolve into
the modern definition of *infantry*? Originally, Latin *infāns* referred to a baby
or young child who had not yet begun to speak—the source, of course, of
English *infant*. But as the Latin language grew, so too did the child denoted
by *infāns*, and soon *infāns* referred to any child, regardless of age or ability
to speak. Then, when Latin *infāns* passed into Old French as *enfant* and into
Old Italian as *infant*, these words came to refer not only to a child but, more
specifically, to a teenage boy and, in time, to those teenage boys who followed and attended a mounted knight *on foot*. And thus in Old Italian,
infanteria arose to designate a "band of young men on foot"—and from here
it was but a simple transition to a "band of young fighting men on foot" and,
hence, English *infantry*, 81
infidel, 206
Infinitives, 214-17
infix, 198, see also under -AN
inflammable, 94
INFLAMMATION OF, THE (**-ITIS**), 66–68
influentia, 132
influenza, *132*, see also under -ENZ- and -A³
infomercial, 131
informal, 82
-ing, *73*, *82*, *85*, *89*, **105**, *121*, *132*, *155*, see also under -ANT and -ENT
-inger, *107*
in**gress**, *80*, **106**
inhabit, 220
inhabitable, 94, 221
initial, see under VOLITION
in memoriam, 148
innocuous, see under NOCENT
insane, 94, see also under NOCENT
inscribe, 215
insect, 142, see under ENTOM-
insect(um) (animale), 142
INSENSATE (in·sen´sāt´, -sit) *adj.* lacking feeling, sensation, compassion, or
sense of reason. **[in- + sens- + -at- + -e]** < L *in-*: not, without + *sēns(us)*:
sensation, feeling, understanding + -*āt-* (base of -*ātus*): ppl. suffix with the
inflectional meaning: having been or having had; in E. (without the macron),
also meaning: having, possessing, or charact. by + E. -*e*: silent final letter.
RECON: *not* (**in-**) *having had* (**-at-**) *sensation* (**sens-**). SEC. DISS: [in- + sens-
+ -**ate**] Note: L. -*āt-* (base of -*ātus*): having been, having had + E. -*e*: silent
final letter > the E. *adj*-forming suffix -ATE, having, in this entry, the basic
meaning: having, having been, possessing, or charact. by. SEC. RECON: *not*
(**in-**) *having* (**-ate-**) *sensation* (**sens-**), 79
INSOMNIA (in·säm´nē·ə) n. difficulty in falling or remaining asleep, esp. when
chronic. **[in- + somn- + -ia]** < L *in-*: not, without + *somn(us)*: sleep + -*ia*:
the state, condition, or result of. RECON: *the state, condition, or result of*
(**-ia**) *not* (**in-**) *sleeping* (**somn-**), 53, 94, see also under -IA
instant, see under STA-¹
intendant, see under -ANT,-ENT, and SUPERINTENDENT
intensives, 181, 238
inter-, *108*, *108*, *107*, *107*, *114*, *122*
inter**action**, *89*, **108**
interfenestral, 114
interhabitation, 222
INTERIOR DESIGN, 121
interjacent, see under JAC-²
interjaculate, see under JAC-¹
inter**locution**, *83*, **107**
inter**locutor**, *83*, **107**
inter**locutory**, *83*, **107**
international, see under -AL
internuncial, see under CADUCEUS
intervention, 122
in the catbird seat, 151
in the lineup, 152
in there pitching, 152
intra-articularly, see under HYPODERMIC NEEDLE
intramuscularly, see under HYPODERMIC NEEDLE

intransigent, 89, see also under -IG-

intraspinally, see under HYPODERMIC NEEDLE

intravenously, see under HYPODERMIC NEEDLE

intro- < L. *intrō-* (a prefixal form of the adverb *intrō*): in, into, within: INTRO-DUCTION, *introspection* (a contemplation or self-examination of one's inner feelings, attitudes, beliefs, and other emotional, rather than intellectual, states), *intromission* (the act or process of introducing or permitting to enter; also, the insertion or placing of something within something else), *1*

INTRODUCTION, 1-41

Introduction, xi, 1

introduction, 1, 76, see also under INTRO-

introduction, xi, 1

intromission, see under INTRO-

introspection, see under INTRO-

Inuit, see under IGLOO

-īn(us), 106, see also under -IN-

inveigh (in·vā΄) *v.* to protest vehemently (vĕ΄ə·mənt·lē; intensely and passionately) or criticize harshly; rail (usu. followed by *against*): *to inveigh against social injustice.* **[in- + veigh-]** < L. *in-*: in, into, within, on + *veh(ere)*: to carry, to convey, to drive. RECON: *to drive* (**veigh-**) *into* (**in-**). When we harshly criticize someone or something, we verbally "drive into" that person or thing; cf. AGGRESSION and INTRANSIGENT, 55

-iō, 75, 72, 78, 84, 88, 97, *passim*

iodine, 147

iodine, 245, see also under -INE²

-ion, *xix*, 58, 72, 73, **75**, 75, **78**, 78, 79, 82, 83, **84**, 84, **88**, 88, 89, **97**, 97, **107**, *107*, **109**, *123*, *passim*

-iōnis, 72, 75, 88, 97, 78, 84, 109, *passim*

I perish for her touch, 64

Iranian, see under INDO-EUROPEAN

irid- < G. *irid-*, base of *iridos*, gen. of *iris*: rainbow, goddess of the rainbow, iris (both of the eye and the flower), 121

iridescent, 121, see also under -SC-

iridium, 121

Iris, 121

iris, 121

irrational, see under IN-²

irreversible, see under IN-²

irrigation, see under IN-¹

irruption, see under IN-¹

-is-, 81

is-¹ < G. *is-*, base of *isos*: equal: *isotherm* (ī΄sə·thûrm΄; a line on a weather map, graph, etc., connecting points of equal temperature), *isobar* (ī΄sə·bär΄; a line on a weather map, graph, etc., connecting points of equal barometric pressure), PANTISOCRACY, **101**

is-² < G. *(e)is-*: into: ISAGOGE, ISAGOGICS, *isagogical*, **103**

isagoge, 47, 101, see also under IS-² (preceding entry)

isagogical, see under is-²

isagogics, 47, 101, 126, see also under IS-²

-isc, 101

-ish (ish) a native E. *adj*-forming suffix having a variety of associated meanings: **1.** having the qualities or characteristics of, like: *sheepish, boyish.* **2.** tending or inclined to: *thievish, devilish.* **3.** somewhat; rather; slightly: *greenish, sweetish.* **4.** approximately (but usu. somewhat over): *thirtyish, fiftyish.* **5.** of, belonging to, or characteristic of that country, people, tribe, etc. (specified by the preceding base or elements): *English, Spanish, Frankish.* **[-ish]** < OE. *-isc*: -ish, but do not confuse with Fr-derived *-ish* (see under ANTIDISESTABLISHMENTARIANISM), **101**

-ism (iz΄m) a G-derived *n*-forming suffix having a wide variety of sometimes vaguely associated meanings: **1.** the quality, state, or condition of: *pauperism* (the state of being penniless or of living on welfare or charity), *hypnotism* (see HYPNOSIS). **2.** the act, practice, or result of: SOMNAMBULISM, *nepotism* (favoritism shown to relatives, esp. in appointing them to political or other positions). **3.** the beliefs, theory, school, or doctrine of: SOCIALISM, SOLIPSISM, ANTIDISESTABLISHMENTARIANISM. **4.** adherence to or display of (a particular belief, doctrine, or attitude): *nationalism, sexism.* **5.** a distinctive usage or characteristic of, esp. in language: *Latinism, spoonerism* (an unintentional transposition of spoken sounds in one or more words, as "to patch a Hun" for "to hatch a pun"). **6.** an abnormal medical condition, esp. one characterized by an excess of or preoccupation with: *alcoholism, autism* (ô΄tiz·΄m; a psychotic detachment from reality, esp. in children, characterized by a total immersion in self, fantasies, and daydreams). **[-ism]** < G. *-ism(os)*: the act or the result of the act of (< -is-: final letter of the base of denom. verbs ending in *-izein* + *-m(os)*: the act or the result of the act of), 86, **101**, *101*, **107**, *107*, **109**, *109*, 126

I smell a rat, 151

-ism(os), *61*, *101*, see also under -ISM

isobar, see under IS-¹

is(os), 103

isotherm, see under IS-¹

-ist (ist, əst) a G-derived *n*-forming suffix generally corresponding to nouns ending in -ISM (and, less frequently, verbs ending in *-ize*), having two classes of broadly associated meanings: **1.** a person who believes in, adheres to, or practices (a specified doctrine, activity, etc.): *fascist, sexist, somnambulist* (a sleepwalker; see SOMNAMBULISM). **2.** a person who is skilled in, works with, performs on, etc. (that which is designated by the preceding base or elements): LINGUIST, *botanist, podiatrist* (a foot doctor), *accordionist*. **[-ist]** < G. *-ist(ēs)*: one who believes in, adheres to, works with, is skilled in, or is otherwise associated with (that which is designated by the previous base or elements)(< -is-: final letter of the base of denom. verbs ending in *-izein* + *-t(ēs)*: one who or that which), *81*, *81*, 101

-istēs, 81

Italic, see under INDO-EUROPEAN

itēs, 66, 67, 102

-iti(a), 107

itinerant (ī·tin΄ər·ənt, i·tin΄-) *adj.* **1.** traveling from place to place, esp. as part of a job or mission; PERIPATETIC: *itinerant farm hands; itinerant preachers.* —*n.* **2.** any person who travels from place to place. **[itiner- + -ant]** < L. *itiner(is)* (gen. of *iter*): a walk, journey (< or akin to *īre*: to go) + *-ant(is)* (gen. of *-āns*): prpl. suffix having the inflectional meaning: being, having, doing, performing, or manifesting (that which is designated by the preceding verb base), equivalent in meaning to E. participles ending in *-ing*, but also having the SUBSTANTIVE meaning: one who or that which (performs the action designated by the preceding verb base); see -ANT for further information. RECON: *walk-* (**itiner-**) *-ing* (**-ant**), 78

-ITIS, 66–68

-itis, 66, 66, 67, 102, 102

-ity (i·tē, ə·tē) a L-derived *n*-forming suffix having the closely related abstract meanings: the quality, state, or condition of: HYPERACTIVITY, *perspicacity* (pûr΄spi·kas΄i·tē; the quality of having or showing penetrating insight and keen understanding, esp. in areas that others find puzzling or inscrutable), *perspicuity* (pûr΄spi·kyo͞o΄i·tē; the quality or result of being clearly expressed and easy to understand, esp. in speech or writing; lucidity of expression). **[-i- + -ty]** < L. *-i-*: conn. vowel + *-tās*: the quality, state, or condition of. For further information and examples see -TY and -ETY; (**101**, **106**, **107**)

-ium, 90, **107**, *107*, see also under MENINGIOMA

-iv- < L. *-īv*, base of *-īvus*: tending to (be), inclined to (be). **Note:** L. *-īvus*: tending to (be), inclined to (be) + E. *-e*: silent final letter > the E. *adj*-forming suffix -IVE (see following entry), *63*, 63, 88, 104, **106**, 108, 109

-ive (īv) a L-derived *adj*-forming suffix having two common meanings: **1.** tending to (be), inclined to (be): *abortive, disruptive,* PROGRESSIVE. **2.** pert. to, charact. by, having the nature of, like: *native, distinctive, massive.* **[-iv + -e]** < L. *-īv(us)*: tending to (be), inclined to (be) + E. *-e*: silent final letter, *63*, (88), (**108**)

-īvus, 63

-īv(us), 97, 108, 109, 106

-izein, 81

jac-¹ < L. *jac-*, base of *jacere*: to throw: *jaculate* (to throw or hurl), *ejaculate* (etymologically, to throw or hurl out of; see E-), *interjaculate* (to blurt out or interject abruptly during a conversation; see INTER-).

jac-² < L. *jac-*, base of *jacēre*: to be thrown, to lie, to rest: *adjacent,* CIRCUMJACENT, *interjacent* (lying between or among others; intervening), **103**

Jacob, see under BENJAMIN

jactat- < L. *jactāt-*, base of *jactātus*, pp. of *jactāre*, freq. of *jacere*, to throw: *jactation* (bragging, boasting; also, a restless jerking of the body during a high fever or other illness); cf. JACTITAT-.

jactation, see under JACTAT-

jactitat- < L. *jactitāt-*, base of *jactitātus*, pp. of *jactitāre*, freq. of *jactāre*, freq. of *jacere*, to throw: *jactitation* (in law, a false claim or boast that causes harm or injury to another); cf. JACTAT-

jactitation, see under JACTITAT- (preceding entry)

jaculate, see under JAC-¹

jalousie, 121

jeans, 135

Jell-O, 133

Jerusalem artichoke, *xviii*

Jesus Christ, 262

Jewish, 230, see also under INDO-EUROPEAN

jihad, 138

Johnson, Samuel, 73, 49

jointure, see under -URE

jov- < L. *Jov-*, base of *Jovis*, used as a gen. of *Jupiter* and its var. *Juppiter*: Jupiter, *136*

jovial, 136, *136*

jūris, 109
juvenile (jōō´və·n'l, -nīl´) *adj.* **1.** young, youthful, or immature. —*n.* **2.** a child or youth. **[juven- + -il- + -e]** < L. *juven(is)*: young, youthful + *-īl(is)*: pert. to, charact. by E. *-e*: silent final letter. RECON: *charact. by* (**-il-**) *youth* (**juven-**). SEC. DISS: [juven- + **-ile**] Note: L. *-īl(is)*: pert. to, charact. by + E. *-e*: silent final letter > the E. *adj*-forming suffix -ILE, also meaning: pert. to, charact. by. SEC. RECON: *charact. by* (**-ile**) *youth* (**juven-**), 213
juxtapose, see under COLLOCATE
juxtaposition, see under COLLOCATION

KAKISTOCRACY (kak´ə·stäk´rə·sē) *n.* government by the worst people. **[kak- + -ist- + -o- + crac- + -y]** < G. *kak(os)*: bad + *-ist(os)*: superl. suffix having the basic meaning: of the highest degree or order; most (cf. L. *-issimus*; and do not confuse G. *-ist(os)* with G. *-ist(ēs)*: one who) + *-o-*: conn. vowel + *krat(os)*: strength, power, rule (> *kratein*: to rule) + E. *-y*: the act, process, condition, or result of (< G. *-ia*). RECON: *the act, process, or result of* (**-y**) *rule* (**crac-**) *by the most* (**-ist-**) *bad* (**kak-**). SEC. DISS: [kakist- + -o- + -cracy] Note: G. *kak(os)*: bad + *-ist(os)*: most > *kakist(os)*: most bad, hence worst. Also note: G. *krat(os)*: strength, power, rule + *-ia*: the act, process, condition, or result of > G. *-kratia*: the act of ruling; hence, a ruling, government > the E. *n*-forming comb. form -CRACY: rule by or government of. SEC. RECON: *rule by or government of* (**-cracy**) *the worst* (**kakist-**). But how did Greek *-kratia* evolve into English *-cracy*? First, Greek *-kratia* passed into Late Latin, in which the Greek *-k-* characteristically became a Latin *-c-*, resulting in Late Latin *-cratia* (see LATINIZATION for an explanation of this process). From here, *-cratia* entered Middle French in which the two syllables of *-tia* gradually ELIDED to form the monosyllabic *-cie*, yielding the Middle French combining form *-(cra)cie*. This form then passed into English in which, because English *-ie* and *-y* often have the same meaning and pronunciation but *-y* is the more naturalized spelling, Middle French *-cracie* (F. *-kratie*) became Modern English *-cracy*, 60, 84

KATHISOMANIA (kath´i·sō·mā´nē·ə) *n.* an overwhelming desire or compulsion to sit; cf. CLINOMANIA. [< G. *kathis(is)*: sitting (< *kat(a)*: down, downward + *his(ma)*: foundation, seat [< *hizein*: to seat]) + *-o-*: conn. vowel + -MANIA] 145
kinesics (ki·nē´siks, kī-) *n.* the study of body movements, gestures, expressions, blushes, etc., as forms of nonverbal communication; cf. *body language*. **[kine- + -s- + -ics]** < G. *kinē-* (base of *kinein*): to move + *-s(is)*: the act, process, condition, or result of + E. -ICS: a *n*-forming suffix, having, in this entry, the modern definition: the art, science, study, or discipline of (< L. *-ic(a)* [neut. pl. of *-icus*]: pert. to, charact. by [< G. *-ik(a)*, neut. pl. of *-ikos*] + E. *-s* [< OE. *-as*]: pl. suffix, used in this context as a substitution for G. *-a*). RECON: *the science or study of* (**-ics**) *the act, process or result of* (**-s-**) *moving* (**kine-**), 120
KINESOMANIA (ki·nē´sō·mā´nē·ə) *n.* an extreme enthusiasm for or compulsion for movement. [< G. *kinē-* (base of *kinein*): to move + *-s(is)*: the act, process, condition, or result of + *-o-*: conn. vowel + -MANIA], 145

kinetics (ki·net´iks, kī-) *n.* **1.** the branch of mechanics dealing with the motion of masses, as planets or satellites, and the forces responsible for producing or altering these motions; dynamics. **2.** the branch of chemistry dealing with the measurement and rates of change of chemical reactions. **[kine- + -t- + -ics]** < G. *kinē-* (base of *kinein*): to move + *-t(os)*: verbal suffix with the inflectional meaning: having been or having had (that which is designated by the preceding verb base) + E. -ICS: a *n*-forming suffix, having, in this entry, the modern definition: the art, science, study, or discipline of (< L. *-ic(a)* [neut. pl. of *-icus*]: pert. to, charact. by [< G. *-ik(a)*, neut. pl. of *-ikos*] + E. *-s* [< OE. *-as*]: pl. suffix, used in this context as a substitution for G. *-a*). RECON: *the science or study of* (**-ics**) *having been* (**-t-**) *moved* (**kine-**), 118, 120, see also under -ICS
klept- < G. *klept-*, base of *kleptēs*: a thief (< *klep-* [base of *kleptein*]: to steal + *-tēs*: one who or that which), 49
klepto- < G. *klepto-* < *klep-* (base of *kleptein*): to steal + *-t-* (< *-tēs*): one who or that which + *-o-*: conn. vowel, 144
KLEPTOMANIA (klep´tō·mā´nē·ə, klep´tə-) *n.* a compulsion or irresistible urge to steal things, arising from psychological, rather than economic, need. **[klep- + -t- + -o- + man- + -ia]** < G. *klep(tein)*: to steal + *-t(ēs)*: one who or that which + *-o-*: conn. vowel + *ma(i)n(esthai)*: to rage, to go mad + *-ia*: the act, process, condition, or result of. RECON: *the act or condition of* (**-ia**) *one who* (**-t-**) *rages* (**man-**) *to steal* (**klep-**). SEC. DISS: [klepto- + -mania] Note: G. *klep(tein)*: to steal + *-t(ēs)*: one who or that which + *-o-*: conn. vowel > G. *klepto-*: one who steals; thief > the E. comb. form *klepto-*: thief, theft, stealing. Also note: G. *ma(i)n(esthai)*: to rage, to go mad + *-ia*: the act, process, condition, or result of > G. *mania*: madness > the E. *n*-forming comb. form -MANIA, having the modern medical meaning: a mental disorder or aberration charact. by an extreme enthusiasm for, preoccupation with, or compulsion for (that which is designated by the preceding base or elements). SEC. RECON: *a compulsion for* (**-mania**) *stealing* (**klepto-**), 36, 49
KONIOPHOBIA (kō´nē·ə·fō´bē·ə) *n.* an abnormal dislike or aversion to dust, as in a mine; AMATHOPHOBIA. [< G. *koni(s)*: dust, ashes + *-o-*: conn. vowel + -PHOBIA], 143

l' (Fr.): the definite article *the*, a contraction of *le* (masc.) (< L. *ille*: that) or *la* (fem.) (< L. *illa*: that) used before words beginning with a vowel or *h*, *138*
labi-, 108
lab(ium), 108
laboratory, 265
LACKING, NOT, WITHOUT (A-, AN-), **69–71**
lacrimation, see under PHOTOPHOBIA
lacteous circle, see under GALACTIC
LALIOPHOBIA (lal´ē·ə·fō´bē·ə, lā´lē-) *n.* an abnormal fear or dread of speaking, as in public or by one who stutters. Many people experience a touch of laliophobia when they make a phone call and get someone's answering machine. [< G. *lal(ein)*: to babble, chatter, prattle + *-i(a)*: the act, state, condition, or result of + *-o-*: conn. vowel + -PHOBIA], 143
land of Nod, 137
language (lang´gwij) *n.* **1.** a system for communicating thoughts and feelings through combinations of vocal sounds and other symbols, generally understood by members of the same nation, geographical area, ethnic stock, etc. **2.** a particular style or type of verbal expression: *coarse, vulgar language.* **3.** the specialized terminology of a particular science, profession, or group: *the language of medicine.* [**langu-** + **-age**] < OF. *langu(e)* (< L. *lingua*): tongue, speech, language + *-age*: the quality, state, condition; act, means, result, or process of (< L. *-āticum*, neut. of *-āticus*: pert. to, charact. by, having [< either *-āt(us)*: having been, having had + *-icus*: pert. to, charact. by OR < L. words ending in *-ā* (cf. -A-¹) + *-ticus*: pert. to, charact. by]). **RECON:** *the act, result, or condition of* (**-age**) *speech* (**langu-**), *92*
lapid-, 109
lapidary, see under -ARY
lapidification, 98, **109**
lapid(is) (lapis), 109
lapis lazuli, 115
"Largest Racecourse," see under CIRCUS
laryng-, 104
laryngeal, 254
laryngitis, 68, **104**, *254*
laryngologist, 254
laryngology, 254
laryngopharyngeal (lə·ring´gō·fə·rin´jē·əl) *adj.* pertaining to the LARYNX and PHARYNX. [**laryng-** + **-o-** + **pharyng-** + **-e-** + **-al**] < G. *laryng(os)* (gen. of *larynx*): upper windpipe, larynx + *-o-*: conn. vowel (in this context rep. "and") + G. *pharyng(os)* (gen. of *pharynx*): throat, gullet, pharynx + L. *-e(us)*: pert. to + *-āl(is)*: pert. to, charact. by. **RECON:** *charact. by* (**-al**) *pert. to* (**-e-**) *the upper windpipe* (**laryng-**) *and throat* (**pharyng-**) OR (when attributing "and" to *-o-*) *charact. by* (**-al**) *pert. to* (**-e-**) *the upper windpipe* (**laryng-**) *and* (**-o-**) *throat* (**pharyng-**); cf. HEPATOCYSTIC, CERVICOFACIAL, and NEPHROCARDIAC, *254*
laryng(os) (larynx), 104
laryngoscopy (lar´ing·gäs´kə·pē) *n.* a visual examination of the interior of the LARYNX with a laryngoscope (lə·ring´gə·skōp´; a long, slender optical instrument equipped with a telescopic lens, light, and surgical cutter, used for examining and performing local surgery on the larynx). [**laryng-** + **-o-** + **scop-** + **-y**] < G. *laryng(os)* (gen. of *larynx*): upper windpipe, larynx + *skop(ein)*: to look, to see, to behold + E. *-y*: the act, process, condition, or result of (< G. *-ia*). **RECON:** *the act, process, or result of* (**-y**) *seeing* (**scop-**) *the upper windpipe or larynx* (**laryng-**). **SEC. DISS:** [laryng- + -o- + **-scopy**] **Note:** G. *skop(ein)*: to look, to see, to behold + E. *-y*: the act, process, condition, or result of > the E. *n*-forming comb. form *-scopy*, having, in this context, the modern medical meaning: a visual examination of (that anatomical structure or part specified by the preceding base or elements). **SEC. RECON:** *a visual examination of* (**-scopy**) *the upper windpipe or larynx* (**laryng-**), *254*
lasagna, see under VERMICELLI
laser, 130
LATIN, 175–228
LATIN, UNDERSTANDING, 187-90

lob-, 103
lob(os), 103
LOBOTOMY (lə·bät′ə·mē, lō-) *n.* the surgical cutting or incision of a lobe of the brain, esp. the prefrontal lobe. **[lob- + -o- + tom- + -y]** < G. *lob(os):* lobe, vegetable pod + *-o-:* conn. vowel + *tom(ē):* a cutting (< *temnein:* to cut) + E. *-y:* the act, process, condition, or result of (< G. *-ia).* RECON: *the act, process, or result of* **(-y)** *cutting* **(tom-)** *a lobe* **(lob-).** SEC. DISS: [lob- + -o- + -tomy] Note: G. *tom(ē):* a cutting + *-ia:* the act, process, condition, or result of > G. *-tomia:* a cutting > the E. *n*-forming comb. form -TOMY, having, in this entry, the modern medical meaning: the surgical cutting or incision of (that anatomical structure or part specified by the preceding base or elements) *without* the removal of that which is cut; cf. PHLEBOTOMY. SEC. RECON: *the surgical incision of* **(-tomy)** *a lobe* **(lob-),** 52, 70, see also under -TOMY, -STOMY, and -ECTOMY
loc-,
locale (lō·kal′) *n.* **1.** the place or location with which a particular event, condition, or set of circumstances is associated: *What is the locale of the Summer Olympics?* **2.** the scene or setting, as of a movie, play, novel, etc. **[loc- + -al- + -e]** < L. *loc(us):* a place, site + *-āl(is):* pert. to, charact. by + E. *-e:* silent final letter. RECON: *pert. to* **(-al-)** *a place or site* **(loc-).** In this word, the *-al-* was converted in French from an adjective-forming suffix to a noun-forming suffix before the addition, in the early 19th century, of English *-e, 81*
locus, 81
LOCUT- (LOQU-), 81–83
locut-, *81, 81, 82, 83,* **103,** *123*
locution, 83, **107**
locution**ary,** 83, **107**
locut**ory,** 83, **107**
locutus, 81
locūt(us) (loquī), 103
log-, *61, 81,* **101**
LOGICAL (läj′i·k′l) *adj.* rationally and sensibly thought out. **[log- + -ic- + -al]** < G. *log(os):* word, speech, thought, reckoning (< *legein:* to gather, to choose, to speak) + *-ik(os):* pert. to, charact. by + L. *-āl(is):* pert. to, charact. by. RECON: *charact. by* **(-al)** *pert. to* **(-ic-)** *thought or reckoning* **(log-),** 78
LOGOMANIA *n.* a compulsion for nonstop, repetitive talking, often seen as part of a manic state; excessive LOGORRHEA. [< G. *log(os):* word, speech, discourse (< *legein:* to gather, to choose, to speak) + *-o-:* conn. vowel + -MANIA], 145, see also under MAN-²
logophilia, 61
logorrhea, 61, 155
log(os), 61, 101
-LOGY (lə·jē) a G-derived *n*-forming comb. form having two clearly differentiated meanings: **1.** the science, study, theory, or doctrine of: BIOLOGY, GYNECOLOGY, *mycology* (the scientific study of fungi < G. *myk(ēs):* mushroom, fungus + *-o-:* conn. vowel + *-logy).* **2.** a writing or speaking (in the manner specified by the preceding base or elements): EULOGY, *trilogy, tetralogy* (a series of four related plays, novels, operas, etc.). **[log- + -y]** < G. *-log(os):*

word, thought, reason, reckoning, speech, discourse; also, one who deals with, treats, or studies (< *legein:* to gather, to choose, to speak) + E. *-y:* the act, process, condition, or result of (< G. *-ia).* RECON: *the act or process of* **(-y)** *thought* **(log-)** *about* [*that which is designated by the preceding base or elements*]. For a suffix with a similar meaning, see -ICS; 52, (70)
-log(y), 139, see also under -LOGY (preceding entry)
looked, see under PURPORTEDLY and SOPHISTICATED
LOQU-, LOCUT-, 11, 81–83
loqu-, 81, 81, 82
loqu**acious,** 83, **107**
loquī, 81
loqu(ī), 81
loran, 130
Louis XVI, *134*
Louis, Dr. Antoine, *134*
Louisette, La, 134
louse (sing. of *lice*), see under PED-³
lucidity, see under -ITY
ludicrous, 196
luminescent, see under -SC-
LUNAR (loō′nər) *adj.* **1.** of or relating to the moon: *the lunar landscape.* **2.** like or resembling the moon; circular or lunate (crescent-shaped): *a lunar design.* **[lun- + -ar]** < L. *lun(a):* moon + *-ār(is):* pert. to, charact. by. RECON: *pert. to* **(-ar)** *the moon* **(lun-),** 92
lunate, see under LUNAR
lunatic, see under -IC
lupicide, 56
lupine, 148
lupus, 56
lute-, 109
lūte(us), 109
-ly¹ (lē) a native E. *adj*-forming suffix having two common meanings: **1.** having the qualities or nature of, like: *brotherly, heavenly.* **2.** happening or occurring at or during (a specified time or time period): *yearly, daily* (as in the phrase, "a daily occurrence"). **[-ly]** < OE. *-līc:* having the form or shape of (a suffixal form of *gelīc:* like).
-ly² (lē) a native E. *adv*-forming suffix having a variety of closely associated meanings: **1.** with regard or respect to: PHONETICALLY, ORTHOGRAPHICALLY. **2.** in the manner of: *gladly, generally.* **3.** to the degree of: *greatly, badly.* **4.** in the direction of or from: *northwardly, southwardly.* **5.** in the sequence of: *firstly, secondly.* **6.** at the time of, or during the time interval of: *recently, daily* (as in the sentence, "The trains run daily"). **[-ly]** < OE. *-līce* (< *-līc:* adj. suffix + *-e:* adv. suffix), **101, 105,** *259*
lycanthropy, 155
Lyceum, see under ANALECTS and PERIPATETIC
lyein, 259
Lynch, William, see under EPI-
lynch, epi-1
LYSSOPHOBIA (lis′ō·fō′bē·ə) *n.* an irrational fear or dread of insanity. [< G. *lyss(a):* madness, rage, fury, rabies + *-o-:* conn. vowel + -PHOBIA], 143

---

macropicide, 56, **102**
Mae West, *134*
magn-, 107
magn**iloquent,** 83, **107**
magn(us), 107
maieusophobia, 142
maieutic, 126
ma(i)n(esthai), 101
TO MAKE, TO DO **(FACT-, -FECT-, FAC-, -FIC-, -FY), 96–98**
make a clean break, *153*
make a comeback, *153*
mal, 84, 84, 86
MAL-, MALE- (MAL, MALUM), 84–86
mal-, 84, 85
mala aria, 86
mal**adroit,** 86, **107**
mal**aise,** 86, **107**
malaria, 85, *86*
mal' aria, 86
malariology, 86
mal de la **rosa,** 86, **107**
mal del **pinto,** 86, **107**
mal de mer, 84, 86
mal du **pays,** 86, **107**
mal du **siècle,** 86, **107**
male-, 84, 84, 85
male¹ (E.), *84*
male² (L.), *72, 84*

mal(e) chauvinist pig, 84, *84*
malediction, *72,* **84**
malefactor, *72,* **84,** *85*
malefic, *72,* **85,** *85*
malevolent, *72,* **84,** *85,* see also under VOL-¹
mal**feasance,** 86, **107,** *122*
mal**function,** 86, **107**
mal**icious,** 86, **107**
mal**ign,** 86, **107**
mal**ignant,** 86, **107**
mal**ignity,** 86, **107**
mal**inger,** 86, **107**
mal**ism,** 86, **107**
malison, 72
mal**nutrition,** 86, **107**
mal**occlusion,** 86, **107**
mal**odorous,** 86, **107**
mal**practice,** 86, **107**
malum, 84
malum coxae, 86, **107**
malum coxae senilis, 86, **107**
malum venereum, 84
malus, 84
mama, see under BONBON
mammae (mam′ē) *pl. n., sing.* mamma (mam′ə). the milk-secreting glands present in all mammals but only functional in the female; breasts; udders. **[mamm- + -ae]** < L. *mamm(a):* breast, mother + *-ae:* pl. suffix. RECON: *breast-* **(mamm-)** *-s* **(-ae),** 47

mammoplasty, 264

man-¹ < L. *man-* or *manu-*, bases of *manus*: hand: MANUSCRIPT, MANACLE, EMANCIPATION PROCLAMATION, **108**

man-² < G. *man-*, base of *mainesthai*: to rage, to go mad: *maniac*, LOGOMANIA, BIBLIOKLEPTOMANIA, **101**, *144*

manacle, 204, see also under MAN-¹

manc- < G. *mant-*, base of *manteia*: divination, prophecy < *mant-* (base of *mantis*): prophet, seer + *-eia*: the act, process, condition, or result of. Greek *-manteia*, the combining form of *manteia*, became *-mantía* in Latin. This form then passed into Old French in which the DISYLLABIC *-tía* ELIDED into the monosyllabic *-cie*, thereby converting *-mantía* into *-mancie*. From here *-mancie* passed into Middle English where the *-ie* became *-y*, resulting in Modern English *-mancy*, 150

-MANCY, PROPHETIC WORDS ENDING IN, 150

mandate, see under -ATE

-mania (mā′nē-ə, mān′yə) a G-derived *n*-forming suffix having the modern medical meaning: a mental disorder or aberration characterized by an extreme enthusiasm for, preoccupation with, or compulsion for (that which is designated by the preceding base or elements): KLEPTOMANIA, HIPPOMANIA, GYMNOMANIA, and *tulipomania* (an obsession with tulips, esp. prevalent in 17th century Holland). **[-man + -ia]** < G. *ma(i)n(esthai)*: to go mad + *-ia*: the act, process, condition or result of. **RECON:** *the act, condition, or result of* (**-ia**) *raging or going mad* (**-man**) *about* [*that which is designated by the preceding base or elements*]. For a semantically similar suffix, see the extended meaning of -ITIS; (49), *66*, *144*, *(145)*

maniac, see under MAN-²

MANIAS, 144

MANIAS, SIXTY-SIX, 145

manicure, 204

mannequin, 119

manual, 203

manualism, 203

manu<u>facture</u>, <u>98</u>, **109**, *204*

manumission, 204

man(us), 108

manuscript, 204, see also under MAN-¹

mar- < L. *mar-*, base of *maris*, gen. of *mare*: sea, *115*

march (borderland), see under DUKE

marchioness, see under DUKE

margrave, see under DUKE

Mariana Islands, see under MICRONESIA

mariticide, 55

marītus, 55

mark (borderland), see under DUKE

marquee, see under DUKE

marquess, see under DUKE

marquis, see under DUKE

marquisate, see under DUKE

marquise, see under DUKE

marquisette, 119, see also under DUKE

marsh fever, 86

Marshall Islands, see under BIKINI and MICRONESIA

maser, 130

masochism, 134

massive, see under -IVE

mast , 104, 105, 108

mast<u>itis</u>, <u>68</u>, **104**

mast(os), 104, 105, 108

māter, 55

matriarchy (mā′trē-är′kē) *n.* **1.** a form of social organization in which the mother or a revered female is head of the family, clan, or tribe, and in which descent and kinship are reckoned through the female line; cf. PATRIARCHY. **2.** a family, clan, tribe, or state governed by women or a woman. **[matr- + -i- + arch- + -y]** < L. *mātr(is)* (gen. of *māter*): mother (akin to G. *mētr(os)* [gen. of *mētēr*]: mother) + *-i-*: conn. vowel + G. *arch(os)*: first, chief, ruler (< *archein*: to rule, orig., to be first, to begin, to take the lead) + E. *-y*: the act, process, condition, or result of (< G. *-ia*). **RECON:** *the act, condition, or result of* (**-y**) *the mother* (**matr-**) *ruler* (**arch-**). **SEC. DISS:** [matr- + -archy]. **Note:** G. *arch(os)*: first, chief, ruler (< *archein*: to rule) + *-ia*: the act, process, condition, or result of > G. *-archia*: the act of ruling; hence, a ruling, government > the E. *n*-forming comb. form -ARCHY: rule by or government of. **SEC. RECON:** *rule by or government of* (-**archy**) *mothers* (**matr-**), *60*, see also under -ARCHY

matricide, 55

maudlin, 137

maximal, 212

mazel tov, 138

McCarthy, Cormac, 135

McKay's snow bunting, 65

meatus, see under FORESKIN

meddlesome, see under OFFICIOUS

MEDICINE, 124

medicine, see under -INE²

MEDITATION (med′i·tā′shən) *n.* the process of engaging in deep thought or contemplation. **[medit- + -at- + -ion]** < L. *meditā(rī)*: to contemplate, meditate + *-āt-* (base of *-ātus*), ppl. suffix with the inflectional meaning: having been or having had; in E. (without the macron), also meaning: having, possessing,

or charact. by + L. *-iōn(is)* (gen. of *-iō*): the act, means, or result of. **RECON:** *the act or result of* (**-ion**) *having been* (**-at-**) *contemplated* (**medit-**), 79, see also under TRANSCENDENTAL MEDITATION

meet your match, 153

Mefit(ei), 104

megalith, 238

megalomania, 144

melancholy, 147

Melanesia (mel′ə·nē′zhə, -shə) *n.* one of the three principal divisions of the central and western Pacific, constituting the region northeast of Australia, including the Solomon Islands, the Santa Cruz Islands, Vanuatu (vän′wä · tōō′; formerly, New Hebrides), and New Caledonia; cf. MICRONESIA and POLYNESIA. **[mela- + nes- + -ia]** < G. *mela(nos)* (gen. of *melas*): black + *nēs(os)*: island + *-ia*: the act, process, state, condition, or result of, but used in this context as a placename-forming suffix, having the related meanings: the country, land, territory, region, or place of. **RECON:** *the region of* (**-ia**) *black* (**micr-**) *islands* (**nes-**). Because of its proximity to New Guinea and aboriginal Australia, Melanesia is inhabited predominantly by people with dark skin, 147

Melanie, 147

meliorated, 98

Melissa, 148

MELISSOPHOBIA *n.* an intense and sometimes irrational fear or dread of bees, as by one who is allergic to bee stings; APIPHOBIA. [< G. *meliss(a)*: honeybee (var. of *melitta* < *meli*: honey) + *-o-*: conn. vowel + -PHOBIA], 143

mellifluous, see under SUPERMAN

MELOMANIA (mel′ō·mā′nē·ə) *n.* an extreme enthusiasm for, preoccupation with, or devotion to music. [< G. *mel(os)*: limb, musical piece, song + *-o-*: conn. vowel + -MANIA], 145

memo, 132

memoranda, 228

memorandum, 228

Memory Aid (how to use and benefit from), **5-6**, *32*

Mencken, H. L., see under EX-²

mening-, 104

meningeal (mə·nin′jē·əl) *adj.* of or relating to the MENINGES; cf. MENINGITIC. **[mening- + -e- + -al]** < G. *mēning(os)* (gen. of *mēninx*): membrane, brain membrane + L. *-e(us)*: pert. to + *-āl(is)*: pert. to, charact. by. **RECON:** *charact. by* (**-al**) *pert. to* (**-e-**) *the brain membrane* (**mening-**), 254

mēning(es), 104

meningioma (mə·nin′jē·ō′mə) *n.* a solid, slow-growing tumor in or along the MENINGES or other central nervous system structures. **[mening- + -i- + -oma]** Etymologically and orthographically (with regard to spelling), *meningioma* is a contraction of English *meningothelioma* (mə·ning′gō·thē′lē·ō′mə). Hence, *meningioma* is ult. < G. *mēning(os)* (gen. of *mēninx*): membrane, brain membrane + E. *(thel(i)um)*: a cellular tissue that covers a body surface or lines a cavity (< G. *thēl(ē)*: nipple, papilla [pə·pil′ə; any small nipplelike structure or projection] < NL. *-ium*: a scientific suffix used to form the name of chemical elements, ions, plant structures, anatomical parts, cellular tissues, etc. [< L. *-(i)um*: neut. sing. ending < G. *-(i)on*]) + E. *-oma*: a tumor or swelling of (< L. *-ō-*: conn. vowel [tech., the final letter of the base of denom. verbs ending in *-oun*] + *-ma*: the result of). **RECON:** *a tumor of* (**-oma**) *cellular tissue that covers or lines* (**-i-**) *the brain membrane* (**mening-**), *254*, see also under -O-³

meningitic (men′in·jit′ik) *adj.* of, relating to, or having MENINGITIS; cf. MENINGEAL. **[mening- + -it- + -ic]** < G. *mēning(os)* (gen. of *mēninx*): membrane, brain membrane + *-itis*: the inflammation of (< L. *-itis*): [understood to mean] the disease of [orig., abstracted from the phrase, *hē arthritis nosos*: the disease of the joint], fem. of the *adj*-forming suffix *-itēs*: of, relating to, belonging to, or having the characteristics of) + *-ik(os)*: pert. to, charact. by. **RECON:** *pert. to* (**-ic**) *the inflammation of* (**-it-**) *the brain membrane* (**mening-**), 254

mening<u>itis</u>, <u>68</u>, **104**, *254*

meningococcus (mə·ning′gō·käk′əs) *n.* a spherical or reniform (ren′ə·fôrm′, rē′nə-; kidney-shaped) bacterium that causes cerebrospinal meningitis (an acute form of meningitis affecting both the brain and spinal cord). **[mening- + -o- + -coccus]** < G. *mēning(os)* (gen. of *mēninx*): membrane, brain membrane + *-o-*: conn. vowel + NL. *coccus*: a spherical bacterium of (< G. *kokkos*: grain, seed, berry). **RECON:** *a spherical bacterium of* (**-coccus**) *the brain membrane* (**mening-**), 254

mē(n)s(is), 108

ment- < L. *ment-*, base of *mentis*, gen. of *mēns*: mind, **105**

-ment < L. *-ment*, base of *-mentum*: the act, means, or result of, *106*, *119*

ment(is) (*mēns*), 105

MENTULOMANIA (men′tyōō·lə·mā′nē·ə) *n.* a compulsion for or addiction to masturbation. [< G. *mentul(a)*: penis (cf. PHALLIC) + *-o-*: conn. vowel + -PHOBIA]. The etymology of this word suggests which sex is more prone to this disorder, 145

-ment(um), 106

mephit-, 104

mephit<u>is</u>, <u>68</u>, **104**

mer < Fr. *mer*: sea (< L. *mare*: sea; akin to OE. *mere*, as in MERMAID and MER-MAN), *86*

mercerization, 119

Mercury, see under CADUCEUS

mercy killing, see under EUTHANASIA

merit-, 103

meritocracy, 62, **103**
merit(um), 103
merkin, 155
MERMAID (mûr´mād´) *n.* an imaginary sea creature having the head, arms, and torso (the body of a person or animal excluding the head and limbs) of a woman and the tail of a fish; cf. MERMAN. [**mer-** + **maid**] < OE. *mer(e)*: sea, lake, pond (akin to Fr. *mer* as in MAL DE MER) + *mæ(g)d(en)*: young girl, virgin. **RECON:** *sea* (**mer-**) *virgin* (**maid**), 86
MERMAN (mûr´man´) *n.* an imaginary sea creature having the head, arms, and torso (the body of a person or animal excluding the head and limbs) of a man and the tail of a fish; cf. MERMAID. [**mer-** + **man**] < OE. *mer(e)*: sea, lake, pond (akin to Fr. *mer* as in MAL DE MER) + *man(n)*: human being, adult human male, man. **RECON:** *sea* (**mer-**) *man* (**maid**)
mes-, **108**
mesmerism, see under MESMEROMANIA (following entry)
MESMEROMANIA *n.* an extreme enthusiasm for or preoccupation with hypnotism. [< E. *mesmer(ism)*: hypnotism, "animal magnetism" (a former term for hypnotism, now generally restricted to a person's charm or power to attract or influence others, either through sex appeal or through one's overpowering presence) + *-o-*: conn. vowel + -MANIA]. *Mesmerism* was named after Dr. Franz Mesmer, an 18th century practitioner of what we now know to be hypnotism who, himself, believed that his effect upon subjects was caused more by his use of magnets than by his mastery of the art of inducing trances—hence, his focus upon animal (i.e., the lower, baser forms of human nature) magnetism, 145
mesohippus, 16, 246
mesomorph, 117
met-, **106**
metall-, **108**
metall(on), 108
metamorphosis, 244, see also under -OSIS
metaphor, 123
"metaphorical shift," see also under INCIDENT
metastasis, see under STA-²
metathesis (mə·tath´ə·sis, *not* met´ə·thē´sis) *n.* the transposition of sounds, letters, or syllables in a word, as in the shift from Old High German *hros* to Old English *hors*, yielding Modern English *horse*, or in the change of pronunciation of *ask* to the substandard "aks"; cf. METASTASIS. [**meta-** + **the-** + **-sis**] < G. *meta-*: with, after, between (but generally used in English with the meanings: changed in position, reversed; after, behind, beyond) + *the-* (base of *tithenai*): to put, to place + *-sis*: the act, process, condition, or result of. **RECON:** *the process or result of* (**-sis**) *placing* (**the-**) *after* (**meta-**), *xix,* see also under TONGUE and THE-²
metempsychosis, 126
methanol, see under ALCOHOL
metonymy, 123
metr-¹ < G. *metr-*, base of *metron*: measure: SYMMETRICAL, *metric system, metrology* (mi·träl´ə·jē; the science of weights and measures; cf. -LOGY), **104**
metr-² < G. *mētr-*, base of *mētra*: uterus: METRITIS, *metralgia* (mi·tral´jē·ə; pain in the uterus; cf. ALG- and -IA), *endometriosis* (en´dō·mē´trē·ō´sis; the appearance and growth of uterine lining in nonuterine parts of the body, as the ovaries, often resulting in pain and other pathological conditions; cf. END- and -OSIS)
mētr(a), 104
metralgia, see under METR-²
metric system, see under METR-¹
metritis, 68, **104,** see also under METR-²
metro, see under SUBWAY
Métro, see under SUBWAY
metrology, see under METR-¹
metr(on), 104, 106
micr- < G. *mikr-*, base of *mikros*: small, *xviii,* 120
microcephalus, xviii
Micronesia (mī´krə·nē´zhə, -shə) *n.* one of the three principal divisions of the central and western Pacific, constituting the region north of the equator and east of the Philippines, including the Mariana Islands, the Caroline Islands, the Marshall Islands, and the Gilbert Islands; cf. MELANESIA and POLYNESIA. [**micr-** + **-o-** + **nes-** + **-ia**] < G. *mikr(os)*: small + *nēs(os)*: island + *-ia*: the act, process, state, condition, or result of, but used in this context as a place-name-forming suffix, having the related meanings: the country, land, territory, region, or place of. **RECON:** *the region of* (**-ia**) *small* (**micr-**) *islands* (**nes-**). Micronesia is noted for its vast number of tiny islands. The Caroline Islands, for example, comprise almost a thousand pinpoints of land spanning an area of over 1,500 miles. Yet if put all together, they would scarcely equal the area of Los Angeles.
microscope, xviii
Middle English, 163-64
midriff, see under SCHIZOPHRENIA
milieu, see under PHATIC
milked, see under UNDAUNTED
Milky Way, see under GALACTIC
mille, 91
millennia, *pl.* of MILLENNIUM, see also under ALCOHOL
millennial < L. *mill(e)*: thousand + *-enn-* (comb. form of *annus*): year + *-i(um)*: orig., a *n*-forming suffix, but serving in this entry as a conn. vowel (cf. MILLENNIUM) + *-āl(is)*: pert. to, charact. by, *91*
millennium < L. *mill(e)*: thousand + *-enn-* (comb. form of *annus*): year (cf. CEN-

TENNIAL and BICENTENNIAL) + *-i(um)*: *n*-forming suffix (tech., the neut. sing. ending of L. nouns and adjs. of the second declension [< or akin to G. *-ion*], *91,* 146
millinery, 119
Milton, John, 46, 55
mimeograph, 133
(mi)mnē(skesthai), 105
ming- < L. *ming-*, base of *mingere*: to urinate, 155
minimal, 212
minimal brain dysfunction, see under HYPERACTIVITY
minimal chronic brain syndrome, see under HYPERACTIVITY
minimus, 212
minyan (min´yən, min·yän´, mēn·yän´) *n.* in Jewish law, the minimum number of persons required to be present for a public religious service, traditionally set at ten Jewish males above the age of thirteen. [**minyan**] < Heb. *minyān*: number, quantity, quorum, 46
mis-¹ < OE. *mis-* < *misse,* bad, wrong: mistake, misfortune, miscarriage, **106**
mis-² < G. *mis-*, base of *misein*: to hate, or *misos*: hatred: *misogyny* (mi·säj´ə·nē; hatred, fear, or mistrust of women), *misandry* (mis´an·drē; hatred, fear, or mistrust of men), *misogamy* (mi·säg´ə·mē; hatred, fear, or disgust of marriage), *misopedia* (hatred or dislike of children; cf. PEDOPHILIA)
misandry, see under MIS-²
miscarriage, see under MIS-¹
misconduct, 77, **106**
misericord (miz´er·i·kôrd´, mi·zer´ə·kôrd´) *n.* **1.** a temporary relaxation of discipline in a monastery, esp. a suspension from fasting. **2.** the room set aside in a monastery for monks breaking their fast or otherwise taking recess from strict discipline. **3.** a small ledge or projection on the underside of a hinged seat in a church stall, which, when the seat is lifted, furnishes support to a person standing in that stall. **4.** a medieval dagger, used to give the *coup de grâce* (kōō´də·gräs´; *not* -grä´; death blow) to a mortally wounded knight. [**miser-** + **-i-** + **cord-**] < L. *miser(ēre)*: to pity (< *miser*: pitiful, wretched) + *-i-*: conn. vowel + *cord(is)* (gen. of *cor*): heart. **RECON:** *to pity* (**miser-**) *the heart* (**cord-**). If you think about it, the one thing all four definitions of *misericord* have in common is the offering of pity—pity for the bearer of monastic discipline, pity for those not permitted to sit down, and pity for the mortally wounded knight in the throes of death, *51, 93*
misfeasance, 122
misfortune, see under MIS-¹
misogamy, see under MIS-²
misogyny, see under MIS-²
misopedia, see under MIS-²
mis(se)-, 106
mistake, see under MIS-¹
mit-, **108**
Mithridates the Great, *249*
mitigate, 89, **108**
mīt(is), 108
mitochondria, 117
mne-, 105
mnemonics, 5
modern definition, xvii, cf. RECONSTRUCTED MEANING
Modern English, 164-65
moiety, see under -ETY
mōnath, 108
monetary, see under -ARY
moniliform, 149
monochromatic, 127
monokinis, see under BIKINI
monolith, 238
MONOMANIA *n.* an abnormal preoccupation with or fixation on one subject or idea; cf. OLIGOMANIA. [< G. *mon(os)*: single, alone + *-o-*: conn. vowel + -PHOBIA], 145
monosome, 250
monozygotic (män´ə·zī·gät´ik) *adj.* developed from a single fertilized ovum (ō´vəm: egg cell), as identical twins; cf. DIZYGOTIC. [**mon-** + **-o-** + **zyg-** + **-o-** + **-t-** + **-ic**] < G. *mon(os)*: single, alone + *zyg(oun)*: to join together, to yoke (< *zygon*: a yoke) + *-o-*: conn. vowel + *-t(os)*: verbal suffix with the inflectional meaning: having been or having had (that which is designated by the preceding verb base) + *-ik(os)*: pert. to, charact. by. **RECON:** *charact. by* (**-ic**) *one* (**mon-**) *having been* (**-t-**) *joined* (**zyg-**). The "joining" is of one spermatozoon (sperm cell) with one ovum, resulting in one fertilized egg, which subsequently splits into two potential individuals, 37, see also under ZYG-
month-, **108**
monument, 215
monumental, 215
moon, 139
moondog, see under PARA-
mor-, **105**
mōr(is) (mōs), 105
mōros, 50
morph-, **105**
morph(ē), 105
morphē, 47, see also under LINGUISTICS
Morpheus, 47
MORPHINE (môr´fēn) *n.* a narcotic ALKALOID derived from opium. [**Morph-** + **-in-** + **-e**] < L. *Morph(eus)*: the Roman god of dreams (< G. *morph(ē)*: form,

shape + L. *-eus*: pert. to, charact. by; also, one who or that which) + *-īn(a)* (fem. of *-īnus*): pert. to, charact. by; also, a fem. abstract *n*-forming suffix having the basic meaning: the quality, state, or condition of + E. *-e*: silent final letter. **RECON**: *pert. to* (**-in**-) *the Roman god of dreams* (**Morph**-). **SEC. DISS**: [Morph- + -**ine**] **Note**: L. *-īn(a)*: the quality, state, or condition of + E. *-e*: silent final letter > the E. *n*-forming suffix -INE², having, in this entry, the medical and scientific meaning: an alkaloid or nitrogenous base of (that which is designated by the preceding base or elements). **SEC. RECON**: *an alkaloid of* (**-ine**) *the Roman god of dreams* (**Morph**-). Morphine was named for its soporific (sleep-inducing) qualities, 25, 47, *244*

MORPHOLOGY (môr·fäl´ə·jē) *n.* the scientific study of form and structure, as in biology, linguistics, geography, and other disciplines. [**morph-** + **-o-** + **log-** + **-y**] < G. *morph(ē)*: form, shape + *-o-*: conn. vowel + *log(os)*: word, thought, reason, reckoning, discourse (< *legein*: to gather, to choose, to speak) + E. *-y*: the act, process, condition, or result of (< G. *-ia*). **RECON**: *the act, process, or result of* (**-y**) *thought* (**log-**) *about form or shape* (**morph-**). **SEC. DISS**: [morph- + -o- + -**logy**] **Note**: G. *log(os)*: word, thought, reason, reckoning, discourse + *-ia*: the act, process, condition, or result of > G. *-logia* > the E. *n*-forming comb. form -LOGY, having, in this context, the scientific and literary meaning: the science, study, theory, or doctrine of. **SEC. RECON**: *the science of* (**-logy**) *form and shape* (**morph-**), 25, 47, *244*, see also under LINGUISTICS

m(os), 94
motel, 131
mother, 139
motif, 37
motor (in medicine), see under SCHIZOPHRENIA
mouth, 139
movieitis, 66
Much Ado About Nothing, 74
mult- < L. *mult-*, base of *multus*: much, many, **107**, *119*
multifilamentous, **119**
multiloquent, 83, **107**
multiparous, 77, see also under PAR-²
multiple personality, see under SCHIZOPHRENIA
mult(us), 77, 107
mural, see under -AL
murder, 154
murmuration, 154
musca, **102**, *102*
muscacide, 56, **102**
muscle, 148

MUSCULAR (mus´kyə·lər) *adj.* **1.** of or pert. to a muscle. **2.** having well-developed muscles; strong; brawny. [**mus-** + **-cul-** + **-ar**] < L. *mūs* (gen: *mūris*): mouse + *-cul(us)*: a dim. suffix having the basic meaning: small, little, tiny + *-ār(is)*: pert. to, charact. by. **RECON**: *charact. by* (**-ar**) *a little* (**-cul-**) *mouse* (**mus**). The ancient Romans fancied that certain rippling muscles looked as though a little mouse were running beneath the skin, 70, see also under -CUL-¹

MUSCULAR DYSTROPHY (mus´kyə·lər dis´trə·fē) a chronic, hereditary disease charact. by a progressive degeneration of the muscles. [**muscular** (+) **dys-** + **troph-** + **-y**] < E. MUSCULAR (see preceding entry) (+) G. *dys-*: bad, difficult; in E., also meaning: abnormal, dysfunctional, impaired + *troph(ē)*: food, nourishment (< *trephein*: to feed, to nourish) + E. *-y*: the act, process, condition, or result of (< G. *-ia*). **RECON**: *the condition or result of* (**-y**) *impaired* (**dys-**) *nourishment* (**troph-**), 70

Muses, 148
museum (Anglicization of L. *mūsēum*), 136, 236, see following entry
mūsēum (Latinization of G. *mouseion*), 236, see preceding entry
MUSOPHOBIA *n.* an irrational fear or dread of mice. [< L. *mūs* (gen: *mūris*): mouse + G. *-o-*: conn. vowel + -PHOBIA), 143
Mussolini, Benito, see under IL DUCE
mutating, see under AURORA BOREALIS and AURORA AUSTRALIS
mutation, 224
mutual, 224
my-, **102**
mycology, see under -LOGY
myel-, **66**, 67
myelos, 66
myocarditis, 53, **102**
myocardium, 53, **102**
myomancy, 150
my(os) (*mys*), 102
MYRMECOPHOBIA *n.* an irrational fear or dread of ants. [< G. *mymēk(os)* (gen. of *mymēx*): ant + *-o-*: conn. vowel + -PHOBIA], 143
mys, 66, *(102)*
MYSOPHOBIA *n.* an abnormal dislike or aversion to dirt. [< G. *mys(os)*: filth, defilement + *-o-*: conn. vowel + -PHOBIA], 143
myst-, **101**
mystagogue, 47, **101**
myst(ēs), *101*
MYTHOMANIA *n.* a pathological tendency or compulsion to tell tall tales or lies. [< G. *myth(os)*: word, speech, story, fable, myth + *-o-*: conn. vowel + -MANIA], 145

NAFTA, 130
narcohypnia, 124
nat-, **103**
nat(āre), 103
nationalism, see under -ISM
NATIVE TABLES (in addition to the following tables, see entries beginning with "ENGLISH")
NATIVE / FRENCH-DERIVED SYNONYMS (table), 163
NATIVE ADJECTIVE-FORMING SUFFIXES (table), 173
NATIVE NOUN-FORMING SUFFIXES (table), 174
NATIVE PREFIXES (table), 172
NATIVE VERB-FORMING SUFFIXES (table), 174
native, see under -IVE
NATO, 130
natr-, **104**
natr(ium), 104
nav-, **57**, *57*
NAVIGATE (nav´i·gāt´) *v.* to steer or direct a ship, aircraft, submarine, etc. [**nav-** + **-ig-** + **-at-** + **-e**] < L. *nāv(is)*: ship + *-ig(ere)* (comb. form of *agere*): to do, to act, to drive + *-āt-* (base of *-ātus*), ppl. suffix with the inflectional meaning: having been or having had; in E. (without the macron), also meaning: having, possessing, or charact. by, but often used as a verbal suffix with the senses described under "NOTE" below + E. *-e*: silent final letter. **RECON**: *having had* (**-at-**) *driven* (**-ig-**) *a ship* (**nav-**). **SEC. DISS**: [nav- + -ig- + -**ate**] **Note**: L. *-āt-* (base of *-ātus*): having been, having had + E. *-e*: silent final letter > E. -ATE, used in this entry as a *v*-forming suffix, having the related meanings: to cause, to become, to cause to become, to make, to do, to form, to function, to manage, etc. **SEC. RECON**: *to function or manage* (**-ate**) *to drive* (**-ig-**) *a ship* (**nav-**), 88, see also under -ATE
nāvis, 57
ne-, 61
Neanderthal, 265
necromancy, 150
NECROMANIA *n.* a morbid preoccupation with corpses and death. [< G. *nekr(os)*: dead person, corpse + *-o-*: conn. vowel + -MANIA], 145
NECROPHOBIA *n.* a morbid fear or dread of corpses. Many people fear even

looking at cadavers. If you're a medical student, you have a problem. [< G. *nekr(os)*: dead person, corpse + *-o-*: conn. vowel + -PHOBIA], 143
negative, 127
nem-, **102**
nēm(a) [*nēmatos*], *102*
neocracy, 61
neologism, 61
neo-Nazi, 61
neophyte, 61
ne(os), 61
NEPHOPHOBIA *n.* an abnormal fear or dread of clouds, esp. those associated with rain. [< G. *neph(os)*: cloud, mass of clouds + *-o-*: conn. vowel + -PHOBIA], 143
nephr-, **102**
nephritis, 66
nephrocardiac (nef´rō·kär´dē·ak´) *adj.* pertaining to the kidneys and heart. [**nephr-** + **-o-** + **cardi-** + **-ac**] < *nephr(os)*: kidney, kidneys + *-o-*: conn. vowel (in this context rep. "and") + *kardi(a)*: heart + *-ak(os)* (var. of *-ikos* used after *i*; see -AC): pert. to, charact. by. **RECON**: *pert. to* (**-ac**) *the heart* (**cardi-**) *and kidneys* (**nephr-**) OR (when attributing "and" to -o-) *pert. to* (**-ac**) *the heart* (**cardi-**) *and* (**-o-**) *kidneys*; cf. HEPATOCYSTIC, LARYNGOPHARYNGEAL, and OCULOGASTRIC, 52, see also under -O-²
nephrolithotomy, 124
nephr(os), 66, *102*
nepotism, see under -ISM
Netherlands, see under DUCHESS
neurosis, see under -OSIS
neut(e)r, 103
neutr-, **103**
New Caledonia, see under MELANESIA
New Hebrides, see under MELANESIA
newscast, 131
nicotine, 134
nid-, **109**
nidification, 98, **109**
nīd(us), *109*

NIMBY, 130
NINETY-NINE PHOBIAS, 143
nitr-, 104
nitr(ogen), 104
nitwit, see under SUPERMAN
Nixon, Richard, 68
Noah, see under SEMITIC
NOCENT (nō´s'nt) *adj.* harming or tending to harm; injurious (in·jeor´ē·əs, *not* in´jeor·əs); noxious (harmful to one's physical or mental health). **[noc-,** **-ent]** < L. *noc(ēre)*: to harm, to injure + *-ent(is)* (gen. of *-ēns*): prpl. suffix having the inflectional meaning: be*ing,* hav*ing,* do*ing,* perform*ing,* or manifest*ing* (that which is designated by the preceding verb base), equivalent in meaning to E. participles ending in *-ing*; see -ENT for further information. RECON: *harm-* **(noc-)** *-ing* **(-ent).** An additional, largely archaic sense of *nocent* is "guilty," or the opposite of *innocent* (< L. *in-*: not, without + *noc(ēre)*: to harm, to injure + *-ent(is)* (gen. of *-ēns*): prpl. suffix equivalent in meaning to E. *-ing*; hence, "without harming"). This *nocent–innocent* antonymy (an·tän´ə·mē; the state or condition of being antonymous or constituting or relating to antonyms, i.e., words opposite in meaning; cf. *syn-onym, synonymous, synonymy)* is both surprising and not surprising. In English, thousands of words exist in which the prefix *in-*, "not, without," (or an assimilated or variant form of this prefix; see IN-²) is routinely added to a base word to create that word's opposite—hence, *sane–insane, compatible–incompatible, convenient–inconvenient,* and *literate–illiterate.* But occasionally, as with *nocent–innocent,* the base word is much less common than its derivative form, e.g., *evitable–inevitable, advertent–inadvertent, peccable–impeccable,* and *nocuous–innocuous.* What is then surprising about these pairs is how, over the centuries, the base form has all but vanished from common use while its derivative form continues to thrive and flourish. But what is perhaps even more surprising is that most speakers of English never stop to consider that a word beginning with *in-* "not, without," (or one of its variant or assimilated forms) might very well have an antonym that simply omits that prefix, 82
NOCTIMANIA *n.* an extreme enthusiasm for or preoccupation with night and darkness. [< L. *noct(is)* (gen. of *nox*): night + *-i-*: conn. vowel + -PHOBIA], 145
nocturnal, 206
nocuous, see under NOCENT
nom-, 105
Nominative, 189-90
nom(os), 105
non- (nän) a L-derived prefix having three common meanings: **1.** not, without (generally used without intensity; cf. A-¹, UN-, and IN-): *nonporous, noncompliance, non-American.* **2.** (of a person or thing) excluded from a particular category: *noncombatant, nonjuror, nonfiction.* **3.** (of a person or thing) lacking that which is necessary to qualify for status in a particular field or area: *nonfact, nonsubject, nonevent.* **[non-]** < L. *nōn-* (a prefixal form of the adv. *nōn)*: not (< OL. *noenum* [< *ne-*: not + *oinon,* neut. of *oinos*: one]), 69
nonagenarian, 146
non-American, see under NON-

noncombatant, see under NON-
noncompliance, see under NON-
nonevent, see under NON-
nonfact, see under NON-
nonfeasance, 122
nonfiction, see under NON-
nonjuror, see under NON-
nonporous, see under NON-
non sequitur, 138
nonsubject, see under NON-
norma, 64
Norman Conquest, 162, *234*
Norman-French, 162
normotensive, 64
northern lights, see under AURORA BOREALIS
North Pole, 237
northwardly, see under -LY²
nose, 139
nosism, 155
no skin off my nose, 153
nosos, 66, 67
NOSTALGIC (nä·stal´jik, nə-) *adj.* sentimentally longing to return to one's home or to a former time and place in one's life, as one's youth, when things were happier and usually simpler, too; homesick. **[nost-** + **alg-** + **-ic]** < G. *nost(os)*: a return home + *alg(os)*: pain, distress, suffering (< *algein*: to feel pain or distress; suffer) + *-ik(os)*: pert. to, charact. by. RECON: *charact. by* **(-ic)** *the pain of* **(alg-)** *returning home* **(nost-).** The "pain" is not caused by returning home, but by *thinking* about returning home and not being able to do so, 10, 52
nostomania, 144
NOT, WITHOUT, LACKING (A-, AN-), 69–71
notoriety, see under -TY
nova, 116
novelty, see under -TY
novem (L. nine), *91*
*novicentennial < L. *nov-,* base of *novem*: nine + *-i-*: conn. vowel + CENTENNIAL, *91*
noxious, see under NOCENT
nudophobia, see under GYMNOPHOBIA
nulliparous, 77
nūll(us), 77
NUMBERS, WORDS WITH, 146
nūt(āre), 103
nutrit-, 107
NUTRITION AND DIETETICS, 125
nūtrit(us) (nūtrīre), 107
NYCTOPHOBIA *n.* an abnormal fear or dread of night, generally because of what lurks in the dark. [G. *nykt(os)* (gen. of *nyx*): night + *-o-*: conn. vowel + -PHOBIA], 143
nymphomania, see under SATYRIASIS

-o-¹ < G. *-o-*: conn. vowel: ANTHROPOLOGY, HYDROPHOBIA, GYNECOCRACY; **48,** *49,* **60,** *93, 120, 144, passim*
-o-² < G. *-o-*: conn. vowel (in this context rep. "and"): CARDIOVASCULAR, NEPHROCARDIAC, CERVICOFACIAL; *51, 51–52*
-o-³ < G. *-ō-*: final letter of the base of denom. verbs ending in *-oun* (often functioning as a conn. vowel): HEMATOMA, HYPNOSIS, MENINGIOMA
ob- (äb, əb) a L-derived prefix having six common meanings: **1.** to, toward: *obtrusive, obvert* (to turn or change the position of something so as to display another side of it). **2.** before, in front of: *obvious* (< L. *obvius*: before the road; hence, lying in the way; hence, clearly visible < *ob-*: before + *vi(a)*: road, way + *-us*: adj. suffix; cf. PROBLEM), OBSTETRICS. **3.** against, in opposition to: *objection, obloquy* (äb´lə-kwē; abusive language or harsh criticism directed at a person or thing, especially by the public or a large number of people). **4.** over, upon: *obfuscate* (to make unclear; cloud over; muddle), *obnubilation* (a clouding over or upon; obfuscation). **5.** completely, thoroughly: *oblivion, obstipation* (severe and unyielding constipation). **6.** inverse, inversely, opposite to: *obovate* (äb-ō´vāt; egg-shaped, with the narrow end attached to the base, as certain leaves), *obcordate* (äb-kôr´dāt; heart-shaped, with the narrow end attached to the base, as certain leaves). **Note:** *ob-* is ASSIMILATED in the following manner: *ob-* becomes *oc-* before c: *occasion,* OCCIDENT; *of-* before f: OFFER, *offense;* and *op-* before p: *opponent, oppose* (cf. *appose* under AD-). Also, *ob-* becomes *o-* before *m* but only in one family of English words: *omit, omission, omissive* (of or characterized by omission), *omissible* (permitted to be or capable of being omitted; cf. *admissible),* etc. **[ob-]** < L. *ob-* (a prefixal form of the prep.): to, toward, before, against. However, *ob-* in the sense of "inverse, inversely, opposite to" (see def. 6) is abstracted from the NL. adverb *ob(versē)*: obversely (< L. *obvers(us)* [pp. of *obvertere*: to turn toward < *ob-*: to, toward

+ *vertere*: to turn] + *-ē*: adv. ending). For semantically similar suffixes, see L. *ad-* and *contrā-*, and G. *pros-* and *epi-*; **106,** *106,* **107,** *107*
obcordate, see under OB-
obdormition, 124, *220*
obduction, 77, 106
obfuscate, see under OB-
obfuscating, see under OLIGEMIA
obituary, see under VOLITIVE
objection, see under OB-
oblique stems, 39, see also following entry
oblique cases, 194, see also preceding entry
oblivion, see under OB-
obloquy, **83, 107,** see also under OB-
obnubilation, see under OB-
obovate, see under OB-
obstetrics (äb-ste´triks, əb-) *n.* the branch of medicine dealing with the care and treatment of women during pregnancy, childbirth, and the period following delivery. **[ob-** + **ste-** + **-tr-** + **-ics]** < L. *ob-*: before, in front of + *ste-* (var. of *sta-,* base of *histanai*): to set, to stand + *-tr(icis)* (gen. of *-trīx*): a female (of) or she who (performs the action designated by the preceding base or elements) + E. *-ics*: a *n*-forming suffix, having, in this entry, the modern definition: the art, science, study, or discipline of (< L. *-ic(a)* [neut. pl. of *-icus*]: pert. to, charact. by [< G. *-ik(a),* neut. pl. of *-ikos*] + E. *-s* [< OE. *-as*]: pl. suffix, used in this context as a substitution for G. *-a).* RECON: *the art, science, or discipline of* **(-ics)** *she who* **(-tr-)** *stands* **(ste-)** *before or in front of* **(ob-).** The midwife or doctor stands before or in front of the PARTURIENT woman; see also under OB-
obstipation, see under OB-

obtrusive, see under OB-

obvert, see under OB-

obvious, see under OB-

occasion, see under OB-

occident (äk´si·dənt´, -dint) *n.* **1.** the west or western regions, as of a country or land (preceded by "the"). **2.** [O-] the continents and territories west of Asia, particulary Europe and the Americas; the West (preceded by "the"). **[oc- + -cid- + -ent]** < L. *oc-* (assim. form of OB-): to, toward, before, against (in this context signifying "down") + *-cid(ere)* (comb. form of *cadere*): to fall + *-ent(is)* (gen. of *-ēns*): prpl. suffix having the SUBSTANTIVE meaning: one who or that which (performs the action designated by the preceding base or elements); see -ENT for further information. RECON: *that which* (-**ent**) *falls* (-**cid-**) *down* (**oc-**). The allusion here is to the sun "falling down" or setting; and since the sun sets in the west, *occident* has come to mean "west" or, more specifically, "the West." For a more extensive etymological discussion, see INCIDENT; *54*

occultation, 116

ochl-, 103

ochlocracy, *62*, 103

OCHLOPHOBIA (äk´lə·fō´bē·ə) *n.* an irrational or intense fear or dread of crowds. [< G. *ochl(os)*: a crowd, mob + *-o-*: conn. vowel + -PHOBIA], 143

ochl(os), 103

octō- (L. eight; akin to G. *oktō-*), *91*

octocentennial < L. *octō-*: eight + CENTENNIAL, *91*

octopus, 146

ocul- < L. *ocul-*, base of *oculus*: eye, *92*

ocular, see under OCULIST, OPHTHALMOLOGIST, OPTICIAN, and OPTOMETRIST

OCULIST (äk´yə·list) *n.* a former term for an OPHTHALMOLOGIST; cf. also OPTOMETRIST and OPTICIAN. **[ocul- + -ist]** < L. *ocul(us)*: eye + G. *-ist(ēs)*: one who believes in, adheres to, works with, is skilled in, or is otherwise associated with (that which is designated by the previous base or elements) (< -is-: final letter of the base of denom. verbs ending in *-izein* + *-t(ēs)*: one who or that which). RECON: *one who works with* (-**ist**) *the eyes* (**ocul-**), *92*

oculogastric (äk´yə·lō·gas´trik) *adj.* pertaining to the eyes and stomach. **[ocul- + -o- + gastr- + -ic]** < L. *ocul(us)*: eye + G. *-o-*: conn. vowel (in this context rep. "and") + *gastr(os)* (gen. of *gastēr*): stomach + *-ik(os)*: pert. to, charact. by. RECON: *pert. to* (-**ic**) *the stomach* (**gastr-**) *and eyes* (**ocul-**) OR (when attributing "and" to *-o-*) *pert. to* (-**ic**) *the stomach* (**gastr-**) *and* (-**o-**) *eyes* (**ocul-**); cf. HEPATOCYSTIC, NEPHROCARDIAC, LARYNGOPHARYNGEAL, *52*

odontiasis, see under -IASIS

ODONTOPHOBIA *n.* an abnormal or intense fear or dread of teeth, as those of a dog. [< G. *odont(os)* (gen. of *odōn* or *odous*): tooth + *-o-*: conn. vowel + -PHOBIA], 143

odontoprisis, see under BRUXOMANIA

odor, 107, *107*

ODYNOPHOBIA (ō·din´ə·fō´bē·ə, äd´´n·ō-) *n.* an abnormal fear or dread of pain; ALGOPHOBIA. [< G. *odyn(ē)*: pain + *-o-*: conn. vowel + -PHOBIA], 143

oeconomia (Latinization of G. *oikonomia*), 236

-o(e)id(ēs), 18, 19, *102*

oenology, see under OINOMANIA

oenophile, see under OINOMANIA

off base, 152

offense, see under OB-

OFFER (ô´fər) *v.* **1.** to present for acceptance, rejection, or other consideration; tender; proffer: *We offer you two alternatives.* **2.** to propose as a payment or bid for: *I offer you fifty dollars.* **3.** to give or render: *We offer you our thanks.* **4.** to make a formal declaration or presentation of: *I offer my resignation.* **5.** to express one's willingness to do something; volunteer: *Will you offer to take part in the experiment?* **6.** to put forth or put up: *to offer resistance.* —*n.* **7.** the act or result of offering (see defs. 1-6). **[of- + fer-]** < L. *of-* (assim. form of OB-): to, toward, before, against + *fer(re)*: to bear, to carry. RECON: *to bear or carry* (**fer-**) *to, toward, or before* (**of-**), 58

officious (ə·fish´əs) *adj.* offering unrequested and unwanted help or advice, often in a presumptuous and supercilious (soō´pər·sil´ē·əs; disdainful and contemptuous) manner; meddlesome. **[of- + -fic- + -i- + -ous]** < L. *of-* (an unusual assim. form of *op(us)*: work, labor, task + *fic(ere)* (comb. form of *facere*): to make, to do + *-i-*: conn. vowel + E. *-ous*: full of, abounding in, charact. by, like (< L. *-ōsus*). RECON: *full of or charact. by* (-**ous**) *making* (-**fic-**) *work* (**of-**). Originally, *officious* meant ready and eager to serve or help, but by the 17th century it had acquired a negative sense of offering help when it is neither requested nor wanted—a sense that has long since supplanted its earlier, laudatory (containing or expressing praise, esp. high praise; commendatory; extolling) sense, *96*

ogre, see under -ESS

ogress, see under -ESS

-oid, 18, *102*

OIKOPHOBIA *n.* an abnormal fear or dread of houses, homes, or common objects found in homes. If you have an intense fear of bathtubs and kitchen sinks, you're an oikophobic. [< G. *oik(os)*: house, household, management; cf. ECONOMY + *-o-*: conn. vowel + -PHOBIA], 143

OINOMANIA *n.* an extreme enthusiasm for, preoccupation with, or compulsion to drink wine. An *oenophile* is a lover or connoisseur of wines, and *oenology* or *enology* is the scientific study of wines and winemaking. [< G. *oin(os)*: wine + *-o-*: conn. vowel + -MANIA), 145

oktō- G. eight; akin to L. *octō-*

-ol < E. *-ol* (abstracted < (ALCOH)OL): a chemical suffix denoting an alcohol or phenol (any of a class of caustic organic compounds, esp. carbolic acid, that contains at least one hydroxyl group attached to a benzene ring); cf. -ENE, *125*

olfactory, 6

oligarchy, see under -ARCHY

oligemia (äl´i·gē´mē·ə) *n.* a medical condition caused by a reduction in total blood content. **[olig- + -em- + -ia]** < G. *olig(os)*: small, few, little + E. *-em-*: blood (< G. *(h)aim(a)*: blood) + G. *-ia*: the state, condition, or result of. RECON: *the state, condition, or result of* (-**ia**) *little* (**olig-**) *blood* (-**em-**). SEC. DISS: [olig- + -emia] Note: G. *(h)aim(a)*: blood + *-ia*: the state, condition, or result of > G. *-aimia* > the E. *n*-forming comb. form -EMIA, having the modern medical meaning: a disordered or diseased condition of the blood charact. by (that which is designated by the preceding base or elements). SEC. RECON: *a disordered or diseased condition of the blood charact. by* (-**emia**) *little* (**olig-**). But this secondary reconstruction, rather than elucidating (i·loō´si·dā´ting; shedding light upon; making clear; clarifying) the etymology and meaning of *oligemia*, is obfuscating (making unclear; clouding over; muddling) it. Thus, for most *-emia* words, we can obtain a clearer understanding of their definitions by re-dissecting *-emia* into *-em-* and *-ia* and, after defining *-em-*, attributing to *-ia* the medical meaning, "a disordered or diseased condition of," and then reconstructing the meanings of the roots in each respective word in the following sequence: *-ia* + (the specific root or roots at the beginning of the word) + *-em-*. Hence, in this entry our reconstruction would be: *a disordered or diseased condition of* (-**ia**) *little* (**olig-**) *blood* (-**em-**). For a slightly different approach to the same reconstruction, see -EMIA; and for a step-by-step analysis of how Greek *haima* evolved into English *-em-*, see ANEMIA; *70*

OLIGOMANIA (äl´i·gə·mā´nē·ə) *n.* an extreme enthusiasm for, preoccupation with, or fixation on a few subjects or ideas; cf. MONOMANIA. [< G. *olig(os)*: small, few, little + *-o-*: conn. vowel + -MANIA], 145

oligos, 70

OMBROPHOBIA *n.* an abnormal fear or dread of rain. [< G. *ombr(os)*: a shower, rain, rainstorm + *-o-*: conn. vowel + -PHOBIA], 143

omissible, see under OB-

omission, see under OB-

omissive, see under OB-

omit, see under OB-

OMMATOPHOBIA (ə·mat´ə·fō´bē·ə, äm´ə·tə-) *n.* an abnormal fear or dread of eyes, not to be confused with the fear of being looked or stared at, which is SCOPOPHOBIA. [< G. *ommat(os)* (gen. of *omma*): eye + *-o-*: conn. vowel + -PHOBIA], 143

omnipotent, see under CREATOR

omniscient, see under CREATOR

omphalomancy, 150, see also under RHABDOPHOBIA

omphalopsychite, 155

one down, two to go, 152

oneir- < G. *oneir-*, base of *oneiros*: a dream, *150*

oneirism, *150*

oneirocrisy, *150*

oneirocritic, *150*

oneirocriticism, *150*

oneirodynia, *150*

oneirologist, *150*

oneiromancy, 150, *150*, see also under RHABDOPHOBIA

oneiromantic, *150*

ONEIROPHOBIA (ō·nī´rə·fō´bē·ə) *n.* an abnormal or irrational fear of dreams or of dreaming. If you experience oneirophobia, you probably also experience HYPNOPHOBIA. [< G. *oneir(os)*: a dream + *-o-*: conn. vowel + -PHOBIA], 143

oneiropompism, *150*

oneiroscopist, *150*

oneiroscopy, *150*

One-Root Infinitives (Greek), **263-64**

one-two (punch), 153

ONIOMANIA (ō´nē·ə·mā´nē·ə) *n.* an irresistible impulse or compulsion to buy things, often with little bearing on one's needs. [< G. *ōni(os)*: to be purchased, for sale (< *ōnos*: price) + *-o-*: conn. vowel + -MANIA], 145

ONOMATOPHOBIA (än´ə·mat´ə·fō´bē·ə) *n.* an irrational fear or dread of names. The ancient Hebrews feared to say the name of God and substituted the initials YHVH, which was eventually corrupted into *Jehovah*. [< G. *onomat(os)* (gen. of *onoma*): name + *-o-*: conn. vowel + -PHOBIA], 143

on the ropes, 153

"ontogeny recapitulates phylogeny," 261

ontology, 126

onych-, 105

onychocryptosis, 124

onycholysis, 259

onychophagist, 155, *259*

onych(os) (*onyx*), 105

onym-, 105

onym(a), 105

on your toes, 153

oo- < G. *ō(i)o-*: comb. form of *ōion*: egg, 68, *124*

oophor-, *124*

oophorectomy, **124**

oophoritis, **68**

opalescent , see under -SC-

OPEC, 130

operate, 16, 201

neut. of *-ārius*: pert. to, charact. by, having the nature of, like; see -ARY for further information). RECON: *a place for* (**-ary**) *eggs* (**ov-**), 76

ovary, 76

ovate, see under -ATE, CORDATE, and SAGITTATE

OVER, ABOVE, BEYOND; ABNORMALLY HIGH; EXCESSIVELY (HYPER-), 63–65

overlearning, 38, see also REVIEW OF LITERATURE

overlegislate, 201

oviduct, 76, 76

oviform¹ (ō′və·fôrm′) *adj.* egg-shaped; ovoid. [**ov-** + **-i-** + **-form**] < L. *ōv(um)*: egg + *-i-*: conn. vowel + *-fōrm(is)*: having the form or shape of (< *fōrma*: form, shape). RECON: *having the form or shape of* (**-form**) *an egg* (**ov-**), 149

oviform² (ō′və·fôrm′) *adj.* shaped like a sheep; sheeplike. [**ov-** + **-i-** + **-form**] < L. *ov(is)*: sheep + *-i-*: conn. vowel + *-fōrm(is)*: having the form or shape of

(< *fōrma*: form, shape). RECON: *having the form or shape of* (**-form**) *a sheep* (**ov-**), 149

oviparous, 77

ovoid, see under OVIFORM¹

ovoviviparous, 77

ovulates, 76

ovules, see under OVARY

ovum, 76, 198, see also under OVARY, DIZYGOTIC, and MONOZYGOTIC

ōv(um), 76

ox-, 104

oxeye daisy, 147

oxymora, 50

oxymoron, 50, 82, 123

oxys, 50

ox(ys), 104

p- (abstracted from G. *pous*), **102**
pac-, 109
Pacific, see under -IC
pacific, 98, 109
pacify (pas′ə·fī′) *v.* **1.** to calm down, soothe, or appease: *to pacify a screaming child.* **2.** to restore peace or tranquility to, esp. by military intervention: *We must pacify the countryside.* [**pac-** + **-i-** + **-fy**] < L. *pāc(is)* (gen. of *pāx*): peace + *-i-*: conn. vowel + E. *-fy*: to make, to do (< L. *-ficāre*: to make or do repeatedly [< *-fic(us)*: making, doing, causing, producing + *-āre*: first conj. verb ending; cf. -A-¹ and -ATE] < *facere*, comb. form of *facere*: to make, to do). RECON: *to make* (**-fy**) *peace* (**pac-**), 96
pāc(is) (*pāx*), 109
pack a wallop, 153
paed-, 46
pagan, 193
paid-, 34, 46
paidagōgos, 8, 46
paidos, 8, 34, 45
pais 8, 34, 45, 46
palace, 265
Palātium, 265
paleontology, 117
palingenesis, 126
palūd(is), 86
paludism, 86
pan-, 102, *102*
pancard**itis**, 53, **102**
pancreat**itis**, 68, **104**
PANHYSTEROSALPINGO-OOPHORECTOMY (pan·his′tə·rō·sal·ping′gō·ō′ə·fə·rek′tə·mē, -ō′ äf·ə·rek′tə·mē) *n.* the surgical EXCISION of the uterus, cervix, OVARIES, and FALLOPIAN TUBES. [**pan-** + **hyster-** + **-o-** + **salping-** + **-o-** + **oo-** + **phor-** + **ec-** + **tom-** + **-y**] < G. *pan-*: all, every, entire, universal (< *pan*, neut. of *pas*) + *hyster(a)*: uterus + *-o-*: conn. vowel + E. *salping-*: the fallopian tube or, less frequently, the EUSTACHIAN TUBE (< G. *salping(os)* [gen. of *salpinx*]: trumpet—the fallopian tubes and Eustachian tubes are roughly shaped like the upper tube and bell of a trumpet) + G. *-o-*: conn. vowel + *ō(i)o(n)*: egg + *phor(os)*: bearing, carrying (< *pherein*: to bear, to carry) + *ek-* (var. of EX-¹ used before a consonant): out of, from, forth + *tom(ē)*: a cutting (< *temnein*: to cut) + E. *-y*: the act, process, condition, or result of (< G. *-ia*). RECON: *the act or process of* (**-y**) *cutting* (**tom-**) *out* (**ec-**) *the entire* (**pan-**) *uterus* (**hyster-**), *the fallopian tubes* (**salping-**), *and that which bears* (**phor-**) *the egg* (**oo-**). SEC. DISS: [pan- + hyster- + o- + salping- + -o- + **oophor-** + **-ectomy**] Note: G. *ō(i)o(n)*: egg + *phor(os)*: bearing, carrying > the E. comb. form oophor-: that which bears the egg, hence egg-bearer, hence ovary. Also note: G. *ek-*: out of, from, forth + *tom(ē)*: a cutting + *-ia*: the act, process, condition, or result of > NL. *-ectomia*: a cutting out of > the E. *n*-forming comb. form -ECTOMY, having the modern medical meaning: the surgical removal or excision of (that anatomical structure or part specified by the preceding base or elements). SEC. RECON: *the surgical excision of* (**-ectomy**) *the entire* (**pan-**) *uterus* (**hyster-**), *the fallopian tubes* (**salping-**), *and the ovaries* (**oophor-**). The cervix is not mentioned in this etymology because, technically speaking, it is part of the uterus, constituting its "neck" (cf. CERVICOFACIAL), and a total (*pan-*) hysterectomy (excision of the uterus) would necessarily include it, 68, *171*

panic, 136
panis, 91
panis bis coctus, 91
pan out, 151
pantheism, 126
pant**iso**cracy, 62, **103**, see also under IS-¹
pantophobia, 142
pants, 132
papa, see under BONBON

papilla, see under MENINGIOMA
papyrus, 48
par-¹ < G. *par-*, var. of PARA- (used before a vowel or *h*): beside, alongside; in E., also meaning: beyond, amiss, in a secondary capacity, medically dysfunctional or diseased, like or resembling: PARODY, PAROTITIS, PARHELION, **101**, see also under PARA-
par-² < L. *par-*, base of *parere* (pp: *partus*): to bring forth, bear, beget, give birth to: *parent* (but not *transparent*; see under PAR-⁴), PARTURIENT, MULTIPAROUS, **102**
par-³ < L. *par-*, base of *parāre* (pp: *-parātus*): to prepare, get ready, set in order; arrange, furnish, equip: *prepare, apparatus, separate*
par-⁴ < L. *pār-*, base of *pārēre* (prp: *pārēns* [gen: *pārentis*]; pp: *-paritus*): to show, appear, be visible: *transparent* (but not *parent*; see under PAR-²), *apparent, apparition* (a ghost or ghostly appearance; specter)
par-⁵ < L. *pār* (gen: *paris*), equal: *comparison, disparage, parity* (equality or equivalence, as in status, prices, securities, currencies, etc.)
par-⁶ < G. *par-*, alter. of PER-: through, throughout (also used intensively, i.e., completely, thoroughly, utterly): PARAMOUR, PARBOIL, see also under PER-
para (par′ə) a G-derived prefix having a wide variety of meanings: **1.** beside, alongside, nearby: *parallel, paraphrase, parauterine* (near the uterus). **2.** beyond, aside from, amiss: *parapsychology, paranormal.* **3.** in a secondary or auxiliary capacity: *paralegal, paramedic.* **4.** medically dysfunctional or diseased: *parasitosis* (par′ə·sī·tō′sis, -sī-; any disease or condition caused by parasites), *paraphilia* (a mental disorder characterized by unusual sexual preferences; cf. PEDOPHILE). **5.** like or resembling: *parapertussis* (par′ə·pər·tus′is; a respiratory disease closely resembling and almost indistinguishable from pertussis [whooping cough]), *paraselene* (par′ə·sə·lē′nē; a bright, moonlike spot sometimes observed in the halo of the moon; moondog). **Note:** *para-* becomes *par-* (see PAR-¹) before a vowel or *h*: *parody, parotitis* (mumps), *parhelion* (pär·hē′lē·ən, -hēl′yən; a bright, sunlike spot sometimes observed in the halo of the sun; sundog). But do not confuse *par-*, var. of *para-*, with PAR-², PAR-³, PAR-⁴, PAR-⁵, and PAR-⁶. [**para-**] < G. *para-* (a prefixal form of the prep. *para*): beside, alongside, (*101*, 101)
par(a)-, *101*, see also preceding entry
PARABLE (par′ə·b′l) *n.* a short, simple story or episode, generally involving basic human relations or common, everyday events, used to teach a moral lesson or reveal a deeper truth: *What lessons can you learn from the parable of the Boy Who Cried Wolf?* [**para-** + **-bl-** + **-e**] < G. *para-*: beside, alongside, nearby + *b(o)l(ē)*: a throwing (< *ballein*: to throw) + E. *-e*: silent final letter. RECON: *a throwing* (**-bl-**) *beside* (**para-**). A parable is a simple allegorical story in which the literal events are "thrown beside" or merely suggestive of a moral lesson or deeper truth, which, unlike a fable or precept (a rule for moral conduct), is never actually stated but only implied, 64
parade, see under PAR-³
paragoge, 47, **101**
paralegal, see under PARA-
parallel, see under PARA-
paralysis, see under -SIS
paramedic, see under PARA-
paramour, see under PER- and PAR-⁶
paranormal, see under PARA-
parapertussis, see under PARA-
paraphilia, see under PARA-
paraphrase, see under PARA-
parapsychology, see under PARA-
paraselene, see under PARA-
parasitosis, see under PARA-
parataxis, 123
parauterine, see under PARA-
parboil, see under PARA- and PAR-⁶
parent, see under PAR-²
parenthetical definitions (rationale), 31
parentic**ide**, 56, **102**

par(ere), 77, 102, see also under PAR-²
paresis, see under -SIS
parhelion, see under PARA- and PAR-¹
parity, see under PAR-⁵
parliament, 154
parody, see under PARA-
parotitis, see under PARA-
parsec, 130
Parthenon, 114
PARTHENOPHOBIA (pär´thə·nō·fō´bē·ə) *n.* an irrational fear or dread of girls, esp. young girls or virgins. [< G. *parthen(os)*: a maiden, virgin + -*o*-: conn. vowel + -PHOBIA], 143
participle, see PAST PARTICIPLE and PRESENT PARTICIPLE
parturient, 31, see also under BENJAMIN and PAR-²
parturition, see under CAESARIAN SECTION
pas, 102, 104
pason, 104
pasōn, 104
passim (pas´im) *adv.* here and there; throughout the text: used in indexes, bibliographical references, and other scholarly works to indicate that a word, name, or other citation occurs frequently in the text. [**pass-** + -**im**] < L. *pass(us)* (pp. of *pandere*: to stretch, to scatter, to spread out) + -*im*: adv. suffix having the various meanings: with respect to, in the manner of, at the time of, etc. RECON: *with respect to* (-**im**) *spreading out* (**pass-**), see under AL-, DENOMINATIVE, ETYMOLOGY, -ION, RE-, *passim*
Past Participles (Latin), **218-20**
pasta, see under VERMICELLI
patein, 78
path-, 105, 102
pathogenic, see under -SIS
path(os), 102, 105
patr- < L. *patr-*, base of *patris*, gen. of *pater*: father, 55
patriarchy (pā´trē·är´kē) *n.* **1.** a form of social organization in which the father or a revered male is head of the family, clan, or tribe, and in which descent and kinship are reckoned through the male line; cf. MATRIARCHY. **2.** a family, clan, tribe, or state governed by men or a man. [**patri-** + **arch-** + -**y**] < G. *patri(a)*: family, clan (< *patr(os)* [gen. of *patēr*]: father + -*ia*: the act, process, condition, or result of) + -*arch(ēs)* (comb. form of *archos*): first, chief, ruler (< *archein*: to rule, orig., to be first, to begin, to take the lead) + E. -*y*: the act, process, condition, or result of (< G. -*ia*). RECON: *the act, condition, or result of* (-**y**) *the family* (**patri-**) *ruler* (**arch-**). In male-dominated Classical Greek society, the "family ruler" was understood to be the father or adult male of the household. SEC. DISS: [**patri-** + -**archy**]. Note: G. *patri(a)*: family, clan (< *patr(os)* [gen. of *patēr*]: father + -*ia*: the act, process, condition, or result of) > the E. *n*-forming comb. form *patri-*: father. Also note: G. *arch(os)*: first, chief, ruler (< *archein*: to rule) + -*ia*: the act, process, condition, or result of > G. -*archia*: the act of ruling; hence, a ruling, government > the E. *n*-forming comb. form -ARCHY: rule by or government of. SEC. RECON: *rule by or government of* (-**archy**) *fathers* (**patri-**), 60, see also under -ARCHY
patricide, 55
PATRILINEAL (pa´trə·lin´ē·əl, pā´-) *adj.* of or designating descent or kinship through the male line or side of the family. [**patr-** + -**i-** + **line-** + -**al**] < L. *patr(is)* (gen. of *pater*) + -*i*-: conn. vowel + *līne(a)*: linen thread, string, line (< *līnea*, fem. of *līneus*: of string, flax < *līnum*: flax [linen thread is manufactured from the slender fibers of the flax plant]) + -*āl(is)*: pert. to, charact. by. RECON: *pert. to* (-**al**) *father's* (**patr-**) *line* (**line-**), 55
Patroclus, see under ARISTOTLE
pauc-, 107
pauciloquent, 83, **107**
pauc(us), 107
pauperism, see under -ISM
pāx, 109-1
pays, 107, 107
pay through the nose, 151
peccable, see under NOCENT
ped-¹ < L. *ped-*, base of *pedis*, gen. of *pēs*: foot: *pedestal*, PEDICURE, *pedometer* (pi·däm´i·tər, pə-; a device carried by a walker or jogger that records the number of steps taken), 34-35 (explanation of features in this entry), 45, 45, **108**, *108*
ped-² < G. *paid-*, base of *paidos*, gen. of *pais*: boy, child: PEDAGOGUE, PEDOPHILE, *pediatrics* (the branch of medicine dealing with the development, care, diseases, and treatment of children), *encyclopedia*, 34-35 (explanation of features in this entry), 46
ped-³ < L. *pēd-*, base of *pedis*: louse (pl: lice): *pediculosis* (the infestation with lice; also called *phthiriasis* [thə·rī´ə·sis]—not to be confused with *psoriasis*, a skin condition charact. by scaly, reddish patches), 34-36 (explanation of features in this entry), **102**
pedagogic, 10
*pedago***gics**, *47*, **101**
pedagogue, 8 (as a guide to understanding the Detailed Example within the COMMON ROOTS entries), 34-35 (as a guide to understanding the choice of cross references within homophonic root entries), **45**
*pedago***guish**, *47*, **101**
*peda***gogy**, *47*, **101**
pedestal, 34-35, see also under PED-¹
pediatrics, 36, 250, see also under PED-²

*pediculi***cide**, *56*, **102**
PEDICULOPHOBIA (pə·dik´yə·lə·fō´bē·ə) *n.* an abnormal or irrational fear or dread of infestation with lice. One of the first symptoms of harboring lice is itching. If the itching is in the genital area, you probably have pubic lice, also known as *crabs*; cf. PEDICULOSIS and PHTHIRIASIS. (< L. *pēd(is)*: louse + -*i*-: conn. vowel + *cul(us)*: a dim. suffix having the basic meaning: small, little, tiny + G. -*o*-: conn. vowel + -PHOBIA), 143
pediculosis, 34, 36, see also under PED-³
PEDICURE (ped´i·kyoor´) *n.* care and treatment of the feet, esp. the toenails. [**ped-** + -**i-** + **cur-** + -**e**] < L. *ped(is)* (gen. of *pes*): foot + -*i*-: conn. vowel + *cūr(āre)*: to take care of (< *cūra*: care, concern) + E. -*e*: silent final letter. RECON: *to care for* (-**cur-**) *the foot* (**ped-**), 34, 35, see also under PED-¹
pediment, 114
ped(is) (*pēs*), 108, see also PED-¹
pēd(is), 102
pedodontics, 250
pedometer, 34, 35, see also under PED-¹
PEDOPHILE (pē´də·fīl´, ped´ə-) *n.* an adult who is sexually attracted to children; cf. PARAPHILIA. [**ped-** + -**o-** + **phil-** + -**e**] < G. *paid(os)* (gen. of *pais*): boy, child + -*o*-: conn. vowel + *phil(os)*: loving, beloved (< *philein*: to love) + E. -*e*: silent final letter. RECON: *loving* (**ped-**) *children* (**ped-**). SEC. DISS: [**ped-** + -**o-** + -**phile**] Note: G. *phil(os)*: loving, beloved + E. -*e*: silent final letter > the E. *n*-forming comb. form -PHILE, having the modern meaning: one who is fond of, likes, loves, or has an abnormal attraction for (that which is designated by the preceding base or elements). SEC. RECON: *one who has an abnormal attraction for* (-**phile**) *children* (**ped-**), 34, 36, see also under PED-² and -PHILE
PEDOPHOBIA (pē´də·fō´bē·ə, ped´ə-) *n.* an abnormal fear, dread, or dislike of children. [< G. *paid(os)* (gen. of *pais*): boy, child + -*o*-: conn. vowel + -PHOBIA], 143
Peeping Tom, 265
peer, see under DUKE
peerage, see under DUKE
peg-, 101
Pegasus, 148
pēg(nynai), 101
pejorative (pi·jär´ə·tiv, -jôr´-; pej´ə·rā´tiv, pē´jə-) *adj.* **1.** belittling, disparaging, or derogatory: *Calling preliterate cultures "illiterate" is mildly pejorative.* **2.** (of a word) becoming increasingly negative or deteriorating in meaning over time: *"Villain," in its original Latin form "villānus," meant "belonging to a country house"* (< L. *vīlla*: country house, farm + -*ānus*: of, pert. to, charact. by, or belonging to), *but, through a series of pejorative developments, has come to mean "a wicked or evil person; scoundrel." —n.* **3.** a belittling, disparaging, or derogatory word or form: *Spare me the superlatives and pejoratives.* [**pejor-** + -**at-** + -**iv-** + -**e**] < L. *pējor*: worse (compar. of *malus*: bad) + -*āt*- (base of -*ātus*), ppl. suffix with the inflectional meaning: having been or having had; in E. (without the macron), also meaning: having, possessing, or charact. by + L. -*īv(us)*: tending to (be), inclined to (be) + E. -*e*: silent final letter. RECON: *having been* (-**at-**) *inclined to* (-**iv-**) *worsen* (**pejor.**). SEC. DISS: [pejor- + -at- + -**ive**] Note: L. -*īv(us)*: tending to (be), inclined to (be) + E. -*e*: silent final letter > the E. *adj*-forming suffix -IVE, having the associated meanings: tending to (be), inclined to (be), charact. by, having the nature of. SEC. RECON: *charact. by* (-**at-**) *tending to* (-**ive-**) *worsen* (**pejor.**), 46, 174
Peletier, 134
pemptē ousia, 146
pend-, 104
pend(ere), 104
pend(ēre), 119
pendulous, see under -UL-²
PENIAPHOBIA (pē´nē·ə·fō´bē·ə) *n.* an irrational and unremitting fear of poverty. [< G. *penia*: lack, need, poverty + -*o*-: conn. vowel + -PHOBIA], 143
pente, 104, *104*
Pentecost, 146
penult, **179**
penumbra, 116
per- (pûr, pər) a L-derived prefix having the basic meaning: through, throughout (though often used intensively, i.e., completely, thoroughly, utterly): PERSISTENCE, PERFUME, perception. Note: per- occasionally becomes *par-*: *paramour* (par´ə·moor´, a lover, esp. of a married man or woman; cf. *enamored* under IN-¹), *parboil* (to boil partially—the shift in meaning from "through, throughout, thoroughly" to "partially" due to confusion of *par-* with *part*). But do not confuse *par-*, var. of *per-*, with PAR-¹, PAR-², PAR-³, PAR-⁴, and PAR-⁵; and do not mistake L. *per-* for G. PERI-. [**per-**] < L. *per-* (a prefixal form of the preposition *per*): through, throughout, by, for, during, by means of, on account of, etc. For semantically similar prefixes, see G. *dia-* and L. *trāns-*; 97
perennial, see under -AL
perfect passive participles, see PAST PARTICIPLES
perfidy, 206
PERFUME (pûr´fyoom´, pər·fyoom´) *n.* **1.** a volatile oil or other substance with a pleasing, fragrant odor, esp. one applied to the body. **2.** the scent of this. — *v.* **3.** to apply such a substance to (the body, bathwater, hairspray, etc.). **4.** to permeate or impregnate with a pleasing, fragrant odor. [**per-** + **fum-** + -**e**] < L. *per-*: through, throughout (in E., also often used intensively, i.e., completely, thoroughly, utterly) + *fūm(us)*: smoke, vapor, fume + E. -*e*: silent final letter. RECON: *to smoke* (**fum-**) *throughout* (**per-**). Originally, perfume

referred to the fumes of a burning substance, such as aromatic leaves or incense, 88, 97, see also under PER-

perfume, 194

peri- < G. *peri-* (a prefixal form of the adv. and prep. *peri*): around, about, surrounding, near, 57, *102, 102, 123,* see also under PERILUNE, PERIMETER, and PERISCOPE

peri**cardium**, *53,* **102**

perigee, 116

perihelion, 116

perilune (per´ə·lōōn´) *n.* the point in a lunar orbit of a satellite or any other object that is closest to the moon; cf. APOLUNE. [**peri-** + **lun-** + **-e**] < G. *peri-*: around, about, surrounding, near + *lūn(a)*: moon + E. *-e*: silent final letter. RECON: *near* (**peri-**) *the moon* (**lun-**)

perimeter (pə·rim´ə·tər) *n.* **1.** the border or boundary of a figure or area. **2.** the length of this border. [**peri-** + **meter**] < G. *peri-*: around, about, surrounding, near + *metr(on)*: a measure (in other contexts > L. *metrum* > OF. *metre* and OE. *meter* > ME. *metre, meter* > E. *meter*). Thus, the *-er* in *perimeter* is not the E. agential suffix *-er,* "one who or that which" (forming the plausible but erroneous dissection: *met(ron)* + *-er*), but was originally an abstraction of OE. and ME. *(met)er,* the latter a METATHESIS of OF. *(met)re* [< L. *(met)rum* < G. *(met)ron*] ult. > E. *(met)er.* For a more conventional usage of *-er,* see BIBLIOGRAPHER and LEXICOGRAPHER. RECON: *measuring* (**meter**) *around* (**peri-**), 57

peripatetic (per´i·pə·tet´ik) *adj.* **1.** roaming about or wandering from place to place; ITINERANT. —*n.* **2.** a person who roams about or wanders from place to place. [**peri-** + **pate-** + **-tic**] < G. *peri-*: around, about, surrounding + *pate(in)*: to walk + *-tik(os)*: pert. to, charact. by. RECON: *charact. by* (**-tic**) *walking* (**pate-**) *around or about* (**peri-**). Originally, the adjective *peripatetic* referred to the teaching methods of Aristotle, who discussed and debated philosophy with his students while walking about the Lyceum (lī·sē´əm), a grove near Athens. The word then became increasingly used as the uppercased noun *Peripatetic* to characterize his pupils and later anyone espousing Aristotelian philosophy. Finally, in English, the common noun *peripatetic* came to designate any person traveling or roaming about, regardless of background or purpose, 78

periphery, 262

peri**phrasis**, *123, 123*

periscope (per´ə·skōp´) *n.* an optical instrument, as on a submarine, consisting of a long vertical tube containing an arrangement of lenses and mirrors by which a person looking through a horizontal eyepiece at the lower end can view objects in direct horizontal line with the upper end. [**peri-** + **scop-** + **-e**] < G. *peri-*: around, about, surrounding, near + *skop(ein)*: to look, to see, to behold + E. *-e*: silent final letter. RECON: *to look* (**scop-**) *around* (**peri-**). SEC. DISS: [peri- + **-scope**] Note: G. *skop(ein)*: to look, to see, to behold + E. *-e*: silent final letter > the E. *n*-forming comb. form *-scope*: an instrument or apparatus for viewing objects or other phenomena (of the type described by or in the manner alluded to by the preceding base or elements). SEC. RECON: *an apparatus for viewing* (**-scope**) *around* (**peri-**). A periscope has the ability to swivel around and view objects in a 360° arc, 57, see also under PER-

perk, 132

PERSISTENCE (pər·sis´təns) *n.* **1.** the act or quality of pursuing steadfastly or stubbornly, esp. when faced with hardship, discouragement, adverse criticism, etc. **2.** continued existence or longevity; endurance; tenacity: *The persistence of the human race is a tribute to the human mind.* [**per-** + **sist-** + **-ence**] < L. *per-*: through, throughout; in E., also used intensively with the basic meaning: completely, thoroughly, utterly + *sist(ere)*: to cause to stand (< *stāre*: to stand) + E. *-ence*: the quality, state, condition; act, means, result, or process of ___ing (< L. *-entia* < *-ent(is)* [gen. of *-ēns*]: prpl. suffix having the inflectional meaning: be(ing, hav(ing, do(ing, perform(ing, or manifest(ing [that which is designated by the preceding verb base; see *-ENT* for further information] + *-ia*: the quality, state, condition; act, means, result, or process of. For a brief analysis of how Latin *-ent-* + *-ia* evolved into English *-ence,* see *-ENCE*). RECON: *the condition, act, or result of* (**-ence**) *caus-* (**sist-**) *-ing* (**-ence**) *to stand* (**sist-**) *throughout* (**per-**). Note: Because English *-ence* combines two meanings derived from two distinct Latin roots, this reconstruction must oscillate between *-ence* and *-sist-* and is somewhat confusing. However, if we reconstruct *persistence* entirely on the basis of its Latin roots, we can reduce this "oscillation" by 50 percent and at the same time be more precise in our isolation and articulation of each root. Hence, our ALT. DISS: [per- + sist- + **-ent-** + **-ia**] < L. *-ent(is)* (gen. of *-ēns*): prpl. suffix having the inflectional meaning: be(ing, hav(ing, do(ing, perform(ing, or manifest(ing (that which is designated by the preceding verb base), equivalent in meaning to E. participles ending in *-ing* + *-ia*: the quality, state, condition; act, means, result, or process of. ALT. RECON: *the condition, act, or result of* (**-ia**) *caus-* (**sist-**) *-ing* (**-ent-**) *to stand* (**sist-**) *throughout* (**per-**), 58, see also under PER-

PERSONS' NAMES, WORDS DERIVED FROM, 134

perspicacity, see under -ITY

perspicuity, see under -ITY

perturbation, 116

pertussis, see under PARA-

perusing, 32

pessimist, 212

pessimistic, 212

pet- < L. *pet-,* base of *petere*: to go toward, seek, *118*

petal-, xviii

petit, 107, *107*

Petite Louison, La, 134

petit mal, <u>86,</u> **107**

petrified, see under TRANSATLANTIC

petrify (pe´trə·fī´) *v.* **1.** to transform wood or other organic (of or derived from living organisms) matter into stone or a stonelike substance by replacing its organic cells with inorganic minerals. **2.** to become or cause to become numb or paralyzed, as from fear, horror, or stunning disbelief; cf. STUPEFY. **3.** to become stiff, hardened, or rigid, either literally or figuratively: *His heart and soul petrified after the death of his wife;* cf. CALCIFICATION. [**petr-** + **-i-** + **-fy**] < G. *petr(a)*: rock, or *petr(os)*: stone + L. *-i-*: conn. vowel + E. *-fy*: to make, to do (< L. *-ficāre*: to make or do repeatedly [< *-fic(us)*: making, doing, causing, producing + *-āre*: first conj. verb ending; cf. *-A-¹* and *-ATE*] < *-ficere,* comb. form of *facere*: to make, to do). RECON: *to make* (**-fy**) *rock or stone* (**petr-**). This word is unusual in that each of its three roots represents a different language, 96

pha-, 81

phag-, 101, *117*

phag(ein), 101

phagein, 117

phagocytosis, 117, see also under -OSIS

PHAGOMANIA *n.* an intense compulsion to eat something; also, an obsessive preoccupation with food or the subject of foods; cf. OPSOMANIA and SITOMANIA. [< G. *phag(os)*: eating, devouring (< *phagein*: to eat, to devour) + *-o-*: conn. vowel + -MANIA], 145

PHAGOPHOBIA *n.* an abnormal or irrational fear or dread of eating; cf CIBOPHOBIA and SITOPHOBIA. [< G. *phag(os)*: eating, devouring (< *phagein*: to eat, to devour) + *-o-*: conn. vowel + -PHOBIA], 143

phalang-, 105

phalang(os) (phalanx), 105

phallic (fal´ik) *adj.* **1.** of, resembling, or suggestive of a phallus or penis. **2.** of or pertaining to phallicism or the worship of the phallus, either as a symbol of male procreative (prō´krē·ā´tiv; having or relating to the ability to beget or bring forth offspring) power, or the generative (jen´ər·ə·tiv, -ə·rā´tiv; creative; conceptive; cf. GENERATE) principle of nature. [**phall-** + **-ic**] < G. *phall(os)*: penis + *-ik(os)*: pert. to, charact. by. RECON: *pert. to* (**-ic**) *the penis* (**phall-**). In ancient Dionysian (dī´ə·nish´ən; of Dionysus [dī´ə·nī´səs], the Greek god of wine and fertility) and Bacchic (of Bacchus, the Greek and Roman god of wine and fertility—a later name for Dionysus) festivals, a giant replica of the phallus was ceremonially carried and worshiped by devotees (dev´ə·tēz´, -tāz´; devoted followers) in procession (a formal and orderly marching or walking together); see also MENTULOMANIA, and do not confuse with PHATIC

phallicism, see under PHALLIC

phallus, see under PHALLIC

phanai, 81

PHANEROMANIA (fan´ər·ə·mā´nē·ə) *n.* a compulsion for picking at growths, as hangnails, blackheads, warts, etc.; cf. TRICHOTILLOMANIA. [< G. *phaner(os)*: visible (< *phainein*: to appear, to show, to be visible) + *-o-*: conn. vowel + -MANIA]. If the growths were not evident or visible, one would not pick at them, 145

PHARMACOMANIA *n.* an abnormal craving for or compulsion to take medicines; also, an abnormal desire to give or administer medicines to others; cf. LETHEOMANIA. [< G. *pharmak(on)*: drug + *-o-*: conn. vowel + -MANIA], 145

PHARMACOPHOBIA *n.* an abnormal fear or aversion to taking drugs. [< G. *pharmak(on)*: drug + *-o-*: conn. vowel + -PHOBIA], 143

pharynx (far´ingks) *n., pl.* pharynges (fə·rin´jēz). the cavity connecting the back of the mouth and nasal passageways with the LARYNX and ESOPHAGUS; loosely, the throat. [**pharynx**] < G. *pharynx*: throat, gullet. RECON: *throat, gullet* (**pharynx**); cf. LARYNGOPHARYNGEAL, (254)

PHASMOPHOBIA *n.* an irrational fear or dread of ghosts. [< G. *phasm(a)*: ghost, apparition (< *pha(inein)*: to appear, to show, to be visible + ?*s(is)*: the act, process, condition, or result of + *-ma*: the result of) + *-o-*: conn. vowel + -PHOBIA], 143

phat-, 81

phatic (fat´ik) *adj.* of or designating speech or conversation expressed to acknowledge another's existence or to create a milieu (mil·yōō´; an environment or atmosphere, esp. of a social or cultural nature) of sociability and interconnectedness rather than to impart useful information: *As the two neighbors briskly passed on opposite sides of the street, one shouted to the other, "How's it going?" And the other yelled back, speaking at almost the same time, "How ya doing?" whereupon they continued walking in their respective directions. Unbeknownst to them, they had just engaged in phatic communion.* [**pha-** + **-t-** + **-ic**] < G. *pha(nai)*: to speak + *-t(os)*: verbal suffix with the inflectional meaning: having been or having had (that which is designated by the preceding verb base) + *-ik(os)*: pert. to, charact. by. RECON: *pert. to* (**-ic**) *having* (**-t-**) *spoken* (**pha-**); *81,* and do not confuse with PHALLIC

PHENGOPHOBIA *n.* an abnormal fear or dread of daylight. Some phengophobics keep their window shutters closed all the time and often don't know whether it's daytime or nighttime; cf. HELIOPHOBIA and PHOTOPHOBIA. (< G. *pheng(os)*: light, moonlight, sunlight, radiance (< *phengein*: to make bright, shine) + *-o-*: conn. vowel + -PHOBIA], 143

phenol, see under -OL

phenomena, 248

phil- < G. *phil-,* base of *philos*: loving, beloved (< *philein*: to love). Note: G. *phil(os)*: loving, beloved + E. *-e*: silent final letter > the E. *n*-forming comb. form -PHILE (see following entry), 49

-phile (fīl, fil) a G-derived *n*-forming comb. form having the related meanings:

one who is fond of, likes, love, or has an abnormal attraction for (that which is designated by the preceding base or elements): *Anglophile* (a person who loves or greatly admires the English), BIBLIOPHILE, PEDOPHILE. **[phil- + -e]** < G. *phil(os)*: loving, beloved (< *philein*: to love) + E. *-e*: silent final letter, **(49)**

philematology, 155

Phillips, Edward, 55

philologists, see under INDO-EUROPEAN

PHILOPATRIDOMANIA (fil´ ō·pat´ri·dō·mā´nē·ə) *n.* an overwhelming and debilitating desire to return to one's home; abnormal home sickness. [< G. *phil(os)*: loving, beloved (< *philein*: to love) + *-o-*: conn. vowel + *-patrid(os)* (gen. of *patris*): one's fatherland (< *patria*: family, clan < *patēr*: father) + *-o-*: conn. vowel + -MANIA], 145

PHILOSOPHY, 126

philosophy, see under -Y

phleb- < G. *phleb-*, base of *phlebos*, gen. of *phleps*: vein, 67

phlebitis, 67

PHLEBOTOMY (flə·bät´ə·mē) *n.* **1.** the therapeutic procedure of surgically cutting and bleeding a person, usually for a relatively long period of time or until a substantial amount of blood is lost; bloodletting; venesection (ven´ə·sek´shən, vē´nə-; not to be confused with *vivisection*, the medical practice of subjecting living animals to experimental surgery and other harmful procedures for scientific research). **2.** the process of directly transferring blood from one person or animal to another; blood transfusion. **3.** the drawing of blood from a person or animal for collection, processing, storage, and redistribution, as at a blood bank. **[phleb- + -o- + tom- + -y]** < G. *phleb(os)* (gen. of *phleps*): vein + *-o-*: conn. vowel + *tom(ē)*: a cutting (< *temnein*: to cut) + E. *-y*: the act, process, condition, or result of (< G. *-ia*). RECON: *the act or process of* (**-y**) *cutting* (**tom-**) *a vein* (**phleb-**). SEC. DISS: [phleb- + -o- + -tomy] Note: G. *tom(ē)*: a cutting + *-ia*: the act, process, condition, or result of > G. *-tomia*: a cutting > the E. *n*-forming comb. form -TOMY, having, in this entry, the modern medical meaning: the surgical cutting or incision of (that anatomical structure or part specified by the preceding base or elements) *without* the removal of that which is cut; cf. LOBOTOMY. SEC. RECON: *the surgical incision of* (**-tomy**) *a vein* (**phleb-**). Phlebotomy or bloodletting, formerly accomplished with the help of a leech or bloodsucking worm attached to a person's flesh, was, prior to the 20th century, widely used in the treatment of a vast array of diseases and symptoms—the belief being that most afflictions are caused by an overabundance of "bad blood," which if removed will restore the individual to health. Allegedly, George Washington was killed by this high-tech procedure, 68, see also -TOMY, -ECTOMY, and -STOMY

phob- < G. *phob-*, base of *phobos*: fear, panic, flight (< *phobein* or *phebesthai*: to flee in fright or terror). Note: G. *phob(os)*: fear, panic, flight + E. *-e*: silent final letter > the E. *n*-forming comb. form -PHOBE (see following entry), 49, 102

-phobe (fōb) a G-derived *n*-forming comb. form having the basic meaning: one who fears, dreads, or hates (that which is designated by the preceding base or elements): *Anglophobe* (a person who hates or fears the English), XENOPHOBE, *agoraphobe* (ag´ər·ə·fōb´; a person who has an intense fear or dread of leaving home and going out to public places). **[phob- + -e]** < G. *phob(os)*: fear, panic, flight (< *phobein* or *phebesthai*: to flee in fright or terror) + E. *-e*: silent final letter, **(49)**

-phobia (fō´bē·ə) a G-derived *n*-forming comb. form having the modern medical meaning: an irrational or intense fear or dread of (that which is designated by the preceding base or elements): HYDROPHOBIA, THANATOPHOBIA, ACROPHOBIA, BRONTOPHOBIA. **[phob- + -ia]** < G. *phob(os)*: fear, panic, flight (< *phobein* or *phebesthai*: to flee in fright or terror) + *-ia*: the act, process, condition, or result of. RECON: *the act, condition, or result of* (**-ia**) *fearing* (**phob-**) [*that which is designated by the preceding base or elements*], (70), *142*, (*143*)

PHOBIAS, 142

PHOBIAS, NINETY-NINE, 143

PHOBOPHOBIA *n.* fear of fear. On March 4, 1933, at the depths of the Great Depression, Franklin Delano Roosevelt proclaimed in his first inaugural address: ". . . the only thing we have to fear is fear itself—nameless, unreasoning, unjustified terror . . . ." [< G. *phob(os)*: fear, panic, flight (< *phobein* or *phebesthai*: to flee in fright or terror) + *-o-*: conn. vowel + -PHOBIA], 143

phob(os), 102, see also under PHOB- and -PHOBE

Phoenicia, see under INDO-EUROPEAN

Phoenician, see under SEMITIC

phōn(ē), see under LINGUISTICS

Phonetic Shift, 217

phonetic (language), 231

phonetically, 96, see also under -LY²

phonograph, 168

phonology, see under LINGUISTICS

phor- < G. *phor-*, base of *phoros*: bearing, carrying (< *pherein*: to bear, to carry), 68, 124

phospholipids, 115

phot- < G. *phōt-*, base of *phōtos*, gen. of *phōs*: light, 127

photalgia, see under PHOTOPHOBIA

photo, 132

PHOTOGRAPHY, 127

photogravure, 127

(*photo*)*gravure*, 127

PHOTOMANIA *n.* an abnormal desire or compulsion for light; also a psychosis

induced by exposure to intense light. [< G. *phōt(os)* (gen. of *phōs*) light + *-o-*: conn. vowel + -MANIA], 145

photons, 130

PHOTOPHOBIA *n.* an abnormal fear or dread of light, often the result of a hypersensitivity to light that results in photalgia (fō·tal´jē·ə, -jə; pain caused by exposure to bright light; cf. ALG-) or lacrimation (excessive tearing); cf. HELIOPHOBIA and PHENGOPHOBIA. [< G. *phōt(os)* (gen. of *phōs*) light + *-o-*: conn. vowel + -PHOBIA], 143

Photostat, 133

phra- < G. *phra-*, base of *phrazein*: to speak, *123*

PHRONEMOMANIA (frän´ə·mō·mā´nē·ə) *n.* a preoccupation with or compulsion for thinking. [< G. *phronēm(a)*: thought (< *phrone(in)*: to think + *-ma*: the result of) + *-o-*: conn. vowel + -MANIA], 145

phthiriasis, 34, 36, see under PED-³

phylum, 247

phyt-, 61

phyt(on), 61

piano, 132

Picturesque Words and Phrases, 15 (overview), **141-55**

pi(c)t(us), *107*

pièce de résistance, *xiii*

pie in the sky, 151

pilaster, 114

piliform, 149

pinch hit for, 152

Ping-Pong, 133

pinn-, 106

pinn(a), *106*

pinnate, see under -ATE

pinnigrade, 80, **106**

pint-, 107

pint(o), *107*

pisc-, 102

piscatory, see under -ORY¹

piscicide, 56, **102**

pisciform, 149

piscine (pī´sēn; pis´īn, -ēn, -in) *adj.* of, resembling, or characteristic of fish or fishes; ICHTHYIC. **[pisc- + -in- + -e]** < L. *pisc(is)*: fish + *-īn(us)*: pert. to, charact. by + E. *-e*: silent final letter. RECON: *pert. to or charact. by* (**-in-**) *fish* (**pisc-**), 154

pisc(is), 102

pisiform, 149

pistil, see under OVARY

pituit-, 104

pītuīt(a), *104*

pixilation, 120

PLACE-NAMES, WORDS DERIVED FROM, 135

plague, 154

plane, 132

plant-, 106

plant(a), *106*

plantigrade, 80, **106**

plas(sein), 93

plastic, see under -IC

Plato, 61, see also under ARISTOTLE

Plectrophenax hyperboreus, 65

pleg-, 102

plēg(ē), *102*

plen-, 107

pleniloquent, 83, **107**

plēn(us), *107*

plethora, 243

plout(os), *103*

plumigerous, 117

plut-, 103

plutocracy, 62, **103**

PLUTOMANIA *n.* a preoccupation with or obsession for acquiring wealth and riches; also, the delusion that one already possesses such wealth. [< G. *pl(o)ut(os)*: wealth, riches + *-o-*: conn. vowel + -MANIA], 145

plutonium, 136, see also under TRANS-

pod, 154

podiatrist, see under -IST

poe-, *xix*

POET (pō´it) *n.* a person who writes or composes poetry. **[poe- + -t]** < G. *po(i)e(ein)* to make + *-t(ēs)*: one who or that which. RECON: *one who* (**-t**) *makes* (**poe-**), *xix*, 49

POGONOPHOBIA (pō´gə·nə·fō´bē·ə) *n.* an intense dislike or dread of beards. This phobia is especially prevalent in young children. [< G. *pōgōn*: beard + *-o-*: conn. vowel + -PHOBIA], 143

pogonotomy, 155, see elements under POGONOPHOBIA (above) and -TOMY

poie-, *xix*, *xviii*

pol-, 101

pōl(ein), *101*

poli-, 66, 67

polio, 67

polioencephalitis, 67, see also under ENCEPHALITIS

polioencephalomyelitis, 67, see also under ENCEPHALITIS

poliomyelitis, 66, *67*
polios, 66
polio vaccine, 67
poliovirus, 67
polish it off, 153
politics, see under -ICS
polyester, 119
polyglot, see under LINGUIST
polyhedra, 114
polymerization, 119
Polynesia (päl´ə·nē´zhə, -shə) *n.* one of the three principal divisions of the central and western Pacific, constituting the region east of MICRONESIA and MELANESIA, including Hawaii, Samoa, the Society Islands (including Tahiti), and Easter Island. [**poly-** + **nes-** + **-ia**] < G. *poly(s)*: much, many + *nēs(os)*: island + *-ia*: the act, process, condition, or result of, but used in this context as a placename-forming suffix, having the related meanings: the country, land, territory, region, or place of. RECON: *the region of* (**-ia**) *many* (**poly-**) *islands* (**nes-**). Polynesia is by far the largest of the three divisions of Pacific Islands and includes "many islands."
polypeptide, 125
polysyndeton, 123
porcupine, 148
PORIOMANIA *n.* an irresistible or impulsive urge to travel or wander about; cf. DROMOMANIA, HODOMANIA, and ECDEMOMANIA. [< G. *por(e)i(a)*: a journey (< *por(os)*: a hole, opening, passage + *eia*: the act, process, condition, or result of) + *-o-*: conn. vowel + -MANIA], 145
porn- < G. *porn-*, base of *pornē*: prostitute, 49, 62
pornocracy, 60, **62** , 155
pornocrat, 62
"pornocratic," 62
pornographer (pôr·näg´rə·fər) *n.* a person who writes, sells, or produces crude sexual literature, drawings, photographs, videos, or related materials. [**porn-** + **-o-** + **graph-** + **-er**] < G. *porn(ē)*: prostitute + *-o-*: conn. vowel + *graph(os)*: drawn, written (< *graphein*: to write, to draw) + E. *-er*: one who or that which (performs the action designated by the preceding base or elements) (< OE. *-er(e)*, akin to or < L. *-ārius*). RECON: *one who* (**-er**) *writes about or draws* (**graph-**) *prostitutes* (**porn-**), 49, 62
portiere, 121
PORTMANTEAU WORDS, 131
positive, 127, *211*
POSSLQ, 130
possum, 132
post meridiem, 206
postbellum , 197
postmeridian, 206
potable, see under ALCOHOL
potam- < G. *potam-*, base of *potamos*: river, 148
POTAMOPHOBIA (pät´ə·mə·fō´bē·ə) *n.* an irrational fear or dread of rivers; cf. LIMNOPHOBIA and THALASSOPHOBIA. [< G. *potam(os)*: river + *-o-*: conn. vowel + -PHOBIA], 143
potter's field, 137
p(ous), *(podos)*, 102
poverty, see under -TY
powers, see under HIERARCHY
prac-, 107
practicable, 16
practical, 16, *263*
Prague, 114
prāk-, 107
prassein, 107
pre- < L. *prae-* (a prefixal form of the adv. and prep. *prae*): before, in front of: *predate, preamble, PRECISION, xv,* xv, *xvi, 1, 122*
preamble, see under PRE-
precept, see under PARABLE
precipice, see under CREMNOPHOBIA
precipitous, see under ARDUOUS
precise, see under -CIS-
precision (pri·sizh´ən) *n.* 1. the quality, state, or condition of being definite or exact. 2. an act or instance of being definite or exact. —*adj.* 3. of, characterized by, or designed for exactness: *precision instruments*. [**pre-** + **-cis-** + **-ion**] < L. *prae-*: before, in front of + *-cīs(us)* (pp. of *-cīdere*, comb. form of *caedere*: to cut, to kill) + *-iōn(is)* (gen. of *-iō*): the act, means, or result of. RECON: *the act, means, or result of* (**-ion**) *cutting* (**-cis-**) *in front of* (**pre-**). The sense development of this word is as follows: that which is "cut in front of" or has its front cut is shortened; that which is shortened is SUCCINCT; that which is succinct is to the point; and that which is to the point is precise, *54,* see also under PRE-
predate, see under PRE-
*pref-, *xvi*
prefabricated, see under OPTOMETRIST
PREFACE, XV–XX
Preface, xi, xv 1
preface, xv, xvi, xvii, 1, see also under -FACE
prefect, see under -URE
prefecture, see under -URE
*prefface, xvi
prelate, see under -URE

prelature, see under -URE
prepare, see under PAR-³
prepuce, see under FORESKIN
prescience, 31, see also under BENJAMIN
prescription, 220
Present Participles (Latin), **222–25**
present active infinitives, see INFINITIVES
present active participles, see PRESENT PARTICIPLES
president pro tempore, see under BENEATH
pressure, 63, see also under -URE
pretty, prettier, prettiest, 211
pretty ugly, 50
prevent, see under VENT-¹
prevention, 122
pride, 154
primal, 214
PRIMARY DECLENSIONAL SIMILARITIES IN LATIN AND GREEK (table), 229
primary, 214
primary hypertension, 64
primate, see under -ATE
primiparous, 77
primogeniture, 122, 146
prīm(us), 77
prince, see under DUKE
principalities, see under HIERARCHY
PRINCIPLES OF LATINIZATION AND ANGLICIZATION OF GREEK WORDS (table), 236
prison neurosis, see under CHRONOPHOBIA
privilege, 201
pro-¹ (prō) a L-derived prefix having a variety of meanings: **1.** forward, forth, to the front of: *produce, propel,* PROGRESSIVE. **2.** before, beforehand: *provide, prohibit,* PROTECTOR. **3.** in place of, on behalf of, substituting for: *pronoun, proconsul* (an appointed administrator of a colony, occupied territory, etc.; cf. *consulate* under -ATE). **4.** favoring, supporting, defending: *pro-American, pro-union.* [**pro-**] < L. *prō-* (a prefixal form of the prep. *prō*): before, in front of, on behalf of, in place of, *76, 88,* **106**
pro-² (prō) a G-derived prefix having two closely associated meanings: **1.** before in time: PROGNOSIS, *prodrome* (a warning symptom of an imminent disease or illness, as a scratchy throat before a cold). **2.** before in place or space: PROLEGOMENON, *prologue, proboscis* (prō·bä´sis; an elephant's or other animal's trunk; lit., in front of where it feeds < G. *pro-*: in front of + *bosk(ein)*: to feed + *-is*: *n.* suffix). [**pro-**] < G. *pro-* (a prefixal form of the prep. *pro*): before, in front of; forward, forth, 240
prō-, 76, 106
pro-American, see under PRO-¹
problem, 262
proboscis, see under PRO-²
procession, see under PHALLIC
proclamation 219
proconsul, see under PRO-¹
procreate, see under GENERATE
procreative, see under PHALLIC
Procrustean, 136
proct- < G. *prōkt-*, base of *prōktos*: anus, 68
PROCTALGIA (präk·tal´jē·ə) *n.* a painful condition of the anus or rectum, or both. [**proct-** + **alg-** + **-ia**] < G. *prōkt(os)*: anus + *alg(os)*: pain, distress, suffering (< *algein*: to feel pain or distress; suffer) + *-ia*: the state or condition of. RECON: *the state or condition of* (**-ia**) *pain* (**alg-**) *in the anus* (**proct-**). SEC. DISS: [proct- + -algia] Note: G. *alg(os)*: pain, distress, suffering + *-ia*: the state or condition of > G. *-algia*: the state or condition of feeling pain or distress in > the E. *n*-forming comb. form *-algia*, having the modern medical meaning: a painful condition of (that anatomical structure or part specified by the preceding base or elements). SEC. RECON: *a painful condition of* (**-algia**) *the anus* (**proct-**). In English, *proct-* has expanded its meaning to include the rectum as well as, or in place of, the anus. Do you know the difference between the two?, 68
proctitis , **66**, 66, 68
proctor (präk´tər) *n.* **1.** a person, usu. a teacher, assigned to monitor students during an examination. **2.** a person assigned or employed to manage the affairs of another; agent; manager; attorney. —*v.* **3.** to monitor students during an examination. [**pro-** + **c-** + **-t-** + **-or**] Etymologically and orthographically (with regard to spelling), *proctor* is a contraction of Middle English *proc(ura)to(u)r* (see PROCURATOR in following entry). Hence, *proctor* is ult < L. *prō-*: forward, forth, in place of, on behalf of + *c(ūrāre)*: to take care of (< *cūra*: care, concern, management) + *-(ā)t(us)*, ppl. suffix with the inflectional meaning: having been or having had; in E., the *-t-* in this root also meaning: having, possessing, or charact. by + *-or*: one who or that which. RECON: *one who* (**-or**) *is charact. by* (**-t-**) *taking care of* (**c-**) *on behalf of* (**pro-**), 66, 66
procurator (präk´yə·rāt·ər) *n.* a person assigned or employed to manage the affairs of another; agent; deputy; attorney (see PROCTOR in preceding entry). [**pro-** + **cur-** + **-at-** + **-or**] < L. *prō-*: forward, forth, in place of, on behalf of + *cūrāre*: to take care of (< *cūra*: care, concern, management) + *-āt-* (base of *-ātus*), ppl. suffix with the inflectional meaning: having been or having had; in E. (without the MACRON), also meaning: having, possessing, or charact. by + *-or*: one who or that which. RECON: *one who* (**-or**) *is charact. by* (**-at-**) *taking care of* (**cur-**) *on behalf of* (**pro-**). In the ancient Roman Empire, a procurator was any of various officials who managed the fiscal or administrative affairs of a lesser province or imperial estate or property

PRODIGAL (präd´i·gəl) *adj.* recklessly wasteful; lavish. [**prod-** + **-ig-** + **-al**] < L. *prŏd-* (var. of *prō-*; see PRO-¹): forward, forth + *-ig(ere)* (comb. form of *-agere*): to do, to act, to drive + *-āl(is)*: pert. to, charact. by. RECON: *charact. by* (**-al**) *driving* (**-ig-**) *forward* (**prod-**), 82, 89

prodrome, see under PRO-²

produce, 76, see under PRO-¹

production, xix, 76

produc**tiv**ity, 77, **106**

Professional Words, 14 (overview), **113-27**

professoriate, see under -ATE

proffer, see under OFFER

progeny, see under PROLIFIC

progesterone, see under OVARY

prognosis, 253, see also under PRO-²

prognosticate, 253

program, 259

prog**ression,** 80, **106**

progressive (prə·gres´iv, prō-) *adj.* **1.** moving forward or onward, either continuously or step by step: *progressive change.* **2.** of or relating to novel and imaginative ideas, theories, experimental methods, etc.: *progressive education; a progressive community.* **3.** favoring or advocating new and enlightened social or political reform, esp. that which is substantially different from the STATUS QUO. **4.** [sometimes P-] of or pertaining to a member of the Progressive party. **5.** designating a successively spreading or worsening medical condition: *progressive heart disease.*—*n.* **6.** a person who espouses or advocates progressive principles or beliefs (see defs. 3 and 4); cf. LIBERAL and CONSERVATIVE. [**pro-** + **gress-** + **-iv-** + **-e**] < L. *prō-:* forward, forth + *gress(us)* (pp. of *gradī:* to step, to walk, to go) + *-īv(us):* tending to (be), inclined to (be) + E. *-e:* silent letter. RECON: *tending or inclined to* (**-iv-**) *step* (**gress-**) *forward* (**pro-**). SEC. DISS: [pro- + gress- + -ive] **Note:** L. *-īv(us):* tending to (be), inclined to (be) + E. *-e:* silent letter > the E. *adj-*forming suffix -IVE, having the associated meanings: tending to (be), inclined to (be), charact. by, having the nature of. SEC. RECON: *tending or inclined to* (**-ive**) *step* (**gress-**) *forward* (**pro-**), 76, 88, see also under PRO-¹

prohibit, see under PRO-¹

prolegomenon (prō´li·gäm´ə·nän´, -nən) *n.* a preliminary statement or discussion, esp. a formal essay introducing a lengthy and complex work; cf. FOREWORD, PREFACE. [**pro-** + **leg-** + **-o-** + **-menon**] < G. *pro-:* before, in front of + *leg(ein):* to gather, to choose, to speak + *-o-:* conn. vowel + *-menon* (neut. of *-menos):* passive prpl. suffix having the inflectional meaning: being or having (that which is designated by the preceding verb base). RECON: *being* (**-menon**) *spoken* (**leg-**) *before* (**pro-**), 81

prŏlēs, 55

prolicide, 55

PROLIFIC (prə·lif´ik, prō-) *adj.* **1.** producing an abundance of children, animals, plants, or other progeny (präj´ə·nē); descendants or offspring); fecund (fē´ kund, fek´ənd; extremely fruitful or fertile); bountiful: *a prolific apple orchard.* **2.** producing or creating anything in large quantities or with great frequency: *a vivid and prolific imagination.* [**prol-** + **-i-** + **-fic**] < L. *prōl(ēs):* offspring, lit., one who or that which is fed or nourished beforehand (< *prŏ-:* forward, forth; before, beforehand + *-(o)l(ēs)* [var. of *-alēs*]: one who or that which is fed or nourished [< *alere:* to feed, to nourish]) + *-i-:* conn. vowel + *-fic(us):* making, doing, causing, producing (< *-fic(ere)* [comb. form of *facere*]: to make, to do + *-us:* adj. suffix). RECON: *producing* (**-fic**) *offspring* (**prol-**), 85

prologue, see under PRO-²

promenade, see under EX-¹

pron-, 106

pronograde, 80, **106**

pronoun, see under PRO-¹

PRONUNCIATION KEY, XXIII–XXIV

prōn(us), 106

propaedeutic, 126

propel, see under PRO-¹

PROPHETIC WORDS ENDING IN -*MANCY*, 150

prophylactic, 249, 257, see also under HERB BENNET

propitiation, see under RHABDOMANCY

PROPRIETARY TERMS, 14, **133,** 265

proscription, 220

prosopopoeia, 123

prostate, 264

pros**ta**titis, 68, **104**

prostrate, 264

protagonist, 146

protean, 136

PROTECTOR (prə·tek´tər) *n.* a person or thing that shields or defends someone or something from danger, injury, loss, insult, etc.; defender; guardian. [**pro-** + **tect-** + **-or**] < L. *prō-:* forward, forth; before, beforehand + *tect(us)* (pp. of *tegere:* to cover) + *-or:* one who or that which. RECON: *one who or that which* (**-or**) *covers* (**tect-**) *beforehand* (**pro-**), 73, see also under PRO-¹

prothalamion, 123

prothetic, see under ANTIDISESTABLISHMENTARIANISM

Proto-Indo-European, see INDO-EUROPEAN (def. 2)

protohippus, 16, 246

protrusile, see under TONGUE

pro-union, see under PRO-¹

---

provenance, 135

provide, see under PRO-¹

provident, 224

pseudocyesis, 155

pseudolegendary, 227

pseudonym, 251

psomophagist, 155

psoriasis, 34, 36, see under PED-³

psych-, 101

psychagogue, 47, **101**

psych(ē), 101, 243

psychokinesis, see under TELEKINESIS

psychosocial, 194

psychosomatic (sī´kō·sō·mat´ik, -sə-) *adj.* **1.** of or relating to a disease or physical disorder that is caused by or exacerbated (eg·zas´ər·bā´tid, ig-; made worse or more intense) by emotional or psychological factors, esp. those in which a person is preoccupied with or overconcerned about that disease or disorder: *a psychosomatic illness;* cf. SOMATOPSYCHIC. **2.** of or involving the mind and body: *psychosomatic medicine.* [**psych-** + **-o-** + **somat-** + **-ic**] < G. *psych(ē):* breath, spirit, soul, mind (< or akin to *psychein:* to breathe, to blow) + *-o-:* conn. vowel + *sōmat(os)* (gen. of *sōma):* body + *-ik(os):* pert. to, charact. by. RECON: *pert. to* (**-ic**) *the mind* (**psych-**) *and body* (**somat-**), 93, 251

PSYCHROPHOBIA (sī´krō·fō´bē·ə) *n.* an irrational dread of or aversion to cold or cold weather; also, an abnormal sensitivity to cold. [< G. *psychr(os):* cold + *-o-:* conn. vowel + -PHOBIA], 143

ptoch-, 103

ptochocracy, 62, **103**

ptōch(os), 103

ptomaine (tō´mān) *n.* any of a class of fetid (fet´id, fē´tid; stinking) ALKALOIDS produced by the bacterial decomposition and putrefaction (rotting) of protein, formerly believed to cause food poisoning. [**pto-** + **-ma** + **-in-** + **-e**] < G. *ptō-* (base of *piptein*): to fall + *-ma:* the result of + L. *-īn(a)* (fem. of *-īnus):* pert. to, charact. by; also, a fem. abstract *n-*forming suffix having the basic meaning: the quality, state, or condition of + E. *-e:* silent final letter. RECON: *the condition of* (**-in-**) *the result of* (**-ma**) *falling* (**pto-**). But what does "falling" have to do with ptomaine? The answer becomes clear when we consider the SEC. DISS: [ptoma + -ine] **Note:** G. *ptō-* (base of *piptein*): to fall + *-ma:* the result of > *ptōma:* dead body, corpse. Also note: L. *-īn(a):* the quality, state, or condition of + E. *-e:* silent final letter > the E. *n*-forming suffix -INE², having, in this entry, the medical and scientific meaning: an ALKALOID or nitrogenous base of (that which is designated by the preceding base or elements). SEC. RECON: *an alkaloid of* (**-ine**) *a dead body* (**ptoma**); cf. CADAVERINE for a parallel but primarily Latin-derived secondary reconstruction

pubescence, see under -SC-

pugilist, see under RECUMBENT

pulic-, 102

pulicicide, 56, **102**

pulic(is) (*pulex*), 102

pull no punches, 153

pulmon-, 102

pulmōn(is) (*pulmō*), 102

pulsar, 116, 131

purportedly (pər·pôr´tid·lē) *adv.* according to what is or has been professed or claimed but not verified; allegedly; reputedly. [**pur-** + **port-** + **-ed** + **-ly**] < NormFr. *pur-:* before, in front of; forward, forth (< L. *prō-;* see PRO-¹) + L. *port(āre):* to carry (< OE. *-d, -ed, -ad,* or *-od*): ppl. suffix with the inflectional meaning: having been or having had (not to be confused with E. *-ed* [< OE. *-de, -ede, -ade,* or *-ode*], past tense suffix, as in *walked* or *looked*) + E. *-ly* (< OE. *-līce*): adv. suffix having the various meanings: with respect to, in the manner of, at the time of, etc. RECON: *in the manner of* (**-ly**) *having been* (**-ed**) *carried* (**port-**) *forth* (**pur-**), 95

putr-, 109

putrefaction, see under PTOMAINE

putrefactive, 98, **109**

putr(ēre), 109

pygalgia, 155

pyloric, see under CARDIOPYLORIC

pylorus (pī·lôr´əs, pi-) *n., pl.* pylori (pī·lôr´ī, pi-). the SPHINCTER between the outlet of the stomach and the inlet to the duodenum (dōō´ə·dē´nəm, dōō·äd´ ´n·əm; the first portion of the small intestine, originally considered to measure twelve fingerbreadths or *duodēnum digitōrum*); cf. CARDIA (def. 1). [**pyl-** + **-orus**] < G. *pyl(ē):* gate + *o(u)ros:* guard, watcher (< or akin to *horan:* to see, to view). RECON: *the gate* (**pyl-**) *watcher* (**-orus**). The pylorus is perched atop the opening to the intestines and from this standpoint is the "gate watcher" for the remainder and better part of the digestive tract, (52), see also CARDIOPYLORIC

PYREXIOPHOBIA (pī·rek´sē·ō·fō´bē·ə) *n.* an abnormal or irrational fear or dread of fever; FEBRIPHOBIA; cf. PYROPHOBIA. [< G. *pyrex-* (< *pyressein*): to be feverish (< *pyretos:* fever < *pyr:* fire) + *-i(a):* the state, condition, or result of + *-o-:* conn. vowel + -PHOBIA), 143

pyrography, 115

pyromancy, 150

pyromania, 144

PYROPHOBIA *n.* an abnormal or irrational fear or dread of fire; cf. PYREXIOPHOBIA. [< G. *pyr:* fire + *-o-:* conn. vowel + -PHOBIA], 143

quack, 132
quadricentennial < L. *quadr-*, base of *quattuor*: four + *-i-*: conn. vowel + CEN-
TENNIAL, *91*
quadrumanous, 146
quadruped (kwä´drᴏᴏ⋅ped´) *n.* an animal, esp. a large mammal, having four
feet. **[quadr- + u- + ped-]** < L. *quadr-* (base of *quattuor*): four + *-u-*:
conn. vowel (hence, *quadr- + -u- = quadru-*, var. of *quadri-* used primarily
before *p* or *m*) + *ped(is)* (gen. of *pēs*): foot. RECON: *four* (**quadr-**) *feet*
(**ped-**), 80
quarantine, 146
quartan, 86
quartan malaria, 86
quart(us), 86

quasar, 116, 131
quasi-, 84
quattuor (L. five), 91
quincentennial < L. *quīn(que)*: five + CENTENNIAL, *91*
quīnque (L. five), 91
quint- (in QUINTESSENTIAL) < L. *quīnt-*, base of *quīnta*, fem. of *quīntus*: fifth,
the ordinal (a number that designates order, such as *first, second, third*,
rather than amount, such as *one, two, three*, which are cardinal numbers) of
quīnque: five, *146*
quīnta essentia, 146
quintessence, 146, *146*
quoit, see under DISCOPHILE
quotidian, 206

rac-, 108
racemose, 117
Rachel, see under BENJAMIN
radar, 130
radiance, 225
radiograph, 127
radius , 193
rail, see under INVEIGH
raincheck, 152
raise Cain, 137
ramifications, see under CADUCEUS
RATIONALE FOR THIS WORK, 37-38
rat race, 151
razz(a), 108
re- (rē, ri, rə) a L-derived prefix having two basic meanings: **1.** back (as to an
earlier condition): *repay, recoil, recede.* **2.** again, again and again, anew,
repeatedly: *reheat, refinance, reappear, refire.* **Note:** *re-* becomes *red-* before a vowel: *redemption, redact* (to draw up a proclamation; revise; edit),
redound (to accrue to; return to have an effect upon). **[re-]** < L. *re-*: back,
again, *75, 78,* **87**, *87*, 88, 89, **104**, *104*, **106**, *106*, **108**, *108*, passim
reactionary, 87
re**active**, **89**, **108**
re**agent**, **89**, **108**, see also under AG-¹
Real McCoy, the, 153
reappear, see under RE-
RECAPTURE (rē⋅kap´chər) *v.* to take or seize again. **[re- + capt- + -ur- + -e]** <
L. *re-*: back, again + *capt(us)* (pp. of *capere*: to take, to seize) + *-ūr(a)*: the
act, process, condition, or result of + E. *-e*: silent final letter. RECON: *the act
or result of* (**-ur-**) *seizing* (**capt-**) *again* (**re-**). SEC. DISS: [re- + capt- + -**ure**]
Note: L. *-ūr(a)*: the act, process, condition, or result of + E. *-e*: silent final
letter > the E. *n*-forming suffix -URE, also meaning: the act, process, condition, or result of. SEC. RECON: *the act or result of* (**-ure**) *seizing* (**capt-**)
again (**re-**), *89*, see also under -URE
recede, see under RE-
recently, see under -LY²
reclamation, 219
recoil, see under RE-
recombination (genetic), see under SUPERMAN
recondite, see under AB-
reconstructed meaning, *xvii,* cf. MODERN DEFINITION
Reconstruction, 8-9 (of Detailed Example within the COMMON ROOTS), 24 (of a
CROSS-REFERENCE DICTIONARY entry *cadaverine*)
rectifier, 118
RECUMBENT (ri⋅kum´bənt) *adj.* lying down or resting upon a surface; reclining;
leaning: *a recumbent plant; a recumbent pugilist* (pyᴏᴏ´jə⋅list; a person who
fights with his or her fists; boxer). **[re- + cumb- + -ent]** < L. *re-*: back,
again + *cumb(ere)*: to lie, lie down (a nasalized verb akin to *cubāre*: to lie
down; cf. *incubus* [a male demon fabled to engage in COITION with sleeping
women]and *succubus* [a female demon fabled to engage in COITION with
sleeping men]; the offspring of an incubus and succubus is a cambion) +
-ent(is) (gen. of *-ēns*): prpl. suffix having the inflectional meaning: be**ing**,
hav**ing**, perform**ing**, or manifest**ing** (that which is designated by the
preceding verb base), equivalent in meaning to E. participles ending in *-ing*;
see -ENT for further information. RECON: *ly-* (**cumb-**) *-ing* (**-ent**) *back* (**re-**),
73
recusation, 122
red- < L. *red-*, var. of *re-* used before a vowel: back, again, anew, repeatedly:
redeem, redintegrate (red⋅in´tə⋅grāt´, ri⋅din´-; to make whole or complete
again; restore; renew < L. *red-*: back, again + *integr(āre)*: to renew, to restore
+ *-āt(us)-*: having been + E. *-e*: silent final letter), **108**, *108*, see also under RE-
redact, see under RE-

red**actor**, **89**, **108**
redeem, see under RED-
redemption, see under RE-
redintegrate, 184, see also under RE-
redound, see under RE-
reduction, 76
reduplication, 260
re**fectory**, **98**, **109**, see also under -ORY²
refinance, see under RE-
refire, see under RE-
refraction, see under OPTOMETRIST
refrigerator, 265
reg-, 102
regal, 201
re**gicide**, **56**, **102**
rēg(is) (*rēx*), 102
regress, 78
regressive, **80**, **106**
reheat, see under RE-
rejuvenate, 213
reluctant, 216
rem-, 108
re**migate**, **89**, **108**
rēm(us), 108
ren-, 102
Renaissance, 234
rēn(ēs), 102
reniform, 149, see also under MENINGOCOCCUS
repay, see under RE-
reproduction, *xix*, 76
re**productive**, **77**, **106**
resolution, 127
retardate, see under -ATE
retina, see under OPTOMETRIST
retribution, 204
retro- < L. *retrō-* (a prefixal form of the prep. and adv. *retrō*): back, backward,
behind, *xvi,* **106**, *155*
retrō-, *106*, see also under RETRO- (preceding entry)
retroduction, **77**, **106**
retrogression, *xvi,* xvii, **80**, **106**
retromingent, 155
revere, 216
reverend, 227
reverent., 216
REVIEW OF LITERATURE, 41
rhabdomancy, 150, see also under RHABDOPHOBIA (see following entry)
RHABDOPHOBIA *n.* an irrational fear or dread of magic. [< G. *rhabd(os)*: rod,
wand, staff + *-o-*: conn. vowel + -PHOBIA). Archeological finds reveal that
prehistoric peoples, who could not understand natural phenomena, were very
much afflicted with rhabdophobia and other "primitive" phobias, such as
SCIAPHOBIA, SELENOPHOBIA, STYGIOPHOBIA, and BATRACHOPHOBIA. Consequently, they developed religion to explain these phenomena and
employed ritual, prayer, sacrifice, and other forms of propitiation (prə⋅pish´ē
⋅ā´shən; the act of appeasing or making more favorably inclined) to the gods
to make life easier for them. In divination (div´ə⋅nā´shən; the art or practice
of attempting to foretell the future or reveal hidden knowledge by magical,
religious, or other supernatural means), they carefully observed the movement of animals and inanimate substances, such as horses and smoke (see
HIPPOMANCY and CAPNOMANCY), pondered and analyzed various aspects of
human anatomy and pseudo-psychology, such as bellybuttons and dreams
(see OMPHALOMANCY and ONEIROMANCY), and used "magic" wands in a vari-

ety of pursuits, such as searching for water or wealth (see RHABDOMANCY).
For additional prophetic words ending in *-mancy*, see TERMS OF DIVINATION,
143
rhinoplasty, 264
rhododendron, 147, 246
riboflavin, 125
-rie, 101
right off the bat, 152
right up one's alley, 152
rod- < L. *rōd-*, base of *rōdere*: to gnaw, 55
rodenticide, 55
roll with the punches, 153
Roots and Definitions (of the COMMON ROOTS), **5**
ros-, **107**
ros(a)-¹ (L.), *107*
ros(a)-² (Sp.), *107*
ROSEATE (rō′zē·it, -āt′) *adj.* rosy or cheerful. [**rose-** + **-at-** + **-e**] < L. *rose(us)*:
   rose + *-āt-* (base of *-ātus*), ppl. suffix with the inflectional meaning: having
   been or having had; in E. (without the MACRON), also meaning: having,
   possessing, or charact. by + E. *-e*: silent final letter. RECON: *having been*

(**-at-**) *a rose* (**rose-**). SEC. DISS: [rose- + -ate] Note: L. *-āt-* (base of *-ātus*):
   having been, having had + E. *-e*: silent final letter > the E. *adj*-forming suffix
   -ATE, having, in this entry, the basic meaning: having, having been, possessing, or charact. by. SEC. RECON: *possessing or charact. by* (**-ate**) *a rose*
   (**rose-**), see also under -ATE
rostra, *198*
rostrum, *198*
rota, *127*
rotogravure, *127*
Roto(gravur Deutsche Tiefdruck Gesellschaft), *127*
ro(u)l(er), *95*
royal, *201*
royalty, see under -TY
rubeola, 147
rubiginous, 115
rudiments, 16
RULE BY, GOVERNMENT OF (**-CRACY**), **60–62**
rupture, see under -URE
Russian, see under INDO-EUROPEAN
-ry, 101

s

---

sac (sak) *n.* a pouchlike structure in an animal or plant, esp. one containing a
   fluid: *The gall bladder and urinary bladder are sacs.* [**sac-**] < L. *sac(cus)*:
   a bag, sack < G. *sakk(os)*: a bag made out of hair or cloth < an unknown
   SEMITIC word, akin to Heb. *saq*: bag. RECON: *a bag or sack* (**sac-**), 67
sacer, 208
sacr~, 208
sacra, 48
sacrifice, 208
sadism, 134
sagittate (saj′ə·tāt′) *adj.* shaped like an arrowhead: *Small sagittate and* COR-
   DATE *rocks sometimes turn out to be prehistoric arrowheads*; cf. OVATE, PIN-
   NATE, and OBCORDATE. [**sagitt-** + **-at-** + **-e**] < L. *sagitt(a)*: arrow + *-āt-* (base
   of *-ātus*), ppl. suffix with the inflectional meaning: having been or having
   had; in E. (without the MACRON), also meaning: having, possessing, or charact. by + E. *-e*: silent final letter. RECON: *having been* (**-at-**) *an arrow*
   (**sagitt-**). SEC. DISS: [sagitt- + -ate] Note: L. *-āt-* (base of *-ātus*): having
   been, having had + E. *-e*: silent final letter > the E. *adj*-forming suffix -ATE,
   having, in this entry, the associated meanings: possessing, charact. by, resembling, shaped (like). SEC. RECON: *resembling* (**-ate**) *an arrow* (**sagitt-**)
   OR *arrow-* (**sagitt-**) *shaped* (**-ate**), 117
sahib, 138
Saint Thomas, 137
salīre, 221
Salish, see under GWEDUC
salivate, see under -ATE
salping-, **104**
salpingitis, 68, 104
salping(os), (*salpinx*), 104
salt- < L. *salt-*, base of *saltāre*: to jump or leap about, dance (freq. of *salīre*: to
   jump, to leap), *80*
saltant, 221
saltation, 222
saltationism, 222
saltatory, 222
saltigrade, 80, *221*
salud, 138
Samoa, see under POLYNESIA
sandwich, 134
Sandwich, the Fourth Earl of, see under EPI-
sane, see under NOCENT
Sanskrit, see also under INDO-EUROPEAN
sant- (in CORPOSANT) < Port. and Sp. *sant-*, base of *santo*: holy, sacred (< L.
   sānctum, neut. of *sānctus*: holy, sacred < *sānctus*, pp. of *sancīre*: to make
   holy, consecrate, hallow), 95
Santa Cruz Islands, see under MELANESIA
SANTA FE (san′tə fā′) the capital of New Mexico, located in the north central
   part of the state. [**santa + fe**] < Sp. *santa*: holy, sacred (< L. *sāncta*, fem. of
   sānctus: holy, sacred < *sānctus*, pp. of *sancīre*: to make holy, sacred) + *fé*:
   faith (< L. *fidēs*: faith, trust < or akin to *fidere*: to trust, to believe). RECON:
   holy (**santa**) *faith* (**fe**). This oldest state capital in the United States was
   founded circa (about) 1609 by Spanish missionaries who named it, rather
   bombastically (pompously and theatrically), *La Villa Real de la Santa Fé de
   San Francisco de Asis*, "The Royal City of the Holy Faith of Saint Francis of
   Assisi," later shortened to *Santa Fe*. Other *sant-*, "holy," cities in the Americas include the Argentinean *Santa Fé* (note the acute accent above the *-e*),
   Santa Cruz, "Holy Cross," (both in Bolivia and California), and, by one
   reckoning, *Santo Domingo*, "Holy Sunday," the capital of the Dominican
   Republic. But do not mistake Spanish *sant-*, "holy," for its derivative *sant-*,

"saint," which occurs in *Santa Barbara, Santa Monica*, and *Santa Ana* (not
   to be confused with Santa Anna, the Mexican general who vanquished Davy
   Crockett and his band of ruffians at the Alamo in 1836); and do not confuse
   the *sant-* in *Santa Claus* (< Dutch *sint-*, a dialectal var. of Dutch *sant-*) with
   its Spanish and Portuguese cognates, *sant-*, 95, see also under SANT-
sapon-, **109**
saponification, **98, 109**
sāpōn(is) (*sāpō*), *109*
sarcoma, 124
sardonic, 135
satiety, see under -TY
satyr, see under SATYRIASIS (following entry)
SATYRIASIS (sā′tə·rī′ə·sis, sat′ə-) *n.* an abnormally strong and often uncontrollable sexual desire in a man; cf. *nymphomania*. [**satyr-** + **-ia** + **-sis**] < G.
   satyr(os): a satyr (a lecherous mythological beast, part human and part goat)
   + *-ia*: the act, process, or condition of + *-sis*: the act, process, or result of.
   RECON: *the result of* (**-sis**) *the act of* (**-ia**) *satyrs* (**satyr-**). SEC. DISS: [satyr-
   + -iasis] Note: G. *-ia*: the act, process, or condition of + *-sis*: the act, process, or result of > G. *-iasis* > the E. *n*-forming suffix -IASIS, having, in this
   entry, the modern scientific meaning: an abnormal medical condition or disease, often charact. by the presence or infestation of intestinal worms, protozoa, calculi (body stones), crawling insects, or other parasites (as specified
   by the preceding base or elements). SEC. RECON: *an abnormal medical condition charact. by the presence of* (**-iasis**) *satyrs* (**satyr-**), see also under
   -IASIS
SAXONISM, *xv*
saxophone, 134
-sc- < L. *-sc-*, base of *-scere*: an inchoative (in·kō′ə·tiv; in grammar, a verb or
   verb form expressing the beginning of an action, state, or process; inceptive)
   combining form having the essential meaning: to start, begin, begin to be, or
   become (that which is described by the preceding verb base): *crescent,
   pubescence* (the state of reaching or having reached puberty),
   convalescence. In English, *-sc-* in combination with *-ent* has developed the
   additional senses: to reflect or emit light, or to exhibit a display of colors of
   (that type or in the manner suggested by the preceding base or elements):
   luminescent, IRIDESCENT, *opalescent* (ō′pə·les′ənt; exhibiting the milky, iridescent colors of or resembling that of certain varieties of opal), *121*
scalpriform, 149
Scandinavian words, 162
scans- < L. *-scans-*, base of *scansus*, pp. of *scandere*: to climb, *126*
scansorial, 126
scant, see under BIKINI
sceald, 154
-scend- < L. *-scend-*, base of *-scendere*, comb. form of *scandere*: to climb, *126*
-scens- < L. *-scens-*, base of *-scensus*, pp. of *-scendere*, comb. form of *scandere*: to climb, *126*
Schadenfreude, 138
schizophrenia (skit′sə·frē′nē·ə) *n.* any of a number of symptomatically related
   psychoses typically characterized by a profound withdrawal from reality,
   bizarre delusions and hallucinations, disjointed speech, and a variety of motor (of or involving muscular movement) disturbances. [**schiz-** + **-o-** +
   phren- + **-ia**] < G. *schiz(ein)*: to cleave, to split + *-o-*: conn. vowel +
   phren(os) (gen. of *phrēn*): diaphragm, midriff (abdomen), mind + *-ia*: the
   quality, state, or condition of. RECON: *the state or condition of* (**-ia**) *a split*
   (**schiz-**) *mind* (**phren-**). *Schizophrenia*, though etymologically a "split
   mind," is not the equivalent of a "split personality," which is a synonym for
   multiple personality, an entirely different disorder in which an individual
   displays two or more distinct and compartmentalized personalities. *Schizo-*

sinus, 104, *104*
sinusitis, 68, *104*
-sis (sis) a G-derived *n*-forming suffix having two closely associated meanings:
 1. the act, means, result, or process of: SYNTHESIS, METATHESIS, GENESIS. **2.** the state or condition of: *paralysis, paresis* (partial paralysis), *sepsis* (a diseased condition caused by the presence of PATHOGENIC [disease-producing] microorganisms in the blood; blood poisoning); cf. -OSIS and -IASIS. **[-sis]** < G. *-sis*: the act, process, condition, or result of, *xviii, xix,* 108, 123
SITOMANIA (sī´tō·mā´nē·ə) *n.* a compulsion or craving for food, sometimes resulting in bouts of *bulimia* (gross overeating followed by self-induced vomiting or diarrhea); cf. OPSOMANIA and PHAGOMANIA. [< G. *sīt(os)*: grain, food + *-o-*: conn. vowel + -MANIA], 145
SITOPHOBIA (sī´tō·fō´bē·ə) *n.* an abnormal dread of or aversion to eating; cf CIBOPHOBIA and PHAGOPHOBIA. [< G. *sīt(os)*: grain, food + *-o-*: conn. vowel + -PHOBIA], 143
SIXTY-SIX MANIAS, 145
smog, 131, *131*
soci-, 103
sociocracy, 62, **103**
sol- < L. *sōl-,* base of *sōlus:* alone, sole, solitary, *83,* **107**
soli**loqua**cious, 83, **107**
soliloquy, *22, 83*
SOLIPSISM (säl´ip·siz´´m) *n.* **1.** the philosophical doctrine that only the self exists, or that the self can know of nothing but its own feelings and projections. **2.** the condition or characteristic of being extremely preoccupied with or overly indulgent of oneself, often to the exclusion and detriment of one's responsibilities, interpersonal relationships, and joy of life: *Invalids, dictators, and self-employed artists often develop a solipsism that ultimately leads to their downfall.* **[sol- + ips- + -ism]** < L. *sōl(us)*: alone, sole, solitary + *ips(e)*: self + E. -ISM: a *n*-forming suffix having, in this entry, the modern philosophical meaning: the beliefs, theory, school, or doctrine of (< G. *-ism(os)*: the act or the result of the act of [< *-is-*: denom. base of verbs ending in *-izein* + *-m(os)*: the act or the result of the act of]). RECON: *the theory or doctrine of* (**-ism**) *the solitary* (**sol-**) *self* (**ips-**), *xvii,* 83
SOMERSAULT (sum´ər·sôlt´) *n.* an acrobatic feat in which a person rolls heels over head, either forward or backward, making a complete revolution. **[somer- + -sault]** < MF. *sombre-* (a nasalized alter. of *soubre-* < L. *suprā-*): over, above + *-sault*: a leap (< L. *saltus*: a leap; either < *saltātus*, pp. of *saltāre*: to jump or leap about, dance, freq. of *salīre*: to jump, to leap; or, more likely, directly < *saltus*, pp. of *salīre*: to jump, to leap). RECON: *to leap* (**-sault**) *over* (**somer-**). Originally, a somersault was a standing leap (rather than a "roll") in which an acrobat or gymnast turned head over heels in the air and landed gracefully on his or her feet, 80
somn- < L. *somn(us)*: sleep, slumber, *83*
somn-, 107
SOMNAMBULISM (säm·nam´byoo·liz´´m, -byə-) *n.* the act of getting up and walking around while asleep or in a sleeplike trance; sleepwalking. **[somn- + ambul- + -ism]** < L. *somn(us)*: sleep + *ambul(āre)*: to walk, to travel, to go about + NL. -ISM: a *n*-forming suffix having, in this entry, the related meanings: the act, practice, or result of (< G. *-ism(os)*: the act or the result of the act of [< *-is-*: denom. base of verbs ending in *-izein* + *-m(os)*: the act or

the result of the act of]). RECON: *the act of* (**-ism**) *sleep* (**somn-**) *walking* (**ambul-**), 25, 47, 78
somni**loqua**cious, 83, **107**
somni**loquent,** 83, **107**
somniloquy, 11, 25, 47, **83**
son- < L. *son-,* base of *sonus*: sound, *64*
-son (contraction and alteration of *-diction-*), *73*
SONOGRAM (sän´ə·gram´) *n.* **1.** a medical image or picture, resembling an X-ray, produced by reflected sound waves from an internal organ, structure, fetus, etc., forming the foundation for a diagnostic ultrasound examination; echogram **2.** any image or picture representing or derived from sound waves, as of a person's voice. **[son- + -o- + -gram]** < L. *son(us)*: sound + G. *-o-*: conn. vowel + *gram(ma)*: that which is written or drawn (< *graphein*: to write, to draw). RECON: *written or drawn* (**gram-**) *sound* (**son-**), 64
soph- < G. *soph-,* base of *sophos*: wise, clever, skillful, *49, 50*
SOPHISTICATED (sə·fis´tə·kā´tid) *adj.* **1.** knowledgeable and cultured in worldly affairs; worldly-wise. **2.** highly complex and intricate: *sophisticated technology.* **[soph- + -ist + -ic- + -at- + -ed]** < G. *soph(os)*: wise, clever, skillful + *-ist(ēs)*: one who (< *-is-*: final letter of the base of denom. verbs ending in *-izein + -t(ēs)*: one who or that which; cf. -IST) + *-ik(os)*: pert. to, charact. by + L. *-āt-* (base of *-ātus*), ppl. suffix with the inflectional meaning: having been or having had; in E. (without the macron), also meaning: having, possessing, or charact. by + E. *-ed* (< OE. *-d, -ed, -ad,* or *-od*): ppl. suffix with the inflectional meaning: having been or having had (not to be confused with E. *-ed* [< OE. *-de, -ede, -ade,* or *-ode*], past tense suffix, as in *walked* or *looked*). RECON: *having been* (**-ed**) *charact. by* (**-at-**) *pert. to* (**-ic-**) *one who* (**-ist**) *is wise or clever* (**soph-**). *Sophisticated* is an unusual word in that the reconstruction of its roots suggests that its meaning has not changed very much over the MILLENNIA. In point of fact, after the coalescing in ancient Greek of *soph(os)* and *-istēs* into *sophistēs,* "one who is wise," this term came to refer to a group of Greek philosophers, the Sophists, who flourished in the 5th century B.C. However, because these philosophers increasingly used specious (plausible but purposely misleading) and devious reasoning—and through the later association of ML. *sophisticātus* with the impure mixtures of the medieval alchemists—the English derivative *sophisticated* first came to mean "adulterated or corrupted." And not until the end of the 19th century did it ameliorate (ə·mēl´yə·rāt´, ə·mē´lē·ə·rāt´) (elevate or become more positive in meaning), characterizing one who or that which is "cultured and worldly-wise." Finally, after World War II *sophisticated* developed its most EXALTED sense of "highly complex and intricate," as often used to describe state-of-the-art technology, 49
TO SPEAK (**LOQU-, LOCUT-**), 81–83
Speaker of the House, see under BENEATH
Specialty Words and Phrases, 14 (overview) **129-39**
spect-, 103
sperm-, 102
spermicide, 56, **102**
SPHINCTER (sfingk´tər) *n.* an annular (ring-shaped—not to be confused with *annual*) muscle that encircles the inner surface of a passageway or opening in the body and is normally in a contracted state, closing off that passageway or opening: *The external anal sphincter is the best known, and to most people the most important, sphincter in the body;* cf. CARDIA, PYLORUS, CARDIOPYLORIC. **[sphinc- + -ter]** < G. *sphing(ein)*: to draw close, hold tight, squeeze + *-tēr*: one who or that which. RECON: *that which* (**-ter**) *draws close or holds tight* (**sphinc-**)
sphyx-, 105

sphyx(is), 105
Spir(aea), 133
spir(säure), 133
splatter, 131
"split personality," see under SCHIZOPHRENIA
spoken, see under -ATE
spoonerism, see under -ISM
spring, 139
st- < L. *st-*, base of *stāre*: to stand: *state, instant, substantive* (sub´stən·tiv—*not* sub·stan´tiv; in grammar, a noun, or a word or phrase used as a noun; also an adjective having the meaning: pertaining to or having the characteristics of a noun; in addition, the verb "to be" is known as "the substantive verb" because of its capacity to express existence), **103**, see also SUBSTANTIVAL
sta- < G. *sta-*, base of *(hi)sta(nai)*: to set, to stand, to place: *ecstasy, metastasis* (mə·tas´tə·sis; the spread of disease, esp. cancer, from one part of the body to another, often remote part, generally caused by the dissemination of abnormal body cells or other disease-producing agents through the blood or lymph—not to be confused with METATHESIS), *catastasis* (kə·tas´tə·sis; the climax or heightened part of a drama, immediately preceding the catastrophe), **104**
staff of Aesculapius, see under CADUCEUS
sta(nai), 104
staphyl-, **102**
staphyl(ē), 102
staphylococ<u>cide</u>, <u>56</u>, **102**
star, 139
stā(re), 103
state, see under STA-¹
status quo, see under ANTIDISESTABLISHMENTARIANISM
St. Benedict, 74
stelliform, 149
St. Elmo's fire, 95
stentorian, 136
TO STEP, TO WALK, TO GO (**GRAD-, GRESS-**), **78–80**
-ster, 174
ster- < G. *ster(e)*-, base of *stereos*: firm, hard, solid, , **104**, *125*, 174
stereo, 132
ster(eos), 104
stern, see under ASTERN
stimulating, 17
stom-, **105**
stom(a) [*stomatos*], 105
-STOMY (stə·mē) a G-derived *n*-forming comb. form having the modern medical meaning: the surgical construction of an artificial "mouthlike" opening or channel, either passing to the outside of the body from (that anatomical structure or part specified by the preceding base or elements) or joining two hollow parts or organs within the body: COLOSTOMY, *tracheostomy* (trā´kē·äs´tə·mē; the surgical construction of an opening from the trachea or windpipe to the outside of the throat, enabling an injured person or one who has undergone major throat surgery to breathe; cf. TRACHEOTOMY), *colo-colostomy* (kō´lō·kə·läs´tə·mē; a surgical joining of two separate sections of the colon, as when an intermediate section has been removed due to cancer; cf. COLOSTOMY). [**stom-** + **-y**] < G. *stom(a)*: mouth + E. *-y*: the act, process, condition, or result of (< G. *-ia*). RECON: *the act, process, or result of* (**-y**) [*forming*] *a ___* ( ) *mouth* (**stom-**) [the parentheses to be filled in with the base preceding **stom-**, and its definition to be placed on the line; see COLOSTOMY for an example] OR *the act, process, or result of* (**-y**) [*forming*] *a mouth* (**stom-**) [*from that anatomical structure or part specified by the preceding base or elements*]. Note: the English medical comb. form *-stomy* in conjunction with the preceding conn. vowel *-o-* is commonly represented as *-ostomy* and should not be confused with "(O)TOMY, "the surgical *incision* of ": LOBOTOMY, PHLEBOTOMY, TRACHEOTOMY; and neither *-ostomy* nor *-otomy* should be confused with -ECTOMY, "the surgical *excision* of": TONSILLECTOMY, APPENDECTOMY, CHOLECYSTECTOMY, see also under -TOMY and -ECTOMY
strat-, **103**
strato<u>cracy</u>, <u>62</u>, **103**
strat(os), 103
strept-, **102**
streptococ<u>cide</u>, <u>56</u>, **102**
strept(os), 102
stri-, **109**
stri(a), 109
strike out, 152
stripteaser, see under EX-²
student, see under -ENT
student teacher, 50
St. Ulmo's fire, 95
stult-, **107**
stulti<u>loquent</u>, <u>83</u>, **107**
stult(us), 107
stup-, **96**, 97
stupefacient, 97
stupefaction, **97**, 85
stupefac<u>tive</u>, 97
stupefy, 97
stupefying, 97

stupendous, see under -OUS
stupēre, 96
STYGIOPHOBIA (stij´ē·ə·fō´bē·ə) *n.* an irrational fear or dread of hell; hadephobia (hā´də·fō´bē·ə, named after *Hades* [hā´dēz; in Greek mythology, the underworld inhabited by the dead]). [< G. *Styg(os)* (gen. of *Styx*): in Greek mythology, a river encircling Hades over which the dead were ferried by Charon + *-i(os)*: pert. to, charact. by + *-o-*: conn. vowel + -PHOBIA], 143, see also under RHABDOPHOBIA
sub-, *63*, 106, *106*, 108
subcutaneously, see under HYPODERMIC NEEDLE
subdefinitions (rationale), 31
sub<u>duction</u>, <u>77</u>, **106**
subfuscous, 115
SUBJECTS, **14-15** (organization of), 26 (explanation of features of "Example"), **111–55**
sublimate, see under ALCOHOL
subrogation, 122
SUBSCRIBE (səb·skrīb´) *v.* **1.** to pay for or agree to pay for and receive a specified number of magazine issues, theater tickets, commuter passes, etc. **2.** to sign or write one's name on a contract or other document to signify one's approval or assent: *Did she subscribe her name on the deed?* **3.** to pledge to pay or contribute a certain amount of money, as to a charitable organization: *He subscribed $150 to the public radio station.* **4.** to express agreement with or approval of; sanction; support: *I subscribe to your cause.* [**sub-** + **scrib-** + **-e**] < L. *sub-*: under, below, beneath + *scrīb(ere)*: to scratch, to incise, to write + E. *-e*: silent final letter. RECON: *to write* (**scrib-**) *beneath* (**sub-**). When you sign a contract or subscribe to a publication, you generally write your name beneath a statement of terms and obligations, 58, *63*
subscription, 220
substantival (sub´stən·tī´vəl) *adj.* of, pertaining to, or having the characteristics of a SUBSTANTIVE. [**sub-** + **st-** + **-ant-** + **-iv-** + **-al**] < L. *sub-*: under, below, beneath + *st(āre)*: to stand + *-ant(is)* (gen. of *-āns*): prpl. suffix having the inflectional meaning: being, having, doing, performing, or manifesting (that which is designated by the preceding verb base), equivalent in meaning to E. participles ending in *-ing* (see -ANT for further information) + *-īv(us)*: tending to (be), inclined to (be) + *-āl(is)*: pert. to, charact. by. RECON: *charact. by* (**-al**) *tending to be* (**-iv-**) *stand-* (**st-**) *-ing* (**-ant-**) *below* (**sub-**). That which stands below often serves as a support or foundation and therefore has "substance," see under -AL, AMBIVALENT, -ANT, -ARY, DICTIONARY, -ENT, -IC, SUPERINTENDENT, *passim*
substantive, see grammatical definitions under ST- and etymology under SUBSTANTIVAL; and for examples, see under -AL, AMBIVALENT, -ANT, -ARY, DICTIONARY, -ENT, -IC, SUPERINTENDENT, *passim*
subway (sub´wā´) *n.* an electric railway running wholly or partly beneath the streets of certain metropolitan areas, serving as a mode of local transportation. [**sub-** + **way**] < L. *sub-*: under, below, beneath + E. *way* (< OE. *weg*): road, course, passage. RECON: *passage* (**way**) *below* (**sub-**). In Paris, Montreal, Washington, D.C., and certain other cities, the subway is called the *Métro* or *metro*, a contraction, ultimately, of French (*chemin de fer*) *métro(politain)*, "metro(politan railroad)." In London, however, the subway is called the *Underground* or *tube*—*subway* being reserved for an underpass or short underground passageway, generally used by pedestrians or bicyclists. But this British underground railroad should not be confused with the erstwhile (former) American *Underground Railroad*, a network in existence prior to the abolition of slavery in 1863 for helping fugitive slaves escape to safety in the northern Free States and Canada—a network having absolutely nothing to do with railroads, subways, underpasses, or subterranean passageways, *63*, see also SIDERODROMOMANIA and the facetious *bathysiderodromophobia* (< G. *bathys*: depth + *siderodromophobia*)
succubus, see under RECUMBENT
suck the hind teat, 151
suf-, **108**
suf<u>fumigate</u>, <u>89</u>, **108**, see also under -IG-
"sui", 55
sui, *54*, 55
suī, 55
suicide, **54**, *55*
suid, 55
Suidae, 55
suiform, 55
suigenderism, 55
suimate, 55
su(is), 55
summer, 139
sun, 139
sundial, 206
sundog, see under PARA-
sundry, 39
sunflowers, *xvii*
super-, *63*, 106, *106*
supercilious, see under OFFICIOUS
superimpose, 120
superin<u>duction</u>, <u>77</u>, **106**
SUPERINTENDENT (sōō´pər·in·ten´dənt) *n.* a person in charge of or responsible for maintaining a building or other establishment; intendant (not to be confused with *attendant*). [**super-** + **in-** + **tend-** + **-ent**] < L. *super-*: over, above, beyond + *in-*: in, into + *tend(ere)*: to stretch, to extend + *-ent(is)* (gen.

of -*ēns*): prpl. suffix having the SUBSTANTIVE meaning: one who or that which (performs the action designated by the preceding verb base; see -ENT for further information). RECON: *one who* (**-ent**) *stretches* (**tend-**) *in* (**in-**) *over* (**super-**). *A superintendent oversees all building operations,* 55, 63, 89, see also under -ENT and -ANT

superlative, 211

superman (soo′pər·man′) *n.* **1.** a man of extraordinary or superhuman abilities or accomplishments. **2.** a genetically superior person, esp. one conceived through cloning (a form of asexual reproduction in which one isolated cell is removed from an individual and grown in a controlled environment, resulting in an offspring genetically identical to its parent) or genetic engineering (any of various forms of gene splicing and recombination designed to alter the genetic code of an individual and produce an offspring—or new life form—with different and, one hopes, improved genetic characteristics). **[super- + man]** < L. *super-*: over, above, beyond (in this entry, a Latin loan translation of Ger. *über*: over, above, beyond) + E. *man* (in this entry, an English loan translation of Ger. *Mensch*: man). RECON: *over or beyond* (**super-**) *man* (**man**). In 1891, the German philosopher Friedrich Nietzsche completed *Also sprach Zarathustra* in which he elaborated upon his conception of the *Übermensch*, an intellectually transcendent human being who completely masters himself, forgoes frivolous pleasures, spurns Christian "herd morality," and embodies human evolutionary potential and creative mastery. Twelve years later, the English dramatist George Bernard Shaw, in attempting to recast and popularize this character in a play he was writing, took on the task of translating *Übermensch* into English. But, evidently, he did not find the native rendering of *overman* or *beyondman* sufficiently mellifluous (sweet and melodious) and instead translated the first German element *über* into its Latin equivalent, creating for his new work and all posterity that immortal loan translation . . . *Superman!*

> *Faster than a speeding bullet!*
> *More powerful than a locomotive!*
> *Able to leap tall buildings at a single bound!*
> *Look! Up in the sky!*
> *It's a bird!*
> *It's a plane!*
> IT'S *ÜBERMENSCH*!

Yes, it's *Übermensch*, strange visitor from another wagwit (joker, clown; cf. *nitwit*), 63

supreme, 212

sus, 55

suturing, see under CAESARIAN SECTION

SWAK, 130

swamp fever, 86

Swedish, see under INDO-EUROPEAN

sweetish, see under -ISH

swindle, see under AMBIVALENT

swindler, see under AMBIVALENT

sword of Damocles, 119

sy- < G. *sy-,* var. of *syn-* (used before *st, z,* and certain other letter combinations): with, together, *116,* see also under SYN-

Syllabic Consonants, xxiv

syllable, see under SYN-

syllepsis, 123

syllogism (sil′ə·jiz′m) *n.* a classical form of deductive reasoning in which a major and minor premise are stated, followed by a logical and inescapable conclusion. Ex: *All human beings will die* (major premise); *John is a human being* (minor premise); *therefore, John will die* (logical and inescapable conclusion). **[syl- + log- + -ism]** < G. *syl-* (assim. form of SYN-): with, together + *log(os)*: word, thought, reason, reckoning, discourse (< *legein*: to gather, to choose, to speak) + *-ism(os)*: the act or the result of the act of (< *-is-*: denom. base of verbs ending in *-izein* + *-m(os)*: the act or the result of the act of; see -ISM). RECON: *the act or the result of the act of* (**-ism**) *reasoning* (**log-**) *together* (**syl-**), xii, see also under SYN-

sym- < G. *sym-,* assim. form and var. of SYN- (used before *m, p,* and *b*): with, together (sometimes used intensively, i.e., completely, thoroughly, throughout, utterly): *symmetrical, sympathy, symbol,* **1,** *105, 105,* see also under *symbiosis,* see under SYN- and -OSIS

symbol, see under SYM-

SYMBOLS AND ABBREVIATIONS, XXI–XXII

symmetrical, see under SYM- and METR-¹

symmetry, see under SYN-

sympathy, see under SYM- and -Y

symptom, see under SYN-

syn- (sin) a G-derived prefix having the associated meanings: with, together, together with, at the same time (sometimes used intensively, i.e., completely, thoroughly, throughout, utterly): SYNTHESIS, *syndicate, synergism* (a synthesis or interaction of factors in which the whole is greater than the sum of its parts). *Note: syn-* is ASSIMILATED in the following manner: *syn-* becomes *syl-* before l: *syllable,* SYLLOGISM; and *syn-* becomes *sym-* before m: *symmetry, asymmetrical.* Also, *syn-* becomes *sym-* before p and b: *symptom, symbiosis* (sim′bē·ō′sis, -bī-; the cohabitation of two dissimilar organisms; see also under -OSIS); and *syn-* becomes *sy-* before *st, z,* and certain other letter combinations): *system,* SYSTOLE (sis′tə·lē′), SYZYGY (sis′ə·jē). **[syn-]** < G. *syn-* (a prefixal form of the prep. *syn* [< *xyn*]): with, together, together with. For a Latin prefix with an almost identical meaning, see *com-; 46, 105, 116,* see also under SYM-

synagōgē, 46

synagogical, *47,* **101**

synagogue, 46

syndicate, see under SYN-

synergism, see under SYN-

synonym, 251, see also under ANA- and NOCENT

synonymous, see under NOCENT

synonymy, see under NOCENT

syntax, see under LINGUISTICS

SYNTHESIS (sin′thə·sis) *n., pl.* syntheses (sin′thə·sēz′). **1.** the combining of parts or elements to form a whole. **2.** the resulting whole made up of these parts or elements. **[syn- + the- -sis]** < G. *syn-*: with, together + *the-* (base of *tithenai*): to put, to place + *-sis*: the act, process, condition, or result of. RECON: *the process of* (**-sis**) *placing* (**the-**) *together* (**syn-**), xix, 46, see also under SYN-, THE-², and -SIS

synthetic (language), 187

syphilis, 84

system, 116, see also under SYN-

systole, 116, see also under SYN-

syzygy, 116, *116,* see also under SYN- and -Y

T

-t- < G. *-t(ēs)*: one who or that which, *37, 48, 144*

ta biblia, 48

tach-, 102

tach(os), 102

tachy- < G. *tachy-,* base of *tachys*: fast, swift, rapid, *52*

tachycardia, 52, 257

tachymeter, 257

TACHYPHAGIA (tak′i·fā′jē·ə) *n.* abnormally rapid eating; cf. BRADYPHAGIA. **[tachy- + phag- + -ia]** < G. *tachy(s)*: fast, swift, rapid + *phag(os)*: eating, devouring (< *phagein*: to eat, to devour) + *-ia*: the act, process, condition, or result of. RECON: *the act or process of* (**-ia**) *eating* (**phag-**) *fast* (**tachy-**), 52

tachyphagia, 257

tachyphylactic, 249, 257

tad, 11

taenia, 102

taeniacide, *56,* **102**

taeniasis, 124

taeniophobia, 142

Tahiti, see under POLYNESIA

tainia, 102

take heart, see under COURAGE

take your lumps, 153

Tale of Melibee, The, see under DOGGEREL

tantalize, 136

taph-, 101

taph(os), 101

tapinosis, 64

tarantula, 135

tard-, 106

tardigrade, *80,* **106**

tard(us), 106

-tās, 101, 105, 106, 107, 109, *passim*

tax(is), see under LINGUISTICS

taxonomy, see under LINGUISTICS

techn-, 103

techn(ē), 103

Technical Information of COMMON ROOTS (explanation of features), **7-8,** 22, 30

Technicolor, 120

technocracy, **62,** **103**

Teflon, 133

tele-, 102

tēle-, 102

telecardiophone, *53,* **102**

telegnosis, 126

telekinesis (tel′i·ki·nē′sis, -kī-) *n.* the purported (see PURPORTEDLY) ability to move, bend, or otherwise deform objects, as paper clips or silverware, with the power of the mind; psychokinesis. **[tele- + kine- + -sis]** < G. *tēle-*

(comb. form of *tēle*): far, far off, afar + *kinē-* (base of *kinein*): to move + *-sis*: the act, process, condition, or result of. **RECON:** *the act or result of* (**-sis**) *moving* (**kine-**) *afar* (**tele-**), *120*

teleology, 126

telephone, 168, see also under LINGUISTICS

telethon, 131

Teletype, 133

tenacity, see under PERSISTENCE

tender, see under OFFER

tendere, *63*

tens-, **63**, *63*

tension, *63*

tēnsus, *63*, *64*

tequila, 135

TERMS OF DIVINATION, 150, see also under RHABDOPHOBIA

terpsichorean, 136

terr- < L. *terr-*, base of *terrēre*: to frighten, to scare, to terrify, *97*

terra firma, 208

terrific, 96, *97*

TERRIFY (ter´ə·fī´) *v.* to fill with terror or intense, overpowering fright. **[terr-** + **-i-** + **-fy]** < L. *terr(ēre)*: to frighten, to scare, to terrify + *-i-*: conn. vowel + E. *-fy*: to make, to do (< L. *-ficāre*: to make or do repeatedly [< *-fic(us)*: making, doing, causing, producing + *-āre*: first conj. verb ending; cf. *-A-¹* and *-ATE*] < *-ficere*, comb. form of *facere*: to make, to do). **RECON:** *to make* (**-fy**) *frightened* (**terr-**), *97*

tertian, *86*

tertian malaria, *86*

tertiary, 23, see also under CARDINAL

terti(us), *86*

-tēs, *49*, *81*

tessaron, 104

tessarōn (tessares), *104*

testaceous, 115

têt-à-têt, 121

tetralogy, see under -LOGY

thalass-, **103**

thalass(a), *103*

thalassocracy, *62*, **103**

THALASSOMANIA (thə·las´ə·mā´nē·ə) *n.* an extreme enthusiasm for or preoccupation with sailing or the sea. [< G. *thalass(a)*: sea + *-o-*: conn. vowel + *-MANIA*], 145

THALASSOPHOBIA (thə·las´ə·fō´bē·ə) *n.* an abnormal fear or dread of the sea; cf. LIMNOPHOBIA and POTAMOPHOBIA], 143

THANATOMANIA *n.* a morbid preoccupation with or compulsion for death. [< G. *thanat(os)*: death + *-o-*: conn. vowel + -MANIA], 145, cf. THANATOPHOBIA in the following entry for a more detailed etymology

THANATOPHOBIA (than´ə·tə·fō´bē·ə) *n.* an irrational, intense, and persistent fear of death. **[thanat-** + **-o-** + **phob-** + **-ia]** < G. *thanat(os)*: death + *-o-*: conn. vowel + *phob(os)*: fear, panic, flight (< *phobein* or *phebesthai*: to flee in fright) + *-ia*: the act, process, condition, or result of. **RECON:** *the act or condition of* (**-ia**) *fearing* (**phob-**) *death* (**thanat-**). **SEC. DISS:** [thanat- + -o- + **-phobia**] Note: G. *phob(os)*: fear, panic, flight + *-ia*: the act, process, condition, or result of > G. *-phobia* > the E. *n*-forming comb. form -PHOBIA, having the modern medical meaning: an irrational or intense fear or dread of. **SEC. RECON:** *an irrational or intense fear or dread of* (**-phobia**) *death* (**thanat-**), 25, 47, 142, see also under -PHOBIA

Thanatos, 47

thanatos, *47*

thane, see under DUKE

"the afterborn," 261

the-¹ < G. *the-*, base of *theos*: god: *theology*, ATHEIST, *theomachy* (thē·äm´ə·kē; a battle or conflict with or among the gods < G. *the(os)*: god + *-o-*: conn. vowel + *mach(ē)*: battle + E. *-y*: the act, process, condition, or result of [< G. *-ia*]), *103*

the-² < G. *the-*, base of *tithenai*: to put, to place: *thesis*, SYNTHESIS, METATHESIS, **104**

the Big Apple, 151

The bigger they are, 153

the big leagues, 152

theca-, **101**

thēkē, *101*

thel-, **104**

thēl(ē), *104*

thelitis, **68**, **104**

the main event, 153

theocracy, *62*, **103**

Theodora, 62

Theodore, see under ARISTOTLE

theology, see under -THE-¹

theomachy, see under -THE-¹

THEOPHOBIA *n.* an irrational fear or dread of god. The Bible is rife with injunctions that people should be god-fearing. [< G. *the(os)*: god + *-o-*: conn. vowel + -PHOBIA], 143

the(os), *103*

theosophical, 126

therap-, **101**, **102**

therap(euein), *101*, *102*

the Real McCoy, 153

therm-, **104**

therm(ē), *104*

thermocouple, 118

THERMOPHOBIA *n.* an abnormal fear or aversion to heat, such as hot weather or overheated rooms. [< G. *therm(ē)*: heat OR *therm(os)*: hot + *-o-*: conn. vowel + -PHOBIA], 143

thermos, 133

therm(os), *104*

thesaurus, 245

thesis, see under THE-²

thievish, see under -ISH

thiosulfate, 127

thirtyish, see under -ISH

Thirty Years' War, 114

Thomas, Saint, 137

Three-Root Infinitives (Greek), **261-62**

thrice, see under CADUCEUS

thrombus, 68

thrones, see under HIERARCHY

throw in the towel, 153

thur-, **109**

thurification, **98**, **109**

thūr(is) (thūs), *109*

thyr-, **104**

thyr(eos), *104*

tickled pink, 151

tiglon, 131

"Tigress" (tī´gris) *n.* a female tiger. **[tigr-** + **-ess]** < ME. *tigr(e)*: tiger (< OF. *tigre*: tiger AND OE. *tigr(as)*: tigers, both < L. *tīgris, tigris*: tiger < G. *tigris*: tiger, prob. from an Iranian or Oriental source) + E. *-ess*: a female (of) (< L. *-issa* < G. *-issa*). **RECON:** *a female* (**-ess**) *tiger* (**tigr-**). Note: Because L. *tīgris*, "tiger," ends in *-s*, this word was probably assumed in OE. to be a plural form, resulting in the creation of the erroneous *s*-less singular form, *tigra* > (in conjunction with OF. *tigre*) ME. *tigre* and ult. E. *tiger*, 79

-tik(os), *61*

tim-, **103**

tīm(ē), *103*

timidity, see under COURAGE and -TY

timocracy, *62*, **103**

titanic, 136

(ti)the(nai), *104*

tithes, see under ANTIDISESTABLISHMENTARIANISM

"To The Egress," 79

toady, 32

tocopherol, 125

TOCOPHOBIA *n.* an abnormal or intense fear or dread of childbirth, esp. by expectant, NULLIPAROUS women. [< G. *tok(os)*: childbirth (< *tiktein*: to bear, to beget) + *-o-*: conn. vowel + -PHOBIA], 143

tom- < G. *tom-*, base of *tomos*: divided, cut, cutting AND *tomē*: a cutting (both < *temnein*: to cut), 70, 124, 142

TOMOMANIA *n.* an abnormal desire or compulsion to have surgery; also, an abnormal desire to perform surgery. [< G. *tom(os)*: cut, cutting (< *temnein*: to cut) + *-o-*: conn. vowel + -MANIA], 145

-TOMY (tə·mē) a G-derived *n*-forming comb. form having two meanings: **1.** a division or dissection of, into, or related to (that which is designated by the preceding base or elements): *anatomy, dichotomy* (a division into two often sharply opposed or mutually exclusive parts, groups, ideas, etc.). **2.** the surgical cutting or incision of (that anatomical structure or part specified by the preceding base or elements) *without* the removal of that which is cut: LOBOTOMY, PHLEBOTOMY, *tracheotomy* (trā´kē·ät´ə·mē; a surgical incision through the front of the neck into the trachea or windpipe, as in preparation for a TRACHEOSTOMY). **[tom-** + **-y]** < G. *tom(ē)*: a cutting (< *temnein*: to cut) + E. *-y*: the act, process, condition, or result of. **RECON:** *the act, process, or result of* (**-y**) *cutting* (**tom-**) *[that anatomical structure or part specified by the preceding base or elements]*. Note: the English medical comb. form *-tomy* in conjunction with the frequently preceding conn. vowel *-o-* is often represented as *-(o)TOMY*, "the surgical incision of," and should not be confused with -ECTOMY, "the surgical excision of": TONSILLECTOMY, APPENDECTOMY, CHOLECYSTECTOMY; and neither *-(o)tomy* nor *-ectomy* should be mistaken for *-(o)STOMY*, "the surgical construction of a 'mouthlike' opening of": COLOSTOMY, TRACHEOSTOMY, COLOCOLOSTOMY, (70), see also under -ECTOMY and -STOMY

ton-, **104**

tongue (tung) *n.* **1.** the protrusile (prō·trōō´s'l, prə-; capable of being protruded or thrust out), muscular organ attached to the floor of the mouth in most vertebrates, used in chewing, swallowing, tasting, and, in humans, the articulation of speech. **2.** a system for communicating thoughts and feelings through combinations of vocal sounds, generally understood by members of the same nation, geographical area, ethnic stock, etc.; LANGUAGE. **3.** a particular style or type of verbal expression: *a coarse, vulgar tongue.* **4.** any object that resembles a human or animal tongue (see def. 1). **[tong-** + **-ue]** < OE. *tung(e)*: tongue, speech, language + E. *-ue*: silent ending (the *-u* in *tongue* is perhaps a METATHESIS of the *-u* in the ME. var. spelling *tounge*). **RECON:** *tongue* (**tong-**), *92* *ton(os)*, *104*

TONSIL (tän′səl) *n.* one of two prominent masses of lymphoid tissue on each side of the throat. **[tonsil-]** < L. *tōnsill(ae)*: the tonsils (perhaps < a dim. of *tōlēs*: goiter), 70

tonsill-, **104**

tōnsill(ae), *104*

TONSILLECTOMY (tän′sə·lek′tə·mē) *n.* the surgical EXCISION of one or both TON-SILS . **[tonsill- + ec- + tom- + -y]** < L. *tōnsill(ae)*: the tonsils + G. *ek-* (var. of EX-² used before a consonant): out of, from, forth + *tom(ē)*: a cutting (< *temnein*: to cut) + E. *-y*: the act, process, condition, or result of (< G. *-ia*). RECON: *the act or process of* (**-y**) *cutting* (**tom-**) *out* (**ec-**) *the tonsils* (**tonsill-**). SEC. DISS: [tonsill- + -ectomy] Note: G. *ek-*: out of, from, forth + *tom(ē)*: a cutting + *-ia*: the act, process, condition, or result of > NL. *-ectomia*: a cutting out of > the E. *n*-forming comb. form -ECTOMY, having the modern medical meaning: the surgical removal or excision of (that anatomical structure or part specified by the preceding base or elements). SEC. RECON: *the surgical excision of* (**-ectomy**) *the tonsils* (**tonsill-**), 70, see also under -ECTOMY, -TOMY, and -STOMY

tonsillitis, **68**, **104**

toothless, see under -LESS

TOPONYMS, **135**, *225*

torso, see under MERMAID and MERMAN

tortfeasor, 122

torticollis, 124

-t(os), see under LINGUISTICS

touch base, 152

tra-, **106**, see also under TRANS-

trachea, see under BRONCHIAL and -STOMY

trachel-, **104**

trachelitis, **68**, **104**

trachēl(os), *104*

tracheostomy, see under -STOMY, -TOMY, and -ECTOMY

tracheotomy, see under -TOMY, -STOMY, and -ECTOMY

TRADEMARKS THAT HAVE BECOME WORDS, 133

tradition, see under TRANS-

traduction, **77**, **106**

trajectory, see under TRANS-

tran-, see under TRANS-

trans- (tranz, trans) a L-derived prefix having several related meanings: **1.** over, across, through, on the other side of: *transfer*, TRANSATLANTIC. **2.** beyond, surpassing: *transuranic* (tranz′yŏŏ·ran′ik, trans ́-; designating an element having an atomic number [the number of protons in the nucleus of an atom] higher than that of uranium, as plutonium), *trans-Plutonian* (farther from the sun than Pluto). **3.** changing completely or thoroughly: *transform*, *transliterate* (to represent the letters or words of a language that uses one alphabet in the corresponding characters of another language or different stage of the same language that uses a different alphabet, e.g., Greek *crwma* [gen: *crwmatos*] is transliterated as English *chrōma* [gen: *chrōmatos*]; see CHROMOSOME). Note: *trans-* becomes *tran-* before *s*: *transcribe*, TRANSCENDENTAL MEDITATION; and *trans-* is reduced to *tra-* in certain isolated words: *tradition*, *trajectory* (the curve described by a flying bullet, missile, rocket, etc.). **[trans-]** < L. *trāns-* (a prefixal form of the prep. *trāns*): over, across, beyond, 79, 89, 108, *126*

trāns-, *108*

trāns)-, *106*

transaction, **89**, **108**

TRANSATLANTIC (tranz′ət·lan′tik, trans ́-) *adj.* **1.** crossing or extending across the Atlantic Ocean. **2.** on a distant side of the Atlantic Ocean. **[trans- + Atlantic]** < L. *trāns-*: over, across, beyond + E. *Atlantic*: Atlantic Ocean (< G. *Atlant(os)* [gen. of *Atlas*]: Atlas + *-ik(os)*: pert. to, charact. by). RECON: *across* (**trans-**) *the Atlantic Ocean* (**Atlantic**). The Atlantic Ocean was named after the Atlas Mountains of North Africa, which, according to Greek mythology, are the petrified (turned to stone; see PETRIFY) remains of the Greek god Atlas—still holding up the heavens (the sky or space surrounding the earth), 89, see also under TRANS-, -IC, and PER-

TRANSCENDENTAL MEDITATION (tran′sen·den′t′l med′i·tā′shən) a form of Hindu meditation that strives to free adherents from the stresses of daily living, popularized by Marharishi Mahesh Yogi in the 1970s. **[tran- + -scend- + -ent- + -al** (+) **meditation]** < L. *trān-* (a reduced form of *trāns-*): over, across, beyond + *scend(ere)* (comb. form of *scandere*): to climb + *-ent(is)* (gen. of *-ēns*): prpl. suffix having the inflectional meaning: being, having, doing, performing, or manifesting (that which is designated by the preceding verb base), equivalent in meaning to E. participles ending in *-ing* (see -ENT for further information) + *-āl(is)*: pert. to, charact. by (+) E. MEDITATION: deep thought, contemplation. RECON: *pert. to* (**-al**) *deep thought or contemplation* (**meditation**) *that is climb-* (**-scend-**) *-ing* (**-ent-**) *beyond* (**tran-**), 79, see also under TRANS- and MEDITATION

transcendentalism, **126**, *171*

transcribe, 215, see also under TRANS-

transducer, 118

transfer, see under TRANS-

transform, see under TRANS-

transgression, **79**

transition, see under VOLITION

transliterate, 230, see also under TRANS-

trans-Plutonian, see under TRANS-

transuranic, see under TRANS-

travail, 31, see also under BENJAMIN

travelogue, 131

treis (G. three; akin to L. *trēs*)

trenchant, see under INCISION

treponemicide, **56**, **102**

Treppen, 138

Treppenwitz, 138

trēs (L. three; akin to G. *treis*), *91*, *109*

tres- < L. *trēs*: three, **101**

trēs(is), *101*

tri-, **109**, *109*

triathlon, 146

tribadism, 204

tribalism, 204

tribunal, 204

tributary, 204

tribute, 204

tricentennial < L. *tri-*, comb. form of *trēs*: three + CENTENNIAL, *91*

~trices, **105**

-tricēs, *105*

trichorrhea, 124

TRICHOTILLOMANIA (trik′ə·til′ə·mā′nē·ə) *n.* an uncontrollable impulse or compulsion to pluck out one's hair; cf. PHANEROMANIA. [< G. *trich(os)* (gen. of *thrix*): hair + *-o-*: conn. vowel + *till(ein)*: to pluck, to pull out, to tear + *-o-*: conn. vowel + -MANIA], 145

tricorporate, *95*, **109**

trilogy, see under -LOGY

tripod, 127

-trix, *105*, *108*, *108*, cf. also -ESS

troop, 154

troph- < G. *troph-*, base of *trophē*: food, nourishment (< *trephein*: to feed, to nourish), *70*

Trypanosoma, see under TRYPANOSOMIASIS

trypanosomes, see under TRYPANOSOMIASIS and -CUL-¹

trypanosomiasis (trip′ə·nō′sō·mī′ə·sis, tri·pan′ō-) *n.* any of various diseases, as African sleeping sickness, resulting from the infestation and proliferation of trypanosomes (trip′ə·nə·sōmz′, tri·pan′ə-; minute FLAGELLATE protozoa of the genus *Trypanosoma*) in the blood or tissues, usually transmitted from the bite of an insect, as the African tsetse (tset′sē, tsē′tsē) fly. **[trypan- + -o- + som- + -ia + -sis]** < *trypan(on)*: borer, auger (a spindle-shaped tool with a spiral cutting edge for boring holes in wood and other objects) (< *trypan*: to bore [< *tryp(ē)*: hole + *-an*: denom. verb ending] + *-on*: neuter *n*-forming suffix) + *-o-*: conn. vowel + *sōm(a)* (gen: *sōmatos*): body + *-ia*: the act, process, or condition of + *-sis*: the act, process, or result of. RECON: *the result of* (**-sis**) *the act of* (**-ia**) *body* (**som-**) *borers* (**trypan-**) OR *the result of* (**-sis**) *the act of* (**-ia**) *auger* (**trypan-**) *bodies* (**som-**). SEC. DISS: [trypan- + -o- + som- + -iasis] Note: G. *-ia*: the act, process, or condition of + *-sis*: the act, process, or result of > G. *-iasis* > the E. *n*-forming suffix -IASIS, having, in this entry, the modern scientific meaning: an abnormal medical condition or disease, often charact. by the presence or infestation of intestinal worms, protozoa, calculi (body stones), crawling insects, or other parasites (as specified by the preceding base or elements). SEC. RECON: *an abnormal medical condition charact. by the infestation of* (**-iasis**) *body* (**som-**) *borers* (**trypan-**) OR *an abnormal medical condition charact. by the infestation of* (**-iasis**) *auger* (**trypan-**) *bodies* (**som-**). Trypanosomes were named after their auger-shaped bodies, *93*, see also under -IASIS

tsetse fly, see under TRYPANOSOMIASIS

tube, see under SUBWAY

tuxedo, 135

TWO, TWICE, DOUBLE (BI-, BIN-, BIS-), 90–92

Two-Root Infinitives (Greek), **262**

-ty (tē) a L-derived *n*-forming suffix having the closely related abstract meanings: the quality, state, or condition of: *royalty*, *poverty*, *difficulty*. **[-ty]** < L. *-tās*: the quality, state, or condition of. Note: *-ty* is often preceded by the connecting vowel *-i-*, forming the E. suffix *-ity*: ENMITY, TIMIDITY, *absurdity*; and occasionally *-ty* is preceded by the connecting vowel *-e-*, forming the E. suffix *-ety*: anxiety, notoriety, *satiety* (sə·tī′i·tē; the state or condition of being fully satisfied or of receiving or experiencing so much of what one desires that all sense of pleasure and satisfaction is lost, as in overeating). For further information and examples, see -ITY and -ETY; *78*, *101*, *105*, *106*, **109**

typ-, **105**

typewrite, see under AMBIVALENT

typewriter, see under AMBIVALENT

typhlology, 124

typ(os), *105*

tyrann-, **102**

tyrannicide, **56**, **102**

tyrann(os), *102*

tyrann(us), *102*

Xanthippe, 147, 148

XENOMANIA (zen´ə·mā´nē·ə, zē´nə-) *n.* an extreme affection for or attachment to persons of foreign extraction. [< G. *xen₍os₎*: stranger, foreigner + *-o-*: conn. vowel + -MANIA], 145

XENOPHOBE (zen´ə·fōb´, zē´nə-) *n.* a person who fears, dreads, or hates foreigners or that which is foreign. [**xen-** + **-o-** + **phob-** + **-e**] < G. *xen₍os₎*: stranger, foreigner, guest; strange, foreign + *-o-*: conn. vowel + *phob₍os₎*: fear, panic, flight (< *phobein* or *phebesthai*: to flee in fright or terror). **RECON:** *fearing*

(**phob-**) *strangers or foreigners* (**xen-**). **SEC. DISS:** [xen- + -o- + -phobe] **Note:** G. *phob₍os₎*: fear, panic, flight + E. *-e*: silent final letter > the E. *n*-forming comb. form -PHOBE, having the basic meaning: one who fears, dreads, or hates (that which is designated by the preceding base or elements). **SEC. RECON:** *one who fears, dreads, or hates* (**-phobe**) *strangers or foreigners* (**-xen**), 49, see also under -PHOBE

xenophobia, 142

Xerox, 133

-**y** (ē) a G- or L-derived abstract *n*-forming suffix having a variety of closely related and often overlapping meanings: the quality, state, condition; act, means, result, or process of: *philosophy* (G.), *sympathy* (G.: see also under SYM-), *SYZYGY* (G.), *victory* (L.), *agency* (L.), EULOGY (G.). [-**y**] < G. *-ia* or *-eia*; or L. *-ia*; or L. *-ia* < G. *-ia*; *60, 70, 83,* **101**, **101**, *116, 120, 124, 150, passim*

YAVIS, 130

yearly, see under -LY¹

Yiddish, 230, see also under INDO-EUROPEAN

yuppie, 130

zo-, 60

ZODIAC (zō´dē·ak´) *n.* **1.** an imaginary circle in the heavens, extending approximately eight degrees on each side of the ecliptic (the combined paths of the apparent annual movements of the sun, moon, and all the planets save Pluto), that is divided into twelve equal parts or signs, each named after a constellation. **2.** a representation of this circle, used in astrology. [**zo-** + **-di-** + **-ac**] < G. *zō₍ion₎*: animal, living being (< or akin to *zoē*: life) + *-₍i₎di₍on₎*: a dim. suffix having the basic meaning: small, little, tiny + *-ak₍os₎* (var. of *-ikos* used after *i*; see -AC): pert. to, charact. by. **RECON:** *pert. to* (**-ac**) *small* (**-di-**) *animals* (**zo-**). Eight of the twelve zodiacal (zō·dī´ə·k´l) constellations involve animals. But why were these animals said to be "small"? Before it became associated with stellar (star) animals, Greek *zōidion* denoted a small sculpted figure of an animal. This word then passed into the phrase *zōidiakos kyklos,* "circle of little animals," which was applied to and used to conceptualize the constellations of the zodiac. *Kyklos* eventually dropped out, leaving only *zōidiakos,* which in time became English *zodiac.* But *zodiac* never lost its diminutive element *-₍i₎di₍on₎, 52, 60*

zodiacal, see under ZODIAC

zō₍ion₎, 60

zombie (zäm´bē) *n.* **1.** in West African and West Indian voodoo religion, a corpse reanimated by a person or supernatural force into a plodding, mindless creature, usually for the purpose of doing evil. **2.** any person whose movements are slow, lethargic, mechanical, or seemingly without VOLITION

or conscious thought. [**zombie**] < one or more Bantu languages of southwestern Africa, perhaps an Americanization of Kimbundu (a Bantu language of northern Angola) *nzambi,* "god" or an alteration of Kikongo (the Bantu language of the Kongo people of southeastern Zaire and northern Angola) *zumbi,* "fetish," 160

zōna (Latinization of G. *zōnē*), 236

zone (Anglicization of L. *zōna*), 236

zoo, *60,* 132

zoological garden, 60

zoomania, 144

ZOOPHOBIA *n.* an abnormal fear or dread of animals. [< G. *zō₍ion₎*: animal, living being (< or akin to *zoē*: life) + *-o-*: conn. vowel + -PHOBIA], 143; see also the entry, WORDS WITH ANIMALS IN THEM, for a list of specific animal phobias

zoophorus, 114

zwie, 91

zwieback, 91, *91*

zyg- < G. *zyg-,* base of *zygoun* or *zygnynai*: to join together, to yoke (< *zygon*: a yoke); or G. *zyg-* may be derived directly from *zygon*: a yoke, *116,* see also under DIZYGOTIC and MONOZYGOTIC

zygodactyl, 116

zygon, 37, 116

zygote, 116

About the Author

Robert Schleifer is a professional lexicographer with over fifteen years' experience teaching vocabulary and etymology. A lifelong student and scholar of the English language, he has been a general editor of the *Macmillan/McGraw-Hill School Dictionary 3* and has published articles on vocabulary and etymology in popular and linguistics journals. Formerly a teacher of technical writing at Oklahoma State University, he has given presentations in writing, etymology, and scientific nomenclature at professional meetings and symposia throughout the United States and has conducted adult education classes on vocabulary-building on the East Coast. He currently resides in New York City but makes frequent trips to Oklahoma to visit his two young nephews.